SIR JOHN VANBRUGH

SIR JOHN VANBRUGH

__ A BIOGRAPHY __

Kerry Downes

SIDGWICK & JACKSON
LONDON

First published in Great Britain in 1987
by Sidgwick & Jackson Limited

ISBN 0–283–99497–5

Phototypeset by Falcon Graphic Art Limited
Wallington, Surrey
Printed by Butler and Tanner Limited
Frome, Somerset
for Sidgwick & Jackson Limited
1 Tavistock Chambers
Bloomsbury Way
London WC1A 2SG

To Margaret

Contents

Sugar in Chester. The Henthornes. Chester records. Dissenters and sympathisers. Sir Willoughby Aston. The pressure cooker. John Vanbrugh's siblings. Giles's will. Education. The Garencieres. Giles's letter to the Bishop of London.

The wine trade and other family connections. Myths of study in France. London in 1681. An impressionable lad of seventeen.

Lord Clarendon and Lord Huntingdon. The king's shilling. Marching orders. A Catholic army and administration. The Glorious Revolution. An ill-starred journey.

Piecing the story together. True and false accounts. Efforts to obtain release. Transfer from Calais to Vincennes. An appeal to Saint-Germain. The Duliviers. Smuggled letters. The Bastille. Money in prison. Vanbrugh's plan. Further complications in England and France. At liberty in Paris. The effects of imprisonment.

Giles Vanbrugh's death. His children and nephews. The Duchy of Lancaster. Peregrine and other Berties. Whiggism and the Kit-Cat Club. Lord Somers and other members. Vanbrugh at sea and in London.

Ideas about the theatre: licensing and licence. Davenant's operas. The King's and Duke's Companies. Forestage and deep stage: scenery. Women on the stage. Travesty parts. More moral objections. Dryden's *The Kind Keeper*. Seduction in *The Relapse*. Ladies in the audience. Participation. Unruly behaviour.

Colley Cibber. Betterton's secession from the United Com-

comedy written by rules. The limits of regularity. Moral defences of the stage. Steele's *The Funeral. The Lying Lover*. Sentimental comedy.

18 Without Thought or Lecture

The Castle Howard obelisk and Lady Irwin's poem. Patron and client. Changes in remuneration. Hawksmoor at Castle Howard and Blenheim. Talman's lawsuit against Lord Carlisle. Carlisle's patronage of Vanbrugh. Architecture a gentlemanly pursuit. Roger North. Hawksmoor's indispensability. His training and character. William Vanbrugh. The decision to become an architect.

19 When a Design was Chosen and Followed

Dacres and Howards. The Earls of Carlisle. Old Henderskelfe. Carlisle as *Pater Patriæ*. The new Whig palaces. Carlisle's decision to build. Talman's methods and his design. Garden plans. Vanbrugh's introduction. His Christmas letter. The dome. Afterthoughts and responsibility. Earlier domes. A building like an orange-house. State rooms. Diverse messages in architecture. The completion of Castle Howard. The bow window room. The service courts.

20 A Goose Pie

House fires. Old Whitehall. Vanbrugh's request to build in the ruins. His first visible work. London gossip. A vicious attack. Swift's poems. The form of the house. How to make a goose pie. The uniqueness of the house. Vanbrugh appointed Comptroller in place of Talman.

21 Comptroller and Herald

The Comptroller's duties. The end of Vanbrugh's army service. His business abilities. Opposition to his appointment as a herald. His induction. Tonson's purchases in Amsterdam. Julius Cæsar's Works. London life. Vanbrugh the traveller. Barn Elms. The Great Storm. Henry Winstanley. Dissuasives from the playhouse and from building. The Kensington Orangery affair. Vanbrugh and Wren.

22 Towards a New Theatre

The new company of comedians. Vanbrugh's playhouse.

Healing the split. Kit-Cat support. The Italian Opera. Purcell. Addison's *Rosamond*. Opening the theatre. The 1705 spring season. Defects in the new theatre. Illusory vastness: a triumphal piece of architecture. Changes in staging. The auditorium improved. The character of Vanbrugh's building. *The Confederacy* and *The Mistake*.

Chargate. Kings Weston. Chimneys. Plainness as an aesthetic positive. Reasons for preserving Old Woodstock Manor. The Great Bridge.

The Fifty New Churches. Vanbrugh a Commissioner. His proposals and Wren's. Designs for St James's and Kensington. The Woodstock letter: leaked and printed. Attempts at salvage. Loss of the Comptrollership. Away from London. The convenience of Castle Howard. Costumes and properties. Vanbrugh's grant of arms. Loss of the Garter reversion. Political and financial recovery. Grimsthorpe. Return of the Marlboroughs. Correspondence with the Duchess. Her scheme against Vanbrugh. His resignation. Glassmaker Moore.

Surveyor at Greenwich Hospital. Knighthood. The green village. A rented house. York gossip: Lady Mary Wortley Montagu. Mrs Yarburgh. The Heslington Lady. Christmas at Castle Howard. Nottingham Castle. The wedding at York: more premeditated than at first appears. A successful marriage. The lease of a field. Vanbrugh Castle.

A second portrait and its pair. Strokes of philosophy. Reform in the Office of Works. The new Board. William Benson: his appointment as Surveyor. His misconduct and dismissal. The House of Lords. Sir Thomas Hewett. Vanbrugh, approaching sixty, seeks a sinecure. Work at St James's and Hampton Court.

The insecurity of patronage. The Blenheim lawsuits. The Duchess of Marlborough appeals to the Lords. Vanbrugh's *Justification*. Whig aesthetics: Shaftesbury. Faults found with Blenheim. Letters to Newcastle. The Holbein Gate. Dean Jones. More trouble with the mail. The King's Progress of 1722.

Stagnation in the theatre. Steele's *The Conscious Lovers*: a Georgian play. Duelling. Terence and Plautus. *The Spectator* on comedy: its proper subjects. Steele's patent. Selling *The Conscious Lovers*. Dennis's strictures. Humour banished from the stage. Parallel reactions to Vanbrugh's plays and his architecture. *A Journey to London*. Cibber's completion. Vanbrugh's intentions.

List of Plates

List of Text Figures

Preface

The immediate reason for writing this book was that Bridget Sleddon, then of Waterstone's, commissioned me to do so, and my first debt is to her for the idea of a biography of this great and versatile character. Once I began work on the book, it was quite clear that it needed to be written, and that is the ultimate reason for its existence. Having engaged privately in the world of literary studies all my life, I make no apology for entering it publicly; in any case, there is a long tradition of the invasion of art history by students of English Literature, and it is not inappropriate to attempt a return journey for once. But what most surprised me, during the enjoyable year I spent reading Restoration comedies, was the grudging critical acknowledgement accorded by many literary authorities to Vanbrugh's worth as a writer.

I do not believe that any defence is needed for writing – as I have done on other occasions – a second book on the same subject. Rivet-counters will discover exactly what is omitted that was included in the previous book, to which this one is in many ways complementary rather than a replacement. There has, however, been a chance to correct some mistakes, and I beg the indulgence of those who find that I have left out whatever they would most have liked to see included. There are no prizes for identifying those previous writers of whose work I have made the greatest use; the breadth rather than the depth of my reliance is indicated in the endnotes to this book.

For information I am grateful particularly to Neil Rhind, Frank Kelsall, John Bold, Christopher Stell, Edward Chaney, Dr Frances

Harris of the British Library and Marjorie G. Wynne of the Beinecke Rare Book Library at Yale. In Cheshire, Susan and Roger Roycroft, Arthur Walsh and Mrs Rene Baker formed a chain for the transmission of a particularly important question and its answer. Many other friends and colleagues have patiently listened, as if to the Ancient Mariner, to parts of my unfolding tale, but only one has heard the whole, like the White Rabbit's evidence, from beginning to end.

In the palmy days a book of these Vanbrugian dimensions took fifteen years to write, or at least a sabbatical year or two; I do not count the fact that I have worked in this area for nearly forty years. That the writing itself has been done in a much shorter time amid the realities of university life in the 1980s is due more than anything to the devotion of my wife, who in spite of all kinds of obstacles contrived to sustain home and hearth within a machine for living and working in, and who heard, read and discussed with me every single page. She would be the first to agree with me that the work was as enjoyable as it was arduous; the dedication to her of the result is no more – indeed less – than her due.

Kerry Downes
Department of History of Art
University of Reading

April 1987

Acknowledgements

Thanks are due, for permission to publish the letters included or identified in Appendix G, to the Public Record Office (Crown Copyright), the British Library Board, and the Borthwick Institute of Historical Research, University of York. Plates and figures are reproduced by courtesy of the following: Windsor Castle, Royal Library, © Her Majesty the Queen (Pl. 24); National Portrait Gallery (Pls 1, 39); British Library (Pls 4, 16); the Trustees of the British Museum (Pls 20, 23); Public Record Office, Crown Copyright (Fig. A); the Earl of Pembroke (Fig. C); the Board of Trustees of the Victoria and Albert Museum (Fig. H).

Chronology

A Note on Dates

In 1582 Pope Gregory XIII introduced a reform of the calendar, which over many centuries had fallen out of synchrony with the geometry of the earth and the sun. Catholic countries adopted the New Style calendar at once, but Protestant ones were slow to do so. England retained until 1752 the Old Style calendar, in which the year began on 25 March and the date was ten or eleven days behind New Style – ten until 1700, eleven thereafter.

Throughout Vanbrugh's lifetime English resistance often embodied an acknowledgement of the discrepancy, so that dates between 1 January and 24 March were – though not always – given in both years, and in foreign correspondence they were increasingly given with both month dates (e.g. 2/12 March 1709/10). However, in cases where such acknowledgement was not made the historian's vigiliance is needed.

In this book, unless otherwise noted, year dates are given as beginning on 1 January, while month dates are given in Old Style or, where necessary, in both styles.

1664	24 Jan.	Baptized, at home, in the Parish of St Nicholas Acons, City of London; probably born the same day.
1665	18 Jan.	Sister Elizabeth baptized at St Nicholas Acons; last record of the family in London.
1667	Feb.	Father petitions for release of cloth from Customs.
	6 June	Brother Carleton baptized at Richmond, Surrey.
	13 Oct.	Carleton buried at Holy Trinity, Chester; first record of the family there.

1681		Working for William Matthews in London or Westminster.
1682	31 Jan.	Youngest brother Philip baptized at Holy Trinity, Chester.
1683	25 Oct.	Father makes his will.
1685	6 Feb.	Death of Charles II; accession of James II.
	28 Dec.	Writes to Earl of Huntingdon requesting employment.
1686	30 Jan.	Commissioned Ensign in Huntingdon's Foot Regiment.
	20 Aug.	Ambrose Jones commissioned Ensign in his place.
1687	16 Sept.	Freeman of City of Oxford, in the train of Earl of Abingdon; revoked 16 Feb. 1688.
1688	Sept.	Arrested and imprisoned at Calais.
	5 Nov.	William III lands at Torbay.
1689	23 Mar.	Tobias Legros appointed Auditor, Southern Division, Duchy of Lancaster, as Vanbrugh's deputy.
	19 July	Father buried at Holy Trinity, Chester.
1690	Oct.	Mother petitions Privy Council in London for exchange with Archibald Cockburne.
1691	17/27 Apr.	Transferred to Vincennes.
	27 June/7 July	Writes to Henry Browne, Secretary of State to James II at Saint-Germain, pretending to be a supporter.
	30 Oct./9 Nov.	Letter to his mother smuggled from Vincennes.
1692	22 Jan./1 Feb.	Transferred to the Bastille.
	12/22 Nov.	Released on parole.
1693	Mar./Apr.	Returns to England.
	11 May	Takes up sinecure in Duchy of Lancaster.
1694	20 May	Described as intimate friend of Peregrine Bertie in London.
	7/8 June	Sees naval action with Lord Carmarthen in Camaret Bay.
1695	15 Aug.	Lord Berkeley agrees to take Vanbrugh in exchange from Lord Carmarthen's Regiment.
1696	31 Jan.	Warrant for exchange to Lord Berkeley's regiment.
	21 Nov.	Première of *The Relapse* at Drury Lane.
	late Dec.	Première of *Æsop* at Drury Lane.

1697	Apr.	Première of *The Provok'd Wife* at Lincoln's Inn Fields.
	May	*Æsop II* presented at Drury Lane.
	20 Sept.	Peace of Rijswijk signed.
1698	4 Jan.	Whitehall Palace burned down.
	Jan.	Première of *The Country House* at Drury Lane.
	Mar./Apr.	Collier's *Short View*.
	8 June	*Short Vindication* published.
	20 Aug.	Warrant for half-pay as Captain of Marines.
	10 Oct.	Lord Carlisle leases Henderskelfe from March 1699.
1699	July	Visits Henderskelfe, Kiveton, Chatsworth, Burley-on-the-Hill.
	25 Dec.	Writes to Lord Manchester about Castle Howard.
1700	Apr.	Première of *The Pilgrim* at Drury Lane.
	June	Castle Howard model sent to Hampton Court; foundation work on the building.
	22 July	Granted permission to build a house in the ruins of Whitehall, constructed during the following year.
1701	5 Sept.	Death in exile of James II; Louis XIV recognises Prince James Francis Edward as King of England.
1702	Feb.	Première of *The False Friend* at Drury Lane.
	8 Mar.	Death of William III; accession of Queen Anne.
	10 Mar.	Commissioned Captain in new Lord Huntingdon's Foot Regiment (resigned by 15 May).
	20 May	Appointed Comptroller of Works.
	Autumn	East wing of Castle Howard roofed.
1703	15 June	Writes to Duke of Newcastle about Welbeck designs and Talman-Carlisle lawsuit.
	21 June	'Souc'd' as Carlisle Herald.
	June-July	Purchasing site for Haymarket Theatre.
	26–7 Nov.	The Great Storm in the South of England.
1704	Mar.	Made Clarenceux Herald.
	30 Mar.	*Squire Trelooby* by Vanbrugh, Congreve and Walsh played at Lincoln's Inn Fields.
	18 Apr.	Foundation stone of Haymarket Theatre laid.
	Summer	Visits Castle Howard.
	9 Nov.	Writes to Godolphin about Kensington Orangery.
	late Nov.	Queen Anne attends a concert at unofficial inauguration of the Haymarket Theatre.
	14 Dec.	Warrant from Lord Chamberlain to Vanbrugh and Congreve for a new company of actors.

	Dec.	Marlborough approaches Vanbrugh about design of a house.
1705	Feb.	Visits Woodstock with Marlborough.
	9 Apr.	Official opening of Haymarket Theatre with Greber's *Loves of Ergasto*.
	9 June	Vanbrugh's warrant as Surveyor to Blenheim.
	18 June	Lays foundation stone of Blenheim with six others.
	Sept.-Oct.	Blenheim model.
	30 Oct.	Première of *The Confederacy* at Haymarket.
	15 Dec.	Congreve has left Vanbrugh as sole manager at Haymarket.
	27 Dec.	Première of *The Mistake* at Haymarket.
1706	11 May	Leaves London for Hanover.
	14 Aug.	Leases Haymarket Theatre to Swiney for seven years.
1707	22 Mar.	*The Cuckold in Conceit* at Haymarket.
	July	Designs new south front at Kimbolton.
	July-Aug.	Visits Castle Howard.
1708	Jan.	Resumes control of Haymarket Theatre.
	11 May	Swiney again in control of Haymarket.
	Summer	Work at Audley End.
	Dec.-Feb.1709	The Great Frost.
1709	13 May	Leases Chargate.
	11 June	*Reasons for Preserving Woodstock Manor.*
	July-Aug.	Visits Castle Howard.
1710		Designs for Kings Weston.
1711	18 Jan.	Duchess of Marlborough resigns.
	30 Apr.	Duke of Marlborough dismissed.
	13 Aug.	Mother dies at Chargate.
1713	21 Jan.	Writes to Mayor of Woodstock in support of Marlborough.
	15 Apr.	Patent as Comptroller terminated.
	Sept.	In Chester.
1714	15 Apr.	Grant of arms by the College of Heralds.
	1 Aug.	Queen Anne dies.
	18 Sept.	George I lands at Greenwich. Vanbrugh knighted.
	14 Oct.	Earl of Clare buys Chargate.
1715	24 Jan.	New patent as Comptroller.
	15 June	Appointed Surveyor of Gardens and Waters.
1716	Jan.	Visits Bath.

	9 Mar.	Receives one third of Blenheim arrears.
	30 Mar.	Last recorded meeting of Kit-Cat Club.
	July-Sept.	Journey to the North.
	1 Aug.	Succeeds Wren as Surveyor to Greenwich Hospital.
	8 Nov.	Resigns as architect of Blenheim.
1717	30 Apr.	Letter about the Heslington Lady.
	Sept.-Nov.	Visits Bath.
1718	3 Mar.	Leases Biddulph's field at Greenwich.
	26 Apr.	Wren dismissed as Surveyor.
	Dec.	Visits Nottingham; Christmas at Castle Howard.
1719	14 Jan.	Marries Henrietta Maria Yarburgh at York.
	30 Jan.	Lady Vanbrugh arrives at Greenwich.
	17 July	Benson resigns as Surveyor.
	6 Aug.	Appeals for preservation of Holbein Gateway.
	8 Aug.	Stillborn daughter.
	Oct.	Journey to Suffolk.
	31 Dec.	Mortgages Vanbrugh Castle to brother Charles (repaid Oct. 1720).
1720	Mar.	Moves into Vanbrugh Castle.
	20 Oct.	Son Charles born.
1721	23-4 May	Lords reject Duchess of Marlborough's case against Blenheim workmen.
	July-Nov.	Journey to the North en famille.
1722	14 Feb.	Son John born.
1723	28 Mar.	Son John buried at Walton-on-Thames.
	Mar.	Proposals for paving London and Westminster.
	Aug.-Sept.	Journey to the North, including Scarborough.
1724	7 Jan.	Hawksmoor describes Vanbrugh's design for Castle Howard Temple.
	July-Oct.	Journey to the North.
1725	May	Visits Eastbury.
	3 July	Sells office of Clarenceux Herald.
	July	Journey to Stowe; refused entry to Blenheim.
	30 Aug.	Receives Blenheim arrears. Makes his will after an 'asthma'.
1726	11 Jan.	New production of *The Provok'd Wife* with alterations.
	26 Mar.	Dies at Whitehall.
1745	2/12 May	Son Charles dies after battle of Fontenoy.
1776	3 May	Henrietta Maria Vanbrugh buried in St Stephen Walbrook.

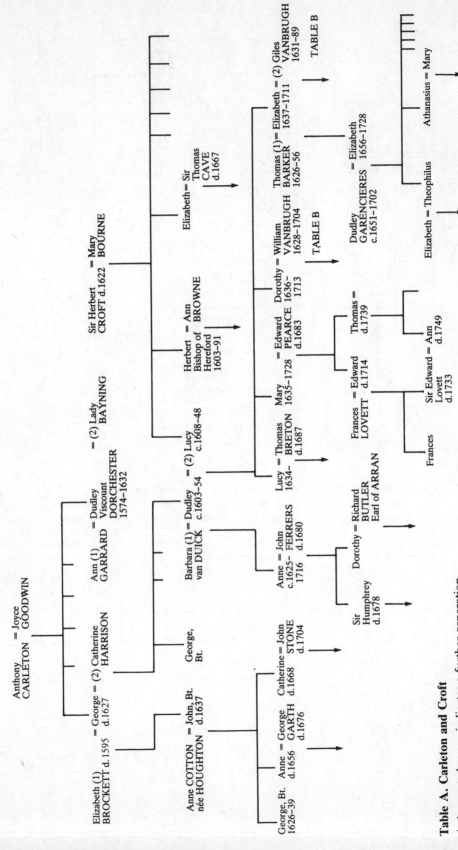

Table A. Carleton and Croft

A downward arrow indicates a further generation

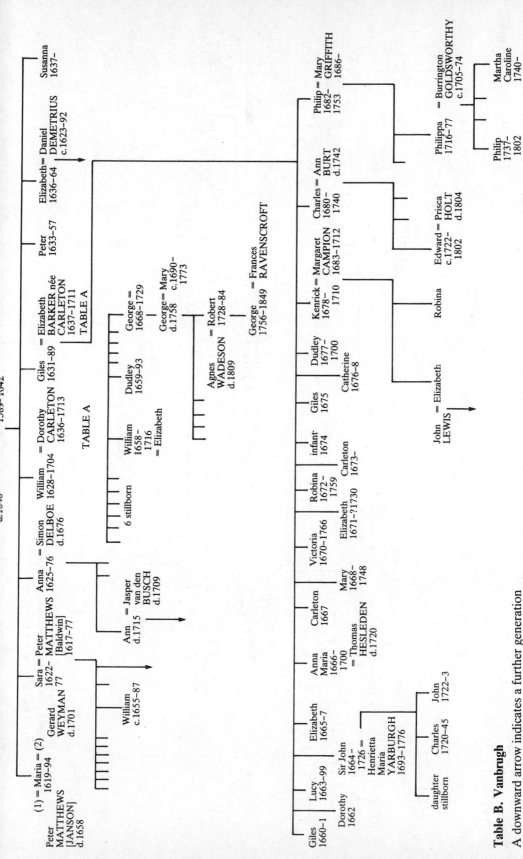

Table B. Vanbrugh

A downward arrow indicates a further generation

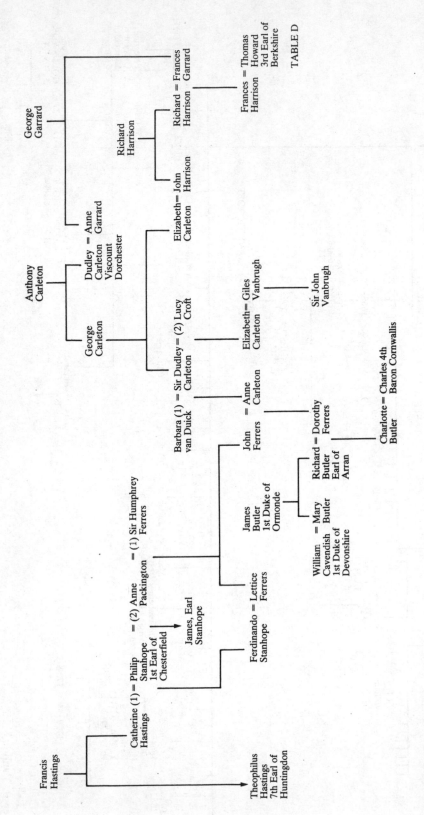

Table C. Carleton Connections

Children are not shown in order of age
Children irrelevant to the connections are omitted
A downward arrow indicates intermediate generations

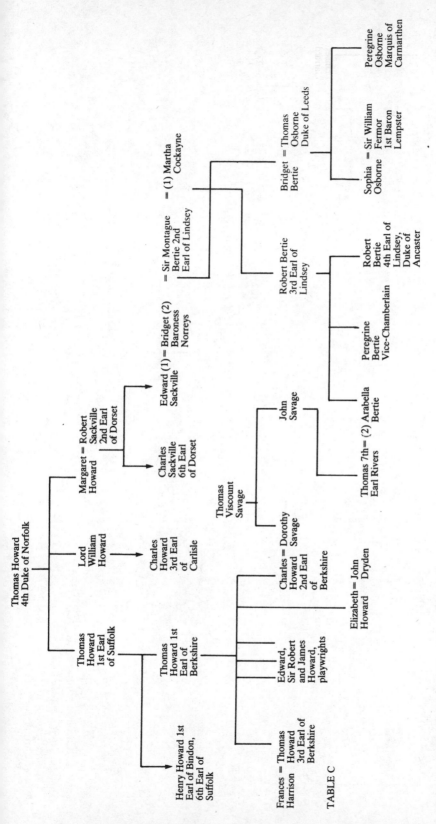

Table D. Howard and Bertie Connections

Children are not shown in order of age
Children irrelevant to the connections are omitted
A downward arrow indicates intermediate generations

1

My Will is This

On the afternoon of Monday, 30 August 1725, Sir John Vanbrugh was at his Whitehall house. August, usually an unsettled month, was coming to an end in 'tollerable harvest weather'. Mortality was not uppermost in his mind, and at sixty-one he was still of an age to live for tomorrow as well as for today. Earlier that particular day he had received at the Exchequer Office the arrears of fees due to him as architect of Blenheim Palace, over £1600. He had resigned nine years earlier, but an incident was still fresh in his memory from a recent excursion, on which he and his wife were barred by his old enemy the Duchess of Marlborough from even entering Blenheim Park. The great house, finished enough for the widowed Duchess to inhabit, was still one of his children; the money he accepted as no more than his due, although it had been necessary to fight for it.

That afternoon Vanbrugh found he could not breathe. The experience, 'an Asthma' or at least 'strong symptomes of one', was new to him; it was unpleasant and it was alarming, but it passed and apparently did not recur. When he had retrieved his breath and his composure he went to his writing desk and took a sheet of paper; he headed it 'My will is this' and proceeded to the disposal of his worldly goods in a sequence of **[A]** neatly written paragraphs.

He must have put the paper away, but the next day, finding himself alive and recovered, he returned to it and wrote a codicil and two postscripts, each of which he signed. Then he put

My Will is This.

[Handwritten manuscript — the first page of Vanbrugh's will]

A The first page of Vanbrugh's will (Public Record Office PRO B1/61).

his will back in a drawer and forgot about it. The following
weekend, from his little country estate at Greenwich, in a letter
to Lord Carlisle, part business and part social, he mentioned
the attack in passing, but it seems that either it left no marked
impression on him or he preferred to try to forget the incident.
It did not occur to him to wonder about its cause, and without
the patient a modern physician would speculate in vain. The
hostility of Nature was familiar, if largely unpredictable.
Bacteria and viruses were unknown, their place in the scheme
of human ills being occupied rather vaguely by bad airs and
vapours. Besides the 'childish illnesses' like measles and the
permanently disfiguring and often fatal smallpox, there were
many ailments attributed to the result of catching cold or being
overheated. The effects rather than the causes of food poison-
ing were distressingly and commonly well known. Beyond
these classes of affliction there lurked in ambush an irregular
host of others, unseen but identified by their effects: fevers,
asthma, quinsy, gout of many kinds, phthisis; like demons they
seized the body, which either succumbed or threw them off
through natural resilience. On the occasion of his asthmatic
attack Vanbrugh did not call a doctor; there is no record of a
consultation until 15 October, and that may well have been for
his wife or his five-year-old son.

Illness struck again in the spring, and Vanbrugh died on 26
March 1726 at Whitehall of 'a quinsey in his throat' (*The
Weekly Journal*, 2 April). The will was found among his papers,
together with sketches for an unfinished play. It was still un-
witnessed, and to obtain probate it had to be authenticated by
the testimony of his cousin George Vanbrugh and George's
servant John Rogers that they had known him personally for a
considerable time and recognized his handwriting. He had
made no additions to it, and indeed we know nothing about his
last illness or of what passed through his mind during it. But
his thoughts can hardly have been as vivid as the kaleidoscope
of memories of the previous August.

At that time he would have remembered his leaving home in
Chester, his early adventures in the London wine trade, his
acceptance of an ensign's commission in the army and his
resignation after a few months. He had been in danger of death
before, in French prisons and in the naval action at Camaret

Bay in 1694. Now he would have heard again the roar of applause that greeted his first successes as a London playwright,
the laughter of Kit-Cat Club dinners in Fleet Street, the exclamation of friends at his first designs for Castle Howard.
More precise images followed in his mind: sitting with his
friends in the fountain basin at Hampton Court one hot July
evening; laying the foundation stone of the Haymarket
Theatre; the Duke of Marlborough asking him to design the
house that became Blenheim; his visit to the future George I
and George II in Hanover; the stopping of work at Blenheim;
dismissal from the Queen's Works and reinstatement and
knighthood by the new king; his first meeting with Henrietta
Yarburgh, courtship and marriage; building the Castle at
Greenwich, the birth and death of children; himself as he was
painted, wearing with satisfaction the badge of office of
Clarenceux Herald; just recently selling the office for £2500
(disposing 'in earnest of a place I got in jest').

These are the bare bones of a life of incident, sometimes of
adventure, usually of success, often of laughter but also on
occasion of stern seriousness. Nearly five years of unjust captivity must have left their mark. Vanbrugh had many friends
within and outside his family circle and, for a man in public
life, few enemies; his enthusiasm, his wit and his candour
were magnetic. Through the mediums of his letters, his plays,
his architecture and the portraits of him it is still possible not
[1]   only to know many very varied things about him, but also to
feel with affection that we have met him. Yet although his
[19]   friends knew collectively much that is unknown to us, it is difficult to say how well any of them really knew him.

There are few, if any, characters in history about whom
more is known than is unknown; this may only be a particular
instance of a general theory about knowledge, but it is important to remember that we always know characters intuitively.
Moreover, the most perceptive or searching of portraitists,
from Van Dyck and Rembrandt to Manet and Cézanne, bring
their sitters to life by a kind of impressionism in which many
marks and patches, in themselves undefined, add up in the eye
of the beholder to a convincing, even a speaking, likeness.

For many years there have been two Vanbrughs, the playwright and the architect. Since in addition to these occupations

he was at times a soldier, a herald and an experienced if not
always conventional businessman, there have been enough
opportunities to see and present him as less than a fully rounded figure.

To say that his architecture is dramatic, or that his plays
have an architecture of their own, is as unhelpful, even if true,
as to pronounce him a businesslike herald. But there are more
meaningful statements to be made. His architectural status
progressed from inspired amateur ('without thought or lecture' in Swift's phrase) to dedicated professional two decades
later. Two of his comedies, *The Relapse* and *The Provok'd Wife*,
are still played to full houses and are among the best of their
period and category, not only because their situations are
amusing but also because their dialogue brings the naturalness of his epistolary style to the stock characters of his stage
and infuses them with life. The artificiality of Lady Fancyfull
and Lord Foppington is offset by the spontaneity of Miss Hoyden and Sir John Brute. The nearly three hundred surviving
letters, addressed to a range of recipients from noble patrons to
clerks of works, from the Treasury Lords to 'Old Jacob' Tonson, cover many of his varied interests, not all at once. They
provide both circumstantial evidence of his movements and
activities and also insights into his thought. Vanbrugh acquired the habit of keeping a journal or day-book of his receipts
and expenses, and the rediscovery of this record for the last ten
years of his life has added enormously to the picture of his
household, both in his later bachelor days and after his
marriage at the age of fifty-five, when he was soon led into the
purchase of pots, cups, lamp and a table for making and taking
the new luxury drink, tea.

Some of his architecture is well documented, especially
Blenheim; elsewhere, evidence is fragmentary or only to be
found in the buildings themselves or in sketches. There is no
shortage of texts of his plays, and much is known about their
original casts and where and how they were staged; on the
other hand, how they should be played and interpreted is by no
means so easy to decide, and whether they tell us anything of
their author and his opinions, as the plays of Shaw and Coward
seem to do, is a question that it may ever be foolish to pursue.

Understanding Vanbrugh is greatly helped both by identifying the society of his friends and patrons and by following the ramifications of his family, which united the backbone of England (church, nobility, army and land) on his mother's side and the international commercial and mercantile community on his father's. Even a name like Vanbrugh is not without pitfalls and ambiguities for the genealogist, for example the Van den Bergh twins who for many years hung uncomfortably but firmly on a branch of the family tree until they were finally dislodged. Caution is always needed in distinguishing the various alternative spellings of the family name from irrelevant strangers of this kind. Vanbrugh's father, Giles, was sometimes described in the Chester period as 'Vanbrough' (perhaps rhyming with *rough* and suggesting that he was experimenting with anglicized forms), and both would sign themselves 'Vanbrook'; these spellings suggest that contemporary pronunciation of the name differed from the modern English '*Van*bruh' or American 'Van*broo*'. Among other strange spellings the cardinal sin, nowadays committed universally by the careless and sometimes passed even by proof-readers, is the transposition of the letters to make 'Vanburgh', a form which was occasionally used at the time but never by any of the family.

All the same, it is a much easier name to trace than Smith. But the two most useful sources of family information are the records of the Dutch Church at Austin Friars in London, with which his father's family maintained contact and in some cases membership, and the burial register of St Stephen's Walbrook, where his grandfather Gillis had bought a funeral vault which continued in use to the end of the eighteenth century.

The Vanbrughs seem to have made little use of banks, but there is much information of value in legal documents and wills. It is from a court case that we learn of the young John's employment by a London cousin in a wine business that failed. In another case one of his uncles, William Vanbrugh, took another uncle, Thomas Breton, unsuccessfully to law for evading the terms of his wife's marriage settlement. When Breton died his will charged William Vanbrugh with the completion Breton had continued to evade, which involved purchasing an estate for Mrs Breton. It also disowned the two youngest children of

Mrs Breton, who was John's aunt Lucy. John's mother gave nothing away in her will either to lawyers or to modern historians, for in a very simple document she left everything to her youngest son Philip, or alternatively to John or their sister Robina, 'to perform whatsoever I have expressed in writing with my own hands'. When she died in 1711 Philip was at sea in the Navy, and her letter of directions therefore went to John for administration. What she had directed is quite unknown, excepting perhaps her burial not in the Vanbrugh vault but at Thames Ditton in Surrey where she had spent some of her childhood.

John Vanbrugh's life spanned five reigns, from Charles II to George I, and the whole architectural career of Sir Christopher Wren. In his boyhood most people, including the King, still believed that the country was ruled by the monarch; by the time he died most people accepted that the country was governed by an elected parliament. He was born in a London that was still virtually a medieval wooden city, and died in one that had been rebuilt in brick and had vastly expanded into the new orderly and spacious streets and squares of Westminster, Bloomsbury and St Marylebone. Both in architecture and the fine arts and in literature and drama he saw great changes in style and taste from the robust vigour of Restoration to the self-conscious Taste and sentiment of Early Georgian. It is simplistic to consider him as belonging merely to either one of these.

_ 2 _

To Giles and Elizabeth, a Son

The small parish of St Nicholas Acons occupied an area no larger than a football pitch: it lay south of Lombard Street and was bisected from north to south by St Nicholas Lane (now Nicholas Lane). The church, which stood west of the lane, originated in the late eleventh century, and the name 'Acons' was probably a corruption of Haakon, an early benefactor. The Royal Exchange and London Bridge were three or four minutes' walk away, the Guildhall and St Paul's Cathedral about twice as far. St Nicholas was one of 107 large and small parishes making up the square mile of the City of London. The church was destroyed in the Great Fire and not rebuilt, the parish being amalgamated with that of St Edmund, Lombard Street.

By the early seventeenth century, when an English 'great town' might comprise no more than a thousand inhabitants, the City (as it is known) already stood out with a population of two hundred times that number. While Westminster, then as now, was an autonomous city and the seat of national government, the City of London was the financial and mercantile capital, as it still is, but with one great difference. Modern city centres are places of work, full of offices, banks and shops; their staff and customers alike live somewhere else. This was still a new idea in the eighteenth century, when the Mansion House was built for the Lord Mayor to live in during his year of office because the Aldermen from whose number he was elected were beginning to live outside the City and travel in to work.

But throughout the seventeenth century most of those who worked in the City lived within its bounds, whether they dealt in money or goods, or made or mended things, or provided other services. Those who were masters of their trades usually lived over their workshops or offices with their families, and 'families' included not only paid household servants but often also distant relatives and employees – assistants, clerks or apprentices.

In the 1660s the diarist Samuel Pepys, Clerk of the Acts to the Navy, lived above the Navy Office in Seething Lane near the Tower of London. This was part of a large rambling house, and contained lodgings for four Principal Officers and their families as well as office accommodation and a porter's lodge. In the years of his diary Pepys and his wife usually had four or five domestic servants, but there was probably little in the way of office staff as we think of them today. The Office also contained lodgings for a clerk, but in the days when bureaucratic paperwork was still quite simple a great deal of business was carried on by word of mouth and by personal visit. The fact that all documents had to be written and copied by hand provided a natural brake on proliferation, although what could be achieved in spite of such obstacles is shown by the career of William Blathwayt. This inspired government servant, who purchased the office of Secretary-at-War in 1683, made a practice of copying every document passing through his hands into his own ledgers, creating in effect what later came to be known as the War Office.

Equal limitations of manpower, accommodation and money applied to private businesses. Many were run singly by the head of the family, but sometimes brothers, brothers-in-law, cousins or acquaintances would form a partnership. When he was about seventeen Vanbrugh worked for one such partnership that failed, but a successful business would often be handed on to a son or son-in-law. It was also not uncommon in the seventeenth century for a widow to carry on her husband's firm, having learned to manage it during his lifetime. Examples of this can be found in the building trades: a widow named Deborah Bushell ran a haulage business in the last years of the century which figures in accounts at Whitehall and Chelsea Hospital, and the bricks for Vanbrugh Castle and the other houses the architect built at Greenwich came by way of Mrs Jane Wright, carrier.*

The unskilled, the illiterate (and many more people could read than write), manual labourers and the unemployed lived in smaller dwellings, poorer buildings, garrets, as well as, increasingly through the century, in the Liberties, areas on the fringe of the City which lacked both the controls and the advantages of the centre within the walls.

Today we think of inhabited town centres as full of shops in which food and goods of all kinds are sold retail to individual customers. In seventeenth-century London most 'shops' were workshops in which wares were sold because they were made there, whether for stock or to order. The main exceptions were bakers, apothecaries and grocers. Beer, wines and spirits were sold in ale-houses, which were often very small but which catered for consumption both on and off the premises. Perishable food and most household wares were sold in daily markets, of which there were several within the City, and by street vendors who carried or wheeled their goods about. Luxury goods – lace and fine cloth for example – were sold in booths in the Royal Exchange and in the New Exchange off the Strand.

The merchants who occupied many of the better houses, often owning rather than renting them, dealt in wholesale goods. In 1601 John Vanbrugh's great-grandfather Peter Jacobs, 'seller of Cloth by great borne at Andwerpe', was arrested by an informer, 'uppon pretence that he retailleth lynnen cloth and other wares which he in no wise doth not'. London, the largest port in England, handled both domestic and foreign trade. Many merchants were importers or exporters, but not all the tall-masted sailing ships that docked between London Bridge and Wapping travelled to Europe – France, the Netherlands, the Baltic and Mediterranean – or to the West or East Indies. Many were coasters, carrying domestic goods in the only way feasible before the development of inland canals in the eighteenth century, railways in the nineteenth and motor roads in the twentieth. After the Great Fire of 1666 the facing stone for Wren's new St Paul's came from Portland around the south coast and Kent to the government wharf at Greenwich,

* p. 381

where it was transferred to barges that could pass under London Bridge and carry it to Paul's Wharf off Thames Street; in 1689 the French fleet, at war with Great Britain, blockaded the English Channel and cut off the supply of stone for some months. By the middle of the seventeenth century London had a smoke and soot problem because large amounts of coal were shipped from Newcastle to be burned in London grates and stoves; there is still a Sea Coal Lane near Blackfriars, and it was a tax on coal coming into London that paid for Wren's cathedral and other rebuilding works after the Great Fire.

Many merchants had extensive stocks of the wares and commodities in which they dealt; often these were stored in warehouses which were conveniently close to the River Thames. Every sort of goods was to be found there, including bolts of wool, linen and silk cloth, pepper and other spices, vegetable oils, pitch, turpentine, and timber of many varieties. In the 1680s Wren recommended the builder of Easton Neston near Northampton to buy his (imported) timber in London and have it shipped around the coast of East Anglia to Wisbech. One of the most spectacular scenes in the Great Fire, and one of the most costly, was the destruction of so many of the City warehouses with their often inflammable contents; the warehouses themselves were little more than wooden sheds and no more secure against fire than the 'half-timbered' dwelling houses whose wooden frames were filled in with wattle and plaster.

But if they were potential fire-traps the merchants' houses were nevertheless commodious and well furnished. One London merchant who made a new will some time after the Great Fire wrote sadly that it was but a shadow of his previous will, such were his losses in the conflagration. Peter Matthews Baldwin, who married one of John Vanbrugh's aunts and who died in 1677, left in his will a set of tapestries woven at the royal tapestry factory at Mortlake, of the pattern known as 'The Flower Pots', which hung in the biggest room of his house and must have been worth several hundred pounds. Imported goods were beginning to include blue-and-white porcelain from China, which was probably seen partly as an investment or at least as a hedge against hard times. Silverware could more obviously be either used or, when necessary, converted into currency. John's uncle Thomas Breton had a collection of plate with the arms of the second Duke of Buckingham which must have come to him in settlement of the Duke's debts. It is difficult to say how far London merchants were involved in financial dealings in money itself, because such affairs were conducted with discretion. But in the 1630s Philip Jacobs, brother of Peter Jacobs the linen merchant, was known as one of the king's jewellers, which meant in fact that he lent money to the Crown.

City houses stood immediately on the narrow streets, but some of the better ones had gardens at the back. The streets and lanes were not only thoroughfares for people, horses and carts but also the only effective drains for rainwater and less wholesome liquids; they were also noisy with traffic and the cries of street sellers. The gardens offered relative quiet, greenery and fresh air, and could have other uses; at the time of the Great Fire Pepys buried his stock of wine and a Parmesan cheese in the garden of the Navy Office. On occasion Pepys would also walk on the 'leads', the flat-roofed back portion of the building, and could talk with neighbours who were provided with similar facilities.

London had many foreign residents. Some were members of the international trading community and represented the interests of foreign producers or buyers, or provided for the exchange of currency. Others had settled in London because of the opportunities the City offered for trade, particularly in foreign cloth. This category overlapped and blurred with another – those who came to avoid religious persecution. Since the 1560s waves of Protestant refugees had been coming from the Southern Netherlands and from France.

They were mainly Calvinists, adhering to a sterner and severer creed and code than the Church of England. Calvin had rejected not only the authority of the Pope, the doctrine of transubstantiation (the real presence of the body of Christ in the materials of the Eucharist) and the doctrine of free will, but also much of the organization and the liturgy of the Catholic Church. Calvinists are presbyterian, not episcopalian: they have no bishops and no hierarchy, and each local church is largely autonomous and administered by presbyters or elders chosen from respected, articulate and industrious members of the church-going community. Authority rested in the elders and in the Bible; moreover, whereas Henry VIII had established the Sovereign as head of the Church of England, Calvin maintained that the Church was entirely independent of the State.

This is a very summary account of the beliefs of the Flemish and French refugees, but what matters for the moment is not so much what they believed as its consequences. They were people of strong principles, preferring exile and other hardships – even death – to compromise. They had a firm sense of responsibility both to their churches and to the secular communities they formed around them. Escape overseas was usually expensive so those who gained freedom for themselves and their families needed to have some economic substance before they could consider the attempt, but often had none when they had achieved it. They were largely from what it is disparagingly fashionable to call the middle class; in other words they were makers, buyers and sellers, and in smaller numbers members of the professions – teachers, lawyers, doctors and engineers. They were well educated, well organized and prepared to offer loyalty to a ruler who allowed them freedom for their belief, conscience and worship. As a result of their combination of theocracy and selective democracy they were seen by the rulers of France and the Spanish Netherlands not only as heretics in defiance of Rome but also as political dissidents from the doctrine of the absolute God-given power of kings.

By 1600 the first series of migrations was over. Henri IV, Protestant King of France, had in 1598 converted to Catholicism but had also, by the Edict of Nantes, established freedom of worship for the Huguenots, the French Calvinists. The Netherlands had been virtually – and by the Twelve Years' Truce of 1609 effectively – divided into the Catholic south, governed by regency from Madrid, and the United Provinces of the north, republican and officially Calvinist, although distinguished by a range of toleration exceptional for the times. Protestants who came to England in the seventeenth century from the Low Countries thus came from the northern provinces – 'Holland' – and were no longer refugees; in France on the other hand the progressive erosion of toleration led to a continued flow of refugees until 1685, when the revocation by Louis XIV of the Edict of Nantes caused an exodus of tens of thousands of Hug-

uenots, mainly to Holland, Germany, England, America and
the Cape of South Africa.

English attitudes to the refugees varied with time and place.
The 'strangers' believed that work was the exercise of a vocation as well as a means of self-discipline, and that a successful
career was a moral duty – what is now known as the 'Protestant
work ethic'. Their industrious application and their skills not
only helped them rebuild the lives they had left for liberty but
also made them useful citizens of their new country. But in
addition they were a potential threat to the jobs of native
Britons, less so in expanding London than around provincial
points of entry such as Norwich, Colchester, Canterbury and
Southampton.

Those who spoke with a marked foreign accent inevitably
invited a certain amount of mistrust, mirth and even harass-
ment. The English bishops, themselves under attack from the
numerous presbyterian elements among their own flocks (collectively known as Puritans), recommended and sometimes
insisted that the newcomers should adopt the Church of
England and its liturgy. By 1660 England had experienced civil
war, waged over the same issues of political authority and religious dissent, culminating in the judicial murder of King
Charles I in 1649 for treason against the State; the war was followed by the establishment of what amounted to a military
theocratic republic. In English political mythology these ex-
periences helped to form the English dislike of extremes, but
what is important is this: Oliver Cromwell had become king in
all but name and crowning, and his death in September 1658
led to passive anarchy because there was nobody who both
could and would succeed him. At the Restoration of Charles II
in May 1660 most of England was in favour of monarchy.

The new King was not well disposed to Puritans in any form,
having endured too many lectures from Scottish presbyterians
in the years immediately after his father's execution. The
'Dutch' and Huguenot communities were, however, not seriously affected, for it was well known that they were politically
stable, hard-working, economically valuable and well behaved. But in spite of social pressures upon them to integrate
themselves completely with their country of adoption, many
continued to attend their own churches, and indeed were

allowed in law, unlike English dissenters, to follow their own forms of worship. It is to the records of these churches that we owe so much of our knowledge about their names, numbers and activities.

Until the Registration Act of 1836 births, marriages and deaths were recorded only in the registers of recognized places of worship. Many went unrecorded: the Duke of Chandos wrote about 1740 that 'not one in ten is registered' in the parish of St Andrew, Holborn. But the London Dutch in the seventeenth century can be divided into those who were registered at the Dutch Church, Austin Friars, those who were registered in Anglican parishes, and those who were recorded in both. Giles Vanbrugh thought of himself as English and a Londoner. In Italy he signed himself *Giles Vanbrook Anglo-Londinensis*; his first name was anglicized from *Gillis,* his father's name. Gillis was both a churchwarden of St Stephen Walbrook and an elder of the Dutch Church; although most of his children were baptized in the latter, two of his sons, William (1628) and Giles (1631) were christened at Walbrook. Both married English women (who in fact were sisters); Elizabeth Carleton was already the young widow of Thomas Barker when she married Giles on 15 October 1659 at All Hallows, London Wall. She was then twenty-two and had a daughter aged three. The couple settled in the parish of St Nicholas Acons, in which ten or twelve infants a year were christened, and their first son, also Giles, was born there on 6 October 1660.

Modern insurance statistics have fostered the idea that longevity is a modern phenomenon, but that is not true: what has changed with better standards of life is the *average* life expectancy, or conversely the number of deaths at an early age. Certainly in the seventeenth century infant and child mortality was very high, and the baby Giles was buried at less than six months old (31 March 1661) in the family vault which Gillis had purchased in St Stephen Walbrook. A second child, Dorothy, was born on 14 February 1662 and, on 27 September, buried in the vault, recorded as 'a young child of Mr Giles Vanbroge'. At least Giles and Elizabeth were spared the misery and frustration that attended his brother William and her sister Dorothy, who had six stillborn babies before the arrival of their son William, who lived to the age of fifty-eight and figures later in our story.

The first two children of Giles and Elizabeth were christened when a week old, at the church; with their third child they took no chances in the cold weather, and asked the parson to come to the house to baptize Lucy, on the very day she was born, 11 February 1663. Whether as a result of this care or the benign favour of Nature, Lucy survived to be, with Elizabeth Barker her half-sister, elder sisters to the next child. On 23 January 1664, as Ralph Josselin of Earls Colne in Essex recorded in his diary, the weather again turned cold after a mild spell, and the following day, Sunday, it snowed continually. So the parson was again called to the house, as the parish register of St Nicholas Acons records, to christen a boy, John, perhaps born that same day. Giles was that year a deacon of the Dutch Church together with his sister's husband Gerrard Weyman, but the boy John was to grow up very English, a master of the English language, the head of the family after Giles died, and second father to the youngest of his brothers. None of that can have been foreseen that cold January day, nor that John would spend his boyhood far from London. Before he was old enough to understand family relationships and occupations, the Giles Vanbrughs had moved to Chester.

3

Lords and Ladies, Merchants and Gentlemen

In London Giles Vanbrugh was a cloth merchant, and the only known reference to his merchandise shows that he dealt in linen. In February 1667 he petitioned with several other City merchants for the release of goods from the Customs; they included silk, dressed flax, calf-skins, locks and sword-blades, but Giles's goods on that occasion were 65 ells (about 74 metres) of linen cloth. His father Gillis had come from a linen town – Haarlem in the Province of Holland – before 1616 when, on 10 December in the Dutch Church, he married Maria Jacobs, daughter of the Peter Jacobs who was wrongly accused of selling linen by retail. Peter Jacobs had come from Antwerp to London in 1573, the year in which the Duke of Alva, after doing his utmost to suppress Calvinism there by force, retired as Governor of Antwerp. For a while the city then seemed safe enough for many Protestants to return there, but three years later Peter Jacobs must have blessed his decision to leave when he did: on 4 November 1576 the occupying Spanish army, who had not been paid for months, mutinied and sacked the city in the mindless outburst of murder and pillage known ever since as the 'Spanish Fury'.

In the early 1580s Antwerp was again officially Calvinist, before becoming finally and even peacefully Catholic in 1585. Thereafter the city even enjoyed a little golden age in the early seventeenth century, the period of the painters Rubens and

Van Dyck, when new churches were built and old ones restored and re-embellished with pictures and sculptures. But in
1627-8 Rubens wrote of his city as slowly dying and devoid of
all trade and industry, and a decade earlier grass was said to be
growing in the streets, a metaphorical if not an actual sign of
the city's economic decline. Antwerp had been an international port in the late Middle Ages, but the silting up of the
River Scheldt during the sixteenth century was worsened by
disuse after the Hollanders blockaded the river mouth. (The
modern port is connected to the sea by a ship canal.) But
manufacture as well as trade declined then. After the settlement of 1585 those Protestants who remained were given four
years either to convert to Rome or to settle up and leave, and
among those who left at that time were some six hundred
textile workers who took their families and their skills to
Haarlem, which became famous for the manufacture of bleached
linen.

In the eighteenth century Peter Le Neve, one of John Vanbrugh's fellow Heralds, put down some rough notes about the
Vanbrugh family, including that 'Gyles Vanbrugh fled from
Flanders in the Duke D'alvas persecution lived in Stevens
Wabrook dyed there – day of – 1646'. If this is so, Gyles (Gillis)
must have been at least eighty when he died, and it is very
likely that Le Neve missed out a generation: that in fact it was
the father of Gillis who fled from Antwerp and went in the first
emigration of textile workers to Haarlem, and that Gillis was
born there and, as we know, came thence to London, leaving
parents and siblings behind in Holland.

When Gillis made his will on 2 February 1646 he mentioned
money, goods and merchandise which he had lent to his sons
William and Giles 'to make them a stocke'; he now bequeathed
his loans in equal shares to them and their younger brother
Peter, who was not yet thirteen when their father died in the
third week of June 1646. Gillis left three houses in Walbrook
Ward, which he had bought from Sir John Sidley, and a property in Battersea which was then a pleasant Surrey market-
gardening village; a certificate of 1641 states that he was living
there for most of the year.

William Vanbrugh was almost eighteen and Giles just fifteen
when Gillis died. How soon they actually set up in business we

do not know; in an era when childhood was seen as a phase to be outgrown more than enjoyed, it is quite probable that they had started under their father's direction. After his death they would have been helped by the husbands of their three elder sisters, Maria, Sara, and Anna: Peter Matthews Janson, Peter Matthews Baldwin, and Simon Delboe. These three were all London merchants. Peter Matthews Janson, of the Dutch Church, described himself in his will (19 February 1658) as of the parish of St Laurence Pountney, which adjoined that of St Nicholas Acons on the south; like his father-in-law he also owned property in Battersea. Peter Matthews Baldwin's father also attended the Dutch Church. He came from Haarlem; in 1612 he was a thread-twister living near St Clement Eastcheap, and he was later described as a merchant. Peter was born in 1617, and at the age of forty became a freeman of the Mercers' Company by redemption, a form of admission which involved a fee but no apprenticeship. The Mercers were originally silk-mercers and dealt in expensive kinds of fabric. In 1671 Peter was Warden of the Mercers' Company, and he was the owner, as already mentioned, of a set of Mortlake 'Flower Pots' tapestries. Simon Delboe was probably a Huguenot; the inhabitants of Elbeuf, a town in the region of Rouen noted for its woollen products, are known as *Elboviens*. Delboe made a will in 1671 before going to the Far East – he died in Siam (Thailand) five years later – and referred in it to a bond made to the East India Company by himself and two other merchants, Francis Lodwicke and Thomas Breton, who was the brother-in-law of Giles and William Vanbrugh.

Their younger brother Peter grew up in this circle, but by the age of twenty-one when he made a will (1654) he was in Smyrna (Izmir) in Turkey. His bequests of over £3000 must have come largely from his inheritance, but once again there are connections with the cloth trade. In the seventeenth century English exports to Turkey included Suffolk and Gloucester woollens as well as kersey, a coarse narrow wool cloth, and also flannel, drugget and fine white cloth from Salisbury, while returning traders brought damasks and camlets. In 1688 the English 'factory' or warehouse in Smyrna burned down after an earthquake, with the destruction of 1000 bales of cloth. Peter Vanbrugh probably died abroad, for his will was proved on 8 March 1658 but he was not buried (in the family vault) until 28 May.

A little is known about the education of Peter and Giles. Their father made a small legacy to Peter's tutor Mr Hermanns, and it may well be that Hermanns had previously taught William and Giles. From Giles's own account (in a letter of 1678) he travelled as a young man in France and Italy 'for my Pleasure and Improvement', including a whole year in Rome. This was in the 1650s; he may have used some of his inheritance to finance his travels, but he was probably also an overseas agent or trader and thus at least partly paying his way. Giles wrote a good clear hand very like that of his close contemporary Sir Christopher Wren; this is a sign of the standard of his education and of the importance he must have placed on proper tuition for his son John. Giles probably spoke good London English, with perhaps a trace of the accent of his father who had remained Dutch enough to be taken for an alien by the Battersea assessor in 1641. Giles's son John's speech would have been completely English, with a gentility of accent derived from his mother and reinforced by his father's ambition to be classed as a gentleman. We do not know what happened to Gillis's house in Battersea, but by the autumn of 1659 William Vanbrugh had followed his father's example and moved into Surrey. The nature of William's trading stock is not known, but the fact that he was able to move progressively further from the City while carrying on his business suggests that it involved money and property – capital, credit and risks – more than particular commodities. He certainly dealt in real estate. In 1646 he had bought, with his brother-in-law Peter Matthews Baldwin (and perhaps partly with a legacy from Gillis), a house in St Laurence Pountney which was in 1661 inhabited by another member of the family (Maria Matthews Janson, née Vanbrugh, and her second husband Gerrard Weyman); after the Great Fire this house, or its site, was sold. William may also, like his kinsmen Simon Delboe and Thomas Breton, have been involved in the financing of trading ships. What can be said with certainty, though not with clarity, is that, in the Vanbrugh and Carleton family circles, from the frequency with which his name appears in legal documents it was a rare pie that was free of William's finger.

By the late summer of 1659, then, William and Dorothy Vanbrugh were living in Morden, where the principal landowner,
George Garth, was married to Dorothy's cousin Anne Carleton.
'A maidservant of Mr Vanbrughs' was buried there on 5 August.
In 1663-4 Morden was certified as William's 'constant habitation' and his house was a substantial one since it was taxed on
fifteen hearths. But by 1668 the family had moved to a dwelling
of about equal size, fourteen hearths, in Walton-on-Thames,
beyond Hampton Court but still handy for the City by water.

William had married Dorothy Carleton at Carshalton,
Surrey, on 21 January 1652. One of the witnesses was Dorothy's cousin Thomas Carleton, gentleman, of Carshalton,
who is elsewhere described as a merchant of London, and a
freeman of the Mercers' Company. Thus it was perhaps
through business associations that William met Dorothy, the
third daughter of Sir Dudley Carleton and Lucy Croft. Their
marriage forged family links between the London Dutch and
not only the native English merchant community but also the
wider social circle of the Carletons. William's younger brother
and Dorothy's younger sister became, as we have seen, the
parents of John Vanbrugh; it would be of great significance for
John, when he was grown up, that he was an indirect descendant and a direct heir of Viscount Dorchester.

Lord Dorchester had been born Dudley Carleton of Bright-
well Baldwin, Oxfordshire, in 1574. He received a knighthood
from James I in 1610 and in the next eighteen years was suc-
cessively ambassador to Venice, The Hague and Paris. In 1628
he was created Viscount Dorchester and appointed Principal
Secretary of State, dying in that office in February 1632. The
heirs to his estate and that of his elder brother George Carleton
of Huntercombe (died 1627) were George's three sons, Sir
John, Bt, Sir George, Bt, and Sir Dudley. The two elder brothers
seem to have inherited the greater part of the Carleton lands,
while Sir Dudley received chiefly money and goods. Sir Dudley
had no sons but was survived by five daughters. The eldest,
Anne (by his first wife Barbara van Duick), married John
Ferrers of Tamworth Castle, to whom there is a fine monument in Tamworth Church, jointly with their son Sir Humphrey Ferrers. Anne outlived both husband and son and was
buried in Westminster Abbey.

Sir Dudley's second wife was Lucy Croft, daughter of Sir Herbert Croft of Croft Castle, Herefordshire; her elder brother Herbert was Dean and (from 1661) Bishop of Hereford. Lucy bore Sir Dudley four daughters, Lucy, Mary, and the Dorothy and Elizabeth who married Vanbrughs. Lucy married the London merchant Thomas Breton, whom we have already met. Mary married Edward Pearce, gentleman, of Parson's Green, Fulham, where Pepys rented a weekend villa in 1677-81; Pearce was also 'of Whitlingham' which is near (and now a suburb of) Norwich. At his death Pearce left two houses on London Bridge as well as land around Whitlingham and stock in the East India Company; the extent to which these families intertwined their finances before the days of investment banks is indicated by the mention in Pearce's will of an indenture made over the Whitlingham estate by the Pearces, John Ferrers and Bishop Croft. Two of the Pearce boys became generals in the British Army; the elder, Edward, married Frances the daughter of Sir Christopher Lovett who traded in Turkey before setting up as a linen merchant in Dublin. The son of this marriage was Sir Edward Lovett Pearce, the Irish Palladian architect, who was both the cousin and probably the pupil of Sir John Vanbrugh.*

Sir Dudley Carleton's will is long and complex not only because it provided for his five daughters but also because his concerns were manifold. To Anne Ferrers he had previously given a good dowry when she married in 1649, so he left her an inlaid cabinet, his signet ring, and unspecified property in the United Provinces where he had been His Majesty's Resident (a lower office than that of ambassador). To Lucy he left £1100 upon her marriage or at the age of twenty-one, and an additional £400 on complicated conditions involving the conveyancing of estates at Walton-on-Thames to Edward Bellamy, fishmonger of London; these estates were the subject of an agreement between Bellamy, Thomas Carleton (witness to Dorothy's marriage) and Sir Dudley. Sir Dudley died in March 1654 and it was at least ten years later that William and Dorothy Vanbrugh moved to Walton-on-Thames; there was perhaps no connection between their property and Sir Dudley's.

* p. 443

To Mary, Sir Dudley left £1500 on marriage or at the age of twenty-one, without further conditions. To Dorothy, who was already married and had received a dowry, he left £20 to buy a mourning ring, while her husband William Vanbrugh received £500 for his pains as executor. After he sold Imber Court, his house near Esher, in 1649, Sir Dudley lived in Clerkenwell, just north of Smithfield, and fifteen minutes' walk from St Paul's. He must have been impressed by the business ability of his young son-in-law, who was then living in the City and was the head of the Vanbrugh family. To Elizabeth, his youngest daughter, Sir Dudley left only £800 in money and some investments which he expected to 'prove troublesome'. The will of her mother, who had died in 1648, was still unsettled, and the portion smaller than those of her sisters may have been allotted in the expectation that the difference would be made up from her mother's estate.

When Elizabeth Carleton married Thomas Barker early in 1655 she was described as of St Stephen Walbrook; she was no more than eighteen and had probably been living, since her father's death, in the Walbrook house of Dorothy and William Vanbrugh. Giles, who would later be her second husband, was then abroad. Like many English visitors to Rome he lunched dangerously with the Jesuits at the Venerable English College, on 6 September 1654. A few months later, the day before the first reading of the Barker-Carleton banns of marriage in London, on 22 January 1655, he signed himself *Giles Vanbrook* in the register of the University of Padua. This was also common practice among English and Scottish travellers; it did not indicate any intention of studying, but provided a useful identification for a stranger in Venetian territory.

Thomas Barker and his two brothers were lawyers. It is as simplistic to say that seventeenth-century marriages were arranged as it is unrealistic to say that they were love-matches. Even today, when Western culture at least believes in the romance of true loves, it does not take much consideration of our own circles of acquaintance for most of us to recall successful matches that grew either from chance or unexpected meetings or from proximity at work or long and casual familiarity. Seventeenth-century City society may have been closely knit but it was not closed. It would be unjust therefore to suggest that Barker was an attractive match for Elizabeth Carleton either because he was prosperous or because a lawyer in the family would be useful, even if we can imagine that at the wedding breakfast someone jocularly put forward the latter reason. Thomas was also the second son of a baronet, Sir John Barker of Grimston, Suffolk, and he was ten or eleven years older than his bride. After graduating at Pembroke College, Cambridge, he had been admitted to Gray's Inn in 1645.

The marriage, however, was short-lived; by May 1656 Thomas had died, leaving an infant daughter, Elizabeth. His younger brother Robert, named as executor in his will, had also died, and probate was therefore granted to their elder brother, Sir John the second Baronet, who thus inherited most of Thomas's estate properties in various parts of England. Thomas left £2000 or its equivalent in property in trust for little Elizabeth until her marriage or majority. To his widow he left provision for their daughter's upbringing and education, out of the income from properties around Croft in Herefordshire that had been part of her marriage settlement and must have come to her in the first place from her mother, Lucy Croft. The new administration of Lucy's will obtained by Elizabeth Barker in December 1655 may have concerned these properties but the timing is very close: this was only about two months before Thomas became ill, making his will on 25 February 1656. Thomas was buried at Grimston and his widow probably returned with their baby daughter to the care, if not indeed the London house, of William and Dorothy Vanbrugh. Some time later Giles Vanbrugh returned from his foreign travels; he and Elizabeth were married, as we have seen, on 15 October 1659 when she was still only twenty-two.

Every large family has one aunt who knows who everyone is and how they are all related; the rest of the family have a vaguer knowledge of a range of uncles, aunts and cousins. Young John Vanbrugh's imagination must have been caught by Uncle Simon who died in Siam and Uncle Peter who went to Turkey, if not by Great-Uncle Herbert the bishop, the Caves of Stanford, the Verneys of Claydon, the Ferrers of Tamworth, or the Earl and Countess of Arran. Only perhaps when he began to seek advancement in the wide world would the more distant but loftier connections become of any interest to him; then he would claim his kinship with the seventh Earl of Huntingdon and acknowledge that with the Berties, Earls of Lindsey.

These connections are too complicated to describe in words and only make sense in a rather elaborate diagram. They are so obscure that, although quite genuine, their existence was not suspected until the discovery of the letters in which Vanbrugh mentioned them. They involve second marriages and connections with those daughters and younger sons whom compilers of peerage handbooks usually ignore. But since Vanbrugh was aware of these, he certainly knew that his kinsmen included the Earls of Berkshire, Carlisle, Dorset and Suffolk, Earls Rivers and Stanhope, and Baron Cornwallis – a list in which we find both some of his architectural patrons and some of his associates in the Kit-Cat Club. An appeal to Lord Huntingdon obtained his entry to the army; his association with the Berties led not only to the society life of Westminster but also to a French prison. The third Earl of Carlisle was both a Kit-Cat member and Vanbrugh's most constant patron. The facts that his Yorkshire palace, Castle Howard, is Vanbrugh's apprentice work in architecture, and that Carlisle obtained for him the offices of both Comptroller of Her Majesty's Works and Clarenceux Herald, are a little easier to understand once we know of the family connection.

4

Exodus

On Wednesday 7 May 1665 Samuel Pepys saw with alarm 'a sad sight ... being the first of the kind that, to my remembrance, I ever saw': in Drury Lane were 'two or three houses marked with a red cross upon the doors, and "God have mercy upon us" writ there'. Bubonic plague had been smouldering in London and south-east England since the last two serious outbreaks of 1603 and 1625, although the number of deaths reported in the capital had recently declined from twenty in 1661 to only five in 1664. Already in May 1665, however, there were forty-three fatalities and a smaller number of recoveries. In the first six days of June alone there were another forty-three deaths. Pepys suddenly felt that he smelled bad; he had to buy some tobacco – believed to be a prophylactic – to smell and chew 'which took away the apprehension'.

By 28 June the week's total was 267, and John Evelyn recorded in his diary that because of the increase the Royal Society had decided to close its programme of weekly meetings (at Gresham College in Bishopsgate) earlier in the summer than usual. Dr Christopher Wren had already arranged a trip to Paris, ostensibly to meet French scientists but certainly with the intention of seeing the architect François Mansart and the great Italian sculptor and architect Gianlorenzo Bernini who was in France that summer. Increasingly those who had somewhere else to be and the means to be there were judging it prudent to leave London.

We know today that, unlike the pneumonic plague of the

Black Death in the fourteenth century, which was spread by droplet to the lungs and was almost always fatal, the bubonic variety was a disease in rats transmitted first to humans by the bites of rat-fleas and thence easily from person to person by the common flea. Thus it was the poor and the overcrowded who were most at risk, and the affluent and the fastidious who were, even if infected, most likely to be among the 30 per cent who recovered. The areas outside the City walls and the East End were worse affected than the City itself, though this outbreak seems to have started in Westminster and spread eastwards along Holborn and the Strand. This detracts nothing from the dedication of those City aldermen, doctors, clergymen and others who stayed at their posts and tried to keep a semblance of normality in London life. Such a one was Dr Robert Breton, Evelyn's parson at Deptford and Thomas Breton's nephew.

On 1 July Pepys heard of seven or eight houses in Basinghall Street near the Guildhall 'shut up of the plague'. Since it was believed to be spread by contagion or through the air, once a house had one case of the sickness it was sealed up with the rest of its unfortunate occupants inside. The following day the King and Court left Whitehall for Hampton Court; on 5 July Pepys found St James's Park 'quite locked up'. The weekly Bills of Mortality printed by the Parish Clerks' Company ensured that the number of deaths was public knowledge, but did nothing to dispel rumours like the 'odd story' related by Pepys of 'Alderman Bence's stumbling at night over a dead corps in the streete, and going home and telling his wife, she at the fright, being with child, fell sicke and died of the plague'.

By 16 August the weekly toll had reached 3880: Pepys noted 'the streets empty of people', the Royal Exchange deserted, 'and about us two shops in three, if not more, generally shut up'. In September the figures reached 7000, both Pepys and Evelyn believing the true number nearer ten thousand 'partly from the poor that cannot be taken notice of, through the greatness of the number, and partly from the Quakers and others that will not have any bell ring for them'. The parish bell was rung both at the hour of death and at the time of a funeral, and at the height of the plague all the other sounds of the City were thrown into mournful relief by the nearly continuous tolling of bells. Walking from Southwark to St James's, Evelyn found the streets full of coffins and 'thin of people, the shops shut up, and all in mournefull silence, as not knowing whose turn might be next'.

On 5 January 1666 Pepys observed that the City was 'full, compared with what it used to be', but 'Covent-Garden and Westminster are yet very empty of people, no Court nor gentry being there'. But although deaths were below 100 a week and Pepys's office and family had returned to Seething Lane the plague was by no means exhausted, and its persistence through the depths of winter was taken to mean that it would continue and flare up again in the spring. The Royal Society meetings began again on 21 February, but London, which lost altogether a quarter of its population to the epidemic, was by no means yet back to normal.

The last record of Giles and Elizabeth Vanbrugh in London is on 18 January 1665, when a daughter, Elizabeth, was christened at St Nicholas Acons; it is very unlikely that they remained in the City after midsummer 1665, although we do not know where they went. On 1 February 1666 Francis, son of Thomas and Lucy Breton, was baptized at Morden; perhaps the Bretons had even taken refuge there in William Vanbrugh's house of fifteen hearths. Some similar arrangement must have been made by Giles and Elizabeth, but if they went first to Morden they did not stay there. For we know that during the first half of 1666 Elizabeth bore another daughter, Anna Maria; she was not registered at Morden and the family must have been elsewhere.

If the situation in London did not press Giles to return, the fact that England was at war with the Dutch, on the direct issue of overseas trade, may have added to the inertia of even so anglicized a merchant as he had become. Whatever the reason, it was to be compounded by the disaster of September 1666.

Fires in the largely wooden city were common enough not to attract more than very local notice. At about three o'clock in the morning of Sunday 2 September Pepys and his wife were woken by one of their servants, who had been preparing overnight for a feast, 'to tell us of a great fire they saw in the City'. From the window Pepys estimated it 'far enough off' and went back to bed. He rose again at about seven and, as daylight competed with the fire-glow, he thought it 'not so much as it was and farther off'. His mistake was soon apparent although, as there was a driving east wind, the fire that had started in a bakery in Pudding Lane near London Bridge moved west-wards and away from his house.

Public servant that he was, Pepys took a boat up river to Whitehall, noting as he passed that the steeple of St Laurence Pountney had already fallen. He told the King and the Duke of York that only demolition in the path of the fire could stop its progress. This was a common practice, and great hooks on poles were kept in churches for pulling down local house frames in an emergency. King Charles accordingly gave Pepys orders to the Lord Mayor for any demolition that might be necessary. But few people as yet appreciated how far from the ordinary this fire was; even so the Lord Mayor had not waited on orders but had given his own. He told Pepys, who met him in Cannon Street, that people would not obey him and in any case the fire was moving too fast. Pepys walked home, seeing people distracted and helpless as the warehouses towards Thames Street hissed and roared with burning pitch, tar, brim-stone, sugar, oil, and brandy. Churches were being filled with goods 'by people who themselves should have been quietly there at this time'. The streets were full of horses and carts, and people who were removing belongings to one house and then again to another as the heat and flames drew nearer. The river was 'full of lighters and boats taking in goods, and good goods swimming in the water, and only I observed that barely one lighter or boat in three that had the goods of a house in, but there was a pair of Virginalls in it'.

By mid afternoon the fire was leaping whole blocks, sparks and the hot wind being enough to start a new flame. After nightfall Pepys began to pack up his own goods, and at day-break on Monday a cart was arranged for him to take his money and plate 'and best things' to Sir William Rider's at Bethnal Green, a couple of miles away to the north. He spent much of Monday and also Tuesday morning moving not only personal effects but the contents of the Navy Office, many of them to a barge near Tower Hill. With two colleagues he dug a pit in the garden for their wines, his cheese and some other things. On Wednesday morning he sent his wife, two servants and his gold — about £2350 — in a boat down river to Woolwich, although as it turned out his precautions were unnecessary.

The smoke drifted as far as Oxford. On Tuesday St Paul's was alight, the stones flying, as Evelyn wrote, like grenades, molten lead from the roof streaming down the streets towards the river. In this fierce heat the churches into which people had taken their goods acted as brick and stone ovens until their roofs caught fire and consumed everything below them; fortunately for historians many parish officers had the presence of mind to rescue their registers.

By Thursday the wind had changed and abated; desperate measures involving the blowing up of houses had at last been effective, and the fire was dying. A mass of timber baulks was floating in the river between the current and the tide; it was the stock of the King's Works at Whitehall which had been thrown into the Thames in case the fire should reach that far. The King rode out to Moorfields and addressed the crowd of refugees and others gathered there. He denied the various rumours that the French or the Dutch or the Catholics had started the fire and declared it an Act of God. A week later he issued a proclamation: a new city would be built of brick and stone, with streets wide enough to break fire. London was in fact rebuilt mostly on the old street pattern, to save time and get the City back in business as quickly as possible. But the Building Act of 1667 laid down legal standards for fire-resistant building materials, the thickness of walls and the raising of party walls as fire-breaks through roofs. Few lives had been lost, but three-quarters of the City had been destroyed: 13,000 houses, 44 company halls, 87 churches, St Paul's, and most other public buildings.

Such were the will of the people and the resilience of the City that five years later the population had almost recovered in numbers: the registers of St Stephen Walbrook had returned by 1672 to the pre-fire statistics, but the family names were quite new ones. Only among the burials would the Vanbrughs and their relatives by marriage continue to be entered as one generation followed another to the vault purchased by old Gillis.

In February 1667 Giles Vanbrugh was probably in London when he petitioned for the release of his linen cloth from Customs. Four months later Elizabeth bore him a son, christ-

ened Carleton Vanbrugh at Richmond, Surrey on 6 June. But by
the autumn the family had moved to Chester, where the little
boy was buried at Holy Trinity on 13 October. Within thirty
years of John Vanbrugh's death, Theophilus Cibber's *Lives of
the Poets* (1753) would say that he was 'descended from an ancient family in Cheshire, which came originally from France;
though by the name it would appear to be of Dutch extraction'.
Theophilus Cibber was the son of the playwright Colley
Cibber, who was certainly intimate with Vanbrugh in the late
1690s. But Theophilus was only twenty-three when Vanbrugh
died, and the *Lives* were mainly compiled by Dr Samuel Johnson's amanuensis Robert Shiels. More of his brief biography
can be disproved than can be credited, but Giles would no
doubt have been pleased at the thought of a Cheshire ancestry.

Blome's *Britannia* (1673), which lists the nobility and gentry
in each county, includes 'Giles Vanbrough of Chester, gent',
and he was one of the most prosperous Chester citizens of the
time, although little is known of his activities and nothing of
the source of his prosperity. The 1812 edition of David Erskine
Baker's *Biographia Dramatica* adds nothing of moment, but
Chalmers's *General Biographical Dictionary* (XXIX, 1816) is
more significant. It quotes Blome and tells us that Giles was, 'it
is supposed, a sugar-baker, where he acquired an ample fortune'. This supposition seems to be the speculative source of
the one thing everyone today knows about Giles Vanbrugh:
that he was a sugar-baker. What happens next is instructive.
Allan Cunningham (*Lives of the Most Eminent British Painters,
Sculptors and Architects*, IV, 1831) is cautious:

> Of the senior Vanbrugh it is said, I know not on what authority,
> that he was a sugar-baker, and lived in the city of Chester. The
> first of these assertions is unlikely to be true; such a trade was
> better fitted for London than Chester – besides, Blome in his
> Britannia writes him gentleman, and he is elsewhere styled
> esquire.

In Cunningham's next paragraph Giles's career is still confused with that of his nephew the younger William Vanbrugh.
But literary biographers of the nineteenth century did not
share Cunningham's scepticism. Leigh Hunt, in the preface to

his one-volume edition of plays by Wycherley, Congreve, Vanbrugh and Farquhar (1840), repeats merely that Giles 'is reported to have settled in Chester as a sugar-baker, and to have acquired such a fortune as appears to have lifted him into the ranks of gentry'. In subsequent accounts the report becomes a certainty, the picturesque appeal of the idea no doubt helped by vague memories of continental *patissiers* and confectioners, although it later came to be understood that sugar baking in the late seventeenth century was not the making of sweets but the refining of raw sugar.

Since even unlikely historical suppositions often embody a grain of truth and no previous biographer seems to have explored the subject, it may be worth doing so. The English sugar refiners stated in 1671 that the number of sugar houses had grown in twenty years from eight to nearly thirty, chiefly from the increased importation of raw sugar, 5000 tons in that year, from British plantations in New England and Barbados. Three pounds of brown sugar yielded less than one pound of the refined product, and the refiners were already facing competition from Dutch, French and Portuguese producers. Competition and an expanding market were reducing the price. The household accounts of the Earls of Bedford at Woburn show that in 1671 ordinary refined sugar cost 6d. a pound, as against 8¼d. in 1655, while a 'double refined' grade cost 1s. 3d. instead of 2s. There were at least three other grades, including 'smooth' which in 1655 cost 4s. a pound and white candy at 2s. 6d. During the 1670s and 1680s prices dropped further.

Ports, especially those on the west coast, were the obvious locations for refineries, which after the Industrial Revolution would come to be concentrated in London and Liverpool. In the 1670s Allyn Smith ran a refinery in partnership with John and Samuel Danvers at Battersea. That was the village where old Gillis Vanbrugh had had his suburban residence; after the Restoration Battersea and Vauxhall to the north-east saw the arrival of several industries which were best situated outside the city because of their smoke or their smell: these included the manufacture of chemicals, lime, glass, and pottery, while sugar processing also used a great deal of fuel. Allyn Smith had previously negotiated for the establishment of a sugar-house

in Liverpool on property belonging to Edward Moores of Bank
Hall. Moores drew up an annotated rent-roll of his Liverpool
properties in 1667-8; among them was one which he called
'sugar-house close' because 'one Mr Smith, a great sugarbaker
at London, a man, as report says, worth forty thousand pounds,
came from London on purpose to treat with me'. Smith proposed to build along the whole frontage of twenty-seven yards
'a stately house of good hewn stone, four story high, and then to
go through the same building with a large entry: and then, on
the back side, to erect a house for boiling and drying sugar,
otherwise called a sugar baker's house'. Moores estimated that
the building would cost £1400 and that the project would bring
£40,000 a year in trade from Barbados.

Besides the Danvers–Smith refinery there was one in
Vauxhall. This had been built by an engineer named Gaspar or
Caspar Kalthof or Colthoffe, who in 1664 was assessed on
twenty-seven hearths; his son-in-law, one Peter Jacobson, was
granted leases from the Duchy of Cornwall for the property in
the parish on 26 October 1666 and 23 February 1667. Jacobson
claimed that his outlay on construction and improvement had
amounted to £7600. In 1675 the factory seems to have been acquired by the inventor and hydraulic engineer Sir Samuel
Morland, who put it to other uses.

The sparse documentation of the Vanbrughs in Chester
offers nothing to suggest that Cunningham's scepticism was
unjustified although, as we shall now see, there was indeed a
sugar refiner who was a neighbour and associate of Giles.

— 5 —

Numbers

The Chester sugar business was in the hands of the Henthornes, who occupied a group of buildings on the east side of
Weavers Lane, between Common Hall Lane and Whitefriars
Lane, incorporating part of the medieval Whitefriars, which at
the Dissolution of the Monasteries had been acquired by the
[B] Egerton family. On Alexander De Lavaux's large city plan of
1745 the sugar house itself is marked as a building equidistant

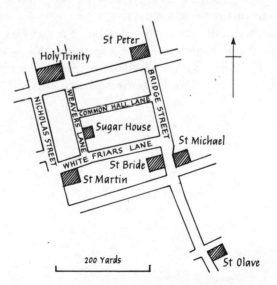

B   Chester. The area round the Sugar House. Based on Alexander de Lavaux's
map of 1745.

from Common Hall and Whitefriars Lanes. In an early
eighteenth-century view of Chester from the south, at Wilton
House, the building can be seen rising above its neighbours   **[C]**
between the steeples of St Olave's and Holy Trinity, smoke curling from its several chimneys.

Records are sparse, but it appears that in 1651 all or part of
the premises was leased from John Egerton, second Earl of
Bridgwater and his co-owners by Richard Harrison, a Chester
beer-brewer; subsequently Harrison, who was sherriff and
alderman in 1662 and Mayor in 1667-8, both bought and sold
leases on parts of the property. Finally in September 1679, the
year before his death, Harrison sold his interest in the 'White
Friars' and the other messuages adjoining it to Anthony Henthorne, but the latter seems to have already rented the principal dwelling house on the site since at least 1672. In that year
it was used for non-conformist meetings conducted by William
Cooke, after he had been ejected from the living of St
Michael's, Chester. Cooke was given a licence on 8 May 1672 to
use a house described as 'the Grey Friars' and identified as
Presbyterian, but another document of 16 May refers to him as
Congregationalist and in the house of Anthony Henthorne, in
other words Whitefriars. In 1678 Henthorne was made a freeman of the city, and contemporary records leave no doubt at all
that his business was sugar refining. In January 1686 his son
Samuel was described in a marriage contract as half-owner of
'The Friars'. Samuel became a freeman in July of that year (the
printed register calls him *Hawborne*) as did his brother John in
December 1688.

One of the difficulties, however, in tracing the relation between properties and occupiers in the Whitefriars area is that
it was divided between the parishes of three churches: Holy
Trinity opposite the north end of Weavers Lane, St Martin's at
the south end, and St Bride's (or Bridget's) to the east at the
corner of Whitefriars Lane and Bridge Street. In 1680
Henthorne was assessed for tax on his house, sugar house and
garden in St Bridget's, and in 1685 for the 'Fryary' in St
Martin's.

Chester Hearth Tax records are fragmentary, but they show
that in 1671-2 Giles Vanbrugh was taxed on a house of nine
hearths in St Martin's and one of seven hearths in St Bridget's.

In 1673-4 the latter had passed to Henthorne, and it is perhaps through a misreading of such evidence that Giles was first thought to have been a sugar-baker. There are no assessments showing the Vanbrughs in Holy Trinity, the third parish, but the church records show that they lived there consistently, from the funeral of the infant Carleton on 13 October 1667 to Giles's own burial on 19 July 1689, and including the christening of the twelve children Elizabeth Vanbrugh bore in Chester. It was not a matter, either, of living in one parish and worshipping in another, for Giles paid the poor rate to Holy Trinity. In 1669 his charge for this was 16s., the same amount as his neighbour Sir Peter Pindar, collector of customs. The charge varied from one year to the next, but Giles was always among the highest rated and therefore the best accommodated. In 1675, like Pindar, he paid 13s. in a total rate, from 111 occupiers, of £17. 5s. He paid 9s.9d. in 1680 and 21s. in 1688. (The year after his death 'Madam Vanbrugh' paid 6s. and by 1691 she had evidently left the parish.)

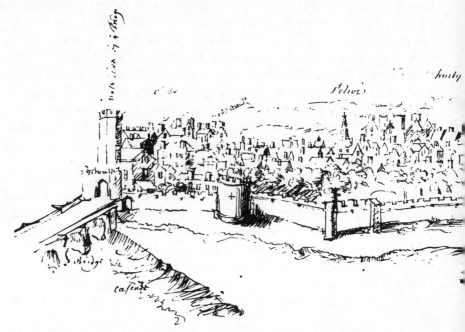

It was also in respect of his house in Holy Trinity that Giles brushed with the law on the only known occasion. The Quarter Sessions summons lists offer a constant picture of a community corporately house-proud but individually opportunist. The commonest misdemeanours were selling beer and ale without a licence, keeping hogs, and having broken pavements or gutters; there were occasional charges of keeping a house of bad – in one case very bad – repute, and a man was taken to court for not only having had 'carnal copulation' with two women on the same day but also bragging about it. One summons was 'for keeping 7 loads of gorse in his back side', a charge less strange than it sounds to modern ears, since gorse was grown as a crop and had, among many other uses, that of fuel for bakers' ovens. 'Muck hills' were not uncommon, and on 18 September 1679 in Holy Trinity Ward 'Mr Vanbrough for a Dunghill' was listed. We do not know what penalty he incurred.

Giles was to have other associations with Anthony Hen-

C Chester from the south-east c.1700 (The Earl of Pembroke). The Sugar House is the building to the right of St Olave's, with smoke issuing from the chimneys. However, it should be noted that the draughtsman hás taken considerable liberties with distance and perspective. As the plan (Fig. B) shows, St Olave's, St Bride's and St Michael's are much nearer to the viewpoint of the drawing than the Sugar House, Holy Trinity and St Peter's.

thorne. The latter witnessed Giles's will in 1683, and the non-
conformism which led him to give shelter to the preacher
William Cooke produced another connection through the
famous dissenting minister Matthew Henry. William Tong's
biography of Henry (1716) tells how Henthorne, 'always forward to promote the Gospel in Chester', offered the dissenting
congregation the use of his house. As the numbers grew, they
moved to a large out-building of the Friary which belonged to
Henthorne, and converted it into a chapel in the space of a
week. It was also, according to Tong, Henthorne who 'having
occasion to go up to London brought along with him the
Wishes of all of the People' and invited Henry to Chester,
where he arrived in June 1687. Tong continues:

> Several worthy Gentlemen that had their Habitations there ...
> were not altogether Strangers to Mr. *Henry* before he came to
> live among them, but now they came to be his very intimate
> Acquaintance; some of these, as Alderman *Mainwaring* and Mr.
> *Vanbrugh*, Father to *Sir John Vanbrugh*, were in communion
> with the Church of *England*, but they heard Mr. *Henry* on the
> Week-day Lectures, and always treated him with great and
> sincere Respect.

Other moderate dissenters in Chester, according to Tong, were
George Booth, a lawyer related to the Earl of Warrington, and
Richard Kenrick, Esq., 'a Gentleman of very good Sense,
pleasant and instructive Conversation, and truly Religious,
happy in his Yoke-fellow and Children, a true lover of Mr.
Henry's Ministry'. Both were Giles's neighbours. Booth is listed
as Esquire in Blome's *Britannia*. Giles named one of his
children Kenrick (b. 1678) after this happy gentleman, and
both Giles and Kenrick are mentioned in the diary of Sir
Willoughby Aston of Aston, Bt. Much of Aston's four folio
volumes concerns his health, and his handwriting is atrocious,
but he met Giles several times and the diary adds to our knowledge of the Chester circle. In August 1685 Aston consulted
Giles and Mr Kenrick about apprenticing his son Willoughby
to an India merchant.

On 15 February 1682 at a coffee-house Vanbrugh showed
Aston 'the booke of the new digestorie which I afterwards

bought one of in Town'. This was *A New Digester or Engine for Softening Bones*, published in 1681 by Denis Papin (1647-1712?), an inventor and pneumatic engineer born in Blois, who came to England in 1675. On 3 July 1679 Papin had demonstrated his digester to the Royal Society, of which he was elected a Fellow the following year and to which he dedicated his book. Evelyn saw the demonstration, and believed that the secret was 'a liquor, in which flesh or fish being boiled, the bones were rendred as soft as marrow'. On 12 April 1682 Evelyn went with other Fellows to a supper cooked in the device, and wrote in his diary an enthusiastic and indeed rather exaggerated account of its capacity for making the hardest bones 'as soft as Cheeze' without water or other liquor and on the heat of only a little charcoal. 'This Philosophical Supper', he concluded, 'raised much mirth amongst us, & exceedingly pleased all the Companie.' History does not relate how soon the pressure cooker – for such it was – reached Chester, but Giles's interest in the latest technology was evidently strong enough for him to make a convert in Sir Willoughby. Did young John, in London in 1681, buy a copy of Papin's book and bring it home with him?

The accidents of family history are fascinating. The first four children born to the Vanbrughs in Chester were all girls. Three of them lived to be eighty or over, the other to nearly sixty: Mary (b. 3 November 1668), Victoria (bapt. 25 January 1670), Elizabeth (bapt. 4 May 1671) and Robina (bapt. 22 September 1672). Then followed a run of mainly boys: Carleton (bapt. 18 September 1673), an infant buried unnamed on 31 August 1674, Giles (bapt. 3 September 1675), Catherine (bapt. 9 October 1676, buried 22 March 1678), Dudley (b. 21 October 1677), Kenrick (bapt. 21 November 1678), Charles (bapt. 27 February 1680), and Philip (bapt. 31 January 1682). Carleton and the last four boys lived into adulthood or beyond. Then after a total of twenty confinements in twenty-two years either Nature or Mrs Vanbrugh cried 'no more'.

Coincidence is the ground base of fiction and, for that very reason, the quicksand of historical writing. But it is also part of all our experience of life. Although most do not, some coincidences turn out to be capable of supporting useful hypotheses; since history advances by hypothesis as much as does any other science, no coincidence observed should be rejected out of hand without private thought if not exploration. Even so, some of the most promising enquiries lead to a dead end. There seems to be, for example, no good ascertainable reason why Giles moved as far as Chester, over two hundred miles from London. As a port it was not only small but in decline, and travellers to Ireland often went on to Holyhead to embark. The sugar trail seems to be quite false. In twenty-two years Giles never became a freeman of Chester, and that is surely because as a *gentleman* he lived by financial business rather than by trade or industry. The sensibility to social distinctions which John Vanbrugh displayed in later life would have been nurtured by his father's aspirations as well as his mother's kinship with gentry and nobility. We might speculate that some local if obscure connection with the Carletons led Giles and Elizabeth to Cheshire, or that Giles went to manage some enterprise financed by his brother William. Giles had previously dealt in linen. In 1665-6 James Butler, Duke of Ormonde, had put through the Irish Parliament a bill to promote the linen industry in Ireland. His younger son Richard, Earl of Arran, married the daughter of Anne Ferrers, Elizabeth Vanbrugh's half-sister. In later years the William Vanbrughs, father and son, had unspecified business in Ireland, and in the eighteenth century Chester imported Irish linen for local trade.

But none of this can be supported. We only know that in 1686 Giles took a twenty-one-year lease of the land known as the Salt Grass down by the river west of the city, and that a few years earlier he had some commercial dealings with Sir Thomas Grosvenor's estate at Eaton Hall. There are two entries in the accounts of Thomas Burton, Grosvenor's steward; the first implies that Giles was buying lead from Grosvenor's Flintshire mines:

Recd on the demaine account the sum of twenty pound July the 24th: 1678 which money came from Mr Vanbrought of lead money.

As a rough guide to the amount, this would have been enough lead in sheet form to roof a church the size of St Mary-le-Bow in London. Three years later Giles was among a number of vendors of grain of various kinds to the Grosvenor estate:

pd Mr Vanbrought decr the 21st 1681 for 3 Bushill of old oats att 8s.2 the bushill is 01 04 06.

Giles's will, made on 25 October 1683 (six years before his death), is suggestively but unspecifically comprehensive, especially in comparison with that of his father:

> Item I will that my Whole Estate wither houses Land or Mortages, Leases or Goods bonds or Moneys be all valewd or such part Sold as is judged convenient by My Executor, and then Equally devided into fourteen parts; whereof two parts I Give and bequeath unto My Eldest son John; one part to Lucy, one part to Anna Mary, one part to Mary, one part to Victoria, one part to Elisabeth, one part to Robina, one part to Carleton, one part to Giles, one part to Dudley, one part to Kendrick, one part to Charles, one part to Philip; and if any one of the younger children dye before the Age of Seaventeen, then his or her portion or Divident to bee Equally devided betwixt My four Eldest children herein now nominated.

John Vanbrugh's education also remains a mystery. It has usually been assumed, just because it was there, that he went to the King's School in Chester. But the assumption seems not to have been made until the nineteenth century and there is no mention in the school's records either of him or of Dudley, who went up to Oxford, or of any of the other brothers. It is therefore more likely that some of the boys were sent to school elsewhere or that with their sisters they had a tutor, as their uncle Peter Vanbrugh had done. Certainly the size of the family would have made this worthwhile. When John was seven his half-sister Barker was already fourteen; by the time John was fourteen Elizabeth Barker was married and there were five siblings aged seven or over and five younger. It is hardly possible to guess who their tutor or tutors might have been, but coincidence offers one possible candidate in the person of Dudley Garencieres.

Dudley was born about 1651, went to Westminster School and then in 1669 to Trinity College, Cambridge, where he graduated in 1673. He took Holy Orders, and was in Chester by May 1675 when he officiated at a wedding. Two years later he became a minor canon of the cathedral at an annual salary of

£20 and Rector of Waverton, but his 'mutining' nearly lost him the canonry at the start and he was fined £10 'for his neglect and contumacy' with the threat of expulsion if he did not reform. Evidently he did, for he went on to become Rector of Handley in 1684 and prebendary of Chester in 1696. In 1675 Elizabeth Barker was nineteen and four of her half-siblings were seven or older. A young and impecunious parson might be both tutor and suitor in the Vanbrugh household, and he was certainly the latter. On 3 May 1678 Peter de Garencieres of St Margaret, Westminster, applied for a marriage licence between Dudley de Garencieres of St Oswald, Chester, and Elizabeth Barker *alias* Vanbrugh and, although no record has been found of it at St Oswald's, Dudley and Elizabeth were married. Five of their sons did go to the King's School. Dudley was buried in Chester Cathedral on 8 April 1702. John Vanbrugh and his mother were among his executors, and his widow (*Sis: Garencieres* in Vanbrugh's account book) lived until 1728.

The eldest son of Dudley and Elizabeth became a parson like his father, and he was christened Theophilus. Neither this nor Dudley is a rare name in the seventeenth century, but their conjunction with Garencieres is suggestive of two connections. Dr Theophilus de Garencieres (1610-80) received his degree in medicine at Caen in 1636 and subsequently accompanied the French ambassador to London as his physician. He settled in England, and was incorporated M.D. at Oxford in 1657, shortly after 'relinquishing the Roman Church' in Anthony Wood's phrase. He published books on pulmonary phthisis (1647) and the plague (1665); the latter work, whose preface is dated 14 September, recommended as an antidote Venice treacle, a mysterious compound widely used at the time for all sorts of malady, which Pepys mentions taking on two occasions (9 February 1663 and 11 June 1665). The doctor wrote two other treatises of equally little value; that on *The Admirable Virtues and Wonderful Effects of Coral in Physick* (1676) was, according to Wood, an indirect cause of his death in poverty in Covent Garden. This little book was issued, according to the colophon, *From my House in Clerkenwell Close, the Second on the Left-hand*, and dedicated to Sir Walter Long. Wood wrote that the doctor's death was 'occasioned by the unworthy dealing of a *certain Knight*, which in a manner broke his Heart'. For:

Sir Walter Long of Wilts gave Garencieres 2 farthings wrapt up in a paper, instead of two guineas, as a reward for a book, which he taking very ill, occasioned sickness, and sickness death.

His name is not to be found in any of the likely parish registers, and there is no record of a marriage. But it would be reasonable to suppose that Dudley was his son and Theophilus his grandson. He was living in Clerkenwell near St James's church by 1665, perhaps earlier.

Moreover the connections with Clerkenwell and Covent Garden can be extended. On 30 November 1669 a licence was issued for the marriage at the Savoy Chapel between Paul Festeau, widower, of St Paul's, Covent Garden, aged about thirty-eight, and Mary de Garencieres of St James's, Clerkenwell, spinster, aged about twenty-four and at her own disposal. Festeau was a teacher and the author of a lively and comprehensive English grammar for French-speakers which ran to several editions and was eventually combined with a similar book, for English-speakers learning French, by Claude Mauger. The 1675 edition of Festeau's grammar contains a laudatory poem signed by Dudley Garencieres. And it is at least worth asking whether the Clerkenwell connection can be taken even further. In 1654 Sir Dudley Carleton died in Clerkenwell where he had moved after the sale of Imber Court five years previously. Dudley Garencieres was born about 1651; can he have been named after Sir Dudley Carleton, and is that the connection which took him to Chester?

At the end of 1678 Giles wrote a remarkable letter which reveals his orthodox Protestant allegiance, his respect for learning, and a degree of fantasy which would later be expressed in a very different way by his eldest son. From late September onwards London, and later the provinces, were gripped by the unfolding revelations of Titus Oates, a twenty-nine-year-old congenital liar of disreputable but evidently charismatic personality; these traits were compounded by his practising homosexuality and, in 1677, his wayward conversion to Roman Catholicism. His story was of a Jesuit plot, mas-

terminded by the Pope, endorsed by English Catholic noblemen and implicating in the later stages of its embroidery not
only members of the royal household but the Catholic Queen
herself: to kill Charles II, overthrow the government and restore Popery. When the Protestant magistrate Sir Edmund
Berry Godfrey was found dead on Primrose Hill on 17 October
– having been run through with a sword after death – public
apprehension turned to panic. This incident, which is still un-
explained today, probably had no connection with Oates, but it
provided the necessary 'evidence' to support his story. The
King was both astute enough not to believe a word of Oates's
account and cynical enough to allow matters to take their
course in the hands of a Parliament and a public ready to accept almost anything when faced with the spectre of Popery.

Over the winter of 1678-9 several priests and Catholic noblemen were tried and convicted on the perjured evidence of
Oates and his allies, and some were put to death, before the
nation, tiring of the affair, came to see Oates's fraudulence. On
the wave of feeling which reached the provinces towards the
end of 1678 Giles Vanbrugh wrote on 28 December, 'though I
am unknowne to yr Lordsh:', to Henry Compton, Bishop of
London, who passed the letter on to the Secretary of State:

My Lord the Horrid plott lately discoverd against his Majestye
the Kingdome and protestant Religion and certainly knowne to
have been hatch'd at Rome, and cheifly furthred by the Pope
himselfe has renew'd in my thoughts, what I have often wish'd
and judg'd easily feasible; But I doubted the proposition would
have been rejected and thought a little dishonnorable to attaque
a prince in his owne Dominions & without a just pretence or
provocation. But, that objection being now remov'd, I shall acquaint yor Lordsh. with what I thinke not only warrantable but
honnorable, and may much advantage the Protestant religion. It
is in short, my Lord, the assaulting the citty of Rome on that side
where the Vatican Palace stands and bringing away the Library.
And pray My Lord before yu censure my proposall, I desire yr
Lordsh to consider what reasons I have to beleeve the thing not
only possible but easy to be Effected.

Having spent a year in Rome, Giles went on, he knew that the
inhabitants were:

not warrlike, like their Ancestors, but of a poor spirit, kept under by the clergye and prone to their superstitious worship rather than fighting.

He proposed the despatch of an invasion fleet to the port of Ostia with 4000 'briske active men, well armed and provided with scaling ladders and other Instruments'. Such an exploit would not only retrieve valuable manuscripts of the Palatine and other libraries, the printing of which would serve 'towards defending ours and Impugning their own Religion'. It would also 'make such an open Breach between us and them, as would occasion a more strict union, and close confederacy between all other Protestant Princes and ours'. To encourage the troops he suggested that instead of Rome the sanctuary at Loreto should be sacked and its treasures carried away. He chose the Bishop to reveal his plan, 'although of martiall concern', because he could trust to secrecy 'a true protestant and zealous prosecutor of what your Lordsh is convinc'd may conduce to the good of Church & State'.

John was nearly fifteen at this time. His father will not have confided so secret a project to him, but the strength of his feelings in general he will not have hidden. John grew up to be not only a true Protestant but also an active Whig, a supporter of the Protestant succession to the throne. Giles may have believed that the Great Fire was started by Papists; we do not know what property he lost by it, but his son's convictions were to be sharpened and hardened by personal experience and hardship.

A Journey to Nowhere

In 1681 John Vanbrugh found himself in London. He was seventeen, the age at which his uncle William had been set up in business by old Gillis, and the age too at which, unusually early, his father Giles would, when making his will in 1683, consider his children old enough to claim their inheritance. Ten years earlier his first cousin William Matthews, son of Peter Matthews Baldwin (of the flower pots) and aunt Sara Vanbrugh, had been apprenticed to Peter his father, who was then Warden of the Mercers' Company. But William Matthews never became a freeman mercer; by about 1676 he was carrying on a trade in London, with John Vanhattem, in wines and brandies. The business seems to have been badly run, for Vanhattem received all the profits and Matthews paid all the expenses; the resulting cash-flow problem led to Matthews's being bankrupt in 1682.

At that point William Vanbrugh, head of the family, tried to gain redress by suing Vanhattem for what he owed Matthews. Vanhattem denied any debt to his partner, and although we know this much from surviving documents of the case, we do not know the outcome; William Matthews died at the end of 1687 and was buried in the vault at St Stephen Walbrook. But the Chancery records contain some rough accounts of cash transactions in 1681, including sums of up to £100 passing through the hands of John Vanbrugg, described as Matthews's servant, and on one occasion as being at the White Hart. In 1695 John's younger brother Carleton was described as servant in the household of *his* first cousin Ann Delboe's husband Jasper Van den Busch, in the parish of All Hallows the Less, and this kind of arrangement among families was not uncommon.

When William Matthews could no longer employ or even board him, John must have left, having learned something about trade and a good deal about people, but perhaps not yet very much about himself. At eighteen he could have had the world before him, if only he knew how. For the next four years there are no records of him. There is a persistent story (stated as fact, for example, in the *Dictionary of National Biography* and elsewhere) that he went to France; variations of this basic supposition include that he stayed for three years, that he studied architecture there, or even that he went with that express intention.

Attractive though these ideas may be in a vacuum, there has never been a shred of evidence for any of them. As far as studying architecture is concerned, Laurence Whistler pointed out nearly fifty years ago that at home 'there were plenty of openings in that profession for a young man of talent'. Moreover, the discovery in 1951 of the early drawings for Castle Howard showed that around 1700 Vanbrugh still drew like a novice, whereas the first thing one would learn in a French architect's office would be the proper way of setting out and carrying on a drawing. In fact, though he later learned to draw quite expressively, Vanbrugh's drawing was never professional and **[H]** his technique, such as it was, derived from his own observation and the helpful hints of others. In his own practice he relied on professional draughtsmen, first on Hawksmoor, later on the mysterious Arthur and others.*

It is true that at a little over twenty his father Giles had gone off to France and Italy for three years, but then Giles had been fortified by his father's legacy and his brother William's support. When his own son's turn came the situation was rather different, for in 1682 Giles had twelve other children to support, and his substance was tied up, as his will of the following year shows, in houses, land, mortgages, leases, goods and bonds. If John had shown any particular aptitude or inclina-

* p. 442

tion, his father might have found the means for him to follow it, but there is no reason to suppose that this was the case.

The supposed study in France seems to go back to a statement in Theophilus Cibber's *Lives** that:

> in some part of our author's life (for we cannot justly ascertain the time) he gratified an inclination of visiting France ... His taste for architecture excited him to take a survey of the fortifications in that kingdom.

There follows a touching account of how Vanbrugh was arrested while drawing a fort and how his charm gained him 'liberty some days before the sollicitation came from England'. Now Vanbrugh himself wrote in 1725 of having begun his days in a French prison, a remark which Isaac D'Israeli, in *Curiosities of Literature*, took literally, but which we know to be figurative; we know also when and why he was in a French prison. It was from 1688 to 1692 and it was not for drawing fortifications. The unfortunate Englishman arrested for drawing the gate of the Citadel at Calais was not Vanbrugh anyway but the painter William Hogarth in 1748 – just long enough ago for Shiels to be able to adapt the story for Theophilus Cibber.

Vanbrugh's own remark indeed implies that he had not previously been a student in France, but it also maybe tells us more. Surely it was in those years of confinement – in the late, not the early 1680s – that (in St Paul's phrase) Vanbrugh 'became a man ... put away childish things'. The very certainty and success of his maturity are indeed related to the uncertainty of his youth. The modern cult of youth and spontaneity has no place for the slow developer; yet in history young prodigies have been relatively rare and genius has often developed at a leisurely pace. Vanbrugh's first play was produced when he was thirty-two, his first building was begun when he was thirty-five, but thereafter he never looked back.

Indeed there had been impressions enough for an impressionable seventeen-year-old in London in 1681. In the fifteen years since the Great Fire, the City itself had been virtually rebuilt, and although the streets followed the same pattern as

* p. 31

before the houses were neat and regular, built of brick with rectangular windows set back into the walls. The Royal Exchange and the halls of the Livery companies had been rebuilt. Many of Wren's new churches were finished, and the magnificent stone steeple of St Mary-le-Bow gleamed newly white above Cheapside. St Nicholas Acons had disappeared, leaving only the little churchyard, but the new St Stephen Walbrook was complete and in use. The family vault under the north aisle probably did not mean much to the lad, but if he paid even a nodding visit he would have seen the beautiful interior of the church with its plaster dome freshly white and the whole space flooded with light. Of St Paul's Cathedral the most impressive part was the ruined old west end, charred and roofless but not yet demolished, with the forty-foot Corinthian columns of Inigo Jones's western portico. The new choir was scarcely one storey high and could only be glimpsed through the wattle screens that enclosed the wooden scaffolding. The mapmaker William Morgan was indeed preparing to offer an engraved view of the building under construction, but he was obliged to admit that most of what he showed was 'according to the best information we could get hoping it may not be very unlike when finished'. He was an optimist.

Westward along the Strand the great noblemen's palaces John's father would have described to him remained much the same – Arundel, Bedford and Northumberland Houses and the royal buildings of Somerset House and the Savoy. In the growing court city of Westminster the Earl of Bedford's example of fashionable new development at Covent Garden in the 1630s was becoming popular and imitated. Lord Southampton had laid out a square of houses behind his own, today Bloomsbury Square. Soho Square, laid out by the Earl of St Albans, was no more than lines on a map, but St James's Square, which he had begun soon after the Restoration, was already surrounded by other streets of desirable standard residences; many of the new houses had, instead of the traditional hinged casement windows, the new sash-windows invented ten or twelve years earlier, with the frames sliding vertically in grooves against counterweights concealed in the wall. The neighbourhood church of St James, Piccadilly, designed by Wren, was nearing completion. Many years later John Vanbrugh would for a time have a house in Duke Street, St James's.

In comparison with all this, the wooden houses which still
made up most of Chester and even the mile-and-three-quarter
circuit of its fortified wall must have seemed small and old-
fashioned, but London had another attraction. Elsewhere
plays were presented by occasional travelling companies of
actors in makeshift halls or out of doors, but London offered
two modern theatres which, although small by European
standards, competed with each other in using all the refine-
ments of seventeenth-century technology on a permanent
stage, with a proscenium arch, wonderful scenery with fantastic effects of lighting, perspective and transformation.
Moreover there were many different plays in a year, because
the two repertory companies constantly needed new plays or
productions in order to stay in business when a run of four
nights or so could accommodate the whole of the London
theatre-going classes.

In his *Short Vindication* of 1698, Vanbrugh's bantering answer to Jeremy Collier's attack on the stage, he remarked that
The Provok'd Wife 'was writ many years ago, and when I was
very young'. It is impossible to say exactly what those phrases
would mean to a man of thirty-four at the end of the seventeenth century, but they do suggest something rather earlier
than the accepted story that the play was first sketched in the
Bastille in 1692. They suggest, in fact, that Vanbrugh was
stage-struck at the age of seventeen although it was many
years before he had both an understanding of what had happened and an opportunity to gather its fruits.

Recent studies have shown that the idea of Restoration audiences as consisting mainly of courtiers, rakes and the *demi-
monde* is based on a misreading of the evidence. Pepys's diary
is particularly informative, because he was a professional civil
servant and not a courtier and, for all his very human lapses, a
man of basically puritan attitude. In the first eight months of
1668 he went to the theatre seventy-three times, taking his
wife on nearly half his visits; on other occasions she went by
herself. His frequent scruples about his attendance derived not
from immoral associations of the stage, plays or players but
from his fear of wasting money and neglecting his work. There
will be more to say about theatres and their audiences when

we come to consider Vanbrugh's own plays; it is enough at this point to say that if he could afford the shilling ticket the entertainment was open to him – indeed it was possible to get in for one act without paying – and that, as Pepys often did, he would have been able also to read the many published scripts of both contemporary and earlier plays.

It is not possible to identify the White Hart at which John was in 1681; it may have been an inn near St Botolph's church in Bishopsgate, or it may have been in the new West End. Ogilby and Morgan's map of 1681-2 shows a White Hart between the east end of Jermyn Street and the market that served the new St James's area, and another near Covent Garden in Hart Street (modern Floral Street). This would have been almost on the doorstep of the Theatre Royal in Drury Lane, but both the others were within easy walking distance of this theatre and the rival one in Dorset Garden, which stood near the river just west of Blackfriars (roughly on the site of John Carpenter Street). By the time of his successes in 1697 Vanbrugh must have seen many plays and read many more, good, bad, and indifferent. He may have read some of those written and published in the 1660s and 1670s by Edward, Sir Robert, and James Howard, three of the younger sons of the first Earl of Berkshire – brothers-in-law of the poet and dramatist John Dryden and also, through marriage ties with the Harrisons of Hurst in Berkshire, kinsmen of Vanbrugh's mother.

In *This Time Next Week* the novelist Leslie Thomas describes the schoolroom experience that at the age of thirteen changed his life. Called one morning in his turn to read aloud a passage from the Bible, he began to read 'as we had always read it, gabblingly fast, the quicker the better'. But then something happened: 'Suddenly I knew what words were; that put together they sang like a song. I stumbled, then started again. But more slowly.' He had made a miraculous discovery. 'I knew about words, and I went on seeking them, discovering them, and wondering and delighting in their shape and beauty.' We know too little about Vanbrugh's education to be able to say when it was he came to know about words – for he certainly did so. By the end of 1685 he must have read widely, and he must have been touched by some of what he read. He still had the uncertainty of youth, by turns blustering or diffident, high-spirited or deeply withdrawn, carefree or fragile. Wherever he had been and whatever he had been doing, he was now back at home in Chester and at a loose end. He decided to write a letter to his noble kinsman.

7

Creditable Stations

On 16 December 1685 Henry Hyde, second Earl of Clarendon, brother-in-law of King James II, set out from London to Chester on the first stage of the journey to Dublin in order to take up his appointment as Lord Lieutenant of Ireland. He was accompanied, as Narcissus Luttrell reported, 'by many of the nobility and gentry'. His party reached Chester just before Christmas, and were lodged in the Castle. This was a group of fortified and domestic buildings just outside the city wall, which were in a moderate state of repair; although officially a residence of the Prince of Wales, the Castle was in practice (there being no Prince at this time) the seat of a garrison, stores and lawcourts. Clarendon was 'very respectfully treated' as Vanbrugh wrote on the day the Earl left Chester; he did not sail direct for Ireland but instead, the party now being reduced to three carriages and a wagon for luggage, went overland to Holyhead, whence they reached Dublin on 9 January 1686. Lord Clarendon was in an unenviable position as a committed Protestant appointed by a Catholic king to govern a fiercely Catholic dependency, and his authority was undermined by the behaviour of both James II in London and of the commander-in-chief of the army in Ireland, the Earl of Tyrconnel. Exactly a year after his arrival in Dublin, Clarendon was recalled and his post was awarded to Tyrconnel.

As Clarendon drove away from Chester on 28 December 1685 John Vanbrugh was writing to his kinsman Theophilus Hastings, seventh Earl of Huntingdon, at his house in Gerrard

Street, Westminster. Huntingdon had already, he wrote, helped him (in some way unknown to us), and Vanbrugh was thus encouraged to presume 'that if you see it convenient yr Lordship will graunt my request'. Perhaps His Lordship would write a line or two to My Lord Lieutenant of Ireland, 'if I may be admitted into such a station as may be at present creditable, and may have reason to expect a suitable advance as my behaviour may prove'. Having thus lodged his request and asked pardon for his presumption, Vanbrugh proceeded to what a more experienced writer of begging letters would have placed first — Huntingdon's own appointment as Warden and Chief Justice in Eyre of Royal Forests South of the Trent. This appointment was reported by Luttrell on the same day that Clarendon had set out for Chester, and the news probably arrived there at about the same time as he did. As a second string to his bow Vanbrugh offered to serve Lord Huntingdon in some capacity, although 'what sort of servants yr Ldship may need to assist you in this new business, I cannot tell'.

After some chatty remarks about Clarendon's arrival and departure, Vanbrugh again asked pardon 'for the trouble I give you' and subscribed himself 'as in duty bound, Yr Lordships most oblieged kinsman & faithfull servant'. Huntingdon's new post was a virtual sinecure, but originally it had been connected with the administration and leasing of Crown forests and estates, and on occasion he was called on to exercise his judicial powers. The *Calendar of State Papers* for 1686-7 mentions the reference to Huntingdon of the petition of James Skrymshere and Carolina his wife, who had inherited from her father Sir Baynham Throckmorton the office of Forester of the Forest of Dean. This office entitled her, in lieu of fees, to 'the right shoulder of every deer killed within the Forest' and ten bucks and ten does a year, and the Skrymsheres were seeking confirmation of their ancient right to these rewards. Vanbrugh can have had only the vaguest idea of what was entailed, and he must have hoped by one route or another to gain entry to the world of court patronage which provided a living, if not always an occupation, for young gentlemen and noblemen. But even he cannot, as has recently been suggested, have supposed that the itinerant judiciary of forests had anything to do with landscape gardening. On the other hand, he is not very likely to have expected the kind of employment that was offered him.

Huntingdon was also the colonel of a foot regiment which had been formed in July 1685 to help fight the Duke of Monmouth's rebellion — Monmouth, the illegitimate son of Charles II, had claimed the throne on his father's death. On 30 January 1686 Vanbrugh was commissioned as an ensign in this regiment. Perhaps his patron's response had been to send for him to London and make him the offer on the lowest rung of the commissioned ladder, equivalent to a modern second-lieutenant. The gift of a commission was valuable: unless it was given as a reward for some service or as a favour, it cost several hundred pounds and it could subsequently be sold on resignation if another suitable man was willing to buy it. Huntingdon sent the young man to Hull with a letter for his captain, Owen Macarty, who acknowledged its delivery on 19 February.

In peacetime he could expect to lead a fairly relaxed life within the limits of a garrison. As a very junior officer he would both be waited upon and also wait on others of higher rank; as ensign it was his duty to carry the Colour, the flag of his company, and he would wear the bright uniform of his regiment: a round hat with a broad brim, turned up on the right and a yellow riband, a scarlet thigh-length coat lined with yellow, yellow knee-breeches, grey stockings, and an orange sash. There were more distant and less distinct prospects: promotion, travel, maybe abroad, adventure, active service, distinction in battle, and remotest of all, death, perhaps more painful than glamorous. But death was the loser's ticket in a lottery which only the quixotic and the desperate expected to lose.

On 13 April 1686 the regiment was ordered south to Ware in Hertfordshire, a march of nine days interspersed with three rest days; a month after arriving there it proceeded to Hounslow Heath to join a great gathering of troops, estimated at between 13,000 and 16,000, which was forming a camp there. Uncertainty about the object of this show of strength disquieted many in the nation: was it strength against a foreign power, against another possible pretender like Monmouth, or against those at home who disagreed with King James's policies? Charles II had held a general review in June 1673 of 'the formal, & formidable Camp, on Blackheath, raised', in Evelyn's words, 'to invade Holland, or as others suspected for another designe', namely to assert the King's authority over London and over a Parliament that not only feared but had refused to sanction a standing army in peacetime.

Now, thirteen years later with a camp on the other side of London, some of the disquiet was expressed through rumours of soldiers falling ill and dying in the poor weather conditions, first very wet and then very hot; these rumours were strong and widespread enough to be officially denied in the *London Gazette* of 17 June. Evelyn had referred to them at the beginning of June, but on the 9th he mentioned both sickness and 'greate feasting' as well as 'many jealosies & discourse what the meaning of this incampment of an army should be'. On 5 July, returning to London from Windsor, he saw the camp and 'was in the Generals Tent'. But by then its official purpose had been served. The immediate object of the show was the army itself, since it was important that the King and his forces should have met and identified each other. On 30 June James reviewed his massed troops in what Luttrell called 'a generall rendevouze', and in the next few weeks the regiments began to disperse to resume duties in garrisons throughout the country.

In the second week of August Huntingdon's regiment received marching orders to York and Carlisle. But Vanbrugh was not among them, for by the 20th his place had been taken by Ambrose Jones, whose commission as ensign of Macarty's company bears that date. There is no substance in the story that he left because his regiment was being posted to Guernsey and consequently to inertia and oblivion. Probably the reasons for Vanbrugh's resignation were personal, and there are some clues to them in the *Calendar of State Papers*. In January 1686 dispensations were given to various officers in various regiments from the oaths and tests intended to disqualify Roman Catholics from holding office; among the officers were Vanbrugh's captain, Owen Macarty, and Sir Edward Hales, the colonel of another foot regiment. The grant of these dispensations was one of the many signs of the liberalism extended by the Catholic James II to his loyal Catholic subjects and servants; in June 1686 Hales's dispensation became a test case in the King's Bench Court, and on 21 June a majority of the judges found in favour of Hales.

Not only Vanbrugh's Irish captain but also his colonel, Huntingdon himself, was a Catholic. In November 1688 at the Revolution the Protestant officers of the regiment would declare allegiance to William of Orange and would arrest and then dismiss Huntingdon and the Catholics on his staff, and Huntingdon would retire and be succeeded as colonel by his son. Vanbrugh was later to display both courage and physical endurance, and it is hard to suppose that he simply could not face the march back to the North. Little though we know about the origins of his feeling for the theatre, as standard-bearer for his company he cannot but have been impressed and moved by the pageantry of the great 'rendevouze' on Hounslow Heath. But as a Catholic chapel was set up in the camp and priests came and went freely the grave warning voice of his true Protestant father must have resounded in his inner ear. It began to come home to him that, whatever the allegiance of the rank and file, he was a junior officer in a company, and a regiment, increasingly under the influence of popish officers on behalf of a popish king. By a curious turn of events his cousin Dudley was commissioned ensign in Hales's regiment on 1 April 1687, but Dudley's fortune would be very different.

Two other officers in Lord Huntingdon's Foot who would reappear later in Vanbrugh's life were Captain John Tidcombe and Captain Thomas Skipwith. Tidcombe remained a professional soldier and was a member of the Kit-Cat Club; Skipwith's service in the regiment was almost as brief as Vanbrugh's and we do not know why he resigned. He was commissioned on 20 June 1685, the day the regiment was formed, and on 12 June 1686 he was replaced by another captain. But in the five months they shared in the army Vanbrugh incurred an obligation of some sort to Skipwith, for knowledge of which we only have Colley Cibber's account of the origin of *The Relapse*:

> In his first Step, into publick Life, when he was but an Ensign, and had a Heart above his Income, he happen'd somewhere, at his Winter-Quarters, upon a very slender acquaintance with Sir *Thomas Skipwith*, to receive a particular Obligation from him, which he had not forgot at the Time I am speaking of: when Sir *Thomas's* Interest, in the Theatrical Patent (for he had a large Share in it, though he little concern'd himself in the Conduct of

it) was rising but very slowly, he thought, that to give it a Lift, by
a new comedy, if it succeeded, might be the handsomest Return
he could make to those his former Favours.

If Cibber is right about the winter quarters the incident must
have been in the first two months of Vanbrugh's service. But
how Skipwith helped him, and even whether money was involved, is still unknown.

Travel, adventure, war and distinction were to come later,
but for the moment Vanbrugh turned for help and alliance to
another branch of his kinship: the Bertie family. Robert, Lord
Willoughby, later fourth Earl of Lindsey and first Duke of
Ancaster (1660-1723), was almost four years his senior. Two of
Robert's younger brothers were Peregrine (d. 1711) and
Charles. Their uncle (their father's half-brother) was James,
Lord Norreys of Rycote, Earl of Abingdon, and Lord Lieutenant
of Oxfordshire from 1674 to 1687. Already in February 1687
there was daily news, as Sir John Reresby wrote soon afterwards, of 'gentlemen laying down their appointments and
papists for the most part being put in their places'. The deliberate and provocative policies of the King had gone so far by
Whitsun that, although his fears for himself were groundless,
the moderate and apolitical Sir Christopher Wren was writing,
'wee are bound to our good behaviour, uncertain wch way the
next wind may tosse us'. The King now wished to obtain from
Parliament the repeal of the Test Acts and other penal laws
against Roman Catholics; this needed a majority of Catholics
and dissenters (whom the Test Acts also affected) in the House
of Commons. James began to ask Members of Parliament,
magistrates, and other office holders whether they would vote
for, or otherwise support, repeal and legal toleration. When he
went on in the early autumn of 1687 to depute this inquisition
to the Lords Lieutenants of the Counties, about half of them
merely refused to question their gentry and were consequently
dismissed. Lord Abingdon was one of these: he told the King on
18 November, as he recorded, that 'I knew not what was done
in other countries, but for my own I could answer, that all this
noise of persecution was like shearing of hogs, a great cry and
little wool'.

However, on 16 September 1687 Abingdon had been installed by the City of Oxford as its High Steward, and on that occasion the freedom of the city was given to several members of his retinue, including his nephews Robert, Peregrine and Charles, and (as the Council Acts record) John Vanbrooke. In due course the King's displeasure extended to these honours, which were revoked with the Earl's stewardship on 16 February 1688. The implication for Vanbrugh, however, is that he was, with the nephews, attached to Lord Abingdon's household: that they were all his servants, although on a higher social level than Vanbrugh had been to his cousin Matthews in 1681.

The lines were being drawn in politics between Whigs and Tories, whose nicknames, originally abusive, became accepted. The Civil War had not solved the central problems of how the country could be governed and how government was to be paid for. In the simplest of terms, the King's problem was that taxes, which paid for both the royal household and the central government, could only be imposed by Act of Parliament, and Parliament would only agree to vote for taxes in exchange for a share in the making of policies and the spending of money. Unless the King could raise money he could not do what he thought best for the country. Parliament – or the House of Commons – saw matters differently. The Tudors in the previous century had increased the power of the Commons as a buffer between themselves and the House of Lords; that power the Stuarts now found turned against themselves. The Commons formed a very clear idea of the desirable limits to royal prerogative and power, and the purse-strings of the state proved an effective way of confirming those limits, although Stuart kings did their best to raise money from other sources outside the control or even the knowledge of Parliament.

But the House of Commons of Charles II's reign differed from previous parliaments in several respects. First, in the second Charles they had a shrewder and more successful adversary than in the first. Secondly, the bitter and bloody mistakes of the Civil War and the execution of Charles I gave the moral advantage, at the Restoration, to the King. Thirdly, the suspicion or fear that Charles II would declare himself a Roman Catholic, and the virtual certainty that James, Duke of York, who had already done so, would if he ever came to the

throne attempt to restore the national allegiance to Rome,
made the succession itself contentious. The Commons attempt-
ted to pass an Act disqualifying James from the throne; they
failed, but arguments about money and power were compounded by ones about religion and the nature of kingship.
Fourthly, partly alongside these matters and partly as a consequence of them, the centre of contention shifted, so that increasingly the House of Commons included a group, and later
a party, who supported the King, his traditional authority and
the succession on Charles's death, in default of any legitimate
child of his (thus excluding Monmouth whom he had
expressly refused to recognize) by his younger brother James.
Thus the opposition came to be not between King and Parliament but between two parties in Parliament: between the
Tories, the hereditary owners of land, supporters of royal prerogative and the established Church, and the Whigs, the
exploiters of money, supporters of parliamentary privilege,
Protestant non-conformity, and a Protestant succession.

By the end of May 1688 the question in most minds was not
whether James II would lose the throne but how soon, for, full
of his own rightness, he had set himself in opposition to most of
his subjects in every sphere of activity. Princess Mary, his elder
daughter (by his first wife Anne Hyde), had married William
III, Prince of Orange and Stadholder (roughly hereditary pres-
ident) of the United Provinces. William was, through his
mother, as Mary was through her father, a grandchild of
Charles I, and although William professed not to be very interested, a strong case could be – and was – put forward for their
succeeding jointly to the throne of England. But on 10 June
1688 James's Queen (his second wife Mary of Modena) gave
birth to a son, James Francis Edward.

Attempts were made by interested parties first to cast doubt
on the reality of the Queen's pregnancy and then to suggest
that she had borne a daughter, and that the little boy so tri-
umphantly displayed was of humbler origin and had been
smuggled into St James's Palace in a warming pan. But there
was never any real doubt, and James Edward would as a male
child take precedence over his adult half-sisters Mary and
Anne. While James II rejoiced in the prospect of a Catholic
Great Britain extending through the next century, others acted

swiftly and secretly. On 30 June a coded letter was sent to William and Mary at The Hague, signed by six noblemen and the Bishop of London (to whom Giles Vanbrugh had written ten years previously), inviting William to come to protect the British People – in effect asking him to bring an invasion force and, with his many supporters in Britain, to depose his father-in-law.

When in the late autumn James accepted the inevitable, at least for the moment, and fled to France, considerable care was taken to see that he got away safely, as nobody wanted a second royal martyr. But until the eleventh hour he had attempted to secure his position by securing his friends and servants. Thus it was that back in December 1685, while Catholic officers in his army were being exempted from the law, a group of 'several Parliament men and others' had been discharged from the army, including Robert, Lord Willoughby (from Lord Peterborough's Regiment of Horse) and two other Berties. The dismissal of Lord Abingdon and his party from Oxford in February 1688 can have surprised none of them.

Soon after that incident, in March, Robert and Peregrine Bertie were planning to meet in Paris, and later in the year Robert was apparently in The Hague, and John Vanbrugh was probably with him. We know of this journey from a letter Vanbrugh wrote in 1692, describing how the English ambassador in Paris, Bevil Skelton, told the French War Minister, the Marquis de Louvois 'that I had been at the Hague in my Lord Willoughby's Company; That I was his Relation, and that (as he was pleas'd to say) I lead all the Bertue family, wch way I wou'd' (Bertie was usually pronounced Bartie and sometimes written Bartue or Bartew). Since Vanbrugh was writing secretly to William Blathwayt, Secretary of State for War, about the ill-treatment he had received as a result of this report, it seems likely that he would have denied any parts of it which were untrue, and his kinship with the family has been established from other sources.

Again, we do not know what Willoughby and Vanbrugh were doing in The Hague: whether for example they carried a letter from Lord Abingdon to William of Orange. Nor do we know what led them so fatefully to France. In the last week of August it was known in London that the Dutch were preparing an invasion force and the French a fleet to intercept it. Narcissus Luttrell reported on the 27th that ''tis certain a war must ensue' and on 8 September that France had declared war on the Dutch. On the 17th Skelton, who had been recalled from Paris, was arrested in London, because James resented the interference of Louis XIV; according to Luttrell, Skelton had 'exceeded his commission' in Paris. Skelton was released when the scale of William's plans became known in London. But by then Vanbrugh, though not Willoughby, was a prisoner in the citadel at Calais.

— 8 —

Prison

The story of Vanbrugh's captivity has to be pieced together
from many sources, but the available evidence is such that it
reads like one of those modern investigative newspaper articles in which several journalists pool their efforts. The official
French version of his capture, written nearly three years later
when he had become one cog among many in the security
machine, is given in a letter of 10 July 1691 from the Marquis
de Barbezieux to Louis Phélypeaux, Sieur de Pontchartrain.
The latter had become Minister for the Navy upon the death in
November 1690 of the Marquis de Seignelay, who undoubtedly
had known the facts of the case. Pontchartrain on the other
hand was in ignorance, and therefore wrote for information to
Barbezieux, who was the son of the Marquis de Louvois, the
Minister for War, and who would succeed him in that office
when Louvois suddenly died about a week later. Barbezieux
made enquiries about the Englishman with the Dutch name,
and was told that Vanbrugh had been arrested for attempting
to leave France without a passport in wartime, that is after May
1689 when hostilities were declared between France and England. Barbezieux was also told that Vanbrugh had procured a
Parisian woman for 'un my Lord' who had Vanbrugh's release
very much at heart.

Barbezieux ended his reply with 'this is all the light I can
shed for you on the subject of Vanbrugh'. All this was a good
story, but it was based on hearsay — rather than on malice — and
little of it was correct. Until the rediscovery of documentary re-

ferences earlier than September 1690 it was assumed that the
arrest took place in the summer of 1690; in fact it was almost
two years earlier. Only Vanbrugh's own letter to Blathwayt,
discovered some years ago in the Finch Papers, reveals the
true time and circumstances of his arrest.

On 16/26 August 1692 Vanbrugh wrote that he had 'been
near four years' in prison, having been arrested 'about the time
the Warr broak out, accus'd of speaking somthing in favour of
the enterprize the King was then upon the point of executing
upon England'. By this of course he meant the war between
France and Holland; this agrees with his estimate of the length
of his captivity as well as with another, of 'allmost 3 yeares',
which he gave in a letter of July 1691. Skelton's opinion, given
before his recall to London (or just possibly when he returned
to Paris in December 1688 with the fugitive James II) was dam-
ning, not because it identified Vanbrugh as a supporter of the
Prince of Orange but because it exaggerated his value as a hostage through the suggestion that he was of noble family. Pro-
tests that he was a mere Chester businessman's son would not
be credited; Martin de Forval, a Norman gentleman for whom
Vanbrugh eventually became the hostage, claimed, when app-
rehended in London, to be no more than a valet who had fled
after fighting a duel, which was illegal in France.

But there is no reason to doubt the rest of Barbezieux's report, which says that a French spy, Monsieur du Clos Chrétien,
bound for London, had asked for Vanbrugh to be confined at
Calais as a hostage until Chrétien's safe return. When Chrétien
proved to be a double agent the French left him to fend for himself, and it was decided to keep Vanbrugh for some other exchange. Early in 1690 Forval was sent over, under the alias of
Martin Bertillier, to explore areas of English discontent with
King William, who had by then made it clear to the English that
he was his own man. Forval was arrested in Kent in May 1690;
his story was not believed but he preserved his cover and was
therefore committed to Newgate gaol instead of the socially
superior prison in the Tower of London. In August he was re-
committed to Newgate, and on 8/18 September the commandant of Calais was instructed in consequence to have Vanbrugh more closely guarded so that there would be no chance
of his escaping.

The court of James II in exile at Saint-Germain-en-Laye now approached Vanbrugh's mother, suggesting the exchange of her son with Archibald Cockburne, a young Scot captured at sea by King William's forces after the Battle of the Boyne. Mrs Vanbrugh's petition to the Privy Council in London in October 1690 was granted, but the French were determined that Vanbrugh be exchanged only for 'a French gentleman who is similarly a prisoner in London', by which they meant Forval, who was far more valuable than a young Jacobite officer. But on 1 January 1691 the Calais commandant was ordered to have Vanbrugh well treated and given every assistance, provided that he was securely guarded. Either guile or charm or misery touched the commandant, for six weeks later he had another letter from Versailles. Vanbrugh had, it was heard, been allowed to walk about Calais for three days, but 'he is an Englishman whose word must not be so completely trusted'. Again he was to be well treated, but with no possibility whatsoever of his being able to escape. For 'if we lose him, we have few means of retrieving from the prisons of England the gentleman who you know went there in the King's service'. Calais, although a walled town with a moated castle, was after all almost within sight of Dover, and an inland confinement might well be less strict. Moreover, the castle was four centuries old and undoubtedly damp. The young prisoner was by turns impatient and despondent, and by April 1691 after two and a half years his health was deteriorating. On the 27th the commandant was instructed to send him with a trustworthy guard to Vincennes, four miles east of the centre of Paris.

The journey in a closed coach would have taken several days, and it was stressed that Vanbrugh must still be kept safely either for exchange or for reprisals on account of the 'French gentleman' as Forval is always called. In the thirteenth century Vincennes had been a suburban royal house; in the fourteenth it was turned into a fortress, a quarter-mile-long enclosure inside a massive moated curtain wall with tall towers at the corners and along the sides, and a huge gatehouse in the centre of the north end. Near the middle of the west side a smaller walled enclosure still stands partly proud of the main fortress, and in the middle of this is the *donjon* or keep. Vincennes was occasionally useful as a hunting lodge for the

[15]

[14]

nearby forest of the same name, and in the 1650s Louis Le Vau, the most successful house designer of the time, was commissioned by Cardinal Mazarin, the young Louis XIV's Italian First Minister, to build new lodgings for a king and queen – two impressive stone-fronted pavilions – and a new triumphal gateway at the south end. It was in the new Pavillon du Roi that Mazarin died on 9 March 1661. Louis XIV, now twenty-three, thereupon assumed personal control of his kingdom; seven years later he abandoned Paris as the seat of government and transferred the court to Versailles. Exploiting its strength and rural location, he ordered Vincennes to be converted into a state prison. It was not luxurious, but it was of a higher class that a provincial gaol or a harbour citadel; Louis's unjust steward Nicolas Fouquet had already been confined there in 1662, and later distinguished but unwilling residents included the famous poisoner Madame Voisin and her gang, the philosopher Diderot, the Marquis de Sade, and the revolutionary Mirabeau. Today Vincennes has been put in order as a museum and historic monument; the walls of the *donjon* still bear the carved names of many who were imprisoned in it, and perhaps Vanbrugh's is somewhere among them.

By July 1691 Vanbrugh seems to have guessed that nobody might know or remember the real reason for his arrest. He therefore explored a different avenue: making himself out to be one of its most ardent supporters, he appealed to the Jacobite court, only eighteen miles away at Saint-Germain. The first steps in this masquerade are unknown, but by the beginning of July James II had instructed his Vice-Chamberlain, James Porter, to ask for Vanbrugh's release. On 6 July the prisoner received a 'Charitable visitt' from the septuagenarian courtier Colonel Thomas Napper. 'By that meanes', as Vanbrugh wrote the next day to James's Secretary of State, Henry Browne, he 'came to know I am beholding to you for a favour in speakeing to the King for me'. He pressed his advantage, adding that his 'misfortune to be soe Little knowne to you' made him all the more obliged to Browne; he was of course aware that the less there was known about him the greater was his chance of success. Assuming, therefore, that Browne knew his story but not his person, he forbore to 'trouble you with it my selfe'.

Now the bluff became imaginative; he put forward the fiction – improbable in the extreme in the light of the French insistence on his secure custody – that there was a plan to send him to England on bail to plead himself for the French gentleman's release. Unless James could protect him he would thus be 'reduced either to Lye and Rott in prison or goe throw myselfe at the P: of O's feete for protection and take the Oathes of Allegiance to him'. This was quite a different dilemma from his real one, but it was the one calculated to win sympathy at Saint-Germain. 'They looke upon me as a Partizan of the P of O,' he continued, although 'I never have been accused of anything agt: the King or the State of France the Order to arrest me I finde he knows nothing of'.

On receipt of Vanbrugh's letter Browne contacted the French ministry at Versailles, six miles down the road from Saint-Germain; the resulting enquiries led to Barbezieux's letter of 10 July containing the erroneous account of Vanbrugh's arrest. He had guessed rightly that the true story was lost, and his credibility at Saint-Germain thus survived. But he seemed to be as far as ever from liberty, and all Vice-Chamberlain Porter obtained was that, in principle, Vanbrugh should have the freedom of the courtyard at Vincennes. In fact he obtained nothing, because the prescribed conditions could not be met.

At this point two new characters have to be introduced into the story: the cousins Joseph and Pierre Dulivier. Joseph Dulivier, a French merchant in London, had specialized in contraband silks. He was a Catholic, not a Huguenot, and at the Revolution of 1688 he fled to France in the face of warrants for his arrest, leaving Pierre in charge of the London office. The Duliviers were engaged in several other concerns legal and illegal. They acted, at a profit, as intermediaries in the exchange of English and French prisoners, both officially and privately arranged, and they also transmitted funds for Jacobite agents and the salaries for French spies in England, as well as endeavouring to ensure their safety. Vanbrugh's mother had managed to obtain a bond for £500 from Pierre Dulivier and Gérard Martin for her son's safe return. On 21 October 1691 Pontchartrain actually authorized Vanbrugh's use of the courtyard at Vincennes, on condition of a surety of 10,000 livres (£770) from Joseph Dulivier. But, as Vanbrugh wrote to his mother on 9

November, 'this Rogue has failed me saying 'tis true he promis'd me, but that men don't allwayes keep wt they promis'.

Moreover, Vanbrugh was fairly sure that Joseph had nevertheless 'writ to his Cozen that I have the Castle'. He wrote to his mother as soon as he discovered Dulivier's duplicity, but the first letter was intercepted at Calais. From there it was sent with a translation to Pontchartrain, who on 26 October wrote to the Calais commandant that 'it could cause trouble for M. de Bertillier, who is the gentleman you have sent to England'. Pontchartrain, who incidentally believed that Vanbrugh now had the freedom of the courtyard, was unwilling that Forval, alias Berteillier, should be seen to be reclaimed in the King's name; for that would betray his importance both as a gentleman and as a spy. Accordingly the letter was retained, and a warning was added to the commandant that Vanbrugh would presumably write to his mother again in similar terms. From a further letter of Pontchartrain (31 October) it appears that Pierre Dulivier offered a surety of only 1500 livres (£115); the King believed Vanbrugh would consider such a relatively small sum expendable 'as a sort of ransom' and he was therefore to be 'kept as you have done up to now'.

By 9 November Vanbrugh knew that his first letter had been stopped, and wrote another one which he managed to smuggle out with the help of another Jacobite, Sir Daniel Arthur ('a great Banquer here; all the world know him at London'). Mrs Vanbrugh received this letter and sent it on, as her son had asked, to Lord Nottingham, Secretary of State, at Whitehall. Vanbrugh described Joseph Dulivier's deceit and the daily poorer treatment he was receiving 'upon Bertillers account, for I have now found the whole mystery of his buiseness, & whence it comes that there is so much stickleing for his liberty'. Dulivier had overestimated Vanbrugh's social standing and political importance, and

> has assur'd, that I shou'd be a sure exchang for any prisoner of State that might be taken in England, upon this assurance Bertl: ventures over, and now du Livier finds he had not well inform'd himself of me nor my friends, but this he dares not owne to Mr. de Pontchartran for fear of a reprimand, and so persuades him every day that the thing is ready to be granted. for I can assure

you that Mr. de Pontc: has been once or twice upon the point of
giving me my Liberty, and du Livier still prevents it, and hinders
likwise my having better usage, in hopes the more uneasy I am
the more paines my friends will take to deliver me.

Vanbrugh hoped that this disclosure would persuade Nottingham to free Bertillier; if he refused, Mrs Vanbrugh was to

declare to du Livier & Martin, that if they will not immediatly let
me come over, you'll sue the bond they gave you for 500£ and
declare every perticular of the business to my Lord Nottingham
& to the whole world, by wch it will plainly apear that they play
the Spys in England.

In a postscript Vanbrugh asked his mother to send letters in
future to Sir Daniel Arthur 'as you us'd to do to du Livier'.

But Vanbrugh had still underestimated British bureaucracy,
and he undervalued Bertillier, believing him to be 'a man of no
worth, nor never was more than a Lieutenant in a Privateer, he
had been before, a Vallet de Chamber'. By 21 November
Pontchartrain noted that the King was daily receiving new
complaints from Vanbrugh about his bad treatment, which
now included the refusal of a fire and the withdrawal of
visitors. In order to silence his complaints Pontchartrain ordered him again to be well treated; this long business was by no
means over, but the French were perhaps a little embarrassed
that his counterpart in Newgate both needed and had gained
better treatment. Bertillier had on 28 February 1691 petitioned
for, and received, the liberty of the yard there, on grounds of
his ill health, and on 9/19 December he was removed from
Newgate into the special custody of a Messenger, William
Jones. And on 20/30 January 1692 the order was given for Vanbrugh's transfer from Vincennes to the Bastille, the state prison
of Paris at the east end of the rue Saint-Antoine, the most famous in France and the counterpart of the Tower of London.
He arrived on Friday 1 February at four o'clock in the afternoon.

The Bastille (the word simply means fortress) was founded
in 1370 by King Charles V as a fortress to defend the city walls
and the Porte Saint-Antoine. Its eight towers, four to the east

and four to the west, and the walls connecting them formed a rectangle some 200 by 100 feet in area, and towers and walls alike rose nearly 80 feet high. This massive structure was surrounded by a dry moat 80 feet wide, and the counterscarp around it formed the back walls of buildings facing outwards: stables, guard quarters, stores, and a number of shops rented by local tradesmen. The fortress, which had lost its military functions, had only been a state prison for about seventy years. Besides a number of rooms in the northern half, the eight towers each contained five storeys above the cellars, and as the average complement of prisoners in the reign of Louis XIV was only forty the accommodation was quite spacious. Vanbrugh was installed on the fourth storey of the Tour de la Liberté, which he shared with two gentlemen named de Poncet de Sainte-Praye and Saint-Georges.

It was small comfort to Vanbrugh that his standard of confinement was rising; nevertheless although the upper rooms were hot in summer and freezing in winter the west side was the more temperate and he was to be allowed to walk about, receive visitors, and 'enjoy all the liberty that can be permitted him without compromising the security of his person'. Windows were few and far between, but from the Tour de la Liberté it was possible to look down the rue Saint-Antoine towards the centre of Paris. Prisoners with the means to do so could install their own furniture and keep a servant, and the numerous staff included medical and surgical officers and at one time a midwife. The food was good, and the shops outside the counterscarp near the entrance gate supplied the prisoners with whatever they could afford to buy. A century later, in the French Revolution, the storming of the Bastille by the mob on 14 July 1789 was largely symbolic, as a decision had already been taken to close and demolish the building on grounds of economy, not least because of the enormous expenditure on staff salaries.

Vanbrugh received money from his mother, drawn on Sir Daniel Arthur; in the letter about the Duliviers he asked for a credit for £30 'for my money's gone allmost'. In fact he had a sinecure at home for most of his captivity. In the spring of 1689 he had been appointed in his absence Auditor for the Southern Division of the Duchy of Lancaster; obtaining an income for his unfortunate friend and kinsman was the most practical act that Robert Bertie, Lord Willoughby, managed to execute, on his appointment as Chancellor of the Duchy on 21 March 1689. Among the Vanbrugh papers formerly at Heslington there is a warrant of 23 March 1689 appointing Tobias Legros (who had been Quartermaster to Prince George's Regiment) to the auditorship, with a declaration of the same date by Legros that he was only the deputy of 'John Vanbrough of [blank]'. Sinecures were a common, if to modern sensibilities inequable, form of patronage, and perhaps the sort of thing Vanbrugh had had in mind when he first approached Lord Huntingdon at the end of 1685. They were often made less inequable by the appointment of a deputy who shared the income and did whatever work was entailed. Thus, in theory at least, Mrs Vanbrugh did not have to provide money for her son's needs but only to transmit it.

Now too the letter delivered to Lord Nottingham began to work. In February 1692 seventeen French Catholic merchants in London were arrested on suspicion of spying or smuggling; six of them were held, including Pierre Dulivier, at first by Messengers and from 15 March in the Tower. By then it was known in London, as Luttrell records, that they were 'to be used as Mr North and Mr Vanbroke are in the Bastile'. Luttrell had earlier noted that a third Englishman was 'clapt up' in the Bastille, a student from Angers named Goddard, who in May 1691 had tried to secure an exchange for himself with the same Cockburnc whom the court at Saint-Germain had suggested in return for Vanbrugh the year before. Montagu North, a Turkey merchant, had been imprisoned at Toulon in July 1689 on his way to the Levant, on the assumption that he was an English political agent. North, like Vanbrugh but a few months earlier, had written to King James's Secretary of State for help; he did not profess allegiance to James but nevertheless promised to serve him if he obtained his release.

One of the complications of this whole story is that no prisoner on one side could be equated in value with any one on the opposite side, and this was not only because they were all of diverse kinds – spies, agents, sympathizers, smugglers, and innocents – but also because some were misvalued – in particular both Bertillier and Vanbrugh. Moreover Protestants as well as Catholics, Williamites as well as Jacobites were involved. Thus it was very difficult for either the English or the French to agree among themselves, let alone with each other, on an equable basis for exchange.

The next move was made by France. About 19/29 March several clerks of William Blathwayt, Secretary for War, were captured at sea while on their way over to King William's forces in Flanders, and were taken to Dunkirk, one of the ports noted for this sort of privateering. One of the clerks, James D'Ayrolle, was a Huguenot, who had served on a British embassy to Turkey and later served in Geneva and The Hague. On 5/15 April the commandant at Dunkirk wrote to Blathwayt offering the clerks in exchange for Bertillier, but Blathwayt advised Lord Nottingham nine days later that King William did not 'think it equable that such a one as Bertillier should be exchanged for one of my clerks, but his Majesty does on the other side think fitt that no French prisoners at all be released in England until my people have their liberty if it is true . . . that all prisoners taken at sea are immediately to be released'. D'Ayrolle, who had been sent to the Bastille, was now the centre of Blathwayt's attention; in July he was still telling Nottingham of D'Ayrolle's importance and his superior worth in comparison to Bertillier.

On 10/20 June Joseph Dulivier in Paris wrote, as Vanbrugh had foretold, to complain to the commissioners for the exchange of prisoners. After mentioning the peevishness of some prisoners he referred specifically to Vanbrugh:

It is really very hard service, as well as unjust, that my cousin Peter Dulivier should be kept in a messenger's hands near five months in reprisall of Monsr. Goddard, Vanbrugh and North, who are here prisoners of state and ready to be exchanged with any French prisoners in their circumstances . . . I must tell you more I have done for that most false ungratefull Vanbrugh, all the kind offices that I could be able to do for a brother, and I know it is that villain who has most ungratefully caused all these most false suggestions by his letters which he has since recanted . . . You must certainly know in some measure the services I have done to many in generall and to some in particular, therefore I humbly intreat you to represent it to my Lord Nottingham, who I am sure is falsely prepossess'd by Vanbrugh's

friends; and that if he is rightly inform'd will be pleas'd to consider the hard case of my kinsman.

By now enough had been discovered in London of the activities
and character of the Duliviers for this plea to fall on deaf ears.

On 16/26 August Vanbrugh wrote the letter to Blathwayt
which tells the story of his arrest. He went on to say in it that
North and Goddard had, like himself, been told that they would
be freed if they could procure Bertillier's release. But 'our
friends have not yet been able to get this Bertiller releas't, my
Lord Nottingham thinking it a dishonnour to the Nation, to be
oblieg'd to give a Prisoner of State, arrested in time of Warr, for
men that have been ceas'd in time of peace'. Vanbrugh went on
to describe one of those chance or fated encounters that sometimes occur in prisons. 'By an extraordinary means, (my
Chamber being near the place where he is)', Vanbrugh had
made contact with Count Marlotte or Morlot, who had been
arrested as long ago as 1684 as an agent of William of Orange.
The Count was condemned to death but his sentence was com-
muted to life imprisonment, 'shut up, in a miserable Dungeon,
without leave to see, speak with, or write to any body; no, not so
much as his Daughter'. The Count told Vanbrugh his story and
begged his assistance, 'since unless his Majesty delivers him,
by some suitable Exchange during the warr, he is sure to pass
the rest of his miserable life, in the malancholy condition he is
in'.

Vanbrugh then proposed 'that an Exchange might be made
between him and Bertiller; wch I hope may be found reasonable of all sides, since they are Prisoners, much upon the same
score'. If this were agreed, he had 'good assurance, both Mr
North Goddard & my self shall be releas't. As for Monsr:
d'Ayrole, I don't doubt but he'll procure his freedome by the
same means.' Nine days later Blathwayt, in Flanders with the
King, had read Vanbrugh's letter to him, and sent it on to Lord
Nottingham with the King's agreement to Bertillier's release
'in exchange for them all ... Marlotte included in the number
... leaving it nevertheless to the [Privy] councill to judge
whether such an exchange may be fitt to be made'.

On 2/12 September Nottingham sent Blathwayt a reply
which showed that, like many secretaries of state, he was able,

from an overall view of the situation, to advise caution rather than action. It also showed that Forval's cover had at last been blown:

> Befor what you wrote concerning Bertillier *alias* Forval be put in execution, I am commanded to acquaint you that this man has been a spye for France in most Countrys of Europe and came here for the like errand, and for his dexterity in that treacherous art is much valued by the Court of France. The condition of those gentlemen who are imprisoned in France is much to be pittied, there being no colour for such hardship towards them; whereas Forvall may justly be hanged and would at any time redeem any man who might be sent into France upon the like account. Besides, it may be dangerous to those gentlemen to offer Forvall in exchange for them and Marlotte, for tho' Mr. Vanbruck thinks the proposall would be accepted, yet he is not sure of it, and it might give a fair praetext to France to treat them as spyes, tho' hitherto there be no ground for the suspicion, since Forvall certainly is so. But if the King thinks it fitt his orders shall be speedily obeyed.

The King's reaction, communicated by Blathwayt on 8/18 September, was to delay further consideration of the matter until his return to England; this was in the event not until 20/30 October. Meanwhile the French had indicated that D'Ayrolle was not negotiable, being a French national (and a heretic).

Now a move – apparently decisive – was made by two Jacobites. Thomas Bruce, second Earl of Ailesbury (who was also, through the Ferrers family, a remote kinsman of Vanbrugh) and Major-General Thomas Maxwell were protégés of the Earl of Melfort, James II's secretary. Maxwell and another general named Dorrington had been captured at Athlone in 1691 and were imprisoned in the Tower of London, regarded awkwardly neither as prisoners of war nor as traitors. Many years later Lord Ailesbury referred to the two generals in his *Memoirs*; his account is faulty in some of the details, but it seems clear that he then suggested to Nottingham that Maxwell, who had been released on bail on 23 August 1692, should be balanced against Vanbrugh, North and Goddard. Nottingham agreed, the arrangements in Paris were made by Melfort from Saint-Germain, and on 22 November 1692, at eleven o'clock in the morning,

Vanbrugh was driven out of the Bastille in the customary official coach, on bail of 1000 pistoles (£800) offered by the Abbé de Lagny, the *fermier-général* who dealt – more officially than Joseph Dulivier – with the exchange of prisoners. His first destination was de Lagny's house to make formal expression of his thanks and thereby indicate the fact of his release.

Vanbrugh now had the freedom of Paris, and on 5 December Melfort wrote to Maxwell that the exchange had been accepted, but it was March 1693 before Vanbrugh left France. He was not free to go until all formalities had been completed, and he no doubt took his time to see the sights he had hoped to see four and a half years earlier. If he had yet more than a tourist's interest in buildings we know nothing of it, but as a tourist he would have seen and admired the domed churches, Nôtre-Dame, the vast complex of the Louvre and Tuileries palaces, Le Vau's College of the Four Nations on the left bank, and the many fine houses, especially those in the Marais and on the Ile Saint-Louis, fronted with the local sandstone. As the holder for **[13]** a few months of an ensign's commission he would have gone to see, and wondered at, the courts, arcades and carved military trophies of the Invalides, the old soldiers' home that far outstripped the Chelsea Pensioners' in size and grandeur. When he was fully at liberty he would surely have visited Versailles, the country palace that had become a town in itself as the seat of Louis XIV's government, through whose ledgers his own name had so recently, painfully and unmemorably made its passage. Whether he yet knew what he was seeing or not, all these buildings represented an architecture as yet unparalleled in England for scale, ostentation, richness, taste and sophistication. The branch of art-historical method known colloquially as source-hunting is based on the assumption that what an artist borrows from the past is precisely identifiable. As often as not, this assumption cannot be supported; nevertheless the Paris of the early 1690s must have left its mark on the twenty-eight-year-old Vanbrugh in more ways than he was yet ready or able to recognize.

Modern editors of Vanbrugh's plays have found a multitude of allusions in them not only to events of his day but to situations or phrases in other stage or literary works. In the years covered by the Account Book he recorded few purchases of books, but he belonged to a subscription library and perhaps had always been a borrower rather than an owner of books; the urgency conveyed by temporary possession means that borrowed books are more often read than owned ones. Reading must have been Vanbrugh's salvation in the years of confinement, and he will have read anything he could lay hands on; most if not all of it will have been in French. Lord Ailesbury, who was interested in the theatre, is the only source to identify by name *The Provok'd Wife* as the play Vanbrugh is thought to have sketched out while in the Bastille. This is a neat and tidy idea, because it seems not only to explain the play's eccentricities as the result of inexperience but also to answer the question of how he occupied his time. But Vanbrugh's own defence of this work implies, as we have seen, that it was conceived much earlier, when he was 'very young'. It may well have been another play, of which we now know nothing, that was sketched out in the Bastille.

Maybe it does not matter very much; more important is the effect of his experience on Vanbrugh's character. 'The more one's alone, the more one thinks', says Corinna in *The Confederacy*. When he drove out of the Bastille, Vanbrugh had spent half his adult life so far in captivity, in a foreign and hostile country, without trial and on charges whose nature nobody could remember. He had known hope and despair. He had accepted his keepers as friends in default of others; in 1716 he sent, by way of Sir James Thornhill, good wishes to a Mr Janse at Calais. He had acquired a taste for the comic dramatists and the architecture of France and an equal distaste for her political system. He had learned to say less than he meant or knew, to confide in few and to believe nobody, and to act a part. He had learned much about people, and about himself. For the next year or two he would exult in his freedom and the music that is one's native tongue after a long time abroad. But since after that he sought fresh adventures at sea, even in the face of the French, it seems that he was still not sure who he was, or what he wanted to do.

At the end of March 1693 Vanbrugh and Goddard crossed the English Channel and landed in Kent; they had no papers and were promptly arrested.

— 9 —

Distinguished Service

Giles Vanbrugh was buried at Holy Trinity, Chester, on 19 July 1689. From a memoir written in 1710 by the preacher Matthew Henry we know that he succumbed, 'a zealous good man', together with 'many others of note in the Congregation', to 'a contagious fever'. His widow moved away from the parish, presumably selling the houses and other interests as directed by Giles's will. In later legal document she is described variously as of Chester and of London. We know that John spent about a week in Chester in 1700, but the story repeated from *Notes and Queries* of 1856, that Vanbrughs remained in the city until the end of the eighteenth century, must relate to another branch of the family. For they were descended from George (d. 1758) who was the son of one of John's first cousins, children of his uncle William; either George (1668-1729) who certified his will or possibly William (1658-1716) to whom we shall return presently.

The George who died in 1758 has his own small place in history as a bass singer and a composer of songs. Although nothing is known of his early life, about 1720 he was one of the Duke of Chandos's resident musicians at Cannons. Some years later he went to Canterbury where he seems to have been a lay clerk in the cathedral choir; he was buried in the cathedral precinct. He sent his son Robert (1728-84) to Sedbergh School and then on a scholarship to Eton; Robert then went to Cambridge, took Holy Orders, and became headmaster of the King's School in Chester and in 1780 a minor canon of the cathedral there. He died elsewhere in 1784, but his mother Mary was buried in the cathedral in 1773 and his son, also George (1756-1847), became a minor canon in the same year as Robert and in 1789 married at Chester a daughter of an old and wealthy family of the city, Frances Ravenscroft. By this time the youngest George was rector of Aughton, near Ormskirk, retiring in 1834 to the seaside near Liverpool. In 1813 he had published a cantata, *Lysander*, composed by his grandfather, but already the family history and fortunes were sufficiently confused for him to put Sir John Vanbrugh on the title page. It is a spirited piece in the style of Handel, but the parsimony of the words confirms that they had nothing to do with the playwright.

The only member of Giles's family known to have remained in or returned to Chester was the architect's sister Mary. She was buried in Holy Trinity churchyard on 2 March 1748 and became briefly and locally famous because a tree began to grow out of her coffin.

The letter which Vanbrugh smuggled out of Vincennes by Sir Daniel Arthur (9 November 1691) is addressed to his mother at the house of his cousin Gerrard Weyman in Thames Street, London, but this may have been no more than a convenient City address for Arthur to deliver it. Weyman's next-door neighbour was another cousin, Jasper Van den Busch, also a merchant; in 1695 John Vanbrugh's brother Carleton, then twenty-two, was listed in Jasper's house as one of his servants. By that time a younger brother, Dudley, was eighteen and an undergraduate at Merton College, Oxford; he graduated in 1697 and received his MA in July 1700, but before the autumn he was dead and buried in the college. John Vanbrugh's half-sister Elizabeth Garencieres was still in Cheshire, but we do not know the whereabouts of any of his six unmarried sisters aged between twenty and thirty; his three youngest brothers must have remained with their mother. John will certainly have sought her out on his return from France, and the teen-age lads will have listened open-mouthed to the story of his adventures abroad.

His mother will in turn have told John as much as she knew of another Dudley Vanbrugh, the brother of William and George. On 24 June 1685 this Dudley had been commissioned ensign in Henry Vaughan's company of Sir Edward Hales's Foot Regiment, and the rest of his short life was spent, as far as historians are concerned, being confused with his cousin John. On 13 April 1686 three companies of Hales's regiment were ordered to Hull to replace Lord Huntingdon's troops, and if Dudley's was among them the cousins may possibly have met briefly during the change-over. On 22 August two of Hales's companies were ordered to Jersey. We know that Dudley's was not one of them, but this may be at the root of the chain of confusions that produced the legend of John Vanbrugh's leaving the army rather than go to *Guernsey*.

On 6 November 1688 Dudley was promoted to lieutenant in Sir George Berkeley's company of the same regiment, and on 28 February 1689 to a captaincy in a newly established regiment of foot commanded by Colonel William Beveridge. (The John Brook commissioned captain in Beveridge's regiment the same day was of course not John *Vanbrook*.)

We know little more about Captain Dudley until November 1692 when he was involved in a tragic incident in Flanders which is still occasionally misattributed to his cousin John. On the 22nd Luttrell reported that 'Ostend letters say, Collonel Beveredge of the Scots regiment being at dinner with Captain Vanbrook of the same, words arose and swords were after drawn, and the collonel was killed, having given abusive language to the captain first and shook him.' On 13 February 1693 Dudley was court-martialled, but acquitted on grounds of provocation from his commanding officer. How these events might have affected his career we cannot say, for a few months later, on 29 July 1693, Dudley died in the battle of Landen.

John Vanbrugh's activities after his return from France evidently centred on his Bertie connections. On 11 May 1693 he took up the Duchy of Lancaster sinecure which Tobias Legros had been keeping warm for him, and which he would retain until 1702. It is picturesque but mistaken to imagine him sitting in a little office in Lancaster checking accounts; whatever filled his days took place in London and close to the Berties, and Duchy papers of the time are signed *Richard Husband, Deputy Auditor*. Accident has preserved one relevant document, mixed up in State Papers in the Public Record Office, a private letter which reads in its tantalizing obscurity like the kind of paper that is delivered to a stage character somewhere in the second Act. It is a letter of 20 May 1694 from E. Smith to Henry Tomlin 'at Mr Friths over against the Red Lyon in Bromley Street Drury Lane', enclosing another letter (which does not survive) to a Mr Hobes in a cover addressed to Mr Vanbrugh. This 'will certainly come safe to him', says E. Smith (who seems to be a young woman), for 'that Gentellman you may hear of by any of My Lord Lindsees servants: or elce to be sure by his second son, who is his intimate friend'.

The third Earl of Lindsey's second son, Lord Willoughby's younger brother, was Peregrine Bertie, who had been appointed Vice-Chamberlain of the Household early in 1694. It must be this Peregrine, rather than his uncle who was nearly sixty, who in August 1690, according to Luttrell, had 'upon a wager run the Mall in St James Park 11 times in less than an hour'. The total distance was about 10,000 metres, so the time taken would be roughly twice that of a modern trained athlete. What was unusual was less the feat than the performer, since wagers of this kind were more commonly laid on a running footman. Certainly if he had been at liberty Vanbrugh would have been in the Mall that day to cheer on his friend.

The prison years had sharpened and hardened Vanbrugh's character but, even if by 1694 he may have begun to sense the direction in which to seek them, the paths by which he would find identity – and excellence – still lay some way ahead. The story of the child whose first words, long after their appointed time, form a perfect and perceptive sentence, is part folklore and part real experience. The study of human endeavour often has to proceed by anecdote and intuition because other means simply do not exist; in Richard Feinman's wise words about learning in general, more is known than can be proved. If it is a mystery how *The Relapse* and Castle Howard came to be at once both apprentice works and masterpieces, the only clues must lie in the hidden years of the mid-1690s. Nevertheless two other matters must have preoccupied Vanbrugh in that period: Whiggism and revenge.

Vanbrugh's life-long Whiggism is bound up with the early and obscure history of the Kit-Cat Club, a society which combined political, literary and convivial interests under the **[1]**   secretaryship of the publisher Jacob Tonson. Sir Godfrey Kneller's portrait of Vanbrugh was probably painted about 1705, as one of the long series of portraits of Kit-Cat members, commissioned by Tonson but paid for individually by the sitters. The forty-one surviving canvases remained in the hands of Tonson's heirs until their purchase in 1945 for the National Portrait Gallery. With the exception of the double picture of the Earl of Lincoln and the Duke of Newcastle, each canvas measures 36 x 28 inches (91·5 x 71 cm) and the format, which has both practical and aesthetic advantages in allowing the hands to be included in a life-size image, has come to be known as Kit-Cat from its extensive use in Tonson's series.

It is of the nature of clubs to be essentially exclusive, self-regulating and self-censoring; they lose their character as soon as outsiders are party to their deliberations. But exclusiveness arouses among the excluded curiosity, suspicion, sometimes fear or envy, and in the case of the Kit-Cat the result was a number of publications either purporting to reveal or intended to ridicule the club's activities. Undoubtedly a certain section of society read these works eagerly, but for historians they say very little. The earliest of them is Tom Browne's long-winded satirical poem, *A Description of Mr D----n's Funeral* (1700). In May 1700 the club took charge of Dryden's burial in Westminster Abbey in what has become known as Poet's Corner; Kneller's portrait of Dryden at Trinity College, Cambridge (1697) is of Kit-Cat format, and he may have been a member. A dozen lines will show the limits of Browne's composition as either a work of literature or a historical source:

A Troop of Stationers at first appear'd,
And *Jacob T----n* Captain of the Guard . . .

Next these the Play-house Sparks do take their Turn,
With such as under *Mercury* are born,
As Poets, Fidlers, Cut-purses, and Whores,
Drabs of the Play-house, and of Common-shores ...

A Crowd of Fools attend him to the Grave,
A Crowd so nauseous, so profusely lewd,
With all the Vices of the Times endu'd,
That *Cowley*'s Marble wept to see the Throng,

Old *Chaucer* laugh'd at their unpolish'd Song,
And *Spencer* thought he once again had seen
The Imps attending of his *Fairy Queen*:

Edward Ward's *Secret History of Clubs* (1709) promises vastly more than it yields; apart from references to Tonson as organizer and to the 'shoals of Custards' and other food 'fit for Gods or Poets' consumed by the club, Ward tells us that the name *Kit-Cat* came from a caterer named Christopher (Kit) whose sign was the Cat and Fiddle; other writers however imply that the man's name was Christopher Catt, which may also be true, although a portrait exhibited over his name in 1867 seems to have been titled in error.

The papers acquired by the National Portrait Gallery with the Kneller pictures include a receipted bill of 1689 for 'meat and fruit by arrangement', thirty gallons of wine and various sundries including 7s. 6d. for broken glasses. The bill was paid by Tonson and three others, and may therefore be the earliest dated document of the club, even though the caterer's name is not Catt but Laurens Renaut. On the other hand, the prodigious quantity of alcohol supplied seems excessive for the earliest days of a club that was never very numerous, even bearing in mind the drinking habits of the age: according to Joseph Spence, Wycherley's usual supper was a pint of sherry, a pint of port and two or three apples. Moreover, the Kit-Cat was not a tippling club, and the practice in its later more social years of toasting young ladies was a courtly rather than a rowdy one, as a letter to Lady Granby in November 1703 confirms:

The last 4th of this month was King William's Birthday. 'Twas kept with eluminations &c in the chief streets all over the town, and Lord Orford, Lord Sunderland made bonfires there. The glass sent down was to the immortal memory of King William. They had all new cloaths &c, and now I am on the Kitcat, 'tis proper to tell your Ladyship that a great number of glasses are chose and a sett number of ladys names are writ on them, and as an addition some fine thing is to be said on every lady, and writ there to. For your Ladyship must know that at this famous meeting they sometimes refresh themselves with a glass of wine, but with great moderation 'tis said.

The principal source for the club's existence at an earlier date is John Oldmixon, a Whig historian who knew many of those involved. In his *History of England* (1735) he says that the club grew

> from a private Meeting of Mr Somers, afterwards Lord Chancellor, and another lawyer ... and Mr Tonson ... who before the Revolution met frequently in the Evening at a Tavern, near Temple Bar, to unbend themselves after Business, and have a little free and chearful Conversation in those dangerous Times ... a Mutton Pye a piece, made by a pastry-Cook in that neighbourhood, who became famous for his Excellence in that way.

Another significant remark is much later: writing of Kneller, Horace Walpole, whose father was a Kit-Cat, referred to the club as 'generally mentioned as a set of wits, in reality the patriots that saved Britain'. In its early days the club's serious purpose was the promotion of Whig objectives: a strong Parliament, a limited monarchy, resistance to France, and most important the Protestant succession to the throne. The first succession crisis, on the abdication of James II, ended with the arrival of William and Mary; those of 1702 (on the death of William) and 1714 (on the death of Queen Anne) were less acute, and in any case the club's political value would have been greatest before it became publicly known, let alone fashionable.

Lord Somers (1651-1716) was a lawyer who made his name as the brilliant junior counsel for the Seven Bishops at their trial in June 1688. In April James II had issued, illegally in the view of Parliament, a second Declaration of Indulgence, which not only confirmed the freedom of worship granted to both Dissenters and Catholics in his first declaration of the previous April but also boasted of the appointment of Catholics to positions of civil and military authority. The clergy were ordered to publish the declaration from their pulpits; the Archbishop of Canterbury and six of his bishops decided to draw the King's fire by a petition against this order. James accordingly took them to court on a charge of seditious libel, but they were acquitted on 30 June, the same day (and three weeks after the birth of the Prince of Wales) on which the invitation was signed by another group of seven (six noblemen and the Bishop of London) to William of Orange.

Somers was a cultured man with aspirations to the patronage of literature and an interest in the visual arts; Kneller's portrait shows him holding the new edition of Spenser's *Faerie Queen* which he sponsored. Tonson (c. 1656–1736) was the most enterprising and most successful publisher of his day. His origins were not exalted – his father was a City surgeon; he was a man of great energy and good business sense. He never married, and when Vanbrugh at last left the bachelor state in 1719 Tonson was the last to be told, with a jocular warning that his turn might yet come. He was, from its misty origins to its last known meeting in 1717, the secretary and the leading light of the club. Kneller's portraits are the principal and most reliable documents for the club's membership, not only in default of others, but also because they have a permanence and a public character rare in the history of private societies. According to Macky (1714) another early member was certainly the sixth Earl of Dorset, who was among Vanbrugh's vast Carleton kinship, had connections with the stage, and was one of the first to present his portrait.

The importance of the club can not only be inferred from the secrecy that surrounds its early years but also demonstrated by the names and likenesses of its members painted by the senior portraitist of the day. They included (besides probably Dryden) the writers Congreve, Addison, Steele, and Walsh, soldiers like Lords Stanhope and Cobham and John Tidcombe, Lord Halifax the founder of the Bank of England, the diplomat Lord Manchester, the physician and poet Sir Samuel Garth and Thomas, Marquess of Wharton who, as an atheist and a rake respectively, were among the more obvious targets of invective against the club. Thirty members – about two-thirds – were peers, three became knights; there were also country gentlemen. We do not know how soon after his return in 1693 Vanbrugh became a member, or who introduced him; none of the Whig Berties is known to have belonged, but since the fullest list of names is that of the portraits the possibility cannot be entirely excluded. The importance of the club for Vanbrugh is sufficiently indicated by the presence in the list of five of his future architectural patrons.

Vanbrugh seems to have felt he had not finished with the French, for the summer of 1694 saw him as a volunteer at sea. While William III was fighting France on land in Flanders, in the defence both of his Dutch territories and of his title to the throne of England, a slower war was taking place in the English Channel, the Bay of Biscay and the approaches to the Mediterranean. In 1692 Louis XIV gathered a huge army near the coast, and an invasion fleet at Brest; at the battle of La Hogue (19 May 1692) his fleet was so severely damaged that Louis abandoned the idea of an invasion. But in late June 1693 a long-prepared British merchant convoy bound for Smyrna was savaged by the French fleet in the Gulf of Cadiz. Evelyn reported the loss of sixty merchant ships and two men-of-war. He attributed the disaster, which had been expected for some time, to imprudence or treachery, and called it 'the greatest Blow was ever given the Citty since the fire, & affecting the whole nation'.

Gradually King William's commanders evolved a policy of attacking harbours, installations and shipping with cannon and mortar fire, both to inflict damage and in the hope of diverting French troops from Flanders. In November 1693, for example, Captain Benbow bombarded St Malo for three days. The Camaret Bay action of 7-8 June 1694, the brain-child of Lieutenant-General Thomas Tollemache, related to this campaign, but it was also an attempt to redress the balance both between the opposing powers and in political eyes at home. It failed, with considerable loss of lives.

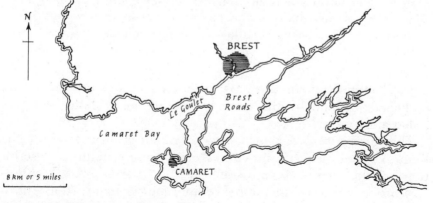

D   Camaret Bay and the Port of Brest.

The fleet left Portsmouth on 30 May. Forty-seven English
and Dutch warships under Admiral Russell proceeded towards
the Mediterranean; a second squadron of twenty-nine ships of
the line, led by John, Lord Berkeley of Stratton, detached itself
on 5 June and made for Ushant. There were also numerous
support ships, and six thousand land soldiers were carried, including companies from Vanbrugh's old regiment.

[D]   Camaret Bay faces south-west on the west coast of the
Breton peninsula; the port of Brest lies within a sound which is
connected with the bay by a throat of water (the *Goulet*) about
a mile wide. Camaret Fort is on the south side of the bay, and
the plan was to capture this with an invasion force, so as to deprive the French of fire power across the *Goulet*; the sound and
the port of Brest would then lie open to naval attack.

On the evening of 7 June Berkeley's ships anchored in the
bay, keeping out of shot of the shore but, as an observer put it,
'entertained with [mortar] bombs from the land on Camaret
side, also from both sides going into Brest Sound and along the
north shore almost as far as St Matthew's Point'. In spite of a
great deal of gunfire the extent of French preparedness was
not realized that evening. The next day, 8 June, seven frigates
led by the Marquis of Carmarthen formed a cover for the landing of several hundred soldiers near Camaret Fort. But

> they were so warmly received by the enemy, that Tolmach was
> shot through the thigh, and with difficulty was brought off; and
> the rest, not being able to advance by reason of the intrench-
> ments and fortifications and numbers of horse and foot upon the
> shore, insomuch that most of our men that landed were either
> killed or taken prisoners, the rest of our soldiers returned on
> board.

Several landing boats were left grounded as the tide went out,
and were burned by the French; one of the frigates also was
holed and sunk.

This account so far is based on manuscript reports of the
time. A more local but much longer and more detailed description of the action is provided in the *Journal of the Brest-
Expedition* written and published in London before the end of
June by Lord Carmarthen, evidently in an attempt to defend in

public his own actions and maintain his reputation as a commander. During the invasion attempt itself he had no sooner gone on board the leading frigate, the *Monk*, than the wind dropped. 'I was forc'd to get Boats to tow us on our way, and as soon as we were separated a little from the Fleet, the Enemy began to throw their Bombs very fast upon us.' The *Monk* was damaged by one bomb, two marines were killed and a third injured; then the battery at Camaret Fort opened up 'for a considerable time having the opportunity of Raking us fore and aft'. Carmarthen seems to have spent most of the time of the actual landing going from one frigate to another, repositioning each ship in an attempt to give fire cover for the troops in the face of a French defensive power which had been greatly underrated. These manoeuvres also involved the towing of ships into position, and between those soldiers who had landed and were killed or wounded and those who had lost their boats and were floundering in the water the chaos was general. The gunners on Carmarthen's flagship, the *Charles*, were vigorous but 'so undisciplin'd and such ill Marksmen' that their fire had little effect on the fort. When the retreat was sounded on shore the conditions on board were near to panic.

Carmarthen showed not only great energy but considerable bravery, taking his twenty-oared boat under enemy fire to pick up retreating troops from the water. Much of the rigging of the cover ships had been shot away, and he once more had to go from boat to boat directing towing operations until ship-to-ship tows could be secured. Matters were made even more difficult by the indiscipline of the boat crews, who 'gave over towing, and ran all of a huddle under the shelter of the ship, notwithstanding all the Officers could say or do to encourage them'. The boats to left and right of Carmarthen's were hit, four men were killed and one boat sunk;

> this so disincourag'd my Men, that they all gave over towing, and began to get under the shelter of the Ship again, so that I was forc'd my self to fire a Musquet at them, and to take up another to do the same, before I could make them return to their work.

By this time the exploit was effectively at an end. At an evening council held in the bay it was decided that no other landing could be attempted, and a proposal to sail into the sound and bombard Brest was ruled out as unrealistic 'unless we could be certain we could ride without reach of their bombs'. On 9 June the fleet weighed anchor and sailed for Spithead; Lieutenant-General Tollemache died of his wound three days later. On 15 July Evelyn recorded that

> My Lord Berkley burnt Dieppe & Haverdegrace [Le Havre] with the bombs in revenge of the defeate at Brest: This manner of destructive warring begun every where by the French, tho' it be exceeding ruinous, especialy falling on the poorer people, & is very barbarous, dos not seeme to tend to make any sooner end of the Warr but rather to exasperate, & incite to revenge.

Lord Carmarthen's *Journal* has long been known to naval historians, but only recently has the significance been realized of one of the names mentioned in it. On the evening of 7 June, he writes,

> A little before we came to an Anchor, My Lord *Cutts*, and my self, agreed to go on Board my Galley, and look into *Camarett*-Bay, taking along with us Sir *John Jacobs*, Captain *Pitman*, Captain *Hammond*, Mr *Vanbrooke*, &c. that were on Board the *Royal William* . . . having stood well into the Bay, so as to gain a good View of it, we were warmly fir'd at by *Camarett*-Fort; but by the assistance of those few little Guns we had in the Galley, and the good Sailing of her, we made a shift in our own Smoke to get out again, without any Damage.

Mr Vanbrooke (the title *Mr* is used by sailors even of an admiral) received a second mention in the remarks at the end of Carmarthen's narration:

> Most of the Volunteers on Board the Royal *William* offered me their Service, which I accepted of, and they all behaved themselves extraordinarily well, and were most of them of great use to me, particularly Mr *Vanbrooke*, Captain *Chasseloup*, Mr *Bonard*, and Mr *Dixon* (my Secretary).
> Mr *Vanbrooke* during all this Action, stuck very close to me, and in a great many things, was extremely Serviceable both by his advice and otherwise.

In the light of Carmarthen's account of his own actions, Mr Vanbrooke must have been in very considerable danger, and his assistance was evidently both energetic and intelligent. If the whole *Journal* had been intended as a roundabout testimonial for him it could not have been better composed, but of course that was not its purpose. The question whether this Mr Vanbrooke was our subject or another member of the family can be answered positively and with certainty.

Peregrine Osborne was born in 1659 and succeeded to the title of Marquis of Carmarthen early in 1694 when his father was created Duke of Leeds. In 1690 he was a captain in the Royal Navy and became the colonel of the Marine Regiment, the first ever formed specifically of soldiers fighting at sea. His mother was Bridget Bertie, sister of the third Earl of Lindsey, and he was thus a first cousin of Vanbrugh's friends Lord Willoughby and Peregrine Bertie the Vice-Chamberlain. The next significant reference is in a letter of 15 August 1695 from Lord Berkeley, the commander in the Brest action, to William Vernon:

> I never preferred any officer upon Lord Carmarthen's recommendation, but promised to make one Mr Vanbrook, a gentleman at sea with him last year, a captain in my regiment, if there was a vacancy in his regiment, and any of my captains willing to go to him; so now I will agree to take him, provided Captain Rodney of my regiment be put into his.

This arrangement seems to have fallen through, and Mr Vanbrook evidently remained with Lord Carmarthen until the New Year. We do not know if he saw further action: a typical instance of warfare in the English Channel is given by Evelyn a month after this letter (15 September 1695):

> My good & worthy friend Cap: Gifford, who that he might get some competency to live decently, adventured all he had in a Voyage of 2 years to the *E. Indies*, was with another greate ship, taken by some French Men-of-Warr, almost within sight of England, to the losse of neere 700000 pounds: to my greate sorrow, & pity of his Wife: he being also a valiant & industrious man: The losses of this sort to the Nation has ben immense; & all thro the negligence & little care of the Government, to secure

the same neere our owne Coasts, of infinite more concernment to the publique than spending their time in bombing & ruining two or three paltry Towns, Calais, St Malo &c in which so many poore Creatures are destroyed, without any benefit, or weakening our Enemys, who, tho' they began, ought not to have ben imitated by an hostility totally averse to humanity, & especialy to Christianity.

The sparse documents of the marine officers in this period give the impression that in the winter months most of the fleet was laid up, that even for much of the summer many officers were ashore, and the senior officers spent much of their time in London. We shall see that Vanbrugh was increasingly in London as time went on, but that it was he who assisted Carmarthen in the Brest attack is finally confirmed by two warrants, one of 31 January for John Brooke Esq. to be captain in Lord Berkeley's marine foot regiment in place of Richard Courtenay, the other of 20 August 1698, after the end of the war, for half-pay to a number of marine officers including Captain John Vanbrook. But between the issuing of those two orders Vanbrugh had effectively left the theatre of war to achieve personal victory on another stage.

_ 10 _

The Restoration Stage

The Puritan objection to the stage does not stem simply from the view that neither actors nor the characters they portray are, in Fletcher's phrase, better than they should be. In fact both the tendency of plays to 'containe much Matter of Prophanation and Scurrility' and also their capacity for 'the Debauchinge of the Manners of Such as are present at them' and for being 'very Scandalous and offensive to all pious and well disposed persons' were used as the pretext for licensing the theatres of Restoration London by royal warrant. These phrases occur in the patent given on 21 August 1660 to Thomas Killigrew and Sir William Davenant for the right to build playhouses and employ actors, to the exclusion of all others in London, Westminster and their suburbs. These two courtiers were also authorized to read plays and to 'expunge all Prophanesse and Scurrility' before they were performed, a task which they seem to have discharged with considerable liberality of mind.

Many of the documents about the restoration of the theatre in 1660 have disappeared since they were printed by nineteenth-century writers; they came from the papers collected by Sir Henry Herbert, Master of the Revels for over forty years, in the cause of his petitions and suits against Killigrew and Davenant whom, he claimed, the King had unlawfully allowed to assume functions and divert monetary rewards that belonged to the Office of the Revels. Not for the first or for the last time, licensing was used both in order to control the content and the 'representation' of plays, and to extract a certain amount of revenue from entertainment.

On the other hand the royal patent also included the more optimistic statement that 'if the Evill & Scandall In the Playes that now are or have bin acted were taken away, the same might serve as Innocent and Harmlesse divertisements for many of our Subjects'. Indeed, moreover, 'such Kind of Entertainments . . . if well Mannaged, might serve as Morrall Instructions in Humane life'. These ideas were unacceptable to Puritans because the basis of their objection to the stage was Calvin's equation of fictions with lies: plays were forbidden because they were not true.

A very different view of the theatre is the one that it is about life and is therefore not fiction at all but in some way a kind of truth. Aristotle had defined poetry as a generalized representation of reality, as opposed to the particularized representations offered by history. He saw the drama as occupying a world with its own validity but distinct from that of everyday life; because the two worlds are parallel, that of fiction can instruct as well as entertain, conveying truth as in a mirror. The extreme view nowadays is that, since art is about life, anything imaginable in life, however mundane or however disturbing, may or even ought to be represented in the theatre. This attitude is neither more nor less reasonable than Calvin's, and it is quite important to remember that a mirror is one of the attributes of a virtue often forgotten today, particularly in artistic matters — that of prudence.

Prudence often tells us, both in life and in art, that there are reasons for not displaying all that we know. In the drama a good and sufficient reason lies in the nature of the art itself, in which the combined effect of actions and words on our imagination enables much more to be suggested than is actually shown. Just how powerful the inner world of the imagination can be, without the aid of any external stimulus at all, is confirmed by the contemporary therapist's advocacy of fantasy as a method for dealing with problems of character or behaviour. But the only novelty in this is the therapist's status: the ancient Greeks after all recognized the restorative properties of a good cry or a good laugh. Moreover while not all plays can be called literature many are that to a greater or lesser extent, and the power of words alone is remarkable. A blind man can enjoy a play or even a farce, and a broadcast play can be totally real in the hearer's imagination.

Plays are written to be acted, and the greatest playwright of the English language never bothered much about the printing of his plays. But printed they were, though many a student grappling with the mysteries of *Hamlet* has wished that they were not. The reading of plays demands more from the imagination than the hearing of them, but by Pepys's time plays were not only commonly printed as soon as acted, if not before, but also, as his diary shows, widely read with enjoyment. Indeed they occupied the place in the imagination later filled by novels, and like novels they were, and are, judged as good, bad or indifferent not only by experts and critics but, in plainer language, by ordinary readers; Pepys was not alone for his day in noting plays as excellent, good, dreary, silly or bawdy. A generation later Vanbrugh will have done the same for some time before venturing from the company of the judges to that of the judged. When on 21 November 1696 the curtain rose on *The Relapse* he ceased to be one of the myriad particularities of history and became what he has been ever since, an object of study in his own right.

The Puritan ban did not extend to music. Several masques were performed in the Inner Temple in the early 1650s, and in May 1656 Sir William Davenant staged at his own residence, Rutland House, Aldersgate, an opera or 'Entertainment by Musick and Declarations'. This was followed in September by *The Siege of Rhodes*, which was noted for the elaboration of the movable scenery contrived by the architect John Webb for such a small hall. In the middle of the 1650s a number of illicit performances of plays were attempted, at the Red Bull in Clerkenwell and elsewhere; the vigour of the illegal theatre is suggested by the frequency of the orders banning it, but by 1659 'Tollerances' were being issued to producers for the fitting up of playhouses. The Restoration brought the recognition of the theatre, the licensing of companies, and momentous changes in the production of plays which affected playhouses, players and audiences alike. During the 1660s, as Pepys's record shows, several theatre buildings were in use in London and the West End, but before the end of 1660 there were only

two companies, who shared between them the exclusive right
to erect theatres and perform plays.

Two companies were as much as, or indeed rather more
than, the size of the theatre-going public could support, and
from 1682 to 1695 they were amalgamated into a single organization, the United Company. But the joint monopoly of
1660 gave the seal of royal approval, and Charles II and his
brother took a great interest in the theatre. Royal support also
gave the hope or illusion of a permanent future for the London
stage, and in the two decades between the Restoration and the
amalgamation an element of competition led to constructive
as well as to some meretricious innovations.

Killigrew's group, the King's Company, opened at the Vere
Street Theatre (near what is now the southern end of Kings-
way) on 8 November 1660. The theatre was a long but not very
large rectangular building shaped like a tennis court, which
indeed is what it had been. Killigrew had the advantages of a
band of experienced actors and the exclusive right to perform
almost all the best existing plays. The theatre's limited width
and the impossibility of expansion meant that there was no
room to operate the moving scenery of sliding shutters which
had characterized both the old court masques and Davenant's
Siege of Rhodes. Killigrew had, as the preface to his *Comedies
and Tragedies* (1664) puts it, suffered 'Twenty Years Banish-
ment', although he was in London for part of the early 1640s.
The plays in that volume are specified as having been written
variously in Naples, Basle, Paris, Turin, Florence, Madrid,
Venice, Rome, and one in London, and as a life-long man of the
theatre Killigrew will during his travels have taken a keen and
professional interest in the elaborate scenic contrivances of
foreign theatres. If only for scenic reasons Vere Street could be
no more than temporary, and on 7 May 1663 the King's Company moved to a newly built playhouse, the Theatre Royal in
Bridges Street (now Catherine Street).

Killigrew's adroitness in securing the rights to the existing
repertory left Davenant with a shortage of ready material;
moreover, when the Duke's Company opened, also in November 1660, they were much less experienced than the King's.
They started in a converted barn at Salisbury Court, south-
west of St Bride's, Fleet Street, but on 28 June 1661 they moved

E   Reconstruction of Drury Lane Theatre in 1674, showing what is reasonably certain.

to more satisfactory accommodation in another refurbished tennis court – Lisle's in Lincoln's Inn Fields, opening with *The Siege of Rhodes*. Pepys noted on 4 July that the rival King's Theatre, still then crammed into Vere Street, was 'empty since the opera begun', and Davenant's production ran for an unprecedented twelve days. The scenery and costumes contributed greatly to its success. Davenant's advantages were those born of necessity: determination to succeed, attention to good management, experience with moving scenery in small spaces, and the need to develop a new repertory and exploit new kinds of play, both heroic and what we should call farcical. Finally in 1671, after Davenant's death, the Duke's Company moved to a new and more commodious theatre at Dorset Garden* furnished with the latest in stage machinery. During the period of amalgamation (1682-95) Dorset Garden was used generally for operas and spectacular plays rather than for comedies and the simpler tragedies.

The emphasis on spectacle and scenery brought about a lasting change from the permanent sets and open stages of Elizabethan and early Stuart theatres. The typical playhouse of the later Restoration is assumed to be the new Theatre Royal – not the one in Bridges Street, which burned down in January 1672 but its replacement on roughly the same site, purpose-

* p. 51

built for Killigrew and approached from Drury Lane from
which it took its name. The attention of theatre historians has
been concentrated on this building in the belief that we know
what it originally looked like, although before it was completely rebuilt in 1791 it had been altered more than once.
There is a lengthwise sectional drawing of a theatre among the
Wren drawings at All Souls, Oxford, whose dimensions are sufficiently close, and it is probably safe to accept both that Christopher Wren was therefore its architect and that in general the
interior as it was in 1674 can be reconstructed from this draw-
[E]   ing. Among theatre scholars only Richard Southern seems to
have noted with caution what should surprise no historian of
architecture: that a surviving drawing is likely to represent a
preliminary or penultimate design rather than the final one.
Nevertheless the study of stage directions in published plays
and in prompt books confirms the main features of this type of
playhouse.

What distinguished the late Restoration playhouse from the
pure picture-frame stage of the eighteenth and nineteenth
centuries was the large extent of the *proscenium* or forestage
in front of the proscenium arch. It was here, as in Shakespeare's theatre, that the greater part of the action took place, so
that the actors' world extended spatially into that of the
audience. In the All Souls drawing this extension is expressed
architecturally: the forestage is bounded at the sides by the
same system of pilasters and arches as that through which the
side boxes look into the auditorium. The two doors on either
side of the forestage are framed by this same architecture; they
were used for entrances and exits as well as for concealing one
character from the others but not from the audience. There
was also a convention by which an exit through one door and a
re-entrance through the adjacent one could accompany, or
even signify, a change of scene. In addition, the openings
above the doors were used by the characters for window and
balcony scenes.

Behind the proscenium arch was a deep stage for scenery: it
speaks for the importance of the new scenery that in spite of
the high value of land in an inner-city area so much of the site
was taken up by space which brought no direct return from the
sale of seats. This 'vista stage' was crossed from side to side by

a number of grooves, in which were inserted sliding shutters, painted with whatever scene was required, lubricated with soap, and framed by cut-out wings at the sides and borders above, which remained the same for one whole production but could be changed for the next. The wings and borders were set in echelon, identical or similar motifs being repeated in diminishing size, so as to exaggerate the perspective depth of the stage. This meant that the far upstage would have made the actors look like giants if they had appeared there; but in any case problems both of lighting from the front and of vocal projection precluded its use in this way except for special effects. On the other hand it is not unusual to find a direction that after an episode in front of a house 'the scene opens' to reveal the inside of the same house, or, as in the last Act of Vanbrugh's *The Confederacy*, that the scene opens from one room to an inner chamber. The front, downstage, part of the vista stage was thus part of the actors' world but was quite separate from that of the audience; the far upstage belonged only to the scenery.

Macky in 1722 explains one of the differences between English and foreign theatres of this time. The latter were

> composed of Rows of small Shut-Boxes, three or four Stories in a Semi-Circle, with a *Parterre* below, whereas here the *Parterre* (commonly call'd the *Pit*) contains the Gentlemen on Benches; and on the first Row of Boxes sit all the Ladies of Quality; in the second, the Citizens Wives and Daughters; and in the third, the common People and Footmen.

Moreover, in the London theatre during the progress of the play

> the whole is illuminated to the greatest Advantage: whereas abroad, the Stage being only illuminated, and the Lodge or Boxes close, you have the Pleasure of seeing the Company.

Thus those who preferred to do so could watch the audience rather than the players.

Sometimes a play would be announced as having new scenery; this was an added attraction because many of the sets

were very familiar to regular play-goers, being used again and
again. This was especially the case in comedies of human
behaviour, which are usually set in streets, squares, parlours,
bedrooms, gardens and parks. But in comedy the quick
changes made possible by the shutters could be exploited to
especially good effect. In Act III of Vanbrugh's *The Relapse* the
scene changes from a London garden to the outside of Sir Tunbelly's country house, two and a half minutes later to a room
inside, and after another minute to a different room.

The second great difference between the Restoration theatre
and that of the preceding age was in the performers. Pepys, not
yet then a frequent theatre-goer, first noted women on the
stage when he saw Fletcher's *Beggars' Bush* at Vere Street on 3
January 1661. The following day he saw, also at Vere Street,
The Scornful Lady by Beaumont and Fletcher 'acted very well',
but on 12 February he saw it again with the title part 'now done
by a woman, which makes the play appear much better than
ever it did to me'. Although women had previously appeared in
court masques and in Davenant's operas, the rule in plays before 1660 was that female parts were taken by boys. In foreign
theatres, on the other hand, women acted with men as a matter
of course; courtiers and others who travelled abroad became
used to this practice and evidently liked what they saw. It was
more realistic, as Pepys was not slow to note, although on 7
January he had seen 'the boy', Edward Kynaston, in Ben Jonson's *The Silent Woman* first 'as a poor woman in ordinary
clothes', then as 'clearly the prettiest woman in the whole
house' and lastly as 'the handsomest man in the house'.
(Kynaston was in fact about twenty then but continued, according to Colley Cibber, to play travesty roles with great success; he always shaved immediately before the performance.)

In fact the replacement of boys by women seems to have
been linked to the establishment of the two licensed theatre
companies in 1660, and it is specifically mentioned in two of Sir
Henry Herbert's papers. One is a petition from Michael Mohun,
Charles Hart, and others, dated 13 October [1660]; their company was in fact to be taken over by Killigrew's, but the
measures the latter had already introduced obliged them 'by
covenant . . . to act with woemen, a new theatre, and habbits
according to our sceanes'. The other is an agreement of 5 Nov-

ember 1660 between Davenant, Thomas Betterton and other actors, and a scene-painter named Henry Harris, by which the actors would 'Joyne with the said Henry Harris, and with other men and women provided or to be provided by the said Sir Wm. Davenant.'

The change was swiftly and generally accepted for three reasons. First, once made it was seen to be successful at the box office, and there could be no return to the old artificiality; in Colley Cibber's words, 'the additional objects then of real, beautiful Women, could not but draw a proportion of new Admirers to the Theatre'. Women as much as men like to see attractively dressed and made-up ladies on the stage. Secondly, the system by which males learned their stagecraft by playing women before their voices broke had been interrupted, few if any boys being surreptitiously trained in the 1650s; this also meant that at the Restoration young women starting their training in competition with boys had the advantages of greater maturity both physically and emotionally.

Thirdly, the change replaced the ambiguity of gender between the boys and the female parts they played by an irony in the correspondence between the actresses and the characters they portrayed. Some members of the new profession were rightly renowned for their virtue, and Mrs Rogers who played Amanda in Vanbrugh's *The Relapse* was prudish. But it was also well known that, in Cibber's judicious phrase, 'more than one of them had charms sufficient at their leisure Hours, to calm and mollify the Cares of Empire'. At the end of Dryden's *The Tyranny of Love, or the Royal Martyr* (1670) Nell Gwynn rose from the bier to address the bearer:

Hold, are you mad? you damn'd confounded Dog,
I am to rise, and speak the Epilogue.

She ended it with these lines:

Here *Nelly* lies, who, though she liv'd a Slater'n,
Yet dy'd a Princess, acting in *S. Cathar'n.*

Thus was the audience recalled from the representation of a heroic martyrdom to the ironic reality of the King's cockney girl-friend (to use a modern term) playing the virgin saint.

Irony to this extent had perhaps not been anticipated in the framing of the 1660 patents to the two companies, but it was soon explored in other ways. On 4 and 11 October 1664 Pepys noted, but did not see, 'a bawdy loose play' by Killigrew, *The Parson's Wedding*, 'acted by nothing but women'. This was an unnecessary innovation in a play in which seven of the principal characters are men, and there is no evidence that it had occurred to Killigrew when he drafted the play over twenty years earlier. Once the novelty of such an experimental casting had worn off it was apparent that it had no other virtues, although over forty years later some performances of Congreve's *Love for Love* were given at Vanbrugh's new Haymarket Theatre in 1706 'Acted all by Women'. On the other hand travesty roles in smaller numbers remained in vogue for more than one reason. They are part of the tradition of farce, as they are of the much-loved English family entertainment, the Christmas pantomime, in which – at least until the field was invaded by the pop groups – the hero or principal boy was always played by a young woman, and his old mother, the dame, was always played by a man. Plays with more serious and consequential plots often required disguise or deception, so that the heroine might travel or act in ways not open to a woman, as Alinda and Juletta do in Fletcher's (and Vanbrugh's) *The Pilgrim*, impersonate a lost brother or, like Florimell in the last Act of Dryden's *Secret Love* compromise an inconstant lover. Travesties of this kind are a standard device of the stage, and there are several examples in Shakespeare. But the final revelation of the heroine's identity became all the more affecting when it could be expressed in flowing locks and a degree of decolletage. In the final scene of Vanbrugh's *The Mistake* Camillo, revealed as Leonora's sister, *Kneels and lets her Perriwig fall off*.

The attractions of a 'breeches part', however, were often more physical when women of all ranks normally wore floor-length dresses. On 28 October 1661 Pepys saw a revival of Henry Glapthorne's *Argalus and Parthenia* in which 'a woman acted Parthenia, and came afterward on the stage in man's clothes, and had the best legs that ever I saw, and I was very well pleased with it'. A woman thus attired speaking the epi-

logue became a favourite ending to a play, and it should not be
forgotten that there was an element of exhibitionism in the
character of many of the early ladies of the theatre. They tended to be quick-witted, engaging, pert and natural mimics. And
whereas it would have been demeaning for a born lady of
quality to go on the stage, it was not unknown, as in later ages,
for actresses to marry into a higher class. Nell Gwynn, though
her final place in society was equivocal as well as exceptional,
and her alliance irregular, was of this type; she excelled in the
part of Florimell, a tomboy or 'mad girle', which was probably
written expressly for her. Pepys, who admired a good figure
however it was dressed, wrote enthusiastically of this performance on 2 March 1667.

By the time of the first production of *The Relapse* audiences
were too familiar with women on the stage to have needed to
attach any special significance to the casting of Mary Kent as
Young Fashion, although this gave a particular flavour to the
reprobate Coupler's attempt to put his hand in the young man's
bosom.*

The liberal attitudes of the late twentieth century, which
allow the discussion in mixed company and daily newspapers
of matters long reserved to the analyst's couch, have at least
made it possible to look freshly at what older critics called the
indecency of the Restoration stage but could not allow themselves to describe; they concentrated instead on the loose
morals of the courtiers and loungers whom they believed
(often against the evidence) to have made up most of the audience. As we have seen,† its composition was far more varied,
and this destroys the traditional picture of the Restoration
stage as a mirror of the immorality of a courtier audience.

Fornication and adultery and their preliminaries have been
fairly common in most ages, although more openly in some
than others. To those concerned they are often matters of
tragedy, but exactly because sex is human and not angelic the
adventures, especially of those whose indulgence is in some
way irregular, are very often laughable. In the small London
society of the time, figures in public life and the world of enter-

* p. 122
† p. 50

tainment were known and watched at first hand as keenly as
today they are known and watched by the whole nation
through newspapers and television; Pepys observed and even
dreamed erotically about the King's mistress, Lady Castle-
maine. Theatre people are certainly no less prone to temptation than other mortals, and the mixture of reality and illusion
that makes a play does tend to spread from the stage into the
dressing room and beyond. But it has recently been suggested
that the Restoration period was not exceptionally lax in morals,
on the basis of a somewhat lower, not higher than average rate
of illegitimate births. This might mean that, with notable and
much-discussed exceptions, more people played with fire than
burned their fingers, or that a great deal more was talked about
than actually done. Both these conclusions apply at any rate on
the stage, and the same critics who forbear to quote from
Dryden's *Secret Love* or to describe his *The Kind Keeper* note
almost as if with regret how seldom stage characters actually
get each other into bed.

In fact it is not easy now to see what the fuss was about. In
Secret Love Florimell and Celadon, having made up their
differences, agree on the latitude acceptable to each in their
contract of marriage, and the word *cuckold* is used. In his Preface Dryden defended on dramatic grounds a different kind of
'indecorum' in that these two secondary characters, a maid of
honour and a courtier, 'are treating too lightly of their marriage in the presence of the Queen, who likewise seems to stand
idle while the great action of the *Drama* is still depending'. *The
Kind Keeper* is, as its title suggests, about a kept mistress. It is,
in twentieth-century terms, a bedroom farce set in a low lodging house near Covent Garden, with a considerable amount of
stage business in which people are obliged to hide in chests
and under beds. There is allusion to sexual incompetence, a
subject which is at least as old in literature as Ovid's *Amores*
but has always troubled editors – although it appears often
enough in modern farces of the Feydeau type. The anti-hero
Woodall is totally immoral but, again as in modern farce, he
never manages to get into bed with any of the women and at
the end of the play he is married off to one of them. It is very
funny and the situations of concealment and discovery are
breathtaking. But unlike modern farce, in which the char-

acters are brought to a point of irresolvable chaos and left there, Dryden's play ends neatly.

Vanbrugh has sometimes been singled out for mention in respect of 'indecency', for the episode in the middle of Act IV of *The Relapse* in which by his adultery Loveless actually justifies the play's title. Berinthia, a pretty young widow who has been trying to steer Loveless's wife, her cousin, into having an affair with her, is in her own chamber with nothing to do, and wishes '*Lovelace* were here to badiner a little'. A moment later she discovers him hiding in the closet, and after some badinage she finds him to be more serious. The scene ends in the following manner:

Ber. Heavens, what do you mean?
Lov. Pray what do you think I mean?
Ber. I don't know.
Lov. I'll show you.
Ber You may as well tell me.
Lov. No, that wou'd make you blush more than t'other.
Ber. Why, do you intend to make me blush?
Lov. Faith I can't tell that, but if I do, it shall be in the dark.
                                                      [*Pulling her.*
Ber. O Heaven! I wou'd not be in the Dark with you for all the World.
Lov. I'll try that.   [*Puts out the Candles.*
Ber. O Lord! are you mad, What shall I do for light?
Lov. You'll do as well without it.
Ber. Why, one can't find a Chair to sit down?
Lov. Come into the Closet, Madam, there's Moon-shine upon the Couch.
Ber. Nay, never pull, for I will not go.
Lov. Then you must be carryed.   ·   [*Carrying her.*
Ber. Help, Help, I'm Ravish'd, ruin'd, undone. O Lord, I shall never be able to bear it.   [*Very softly.*

Loveless's downfall began in the theatre. Reformation was easy in the country, less so in town. The plays, says his wife Amanda at the beginning of Act II, 'have some small Charms, and wou'd have more, wou'd they restrain that loose obscene encouragement to Vice, which shocks, if not the Virtue of some Women, at least the Modesty of all'. The previous evening Loveless had

happen'd in the Play to find my very Character, only with the
addition of a *Relapse*; which struck me so, I put a suddain stop to
a most harmless Entertainment, which till then, diverted me between the Acts. 'Twas to admire the workmanship of Nature, in
the Face of a young Lady, that sate some distance from me, she
was so exquisitely handsome.

But he insists his resolve is not in danger:

for observing in the Play, That he who seem'd to represent me
there, was by an accident like this, unwarily surpriz'd into a Net,
in which he lay a poor intangl'd Slave, and brought a Train of
mischiefs on his Head; I snacht my Eyes away: they pleaded
hard for leave to look again, but I grew absolute, and they
obey'd.

The real trouble begins shortly afterwards when Berinthia,
'the very Woman', walks in to call on Amanda. Theatres, like
public gardens, have always been places to which some people
go to see and be seen, and to hunt and be hunted; but closing
places of entertainment has never served to protect public
morality, only to divert its breach somewhere else.

Vanbrugh's neat irony in describing his own play within
itself relies on the play-goer's knowledge both of the theatre's
dubious reputation and of his own probity. Vanbrugh engages
in a similar game with his audience in *The Provok'd Wife*
(III.iii) when Lady Brute and her niece Bellinda discuss the
theatre. They agree on the need, as Lady Brute says, to

sit in the Fore-front of a Box. For if one sits behind, there's two
Acts gone perhaps, before one's found out. And when I am there,
if I perceive the Men whispering and looking upon me, you must
know I cannot for my Life forbear thinking they talk to my
Advantage.

They talk about practising intelligent expressions in the
mirror. But, says Bellinda,

my Glass and I cou'd never yet agree what Face I shou'd make,
when they come blurt out, with a nasty thing in a Play: For all the
Men presently look upon the Women, that's certain; so laugh we

must not, though our Stays burst for't, Because that's telling
Truth, and owning we understand the Jest. And to look serious
is so dull, when the whole House is a laughing.
Lady B. Besides, that looking serious, do's really betray our
Knowledge in the Matter, as much as laughing, with the Com-
pany wou'd do. For if we did not understand the thing, we shou'd
naturally do like other People.
Bell. For my part I always take that Occasion to blow my Nose.
Lady B. You must blow your Nose half off then at some Plays.
Bell. Why don't some Reformer or other, beat the Poet for't?
Lady B. Because he is not so sure of our private Approbation as
of our public Thanks.

Other dramatists were conscious of the ladies in the audience,
and their favour was solicited as early as the 1670s; indeed in
January 1667 at a performance in the Theatre Royal of
Beaumont and Fletcher's *The Custom of the Country*, a tragi-
comedy about the *droit du seigneur*, they made their opinion
clear. Pepys found it 'of all the plays that ever I did see, the
worst — having neither plot, language, nor anything in the
earth that is acceptable . . . fully the worst play that ever I saw
or I believe shall see'. Richard Legh, writing home to his wife at
Lyme, described it as 'soe dam'd bawdy that the Ladyes flung
theire peares and fruites att the Actors'.

There is evidence from contemporary comments, and also
from references in plays, that audiences were often noisy and
inattentive. To some extent their vocal comments were accepted as gestures of lively appreciation towards a cast who performed in their midst rather than behind a frame. One of the
functions of the Prologue spoken on the first three nights was
to warm up the audience, often with topical allusions, while
the Epilogue was designed to return them to the outside world.
But other forms of behaviour were less welcome. On occasion
swords were drawn, and during a performance of that unlucky
play *Macbeth* at Dorset Garden on 28 April 1675 a duel in the
house was mortal to one party. From time to time there was
also trouble with people sitting on the stage, but although this
is usually taken to mean flamboyant young men encroaching
upon the forestage, proclamations such as those of 2 February
1673/4 and 14 November 1689 against persons on the stage
give as the reason the 'vast engine' and other machines used in

the opera: they concern people sitting in the wings backstage, a danger to themselves and others. Another practice which did not brighten the moral image of the theatre was the admission, for a fee or a bribe, of gentlemen to the actresses' 'tyring-room'. Fights between rival lady stars were not unknown, and on one occasion in 1693 the players got drunk on real punch used in stage business and had to close the performance after only three Acts. Vanbrugh was probably not inventing when he described, in the Preface to *The Relapse*, how on the first night 'some indecencies had like to have happen'd, but 'twas not my fault'. George Powell, playing Worthy, had been 'drinking his Mistresses Health in *Nants* Brandy, from six in the Morning, to the time he wadled on upon the Stage in the Evening'. Powell's approaches to the virtuous Mrs Rogers, playing the virtuous Amanda, were so vigorous that there was some danger of a conclusion not in accordance with the text.

Restoration society had enormous problems, though perhaps no greater than those of other periods. The Great Fire and the Plague affected the economy not only of London but of the whole country. The Civil War had not solved the issue of power in the land: King and Parliament were still at loggerheads and even later both William and Anne were resentful of the new powers of Parliament after the Revolution of 1688. Nor had the Restoration solved the issues of dissent and orthodoxy in religion, and the equivocal attitude of Charles II to Roman Catholic Europe gave way to the assertive Catholic stance of his younger brother. Most people not only believed in God but considered themselves Christians and regularly attended church or a dissenting chapel, but there were some subscribers to atheism and to the mechanistic materialism of Thomas Hobbes.

Attitudes to the stage varied from one person to another and indeed within one person; for all his fumbling with maidservants and dreaming about the King's mistresses, Pepys took a highly moral view of events in fiction as well as, indeed, of his own behaviour. Philosophers and teachers were beginning to explore the nature of the intellect and the emotions. The theatre was certainly a cause both of great enjoyment and of great scandal. The Revolution brought unprecedented freedom to dissenters from Anglican orthodoxy, of every variety except the Catholics; it also deprived the stage of the second of its two great protectors, Charles II and James II. It was neither difficult nor expensive (until the Stamp Act of 1712 put a tax on newspapers and pamphlets) to have one's opinions printed and distributed, and the reading public bought pamphlets in much the same way, if on a far smaller scale, that it now buys magazines. In these circumstances it is not surprising that by the 1690s the stage was increasingly subject to the onslaught of those who would reform it in particular and society in general. When the curtain rose on *The Relapse* Vanbrugh walked not only into the hall of fame but also into the arena of controversy.

11

The Triumph of Virtue

Caius Gabriel Cibber, the sculptor of the great bas-relief on the pedestal of the Monument to the Great Fire, came from Denmark by way of the Netherlands in the late 1650s. In 1670 he married as his second wife Jane Colley, who in theory brought him a large dowry of which in practice little ever materialized. Their son Colley was born the following year. In *An Apology for the Life of Colley Cibber* (1740) Colley tells us that he attended school between the ages of eleven and sixteen and learned Latin; thereafter he served for a short time in the army. But the favour of the Earl of Devonshire (for whom his father was working at Chatsworth) did not extend to the opportunity of a commission, only to a place in his London household. Young Cibber had there the chance to make his way on to the stage, and after some small and not very successful parts he substituted for Edward Kynaston ('the boy' in Pepys's Diary) as Lord Touchwood in Congreve's *The Double Dealer* at Drury Lane in January 1694.

The United Company was now in the hands of two businessmen, Sir Thomas Skipwith and Christopher Rich. Skipwith, the principal shareholder, was the captain who helped Vanbrugh in their early army days; he married a cousin of the Duke of Manchester and succeeded to a baronetcy in June 1694. Rich, a lawyer, did most of the management; by 1690 he was cutting down salaries and juggling with money to deal with a dwindling audience. Although Cibber's performance as Touchwood had won him the praise of Congreve, no new opportunities fol-

lowed until after the secession at the end of 1694 of Thomas
Betterton and most of the best actors. They obtained a new licence from the Lord Chamberlain the following March, and on
29 April 1695 they re-opened the Lincoln's Inn Fields theatre
with a new play by Congreve, *Love for Love*. If one company
could not run at a profit it was difficult to see how two could do
so; nevertheless the return of competition in place of a monopoly stirred both companies to new effort and invention.

At first the situation was not unlike that of the early 1660s,
when one company had the plays and the other had the
scenery. Now thirty years later the City had been transformed
and broader London greatly expanded; Court patronage of the
stage was declining while the merchant and official classes
were growing in numbers and importance; there was also in
the audience a gradually increasing number of what can only
be called tourists, some of whose English was not adequate for
the niceties of the dramatists' phrases. Moreover, although the
seceding players had moved to a building that was far from
ideal, Rich's remnant had the run of both Drury Lane and
Dorset Garden. His immediate problem, as Gildon's *Comparison Between the Two Stages* (1702) says, was that

> 'twas almost impossible to muster up a sufficient number to
> take in all the Parts of any Play; and of them so few were toler-
> able, that a Play must of necessity be damn'd that had not extra-
> ordinary favour from the Audience. No fewer than *Sixteen* (most
> of the old standing) went away; and with them the very beauty
> and vigour of the Stage; they who were left behind being for the
> most part Learners, Boys and Girls, a very unequal match for
> them who revolted.

Rich's problems were largely of his own making, for he was an
inept manager. It was in this period, as Cibber recalled in his
Apology, that Rich courted disaster in his aim 'to please the
Majority, who could more easily comprehend any thing they
saw, than the daintiest things, that could be said to them'. For
he pursued this policy so far as

> actually dealing for an extraordinary large Elephant, at a cer-
> tain Sum, for every Day he might think fit to shew the tractable

Genius of that vast quiet Creature, in any Play, or Farce, in the
Theatre (then standing) in *Dorset-Garden*. But from the Jealousy, which so formidable a Rival had rais'd in his Dancers and
by his Bricklayer's assuring him, that if the Walls were to be
open'd wide enough for its Entrance, it might endanger the Fall
of the House, he gave up his Project, and with it, so hopeful a
Prospect of making the Receipts of the Stage run higher than all
the Wit, and Force of the best Writers had ever yet rais'd them to.

Cibber's contribution in this critical period was one which
revealed his own true talents, as well as his vanity and his
willingness to gamble: 'Having then no other Resource, I was
at last reduc'd to write a character for myself.' He wrote *Love's
Last Shift*, and on the recommendation of the playwright
Thomas Southerne, to whom he read it, it was accepted by Rich
and produced at Drury Lane in January 1696. Cibber had by
nature a rather slight high voice, which after early failures he
learned both to project better and to exploit dramatically. He
saw himself in the part of Sir Novelty Fashion which, as he tells
us, 'was thought a good Portrait of the Foppery then in fashion'.
Against the advice of his advocate Southerne (sustained even
as the curtain was about to rise) he took the part himself, and
had the satisfaction afterwards of the Lord Chamberlain Lord
Dorset's opinion 'That it was the best First Play that any Author
in his Memory had produc'd; and that for a young Fellow to
shew himself such an Actor, and such a Writer, in one Day, was
something extraordinary'.

Cibber, like Vanbrugh, had turned from soldier to retainer;
Vanbrugh, like Cibber, was to produce a brilliant first play.
Their early careers are, however, not otherwise closely parallel; yet before they diverged for ever they passed through a
phase of extraordinary proximity, for Vanbrugh's *The Relapse*
was written as a sequel to, and a comment on, *Love's Last Shift*.
As a sequel it includes some of the same characters: Loveless,
Amanda, Worthy and Sir Novelty. In the first production, on the
same stage, Loveless was played by John Verbruggen, Amanda
by Mrs Jane Rogers and Sir Novelty by Cibber, as they had been
in the earlier play. But Vanbrugh transformed Sir Novelty into
Lord Foppington, and in acting this part Cibber rose to the
occasion to make the Vanbrugian enlargement of his original

conception into the role by which he would be best remembered. Indeed Cibber attempted to carry the character forward into his own *The Careless Husband* (1704), but today, when we cannot see Cibber on the stage, we are only too aware that his lines in the latter play lack Vanbrugh's sparkling verbal caricature.

The Relapse cannot be understood without going in some detail into the construction and character of *Love's Last Shift*. When Cibber's play opens Loveless arrives in London with Snap, his servant. Loveless is 'of a debaucht life, grew weary of his Wife in six Months, left her, and the Town, for Debts he did not care to pay; and having spent the last part of his Estate beyond Sea, returns to *England* in a very mean condition'. He believes his wife Amanda has died, and Young Worthy whom he meets in the Park does not disabuse him of this notion. But on the other hand Young Worthy does warn Amanda, 'a Woman of strict Virtue', that her rakish husband is back in town, and he suggests that she should offer herself to Loveless, in disguise, as a mistress. This is the main plot, but as often happens in comedies of behaviour (a term less specific and therefore less open to misinterpretation than 'comedies of manners') there are several sub-plots of a complication which it is difficult to summarize although they are perfectly clear on the stage.

Young Worthy is in love with Narcissa, the daughter of the rich Sir William Wisewoud, but the latter intends Narcissa to marry the firstborn Elder Worthy, 'a sober Gent, of a fair Estate', who in turn is in love not with Narcissa but with Sir William's niece Hillaria. Before the play can be satisfactorily concluded this tangle must be sorted out, and this is done basically by getting Sir William to sign a marriage contract between Narcissa and 'Mr Worthy' without reading first names. Thus each brother gets the lady of his choice, although not without some diversions. In one of them Hillaria, tired for the moment of Worthy, falls for the foppish Sir Novelty, who in turn courts Narcissa; in the other Sir Novelty is deceived into an assignation in the Park with a masked lady whom he believes to be Narcissa. She turns out to be Mrs Flareit, the mistress he has abandoned, played originally by the versatile Mrs Kent. Mrs Flareit boxes his ear, unmasks, and is only just restrained from running him through with Young Worthy's sword.

Meanwhile Amanda is talked out of her scruples about seducing her own husband because, says Hillaria, it is better for him to be unfaithful only in mistaken intention than in fact 'with some Body else in the mean time'. In Act IV this device – which of course is not Cibber's invention but is much older – is successfully employed. A private supper ends in the exit of Amanda and Loveless to bed, and in the last Act Loveless admits that he is well pleased with her and agrees to reform his life:

'Twas heedless Fancy first, that made me stray,
But Reason now breaks forth, and lights me on my Way.

At a lower level in every sense Snap, the servant, who has compromised Amanda's woman servant in some business involving a trap door to a cellar, is commanded to marry her. Thus in both the parlour and the servants' quarters matrimony is confirmed and virtue is restored.

In *The Two Stages* Gildon calls *Love's Last Shift* 'the Philosopher's Stone', adding that very few comedies 'came up to't for purity of Plot, Manners and Moral: It's often acted now a daies, and by the help of the Author's own good action, it pleases to this Day.' It is never easy either to predict in advance or to account in retrospect for the success or failure of a play. No doubt Cibber's 'own good action' in the part of Sir Novelty contributed to his success; he was also much livelier when writing dialogue than when reminiscing about the past in his *Apology*. Gildon, describing the work as a moral play, had something of an axe to grind, and up to the time of his writing *The Two Stages* there were not many performances; however, some modern critics too have seen *Love's Last Shift* as a milestone in the reform of the stage. Others have seen it as the first sentimental comedy, meaning not only that virtue triumphs at the end but that it does so through the development and experience of pure emotions and aspirations in the characters.

Sentimentalism in comedy, wrote Paul Mueschke and Jeannette Fleisher in *A Re-evaluation of Vanbrugh* (1934), is essentially an optimistic falsification of human nature by exalting a standard of impeccable but conventional morality which the audience, moved to tears by the contemplation of virtue in distress, rendered 'sensible' through the emotions of pity and admiration, is to emulate.

It is the growth of such ideas about feelings that led to the development of the novel in the eighteenth century. It is certainly true, on the one hand, that Restoration comedy is described as cynical because the characters, whether virtuous or immoral, are only skin deep, brilliantly manipulated almost like marionettes. The characters of sentimental comedy, on the other hand, although no less artificial, are subject to strong emotions and express them. Halfway through Act I of *Love's Last Shift* we meet Amanda for the first time, still in mourning for her faithless husband's presumed death:

> *Hillaria.* Well dear *Amanda*, thou art the most Constant Wife I ever heard of: Not to shake off the Memory of an ill Husband, after 8 or 10 years absence; nay, to Mourn, for ought you know for the Living too, and such an Husband, that, tho' he were alive, wou'd never thank you for't: why d'ye persist in such a hopeless Grief?
> *Amanda.* Because 'tis hopeless! For if he be alive, he is Dead to me: his Dead Affections not Virtues self can e'er retrieve; wou'd I were with him, tho' in his Grave!
> *Hil.* In my mind you are much better where you are! The Grave! Young Widows use to have warmer wishes. But methinks the Death of a rich old Uncle, should be a Cordial to your Sorrows.
> *Am.* That adds to 'em; for he was the only Relation I had left, and was as tender of me, as the nearest! He was a Father to me.
> *Hil.* He was better than some Fathers to you; for he dy'd just when you had Occasion for his Estate ... For my part, the greatest Reason I think you have to grieve, is that you are not sure your Husband's dead, for were that confirm'd, then indeed there were hopes that one Poyson might drive out another, you might marry agen.
> *Am.* All the Comfort of my Life is, that I can tell my Conscience, I have been true to Virtue.

In the last Act occurs the scene that is said to have moved eighteenth-century audiences to tears. Amanda's 'Disguise of

Vicious Love' has charmed Loveless 'ev'n to a Madness of Impure Desire'; but now she fears lest when she reveals herself 'bare fac'd Vertue shou'd fright him from my Arms for ever'. In reply to her questions Loveless says (as he believes) that his wife has died; then he asks about her circumstances. She claims to be (as of course she is) 'a True, a Faithful, and a Vertuous Wife', and speaks of virtue and of conscience:

Lov. Your Words are utter'd with such a powerfull Accent, they have awak'd my Soul, and strike my thoughts with horrour and remorse---   [*Stands in a fixt posture.*

Am. Then let me strike you nearer, deeper yet:--- But arm your mind with gentle pity first, or I am lost for ever.

Lov. I am all Pity, all Faith, Expectation, and confused Amazement: be kind, be quick, and ease my Wonder.

Am. Look on me well: Revive your dead remembrance: And oh! for pity's sake [*Kneels*] hate me not for loving long, faithfully forgive this innocent attempt of a despairing passion, and I shall die in quiet.

Lov. Hah! speak on!   [*Amazed.*

Am. I wonot be!--- The word's too weighty for my faultring Tongue, and my Soul sinks beneath the fatal Burthen. Oh!---
                                              [*Falls on the Ground.*

Lov. Ha! she faints! Look up fair Creature! Behold a Heart that bleeds for your distress, and fain wou'd share the weight of your oppressing sorrows! Oh! thou hast rais'd a thought within me, that shocks my Soul.

Am. 'Tis done! [*rising.*] The Conflict's past, and Heav'n bids me speak undaunted. Know then, ev'n all the boasted Raptures of your last Nights Love you found in your *Amanda*'s Arms:--- I am your Wife.

Lov. Hah!

Am. For ever blest or miserable, as your next breath shall sentence me.

Lov. My Wife! impossible! Is she not dead! How shall I believe thee?

Am. How Time and my Afflictions may have alter'd me. I know not: But here's an Indelible Confirmation. [*Bares her Arm.*] These speaking Characters, which in their cheerful Bloom our Early Passions mutually recorded . . .

Lov. Oh I am confounded with my Guilt, and tremble to behold thee . . . I have wrong'd you. Oh! rise! basely wrong'd you! And can I see your Face?

Am. One kind, one pitying look cancels those wrongs for ever: and oh! forgive my fond presuming passion; for from my Soul I pardon and forgive you all: all, all but this, the greatest, your unkind Delay of Love.

Lov. Oh! seal my pardon with thy trembling Lips, while with this tender Grasp of fond reviving Love I seize my Bliss, and stifle all thy wrongs for ever.   [*Embraces her.*

Am. No more; I'le wash away their memory in tears of flowing joy.

Lov. Oh! thou hast rouz'd me from my deep Lethargy of Vice! For hitherto my Soul has been enslav'd to loose Desires, to vain deluding Follies, and shadows of substantial bliss: But now I wake with joy to find my Rapture Real. ---Thus let me kneel and pay my thanks to her, whose conquering Virtue has at last subdu'd me. Here will I fix, thus prostrate sigh my shame, and wash my Crimes in never ceasing tears of Penitence.

Thus is Loveless revealed at last as good at heart; thus does Amanda's virtue triumph through her appeal to pity.

Reconciliations of this kind are hardly to be found in the comedies of the previous age. It is true that most Restoration comedies end in a marriage, but in a marriage of dramatic neatness rather than of emotional conviction – for legalized satisfaction more often than for love. Vanbrugh was quite familiar with conclusions and characters of the earlier kind; we shall see that Sir John Brute's marriage before *The Provok'd Wife* opens had been of this kind. In Act II of Vanbrugh's play Sir John reveals that he married his wife 'because I had a mind to lie with her, and she wou'd not let me'; the play itself traces the consequences developed from this simple logic. Yet *The Provok'd Wife* belongs, like *The Relapse*, to another category in which Cibber's play has rightly been included: a group of plays of the 1690s whose principal characters are not suitors or seducers and their sweethearts but infelicitously married couples for whom divorce, although theoretically possible, could only be attained both at great expense financially and at ruinous cost in the loss of social acceptability which would ensue. There are very few quite new plots in comedy, and when Southerne introduced the theme of the ill-matched couple into *The Wives' Excuse* in 1691 he was reviving an old one, not inventing a new one; nevertheless his was the first play of this particular group.

But Cibber, who was certainly an opportunist, has also on the basis of his Epilogue been branded a cynic. Epilogues were often spoken by a young or a very young actress; addressed directly to the audience, they frequently contained phrases and sentiments of a surprising frankness — a kind of irony that was not lost on the hearers or indeed, we may suppose, on even the youngest members of the companies. Cibber's Epilogue to *Love's Last Shift* is no exception, although Miss Letitia Cross, who sang Cupid in the last scene masque, was actually about eighteen; within the year she was to play Miss Hoyden in *The Relapse*. She first reminded the 'Kind City-Gentlemen o'th' middle Row' that 'There's not a Cuckold made in all his Play'. Cibber, she went on, drew his sharp pen rather against the Beaux. But then she turned to that particular section of the audience:

> Now, Sirs to you, whose sole Religion's Drinking,
> Whoring, Roaring, without the Pain of Thinking;
> He fears h'as made a fault you'll ne'er forgive,
> A Crime, beyond the hopes of a Reprieve;
> An Honest Rake forego the Joys of Life!
> His Whores, and Wine! t'Embrace a dull Cast [chaste] Wife.
> Such out of fashion stuff! But then agen!
> He's Lewd for above four Acts, Gentlemen!
> For Faith he knew, when once he'd chang'd his Fortune,
> And reform'd his Vice, 'twas time - - - to drop the Curtain.

And finally from the Beaux she turned to the ladies:

> Four Acts for your Course Pallats was design'd,
> But Then the Ladies Tast is more refin'd,
> They for Amanda's Sake, will sure be Kind.

Moreover, the realism of the scene in Act IV when Amanda fools her unknowing husband into imagined seduction might well affect the suggestible who need protection and those who strive to protect them, right from the moment when she enters clad in a loose gown to the point when her serving woman says, her ear to the inner door, 'Faith, I must listen, if I were to be hang'd for't'. And as the last Act shows, the serving woman's fate was not death but the one proverbially worse, her seducer Snap claiming in mitigation the example of those above stairs.

__ 12 __

Realism and Relapse

On 31 January 1696 Vanbrugh's transfer, promised the previous August, came through; he was given a captain's commission in place of Richard Courtenay in the Second Marine Regiment of George, Lord Berkeley of Stratton. The Entry Book calls him John Brooke, Esq. but he was not the John *Brooks* promoted from ensign to lieutenant in Colonel Farington's regiment the previous Christmas Eve. Vanbrugh's last weeks in the First Marine Regiment under Lord Carmarthen had been spent in London, where he had seen Cibber's play. We do not know much about his movements, and he no doubt read the text of the play, but there can be no question that the part he wrote for Lord Foppington in *The Relapse* was inspired by having actually seen Cibber's performance as Sir Novelty Fashion.

The theatre is one of those closed worlds to which many aspire but proportionately few gain access: it is a world in which there is seldom enough work to go round, and one in which there is no place for the passenger, the ignorant or the unprofessional. The lucky accident is the dream of many who never achieve it; Cibber was one who did when he was asked to substitute for Kynaston, and before that he had got into the theatre by hanging about in the hope of being found useful. We do not know how Vanbrugh made his entry, but we do know that he had useful friends. In 1696 the Lord Chamberlain was still the Earl of Dorset, who in his youth as Lord Buckhurst had been the protector of Nell Gwynn and who in his maturity was an early Kit-Cat; it was he who complimented Cibber so roundly on his success in *Love's Last Shift*. He was related to the Howards, the Berties and the Carletons. The Vice-Chamberlain was Peregrine Bertie, Vanbrugh's kinsman and close friend. Lord Berkeley's connections with the stage are less clear, but it may be significant that when he died in February 1697 he left by a codicil in his will 200 guineas in gold to the actress Anne Bracegirdle, to be paid before any other sums. Any of these three men could have given Vanbrugh an introduction at the stage door.

Cibber says in the *Apology* that Vanbrugh, 'having observ'd, that in *Love's Last Shift*, most of the Actors had acquitted themselves, beyond what was expected of them . . . took a sudden Hint from what he lik'd in that Play'. He says moreover that Vanbrugh completed *The Relapse* at the beginning of April, 'but the Season being then too far advanc'd, it was not acted 'till the succeeding Winter'. Vanbrugh's Prologue says that his play was 'Got, Conceiv'd, and Born in six Weeks space' which seems a very short time; however, an affectation of easy speed was not uncommon. Thomas Shadwell was known for his claims to quick composition; in the early 1670s Edward Ravenscroft and Edward Revet both claimed to have written a play in a fortnight, and the record seems to be held by Henry Nevil Payne in 1672 with 'nine days' work'. Cibber's memory is likely to have been clear in circumstances which concerned him so directly, and Berkeley's fleet, as we know from newsletters, was not active until the last week in April when preparations were made for it to accompany King William to Flanders. But the timing is of material importance.

Cibber implies that Vanbrugh began to set down his thoughts very soon after seeing *Love's Last Shift* at Drury Lane. Again we do not know Vanbrugh's movements, but Lord Berkeley was back in London from early September 1696, and it is possible that Cibber's memory or his information was at fault and that the play was written, albeit with speed, in the autumn after Vanbrugh had had several months to think about it. Yet *The Relapse* seems to have crept into the theatre unheralded. It is now known (that is, it can be deduced) that it opened on Saturday 21 November 1696, two days after a correspondent had predicted that the Theatre Royal 'must break' unless a new

play came out to save it. Confirmation comes from a list of performances attended by Penelope Lady Morley, annexed to a
lawsuit about her shareholding in the Theatre Royal; she saw
The Relapse on Wednesday 25 November, and it may have run
for altogether six nights. It was a success. Lady Morley saw it
again on 5 January 1698 – the night after the Whitehall fire* –
and in February 1700 and January 1701. It was played in 1702,
1705 and subsequent years, and it says more for Vanbrugh than
many critics have acknowledged that this late Restoration
comedy survived not only the attack of Jeremy Collier but also
the whole reform movement. It ran through the first half of the
eighteenth century and, although by then somewhat refined, it
was revived in the 1750s and 1760s. It even acquired a kind of
after-life, bowdlerized and prettily simplified, as Sheridan's *A
Journey to Scarborough* in 1777; Vanbrugh's widow had died
the previous year.

Vanbrugh wrote not only a sequel to Cibber's work but also
an implied criticism of Cibber's psychology; Loveless's conversion, Vanbrugh believed, was too good to be true, and a
remark in *A Short Vindication*, his reply to Collier, should not
be taken to suggest otherwise. He describes there how
Cibber's Loveless comes to be both convinced of the need to
reform himself and determined to do so:

> For my part, I though him so undisputably in the right; and he
> appear'd to me to be got into so agreeable a Tract of Life, that I
> often took a pleasure to indulge a musing Fancy, and suppose
> myself in his place. The Happiness I saw him possest of, I lookt
> upon as a jewel of a very great Worth, which naturally lead me
> to the fear of losing it.

Here are hyperbole and irony, devices which Vanbrugh uses
throughout the *Short Vindication*. But it is clear that it is Loveless, not Cibber, whom he thought in the right. He goes on:

> I therefore consider'd by what Enemies 'twas most likely to be
> attack'd, and that directed me in the Plan of the Works that were
> most probable to defend it. I saw but one danger in Solitude and
> Retirement, and I saw a thousand in the bustle of the World; I

* p. 223

therefore in a moment determin'd for the Countrey, and suppos'd *Loveless* and *Amanda* gone out of town.

So we find them in the country as the play opens; but, argues Vanbrugh, they could not stay there indefinitely. *The Relapse* is a play about what happens when they return to the bustle of the world. In the *Short Vindication* Vanbrugh then explains the principal plot of his sequel and also, since the moral influence of the stage is under discussion, the lessons to be drawn from it. But before we follow him there it is desirable to outline the whole story of *The Relapse* and to show the extent to which it derives from its precursor.

Like many plays, both of these have secondary titles. Cibber's, *The Fool in Fashion*, points directly to the character of Sir Novelty he had created for himself; Vanbrugh's, *Virtue in Danger*, refers to Worthy's unsuccessful attempt on the virtue of Amanda. But what the two plays have more exceptionally in common is the sub-plot of almost equal importance with the main story. Moreover there are ingenious ways in which Vanbrugh's sub-plot relates to Cibber's. He replaces one pair of brothers by another; that is, he replaces Young Worthy by Young Fashion, a younger brother not in parallel but in competition, and this allows him to explore the situation of the younger son in a family and social tradition in which the firstborn inherits everything. His own father had made a compromise between Continental practice, in which the estate was divided equally among the children, and the English, leaving John a double share as the eldest. But Vanbrugh was familiar with the effects of the English practice among his friends and acquaintances. Yet there are also moments in *The Relapse* at which he seems to be writing a revision rather than a sequel.

The Relapse opens with Loveless and Amanda at home in their country house. Loveless is obliged, by 'indispensable' business, to go to London; he will of course be accompanied by his wife, and he is sure that he is now proof against the temptations of the city. The next scene echoes Cibber's opening one in which Loveless and Snap had arrived penniless in town. Vanbrugh shows us Young Fashion arriving, also penniless, with his servant Lory; indeed they are forced to part with their last piece of luggage – an almost empty trunk – as surety to the

waterman who has brought them up from Gravesend to Whitehall Stairs. Young Fashion is the younger brother Vanbrugh
invented for Sir Novelty, now raised to the peerage as Lord
Foppington.

Scene iii takes us to My Lord's dressing room, where Young
Fashion interrupts his elder brother's business with his tailor,
shoemaker, hosier and wigmaker, business which immediately establishes the absurd nobleman as a rounded character.
Lord Foppington receives him with a coolness bred of long
mutual antipathy; his welcome is a Parthian one as he leaves:
'Dear *Tam*, I'm glad to see thee in *England*, stap my Vitals.' The
younger brother therefore immediately begins to 'contrive his
Destruction'. In this he is unexpectedly aided by the entrance
of Coupler, an ageing and wheezing matchmaker whose personal inclinations appear from almost his first lines to Young
Fashion:

> *Coupler.* Ha! you young Lascivious Rogue you.
> Let me put my Hand into your Bosom, Sirrah.
> *Y. Fash.* Stand off, old *Sodom*.
> *Coupl.* Nay, prithee now don't be so coy.
> *Y. Fash.* Keep your Hands to your self, you old Dog you, or I'll
> wring your Nose off.

But Coupler's errand is a professional one, the marriage between Lord Foppington and Hoyden, the daughter of Sir
Tunbelly Clumsey. 'This plump Patridge ... lives in the
Country, Fifty Miles off'; the match will cost Foppington two
thousand pounds, but will bring him in 'Fifteen hundred
Pound a year, and a great Bag of Money; the Match is concluded, the Writings are drawn, and the Pipkin's to be crack'd in a
Fortnight'. However, Coupler is now disenchanted because he
has reason to understand that Foppington will evade payment
of his part in the bargain; Coupler therefore offers to sell the
marriage to Young Fashion.

In Acts II and III, as we have already seen, Loveless tells
Amanda he has eyed a woman at the theatre. When Amanda's
young widowed cousin Berinthia arrives, Loveless recognizes
her as the woman but says nothing to Amanda, who offers her
cousin lodging. When Amanda is propositioned by Lord

Foppington, she boxes his ear and Loveless challenges and wounds him, though far more slightly than he. pretends. Next Amanda is courted by Worthy, which flatters her; observing a confidential scene between Loveless and Berinthia, Worthy confronts the latter and prevails on her to help him gain Amanda.

In Act IV Loveless pretends to stay late from home, giving Worthy the opportunity to press his attentions on Amanda, but in fact Loveless returns to Berinthia's room. He carries her squeaking into the closet; thus Act IV, which in Cibber's play had brought Loveless to an imagined act of infidelity, leads him in Vanbrugh's to a real one. In the last Act Berinthia, in order to help Worthy, tells Amanda that Loveless is unfaithful, but without identifying herself as the cause. No more is seen of Loveless; but Amanda, although she is attracted to Worthy, ends by dismissing him. The relapse is Loveless's; Amanda's virtue is endangered but in the end preserved.

Meanwhile Young Fashion has made a last plea to his elder brother for money and is repulsed. He therefore goes down to Sir Tunbelly's country seat, pretending to be Foppington. Sir Tunbelly is the kind of minor country house owner consistently mocked by the town wits, playwrights and novelists: traditional and rural, not to say old-fashioned and rustic, with horizons no broader than the parish boundaries. His welcome is unpromising: once his daughter is safely locked up he comes out 'with his Servants Arm'd, with Guns, Clubs, Pitchforks, Sythes, &c'. But Coupler's letter of introduction works an instant change; Fashion and Lory are admitted to meet Hoyden, who is mad to be married. Her nurse is prevailed on to bribe the chaplain, Doctor Bull, to marry the girl to the impostor at once.

Halfway through Act IV, as the audience is imagining the embraces of Loveless and Berinthia, the scene changes to Sir Tunbelly's house. Bull has scarcely congratulated the happy couple whom 'it has been my Lott, to join . . . in the Holy Bands of Wedlock', when the real Lord Foppington arrives. Young Fashion of course claims him as an impostor, but the nobleman manages to call upon a neighbour, Sir John Friendly, to identify him. Young Fashion and Lory make a hurried exit, and Bull deems it prudent to forget the ceremony he has just con-

ducted. In the last Act Coupler reads a letter from Foppington:
'The Papers are Seal'd, and the Contract is Sign'd, so the business of the Lawyer is *Achevé*, but I defer the Divine part of the
thing 'till I arrive at *London*; not being willing to Consummate
in any other Bed but my own.' But Coupler, devious and venge-
ful as always, has summoned the parson and the nurse to
London. We gather that their relationship is closer than they
would acknowledge, and a combination of threats and bribes
restores the parson's memory and induces him to admit and
then to reveal to all concerned the first – and therefore the only
– marriage. This startling announcement is, however, preceded by a short masque, a *Dialogue between Cupid and Hymen*,
which parodies the masque of Fame, Love, Reason, Honour,
and Marriage in the very last scene of Cibber's play. Again Vanbrugh imitates his prototype in order to improve on it. Cibber's
language seems stilted beside the easy flow of Vanbrugh's, and
the latter has one more trick up his sleeve. His Chorus is as
follows:

> *For change, W'are for change, to what ever it be,*
> *We are neither contented, with Freedom nor Thee.*
> 　　*Constancy's an empty sound.*
> 　　*Heaven and Earth, and all go round,*
> 　　*All the Works of Nature move,*
> 　　*And the Joys of Life and Love*
> 　　　　*Are in Variety.*

Change is precisely what the characters are about to experience, when it turns out that Miss Hoyden is not going to marry
Lord Foppington because she is already married to his younger brother. Sir Tunbelly and Lord Foppington make the best
of a *fait accompli*, and Hoyden, who has an earthy liking for the
male sex, is pleased to reflect that if her husband achieves a
knighthood she will still be Lady Fashion; moreover, he does
not 'stink of sweets' like his foppish brother.

The two plots have been described separately, but on the
stage they alternate and interweave to good effect, leaving the
audience constantly guessing. Collier was the first critic to
point out that of the two plots that of the Fashions and Hoyden
is the more interesting: he actually complained that the play
was wrongly titled and should have been called *The Younger*

Brother or *The Fortunate Cheat*. But Collier's difficulty was always in distinguishing sensible criticisms from silly ones, and he dismissed Loveless and Amanda as 'Persons of Inferior Consideration' instead of exploring the range of characters portrayed. Amanda, it is true, remains very much the sentimental person created by Cibber, and at the end of the play her state is hardly better than at the start. Loveless instead of being once faithless and dead is still faithless and alive; that, says Vanbrugh, is what would have happened in real life. In that sense Vanbrugh, like Chaucer, was an observer, a realist rather than a cynic. There were, and are, naively nubile girls like Hoyden guarded by ambitious and uncouth fathers, and there are motherly souls like Nurse. Collier was affronted on behalf of his cloth by the portraiture of Doctor Bull, but (as has been more than once remarked) the tragedy is not that there were not parsons like him but that there were.

If these characters seem livelier or more rounded, more realistic, than their precursors, it must to a considerable degree be because of the naturalness of their speech. This of course means not that they talk like twentieth-century people, but that Vanbrugh's ear picked up accurately the speech of all sorts of people of his time. Speech was more formal and gestures were more extravagant then, and his language still has something of a 'historical' ring to modern ears. Following the example of the *Académie* founded by Louis XIV, the Royal Society had ever since the 1660s attempted to 'reform' English speech, encouraging the use of new words and simpler constructions, weeding out antiquated, florid and complex ones, but this process still had a fair distance to run: the language of Pope and Samuel Johnson is to our ears distinctly more 'modern' than that of Dryden or Vanbrugh, beside which Sir Thomas Browne or the Essays of Francis Bacon (one of the spiritual fathers of the Royal Society) seem in their turn old-fashioned.

In Act III.ii. of *The Relapse* Berinthia and Worthy are discussing the latter's strategy in pursuit of Amanda:

Wor. Where there is a necessity, a Christian is bound to help his Neighbour. So good *Berinthia*, lose no time, but let us begin the Dance as fast as we can.

Ber. Not till the Fiddles are in tune, pray Sir. Your Ladies strings
will be very apt to fly, I can tell you that, if they are wound up too
hastily. But if you'll have patience to screw 'em to their pitch by
degrees, I don't doubt but she may endure to be play'd upon.
Wor. Ay, and will make admirable Musick too, or I'm mistaken;
but have you had no private Closet Discourse with her yet about
Males and Females, and so forth, which may give you hopes in
her Constitution; for I know her Moods are the Devil against us.
Ber. I have had so much discourse with her, that I believe were
she once cur'd of her Fondness to her Husband, the Fortress of
her Vertue wou'd not be so impregnable as she Fancies.

It may be suggested that ordinary people do not speak in metaphor, but the truth is that we all speak in the metaphor of our
own time, place and social group: we are like Monsieur Jour-
dain in Molière's *Le Bourgeois Gentilhomme* who learned with
surprise that he had been speaking prose all his life. Perhaps
the best comparisons are to be made with Vanbrugh's own letters. He writes to Tonson in June 1703:

> Your letter I had from Amsterdam. My brother bids me tell you
> he is extremely obliged to you, and desires you will let him be a
> little more so, by improving (as it may ly in your way) the friend-
> ship he has begun with the gentleman at Rotterdam; tho' my
> hopes are, you'll be spueing at sea before this gets halfway to the
> Brill. In short, the Kit-Cat wants you, much more than you ever
> can do them. Those who remain in towne, are in great desire of
> waiting on you at Barne-Elmes; not that they have finished their
> pictures neither; tho' to excuse them (as well as myself), Sr God-
> frey has been most in fault. The fool has got a country house
> near Hampton Court, and is so busy fitting it up (to receive
> nobody), that there is no getting him to work ...
>
> Neighbour Burgess has been too honest; the pease and beans
> ly all languishing upon the earth; not a cod has been gathered.
> There will be a hundred thousand apricocks ripe in ten days;
> they are now fairer and forwarder than what I saw at the
> Queen's table at Windsor on Sunday – and such strawberrys as
> never were tasted; currants red as blood to; and gooseberrys,
> peaches, pairs, apples, and plumbs to gripe the gutts of a nation.

Pope told Swift that Vanbrugh was 'the most easy careless writer and companion in the world ... wrote and built just as his

fancy led him'. He told Joseph Spence that 'none of our writers have a freer, easier way for comedy than Etherege and Vanbrugh' and on another occasion named him as one of a handful of prose writers suitable 'as authorities for familiar dialogues' in the compilation of an English dictionary. Cibber's tribute is fuller:

> Though, to write much, in a little time, is no excuse for writing ill; yet Sir *John Vanbrugh's* Pen, is not to be a little admir'd, for its Spirit, Ease and Readiness ... for notwithstanding this quick Dispatch, there is a clear and lively Simplicity in his Wit, that neither wants the Ornament of learning, nor has the least Smell of the Lamp in it. As the Face of a fine Woman, with only her Locks loose, about her, may be then in its greatest Beauty, such were his Productions, only adorn'd by Nature. There is something so catching to the Ear, so easy to the Memory, in all he writ, that it has been observ'd by all the Actors of my Time, that the Style of no Author whatsoever, gave their Memory less trouble ... which I myself ... can confirm ... And indeed his Wit, and Humour, was so little laboured, that his most entertaining Scenes seem'd to be no more, than his common Conversation committed to Paper ... We see the *Relapse*, however imperfect, in the Conduct, by the mere Force of its agreeable Wit, ran away with the Hearts of its Hearers; while *Love's Last Shift*, which (as Mr Congreve justly said of it) had only in it, a great many things, that were *like* Wit, that in reality were *not* Wit.

Both were first plays: that is, the first works of their authors to be acted and published. History does not relate, nor do archives apparently preserve, what preceded either of them. Vanbrugh's earliest letters do not have the same easy flow, and he must, like any 'born' writer, have done a good deal of practising in the years immediately preceding *The Relapse*. In no other way can he have developed a strange facility which has often been misunderstood. Dryden was not the last to observe that 'the English tongue so naturally slides' into blank verse 'that, in writing prose, it is hardly to be avoided' (Dedication to *The Rival Ladies*, 1694). A famous example is the King James Bible's 'Consider the lilies of the field, how they grow; they toil not, neither do they spin'. But Vanbrugh was well aware of what are going on in his head: *The Relapse* and *Æsop* contain

fairly long metrical passages set as prose, as well as those set in
verse lines.

Some critics have found something particularly unfortunate
or even unbecoming in Vanbrugh's blank verse, whichever
way it is printed, but in literature as in architecture his is the
kind of genius which no aesthetic theory dependent on a rigid
system of categories will accommodate with fairness. Between
the extremes in Restoration dramatic writing – of prose that
cannot be read as anything else on the one hand, and on the
other hand the rhyming verse of prologues, epilogues and
songs in the text – there seems to lie an ill-defined area that
includes both deliberate and unintentional blank verse. In the
curious case of Southerne's *The Wives' Excuse* the printing was
shared by two firms in such a way that half the play was set in
verse-like lines and the other half, including blank-verse passages, was set solid to save space. Vanbrugh seems to have
given his printers a few headaches over his intentions, but
Peter Holland, who has studied the relationship between printed texts and performances, concludes that the way the text
was laid out meant something:

> The more one analyses these passages, the more one is led to
> conclude that some of them represent a division of the speeches
> into speech-units, that is that they are divided up in the way an
> actor might treat the text in order to speak it. The reader is thus
> enabled to recover that pattern of speech.
> Vanbrugh makes ironic use of the tendency for this prose-as-
> verse to hover in some middle ground between ordinary speech
> and heightened heroic diction.

In Cibber's play Loveless's concluding lines after the masque
are, like most of the reconciliation scene with Amanda, almost
entirely in blank verse although set solid:

> Oh! *Amanda!* once more receive me to thy Arms; and while I am
> there, let all the World confess my Happiness. By my Example
> taught let every man, whose Fate has bound him to a married
> Life, beware of letting loose his wild desires ...

So it should surprise us even less that the same character

opens the sequel in verse lines, in which indeed the whole of
Vanbrugh's first scene is written:

> How true is that Philosophy, which says,
> Our Heaven is seated in our Minds?

Perhaps it should not surprise us either that Collier was the
first to talk Vanbrugh on this ground, claiming that in the
final scene of *The Relapse* Worthy 'gives his Periods a turn of
Versification, and talks *Prose* to her [Amanda] in *Meeter*. Now,
this is just as agreeable as it would be to *Ride* with one Leg and
Walk with the other.' As he often does, Collier here overstates
his case, although Worthy does utter lines such as

> If 'tis the Sting of unrequited Love, remove it instantly:
> I have a balm will quickly heal the Wound.
> *Ama.* You'll find the undertaking difficult:
> The Surgeon, who already has attempted it,
> Has much tormented me.

Generally it is the more sentimental characters, Loveless,
Amanda and Worthy, who break into metre. In Act II Vanbrugh
set out some of Berinthia's lines, although they are not metrical, much as an essayist might do to make the sense clearer:

> *Ama.* How did you live together?
> *Ber.* Like Man and Wife, asunder.
> He lov'd the Country, I the Town.
> He Hawks and Hounds, I Coaches and Equipage.
> He Eating and Drinking, I Carding and Playing.
> He the sound of a Horn, I the squeak of a Fiddle.
> We were dull Company at Table, worse abed.
> Whenever we met, we gave one another the Spleen.
> And never agreed but once, which was about lying alone.

But if Vanbrugh himself needed justification he could have
found it in Dryden, who was a poet before he was a critic. In the
Essay on Dramatic Poesy (1668) Dryden wrote:

> Now measure alone, in any modern language, does not con-
> stitute verse; those of the ancients in Greek and Latin consisted

in quantity of words, and a determinate number of feet. But when ... new languages were introduced, and barbarously mingled with the Latin, of which the Italian, Spanish, French, and ours (made out of them and the Teutonic) are dialects, a new way of poesy was practised ... This new way consisted in measure or number of feet, and rhyme ... No man is tied in modern poesy to observe any farther rule in the feet of his verse, but that they be dissyllables; whether Spondee, Trochee, or Iambic it matters not; only he is obliged to rhyme: neither do the Spanish, French, Italian or Germans, acknowledge at all, or very rarely, any such kind of poesy as blank verse amongst them. Therefore, at most 'tis but a poetic prose, a *sermo pedestris*; and as such, most fit for comedies, where I acknowledge rhyme to be improper.

Nevertheless Dryden's view that English naturally slides into blank verse certainly seems to apply to Vanbrugh. Lines from Foppington's first scene such as 'Now by all that's Great and Powerful, thou art an incomparable Coxcomb' or 'Ay, but you are not so good a Judge of those Things as I am' actually seem entirely natural when they are properly spoken, for then the sense overrides the metre.

Recently a French critic has pointed out another instance of the art that underlies Vanbrugh's seemingly artless writing. The device known as *stichomythia* in Greek drama and the plays of Seneca consists of the alternation of lines between two characters in which words and phrases are repeated with a small but significant change. It is unlikely that Vanbrugh arrived without considerable reading in the Classics at exchanges such as the following, between Lady Brute and Bellinda, in *The Provok'd Wife* (I.i):

> *Lady B.* How strong is Fancy!
> *Bell.* How weak is Woman!
> *Lady B.* Prethee, Neice, have a better opinion of your Aunt's Inclinations.
> *Bell.* Dear Aunt, have a better opinion of your Neice's Understanding.
> *Lady B.* You'll make me Angry.
> *Bell.* You'll make me Laugh.

Authors often find that characters take on a life of their own and seem to write themselves. Cibber thought this had happened with Vanbrugh's last unfinished play, *A Journey to London*, although he never got as far as writing it down:

> All I could gather from him of what he intended in the cata-
> strophe, was, that the conduct of his imaginary fine lady had so
> provok'd him, that he designed actually to have made her hus-
> band turn her out of doors.*

This must also have happened when Vanbrugh ennobled Sir Novelty Fashion. His total improbability is made totally cred-ible because he is drawn so very large, with his costive oaths, his coat-pocket 'too high by a foot' and his new periwig 'so long, and so full of Hair, it will serve . . . for a Hat and Cloak in all Weathers', which he decides to wear 'tho' it shew such a manstrous pair of Cheeks: Stap my Vitals, I shall be taken for a Trumpeter'. His famous drawl with its deformed *o*-sounds con-tributes considerably to the effect. The custom of publishing and reading plays meant that the printed word could be, in-deed needed to be, used to convey visually to readers at home what the audience in the playhouse absorbed aurally; one ex-ample of this is the inclusion of the actors' names with the *dramatis personae* so as to indicate for the knowledgeable the way the characters were imagined; another is the use of phonetic spelling for 'non-standard' speech sounds.

With Lord Foppington Vanbrugh's achievement was three-fold. He discovered in real life a mannerism that he could use, he made it the basis of the character, and he wrote down at least schematically the sound of the mannerism. He was not the first playwright to use phonetic spelling, but he was prob-ably one of the first, as Bernard Harris points out in his edition of *The Relapse*, to transcribe the sounds of a real person. Robert Spencer, second Earl of Sunderland (1640-1702), was a man of noted taciturnity in public, but when he did speak he affected, either from nervousness or from some impediment, a nasal drawl in which *o*'s became protracted *a*'s or *aa*'s. An example of this is given by Roger North: 'Whaat . . . if his Majesty taarn out faarty of us, may not he have faarty athers to saarve him as well?'; from this it is but a step to Foppington's 'As Gad shall jidge me, I can't tell; for 'tis passible I may dine with some of aur House at *Lackets*'.

* p. 425

_ 13 _

The Art of Adaptation

The year 1697 saw Vanbrugh increasingly involved with the theatre. Although he was still a serving captain in Lord Berkeley's Marine Regiment there was no longer any significant marine engagement in the war with France; by April the negotiators for a peace had gathered at Rijswijk, although land fighting continued and the treaty ending the Nine Years War was not signed until 20 September. By that date Vanbrugh had seen two new plays staged: _Æsop_ and _The Provok'd Wife_. _Æsop_ was produced at Drury Lane in December 1696 or the following month, for Narcissus Luttrell bought his copy on 20 January and Lady Morley saw a performance given two days later. _The Provok'd Wife_ was staged in April at the seceding company's new theatre in Lincoln's Inn Fields. By September he was probably already considering a third new work, _The Country House_, which we know from Lady Morley's attendance list was staged at Drury Lane in January 1698.

Of all his dramatic works, only _The Relapse_, _The Provok'd Wife_, and the unfinished _Journey to London_ are completely original; all the others are adaptations from other writers. But the promptness and energy with which Vanbrugh addressed himself to adaptation suggests that he was not merely anxious to make money or short of original ideas; he surely believed he could 'make something' out of the originals of Boursault and Dancourt, very much as a performer sees the potential of a role or a piece of music. In his first venture he had at once revised the psychology of Cibber's play and expanded Cibber's own

lead part; in *Æsop* and *The Country House* he would quicken
the pace and naturalize the language and the characters of his
French originals.

Edme Boursault's *Ésope à la Ville* was first produced in Paris
in January 1690 and was fairly successful after a slow start. According to Vanbrugh's Preface to his adaptation, the original
was 'routed' at the first performance, 'People seldom being
fond of what they don't understand, their own sweet Persons
excepted'. On the second evening it rallied, 'the third it
advanc'd, the fourth it gave a vigorous Attacque, and the fifth
put all the Feathers [flops] in Town to the scamper; pursuing 'em
to the fourteenth, and then they cry'd out, Quarter'. It was not
reasonable to expect, wrote Vanbrugh artlessly, that *Æsop*
should gain so great a Victory here, since 'tis possible by fool-
ing with his Sword, I may have turn'd the edge on't'. Most of Act
V was his own invention, and he made other changes, suggesting in justification that

> had I been so complaisant to have waited on his Play word for
> word, 'tis possible even that might not have ensur'd the success
> of it. For though it swam in *France*, it might have sunk in *Eng-
> land*. Their Country abounds in Cork, ours in Lead.

The first (1690) edition of Boursault's play, published as *Les
Fables d'Ésope*, is no larger than a pocket diary, and Vanbrugh
may have picked up a copy in Paris; it would not have bur-
dened the lightest of travellers. The plot is a slight tale about
the course of true love. Learchus, governor of Syzicus, has
broken the engagement of his daughter Euphronia to Oronces,
and is determined to marry her instead to *Æsop*, wise and famous but old and (as tradition has it) ugly, because the connection will make him too a great man. The young couple beg
Æsop to help them, but it is only at the marriage ceremony
itself that the old sage reveals that he is doing so, taking the
bride's hand and placing it in the young man's. Boursault here
presents the self-seeking Learchus as beaming with approval,
and one of Vanbrugh's perceptive amendments is to make
Æsop admonish the governor sternly for his selfish ambition.

Through this simple plot parade a succession of incidental
characters, who by posing problems and questions to Æsop

provide occasions for him to deliver a series of fables of the
kind for which he is traditionally famous. By these means he
gives a number of elementary lessons in citizenship: the need
to levy and pay taxes, the burdens of government, the proper
structure of society, the usefulness of its members, and so on.
The uncontroversial moral messages are conveyed painlessly
through our enjoyment of the varied and picturesque characters who elicit them. Again Vanbrugh translates Monsieur
Doucet, a genealogist who offers to make a pedigree for Æsop
(who as everyone knows was a liberated slave), into Quaint, a
herald; Pierrot, a peasant presumably dressed as his name
suggests, is turned into Roger, a country bumpkin.

Vanbrugh's renaming of persons is in line with the practice
of Restoration comedy; Mr and Mrs Fruitful are the innkeeper
and his wife who want a reward for bringing up fifteen
children, the size of family in which the playwright himself
was raised. Doris, originally the confidant of Euphronia (defined by Dr Johnson, following the French usage, as 'A person
trusted with private affairs, commonly with affairs of love') becomes her nurse ('One who breeds, educates or protects'). Not
only does the change suggest an older woman, but also the
common-sense part seems to be written for a character not too
far from that of Nurse in *The Relapse*. The country gentleman
of Vanbrugh's own invention rejoices in the name of Sir Polidorus Hogstye; he enters 'drunk, in a Hunting Dress, with a
Huntsman, Groom, Faulkner, and other Servants: one leading
a couple of Hounds, another Grey-hounds, a Third a Spaniel, a
Fourth a Gun upon his Shoulder, the Faulkner, a Hawk upon
his Fist, &c'. This colourful episode is both introduced and concluded by Sir Polidorus's battle cry, transcribed as 'Haux, haux,
haux, haux, haux'.

In the French, all the characters from the highest to the
lowest ride easily on rhymed couplets, even when the dialogue
cuts in mid-line from one voice to another. It would be simplistic to say that Vanbrugh dispensed with the artificiality of
verse. Most of his *Æsop* is indeed set as prose, but while the
less elevated characters speak in prose the principals speak
often in blank verse, especially when they treat of virtue,
emotion or wisdom. Learchus's eulogy of Æsop in the very first
scene is exceptionally set in verse:

'Tis true he's plain, but that, my Girl's, a Trifle.
All manly beauty's seated in the Soul.
And that of *Æsop*, Envy's self must own,
Out shines whate'er the World has yet produc'd.

In this play, even if the printer was unsure, that Vanbrugh himself knew what he was doing is evident from the part of
Hortentia, 'an affected Learned Lady'. Much of it is set in
broken lines, in a kind of parody of just metre, appropriate to
'the Wise Lady', as she is introduced at the end of Act I, 'the
great Scholar, that no body can understand'. The fables which
Æsop is always ready to offer are set in rhymes, and in lines
varying in length from verse to verse and from one fable to another. Moreover, all but two are set in Italic, and this combination is surely significant. Italic is a common typographical convention for the songs in a play, and irregular measure is a
common feature of songs. An almost contemporary example of
a stage song, in a well-known setting attributed variously to
Henry Purcell and Jeremiah Clarke, is the Scottish Song from
Act III of Thomas Scott's *The Mock Marriage* (1695), of which
the first stanzas run:

> 'Twas within a furlong of Edinboro' Town,
> In the rosy time of year when the grass was down,
> Bonny Jocky, blithe and gay,
> Said to Jenny making hay,
> 'Let's sit a little, dear and prattle,
> 'Tis a sultry day.'
>
> He long had courted the black-brow'd maid,
> But Jenny ever said,
> She would ne'er consent to wed,
> And with many a Pish and Pooh,
> She cried 'It will not do,   ·
> I cannot, cannot, cannot, wonnot, wonnot buckle to.'

In comparison, Æsop's response to Hortentia runs:

> Once on a time, a Nightingale
>   To Changes prone:
> Unconstant, Fickle, Whimsical
>   (A Female one:)

Who sung like Others of her kind,
Hearing a Well-taught Linnet's Aires,
Had other matters in her mind,
To imitate him she prepares.
Her Fancy strait was on the Wing:
   I fly, quoth she,
   As well as he;
   I don't know why,
   I shou'd not try,
As well as he, to sing.
From that day forth, she chang'd her Note,
She spoil'd her Voice, she strain'd her Throat:
She did, as Learned Women do,
   Till every thing,
   That heard her sing,
Wou'd run away from her ---- as I from you.

[*Exit Æsop, running.*

If the suggestion that the fables were to be sung may appear speculative, confirmation comes from notices of some early performances, which show that the evening's entertainment included music and singing or dancing acts; it would have been no more than good management to use the musicians for the whole evening. There are no details until late in 1703, when on 10 November there were several items of instrumental music. On 21 January 1704 singing and dancing were mentioned, dancing on 27 October, and singing and dancing on 31 March 1705. In a later performance, on 5 December 1715, the Drury Lane vouchers record a payment for two hounds from Knightsbridge for Sir Polidorus Hogstye's scene.

Æsop was probably, as Arthur Huseboe observes, designed to suit the comic talents of the Drury Lane players. Six of them had appeared in *The Relapse*, and the casting of Cibber as Æsop ('I was equally approv'd in Æsop,' he wrote, 'as the *Lord Foppington*') helps not only to explain the success of the production but also to indicate the flair, elegance and imagination demanded in the title role – and indeed in other parts. It was thoroughly good entertainment, with something of the character of a modern 'musical', although it is not entirely an edifying tale. Not all the characters set a good example: Learchus acts from self-interest, and near the beginning of Act V the arranged marriage with Æsop is specified as breaking Euphronia's oath with Oronces. To dwell on such points is to show the absurdity of those critics of Vanbrugh's time who required the theatre to be wholly improving. Nor is the play quite as free from what the critics call 'indecency' as the artless and often quoted lines from the Prologue would suggest:

> Gallants; We never yet produc'd a Play,
> With greater fears, than this we act to day.
> Barren of all the Graces of the Stage,
> Barren of all that entertains this Age.
> No Hero, no Romance, no Plot, no Show,
> No Rape, no Bawdy, no Intrigue, no Beau:
> There's nothing in't, with which we use to please ye:
> With down right dull Instruction, w'are to tease ye.

There are, for example, several references to the powers of generation, and Mrs Forge-Will, a scrivener's widow, seeks bounties for her two daughters so they can marry and escape being 'eaten up with the Green Sickness, as half the young Women in the Town are, or wou'd be, if there were not more helps for a Disease than one'. Readers of Mrs Sharp's popular books on midwifery, and doubtless others in the audience also, knew that this form of melancholy, which sometimes manifested itself in the craving to eat coal, lime or clay, was instantly cured by the consummation of marriage. The fable with which Æsop attempts to dismiss Mrs Forge-Will contains a line with a dash which can only be completed as 'She bid him kiss her Breech', and the sage's advice to the happy young couple at the end of the play is hilarious. 'Be clean in your Cloaths', he says, 'but nicely so in your Persons: Eat at one Table: Lye in one Room, but sleep in two Beds.' Then, 'Turning to the Boxes', he addresses the ladies of the audience in a cautionary fable about two amorous sparrows which settled at last

> In furious haste,
> On a Twigg, with Birdlime spread,
> (Want of a more Downy Bed)
> To act a Scene of Love.
> Fatal it prov'd, to both their Fires.
> For tho' at length, they broke away,

And baulk'd the School-Boy of his Prey,
Which made him weep, the live-long day.
The Bridegroom, in the hasty strife,
Was stuck so fast, to his Dear Wife;
That tho' he us'd, his utmost Art,
He quickly found, it was in vain,
To put himself, to farther pain,
They never more must part.

One wonders how Jeremy Collier managed to miss this play.

In the spring of 1697 Vanbrugh added a one-act after-piece or Part II to his comedy, designed to be played on the same evening; it must have concluded the performance seen by Lady Morley on 24 May, for it was published that month. This had nothing whatever to do with the second *Aesop* play of Boursault, *Ésope à la Cour*, a five-act *Comédie Héroique* which did not appear until 1701. Vanbrugh's piece starts with the entrance of the players as themselves. They tell Æsop that

> we are Stage-Players;
> That's our Calling:
> Tho' we play upon other things too; some of us play
> Upon the Fiddle; some play upon the Flute;
> We play upon one another, we play upon the Town,
> And we play upon the Patentees.

They then have to explain who the Patentees are, and Vanbrugh uses the similes of a shipwreck and a pack of hounds to make fun of the 1695 secession to Lincoln's Inn Fields, where *The Provok'd Wife* had recently opened. In the second episode a country gentleman dissatisfied with the running of the state is shown the virtues of the professional and the expert; the final scene is a dialogue between Æsop and an airy young beau, who outlines his life-style in a series of short exchanges which show how well Vanbrugh understood the importance of timing on the stage:

> *Aes.* Pray what may be your Name?
> *B. Empty.*
> *Aes.* Where do you live?
> *B.* In the Side-Box.

In Thomas Shadwell's *Bury Fair* Wildish tells Mrs Gertrude
that he will 'stare and goggle at you; and never have my Eyes
off you, while I Side-box you in the Play-house' (III.i). In *The
Relapse* Lord Foppington claims that he does not 'pretend to be
a Beau; but a Man must endeavour to look wholesome, lest he
makes so nauseous a Figure in the Side-Box, the Ladies shou'd
be compell'd to turn their eyes upon the Play' (II.i). Æsop's
interrogation continues:

> *Aes.* What do you do there?
> *B.* I Ogle the Ladies.
> *Aes.* To what purpose?
> *B.* To no purpose.
> *Aes.* Why then do you do it?
> *B.* Because they like it, and *I* like it.
> *Aes.* Wherein consists the Pleasure?
> *B.* In Playing the Fool.

And so on: as the piece begins with the actors playing themselves, so it ends with one of them playing a well-known type of
theatre-goer. Thus far Æsop has won most of the arguments,
but the beau has the last word: he answers Æsop's final fable
with one of his own, in which the contest for a lady's heart, between a parson, a solid citizen and a beau, is won by the last:

> It prov'd such Sun-shine weather,
> That you must know, at the first Beck,
> The Lady leapt about his Neck,
> And off they went together.

The Country House, a two-acter which Lady Morley saw at
Drury Lane on 18 January 1698, was not printed until 1715,
when it was described as a *farce*; this offers an opportunity to
explain the way in which the term *farce* has changed since
Vanbrugh's day. The word is French, and comes from *farcir*,
meaning to stuff, as in cooking. In the theatrical sense farce
was in the late Middle Ages an impromptu interlude or filling
in a religious play. It was short and comic or even ribald, and
might consist as much of 'business' or clowning as of word-
play. As complete and more or less composed works, farces
came to England from France and were usually given before or

after the main play or between the acts. The brevity and the frivolous ancestry of the form absolved it from any critical demands that it should instruct, or elicit any more profound response than laughter.

Earlier in our own century the works of Georges Feydeau in France and those of Sir Arthur Wing Pinero and later Ben Travers in England developed a public taste for the modern farce, a full-length play designed to evoke only laughter, economically and wittily written, breathlessly and exactly timed, full of 'business' and exploiting by suggestion rather than representation the comic aspects of human relationships. An appreciation of the farcical element in Restoration comedy is an important factor in its acceptance by modern audiences, even in the face of the continuing strictures of many literary critics. What Feydeau and Pinero did was not to invent farce in the modern sense but to rediscover it. If in the light of this we alter the way we categorize seventeenth-century plays, some of the problems which have worried critics disappear. We shall return to these considerations in a later chapter; for the present it is enough to make it clear that *The Country House* is still a farce in the seventeenth-century sense of a short comic play with no serious intentions or implications.

Florent Carton de Dancourt's *La Maison de Campagne* was first acted on 27 January 1688. It is a prose comedy in one act, divided by Vanbrugh into two and still playing for no more than a fast-moving twenty minutes. Vanbrugh follows his original, in Bonamy Dobrée's phrase, 'not too closely, but as a happy dog accompanies his master on a walk'. Although the setting remains in France and is specified as Normandy, Vanbrugh omits references and allusions which would be meaningless or obscure to an English audience. *Ces porcelaines de Hollande* becomes 'my Lady's China', and the threat of being put into a convent is omitted since there is no equivalent in a Protestant society. But the simplifications allow Vanbrugh, by using more vivid phrases of his own, to build up a character like Charly, a precocious and quite shameless adolescent – 'a forward Boy' in his own words – whose eye is fixed permanently at bosom height. Vanbrugh turns Dancourt's *je ne le connais point* into 'I never saw him in my life before, but for all that, I'll hold fifty pound he comes to dine with me'. Dancourt

makes the servant tell Madame Bernard that his mistress is
plus diable que vous, quand elle s'y met; Vanbrugh makes
Collin say, 'when Madam's in Passion she has the De'il and his
Dam both in her Belly'. Dancourt writes *patois* for some of his
characters; Vanbrugh's consistent use of a kind of phonetic
spelling for Collin shows that his ear was as acute for the rustic
as for the fop. 'Noa, noa', says Collin, 'but in a Coach they ceam
all besmear'd with Gould, with six breave Horses.' If anyone
had asked Collin where *he* came from, the answer would
surely have been either 'New *Castle*' or 'Geateshead'. But Vanbrugh uses the same conventions in *The Relapse* for Sir Tunbelly's men, who are presumably much nearer to London.

Dancourt's little story concerns Monsieur Bernard (Barnard
in Vanbrugh) who discovers that the disadvantage of a country
house is that not only friends but complete strangers call on
him expecting food, drink, and a bed, and otherwise distract
him by their small-talk and other less sociable interruptions.
During the course of the play the stream of invaders includes
an unknown baron whose hawk has escaped and is perched in
a tree in Bernard's garden, two sickly cousins from Paris sent
by their father to take the country air, and 'a Parcel of Fellows
[who] have been hunting about your Grounds all this Morning,
broke down your Hedges, and are now coming into your
House'. Their quarry, a stag, plays a part offstage almost as important as that on stage of Eraste (Vanbrugh curtails the final
e), the suitor of Bernard's daughter Mariane. When the play
opens we learn that Bernard will not allow the young man in
the house, but it becomes evident that his dislike is a particular
case of his general and growing antipathy to visitors. 'Since I
bought this damn'd Country House', he complains almost at
once, 'I spend more in a Summer than wou'd maintain me
seven Year.' In the original Bernard's 'jade of a wife' pushed
him into the purchase; Vanbrugh's Barnard takes responsibility although he is if anything more bearish towards his
lady than the original. When she complains that his ill humour
will soon make normal life impossible he replies in a series of
exchanges entirely Vanbrugh's own:

Mr Barn. Very true; for in a little time I shall have nothing to live
upon.

Madam. Do you know what a ridiculous Figure you make?

Mr Barn. You'll make a great deal worse, when you han't Money enough to pay for the washing of your Smocks.

Madam. It seems you married me only to Dishonour me; how horrible this is?

Mr Barn. I tell ye, you'll Ruin me. Do you know how much Money you spend in a Year?

Madam. Not I truly, I don't understand Arithmetick.

Mr Barn. Arithmetic, O Lud! O Lud! Is it so hard to comprehend, that he who spends a Shilling, and receives but Six-pence, must be ruin'd in the End?

Madam. I never troubled my Head with Accounts, nor ever will; but if you did but know what ridiculous Things the World says of ye ---

Mr Barn. Rot the World --- 'Twill say worse of me when I'm in a Gail. _____

The unhappy house-owner's brother advises him to 'leave this House quite, and go to Town', and finally, since nobody will buy it, to 'do what's done when a Town's a fire, blow up your House that the Mischief may run no further' (again Vanbrugh's version transfigures Dancourt's simple *Je mettrais le feu à la maison*). He puts up a sign reading 'At the Sword Royal, Entertainment for Man and Horse' and adds to the embarrassment of his son by appearing with his brother dressed as tapsters; the three gentlemen brought in by the sign go away when they learn the scale of the tariff.

Bernard is about to be eaten out of house and home; the cook reports that the hunters' dogs, having uprooted the lettuces and cabbages in the garden, got into the kitchen and tore half the roast off the spit, while 'a Crew of hungry Footmen devour'd what the Dogs left'. The dogs had of course been in pursuit of the stag, which came, 'as big as a donkey and quite out of breath' (Dancourt), blundering into the courtyard, as the servant describes. Vanbrugh's Collin is more graphic:

A large and steatly Stag, with a pair of Horns of his Head, Heavens bless you, your Worship might have seen to wear'em, comes towards our Geat a puffing and blowing like Cew in hard labour.

Collin, seeing a felicitous replenishment for the larder, promptly shoots the poor beast, which of course belongs to the King. At the end of the play Erast reminds Barnard that the slaughter 'of one of the King's Stags that run hither for Refuge is enough to overturn a Fortune much better establish'd than yours --- However, Sir, if you consent to give me your Daughter, for her Sake I will secure you harmless'. Barnard is quite willing to give away his daughter, but insists that Erast must take the house too, and adds, 'if you think you've a hard Bargain, I don't care if I toss you in my Wife to make you amends':

> Since all Things now are sped,
> My Son in Anger, and my Daughter wed,
> My House dispos'd of, which was the Cause of Strife,
> I now may hope to lead a happy Life,
> If I can part with my ingaging Wife.

No such simple solution could ever be available to Sir John and Lady Brute.

— 14 —

The Provok'd Wife

Since 'tis the Intent and Business of the Stage,
To Copy out the Follies of the Age;
To hold to every Man a Faithful Glass,
And shew him of what Species he's an Ass.
I hope the next that teaches in the School,
Will shew our Author he's a scribling Fool.
And that the Satyr may be sure to Bite,
Kind Heav'n! Inspire some venom'd Priest to Write,
And grant some Ugly Lady may Indite.
For I wou'd have him lash'd, by Heav'ns! I woud,
Till his presumption swam away in Blood.
Three Plays at once proclaims a Face of Brass,
No matter what they are! That's not the Case,
To write three Plays, ev'n that's to be an Ass.

In these opening lines of the Prologue to *The Provok'd Wife*, spoken by Mrs Bracegirdle (who played Bellinda), Vanbrugh mocked his own success. *The Relapse* had been followed at Drury Lane by *Æsop*; *The Provok'd Wife* was produced at Lincoln's Inn Fields in April 1697 and published in May. Colley Cibber, as we have seen, knew Vanbrugh well at Drury Lane at the time of the production, and his statement that the third play was offered to the rival theatre to repay Sir Thomas Skipwith for an old favour is probably accurate. Shiels, in Theophilus Cibber's *Lives*,* concocted the statement that in their army

* p. 31

days Vanbrugh read the drafts of two plays to Skipwith; his imperfect sources for this statement were Colley's *Apology* and
Vanbrugh's own remark in his answer to Collier that he was
very young when he wrote *The Relapse*. But neither that play
nor *The Provok'd Wife* as we know them can be considered juv-
enilia, and while some of the allusions in the latter play are to
events current in the mid-1680s others refer to topics a decade
later. Nothing less than the discovery of an early draft, such as
there must have been, could reveal how much labour, and of
what kind, went into the development of *The Provok'd Wife*; instead we have to accept the play as it took the stage in 1697,
warts and all. But what are these warts?

Modern writers concern themselves with the dramatic
failings, inconsistencies and improbabilities of Vanbrugh's
play far more than do actors, for whom the criterion is whether
a part is rewarding to play – a question to which the answer
here is generally affirmative. Now in most discussions of plays
a summary of the action is not considered necessary, because
either the text itself is published with the discussion or the
reader is assumed to be familiar with the work. The process of
making a synopsis for readers who may not be already thus
provided for is in itself revealing; for while on stage Vanbrugh's action flows swiftly and easily through changes of
scene and the movement of characters, in the study or the
library a neat synopsis is unusually difficult to write. Whereas
The Relapse interweaves plots which are largely distinct from
each other, the strands that make up *The Provok'd Wife* are far
more closely knitted together in a way which seems to be deliberate and which indeed contributes to the play's dramatic
effectiveness.

In fact the simplest way to give an account of the play is not
by the sequence of events in time but by the almost architectural arrangement of the characters, starting with the most
vividly drawn, Sir John Brute and Lady Fancyfull, who form a
frame for all the others. Sir John, who married for sex and
whose lady wed him for his money, opens the play in misery;
he hates his wife only less than he hates fighting: 'Wou'd my
Courage come up but to a fourth part of my Ill Nature, I'd stand
buff to her Relations, and thrust her out of Doors'. At the start
he is terrified that she will be unfaithful and thus expose him to

ridicule; by the end his fears are compounded by the growing
suspicion that he has cause for them. His name prepares us for
his crusty behaviour, his fierce tobacco smoking, his drunken
rowdiness with Lord Rake and Colonel Bully, and his abuse of
his wife, verbal at first and physical at the beginning of the last
Act. The first Sir John was the leader of the Lincoln's Inn Fields
company, Betterton himself, and Vanbrugh may have had him
in mind for the part. If so, it is significant that Betterton held his
audiences less by gesture, in which he was economical, or his
appearance, which was small, unhandsome and a little bent,
than by his voice, which was fine by nature and used with mas-
tery. The part is one which can be enhanced by a powerful
figure, but ultimately it depends on the lines and their delivery.
From the start he is consistently and laconically vehement:

> *Lady Brute.* What is it that disturbs you?
> *Sir John.* A Parson.
> *Lady B.* Why, what has he done to you?
> *Sir J.* He has married me.   [*Exit Sir* John.

When at the beginning of Act III his wife and her niece Bellinda
pointedly bring their needlework and their 'prittle prattle' into
the same room with him, he proclaims that far from curing his
spleen the noise 'will so increase it I shall take my own House
for a Paper-Mill'. His very last line, in reference to Bellinda, is
an aside: 'Why now this Woman will be married to somebody
too'.

No part could be more different from Lord Foppington, created by Vanbrugh for Cibber. In 1716 Brute was taken by Keen,
in 1719 by Quin, and when in 1726 Cibber played it his Sir John
was, according to Thomas Davies's *Dramatic Miscellanies*,

> copied from Betterton, as far as a weak pipe and an inexpres-
> sive meagre countenance could bear any resemblance to the
> vigorous original. I have seen him [Cibber] act this part with
> great and deserved applause; his skill was so masterly, that, in
> spite of natural impediments, he exhibited a faithful picture of
> this worshipful debauchee.

Davies says that Cibber, and later Garrick, never forgot that
Brute had once been a gentleman, and this is a valuable in-

sight. Towards the end of the play, grotesque though he is in his swearing, tumbling and snoring, when Razor his valet carries him off to bed like a sack of coal we are for a moment moved to pity him. But that does not make the play into a sentimental one; on the contrary it forms the serious relief that gives roundness to the comic caricature.

In the centre of the play are the drinking scene at the Blue Posts with Brute, Rake and Bully, and the episode in Covent Garden in which Sir John robs an earnest tailor of the new gown he is delivering to the parson and, under its cover, assaults the Constable.

The second pillar of the whole edifice is Lady Fancyfull, a kind of female Foppington: 'Lard', she exclaims, as she peppers her speech with French words and phrases. She is affected, overdressed, selfish, increasingly spiteful, unmarried and likely to remain so. She is mocked in particular by Heartfree, who arouses first her scorn and then her jealousy, and flattered by mercenary servants like her singing master Mr Treble and her French maidservant rather than Cornet, her English one;

Madamoiselle. Ah Matam, I wish I was fine Gentleman for your sake. I do all de ting in de World to get leetel way into your heart. I make Song, I make Verse, I give you de Serenade, I give great many Present to *Madamoiselle*, I no eat, I no sleep, I be lean, I be mad, I hang my self, I drown my self. Ah ma Chere Dame, Que je vous Aimerois? [*Embracing her.*
Lady Fan. Well the *French* have strange obliging ways with 'em; you may take those two pair of Gloves *Madamoiselle*.
Madam. Me humbly tanke my sweet Lady.

Enter Cornet

Cornet. Madam here's a Letter for your Ladyship by the Penny-post.
Lady Fan. Some new Conquest I'll warrant you. For without Vanity I look'd extreamly clear last night, when I went to the Park.

In Act I Scene ii she receives a letter of assignation to St James's Park, from 'one who hates you for some things, as he cou'd love you for Others, and therefore is willing to endeavour your Reformation'. Egged on by Madamoiselle, she goes to the park and discovers the writer is Heartfree, 'a profess'd Woman-hater'. The potential of this relationship would be strictly limited were it not that she admits privately that she could like him 'were he but a fine Gentleman', and that in Act III, at the Brutes' house, Bellinda, noticing this partiality, flirts with Heartfree in order to make her jealous. By the last Act Bellinda and Heartfree are in earnest, and Lady Fancyfull almost avenges herself by insinuating, in disguise, to each of them that the other is not free to marry. But the servants let her down and her plot is revealed and foiled. Her predicament, like Sir John Brute's, is no better at the end of the play.

Within this framework run, with a considerable degree of symmetry, the affairs of Heartfree and Bellinda on one side and Lady Brute – the provoked wife – and Constant on the other. As is so often the case in Restoration comedy, names denote character.* Constant first saw Lady Brute at her wedding, to which he was invited by Sir John. She is still young, perhaps only a few years older than her niece. Constant has loved her 'ever since, more than e'er a Martyr did his Soul', and he is prepared to love her, hopelessly, as he tells Heartfree, 'to eternity'.

> O, 'tis in vain to visit her; sometimes to get a sight of her, I visit that Beast her Husband, but she certainly finds some Pretence to quit the Room as soon as I enter.

Heartfree's comment on Constant is no less appropriate for being more generally applicable: 'he adores his Mistriss for being virtuous, and yet is very angry with her, because she won't be lewd'. But Lady Brute is halfway to meet him; after Sir John's first brusque exit she argues with herself thus:

> What opposes? --- My Matrimonial Vow? --- Why, what did I Vow: I think I promis'd to be true to my Husband.
>> Well; and he promis'd to be kind to me.
>> But he han't kept his Word ---
>> Why then I'm absolv'd from mine --- ay, that seems clear to me. The Argument's good betwixt the King and the People, why

* p. 175

not between the Husband and the Wife? O, but that Condition
was not exprest. --- No matter, 'twas understood.
Well, by all I see, If I argue the matter a little longer with my self,
I shan't find so many Bug-bears in the way, as I thought I shou'd.
Lord what fine notions of Virtue do we Women take up upon the
Credit of old foolish Philosophers. Virtue's its own reward,
Virtue's this, Virtue's that, --- Virtue's an Ass, and a Gallant's
worth forty on't.

It is a good thing, Bellinda tells her a few minutes later, that
Constant does not know 'the weakness of the Fortifications; for
o' my Conscience he'd soon come on to the Assault'. The metaphor of siege and battle runs through the play.

Lady B. Ay, and I'm afraid carry the Town too. But whatever you
may have observ'd, I have dissembled so well as to keep him
Ignorant. So you see I'm no Coquet, Bellinda: And if you'll follow
my advice you'll never be one neither.

Before the end of Act III.i. it is clear to both Constant and Lady
Brute what is at stake, and when the lady runs out and Heartfree returns from talking with Bellinda, Constant hugs him for
joy:

Ha, Heartfree: Thou hast done me Noble Service in pratling to
the young Gentlewoman without there; come to my Arms, Thou
Venerable Bawd, and let me squeeze thee [Embracing him eag-
erly] as a new pair of stayes do's a Fat Country girl, when she's
carry'd to Court to stand for a Maid of Honour.
Heart. Why what the Devil's all this Rapture for?
Const. Rapture? There's ground for Rapture, man, there's hopes,
my Heartfree, hopes, my Friend!
Heart. Hopes? of what?
Const. Why hopes that my Lady and I together, (for 'tis more
than one bodies work) should make Sir John a Cuckold.
Heart. Prithee what did she say to thee?
Const. Say? What did she not say? She said that --- says she ---
she said --- Zoons I don't know what she said: But she look'd as if
she said everything I'd have her.

In the last scene of this Act Bellinda advises her aunt to submit
to her feelings although she is still unsure of her own towards
Heartfree:

But if I cou'd make a Conquest of this Son of *Bacchus*, and rival
his Bottle: What shou'd I do with him, he has no Fortune; I can't
marry him; and sure you wou'd not have me commit Fornication.

Lady B. Why, if you did, Child, 'twou'd be but a good friendly
part; if 'twere only to keep me in Countenance whilst I commit
--- You know what.

Bell. Well, if I can't resolve to serve you that way, I may perhaps
some other, as much to your Satisfaction. But pray how shall we
contrive to see these Blades again quickly?

Lady B. We must e'en have Recourse to the old way; make 'em
an Appointment 'twixt jest and earnest, 'twill look like a Frolick,
and that you know's a very good thing to save a Woman's
Blushes.

But at Spring Garden things begin to get out of hand (IV.iv.).
The ladies are skirmishing, in disguise, with the two young
men when Sir John enters; not recognizing his wife and niece,
he takes them to be a couple of whores and seizes them for
himself; they are therefore obliged to reveal themselves to
Constant and Heartfree, though not to Sir John. Cheated of his
catch by the information that they are respectable ladies
known to his young friends, Sir John leaves. Heartfree then
walks off with the niece and Constant turns jest into earnest in
a manner that seems all set for a repetition of Loveless's scene
with Berinthia at the identical point in *The Relapse*.

> *Const.* Forgive me, therefore, since my Hunger rages, if I at last
> grow Wild, and in my frenzy force at least, This from you.
> [*Kissing her Hand.*] Or if you'd have my Flame soar higher still,
> then grant me this, and this, and this, and Thousands more;
> [*Kissing first her Hand, then her Neck. Aside.*] for now's the time,
> She melts into Compassion.
>
> *Lady B.* [*aside*] Poor Coward Vertue, how it shuns the Battle. O
> heavens ! let me go.
>
> *Const.* Ay, go, ay: Where shall we go, my Charming Angel, – –
> into this private Arbour. --- Nay, let's lose no time --- Moments
> are precious.
>
> *Lady B.* And Lovers wild. Pray let us stop here; at least for this
> time.
>
> *Const.* 'Tis impossible: he that has Power over you, can have
> none over himself.
>
> *Lady B.* Ah; I'm lost.

Poor coward virtue is only saved by the irruption of Lady Fan-cyfull and her maid, who have observed the whole scene. But the play ends with Sir John, threatened by Constant and believ-ing, as the audience does, that time and opportunity will at the last make a fool of him:

'Tis well --- 'tis very well --- In spight of that young Jade's Mat-rimonial Intrigue, I am a downright stinking Cuckold --- Here they are --- Boo --- [*Putting his Hand to his Forehead*] Methinks I could Butt with a Bull. What the Plague did I marry her for? I knew she did not like me; if she had, she wou'd have lain with me; for I wou'd have done so, because I lik'd her: But that's past, and I have her. And now, what shall I do with her --- If I put my Horns in my Pocket, she'll grow Insolent --- if I don't, that Goat there, that Stallion, is ready to whip me through the Guts. --- The Debate then is reduc'd to this; Shall I die a Heroe? or live a Ras-cal? --- Why, Wiser Men than I, have long since concluded, that a living Dog is better than a dead Lion.

All his troubles, and hers, remain at the final curtain.

The Provok'd Wife does thus involve, but not resolve, serious issues of its time – the incompatible couple and the younger son. Nor can we be sure that Heartfree and Bellinda will make a more successful marriage than the Brutes, for they are not sure themselves. At the end of Act III Bellinda had told her aunt she could not marry Heartfree because he had no fortune; but at that stage his character was still so true to his name that for anyone to consider marrying him would be unwise. He had told Constant:

I can pass a Night with a Woman, and for the time, perhaps, make my self as good Sport as you can do. Nay I can court a Woman, too, call her Nymph, Angel, Goddess, what you please; but here's the Difference 'twixt you and I: I perswade a Woman she's an Angel; she perswades you she's one.

He went on to explain how he avoided falling in love. He never considered a woman as either dressmakers or poets might do, but

as pure Nature has contriv'd her, and that more strictly than I shou'd have done our old Grandmother *Eve*, had I seen her naked in the Garden; for I consider her turn'd inside out. Her Heart well examin'd, I find there Pride, Vanity, Covetousness, Indiscretion, but above all things, Malice ... Then for her Outside, I consider it merely as an Outside; she has a thin Tiffany covering over just such Stuff as you and I are made on.

As for her deportment:

If you should see your Mistriss at a Coronation, dragging her Peacock's Train, with all her state and insolence about her, 'twoud strike you with all the awful thoughts that Heaven it self could pretend to from you; whereas I turn the whole matter into a Jest, and suppose her strutting in the self-same stately manner, with nothing on her but her Stays, and her under scanty quilted Petticoat.

It is in Heartfree that signs of change first appear. Act IV.ii. shows him alone in his chamber, up and dressed betimes:

What the Plague Ail's me---Love? No, I thank you for that; my heart's Rock still---
Yet 'tis *Bellinda* that disturbs me; that's positive.
--- Well, what of all that? Must I love her for being troublesome? at that rate, I might love all the Women I meet, I gad.
But hold?---tho' I don't love her for disturbing me, yet she may disturb me, because I love her---Ay, that may be, faith.
I have dreamt of her, that's certain---
Well, so I have of my Mother; therefore what's that to the purpose? Ay, but *Bellinda* runs in my Mind waking---
And so do's many a damn'd thing, that I don't care a Farthing for---
Methinks tho', I would fain be talking to her, and yet I have no Business---
Well, am I the first Man, that has had a Mind to do an Impertinent thing?

When Constant arrives, Heartfree gives himself away by a repeated slip of the tongue:

Const. I thought none but Lovers quarrell'd with their Beds; I expected to have found you snoaring, as I us'd to do.

Heart. Why, faith Friend, 'tis the Care I have of your Affairs, that makes me so thoughtful; I have been studying all Night, how to bring your Matter about with *Bellinda.*
Const. With *Bellinda?*
Heart. With my Lady, I mean.

A device that is of course both common in fiction and quite true to real life.

By Act V.ii. the jest has turned into earnest for this couple too: Heartfree and Bellinda are already acquainted when the play opens, but the ensuing accidents and strategems reveal each to the other through new eyes. Lady Brute reminds her niece that Heartfree is 'a younger Brother, and has Nothing'. True, Bellinda replies,

But I like him, and have Fortune enough to keep above Extremity: I can't say, I wou'd live with him in a Cell upon Love and Bread and Butter. But I had rather have the Man I love, and a Middle State of Life, Than that Gentleman in the Chair there [Sir John], and twice your Ladiship's Splendour.

Heartfree finds himself, heartfree no longer, 'in for *Hobs*'s Voyage; a great Leap in the Dark'. Although the phrase does not occur in any of Thomas Hobbes's published works it is recorded by Anthony Wood and others that he used to say 'Death is a leap into the Dark', and the remark must have been well enough known for Vanbrugh to make one of his characters misquote it. Indeed, he later did so in his own voice, writing to Tonson on 1 July 1719, 'I have taken this great Leap in the Dark, Marriage'. He may also have had in mind Bearjest's words in Mrs Aphra Behn's *The Lucky Chance* (1686):

For my uncle, who is a wise man, says matrimony is a sort of a . . . a kind of a, as it were, d'ye see, of a voyage, which every man of fortune is bound to make, one time or other (II.ii).

It would be foolish to identify Vanbrugh's own sentiments in either Heartfree or Constant, or indeed in any other character. We do not know whether his parents' marriage was as happy as it was fruitful; nevertheless the words he gives his characters show that he had thought about matrimony long before he entered into it. A second letter to Tonson contains another echo from more than twenty years before. It is Constant, the eternal romantic, who remains also the cynic. In a passage that shows both sides of him, he tells Heartfree that

> tho' Marriage be a Lottery in which there are a wondrous many Blanks; yet there is one inestimable Lot, in which the only Heaven on Earth is written. Wou'd your kind Fate but guide your Hand to that, tho' I were wrapt in all that Luxury itself cou'd cloath me with, I still shou'd envy you.
>
> *Heart.* And justly too: For to be capable of loving one, doubtless is better than to possess a Thousand. But how far that Capacity's in me, alas I know not.
>
> *Const.* But you wou'd know?
>
> *Heart.* I wou'd so.
>
> *Const.* Matrimony will inform you.

Vanbrugh wrote of his wife to Tonson (18 June 1722) 'she's Special good'. He had found that one inestimable lot, and the fact of his earlier description of it is quite consistent with his own character. It may have been a slow process, but in his choice of career, in politics, in the theatre, in architecture, and eventually in love Vanbrugh came to know his own mind.*

The final components in the architecture of *The Provok'd Wife* are Lady Fancyfull's maid and Sir John Brute's valet, who in the last Act form a kind of festoon between those two framing characters. Madamoiselle is one of a long line of comic francophones stretching back to Katharine and Alice in Shakespeare's *Henry V*; Vanbrugh's outrageous maid is a significant contribution to the genre, and once again his phonetic spelling shows his ear for sounds and accents. Razor, the valet, does not appear in previous Acts and could well be played by an actor who earlier took a minor part such as a guardian of the law or one of Sir John's tavern cronies. No sooner has Razor put the drunken Sir John to bed than the scene changes to Lady Fancyfull's house.

> *Lady Fan.* But, why did you not tell me before, *Madamoiselle*, that *Razor* and you were fond?

* p. 380

Madam. De Modesty hinder me, Matam.

Lady Fan. Why truly Modesty do's often hinder us from doing things we have an Extravagant Mind to. Do you think to Oblige you he wou'd speak Scandal?

Madam. Matam, to Oblige your Ladiship, he shall speak Blasphemy.

Lady Fan. Why then, *Madamoiselle*, I'll tell you what you shall do. You shall engage him to tell his Master, all that past at *Spring-Garden*. I have a Mind he shou'd know what a Wife and a Neice he has got.

Madam. Il le fera, Matam.

But before Madamoiselle can tell her story Razor has declared that 'My Lady has Cuckolded my Master', and that there is a diversionary scheme to marry Bellinda to Heartfree. The latter piece of information is of course relayed to Lady Fancyfull, who in the last scene nearly succeeds in severing what has become a genuine engagement. Madamoiselle gives Razor an account of the Spring Garden episode, in which she acts out Lady Brute's part and finds in the besotted valet a partner quite as ardent as Constant had been. At the conclusion of this parody the infatuated and inflamed Razor agrees to reveal all to his master; he tells his enchantress that he loves her 'more than a French-man do's Soupe', and that, 'in hopes thou'lt give me up thy Body, I resign thee up my Soul'.

Some of Vanbrugh's critics dwell on the improbable elements in his play. Of course the whole of the scene between Razor and Madamoiselle is improbable, starting with the sudden discovery that the two servants are 'fond', a surprise equally to Lady Fancyfull and to the audience. Just as improbable are Razor's triumphant departure to execute his part of the bargain: 'Not be a Rogue? --- *Amor Vincit omnia*', and his sudden repentance two scenes later, when he enters in sackcloth, reveals Lady Fancyfull's malicious schemes and begs the pardon in turn of Lady Brute, Sir John, Constant, Heartfree, and Bellinda. He then drags in Lady Fancyfull and her maid, masked, and blames the whole mischief on

Sathan, and his Equipage. Woman tempted me, Lust weaken'd me,---and so the Devil overcame me: As fell *Adam*, so fell I . . . [*Shewing* Madam.] 'Tis true; This is the Woman, that tempted

me. But this is the Serpent, that tempted the Woman: And if my
Prayers might be heard, her Punishment for so doing, shou'd be
like the Serpent's of Old---[*Pulls off Lady* F's *Mask.*] She should
lie upon her Face, all the days of her Life.

Razor has in cameo very much the same character as the
craven anticking Harlequin in Goldoni's *The Servant of Two
Masters*; they need to be played with the same vigour and they
share a common ancestry in the stock menial characters of the
Commedia dell' Arte. And this is the key to the difference between Vanbrugh in the library and Vanbrugh on the stage. As
James L. Smith remarks of the Razor scenes in his edition of
the play,

> On the stage these problems disappear. When events are so
> funny and move so fast there is no time to think how they arose.

This is certainly true of *The Provok'd Wife* and it is equally and
consistently true of twentieth-century farces, from which
many a journey home has been occupied with the gradual
realization of the preposterous nature of the evening's events.

The symmetries of this play lie in the structure not of its acts
and scenes but of its *dramatis personae*. These symmetries are
used to convey ideas and events which involve at the same
time both serious social comment and imaginative fantasy. If
this begins to sound like an analysis of Blenheim, the parallels
may yet illuminate to advantage both Vanbrugh's dramatic and
his architectural works. On the grounds of its element of
realism in relation to serious issues *The Provok'd Wife* has
more than once been placed within the development of sentimental theatre and fiction, but here again Vanbrugh's play is
more various and manifold in character. In sentimental literature there are always characters who are totally virtuous:
Cibber's Amanda is an early and a relevant instance. There are
no such paragons in *The Provok'd Wife*, and while the Brutes
actually deteriorate morally in the course of the action even
Bellinda and Heartfree leave us uncertain of their future.
Moreover, the way in which Vanbrugh leaves his characters'
problems unsolved is halfway to those modern farces which
end in a state of affairs far worse than at the beginning. And

Vanbrugh's perhaps semi-conscious lapses into blank verse also are closer to parody than to propriety, as when in the Spring Garden scene Constant and Lady Brute edge nearer the brink of misconduct.

Perhaps it is not surprising that *The Provok'd Wife* has always puzzled critics, for it does not fit comfortably into any single category. This is already apparent in contemporary reactions to the play, and two may be mentioned here. One is from a critic and the other from a lawyer. In 1699 Charles Gildon wrote:

> The Design seems to me as just as the Reflections and Wit of it are poignant, the Conversation as lively and genteel; for it rather teaches Husbands how they ought to expect their Wives shou'd make them a Return, if they use them as Sir John Brute did his; such Husbands may learn, that slighted and abused Virtue and Beauty, may be provoked to hearken to the prevailing Motives of revenge . . . it cannot be deny'd, that this Moral is of admirable Use; and offers a Truth to our consideration, which wou'd often prevent the Ruin of Families, which generally begins with the Husbands faults (*Lives and Characters of the English Dramatick Poets*).

The other reaction was unfavourable, but should be considered for its implications rather than for its credibility.

Ben Travers, a modern master of the preposterous, used to tell a story of the days before the abolition in the 'permissive sixties' of the licensing of plays. A gentleman from the Lord Chamberlain's Office objected on one occasion to the inclusion in a play, albeit in the strictly ornithological sense, of the word *cock*. It was no doubt a precursor in office of this gentleman who in 1701 brought to court Betterton, Doggett, Mrs Barry, Mrs Bracegirdle, and others, for presenting *The Provok'd Wife* and another play, and for uttering in the former such phrases as 'woman tempted me lust weaken'd and so the devil overcame me, as fell Adam so fell I'. They pleaded not guilty, and by various delaying applications seem to have run their case out of time. It was neither the first nor the last occasion on which a guardian of the public conscience chose the wrong target, but, as we shall see, the case betokened a change in taste which was to be significant for both Vanbrugh's plays and his architecture.

_ 15 _

The Provok'd Moralist

The best Things here below, are liable to be corrupted, and the better Things are in their own Natures, the more mischievous are they, if corrupted. For that which is superlatively Good in itself, can be corrupted by nothing but extraordinary Malice. Since then the Stage is acknowledg'd by its greatest Adversaries, to be in itself good, and instrumental to the Instruction of Mankind, nothing can be more unreasonable than to exhort People to ruin it, instead of reforming it, since at that Rate we must think of abolishing much more important Establishments. Yet that is apparently the Design of Mr Collier's *Book, tho' his Malice infinitely surpassing his Ability (as it certainly does, whatever some People may think of him) his Performance is somewhat aukward. For in the Introduction to his Book, he gives you Reasons why the Stage in general ought to be commended; in the first Chapters of his Book, he pretends to shew Cause why the* English *Stage ought to be reform'd; and in the sixth and last Chapter, he pretends to prove by Authority, that no Stage ought to be allow'd ...*

If Mr Collier *had only attack'd the Corruptions of the Stage, for my own Part, I should have been so far from blaming him, that I should have Publickly return'd him my Thanks: For the Abuses are so great, that there is a Necessity for the reforming them; not that I think, that, with all its Corruptions, the Stage has debauch'd the People: I am fully convinc'd it has not, and I believe I have said enough in the following Treatise to convince the Reader of it ... but when I found by his last Chapter, that his Design was against the Stage itself, I thought I could not spend a Month more usefully, than in the Vindication of it.*

My Business, therefore, is a Vindication of the Stage, and not of the Corruptions or the Abuses of it. And, therefore, I have no further meddled with Mr Collier's *Book, than as I have had Occasion to shew, That he has endeavour'd to make some things pass for Abuses, either of the Stage in general, or of the* English *Stage particularly, which are so far from being Abuses, that they may be accounted Excellencies ...*

Mr Collier *is so far from having shewn in his Book, either the Meekness of a true Christian, or the Humility of an exemplary Pastor, that he has neither the Reasoning of a Man of sense in it, nor the Style of a Polite Man, nor the Sincerity of a Honest Man, nor the Humanity of a Gentleman, or a Man of Letters.*

John Dennis (1657-1734) is remembered for his voluminous literary criticism rather than for his plays. His *The Usefulness of the Stage* appeared almost simultaneously with Vanbrugh's *Short Vindication* early in June 1698. Both were replies to *A Short View of the Immorality and Profaneness of the English Stage*, which Jeremy Collier had brought out, probably about the last week of April.

Collier (1650-1726) was a non-juring clergyman, that is one who had refused to take the oath of allegiance to William and Mary. Early in 1696 he achieved notoriety by giving absolution on the scaffold to Sir John Friend and Sir William Perkins, condemned to death for complicity in the Assassination Plot against William III. Thereafter he was not only without a benefice but technically an outlaw. One of the first to answer Collier in print, the anonymous author of *A Defence of Dramatick Poetry* and of *A Farther Defence*, offered the most practical of reasons for Collier, a prolific writer, to have undertaken the *Short View*:

For though Religion and Reformation was the Pretence; instead of a Cole from the Altar to inspire Zeal, here was a warmer *Dulcis Odor*, fifty Guinea's Copy-money that animated the cause.

Another early riposte mentioned the sum of fifty pounds and suggested that Collier's 'Dwelling so long on the Subject of Debauchery, argues something of Delight and Pleasure in the case'. Congreve, in *Amendments of Mr Collier's False and Imperfect Citations*, again imputed lewdness and caprice to him and added that 'The corruption of a rotten Divine is the Generation of a sowr Critick'. These strictures on Collier's integrity are understandable, but they are evidently wrong. However, not only did the Archbishop of Canterbury write to congratulate Collier, but the King was pleased enough with the *Short View* to grant him not a pardon for his mutiny but, according to Colley Cibber, an immunity from prosecution.

Dennis believed that Collier's desire was to mislead, but there can be no doubt that he was honest, sincere, bigoted maybe. He was pedantic rather than learned, but the *Short View* is entertaining to read. He was a born controversialist, pugnacious and fearless; one of those men of principle who have the makings of saints and martyrs and who are usually very difficult to live with. He was not a Puritan: his leanings were, if anywhere, towards Rome rather than Geneva. But puritanical he was, and his chief defects were of a sense not of wit but of humour and of proportion. He simply could see no meaning in Dennis's defence of the stage from the charge of corrupting public manners, in which Dennis noted four principal vices of the age – as indeed of almost any age: drinking, gambling, 'unnatural sins' and 'the love of women'.

The first two, Dennis wrote, were made odious and ridiculous on the stage; the third was 'either never mentioned there, or mentioned with the last Detestation' [or by Vanbrugh with ridicule in *The Relapse*]. The fourth he thought in some measure excusable:

1. Because it has more of nature, and consequently more Temptation, and consequently less malice, than the preceding Three, which the Drama does not encourage.
2. Because it has a Check upon the other Vices, and peculiarly upon that unnatural Sin, in the Restraining of which, the Happiness of Mankind is in so evident a Manner, concerned.

Collier attacked principally Dryden, D'Urfey, Otway, Wycherley, Congreve, and Vanbrugh. Not only had he sufficient reason to do so but also his timing was good; indeed at a later stage in the war of paper Dennis pointed out (in *The Per-*

son of Quality's Answer to Mr Collier's Letter, 1704) that he had
held his peace in the golden days of James II:

> You your self, I remember, Doctor, were then at Years of Discre-
> tion; and yet with passive Ears and Tongue, endur'd the Filth of
> *Epsom Wells*, the Bawdy of the *Soldier's Fortune*, and the Beastli-
> ness of *Limber-Ham*. But the time of your Prophetick Mission it
> seems was not yet come, or perhaps you thought it improper to
> fall out with the Play-Houses, before you had fallen out with the
> Government.

(*Limber-Ham* is the alternative title of Dryden's *The Kind
Keeper*.) Dennis had maintained (in the Preface to his 1702
adaptation of Shakespeare's *Merry Wives of Windsor*) that the
education and expectations of audiences had changed since
Charles II's time. In the earlier reign 'a considerable part of an
Audience had those parts, which were requisite for the judging
of Comedy'. That reign

> was a Reign of Pleasure, even the entertainments of their Closet
> were all delightful. Poetry and Eloquence were then their
> Studies, and that human, gay, and sprightly Philosophy, which
> qualify'd them to relish the only reasonable pleasures which
> man can have in the World, and those are Conversation and
> Dramatick Poetry . . . And the Conversation of those times was
> so different from what it is now, that it let them as much into that
> particular knowledge of Mankind, which is requisite for the
> judging of Comedy, as the present Conversation removes us
> from it.

The decades after the Commonwealth were – relatively –
peaceful and secure, leisurely and not over-taxed. But more
recently, said Dennis, 'go where you will, the conversation
turns upon Politicks . . . For all Men are alarmed by the present
posture of affairs, because all men believe they are concerned'.
Moreover, audiences themselves had changed:

> There are three sorts of People now in our Audiences, who have
> had no education at all; and who were unheard of in the Reign of
> King *Charles* the Second. A great many younger Brothers,
> Gentlemen born, who have been kept at home, by reason of the

pressure of the Taxes. Several People, who made their Fortunes
in the late War; and who from a state of obscurity, and perhaps
of misery, have risen to a condition of distinction and plenty.

Dennis's third category is one that has again become familiar
in the age of global tourism and ethnic migration:

> that considerable number of Foreigners, which within these last
> twenty years have been introduc'd among us; some of whom not
> being acquainted with our Language, and consequently with
> the sense of our Plays ... have been Instrumental in introduc-
> ing Sound and Show, where the business of the Theatre does not
> require it.

This analysis is not entirely accurate, and Dennis's hankering
for the good old days was to intensify in later years. But the age
of William and Mary was certainly very different from the days
of the Merry Monarch and his dour younger brother. Whether
or not audiences were less knowledgeable and more severely
taxed, the theatre no longer enjoyed the sovereign's personal
interest and sponsorship. In any case a reaction was to be expected from the sense of unlaced freedom that had followed
the end of the Commonwealth. The duty of the Patentees to expunge scurrility and profanity began to receive new emphasis,
while at court in the early 1690s Queen Mary had taught her
ladies reform, encouraging useful activities like knitting, and
purifying their language. Moreover, partly because of these
changes and partly because of a new liberality towards dissenting Protestants, it was for the first time in over thirty years
safe for the clergy to attack the stage without incurring a taint
of something near to treason.

And finally, a similar argument was already in progress in
France. In 1694 a volume of Boursault's plays was published in
Paris with a prefatory letter on the lawfulness of the stage by
Francisco Caffaro, a Theatine priest from Messina attached to
the church of Ste Anne-la-Royale in Paris. The Theatines were
a Counter-Reformation order who cultivated both poverty and
education, who specialized in preaching and pastoral work,
and who tended towards a practical view of the world in which
humanity was more important than sin. Caffaro argued that

there was no condemnation of the stage in Scripture; moreover he cited St Thomas Aquinas's agreement that moderate diversions are not only not sinful but are in some measure good, and that a wise man needed 'sometimes to unbend his Mind which is too intent upon his Business'. Caffaro's letter drew a prompt response from Bossuet, the greatest French preacher of the day, and the controversy was soon known in England. The letter was translated by Peter Motteux in the Preface to his play *Beauty in Distress* (1698), and by that time unacknowledged but detectable use of it had been made, for his own purposes, by Collier.

Collier's attack was perhaps not unforeseen. 'Why don't some Reformer or other beat the poet?' asks Bellinda in *The Provok'd Wife*, but already in the Preface to the first edition of *The Relapse* Vanbrugh had written:

As for the Saints (your thorough-pac'd ones I mean, with screw'd Faces and wry Mouths) I despair of them, for they are Friends to no body. They love nothing, but their Altars and Themselves. They have too much Zeal to have any Charity: they make Debauches in Piety, as Sinners do in Wine, and are as quarrelsome in their Religion, as other People are in their Drink: so I hope nobody will mind what they say. But if any Man (with flat plod Shooes, a little Band, Greazy Hair, and a dirty Face, who is wiser than I, at the expence of being Forty years older) happens to be offended at a story of a Cock and a Bull, and a Priest and a Bull-Dog I beg his Pardon with all my heart.

The resentment in this passage suggests not merely the kind of pulpit oratory that undoubtedly was heard on the subject at the time, but a personal encounter or attack. Vanbrugh's dislike of the Cloth has been overemphasized; he knew that, between the extremes of Parson Bull and the screw-faced saints, every age has its share of liberal and humane clergy. Back in Chester his half-sister's husband Dudley Garencieres published in 1697 *The History of Christ's Sufferings*, a book of extremely pious meditations on the Passion, prefaced by an invocation to 'God Eternal, the Father of Mercies' and intended to achieve 'an entire Resignation of the Soul to the Will of God'. We may suppose that Dudley would have agreed with many of Collier's sentiments, but we cannot say either that he had a view of the playwright's art or that he in any way resembled the original of Vanbrugh's 'saints'.

Some of Collier's complaints against the theatre of comedy were anticipated in print in 1695 by Sir Richard Blackmore in the Preface to his *Prince Arthur*:

> The *Man of Sense*, and the *Fine* Gentleman ... you will find to be a *Derider* of Religion ... dissolv'd in Luxury, abandon'd to his Pleasures, a great Debaucher of Women ...
>
> The *Young Lady* ... entertains the Audience with confident Discourses, immodest Repartees, and prophane Raillery. She is throughly instructed in *Intreagues* and *Assignations*, a great *Scoffer* at the prudent Reservedness and Modesty of the best of her Sex ...
>
> If a Clergy-man be introduc'd, as he often is, 'tis seldome for any other purpose but to abuse him, to expose his very *Character* and *Profession* ...
>
> And as these Characters are set up on purpose to ruin all Opinion and Esteem of Virtue, so the Conduct throughout, the *Language*, the *Fable*, and Contrivances seem evidently design'd for the same *Noble* End.

But the identity of the 'saints' probably lies in the societies for the promotion of religion and the amendment of manners which grew up in the late 1680s, originally under the leadership of Dr William Beveridge and Dr Anthony Horneck, two clergymen of a more temperate piety than Collier's. Members of the Society for the Reformation of Manners made it their business to inform the magistrates of swearers, drunkards, profaners of the Sabbath, and keepers of lewd houses. In 1694 the society published an extensive black-list of persons prosecuted for 'whoring, drunkenness, Sabbath-breaking, etc.' With more direct relevance, but confusing theatre and reality, they proposed also 'to supplicate their majesties, that the public play-houses may be suppressed' since 'in these houses, piety is strongly ridiculed, the holy reverend and dreadful name of God profaned, and his glory and interest rendered comtemptible or vile'.

The Society had some effect on official behaviour, for on 24 January 1696 the Lord Chamberlain, the Earl of Dorset, noted that

several playes &c are Acted & prologues spoken wherein many
things ought to be struck out and corrected, And ... of Late several new & Revived plays have been Acted ... without any Licence And that of Late the Managers ... have refused to send
such playes to be purused Corrected & allowed by the master of
the Revels.

Accordingly 'all Persons concerned in the Management of both
Companys' were ordered 'to take notis hereof on the Penalty of
being Silenced'; plays were to be submitted 'in due time' and
licence fees were to be paid to Charles Killigrew, son of the
playwright Thomas and successor to him in the office of
Master of the Revels. Killigrew was

> to be very careful in Correcting all Obsenitys & other Scan-
> dalous matters & such as any ways Offend against the Laws of
> God Good Manners or the Knowne Statutes of the Kingdome.

The phrase 'in due time' suggests that plays had sometimes
been submitted too late, on the real or pretended assumption
that licensing was no more than a matter of paying a fee.

Just as in the Commonwealth period, the frequency with
which orders were repeated suggests that they largely failed in
their objectives. A year and a half later, on 4 June 1697, the next
Lord Chamberlain, the Earl of Sunderland with the drawling
voice, issued orders to the two companies 'att your Perill' not to
'presume to Act any new Play till you shall have first brought it
to my Secretary, and Receive my directions from him'. The
reason on this occasion was 'that many of the new plays acted
by both companys ... are scandalously lewd and Prophane,
and contain Reflections against his Majs Government'. After
another eighteen months (18 February 1699) the Vice-
Chamberlain, Peregrine Bertie, reminded Killigrew of his duty
not to license any plays 'containing expressions contrary to
Religion and good manners', and again warned the managers
against failing 'to leave out such prophane expressions, as he
has struck out'. Similar warrants were issued by Lord Jersey on
15 January 1704, when Vanbrugh was preparing to build a
brand new theatre in the Haymarket.

The signatories of two of these sets of orders were Van-

brugh's friends, and the others moved in the same circles.
There seems to be no answer to the question whether blind
eyes were turned to the content of Vanbrugh's plays in particular or whether, on the other hand, those whose business it
was to inspect them considered that there was nothing to see.
But the instances given in Cibber's *Apology* do suggest that
those with eyes to see were looking somewhere else. The Lord
Chamberlain, he wrote, banned Beaumont and Fletcher's *The
Maid's Tragedy* in the reign of Charles II, either because the
killing of the king in that play recalled the death of Charles I or
because the execution of the deed by a repentant mistress
raised embarrassing associations with the life-style of the
reigning monarch. Cibber mentions several other political
cases but no moralistic ones, and in another passage he relates
how he himself suffered from a show of power by Charles Killigrew:

> When *Richard the Third* (as I alter'd it from *Shakespear*) came
> from his Hands, to the Stage, he expung'd the whole First Act,
> without sparing a Line of it . . . and the Reason he gave for it was,
> that the Distresses of King *Henry the Sixth*, who is kill'd by
> *Richard* in the first Act, would put weak People too much in
> mind of King *James*, then living in *France*.

The play remained a ruin, although Cibber had some satisfaction in 1715 when George I issued a patent to Sir Richard Steele
and his assigns, of whom Cibber was one, to be 'sole Judges of
what Plays might be proper for the Stage'. For when the Master
of the Revels continued to demand his fee of forty shillings for
being spared the trouble of perusing a new play, he was asked
by Cibber to produce his warrant, and could not. 'And from that
Time, neither our Plays, or his Fees, gave either of us any farther trouble.'

But the two most important things about Collier's *Short View*
are firstly his capacity for seeing what was not there and secondly the effects of his venture into literary as well as moral
criticism. It is to the substance of Collier's criticisms that we
must now turn: in particular to his criticisms of *The Relapse*
and *The Provok'd Wife*, and to Vanbrugh's *Short Vindication*,
which was published on 8 June 1698, two days after Dennis's
Usefulness of the Stage.

16

A Longer View

Vanbrugh's touch in the *Vindication* is light and his tone is bantering; the main burden of his reply is that Collier's complaints do not deserve to be taken seriously, and that much of what he complains of lies in the critic's own mind rather than in the plays. At first, says Vanbrugh,

I thought his Charges against me for Immorality and Prophaneness were grounded upon so much Mistake, that every one (who had had the curiosity to see the Plays, or on this Occasion should take the trouble to read 'em) would easily discover the Root of the Invective, and that 'twas the Quarrel of his Gown, and not of his God, that made him take Arms against me ...

I easily believ'd, what my Laziness made me wish; but I have since found, That by the Industry of some People, whose Temporal Interest engages 'em in the Squabble; and the Natural Propensity of others, to be fond of any thing that's Abusive; this Lampoon has got Credit enough in some Places to brand the Persons it mentions with almost a bad a Character, as the Author of it has fixt upon himself, by his Life and Conversation in the World.

I think 'tis therefore now a thing no farther to be laught at. Should I wholly sit still, those People who are so much mistaken to think I have been busy to encourage Immorality, may double their Mistake, and fancy I profess it: I will therefore endeavour, in a very few Pages, to convince the World, I have brought nothing upon the Stage, that proves me more an Atheist than a Bigot.

Collier's first target is the 'rankness and indecency' of the play-wrights' language. He gallantly passes over in silence Mrs Aphra Behn and other women dramatists, and his attitude to Wycherley's works of the 1670s is more one of regret than of offence. But Utway, Dryden, Congreve and Vanbrugh receive no quarter. Starting from the premiss that indecent ex-pressions and descriptions inflame the passions, he accuses these writers not only of wicked intentions but of bad manners and lack of invention. They put, he says, indecent expressions into the mouths of women as well as forcing them on the ears of the ladies in the audience; they present women often as mad or silly. They employ double meanings 'so Contrived that the Smut and Scum of the Thought rises uppermost' – Collier seems to be the first to use *smut* in this sense although Van-brugh had already used *smuttiness*. In prologues and epilogues he finds particular offence, and again offence to women who are often called upon to deliver 'such Strains as would turn the Stomach of an ordinary Debauchee, and be almost nauseous in the Stews'. He further contrasts the licence of the Christian writers under his hammer with the moderation of the pagan Ancients; how well, one wonders, did he know his Plautus or his Aristophanes? The protection of public morality is indeed a good and noble end, but if it is to be achieved it must be with intelligence, moderation, and common sense; the larger ques-tion remains whether the ordinary reader either of Collier's time or of ours would find in the plays he cites anything re-sembling the depths of degeneracy he sees in them.

Vanbrugh picks up with approval Collier's observation

> how valuable a Qualification Modesty is in a Woman: For my part I am wholly of his mind; I think 'tis almost as valuable in a Woman as in a Clergyman; and had I the ruling of the Roast, the one shou'd neither have a Husband, nor the t'other a Benefice without it. If this Declaration won't serve to shew I'm a Friend to't, let us see what Proof this Gentleman can give of the contrary.
>
> I don't find him over-stock'd with Quotations in this Chapter: He's forc'd, rather than say nothing, to fall upon poor Miss *Hoy-den*. He does not come to Particulars, but only mentions her with others, for an immodest Character. What kind of Immodesty he means, I can't tell: But I suppose he means Lewdness, because

he generally means wrong. For my part, I know of no Bawdy she talks: If the Strength of his Imagination gives any of her Discourse that Turn, I suppose it may be owing to the Number of Bawdy Plays he has read, which have debauch'd his Taste, and made every thing seem Salt, that comes in his way.

Vanbrugh then follows Collier's reference to *The Provok'd Wife*

as if there were something in the 41st Page of that Play, to discountenance Modesty in Women. But since he did not think fit to acquaint the Reader what it was, I will.

This is the passage in which Lady Brute and Bellinda speak of 'the Smuttiness of some Plays' and Bellinda asks why some reformer does not beat the poet; Vanbrugh then makes her say that it is 'Men's Fantasque' that obliges women to modesty. Vanbrugh continues:

Here are two Women (not over Virtuous, as their whole Character shews), who . . . let fall a Word between Jest and Earnest, as if now and then they found themselves cramp'd by their Modesty. But lest this shou'd possibly be mistaken by some part of the Audience . . . they are put in mind at the same Instant, That (with the Men) if they quit their Modesty, they lose their Charms: Now I thought 'twas impossible to put the Ladies in mind of any thing more likely to make 'em preserve it.

Collier then addresses himself to the subject of profane language. Passing quickly over the stage characters' frequent 'wishes of Hell, and Confusion, Devils and Diseases, all the Plagues of this World, and the next, to each other', he proceeds to the use of oaths 'by all Persons, and upon all Occasions: By Heroes, and Paltroons; by Gentlemen, and Clowns'. Swearing is both irreligious and illegal, unchristian and ungentlemanly; he notes also that in Dryden's *An Evening's Love* Wildblood 'swears by Mahomet'. Vanbrugh remarks that Collier finds his two plays particularly scandalous in this respect:

Wou'd not any body imagine from hence, that the Oaths that were used there, were no less than those of a Losing Bully at

Baggammon, or a Bilk'd Hackney-Coachman? Yet after all, the stretch of the Prophaneness lies in Lord *Foppington's Gad*, and Miss *Hoyden's I-Cod*. This is all this Gentleman's Zeal is in such a Ferment about.

Now whether such Words are entirely justifiable or not, there's this at least to be said for 'em; That People of the Nicest Rank both in their religion and their Manners throughout *Christendom* use 'em . . . we meet with an Infinity of People, Clergy as well as Laity, and of the best Lives and Conversations, who use the Words *I-Gad, I-faith, Codsfish, Cot's my Life*, and many more, which all lye liable to the same Objection.

In this context it is perhaps worth recalling that Charles II was known for the moderation of his tongue, his customary exclamation being *Oddsfish*.

Collier now turns to the abuse of religion and Scripture, and Vanbrugh asks whether he would prohibit mention on the stage of any story or expression whatsoever from the Bible. He answers Collier's objection to the statement by Razor *That woman having tempted him, the Devil overcame him* (one of the passages that would, a couple of years later, earn the actors a summons) as follows:

How the Scripture is affronted by this, I can't tell; here's nothing that reflects upon the Truth of the Story: It may indeed put the Audience in mind of their Forefather's Crime, and his Folly, which, in my Opinion, like *Gunpowder-Treason*, ought never to be forgot.

The Line in *Rasor's* Confession, which Mr *Collier's* Modesty ties him from repeating, makes the Close of this Sentence: *And if my Prayers were to be heard, her punishment for so doing shou'd be like the Serpent's of old, she shou'd lye upon her face all the days of her life.*

All I shall say to this, is That an Obscene Thought must be buried deep indeed, if he don't smell it out.

Collier's claim that the most convincing examples are too scandalous to quote sets a precedent for trial by whisper which has continued, as we have seen in the case of Dryden's *The Kind Keeper*,* well into our own century. One such passage is in

* p. 102

Miss Hoyden's part in *The Relapse*, where according to Collier,

> She swears by her Maker, *'tis well I have a Husband a coming, or I'de Marry the Baker, I would so. No body can knock at the Gate, but presently I must be lock'd up; and here's the young Grayhound ----- can run loose about the House all day long, she can, 'tis very well!*
> Afterwards her language is too Lewd to be quoted.

Hoyden's swearing by her Maker amounts to an *Icod*; the unspeakable word replaced by a dash is one that Collier does not hesitate to use in describing a passage in Congreve's *The Mourning Bride* as 'a litter of epithets ... like a bitch over stock'd with puppies'. In fact Vanbrugh's scene continues thus:

> Nurse *without, opening the Door*
> Miss *Hoyden*, Miss, Miss, Miss; Miss *Hoyden*.
> *Miss.* Well, what do you make such a noise for, ha? What do you din a Bodies Ears for? Can't one be at quiet for you?
> *Nurse.* What do I din your Ears for? here's one come will din your Ears for you.
> *Miss.* What care I who's come; I care not a Fig who comes, nor who goes, as long as I must be lock'd up like the Ale-Cellar.
> *Nurse.* That, Miss, is for fear you shou'd be drank, before you are Ripe.
> *Miss.* O don't you trouble your head about that, I'm as Ripe as you, tho' not so Mellow.

Vanbrugh goes on to answer one by one Collier's charges about individual phrases; Lord Foppington's account of his idle behaviour in church, conversational references to Heaven and Providence, Worthy's apostrophe of Amanda as an *Angel of Light*, which Collier conveniently forgets is followed by her addressing him as *Minister of Darkness*. Few things so infuriate an author as being misquoted in print, and Collier is an expert in this method of insult. And it may be added that, when in defence of Holy Scripture Collier finds Dryden guilty of blasphemy in making a devil sneeze because he has been too long from the fire, or in making a character say 'I am Truth', he pushes his case altogether too far.

The next Chapter [writes Vanbrugh] is upon the Abuse of the
Clergy: And here we are come to the Spring of the Quarrel. I
believe whoever reads Mr *Collier*, need take very little pains to
find out, that in all probability, had the Poets never discover'd a
Rent in the Gown, he had done by Religion, as I do by my
Brethren, left it to shift for it self.

Collier's defence of the Cloth echoes Blackmore's when he
writes:

These *Poets* I observe, when they grow lazy, and are inclined to
Nonsence, they commonly get a Clergy-man to speak it. Thus
they pass their own Dulness for Humor, and gratifie their Ease,
and their Malice at once ... How they attack Religion under
every Form, and pursue the Priesthood through all the Subdiv-
isions of Opinion.

Once again he makes a contrast with the Ancients; indeed, he
claims, in all past ages the clergy have been respected. Perhaps
he had not read his Chaucer, as Dryden certainly had and Vanbrugh may have done. Vanbrugh makes the point that the
clergy should not only be, but be seen to be, good examples,
and he devotes some space to the implication that Collier's record, as a Non-Juror and an outlaw, is less than exemplary.
Vanbrugh cannot see – and nor, perhaps, can anyone else –
why *on the stage* Sir John Brute's escapade of dressing up as a
parson should give offence. *In reality* it

wou'd be an Abuse and a Prejudice to the Clergy. But to expose
this very Man upon the Stage, for putting this Affront upon the
Gown; to put the Audience in mind, that there were laymen so
wicked, they car'd not what they did to bring Religion in Contempt, and were therefore always ready to throw dirt upon the
Pilots of it:
    This, I believe no body but a Man of Mr *Collier's* heat, could
have mistaken so much, to quote it under the head, of the Clergy
abus'd by the Stage. But Men that ride Post, with the Reins loose
upon the Neck, must expect to get falls.

As for Parson Bull, whom we have already considered, Collier also objects to his reply when summoned by Sir Tunbelly: *I fly, my good Lord*. Vanbrugh is led to

> ask pardon, that I cou'd suppose a Deputy-Lieutenant's Chaplain cou'd be a Blockhead; but I thought, if there was such a thing, he was as likely to be met with in Sir *Tunbelly*'s House, as anywhere.

Vanbrugh's final observation on the clergy neatly turns Collier upon himself. For he says he believes that the quarrel with the clergy need go no farther

> if those who I don't question are still by much the Majority, will to so good an End (as the curbing their Ambitious Brethren, and reforming their Lewd ones) ... agree, that whilst They play their Great Artillery at 'em from the Pulpit, the Poets shall pelt 'em with their Small Shot from the Stage. But since Mr *Collier* is violently bent against this, I'll tell him why I am for it. And 'tis,
>
> Because he has put me in mind, in the first Words of his Book, That the Business of Plays, *is to recommend Virtue and discountenance Vice: To shew the Uncertainty of Human Greatness; the sudden Turns of Fate, and the unhappy Conclusions of Violence and Injustice: That 'tis to expose the Singularities of Pride and Fancy; to make Folly and Falshood contemptible, and to bring every thing that is ill, under Infamy and Neglect.*

From bad language Collier proceeds to bad example, in those stage poets who 'make their Principal Persons Vitious, and reward them at the end of the Play'. One of the principles of the new sentimental comedy will of course be that virtue and vice both get their just deserts at the end of the play, but Collier sees the writers of his time as implicated in a conspiracy to destroy the morality of the age, attacking virtue and encouraging vice of every kind, ridiculing marriage, 'idealizing debauchery, and ... rewarding an Atheistical Bully with a lady and a fortune'. Coming to actual examples, he cites *The Provok'd Wife*, in which '*Constant* Swears at length, solicits Lady *Brute*, Confesses himself Lewd, and prefers Debauchery to Marriage'. Vanbrugh points out that Constant is not rewarded at the end, and has not got even his Mistress yet, he had not, at least, when the Play was last Acted. But this honest Doctor, I find, does not yet understand the nature of Comedy, tho' he has made it his Study so long. For the Business of Comedy is to shew People what they shou'd do, by representing them upon the Stage, doing what they shou'd not.

Turning to Sir John Brute, Vanbrugh writes:

I think there are an Infinity of Husbands who have a very great share of his Vices: And I think his Business throughout the Play, is a visible Burlesque upon his Character. 'Tis this Gentleman that gives the Spring to the rest of the Adventures: And tho' I own there is no mighty Plot in the whole matter, yet what there is, tends to the Reformation of Manners. For . . . tho' his ill usage of [his wife] does not justify her Intrigue, her intriguing upon his ill usage, may be a Caution for some . . . Religion, I own (when a Woman has it) is a very great Bulwark for her Husband's Security: And so is Modesty, and so is Fear, and so is Pride; and yet all are little enough, if the Gallant has a Friend in the Garison. I therefore think That Play has a very good End, which puts the Governor in mind, let his Soldiers be ever so good, 'tis possible he may provoke 'em to a Mutiny.

Collier also makes a bid for the sympathy of persons of quality who as a class, he claims, are degraded by the poets:

They dress up the *Lords* in Nick Names, and explore them in *Characters* of Contempt. *Lord Froth* is explain'd a *Solemn Coxcomb*; and *Lord Rake*, and *Lord Foplington* give you their Talent in their Title. *Lord Plausible*, in the *Plain Dealer*, Acts a ridiculous Part, but is with all very civil.

At this point the argument is a moral one, but Collier also presents it as an aesthetic one. In 1693 Thomas Rymer had censured Shakespeare for presenting Iago as crafty and underhand because a soldier should be lively, fierce, rigorous and sharp. Since the theatre should instruct, it followed also that ladies should be ladylike, noblemen lordly and clergymen spotless. Vanbrugh, however, considers it 'a bungling Piece of Policy, to make the Women and the Nobility take up Arms in his Quarrel'. For if immunity is to be extended from the clergy,

who are God's ambassadors, to the Lords and Ladies, then
eventually 'rather than the Committee of Religion shall be
expos'd for their Faults, all Mankind shall be admitted to Trade
in Sin as they please.' But Collier's attempt to defend the Lords
raises again the question of how well he either read or understood his material. For not only does he consistently mis-spell
Foppington; he also misses the point of the majority of character names in Restoration comedy. Modern farces usually involve characters with names that a modern audience will find
amusing, suggestive, or ironically appropriate, and although
they are often credible as real names they are carrying on an
old tradition. Restoration comedy abounds in names like
Witwood, Fainwood, Wishfor[i]t, Loveless, Amanda, Hillaria,
and Flareit – names more artificial than their modern counter-
parts and therefore quite unequivocally as well suited to the
characters as they are detached from the real world of the
audience and beyond. Whereas characters in serious plays
with names like Antonio or Lysander may claim our recognition as real people, those in the comedies are by their names
placed in a different category. Of course the categories were
sometimes amusingly blurred in real life, as when in 1735 the
secretary of the Radcliffe Trustees in Oxford referred to the
well-known joiner and architectural model-maker John
Smallwell as 'Mr Waitwell', the name of a character in Congreve's *The Way of the World*.

The impact of Collier's book on the London stage and on
those involved with it is indicated by the number of publications in opposition to or in support of it – nineteen before
the end of 1698 and a further fifteen in the next two years. But
the number also reflects the state of critical writing of the time.
Looking back over the seventeenth century, Thomas Rymer
wrote that Ben Jonson was the only critic in the first half; the
second half saw not only the increasing use of prefaces and
dedicatory letters to justify an author's view of his art but also
the growth, in England and in France, of a class of purely critical literature. The opening paragraphs from Dennis's refuta-
tion of Collier which introduced the previous chapter would
not, in either their construction or their tone, seem out of place
in the review pages of a modern literary magazine. Moreover,
in proclaiming Collier's shortcomings as a man of sense, a po-

lite man, and a man of letters, Dennis identifies the wider
arena in which Collier took his stand. For Collier extended his
ground from morals and polemic to literary criticism, and he
was in fact the first to see, rightly or wrongly, certain def-
iciencies in Vanbrugh's two most famous plays.

Collier's approval of the Ancients may be seen in the context
of the famous cultural controversy of the 1690s, between the
'Ancients' and the 'Moderns'. The 'Ancients' held that the
achievements of Classical Antiquity, in whatever field, could
be emulated but, if ever equalled, never surpassed; the 'Moderns' on the contrary believed that progress and improvement
were possible and actual. That was, however, of no great concern to Collier, for in his concluding chapter he reveals, as
Dennis was among the first to observe, that he desires not so
much a reformed stage as no stage whatever. But whether he
knew his poets or not, Collier was well versed in neo-
Aristotelian dramatic theory. *The Relapse*, he says, does not
satisfy the requirements of Classical theory, in respect of the
Unities of Time, Place and Action.

Whereas 'to be exact, the Time of the History, or *Fable*,
should not exceed that of the *Representation*', and twenty-four
hours is a reasonable extension, Vanbrugh's play takes up a
week, or five days at the least. The rule of Place is no better
observed than that of Time, for 'In the Third *Act* the *Play* is in
Town, in the Fourth *Act* 'tis stroll'd Fifty Miles off, and in the
Fifth *Act* in *London* again.' According to the rules Collier is
quite right, but a 'Modern' could argue with reason that, as
with everything else in the heritage of Antiquity, the rules
should be a stimulus to invention rather than a brake on it. Collier's attitude to the rule of Action is perverse, for he not only
disregards the comic tradition of double plots but also, by re-
versing the balance between the two plots, relegates Loveless,
Amanda, and Berinthia to 'no share in the main Business'.

Collier further attacks Vanbrugh's stagecraft by appealing to
René Rapin's remark that 'without probability every Thing is
lame and Faulty'. He finds it incredible that Lord Foppington
had never met Sir Tunbelly or his daughter, over a mere fifty
miles' distance; that the nobleman 'should leave the choise of
his Mistress to *Coupler*' since 'to court thus blindfold and by
Proxy does not agree with the Method of an Estate nor the

Niceness of a *Beau*'. Nor can he believe in the happy accident of
Sir John Friendly's being on hand to identify the real Mylord
(he ignores the coincidence that Sir John *Friend* was one of the
condemned to whom he gave absolution). Collier quarrels at
length with the character and behaviour of Sir Tunbelly and
more briefly with those of his coltish daughter. His inability to
accept the distinction between the theatre and the outside
world would scarcely be worthy of comment if it were not that
modern critics also have censured Vanbrugh for improbability. According to Arthur Huseboe *The Relapse* is 'marred by
improbable coincidences and faults in character motivation';
perhaps 'the most severe strain on the audience's credulity', he
says, is the failure to disclose the nature of the business that
called Loveless back to London.* He comments that the
circumstances of the marriage between Young Fashion and
Hoyden follow stage conventions and not the law of the land.
But he also asks why Amanda invites the pretty Berinthia to
stay, and why in Act V.ii. she does not identify Berinthia as
Loveless's new mistress, especially when she describes her as
'about my height, and very well shap'd'. He also points out that
Loveless calls Berinthia 'the only one on earth' in Act III.ii. but
a few minutes later Amanda says that he has been ogling other
women. The answer to the last question is surely that their
relationship was so insecure that Amanda would voice such
suspicions; the more general answer is that if these things did
not occur *The Relapse* would be a different play and perhaps no
play at all.

It does not require a deep understanding of Shakespeare to
recognize that his *plots* are full of improbabilities. What matters to us, however, is that the *characters* are — or can be made
to be — coherent and convincing. Given the situations in which
we find them, they behave as we believe human beings would
behave, and it is for this (setting aside for the moment his
poetic genius) that we revere Shakespeare, as much as for his
capacity for telling a good story. A play is a hypothesis the
validity of which is limited to the duration of the action. We all
make such limited and conditional hypotheses in daily life,
almost from infancy when the kitchen table becomes a house

* p. 121

or a chair becomes a horse. Later we learn to say and accept
'let x equal 3 and let y equal 2' or 'let AB equal the distance to
the Moon'; still later the salt and pepper pots become two
houses or colliding vehicles or opposing armies. All these
things are what we say they are, until the end of the discussion,
and what matters is not whether our conclusions have any
absolute validity but that they should follow from our premisses, however unlikely those may be. The application of
these principles to Razor's behaviour in Act V of *The Provok'd
Wife* has already been examined, and the farcical behaviour of
Young Fashion at Tunbelly Hall is another apt example. Moreover, the use of so many contrived names in Restoration
comedy should remind us that, however realistic the characters may be, they are not real.

Vanbrugh's first stage work after Collier was a modernized
version of an eighty-year-old play, *The Pilgrim* by John
Fletcher. It was produced at Drury Lane in the last days of April
1700, for the honour and profit of Dryden; the great poet added
a masque in the last scene and also a Prologue and Epilogue
which were written after 11 April and are among the last lines
from his pen: he was already a sick man, and he died on 1 May.
The Pilgrim is set in a Spain full of outlaws and warring factions, and concerns the wanderings of Don Pedro, disguised as
a pilgrim in order to escape from his enemies. The play is full
of disguises and recognitions; Pedro's life is saved by his
sweetheart Alinda, who has gone to look for him in the disguise of a boy, and later he saves the life of his enemy Roderigo,
who in gratitude gives up his feud and his claim to Alinda.
Alinda's maid Juletta, 'a smart Lass', also disguised as a boy,
helps in Puckish and other ways to lead the characters about
and sort them out; most of them are at some time or other shut
up in a lunatic hospital in Segovia. The antics of the more permanent inhabitants of this 'madhouse are for the most part to
be found in Fletcher's original, and in general Vanbrugh
follows Fletcher closely. However, he consistently shortens,
prosifies, clarifies and brings up to date the language. He also
purifies it, replacing 'You juggle, and ye fiddle; fart upon ye' by
'Damn Accidents: You're a Juggler'.

The Welsh madman in Act IV is taken from Fletcher, including his splendid opening lines:

> Give me some Cheese and Onyons; give me some Wash-prew; I have hunger in my pellies: give me apundance. *Pendragon* was a Shentleman, mark you, Sir? And the Organs at *Wrexham* were made by Revelations; there is a Spirit plows and plows the Pellows, and then they Sing.

The organs in Wrexham church were famous in the early seventeenth century; Fletcher's phonetics are different from Vanbrugh's, the place being spelled *Rixum* in the original. One of Vanbrugh's few total inventions is the scene with the two servants, one a stammerer and the other hopelessly drunk since he has been to look for Alinda in the wine cellar and found other attractions there.

According to Colley Cibber it was Vanbrugh who 'had the Disposal of the Parts': he offered Cibber his pick, and Cibber chose the Stuttering Cook and the Mad Englishman, while Vanbrugh cast the young Ann Oldfield as Alinda, after she had joined the Drury Lane company on his recommendation in 1699 but 'remained about a Twelvemonth almost a Mute, and unheeded'.

The fascination of peninsular Spain for the English – indeed for the rest of Europe – has been fairly consistent over many centuries. Its remoteness and cultural differences lend the country and its people an enchantment particularly appropriate to works of fiction, and many English and French plays of the seventeenth century deal with Spanish settings, themes and characters. Vanbrugh's next adaptation, *The False Friend*, was again set in Spain and was derived from Le Sage's *Le Traître Puni*, itself a free adaptation of Francisco de Rojas Zorilla's *La Traicion busca el castigo*. It is described as a comedy, and since only the villain is killed at the end it could scarcely be considered a tragedy. But apart from the antics of the servants Lopez and Jacinta it is a serious story on conventional themes of love, honour and betrayal.

Three noble gentlemen are in pursuit of the same young lady, Leonora: Guzman, her sweetheart, Pedro, the husband chosen by her father, and the lecherous John, whom Vanbrugh clearly identified with the archetypal Don Juan by re-allocating the names of Le Sage's characters. Immediately after the wedding of Leonora to Don Pedro the latter is called away to his father's deathbed, although when Lopez says (aside), '*Don Pedro* is mounting for his Journey' he speaks so prematurely as to mislead the audience. The sense of the action requires that he tarries long enough to pack his baggage and prepare his horse so that he may take part in the rest of the play. Charles Gildon, in the *Comparison Between the Two Stages* (1702), was the first to comment on the 'incredible surprize' of Don Pedro's reappearance when the audience believe him to have departed on a long journey. Gildon found Vanbrugh 'a Man of that able Sense, that he wou'd not run into an absurdity without very great temptation', and believed that Pedro's 'coming in, in the Crisis of so terrible a Scene, tho' it was irregular, yet it gave the Audience infinite astonishment, and indeed for the sake of that beauty we may forgive him the breach of Unity'. Don Pedro commits his bride to the care of Don John, the false friend, who loses no time in attempting Leonora's virtue. In the midnight confusion that follows her cry of alarm Don John puts the blame on Don Guzman, her faithful and beloved admirer; he also persuades Don Pedro, who has still not left, that revenge would by a fine irony be best taken in the dark. In the last Act, by a double irony, Don Pedro stabs not the maligned Guzman but the villain, Don John.

The intrigues, deceptions and changes of mind among the characters make an effective and fairly short play, carried on Vanbrugh's easy and often metrical speech. There are occasional exclamations of 'I'faith' and 'By my troth', and at one point Jacinta checks herself:

> Oons---Now Heaven forgive me, for I had a great Oath upon the Very tip of my Tongue; You'd make one mad with your Impossibles and your Innocence, and your Humilities. 'Sdeath Sir d'you think a Woman makes no distinction between the Assaults of a Man she likes and one she don't? My Lady hates *Don John*, and if she Thought 'twas he had done this Job, she'd hang him for't in her own Garters; She likes you, and if you shou'd do such an other, you might still die in your Bed like a Bishop, for her.

The False Friend was produced at Drury Lane early in

February 1702 and ran for four performances; it was revived briefly in 1710 and 1715 and thereafter every decade or so until late in the century. In the original production Cibber played the villain and Penkethman (who played several of the comic visitors in *Æsop*) took the part of Lopez. Mrs Rogers (the original Amanda) was the virtuous Leonora, Mrs Kent (the original Young Fashion) her friend Isabella, and Ann Oldfield her servant Jacinta.

The audience will have relished the unspoken great oath, for it was an audience made up of those who believed themselves more sensible than Collier. The Prologue, spoken by Captain Griffin who played Leonora's father, began by apostrophizing the reformers:

> *You Dread Reformers of an Impious Age,*
> *You awful Catta-nine-Tailes, to the Stage,*
> *This once be Just, and in our Cause engage.*

> *To gain your Favour, we your Rules Obey,*
> *And Treat you with a Moral Piece to Day;*
> *So Moral, we're afraid 'twill Damn the Play.*

The play itself ends swiftly, even abruptly:

> *Don Pedro.* 'Tis I, have been the Actor in't, my Poignard, *Guzman* I intended in your Heart; I thought your Crime deserv'd it, but I did you wrong, and my Hand in searching the Innocent, has by Heaven's Justice been directed to the Guilty. *Don John*, with his last breath, confest himself the Offender. Thus my Revenge is satisfied, and you are clear'd.
> *Don Guzman.* Good Heaven, how equitable are thy Judgements?
> *Don Ped.* [*To* Leonora.] Come, Madam, my Honour now is satisfied, and if you please my Love may be so too.
> *Leo.* If it is not
>
> > *You to your self alone, shall owe your smart,*
> > *For where I've given my hand, I'll give my heart.*

But the Epilogue, spoken by Mrs Oldfield, archly invites the audience to doubt the finality of this conclusion:

What say you, Sirs, d'ye think my Lady'll 'scape,
'Tis dev'lish hard to stand a Fav'rite's Rape?
Shou'd Guzman, *like* Don John, *break in upon her,*
For all her Vertue, Heaven! have Mercy on her;
Her strength, I doubt, 's in his Irresolution,
There's wond'rous Charms in Vig'rous Execution.

In defending his own work against Collier, Vanbrugh used the same gifts as in his plays – wit, ridicule, style, and common sense. The nearest he came to a theory of comedy was his remark that its business was to show people how to behave 'by representing them upon the Stage, doing what they shou'd not'. What he could not anticipate was the faint praise of posterity; to do him justice, therefore, it is necessary even today to turn to some of his colleagues in the theatre whose critical writings are relevant.

17

Intermezzo: How to Write a Comedy

Jeremy Collier, seeking a stick to beat the comic poets, insisted that the theatre, as a branch of poetry, should teach, and that delight or enjoyment was secondary and no more than sugar on the pill; as authorities for this view he pointed to Aristotle and Rymer. But nearly thirty years earlier Dryden, in the Preface to *An Evening's Love* (1671), had claimed otherwise:

> But in Comedy it is not so; for the chief end of it is divertisement and delight . . . At least I am sure [instruction] can be but its secondary end: for the business of the Poet is to make you laugh: when he writes humour he makes folly ridiculous; when wit, he moves you, if not always to laughter, yet to a pleasure that is more noble. And if he works a cure on folly, and the small imperfections in mankind, by exposing them to publick view, that cure is not perform'd by an immediate operation. For it works first on the ill nature of the Audience; they are mov'd to laugh by the representation of deformity; and the shame of that laughter, teaches us to amend what is ridiculous in our manners. This being, then, establish'd . . . it may reasonably be inferr'd that Comedy is not so much oblig'd to the punishment of the faults which it represents, as Tragedy. For the persons in Comedy are of a lower quality, the action is little, and the faults and vices are but the sallies of youth, and the frailties of humane nature, and not premeditated crimes . . . But, lest any man should think that I write this to make libertinism amiable . . . I must further declare . . . that we make not vicious persons happy, but only as

heaven makes sinners so: that is by reclaiming them first from
vice. For so 'tis to be supposed they are, when they resolve to
marry; for then enjoying what they desire in one, they cease to
pursue the love of many.

Dryden was rather given to public recantation, as for example
in the *Ode to the Memory of Mrs Anne Killigrew* (1686):

O Gracious God! How far have we
Prophan'd thy Heav'nly Gift of Poesy?
Made prostitute and profligate the Muse,
Debas'd to each obscene and impious use.

But then Dryden was an opportunist and a realist, and his remarks on Collier in the Preface to *Fables, Ancient and Modern*
(1700) should therefore not be seen as a capitulation:

I shall say the less of Mr *Collier*, because in many Things he has
tax'd me justly; and I have pleaded Guilty to all Thoughts and
Expressions of mine, which can be truly argu'd of Obscenity,
Profaneness, or Immorality; and retract them ... Yet it were not
difficult to prove, that in many Places he has perverted my
Meaning by his Glosses; and interpreted my Words into
Blasphemy and Baudry, of which they were not guilty. Besides
that, he is too much given to Horse-play in his Raillery; and
comes to Battel, like a Dictatour from the Plough. I will not say,
The Zeal of God's House has eaten him up; but I am sure it has
devour'd some Part of his Good Manners and Civility. It might
also be doubted, whether it were altogether Zeal, which
prompted him to this rough manner of Proceeding; perhaps it
became not one of his Function to rake into the Rubbish of Ancient and Modern Plays; a Divine might have employ'd his Pains
to better purpose, than in the Nastiness of *Plautus* and *Aristophanes*; whose Examples, as they excuse not me, so it might
be possibly suppos'd, that he read them not without some
Pleasure.

Congreve and Dennis in 1695 engaged in a correspondence,
which was published, on the subject of humour in comedy, but
the best – and most readable – exposition of the principles of
Restoration comedy is still George Farquhar's *Discourse upon*

Comedy of 1702, which deals effectively with many of Collier's literary criticisms:

> 'Tis a wonderful thing, that most Men seem to have a great Veneration for *Poetry*, yet will hardly allow a favourable Word to any Piece of it that they meet . . . The Scholar calls upon us for *Decorums* and Oeconomy; the Courtier cries out for *Wit* and *Purity of Stile*; the Citizen for *Humour* and *Ridicule*; the Divines threaten us for Immodesty; and the Ladies will have an Intrigue . . . every one is a Critick after his own way; that is, such a Play is best, because I like it.

Farquhar goes on to imagine a discussion with a scholar:

> I must first beg one Favour of the Graduate — Sir, here is a Pit full of *Covent-Garden* Gentlemen, a Gallery full of Cits, a hundred Ladies of Court-Education, and about two hundred Footmen of nice Morality, who having been unmercifully teaz'd with a Parcel of foolish impertinent irregular Plays all this last Winter, make it their humble Request, that you wou'd oblige them with a Comedy of your own making, which they don't question will give them entertainment. O Sir, replies the *Square-Cap*, I have long commiserated the condition of the *English* Audience, that has been forc'd to take up with such wretched Stuff, as lately has crowded the Stage: your *Jubilees* and your *Foppingtons*, and such irregular Impertinence, that no Man of Sense cou'd bear the Perusal of 'em. I have long intended, out of pure Piety to the Stage, to write a perfect Piece of this Nature . . .
> So to work he goes; old *Aristotle, Scaliger*, with their Commentators, are lugg'd down from the high Shelf, and the Moths are dislodg'd from their Tenements of Years; *Horace, Vossius, Heinsius, Hedelin, Rapin*, with some half a dozen more, are thumb'd and toss'd about, to teach the Gentleman, forsooth, to write a Comedy: and here is he to be furnished with *Unity of Action, Continuity of Action, Extent of Time, Preparation of Incidents, Episodes, Narrations, Deliberations, Didacticks, Patheticks, Monologues, Figures, Intervals, Catastrophes, Chorus's, Scenes, Machines, Decorations*, &c. a Stock sufficient to set up any Mountebank in *Christendom*: And . . . the Misfortune of it is, he scorns all Application to the Vulgar, and will please the better sort, as he calls his own.

The scholar chooses a simple plot, 'no matter whether it

affords Business enough for Diversion or Surprize. He would not for the World introduce a Song or Dance, because his Play must be one entire Action.' Unity of time means nothing can happen, unity of place means 'perhaps we shall lose the only good Scenes in the Play'.

> But no matter for that; this Play is a regular Play; this Play has been examin'd and approv'd by such and such Gentlemen, who are staunch Criticks, and Masters of Art ... Look'e, Mr *Rich*, you may venture to lay out a hundred and fifty Pound for dressing this Play, for it was written by a great Scholar, and Fellow of a College.

The 'grave dogmatical Prologue' tells us

> that this Play has a new and different Cut from the Farce they see every Day; that this Author writes after the Manner of the *Ancients*, and here is a Piece according to the Model of the *Athenian Dramma* ... Then the Players go to work on a piece of hard knotty Stuff, where they can no more shew their Art, than a Carpenter can upon a piece of Steel. Here is the Lamp and the Scholar in every line, but not a Syllable of the Poet: here is elaborate Language, Sounding Epithets, Flights of Words that strike the Clouds, while the poor Sense lags after, like the Lanthorn in the Tail of a Kite, which appears only like a Star, while the Breath of the Player's Lungs has Strength to bear it up in the Air.

But the audience gets bored after two Acts:

> not finding a true genius of Poetry, nor the natural Art of free Conversation, without any Regard to his Regularity, they betake themselves to other Work; not meeting the Diversion they expected on the Stage, they shift for themselves in the Pit; every one turns about to his Neighbour in a Mask, and for default of Entertainment now, they strike up for more diverting Scenes when the Play is done; and tho' the Play be regular as *Aristotle*, and modest as Mr *Collier* cou'd wish, yet it promotes more Lewdness in the Consequence, and procures more effectively for Intrigue, than any *Rover*, *Libertine*, or Old *Batchelor* whatsoever. At last comes the *Epilogue*, which pleases the Audience because it sends them away.

This was not far from the truth. In March 1711 a director of the Society for the Reformation of Manners wrote to *The Spectator* complaining of the new evil of the 'Midnight Masque'. The 'whole Design of this Libidinous Assembly', he said, 'seems to terminate in Assignations and Intrigues'.

Since the origins of poetry lie in Homer, Farquhar seeks the origins of comedy in Æsop as 'the first and original Author'. Comedy, he goes on,

> is no more at present than a *well-fram'd Tale handsomely told, as an agreeable Vehicle for Counsel or Reproof* . . . Then where shou'd we seek for a Foundation, but in Æsop's symbolical way of moralizing upon Tales and Fables, with this Difference, That his Stories were shorter than ours? He had his Tyrant *Lyon*, his Statesman *Fox*, his Beau *Magpy*, his coward *Hare*, his Bravo *Ass*, and his Buffoon *Ape*, with all the Characters that crowd our Stages every Day . . . *Fondlewife* and his young Spouse are no more than the *Eagle* and *Cockle*; he wanted Teeth to break the Shell himself, so somebody else run away with the Meat – The Fox in the Play, is the same with the Fox in the Fable, who stuff'd his Guts so full, that he cou'd not get out at the same Hole he came in.

If Aristotle had not based his theories on Homer, his pupil's favourite poet, the art of poetry would have been very different. Moreover the rules of English comedy lie elsewhere, 'in the Pit, Boxes, and Galleries'. We should look, as we do to determine a lawsuit, not at the Ancients of Greece and Rome but to our own traditions, to Shakespeare, Jonson and Fletcher:

> We shall find that those Gentlemen have fairly dispens'd with the greatest part of Critical Formalities; the Decorums of time and Place, so much cry'd up of late, had no force of Decorum with them, the Oeconomy of their Plays was *Ad libitum*, and the extent of their Plots only limited by the Convenience of Action.

Farquar is not advocating anarchy or decrying all rules, but in pointing out that an 'irregular' play may yet conform with 'all the Exactness imaginable, in respect of unity in Time and Place', he pleads for common sense:

The poet expects no more you should believe the Plot of his Play,
than old Æsop design'd the World should think his *Eagle* and
Lyon talk'd like you and I.

The critics allow twenty-four hours for the time of action, yet
'that a thousand Years should come within the Compass of
three Hours, is no more an Impossibility, than that two Minutes
should be contain'd in one'. And in respect of place, if the
theatre represents Cairo, which it is not, what is intolerable
about changing the representation thence to Astrakhan?

Books on gentlemanly behaviour maintained throughout the
period that theatre-going was a normal and even an improving
pastime. The 1710 edition of Richard Blome's *The Gentleman's
Recreation* goes so far as to ask, 'who is there in *Tragedy* to
match our *Otway*? Our *Etheridge, Wicherley, Congreve, Vanbrugh* in *Comedy*? . . . and for all sorts of Versification, our immortal *Dryden*?' Nevertheless, Farquhar rightly observes that
the audience cares far less about rules than do the critics.
Audiences want to be entertained, and in his preface of 1702
Dennis had blamed the decline in the quality of audiences for
the popularity of 'Tumbling and Vaulting and Ladder Dancing,
and the delightful diversions of *Jack Pudding*' (a clown) as well
as the introduction of

> Sound and Show, where the business of the Theatre does not
> require it, and particularly a sort of a soft and wanton Musick, a
> delight that has gone a very great way towards the enervating
> and dissolving their minds.

It is unwise, because it is simplistic, to see cause and effect one
way or the other between the decline in court patronage of the
theatre and the development of the sentimental comedy; the
two processes were interdependent in a complex way, and in
any case a study of the history of taste is beyond the scope of a
biography. But when we look at symptoms the part played by
Sir Richard Steele is not so difficult to identify. Steele is best
known today for his authorship, with his close contemporary
Joseph Addison, of the periodicals *The Tatler* (1709-11) and
The Spectator (1711-12), but he was also a playwright and a
politician, a Whig and a Kit-Cat, a Member of Parliament and a

political writer. He was born in 1672, the son of a Dublin attorney. His father died before the boy was five, his mother not very long after, and he was cared for by an uncle, Henry Gascoigne, secretary to the Duke of Ormonde, who was incidentally another of those distant kinsmen of Vanbrugh's mother. The Duke gained for young Steele a place at Charterhouse, where he began a life-long friendship with his schoolfellow Addison. He later went up to Oxford, but left without a degree and joined the army in 1694 as a cadet.

Steele, like Cibber, was younger than Vanbrugh perhaps by just enough to see the world differently. In 1700, when he had become a captain, he fought a duel and nearly killed his adversary; this experience affected him deeply, and was one of the springs of his book *The Christian Hero*, published by Tonson in 1701. Towards the close of that same year his comedy *The Funeral* was produced at Drury Lane. It was performed 171 times in the next seventy-five years, and was justly popular. From its somewhat macabre opening in the offices of a funeral director it develops a tale full of suspense and humour, at the end of which old Lord Brumpton is found to be alive and well, his would-be widow's scheming is exposed, his son is reconciled to father and inheritance and gains the bride of his desire, she having been rescued from house-captivity smuggled out in the coffin supposedly containing his Lordship's corpse.

Steele's action and dialogue are lively and the language vivid, but there is little that Collier could have faulted. And when, in order to liberate another young lady, the French maid is persuaded to change clothes with her, the voyeurs in the audience are disappointed:

Campley. Madam *D'Epingle* I must desire you to comply with a Humour of Gallentry of ours, you may be sure I'll have an Eye over the Treatment you have upon my account, only to Change Habits with Lady *Harriot*, and let her go, while you stay.
Mademoiselle. Wit all my Heart.   [*Offers to undress her self.*
Lady Harriot. What before Mr *Campley*?
Madem. [*Apart to* Harriot.] Oh Oh very *Anglaise*! Dat is so English, all Women of Quality en *France* are Dress and Undress, by a Valet de-Chambre, De man Chambermaid Help Complexion, better Den de Woman.
Lady Har. Nay, that's a Secret in Dress *Madamoiselle*, I never

knew before, and am so unpolish'd an English Woman as to resolve never to learn ev'n to Dress before my Husband, Oh! indecency! Mr *Campley* do you hear what *Madamoiselle* says---
Madem. Oh! Hist---Bagatelle.
Lady Har. Well We'll run in and be ready in an instant.
                    [*Exeunt Lady* Harriot *and Mademoiselle* D'Epingle.

However, *The Funeral* did receive one significant alteration at
its author's own hand. *The Spectator*, no. 51 (28 April 1711) carried a letter from a young lady objecting to the passage in this
play

> where a Confident Lover in the Play, speaking of his Mistress,
> Cries out---*Oh that* Harriot! *to fold these Arms about the Waste of
> that Beauteous strugling, and at last yielding Fair*! Such an
> image as this ought, by no means, to be presented to a Chaste
> and Regular Audience.

A modern editor of *The Spectator* suggests that Steele wrote the
letter himself; at any rate he expressed editorial approval, and
in the second edition of the play, published in the autumn of
that year, he made a point of deleting those words.

Steele's next play, *The Lying Lover*, was a failure, and would
hardly be worth mentioning were it not for his own comment
upon it in the *Apology for Himself and his Writings* which he
published after his expulsion from a Tory House of Commons
in 1714. In *The Funeral*, he wrote there, '(tho' full of incidents
that move laughter) Virtue and Vice appear just as they ought
to do'. But of *The Lying Lover* he wrote:

> Mr *Collier* had, about the Time wherein this was published,
> written against the Immorality of the Stage. I was (as far as I
> durst for fear of witty Men, upon whom he had been too severe)
> a great Admirer of his Work, and took it into my Head to write a
> Comedy in the Severity he required. In this Play I make the
> Spark or Heroe kill a Man in his Drink, and finding himself in
> Prison the next Morning, I give him the Contrition which he
> ought to have on that Occasion

In the Preface to the play he had written:

> Tho' it ought to be the Care of all Governments, that publick

Representations should have nothing in 'em but what is agreeable to the Manners, Laws, Religion and Policy of the Place or Nation in which they are exhibited; yet it is the general Complaint of the more Learned and Virtuous amongst Us, that the English Stage has extremely offended in this kind: I thought therefore it would be an honest Ambition to attempt a Comedy, which might be no improper Entertainment in a Christian Commonwealth.

The anguish Young Bookwit expresses in prison,

and the mutual Sorrow between an only child, and a tender Father in that Distress, are, perhaps, an Injury to the Rules of Comedy; but I am sure they are a Justice to those of Morality: And Passages of such a Nature being so frequently applauded on the Stage, it is high time that we should no longer draw Occasions of Mirth from those Images which the Religion of our Country tells us we ought to tremble at with Horrour.

In fact in order to avoid giving away the story Steele concealed the real conclusion, in which Lovemore turns out not to have been killed but only slightly wounded. All therefore ends happily, but the change of mood in the last Act is as marked as anything in Cibber or Vanbrugh. Four Acts tell an entertaining story of attempts at matchmaking, in the middle of which Young Bookwit fights Lovemore and leaves him for dead. Steele no doubt drew on his own experience, the sobering memory of which must have been one of his motives for writing the play, although it is based on Corneille's *Le Menteur*. But Act V contains not a single humorous line; the serious tone would be more suited to high tragedy than comedy, and much of it is actually in the blank verse that Collier had found so unsuitable for comedy. As a dramatic sermon against duelling it is effective and convincing, but it is not surprising that, after a run of six nights between 1 and 8 December 1703, it was never played again in Steele's lifetime – not in fact until 1746 and never since then.

The characters of sentimental comedy are no less pasteboard figures than those of the preceding style; they are merely different stereotypes. And this ought to make it clear that the real losses to the stage were not the oaths and sexual inn-

uendos and the amoral, cynical, lecherous and riotous characters but the very stuffing, the gusto and the vigour of the
comic theatre, the readiness to experiment, and that sense of
absurdity which Farquhar traced back to old Æsop.

Collier was sincere but misguided. Nevertheless public opinion has generally been on his side; the image of a profligate
court and an immoral stage which he did so much to per-
petuate has in its turn fostered the image of Collier the great,
necessary and beneficial reformer. But the later triumph of
sentimental comedy was to be the accomplishment of Steele, a
member of Vanbrugh's own circle and an altogether better
writer than Collier. But by that time Vanbrugh was making a
name for himself in quite another field.

_ 18 _

Without Thought or Lecture

IF TO PERFECTION THESE PLANTATIONS RISE
IF THEY AGREEABLY MY HEIRS SURPRISE
THIS FAITHFUL PILLAR WILL THEIR AGE DECLARE
AS LONG AS TIME THESE CHARACTERS SHALL SPARE
HERE THEN WITH KIND REMEMBRANCE READ HIS NAME
WHO FOR POSTERITY PERFORM'D THE SAME

CHARLES THE III EARL OF CARLISLE
OF THE FAMILY OF THE HOWARDS
ERECTED A CASTLE WHERE THE OLD CASTLE OF
HENDERSKELF STOOD, AND CALL'D IT CASTLE-HOWARD
HE LIKEWISE MADE THE PLANTATIONS IN THIS PARK
AND ALL THE OUT-WORKS, MONUMENTS AND OTHER
PLANTATIONS BELONGING TO THE SAID SEAT
HE BEGAN THESE WORKS
IN THE YEAR MDCCII
AND SET UP THIS INSCRIPTION
ANNO D: MDCCXXXI

So runs the legend at the bottom of the west face of the great obelisk at Castle Howard, erected in 1714 in honour of the Duke of Marlborough and marking the junction of the approach drive to the house with the York-Slingsby road. There is not a word about Lord Carlisle's architects, nor are they mentioned in the 300 rhyming pentameters of *Castle-Howard*, the

poem composed by one of his daughters, Anne, Viscountess
Irwin, and published anonymously in 1732. When we speak of
artistic patronage we often understand no more than the
choice of, and payment for, works of art by those who can
afford them, but the term *patron* properly implies that a favour
is being conferred on the artist. The word *client* on the other
hand suggests someone who approaches an artist, especially
an architect, as he would approach a member of some other
profession such as a solicitor or an engineer. He pays for professional services but cannot presume upon their being offered.
Lord Carlisle thought of himself as the patron of artists and
architects who worked for him, and in 1737 the distinction between patron and client had to be spelled out to him by the
widow of his second architect, Nicholas Hawksmoor.

Some months after Hawksmoor's death on 25 March 1736
(ten years almost to the day after Vanbrugh's) Mrs Hawksmoor
sent Lord Carlisle a long itemized bill: five guineas for drawing
a temple, two guineas for two drawings of a basement and five
shillings for a letter to explain them, one guinea for 'Drawing a
Basement for the Temple of Belvedere began by Sr John Vanbrugh' and so on. Most of the items were between 1727 and
1735, that is after Vanbrugh's death, but there were also expenses of £31 going back as far as 1711, and £50 for a journey
from London to Castle Howard in 1723. The total was £266. 9s.
6d. Carlisle was extremely surprised, and wrote back on 17 December 1736 to say that he had given Hawksmoor £125 and
had believed that his architect had been satisfied.

Mrs Hawksmoor replied on 5 February 1737 explaining in
detail the various kinds of expenditure and charge. The
journey of 1723, made 'at your own pressing instance', involved '30 days hire of a coach & four at 1£ 5 pr day' plus '14
days on the Road Travell-charges at the least 20/- pr day'
which came to £51. 10s., so that 'you cannot think any thing got
by 50£ which he charges for'. And then there were 'the compli-
ments necessary to your Lordships servants to whom we gave
trouble'. Mrs Hawksmoor went on to explain that in the various letters and drawings supplied 'the time itself is only sett
down to your Lordship having reguard to the days spent by
himself & Clerkes, and nothing is set down for his designing
that being always left to your Lordship to reward him by way of

present as you your self should think fit, and as such he took the 125£ sent by your Lordship'. She concluded with the suggestion that neither Carlisle nor 'any Jury on Earth' would think the £125 'a sufficient recompence' and added a few examples to show 'how little value is set on Mr. Hawksmoors service to what others no way superior in their Abilitys had had'. At St Martin-in-the-Fields, she told him, James Gibbs received 5 per cent of the total cost, and although she was mistaken in this it illustrates the tendency of the time towards the modern percentage basis of architects' fees.

Most of Hawksmoor's work in the years covered by his widow's bill was connected with the outworks or park buildings, including the completion of Vanbrugh's Belvedere Temple and the Mausoleum of his own designing. But in the years before 1711 Carlisle had paid Hawksmoor a fee and expenses annually for his assistance. It was some time in 1700, when foundations had been dug and footings laid, that Vanbrugh told Carlisle,

> I spoak to Mr Hawksmoor about his perticular concern and found him as he us'd to be. so he intended to ask yr Ldship fourty pound a year Sallary & fifty each journey wch mounts to £100 clear.

This was not an excessive remuneration for being the right hand that Vanbrugh needed at the time, although over several years, perhaps ten, it added materially to the costs of building.

In the second big commission in which Vanbrugh was assisted by Hawksmoor, namely Blenheim, relationships were quite different. Although the idea of a house in Woodstock Park designed by Vanbrugh was Marlborough's own, the project was taken over by the Crown as a public gift to the victorious Duke. Vanbrugh was to receive a fixed annual salary, which was supposed to be paid by the Treasury as part of the building costs, for the duration of the work, although much of it he only received in arrears. Hawksmoor as assistant architect and Henry Joynes as clerk of works on the site were paid in the same way. Only when the whole project went seriously wrong was responsibility for his architects' remuneration laid at Marlborough's door. Lord Carlisle's dealings with his architects, on the other hand, were direct, personal and distinctive. What particularly distinguished his relationship with Hawksmoor is the duality of roles in which Hawksmoor cast him, that is both the older patron and the newer client. But what distinguishes his relationship with Vanbrugh is its apparent informality in comparison not only with Blenheim and with Hawksmoor 'but also with other private commissions. And now, therefore, two questions arise. First, was Carlisle as ignorant of practical matters as he gave Mrs Hawksmoor to understand, and second, what was Vanbrugh actually paid for designing Castle Howard?

In fact certain aspects of an architect's rewards had been the subject of a legal case in 1703, whose outcome was recorded in a letter from Vanbrugh to the Duke of Newcastle. Carlisle's first choice of a designer for the new Henderskelfe was William Talman, the leading country house specialist of the 1690s. On Talman's first visit to the site Carlisle 'gave him Fifty Guineas and bore his Charges besides, But was not willing to do so the next time'. On the second visit Carlisle offered him in advance thirty guineas, but when Talman was about to leave he 'Order'd his Steward to give him fourty, intending ten more than he was oblig'd to'. Talman took umbrage and refused the money, but later

> sent his Attorney to him, and demanded money for his Designes besided 50 G[uinea]s for his Journey. My Lord was surpris'd at this demand, having never had anything but two or three little trifleing drawings as big as his hand, which prov'd of no use to him.

For these sketches Carlisle had already given Talman's clerk a couple of guineas. So Talman went to court, and the jury found Carlisle obliged to pay fifty guineas for the journey. 'But for the Designes, the Court allow'd nothing', because Vanbrugh in evidence made a significant distinction, which Lord Chief Justice Trevor and the jury accepted:

> That for Designs only drawn imperfectly, by way of proposition for a house, nothing ought to be reckon'd, any more than if a Shopkeeper shew'd you his goods, which if you buy you pay for,

but not for looking on 'em. But that when a Design was chosen and follow'd the Drawings that wou'd be necessary for the carrying on and executing it must be paid for, being things that took up a vast deal of pains and time.

Here was Vanbrugh, an architect of only four years' standing and no known training, but also a man with a very clear mind, excellent legal and business sense, and a great deal of confidence.

There had never been any love lost between Talman and Vanbrugh, who had supplanted him not only as Carlisle's architect but also, in 1702, as Comptroller of the Queen's Works. Talman's part in the invention of Castle Howard was brief but, as we shall see, important. But the process by which Talman lost the Comptrollership to Vanbrugh was also the result of Carlisle's patronage; so was Vanbrugh's introduction into the College of Heralds. His Account Book only covers continuously the period from August 1715 to his death, and if a substantial payment was made to him about 1712 there is of course now no record of it; we should expect such a payment to have been made because it was then that Carlisle and his family moved into the new house. But on the other hand Vanbrugh's concern continued with the outworks, and the Temple was not designed until the winter of 1723–4.

Carlisle's own papers include the record of a payment of £50 in 1708, but there are no payments from him in the whole ten years of Vanbrugh's Account Book, and not even a payment of arrears after Vanbrugh's death such as that of £275 recorded on 9 July 1726 from George Bubb Doddington in respect of work at Eastbury. But one other commission in the years of the Account Book seems to have been without direct monetary reward, and that was Grimsthorpe, where the work was for Robert Bertie, a kinsman like Carlisle whose friendship, patronage and obligation went back, as we have seen, to the 1680s*. It seems very probable that in both these cases the architect's rewards were in kind, and in Carlisle's case we need perhaps look no further to identify them than the Comptrollership and the office of Clarenceux Herald.

* pp. 58, 71

The story of how Castle Howard came to be designed is inseparable from the story of how Vanbrugh came to be an architect; in both events the details are rather few, though sufficient
to leave no doubt that Vanbrugh persuaded his kinsman and
fellow Kit-Cat to prefer him, untrained and untried though he
was, to Talman. The self-confidence which prompted his letter
from Vincennes to Saint-Germain, which led him through
Camaret Bay with Carmarthen, through which he took the
London stage by storm, did not desert him when he made up
his mind to be a better house designer than Talman. It was an
indispensable asset, but there were others: an eye, a backer,
and Hawksmoor.

The talent and imagination – the artist's eye – which he believed he possessed had to be real and not a delusion; we can
see now that they were indeed real. Architecture only passes
from the drawing board to the building site by way of substantial and purposeful expenditure, and Vanbrugh needed a real
commission from a supporter with both the desire and the
affluence to build. Finally, he was able to turn to positive
advantage the delegative nature of architecture, whose very
name indicates the making of designs by a master which are
carried out by the co-ordinated efforts of others working under
him. The Italians of the early Renaissance had turned the process of designing buildings from a craft based on practical
skills and experience into an art based on intellect, learning
and the capacity to give orders as a master does to his servants
or an officer to his troops.

As a consequence it had become feasible for any gentleman
– or lady – with ideas and confidence to learn how to make
designs. Among those who in this way turned to architecture
and made it their profession, the painter Inigo Jones and the
scientist Sir Christopher Wren had risen to be Surveyor (that is
architect) to the King. But it would also have been possible, at
least in theory, for Carlisle to be his own architect if he had
wished. Roger North, the younger brother of Montagu, Vanbrugh's companion in the Bastille, did this when he undertook
'the repair, or rather Metamorfosis, of an old house in The
Country', Rougham Hall in Norfolk, a process which led him to
compile his *Cursory Notes of Building*.

North recommended 'that a man be his owne surveyor; es-

pecially if it be a limited designe, either for the use of a private
family, or reforming an old house'. But North recognized distinctions of scale in building enterprises; for

> If a palace is to be built intirely new, or any publick edifice, or
> church, townhouse or the like, it is a work proper for a surveyor
> and hath too much drudgery for a man of quality, tho such will
> regulate the *gousto* of a surveyor's invention, which doth often
> fall short of true greatness.

Even in such cases North saw the architect as a necessary evil,
since on the one hand 'you may use a head workman' but then
'you must be content with deminutive skill', while on the other
hand a surveyor 'is very costly, and must be payd like a king's
serjeant'; he will be so busy as to 'leave you either to yourself,
or some underworkman'. Moreover he will do things his way
and not yours, he will underestimate the expense, and not least
is the fact that surveyors

> having viewed many fabricks, in life, and in draught, with the
> ornaments of the antique and moderne invention, have a world
> of crotchetts of their owne, occasioned or built upon them; all
> which they have an itch to put in execution, and it is miraculous
> if they doe it not the first opportunity of building they are im-
> ployed in.

North was perhaps unduly pessimistic, although the Duchess
of Marlborough was to say that architects, like painters and
poets, 'have very high flights, but they must be kept down'. But
the Renaissance transformation of architecture from a mechanical to a liberal art meant that professional as well as
amateur architects needed the help of specialists. Leone Battista Alberti, the archetypal Renaissance architect and the first
authority after the ancient Vitruvius to write at length on his
art, put the problem clearly when he warned those who would
follow in his path that

> you will find it very difficult to avoid being made answerable for
> all the faults and mistakes committed either by the ignorance or
> negligence of other men, upon which account you must take
> care to have the assistance of honest, diligent and severe over-
> seers to look after the workmen under you.

The final factor in Vanbrugh's bargain with Carlisle was thus the 'perticular concern' of Mr Hawksmoor. For it is clear from surviving drawings and documents that Hawksmoor performed three functions of which Vanbrugh was as yet incapable; he made most of the drawings, he designed the detailing, and he negotiated rates with the artificers and craftsmen who were to build the house. In the same letter that refers to Hawksmoor's fee, Vanbrugh described his own discussions with the mason and carpenter:

> I talk't a great deal to 'em both, the morning I came away [from Henderskelfe]; but found 'em very unwilling to come to any abatement ... I ask't Mr Hawksmoor alone, what he really thought on't; he said they were indeed come as low, as he ever expected to bring 'em; and yet perhaps it was not impossible for 'em to work lower, but ... they might take this pretence, to performe the work ten per Cent: worse for five per Cent: they were reduc't ... wheras, if they have the rates they have propos'd, they own themselves engag'd to do as good work as that they receive twice as much for, at London, and by consequence they have no room left for evasion.

Nicholas Hawksmoor was two or three years older than Vanbrugh, the son of a Nottinghamshire yeoman farmer. He seems to have attended grammar school, but by his late teens he was building mad, and a chance meeting with Edward Gouge, the most skilled and inventive plaster worker of the later seventeenth century, led to Gouge's taking him to London and introducing him to Sir Christopher Wren. Wren took him into his household at Scotland Yard in 1679 or 1680 as a clerk, gave him opportunities to learn and develop, taught him all he could, and found him employment in His Majesty's Works and in other architectural concerns of his own such as St Paul's and the Hospitals of Chelsea and Greenwich. By the early 1690s Wren was passing on commissions to his gifted pupil, including the new Writing School at Christ's Hospital School in the City and what became Hawksmoor's first masterpiece, the [9] great stone mansion at Easton Neston in Northamptonshire, designed for Lord Lempster, whose wife was the sister of Lord Carmarthen and first cousin of Robert and Peregrine Bertie.

In society Hawksmoor always showed a certain diffidence

and deference, and he never reached the top of the ladder in the Royal Works. But at the least hint of a building proposal Hawksmoor with pencil in hand became bold, expansive, and unstoppable: asked for a sketch design he might produce six, all different, often supporting his drawings with letters of explanation. In the last forty years he has come to be recognized as one of the greatest of English architects, but the retiring side of his nature can still be seen in the years of devoted work which, as he once put it, like 'the loving nurse that almost thinks the child her own', he put into other men's creations, first Wren's and later Vanbrugh's. Like John Webb before him in relation to Inigo Jones, Hawksmoor was in relation to Wren the true professional, the best trained of his generation, yet taught by a master who in contrast was self-instructed.

We do not know how or when Vanbrugh first met Hawksmoor, but it is possible that it was through Carmarthen's sister since Easton Neston was in building in the second half of the 1690s. Or the introduction may have been through the younger William Vanbrugh, the son of Uncle William the litigious merchant and the elder brother of the unlucky Captain Dudley. William was a court official and an administrator. It was he, not John as is sometimes said, who was a member of the commission in 1702 for stating the late King William's debts. In or before 1698 he was Deputy Comptroller of Accounts of the Treasurer of the Chamber, becoming Comptroller in 1707. On 31 May 1695 he had been made Secretary to the commission for building the Royal Naval Hospital at Greenwich; his nomination for this honorary appointment by Evelyn (who was the honorary Treasurer) is an indication of his respectability and status, the maintenance of which must have depended on more than his meagre salary from the Royal Household. Sir Christopher Wren was giving his services as architect, and on 30 June 1696 he was allowed £50 a year for Hawksmoor to assist him. Two years later (22 July 1698) Hawksmoor was appointed Clerk of Works to the Hospital; he was already showing in respect of Greenwich those valuable qualities that were to make him so necessary to the success of the Henderskelfe venture.

Vanbrugh's earliest reference to architecture is in *The Re-*

lapse, when Tom Fashion and Lory arrive at Tunbelly Hall. This is evidently a building of aspiration rather than fulfilment, since it reminds Tom of 'Noah's Ark, as if the chief part on't were design'd for the Fowls of the Air, and the Beasts of the Field'. But Lory bids him, 'Pray, Sir, don't let your Head run upon the Orders of Building here; get but the Heiress, let the Devil take the House.' Jonathan Swift, lampooning Vanbrugh's little house at Whitehall in 1706, summed up his change of vocation in a way that was not questioned in his lifetime:

> Van's genius without Thought or Lecture
> Is hugely turn'd to architecture.*

Lecture of course means study by reading, and since the printed word was the first channel of instruction for those who would teach themselves the art, Swift's account is over-simple. But the speed and unexpectedness of Vanbrugh's conversion are conveyed, and there is no reason to doubt that in essence Swift was right. Swift also made up a little story to the effect that Vanbrugh looked at little boys making mud pies and at a young miss making a house of cards, and built his Whitehall house to show he could do better. This is the imagery of satire, but the perception within the imagery is again essentially accurate. The traditional interpretation of *The Relapse* as both a sequel and a criticism of Cibber's *Love's Last Shift* is not without relevance. As Comptroller of Works Vanbrugh would put considerable effort into the control or reform of the Office. The moral value of success must have been a frequent theme of his merchant father's conversation, and although in his boyhood he perhaps turned a deaf ear to such preaching, the more serious character that began to form in a French prison cell came at last to realize the virtue of old saws about, for example, a thing being worth doing well if it is worth doing at all.

So in London on half-pay, between the production of one play and the writing of another, Vanbrugh reached two decisions: to be an architect, and to be one to the limits of his capacity. How seriously he saw the effects of these decisions emerges in his scornful comment twenty years later when the

* p. 227

painter Sir James Thornhill made a bid for the office of royal architect (15 August 1719):

> 'Twou'd be a pleasant Joke to the World, to See a Painter made Surveyor of the Works, in Order to Save money; When all the Small knowledge or tast they ever have of it, is only in the Great expensive part, as Collumns, Arches, Bas reliefs &c which they just learn enough of, to help fill up their Pictures. But to think that Such a Volatile Gentleman as Thornhill, Shou'd turn his thoughts & Application to the duty of a Surveyors business, is a Monstruous project.

In 1699 much the same could have been said of a writer of comedies turned surveyor. The scaffolding had been struck from Wren's new ranges at Hampton Court, the choir of his St Paul's was at last in use, and the rest of the new cathedral was finished up to the parapet though still without any sign of the dome and towers. Yet Vanbrugh at thirty-five was impatient. At some moment in the last years of the century the conviction overtook him that he wanted to build real houses, not card ones – but *how*? What Hawksmoor showed him was that, as is claimed for certain postal correspondence courses today, he could start practising his new accomplishment while he was still learning it. By the summer of 1699, in Yorkshire, the exercises were reality.

__ 19 __

When a Design was Chosen and Followed

As well as the obelisk at Castle Howard Lord Carlisle commissioned the Pyramid about a kilometre south of the house and slightly east of the central axis of the gardens. It was built in 1728, designed by Hawksmoor, and its roughly conical interior contains a massive stone bust of Lord William Howard (1563-1640), the founder of the Castle Howard branch of the family. Lord William was the third son of Thomas Howard, fourth Duke of Norfolk, whose scheme to marry Mary Queen of Scots incurred the displeasure of Queen Elizabeth I and in consequence his beheading in 1572. The previous year he had betrothed three of his sons to three daughters of Thomas Lord Dacre, whose widow Norfolk had married in 1566. Arrangements of this kind, joining in matrimony a widower and a widow and also their children by their previous marriages, were not uncommon in the sixteenth and seventeenth centuries; in the small world of the landed and moneyed classes, in a period when arranged matches were usual and those for love exceptional, the social benefits of familiarity were often enhanced and perhaps even outweighed by the financial advantages of keeping property within the family from one generation to the next. In this way Lord William and Elizabeth Dacre were married in 1577, and the Dacre estates in Cumberland, Northumberland and the North Riding of Yorkshire passed to Lord William.

Their great-grandson Charles Howard was born in 1629, fought in his teens for Charles I and was fined heavily for doing so by Oliver Cromwell. Later he changed sides, was wounded fighting on the Parliamentary side at the Battle of Worcester, and became captain of Cromwell's bodyguard. Cromwell as Lord Protector granted only two hereditary peerages, one of them being Howard's as Baron Gilsland and Viscount Howard of Morpeth. After Cromwell's death on 3 September 1658 Howard again changed sides and was imprisoned in the Tower for supporting the exiled Charles II; his reward after the Restoration was in 1661 the Earldom of Carlisle. Lord William had made additions to the Dacre castle at Naworth, a mile south of Hadrian's Wall. Henderskelfe, the Yorkshire house, was described by the antiquary John Leland in about 1540 as 'a fair quadrant of stone having 4 toures builded castelle like, but . . . no ample thing'. In about 1680 the first Earl began to modernize it, spending in 1681 £110 on windows, doors and the like. When he died in February 1685, eighteen days after Charles II, the work can only just have been finished, if at all. His son Edward, second Earl, died in 1692 and was succeeded, at the age of twenty-three, by Edward's son Charles, third Earl, who had recently made the Grand Tour to Italy. Like many English visitors, including Giles Vanbrugh, Charles visited the University of Padua: he signed the book, 'Charles Howard of Morpeth the first day of the year 1690'.

On 14 March 1693 a chimney at Henderskelfe, which still belonged to the Dowager first Countess, caught fire, and the castle was seriously damaged and partly gutted; an inventory made soon afterwards mentions melted silverware. At this time Lord Carlisle was active in London, where he had a house in Soho. Like his father before him he had, when Viscount Morpeth, sat as a Whig in the House of Commons, and his political commitment would continue in the Lords and in the Kit-Cat Club. On three occasions after the turn of the century he would play a brief but significant part in government – at the accession of Queen Anne, after the death of Halifax in 1715, and during the split among the Whigs in 1717 – but by 1698 he had already decided to develop his Yorkshire estates and rebuild the house there for reasons that were both aesthetic and practical.

Lady Irwin's poem* emphasizes the seriousness of her father's retreat from London, his 'gen'rous Mind, to ev'ry Social Act of life inclin'd' and his aim 'To serve Mankind ... and make those happy who on you depend'. The theme of Carlisle's bounty as a landlord was further developed in a long obituary poem (1738) by the York printer Thomas Gent, entitled *Pater Patriæ*, a heroic appellation previously associated with both Cosimo de' Medici and Cicero. The planting of trees for utility as well as the creation of an ideal landscape had been promoted in the 1660s especially by John Evelyn on behalf of the Royal Society. Forestry was of vital importance, for English woodlands had been seriously depleted by centuries of prodigal consumption not only of timber in the building of houses and ships but also of fuel for domestic use and, in the form of charcoal, for the smelting of metal ores.

[6]   But the size and grandeur of the house Lord Carlisle intended to build on his estate were not aimed at mere utility. The main range of Castle Howard consisted mainly of thirteen state rooms on one floor, with relatively few bedrooms. In relation to York, it stood almost like Hampton Court to London or Versailles to Paris, as if Carlisle held court there to the society of York, the most spacious city after London and Norwich though not the most populous. In the 1720s Daniel Defoe found York 'full of gentry and persons of distinction' but 'with no trade indeed, except such as depends upon the confluence of the gentry'. In some ways it occupied the position as a northern metropolis that would, after the 1707 Act of Union, gradually pass to Edinburgh. The city consumed, importing its own wines from France and Portugal and timber from Norway, 'and indeed what they please almost from where they please'. But it produced nothing.

Moreover, since the Glorious Revolution, which replaced a monarch responsible only to God with one answerable to Parliament, the symbolism as well as the balance of power in Britain had begun to change. Of the six laymen who signed the invitation to William of Orange of 30 June 1688, three built themselves palatial houses. One was Thomas Osborne, father of Vanbrugh's Lord Carmarthen and later first Duke of Leeds,

* p. 193

who in 1695 retired to build Kiveton near Sheffield, a house
that no longer exists. The grandest and most lavish of these
houses was Chatsworth, which the fourth Earl and first Duke
of Devonshire began to rebuild in the year before the Revolution. His original reasons were capricious – the Cavendishes
were a building family, and he had left the court in 1685 in
order to evade a heavy fine for duelling. Elizabethan Chatsworth consisted of four ranges built around a square
courtyard, and the rebuilding undertaken in 1687 was con-
fined to the south range. Within a decade this piecemeal pro-   **[8]**
cess had taken in the east range and new terracing for the
western one, and by 1707 when the Duke died the whole house
was new; but already the first range had shown a magnificence
previously associated only with royalty. The decoration of the
chapel, with its illusionist wall and ceiling paintings and its
huge marble reredos, was directly inspired by the chapels of
Charles II at Windsor and James II at Whitehall.

The new Chatsworth was indeed not a king's house but a
kingmaker's, and it set a precedent and a new standard for
noblemen's palaces at a time when royal patronage of building
was beginning to decline. The poet Matthew Prior, on an
embassy to Versailles in 1697, when asked whether the King of
England's palace had any similar decorations to what he saw
there, replied rather smugly, 'The monuments of my master's
actions are to be seen everywhere but in his own house'. Certainly it is true that William III is not to be found at Hampton
Court, as Louis XIV might be supposed to be found at
Versailles, in Prior's phrase, 'galloping in every ceiling' but his
answer must have been given in the context not only of royal
palaces but also of the new noble houses, which albeit vicari-
ously were monuments of the newly established government
of free men by free men. Moreover, the new standards, and the
competition to raise them further, were not restricted to
Whigs: in 1696 Lord Nottingham, no longer Secretary of State,
but at that time still a Tory, began to rebuild Burley-on-the-Hill   **[10]**
near Rutland which he had purchased a couple of years ear-
lier. But Castle Howard was to outshine in splendour all previous houses and palaces.

Carlisle was in Yorkshire in August 1698 and probably stayed
until November when his trunk was sent to London. On 10

October he took a lease of Henderskelfe Castle from his grandmother, to take effect the following March, and as he did not
return to the North until about June 1699 it is probable that
Talman's first visit there was in the autumn of 1698, perhaps at
the time the lease was signed. As the architect of the south and
east ranges of Chatsworth and of other great houses, including
perhaps Kiveton (for which he certainly made designs), Talman would have seemed the obvious choice for an ambitious
peer. At that time Carlisle was unaware that Talman was used
to travelling not in a light carriage or by the public coach but in
his own, accompanied by his own servants, or that while his
services could include all the contracting with his own team of
artificers and decorators the result was that country clients
paid London prices for the work. He may not have known
either that Talman was no longer in the Duke of Devonshire's
employment or that, while his renown as a designer grew, so
did the number of clients who, as Vanbrugh was to tell Newcastle in his account of the Talman–Carlisle lawsuit, 'met with
Vexations' from him.

In fairness it must be said that Talman was an architect of
great originality and knowledge and sometimes of brilliance,
and that the faults were not only on his side. The great noblemen of the period were as human as the rest of society and had
the same virtues and failings; nevertheless many of them displayed an overweening vanity and self-importance which coloured as much their good and noble aspirations as their errors
and lapses. Lord Carlisle was one of these: hence his surprise
at Mrs Hawksmoor's bill and hence too the deference with
which even Vanbrugh addressed him in letters to the end of his
life. Devonshire too was not an easy man to please; he disliked
parting with money, spent more on horse-racing than on
architecture, and changed his mind perpetually about the rebuilding. Talman's trouble was in part an ambition which led
him to quarrel with Wren in the Office of Works, but it was also
in part an estimation of himself as working for clients rather
than patrons – men who might be richer, more fortunate and
prouder than himself but in no way better.

However, Devonshire had learned that Talman's method of
building by comprehensive contract or 'by Great', was expensive. In 1703 his steward observed of the new west front at

Chatsworth, for which Talman was not responsible, that it was 'much more noble and finer ... and very much cheaper'. At Castle Howard, with the recommendation of Vanbrugh and the advice of Hawksmoor, Lord Carlisle 'during the whole Course of his Building managed all that part himself, with the greatest care', as Vanbrugh told the Duke of Marlborough in May 1716. 'And tho' he began with Ignorant Masons at lower Rates, he soon found there was good reason to give more, in order to have his work tollerably done.' This bears out Hawksmoor's remarks about work 10 per cent worse for prices 5 per cent cheaper.*

Among the Talman drawings in the R.I.B.A. there are indeed two little plans, identified in the architect's hand as for Lord Carlisle, and showing big rectangular houses, thirteen bays long, with grand staircases in the middle of the block and therefore probably intended to be lit from overhead lanterns. On the back of one of these drawings is a pencil sketch-plan, also marked *Lord Carlisle*, which shows a house surrounded by gardens and courtyards, in an arrangement very similar to that in one of two garden and park plans which were evidently made by George London of Brompton, the leading garden designer of the time. London was a man of enormous energy, who among other places had been perfecting the gardens at Chatsworth since 1688; Stephen Switzer, who was concerned with layouts at Castle Howard some years later, refers in his *Ichnographia Rustica* (1718) to designs made for Lord Carlisle there by London.

Both the garden plans for Castle Howard show a series of straight planted avenues aligned not on the new house but on a courtyard in front of it, and a cross-shaped arrangement of canals and basins lying downhill to the north, where the Great [F] Lake now is. They also show that Carlisle already intended to move Henderskelfe village;† London drew out a new model village, a dozen houses arranged in a circle round a new church, about a third of a mile south-west of the house, on the hilltop where the Pyramid gate was later to be built. In view of [25] Carlisle's evident fondness for placing monuments on top of

* p. 200
† p. 465

the little hills of his rolling domain, and in the light of his daughter's attribution to him of the whole creation, it may well be that not only the new village but also its dramatic siting on the skyline was the Earl's own idea. It cannot have been Vanbrugh's since it already occurs in the plan with the Talman house. But equally it is unlikely to have been Talman's, for one of the defects of the Talman–London plan is that the house would have missed all the good views. The principal rooms faced east and west along a ridge of parkland, and the downward slopes to north and south could only be seen from the courtyard or from the minor rooms at the ends of the house.

The most significant differences in the second garden plan are that it shows the outline of what is unmistakeably Vanbrugh's Castle Howard at an early stage, and that the house has been turned through ninety degrees to face north and south, as it does to this day. The conjunction of these two differences, to which we may add the way Vanbrugh's house stretches out to take advantage of the lie of the land, suggests very strongly that it was Vanbrugh's idea to turn the house round, the first of the great dramatic strokes that characterize his architecture.

When Lord Carlisle returned to Henderskelfe in June 1699

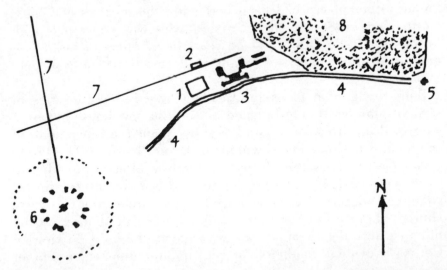

F   Henderskelfe and Castle Howard. 1 Site of Henderskelfe Castle. 2 Church. 3 Castle Howard. 4 The old village street. 5 Vanbrugh's Temple. 6 Proposed new village. 7 Lord Carlisle's new approach roads. 8 Wray Wood.

he wrote to his neighbour Thomas Worsley of Hovingham asking his opinion of masons' and carpenters' estimates. The
dimensions quoted in Worsley's reply of 26 June correspond to
Vanbrugh's earliest known elevation, a drawing actually in
Hawksmoor's hand endorsed *Mr Vanbrooks draft of a great
house*. By this time, therefore, Vanbrugh was at least in competition with Talman, suggesting that (with that useful
draughtsman he had not yet introduced to his Lordship) he
could provide not only a better house than Talman but also a
cheaper one. If this was the occasion of Talman's second visit it
is hardly surprising that he was not especially welcome. In July
1699 George London was at Henderskelfe; it was quite usual to
begin work on the gardens even before the house because a
formal garden takes years to make. But since London's second
garden plan shows not the first draft of Vanbrugh's design but
at least the third, events must have been moving fast. How they
moved is shown by a letter Vanbrugh wrote on Christmas Day
1699 to the Earl of Manchester, who was on embassy to France.

After a great deal of the gossip of theatre and coffee-house,*
Vanbrugh went on, 'I have been this summer at my Ld Carlisle's, and seen most of the great houses in the North, as Ld
Nottings: Duke of Leeds Chattesworth &c. I stay'd at Chattesworth four or five days the Duke being there.' The Duke was
another kinsman by marriage: his brother-in-law Lord Arran
was married to the daughter of Anne Ferrers, half-sister of
Vanbrugh's mother. To judge by later visits, Vanbrugh will
have spent at least a couple of weeks at Henderskelfe, and he
may even have helped to see off Talman. His letter is tantaliz-
ingly vague about 'most of the great houses' he had seen, but
the three he managed to name are significant. Lord
Nottingham's was Burley-on-the-Hill, not yet finished, a great
block of a house whose architect has not so far been   [10]
satisfactorily identified; although not the only possible prototype for the long internal corridors of Castle Howard it is the   [M]
closest in date and location. The Duke of Leeds's, Kiveton, was
newly built and may, as we have seen, have been Talman's
work, as were the two ranges of state rooms so far built at
Chatsworth.

* p. 226

But Vanbrugh was at Chatsworth not only to see but also to
show the Duke of Devonshire 'all my Ld Carlisle's designs',
already an open secret or no secret at all. If few had seen the
drawings, they had talked about them to others. Lord Manchester had seen a design before he left for France in late July,
and had been able to give Devonshire a rather false impression
of 'a plain low building like an orange house'. What Vanbrugh
showed Devonshire in August or September 'was quite another thing, than what he imagin'd from the character yr Ldship gave him. on't'. Devonshire particularly liked the low
wings, which must mean that he saw a tall central block, and
he was surprised and pleased by 'Those Ornaments of Pillasters and Urns, wch he never thought of'. Vanbrugh went on:

> There has been a great many Criticks consulted upon it since,
> and no one objection being made to't, the Stone is raising, and
> the Foundations will be laid in the Spring. The Modell is prepar-
> ing in wood, wch when done, is to travel to Kensington where
> the King's thoughts upon't are to be had.

When Vanbrugh reads like one of his stage characters it is usually for his language rather than for his sentiments, but this
passage does suggest a concerted attempt to take turn-of-the-
century society by storm. Lord Carlisle's designs were the talk
of London, approved by all. It was not unusual to have a
wooden model made, though few have survived: it was a record of the design to which all concerned with the building
work could refer, it was often more explicit than drawings, and
if the architect died or went abroad his intentions remained
clear. It could also be used, as ship models were, for publicity
or, in cases where it was appropriate, to raise money; it was
surely as an advertisement for Vanbrugh that the King's
'thoughts' were sought. The accounts of Carlisle's steward
show that the model was indeed sent not to Kensington but to
Hampton Court in June 1700; what happened to it thereafter
we do not know.

By that time foundations were being dug and probably footings were being laid, at least for the east wing, the first part to
be built; in the letter of June 1703 about the lawsuit Vanbrugh
wrote that Carlisle 'has been Now three Years at Work'.

Hawksmoor had beaten the mason and carpenter down as low as they would go, and quantities of stone were being quarried in the park as well as from the ruined parts of the old castle.

On 26 May 1701 Hawksmoor was on site and wrote to Carlisle in London. Although the late spring had delayed progress – masonry could not be set in the frosty months of the year – he found the work 'to go on with vigour and grt industry'. He concluded with a remark to whose context we have no clue: 'now I shall wish the conclusion of the worke as earnestly as I was for opposing the beginning of it'. A considerable amount of levelling and terracing had to be done to give the site the smooth appearance it still has today; nevertheless the building season of 1702 saw the east wing roofed and the start of work on the main range. At Blenheim in 1705 Vanbrugh would report to Marlborough, four days after the foundation stone was laid, that the drawings he had sent were 'not perfect in little perticulars', one of which he thought worth mentioning: the addition of a clerestory and portico to the hall.* The early drawings for Castle Howard show that additions of about the same magnitude and significance were made to Lord Carlisle's house, and perhaps at a similar stage. The idea of opening the hall into a great domed lantern is absent from the earliest drawings, but it was certainly no later than 1702, for the huge piers on which it stands had to be provided for in the foundations.

There had been cupolas on country houses before, and even on town ones. Coleshill in Berkshire, begun by Sir Roger Pratt about 1657, was probably the first, and certainly the most famous until its destruction by fire in 1952; Pratt's Clarendon House, Piccadilly (1664-7) had a similar cupola which gave the idea a metropolitan prominence until its untimely demolition in 1683. The best-preserved example today is Belton, which was built in the 1680s. In all of these, as in many other Restoration houses, the cupola was a wooden structure rising above the flat central platform of a pitched roof. From the outside the sloping roof, the chimney stacks and the cupola were all important features of the house's outline. But inside these houses the cupola surmounted a spiral staircase rising through the

* p. 296

attic roof space and giving access from it to the roof flat, from
which it was a favourite seventeenth-century pastime to
admire the view; the stair spiral was the only connection with
the house below. Vanbrugh's first 'draft of a great house' has a
cupola which, although probably of masonry, is still similar in
scale to the Restoration type. On the other hand visible pitched
roofs had become old-fashioned by 1690 and the house in the
'draft' bears a silhouette like those of Chatsworth, Burley-on-
[3] the-Hill and other more modern houses, with a flat top ending
in a balustrade which completely hides the roof from below.

What Vanbrugh – and it can have been nobody else – now
introduced to Castle Howard was a much larger dome, a third
of the width and half the depth of the central block and, to the
top of the lantern, as high again as the balustrade. Subjectively
– for there are no rules for this sort of addition – it is dis-
proportionately big for the house, and at close quarters it does
not fit very logically on to the building below. But from a distance it uniquely and dramatically crowns the house and the
[5] ridge on which it sits. No previous house had sported a cupola
of such magnificence and none has done so since. Moreover,
this is not merely a colossal external ornament but an upward
extension of the interior space of the entrance hall. Vanbrugh
would by this time have known the Queen's Staircase at
Windsor Castle, designed by Hugh May twenty-five years earlier, which was lit by a large wooden lantern overhead, and
there was also just time for him to have seen the still
unfinished domed vestibule to the great hall of Greenwich
Hospital; but the mention of these is hardly more than an insurance policy for architectural historians who like to feel that
no 'obvious' source has been overlooked.

Vanbrugh's lack of premeditation must not be misunderstood. There is no evidence that he was an irresponsible
architect, and second thoughts in architecture are even more
expensive than initial ones. He conceived his buildings, be
they large or small, on a broad canvas, and when he changed
his mind the alterations were equally broad. But when we
wake up one morning with a decision clear in our minds, it is
the end of a process of deliberation whose final resolution
comes through 'sleeping on it'. What makes the art-historian's
tracing of sources so perilous is that both decisions of this sort

and those 'inspirations' that come in our waking hours are products of our subconscious, a department of the mind which works by a kind of alchemy on the materials of past experience sometimes beyond recognition, sometimes not so far that the originals cannot still be traced by ourselves or by others.

The hall at Castle Howard with its painted dome has often been compared to the domed crossing of a Baroque church, and ultimately we should probably look for memories of buildings in Paris. The Dome of the Invalides, although it is a church of this kind, is far bigger in size. But nearer to the centre of seventeenth-century Paris there is a building with long flanking wings embracing a shallow forecourt and a domed central block of about the same size as that of Castle Howard: the College of the Four Nations planned by Cardinal Mazarin, designed by Le Vau and begun in 1662 for the education of students from the regions such as Artois and Alsace that had been annexed to France by the Treaty of the Pyrenees. The resemblance is not close – the relationship of the parts in composition and scale is different – but the centre block comprising the chapel carries a domed lantern even bigger in proportion than Castle Howard's. Moreover the College, now the Institut de France, occupies an impressively scenic position on the Left Bank exactly opposite the river front of the Louvre, and there are also, as we shall see, reminiscences of this building in the design of Blenheim. [13]

[9]

Le Vau's sense of occasion was equal to Vanbrugh's and the whole Collège Mazarin is scenic architecture in that it spreads out along the *quai* while the buildings at the back are fitted into an irregular and enclosed site. At Castle Howard of course the site was quite open, but even before the introduction of the dome Vanbrugh's design had developed into a house with not one pair of wings but two. The east wing on which work first began is in fact the north-east; it lies at right angles to the main house and forms one side of the north forecourt. But on the south facing the gardens the central block of two storeys and nine bays stretches out to east and west in one-storey wings of nine bays each. This feature was developed out of the first *draft of a great house,* and must in its simplest form have given rise to the story about the 'plain low building like an orange-house'.

Oranges were sold in the Restoration theatres, the most famous vendor being Nell Gwynn; their foreignness and consequently their cost made them something of a treat, although in the forty years from 1670 to 1710 they fell from sixpence to twopence apiece; the oils in the peel added their note to the mixed odour of perfume, sweat and candle grease that perva-

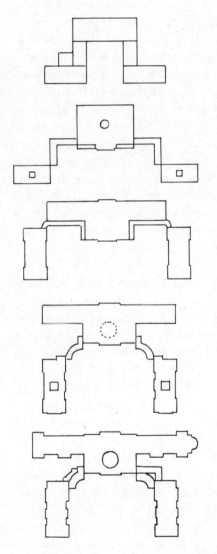

1 Talman's plan was for a long house with parallel wings linked to it. The house faced east and west.

2 *Mr Vanbrook's draft of a great house* was turned to face north and south, but also had wings parallel to it, linked by open corridors. A small cupola surmounted the main house, with turrets over the wings.

3 The first Vanbrugh-Hawksmoor design turned the wings at right angles and placed them at the ends of a second, southern, pair of wings.

4 The north wings were then brought closer together and linked to the house by open quadrants. Later a dome was added to the main block.

5 A closed quadrant was then added on the east, and a right-angled corridor was projected on the west. The west wing was never built to Vanbrugh's design. Cabinets were added at the ends of the south wings.

G   Five stages in the plan of Castle Howard.

ded the house. The accidental coincidence of the name of the fruit with Orange, the Roman Arausio in Provence, led to a fashion not only for the fruit but also for its colour after William of Orange-Nassau became King of England in 1688. It was already well known that in plant-houses, whose thick walls and draughtless windows kept out the frost, these decorative and bright-fruited evergreens could be enjoyed in winter, though not grown on a commercial scale; in the year of Vanbrugh's birth Evelyn noted the orangery at Sir John Shaw's new house at Eltham in Kent and Pepys saw orange trees in the physic garden in St James's Park. Less specifically such buildings were known as greenhouses, a category thus distinct from the glasshouses which only became feasible with the development of cheap industrial glass-making early in the nineteenth century.

Not only do its south wings make Castle Howard look even bigger than it is, exploiting the line of the west-east ridge on which it stands; they also contribute to its thirteen state rooms, and the large south-facing windows take domestic advantage of the sun's warmth with an efficiency that Vanbrugh was to record exactly twenty years after his Christmas 1699 letter. The north sides of these wings consisted of corridors, which insulated the rooms on the cold side.

Another characteristic of the finished house which raises it out of the greenhouse category is its greater degree, as well as greater diversity, of embellishment compared to the early drawings. Many years later Hawksmoor would defend this diversity to Lord Carlisle, worried by Palladian critics, on the ground that the two fronts could not be seen simultaneously – an argument which incidentally would have been endorsed by his master Wren and is perhaps typical of seventeenth-century architects. Originally Vanbrugh and Hawksmoor had proposed a Corinthian pilaster order for both elevations, but by 1702 the north front had been changed to the simpler and sterner Doric with a reduction in the number of window bays. The gravity of this entrance front was increased by the trophies and other martial emblems that appear in the frieze, and the urns, emblems of history, that occupy the end niches. Not all is serious, however, for the central window is flanked by naked boys with garlands and ribbons. All this enrichment not only produces a liveliness of texture and shadowing which are reminiscent of French classical architecture; it also suggests, on careful inspection, a variety of messages about the builder of the house.

The messages of the garden front are equally varied, but both in forms and in associations the effect is softer. The pilasters remain Corinthian, with smaller ones in the wings, and they are fluted. The frieze in the central block is carved with playing boys, heraldic lions, and boys blowing conch shells at seahorses. The boys with seahorses are similar to those on the west front of Chatsworth, which was built in 1700-2, that is between Vanbrugh's visit and the commencement of Lord Carlisle's south front. Not only did the same carver, a Huguenot named Nadauld, work on both façades, but the addition of a pediment to that at Castle Howard, not shown in the early drawing, suggests that Vanbrugh continued to follow developments at Chatsworth with great interest. In both buildings, too, the pediments are enriched with the owner's shield and supporters and martial trophies.

In July 1703 Vanbrugh wrote to Tonson that Lord Carlisle had nearly two hundred men at work. Perhaps as many as half of these will have been engaged on the gardens, in quarrying and in earth-moving, but it is clear that such numbers were involved in order to achieve some speed in such a large undertaking. In 1702 the north-east wing was roofed though by no means completed, the south-east range and the central block by 1706 when the dome was being built. By 1712 Lord Carlisle and his family were able to move into the house, leaving still unbuilt the north-west wing on whose site were as yet the last remains of the old castle. A mason's contract was drafted some time before 1719 for this wing to be built 'after the same manner' as the north-east; the paper in the Castle Howard archives is not dated and the contract was never confirmed. In November 1724 Vanbrugh would still be urging Carlisle to finish the house, but his patron was by then more interested in the outworks.*

According to Macky's *Journey* (1722) Carlisle was leaving the wing to his heir's attention, and although this seems to be a stock phrase — it had been used of Devonshire by an obituarist

* p. 468

– that is what Carlisle did. The result was much to the detriment of the whole, ironically through the employment for the second time of a kinsman as architect. The fourth Earl engaged his brother-in-law Sir Thomas Robinson to make the west side of the house as tastefully and urbanely Palladian as Vanbrugh's architecture was adventurous, innovative and dramatic. Robinson ruined for ever the symmetry of Castle Howard, prevented the completion of another of Vanbrugh's great afterthoughts and caused the destruction of a small one. The larger afterthought was the provision of outer courtyards, the smaller one the bow-window room at the end of the south-west range.

The story of the bow-window room has been widely misunderstood, but it can be unravelled, and the process reveals a little-known aspect of the house.* More than half the state rooms were gutted by a disastrous accidental fire in 1940, and their original disposition has been not only lost but indeed largely forgotten. The plan in *Vitruvius Britannicus* (1715), probably made from drawings prepared in 1707, shows the whole south side of the house as 'the two principal apartments'. The central block contained the domed hall, the saloon or garden room behind it, staircases on either side of the hall which led up to a second saloon above the first, and four other rooms on the upper floor. The rest of the two apartments stretched out through the wings, backed by the 300-foot corridor which is as much a scenic feature as a practical one. References in building accounts to individual rooms as *My Lord's* or *My Lady's* confirm that the arrangement was exactly like that of king's side and queen's side in a royal palace such as Versailles or Hampton Court. My Lord's rooms, lost in the 1940 fire, were on the east and My Lady's on the west. My Lord's rooms were being decorated in 1705–6, including the Grand Cabinet, the last and most private room at the east end, whose three big arched windows received the morning sun before it reached the south front. Over the centre window outside is a relief of Diana hunting.

Meanwhile early in 1705 Vanbrugh had made the first plans for Blenheim, which included in the middle of the east side a room with a semicircular bow window which Vanbrugh later

[N]

* Appendix E

referred to as 'My Lady Duchesses Favourite Bow Window'.*
How fond of it the Duchess of Marlborough really was it is impossible to say, but the half-round bow certainly became one of
Vanbrugh's own favourite motifs. And almost immediately
somebody – either the architect or Lady Carlisle – fancied the
idea of adding a bow window to My Lady's Cabinet at the west
end of Castle Howard. This room, which was destroyed to
make the south end of Robinson's picture gallery, was seen by
the Countess of Oxford in 1745, but otherwise is only known
from the plan in *Vitruvius Britannicus* and from the sketch el-
[4] evation which Hawksmoor made and sent to William Etty, the
consultant clerk of works at Henderskelfe. Lady Oxford's companion mentioned the 'Bow window & 2 Cupalo's', little domes
in the ceiling like those formerly over the Earl's room, and
three tall rectangular windows forming the bow.

The origin of Vanbrugh's larger afterthought, the addition of
outer courtyards and service blocks, is less easy to define, but it
may also follow from developments at Blenheim. The earliest
[6] outline plans for Castle Howard show unspecified service
buildings at the far side of the entrance courtyard, well to the
[H] north of the northern wings. The side courts at Blenheim, containing kitchens, bakery, brewhouse and laundry on the east
and stables on the west, were not part of the original plan of
1705. Since the concept of Blenheim was in many respects
based on Castle Howard this suggests that in that year such
features were not yet parts of the Castle Howard design and
thus were not there to be emulated. On the other hand, in
March 1707 Vanbrugh was using Hawksmoor and Henry
Joynes, the Blenheim clerk of works, to draw out Castle Howard for engraving. If these drawings were the ones used in
the first volume of *Vitruvius Britannicus* (1715) the service
courts and buildings had been designed by 1707.

This is the more likely in that the *Vitruvius* engravings differ
in many respects from the building itself and therefore derive
from drawings made some years before publication. The west
side of course was never built, and Castle Howard had no
adequate stables until Carr of York built the present large
block much further to the west in 1781–4. But Vanbrugh's

* pp. 284-5

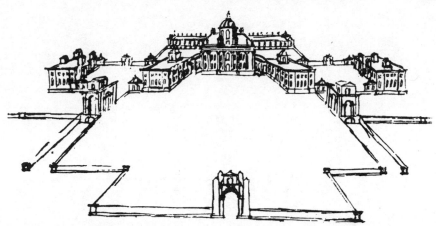

H   Bird's eye view of Castle Howard drawn by Vanbrugh, perhaps the origin of
Plate 6 (Victoria and Albert Museum).

eastern service range adds enormously to views of the house,
especially from the north; its four square towers retain the
image of old Henderskelfe with its '4 toures builded castelle
like'. In other respects the service building is a plain box
without 'ornaments of pilasters'; by the time he designed it the
clearest idea in Vanbrugh's mind must have been the plain box
he had built at Whitehall for his own habitation. Yet that plain
box in its turn derived in essence from the end of the original
north-east wing to which the service building forms a pair.

__ 20 __

A Goose Pie

Fire was perhaps no more common a hazard in the seventeenth century than it is today, but the means of dealing with it
were primitive and the range of causes and locations was
rather different in the absence of such potential modern risks
as gas, oil and electricity supplies. Besides kitchens and
bakeries, the combination of heated glue-pots and copious
wood-shavings made furniture makers' shops particularly
dangerous, and in 1723 a fire was started by an upholsterer in
the Haymarket who was trying to smoke bugs out of furniture.
The principal sources of domestic fires outside workrooms
were chimneys and hearths. The airing of an infrequently used
room could start a fire in the accumulated soot of an uncleaned
chimney, although sometimes the builders were at fault as it
was not unknown for beam-ends to run into the brickwork of
flues; it was a chimney fire of some sort that damaged Henderskelfe Castle in 1693.* Talman's first major building,
Thoresby, was almost burnt down before it was even finished,
the fire being caused by the painters. According to Evelyn the
stables at Burley-on-the-Hill were destroyed in 1705 'by care-
lessnesse of a servant, as most of these accidents happen by'.

Hearth fires usually began with linen bedding or clothing
being left to air by an unguarded grate. The use of brick construction and the establishment of minimum building standards in the City and Westminster after the Great Fire of London

* p. 205

improved matters so far that the idea of insurance began to be entertained and supported, although furnishings and household goods were always inflammable, and at first only the new buildings themselves carried insurance. The insurance companies ran their own fire engines, which of course were horse-drawn and hand-pumped; insured premises were provided with lead plates on their façades, bearing the company's emblem. Some of these plates still survive: their purpose was to help the firemen identify their own companies' clients, since those of rivals would be left to burn.

Montague House in Bloomsbury was destroyed in 1686; this was a modern brick mansion only seven years old, but Evelyn's account of it as 'burnt to the ground' is probably correct since it was immediately rebuilt to a different plan. At the time of the fire it was rented by Lord Devonshire, who was so unfortunate as to lose part of his house in Arlington Street, Piccadilly, in October 1694 – and moreover to be sued by his next-door neighbour for consequential damage. On the other hand, the advice of Vanbrugh and Hawksmoor to Lord Ashburnham on the design and building of No. 3 St James's Square in 1712 saved it from the fire that gutted No. 4 in 1725.

Whitehall Palace was, as a royal residence, a more expensive risk than most. It was also a bad risk, since timber-framed lath-and-plaster additions were still being made to it years after the Great Fire of London; no doubt if anybody had asked about this the answer would have been that regulations did not apply to Crown buildings. There was a fire appliance at Scotland Yard, the headquarters of the Office of Works adjoining the palace on the north; on occasion this was sent to attend incidents within the parish of St Martin-in-the-Fields. A serious fire at Whitehall in 1691 destroyed the south range next to the river including the sumptuous apartment of the Duchess of Portsmouth. But far more serious was the fire started by the airing of linen in the King's Lodgings on the night of Tuesday 4 January 1698. It was soon clearly beyond the neighbourhood's resources, and by morning there was little east of the Whitehall street that could be salvaged. Inigo Jones's Banqueting House was intact, Sir Christopher Wren having mobilized exceptional forces to save it; the brick street gatehouse to the north of it, built in the early 1660s, was also safe.

This gatehouse opened on to a long narrow court, on ground now occupied by Horse Guards Avenue. From the far end of the court a passage led to Whitehall Palace Stairs, the very place at which Young Fashion and Lory landed from the river in Act I of *The Relapse*. The north side of the court was formed by the fronts of houses, offices and kitchens, including a group of rooms occupied in 1669–70 by Sir Henry Wood, Clerk of the Green Cloth. At the time of the Whitehall fire the occupant was another official of the Household, the Vice-Chamberlain, Vanbrugh's friend Peregrine Bertie. Even if the Vice-Chamberlain used his official residence only as an office Vanbrugh is likely to have visited it. He too was at least nominally a court official as Auditor for the Duchy of Lancaster. Whitehall was a desirable address and the surroundings were not unpleasant, although after the fire it required imagination to see what could be made of them. The Vice-Chamberlain's house was a stone's throw from both the Banqueting House and the river, one minute's walk from St James's Park and three from Spring Garden.

Very soon after the fire Sir Christopher Wren made a survey of the site. Whitehall had lost its state rooms and Privy Gallery, the theatre, the Anglican and Catholic chapels, and many lesser parts of its rambling accumulation of courts, houses and workrooms. Some buildings in the south-east corner, near the limit of the 1691 fire, were patched up, and the brick shell of the Queen's Building on the river front, only ten years old, was not demolished for three years. The 'Holbein' gateway and another similar Tudor gatehouse at the south end of the White-hall street towards St James's Park were untouched. Wren was directed to build a council room and five lodgings in a one-storey block immediately south of the Banqueting House.

Wren used one of his outline survey plans to draw out a vast new palace, accompanied by elevations from several aspects. But although Whitehall was already synonymous with central government its atmosphere was too damp for the chesty William III, who soon after the Revolution had bought the Earl of Nottingham's house at Kensington to form the nucleus of a discreet suburban palace while pressing on with the completion of Wren's new buildings at Hampton Court. As for White-hall, King William deferred any consideration of rebuilding, in

Luttrell's words, 'till the parliament provide for the same'. Parliament saw no necessity for a palace which the King would not inhabit, although various architects made unrealistic proposals. The future of English architecture lay not in royal building at all but in great houses such as Chatsworth and Castle Howard.

The King's thoughts on the wooden model for Castle Howard, which he saw about Midsummer 1700, are as lost to us as the model itself. But a few weeks later the promotion of the new Vanbrugh advanced another step. On 22 July 1700 the Earl of Jersey, the Lord Chamberlain, wrote to advise Sir Christopher Wren 'and the rest of the officers of the Works' that His Majesty had 'granted leave to John Vanbrugh, Esq. to build himself a lodging in Whitehall, upon ground where Mr Vice Chamberlain's stood before the Fire'. The Office was therefore 'to give him liberty to bring in his owne workemen to build the said Lodging & to allow him liberty to make use of such brick and Stone out of the Rubbish as they shall have occasion for'. Formulas of His Majesty's service or pleasure were as artificial then as they are now, but the conjunction of the model exhibition, the warrant of the Lord Chamberlain, the previous occupation of the site by his lieutenant, and the latter's friendship with Vanbrugh suggests an unbroken chain.

Wren was somewhat alarmed, and referred the matter, 'being in a frame wholly new', to the Lords of the Treasury. Smarting under a recent reprimand, he reminded them that 'It is incumbent upon me by sev[era]ll letters from your Lps not to permitt any new Foundacions in his Majestys Palaces without yr Lps' directions'. He added that no limits were set either to the use of materials or even to the extent of the site, and that 'It may be a precedent for more of this nature'. Wren was a realist and knew that there was little chance of a new palace on the site, but Vanbrugh did in fact set a precedent, and during the eighteenth century much of the site was leased out for grand private houses. But Wren's representation to the Treasury had some effect. It was read at a meeting on 27 February 1701, and two weeks later William Lowndes, Treasury Secretary, drafted a reply to the Surveyor and his officers which confirmed the authority and imposed the conditions that 'the ground be bounded (before they enter upon the said Building) and that the dimensions of the same do not exceed Sixty four foot in front and Sixty four foot in depth'. On 1 April Lowndes wrote again to the officers of the Works to inform them that 'It is the King's pleasure that you comply with the instructions' of 13 March. There had perhaps been further opposition: Talman, the Comptroller of Works, resentful of the loss of Lord Carlisle's patronage, can hardly have welcomed his rival's new enterprise, although he did not know that worse was to come.

Vanbrugh's permission to build was thus confirmed just in time to make good use of the 1701 building season. He probably used some of the old foundations, and the house will have been roofed before the winter. And with its construction the limelight switched from Yorkshire to London. There was not yet much to be seen of Castle Howard, and thus Vanbrugh's own house was his first visible work in architecture. Even within the palace gates it was soon on display in a way that drawings and models for a distant extravagance were not. The successful playwright, the daring comedian, the witty opponent of Collier, had made a public statement about himself and about his new-found art, and it did not escape comment. In so neatly doing what others might have wished they had thought of, its builder probably caused resentment also.

That Christmas Day letter of 1699 which set rolling the whole Vanbrugh success story contains some fascinating London gossip. One Harcourt 'upon a lawsuit between 'em' sent for Sir John Phillips out of the House of Commons into Westminster Hall and cudgelled him. Thomas Neale, Master of the Mint and the originator of the Seven Dials near Covent Garden (where Neal Street bears his name today) was dead: 'the last word he mutter'd was Salesbury. They say he had made her Sole Executrix. I don't know whether it be true'. The bass Richard Leveridge was 'in Ireland, he Ow's so much money he dare not come over, so for want of him we haven't had one Opera play'd this Winter'. Nevertheless 'the Emperors Crooked Eunuch ... Francisco' had been engaged to sing, at 120 guineas for five nights. A titled widow was caught shoplifting: Lady Ardglass 'for some time under strong Suspicions' was 'catch't stealing four or five fans at Mrs Tooms, who made her refund just as she was getting into her Coach'. This is private talk among friends, and without malice, not public insinuation; here lies the difference between what Vanbrugh gave and what he was to receive.

The anonymous author of *A True Character of the Prince of Wales's Poet, with a Discription of the newly erected Folly at White-hall* abused its creator as a man mean in everything: 'In Conversation, Building, Poetry, He knows no Sense, nor Place, nor Unity.' More specifically the house in the ruins renews 'all the Vice for which 'twas burnt':

> *The Wondrous Gimcrack only stands to tell,*
> *That there was since White-hall, and why it fell.**

Sensational and satirical journalism was still in its infancy, and flourished for the most part not in newspapers or periodicals but in occasional pamphlets and broadsheets; the use of *The character of* as an opening was not uncommon. Writing of this sort exploits the same human tendencies as the comic stage, although often without the redeeming features of theatrical irony. We always know the stage to be partly illusion and, whether only in this knowledge or also in other ways, there is in Restoration theatre a bond of sympathy between actors and audience. The printed word, even over a signature rather than anonymously, is without illusion; it is colder and more detached, a bastion from which the most hurtful shots may safely be fired. We may not be able, as in the theatre, to laugh at ourselves through others; indeed we may be both amused by the foibles and misfortunes of the target and disgusted with the attack.

A few years later Jonathan Swift wrote two more famous and more stylish lampoons on the house: *Vanbrug's House* (1703, revised 1708-9) and *The History of Vanbrug's House* (1706); both were first published in *A Meditation on a Broom-Stick* in April 1710, but from the number of surviving manuscript copies they may have already been circulated. On 7 October 1710 Swift dined with Sir Richard Temple, Congreve, Vanbrugh, and Lieutenant-General Farrington, Lord Willougby's father-in-law. Vanbrugh, Swift wrote in his *Journal to Stella*, 'had a long quarrel with me about those Verses on his House;

* Appendix D

but we were very civil and cold. Lady Marlborough used to
teaze him with them, which had made him angry, though he be
a good-natured fellow.' Already by 1703 the playwright turned
architect, having resigned his captaincy and his Duchy sinecure, had wrested the Comptrollership of the Queen's Works
from Talman and taken on the office of a Herald, and Swift
could write in that year:

> *Van, (for 'tis fit the Reader know it)*
> *Is both a Herald and a Poet;*
> *No wonder then, if nicely skill'd*
> *In each Capacity to Build:*
> *An Herald, he can in a Day*
> *Repair a House gone to decay;*
> *Or by Atchievments, Arms, Device*
> *Erect a new one in a Trice;*
> *And Poets if they had their Due,*
> *By antient Right are Builders too.*

In the revision of 1708-9 Swift changed the last two lines of this
passage to refer in addition to Vanbrugh's new theatre in the
Haymarket:

> *And as a Poet, he has Skill*
> *To build in Speculation still.*

Swift's art lies in the constantly changing metaphor of one idea
for another, and in the revised version he sees the house as a
five-act play:

> *The Building, as the Poet Writ,*
> *Rose in proportion to his Wit:*
> *And first the Prologue built a Wall*
> *So wide as to encompass all.*
> *The Scene, a Wood, produc'd no more*
> *Than a few Scrubby Trees before.*
> *The Plot as yet lay deep, and so*
> *A Cellar next was dug below:*
> *But this a Work so hard was found,*
> *Two Acts it cost him under Ground.*
> *Two other Acts we may presume*

Were spent in Building each a Room;
Thus far advanc't, he made a shift
To raise a Roof with Act the Fift.
The Epilogue behind, did frame
A Place not decent here to name.

This is not really a description of the house, and is not meant to **[I]**
be, although the allusion to unmentionable sanitary arrangements suggests that the small projection, not at the back but on
the east side of the house, was part of the original rather than of
the enlargement of 1719, and may have had – or been thought
to have – this function. The suggestion that this projection was
original is strengthened by the quoining and fenestration it

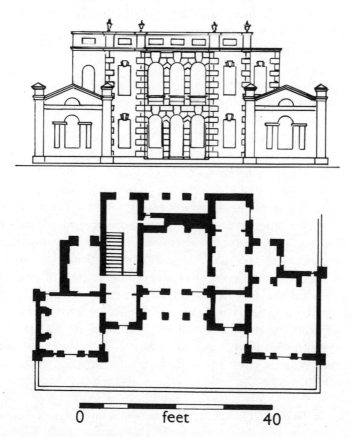

I Vanbrugh's house at Whitehall.

shared with the centre of the house and by its symmetrical position along the east side, which looks like part of Vanbrugh's
original intention.

The History of Vanbrug's House ridicules, as we have already
seen, the way in which, through observation and emulation,
Vanbrugh had turned to architecture and become

> *by due Degrees*
> *For Building fam'd, and justly reckon'd*
> *At Court, Vitruvius the second.*

It also refers to the choice of Vanbrugh to build Blenheim, a
choice which seems to have displeased Lady Marlborough
from the start. But the most accurate, if puzzling, reference to
the house occurs a few lines later in the revised version of the
first poem, *Vanbrug's House.* Poets, says Swift, come looking
for it and cannot find it until

> *At length they in the Rubbish spy*
> *A Thing resembling a Goose Py.*

The house was small, and by 1708 therefore in marked contrast to the enormous and expanding Blenheim. It was also, excluding the eastern annexe, almost a cube about 27 feet high
by 32 feet wide by 28 feet deep. The roof was hidden from
below by a flat parapet with recessed panels. Many years ago
Geoffrey Webb suggested that Swift had in mind what is known
in the trade as a 'raised pie' because in its fabrication the pastry
is raised from the base to form a box containing the filling. Indeed the large oblong cold pork pie made today for the catering
trade looks rather like a pastry castle with a crest or parapet
around the top. Giles Rose, whose *Proper School of Instructions
for the Officers of the Mouth* was published in 1682, describes
under 'cold pyes' first how to make a venison pie: 'make a
Coffin and season your meat and lay it into the Coffin'. For a
duck pie he directs:

> Truss and fit your Ducks ... then give them three or four cuts
> along the Breast, lard them with reasonable small Lard, and
> season them with Pepper, Salt, Nutmegs, Cinamon, and Cloves

between, Bay-leaves, and put them into Paste ... either raised or Flat, made four square ... cover them up and indore the Crust with the Yolks of Eggs ... and Let your Pye bake two small hours.

To bake a Goose

You must make this Pye exactly as you do the Duck Pye, only you should put more Salt, and seed him better with Lard, and let him bake longer, and when he is baked put in at the Funnel a Clove of Garlick.

Half a century later Charles Carter's *Complete Practical Cook* (1730) describes under 'cold baked meats' a 'Goose, Turkey, or Bustard Pie' which could be kept for later use:

First bone your Fowl, and season it with Pepper, Salt, Cloves and Mace; then raise a coffin ... You may put a Goose and a Turkey Together, that is, you may put the Turkey, when bon'd, within the Goose, and lay the Turkey in the Bottom, and the Goose upon it, and the Giblets in the Bottom: You may likewise put a couple of Rabbets cut in Quarters, season'd well, and lard round to fill up the vacant Places; let all be well season'd; cover it with Butter, and close it, and bake it, and give it good Soaking ... and when your Pies are almost cold, fill them up with clarify'd But-ter, first cutting a little Hole in the Side near the Bottom to let out the Gravy, which must be done while hot; when you take it out of the Oven, stop up the Hole again with a Piece of Paste; fill your Pies quite full of clarify'd Butter, and set them by in some dry Place from Vermin, and spend them as Occasion shall serve.

Carter also explains how to make the coffin pastry:

Take a Peck of fine Flower, lay it on your Board, and spread it ready for your Liquor; for a Peck of Flower you must have a Pound and half of Butter; put it in your Liquor, and let it boil, let it cool a little, and then work up your Paste with it, and work it up pretty stiff and close; then put it in a dry Cloath, and let it Sweat a while, and then work it into what you please.

Goose is a seasonal dish (associated with Christmas) because of the bird's breeding time, and hence goose pies also were seasonal; today they are difficult to find. Carter's description of the case as a 'coffin' confirms the oblong shape, and the most famous theatrical example was evidently oblong and large, although it never actually appeared on stage. Vanbrugh's unfinished play *A Journey to London* presents a visiting country family who, suspicious of metropolitan food, bring their own supplies and their cook. They arrive on stage at an inn having been robbed of their hand baggage, and the cook describes how the 'great goose pie' was snatched from under her arm in the street.

Carter also confirms the definition in the *Oxford English Dictionary* as made 'of goose, etc.' This was understood by the Earl of Mar when in 1718 he described a design made for him by an Italian architect as 'full ˙ of trifleing gimcrack insignificant ornaments, worthy of nobody but Vanbruge'. The Italian, he wrote, 'has made a goose pie of my plan and in it raised a modern Gothick superstructure of an order of his own'. The extraordinary and miscellaneous nature of goose pies must have been in Swift's mind too, and Vanbrugh's house was of an order of his own; in strict architectural terms it was of no order at all, being without 'those ornaments of pilasters' that distinguished Castle Howard. Vanbrugh himself enlarged his little house after his marriage in 1719, adding projecting wings at the front and a western annexe roughly matching that on the east. Canaletto's view of Whitehall in 1747 (at Goodwood) is taken from a point whence the house cannot be seen, but the whole area appears tidy and civilized. But originally Vanbrugh's small bachelor home stood on a site of demolition and redevelopment, squat and square and quite unlike any other house.

The references in both the anonymous lampoon and Swift's poems to a mansion or palace are not purely a mockery of the house's small size; they also indicate a departure from the expectations of the time. Street and courtyard houses were normally parts of a terrace or a continuous range of dwellings; only very grand houses in the town centre would have freestanding side elevations. Even today a detached house is commonly considered to be superior to a semi-detached or a terrace one, which is why estate agents have coined for the latter the term 'town house' as something more desirable. In this sense Vanbrugh's house was a diminutive or indeed a pretentious little mansion. Moreover its front elevation, which has its origins in the ends of the north wings at Castle Howard, departed from the usual formula of post-Fire London houses in several other respects. Instead of uniform square-headed windows it had arched openings in the three centre bays, those on the ground floor forming an unglazed loggia or large porch. These bays were also finished with rustication, so that the eye saw a texture not of individual bricks but of groups: blocks of masonry each about five bricks high and two or three bricks wide. This is roughly the scale of the stone rustication of the Banqueting House; thus Vanbrugh's house had a scale and a 'grain' that were large for its actual size. Then the different treatment of the flanking bays from the centre ones suggested a larger scale in a façade composed of three parts rather than of five bays, and finally the top of the house ended in a parapet whereas the typical London house had a pitched roof containing garrets with dormer windows.

Did Vanbrugh choose the site for his house simply for its convenience, or because he knew and liked the setting and the view, or had he something further in mind? In retrospect it is easy to assume that it was all part of a carefully contrived scheme which included his appointment as Comptroller of the Queen's Works on 20 May 1702 in place of Talman.

Talman had been appointed to the post early in the reign of William and Mary, in May 1689, after Wren had managed for five years to dispense with a Comptroller. The job had originally entailed the checking of stores and accounts to keep a control (or a *counter-roll*) on the Surveyor or chief royal architect, but under the regulations laid down by the Treasury and the intelligent guidance of Wren the Office of Works ran reasonably smoothly in the Restoration period and the Comptrollership appears to have become almost a sinecure. For Talman it provided an income and considerable prestige as the background to his country house practice; it also offered him, in the person of Wren, a superior against whom to try his strength. Only a few months after Talman's appointment there was an accident at Hampton Court when part of the new building collapsed and two workmen were killed. Talman tried hard to put the blame on Wren, although without success. Ten years later he made further trouble, not only showing disloyalty but even making a bid for one of the secondary posts held by Wren.

Whatever Wren may have felt about Vanbrugh's entry into either the ruins of Whitehall or the administration of the Works, he can hardly have regretted Talman's departure. Talman is commonly supposed to have owed his appointment to the personal favour of William III, although he is more likely to have had a noble friend at court; the circumstances of his dismissal involve more than the loss of the patron who appointed him.

As the two-party system of English politics became established the working custom grew with it that the Treasury was placed in the charge of the leader of the majority party in the House of Commons. However, in the reigns of William and Anne this system was still scarcely formed, and the Cabinet included members of both parties and was presided over by the monarch in person. The formation of a cabinet from the majority party and the deputation of its leadership by the monarch to the First Lord of the Treasury did not become established practice until the reign of George I; during the eighteenth century the title of Prime Minister, originally a term of opprobrium, gradually came to be accepted for the office of First Lord. Sidney, Lord Godolphin, had been Lord Treasurer during the Tory majority in Parliament from December 1700 to November 1701. The complex political issues which accompany the Tory Godolphin's resignation do not concern our story, but the King's choice of the Whig Carlisle to succeed him is significant both for political history and for the history of architecture.

William III was ailing, and although he had received the support of both parties in the 1701 Act of Settlement (which directed the succession to the throne of Anne and thereafter of the House of Hanover) he feared that after his death Anne might negotiate with her exiled half-brother Prince James Edward Stuart. William in fact died on 8 March 1702, and Lord Carlisle, a committed and respected Whig, proved a strong and effective caretaker during the critical period of the succession. On 6 May Queen Anne reappointed Godolphin in his stead; Godolphin had at first declined, but the Queen pressed him at the express wish of the Earl of Marlborough (created Duke in December 1702). Marlborough and Godolphin were closely allied in public life and were also linked by the marriage of Marlborough's daughter Henrietta to Godolphin's son Francis. Marlborough made Godolphin's appointment the condition of his own military service abroad, which he felt unable to undertake with confidence unless both political and financial control at home were in his trusted friend's hands.

Vanbrugh was appointed Comptroller at a Treasury meeting, attended by the Queen, the Chancellor of the Exchequer and Godolphin, just twelve days after the latter succeeded Carlisle. At that time neither Godolphin nor Marlborough was very interested in architects, and the timing of events was such that the change of Comptroller carrried out by Godolphin must have been prepared for by Carlisle. But the timing is presumably the basis of the confused claim made later, in 1721, by the Duchess of Marlborough (whose view of history was always idiosyncratic) that Vanbrugh owed the post to her husband. (It is, however, possible that she was referring to Vanbrugh's reinstatement as Comptroller in 1715.)* A hundred yards to the north of his own house Vanbrugh now had an official residence in Scotland Yard together with a stable. In accordance with accepted practice, although Wren actually lived in the Surveyor's official house, Vanbrugh rented out the Comptroller's house and stable to a tenant. Minor alterations, however, were made to 'the Comptroller's lodgings' in the winter of 1702–3, when the Works accounts record the building of new walls with old bricks out of the palace ruins, and iron window furniture for a new room.

* p. 386

_ 21 _

Comptroller and Herald

As Comptroller of the Queen's Works Vanbrugh was expected in theory, and when necessary, to attend the daily morning meetings of the officers at Scotland Yard under the direction of the Surveyor, Sir Christopher Wren. He could also be called upon to fix the rates for building work and to examine and check the work books in which accounts were made up each month for work, both 'ordinary' and 'extraordinary', carried out at each royal house. Ordinary work comprised maintenance and minor alterations like partitioning a room into two or re-roofing a shed, while new buildings or additions, usually undertaken on specific contracts with the various tradesmen and craftsmen, were known as extraordinary. The Comptroller would engage in the exchange of memorandums with the Treasury, who controlled the Queen's purse and whose authority, as we have seen, was required for all but the smallest jobs. It was also his duty to check the stores, to ensure that no workmen were retained for whom there was nothing to do, and to make frequent and unexpected visits to sites, especially when the register of workmen was being called. Moreover, it was at least to be hoped that he would in general be as helpful and supportive to Wren as his predecessor Talman had been the reverse.

The appointment was 'at Her Majesty's pleasure', not for life; it was in effect a part-time job, and the pay was not enough to support a gentleman; on the other hand, besides the house in Scotland Yard it entitled him to others at Kensington Palace and Hampton Court, which Vanbrugh also rented out. He could have paid a deputy half his salary to do the necessary work, an early form of job-sharing to which he had been obliged over the Duchy of Lancaster auditorship during his imprisonment in France. But he did not employ a deputy in the Works, and from this time on he began to look increasingly like the true professional who in 1719 found the prospect of a painter's becoming Surveyor a ludicrous one. Whether or not the appointment required him to resign other offices, he did resign them, and the decision not to put in a deputy may have been partly for financial reasons. A successor was appointed to the auditorship on 6 August 1702, but there was also his spasmodic military career. He had been on half-pay from the Second Marine Regiment since August 1698, and Treasury Books and Papers suggest that he received what was due to him up to 24 December 1701 but not for the subsequent period up to 9 March 1702. Moreover in July he petitioned the Treasury for arrears of pay for the *preceding* period, from 1 April 1696 to 20 August 1698; the petition was read on 8 July and he was informed that he would have to apply to the colonel of the regiment, who was now Sir Cloudesley Shovell. But he seems to have been unable to foresee Lord Carlisle's patronage before the very last moment, for he had taken a new commission in the army on 10 March 1702, two days after the accession of Queen Anne and the day before, addressing both Houses of Parliament, she told them of her intention to support the war against France and Spain.

The Entry Books require careful study in order to avoid false trails. On the same day, 10 March 1702, two commissions were entered, one to John Brooks, gentleman, to be lieutenant to Captain Richard Nanfan in Colonel Farington's Regiment, the other to John Vanbrook, esquire, to be captain of a company in the Earl of Huntingdon's Foot, his ensign being John Harris, gentleman; this new regiment was led by the son of Vanbrugh's first commander. Clearly these two cannot relate to the same person, and Lieutenant John Brooks can in fact be traced back several years, having become an ensign in Farington's Regiment on 16 February 1694 and a lieutenant to Captain Cracherode in the same regiment on 24 December 1695. But it was to Captain John Van Brook that a successor was appointed on 15 May 1702, eleven days after the declaration of war. That really was the end of Vanbrugh's military career.

His qualifications for his new post were adequate, whatever wits and journalists like Swift might say. He was educated and well spoken, he wrote a very good hand, and he had some experience both of giving and of executing orders. It was not necessary that the Comptroller should be anything of an architect, and it is only a happy accident that Talman and Hugh May before him had each been the leading domestic designer of his generation. By 1702 Vanbrugh had made his bid to follow in this unofficial role. Wren certainly preferred his staff to have appropriate talents; he was in general not slow to recognize and use them, and he must have been impressed by the readiness of Hawksmoor, his best and most professional pupil and assistant, to work with Vanbrugh, as well as by the Castle Howard model. He may also have been charmed, as were so many others, by Vanbrugh's easy manner, engaging personality and justified self-confidence. On the other side, although on occasion Vanbrugh would not spare his criticism of the Surveyor when he felt it was justified, he developed not only respect but also what he called tenderness towards the great man.

Vanbrugh also must have acquired some knowledge of the way to run a business enterprise, from his father or other members of his family. From his later years the Account Book shows not only his capability in the complex pattern of investment among his siblings, of which he took charge, but also that care over small amounts which is proverbially the mark of good stewardship. The Account Book suggests that he may have known Shelton's method of shorthand (the same as Pepys used) although it would be foolish to fasten too much on the single phrase which appears there on three occasions and reads *my wife*.

There were no spectacular building projects in the Royal Works at this time. Whitehall was rapidly becoming the castle in the air it would for ever remain, but in the first months of her reign the Queen had ordered a new suite of apartments to be built at St James's Palace, while at Hampton Court work continued on the state rooms with the fitting up of the new

Queen's Side in Wren's east range. Vanbrugh's architectural achievement was thus to remain very largely in the private business which Crown servants were not discouraged from accepting.

When he gave evidence for Lord Carlisle against Talman in the spring of 1703 we may imagine that Vanbrugh stood up to cross-examination better than his rival. Moreover, he was able to give what is known as 'expert witness', speaking not merely as the designer of one great house but also as the holder of the same office under the Crown that had previously been occupied by the plaintiff Talman. Kneller's Kit-Cat portrait, probably painted about 1705, shows him holding a pair of dividers [1] and affecting the thoughtful gravity of a forty-year-old who has arrived; in truth the full-bottomed wig covers a very hard head, a mind as sharp as a razor, to which the distinctions between one kind of drawing and another are as clear as the language in which they are described.

In Kneller's portrait Vanbrugh also wears the badge of office of what is perhaps the most misunderstood branch of his career, heraldry, to which he began to make his entry almost exactly a year after his Works appointment. Swift, as we have seen, managed to poke fun with a facetious analogy between building houses and building dynasties, but Vanbrugh's entry into the college of Heralds earned him the displeasure of some of its older members. For he had introduced a comic herald into his play *Æsop*, he was considered to know nothing of heraldry, and he was an outsider; all these statements are true, but they need to be amplified. First, the herald Quaint in *Æsop*: if Vanbrugh had supposed six years earlier that he might become a herald, he could have argued that he was but adapting a character from the original play. Whether anything of his adaptation derives from the third Randle Holme of Chester (1627-99), heraldic painter, antiquary, genealogist, and deputy to Garter Herald in the north-west of England, is a matter of speculation. Holme was certainly a well-known figure in the Chester of Vanbrugh's boyhood, and it is his *Academy of Armory* of 1688 that records Giles Vanbrugh's coat of arms.

Secondly, Vanbrugh probably knew less about heraldry in 1703 than he did about architecture in 1699. The pages of the Account Book suggest not only that the office of Clarenceux

King of Arms was lucrative but also that he discharged it with care and efficiency as well as profit: he was a good learner. Moreover, while clichés abound concerning the dramatic sense of his architecture, it is seldom remarked that heraldry gave him official occasions to put on a costume and act a part. And a magnificent costume it was, at a cost of £185, with a gold crown, a gold collar of S's, a chain, a cap, and 'a coat of Her Majesty's arms' which made him resemble a walking shield, in gold on crimson and blue, lined with crimson satin.*

Thirdly, he was an outsider. Sir Anthony Wagner, a modern Garter Herald, although he found the appointment 'incongruous', yet described Vanbrugh as 'possibly the most distinguished man who has ever worn a herald's tabard' (Heralds of England, 1967) and that perhaps says something about the others. Clarenceux Herald was second only to Garter, and whereas entry to the Works on all but the top step may have been acceptable under Wren's liberal direction, it was a different matter in an institution with a clearly defined order of seniority, into which Vanbrugh's intrusion upset the whole ladder of expectation and promotion. Garter, Sir Thomas St George, had recently died at the age of eighty-eight, and his younger brother Sir Henry, as Clarenceux, would naturally succeed him. Lord Carlisle had the gift of these offices while he acted as Earl Marshal for his cousin the eighth Duke of Norfolk who, even on his coming of age in 1704, was disqualified as a Roman Catholic. Carlisle had met the heralds and perhaps considered them a crusty collection; certainly he showed determination in securing the post for Vanbrugh. For it was indeed not possible for an outsider to proceed directly to the office of Clarenceux, and it was convenient for him and for Vanbrugh that there was an obsolete title of Carlisle Herald which could be revived and given to him. Moreover Carlisle obtained a declaration from the Queen in Council that the Earl Marshal had the right to nominate whomsoever he thought fit for the post of Clarenceux.

Heralds are mindful of historical precedent, and those of Vanbrugh's day will have pointed to an occasion a little over a century earlier when, in October 1597, the author of Britannia,

* Appendix C

the antiquary William Camden, was made Richmond Herald
for one day in order to proceed to the office of Clarenceux,
much to the anger of Ralph Brooke, York Herald. At least Vanbrugh's elevation was less hasty. On 15 June 1703, the same
day as his letter to Newcastle about the Talman–Carlisle lawsuit, Vanbrugh wrote to Tonson that Lord Carlisle

> went homeward yesterday, with wife and children, and has
> made Ld Essex Deputy Earl Marshall; to crown that, Harry St
> George Garter, and me Herald Extraordinary (if the Queen
> pleases), in order to be Clarencieux at his return to towne; but
> whether we shall carry either point at Court, is not yet sure, tho'
> it stands home prest at this moment, and will I believe be known
> tonight.

Four weeks later he explained (13 July) that

> there was a great deal of Saucy Opposition, but my Ld Treasurer
> set the Queen right, and I have accordingly been Souc'd a
> Herald Extraordinary, in order to be a King at Winter. Ld Essex
> was left Deputy to do the feat which he did with a whole Bowle of
> wine about my ears instead of half a Spoonfull. He at the same
> time crown'd Old Sr Harry, Garter.

This was on 21 June; Vanbrugh did not 'become a King' until
March 1704. After selling his office to Knox Ward in July 1725 –
for £2500 – he told Tonson, 'That through great difficultys and
very odd oppositions from very odd folks, I got leave to dispose
in earnest, of a Place I got in jest'. This has been taken as confirmation that he was cynical or insincere about the office in
the first place, but the antithesis *between jest and earnest* is one
that he used on other occasions. Maybe not at first, but at some
time Vanbrugh came to understand the seriousness of the job.
Moreover, it would be unwise to interpret as entirely frivolous
any scheme devised jointly by Vanbrugh and Carlisle. In September 1725 Vanbrugh told Carlisle

> My Parting with that office while I am living, has made your
> Ldps Gift of it to me Still the more Valluable, and for which I
> have therefore the more Acknowledgement to return you.

The three letters to Tonson of June and July 1703 are, apart from that of Christmas Day 1699 introducing Castle Howard, the first to tell us much about Vanbrugh's circle and his activities. The first (15 June) tells in that fruit-filled week of Tonson's house at Barn Elms;* it refers to Vanbrugh's own room there with a bed in it, and a 'compass' (round) window being added. Carpenter Johns is hard at work and 'every room is chips – up to your chin'; Vanbrugh may have been responsible for the alterations, but the famous room at Barn Elms in which the Kit-Cat portraits were hung was not built until after his death and was not his work; Pope told Joseph Spence in 1730 that Tonson was building it. The second letter contains requests to Tonson, still in Amsterdam, for Vanbrugh and on behalf of Lord Halifax. The latter asks Tonson to

> bespeak him a Set of all kinds of Mathematicall Instruments, of the largest sort in Ivory, but adorn'd as curiously as you please, they being more for furniture than any use he's like to put 'em to; He designs to hang 'em up in his Library. He's tould the best in the world are made at Ams. he expects they shou'd cost a good deal of money.

Vanbrugh's own request was cheaper and more practical:

> Tis Palladio in French, wth the Plans of most of the Houses he built. there is one without the Plans, but 'tis that with 'em I would have.

Roland Fréart's translation of 1650 would have been for Vanbrugh the most useful edition of Palladio's *Quattro Libri dell' Architettura*, the most important manual for English architects from Inigo Jones in the early seventeenth century to Lord Burlington in the middle of the eighteenth. He did not know Italian, and the first complete English edition, by James (Giacomo) Leoni, did not begin to appear, in parts, until 1715. Moreover, Fréart's edition was scholarly and authentic to the point of archaism; his publisher Edme Martin managed to use the original wood blocks and a type face similar to that of the original 1570 edition. Vanbrugh's use of Palladio is a subject

* p. 126

for later consideration,* but it is important to say now that this is the only architectural book mentioned in any of his surviving letters. Tonson evidently found him a copy, because he wrote some years later that he had mislaid the book. It is also fairly clear how Vanbrugh first discovered the existence of Palladio in French: Lord Essex's copy survives, with his bookplate dated 1701, and Vanbrugh must have seen it in the library at Cassiobury on the day he was 'souc'd'.

The third letter to Tonson (30 July) is full of London gossip, but also refers to heraldic matters:

> I writ to you about a fortnight Since, and have since spoak more than once to Ld Essex for his Arms . . . I have sent you my Own Coat of Arms, and have written to Ld Carlisle for his: but if you spend much more of your time about 'em in Holland, we all resolve never to subscribe to another Book that must carry you beyond Sea.

Tonson had gone to Amsterdam to buy and commission copperplates for his huge two-volume folio publication of the works of Julius Caesar in Latin, edited by Dr Samuel Clarke of Norwich (1675-1729). This lavish and beautifully printed edition finally appeared in 1712 with a dedication to the Duke of Marlborough, embellished with pictorial initial letters and headings, and illustrated by portraits of the editor, author and dedicatee, seventy-six full- or double-page pictures of battles, primitive people and wild animals described in the text, and reproductions of the nine *Triumphs* by Mantegna then, as now, at Hampton Court. Each engraving is dedicated to a different subscriber, and includes his coat of arms, Plate 62 being Vanbrugh's. Lord Hervey paid £7. 10s. 6d. for the book in July 1712, entered in his Diary as 'Jacob's Commentaries'.

The College of Arms is not, as one might expect, in Westminster, but in the City, south of St Paul's; for the last hundred years or so it has faced Queen Victoria Street, but before that thoroughfare was constructed it stood sandwiched between St Benet's Hill on the west and St Peter's Hill on the east. Some of the Heralds lived there; Vanbrugh had no need and probably

* p. 448

no wish to do so, and in later years his lodgings were occupied
by Robert Dale, Suffolk Herald. But he will have had an office
or a desk at his disposal. Whether or not he saw anything of his
merchant cousins in Thames Street, the College required his
presence in the City from time to time.

'When a man is tired of London, he is tired of life', Dr Johnson told Boswell fifty years after Vanbrugh's death; the reason
that follows is less often quoted: 'for there is in London all that
life can afford'. In Johnson's days the concentration of interests
and facilities in London had not changed greatly from those of
Pepys's time a century earlier, and while it might be convenient to travel by water or by coach almost all business and
social calls could still be made easily on foot, taking in one's
favourite tavern or coffee-house on the way. What is exceptional about Pepys is not where he went but the fact that, as
Robert Hooke did in the decade after him, he kept a record of it.
Much of Sir Christopher Wren's surveyorship of almost fifty
years was based on the territory between Whitehall and his
house in Scotland Yard at one end and St Paul's and the City
churches at the other, with occasional excursions to Kensington, Greenwich, Hampton Court, Windsor, and even less
often to Oxford, Cambridge, or Winchester. But Wren seems
not to have been fond of travelling.

As the Account Book and his letters show, Vanbrugh travelled a good deal and probably enjoyed it, going several times
to south-west England and in most years to the North. He drove
a calash, a light two-wheeled carriage with a removable fol-
ding hood which was, allowing for the drawbacks of hired
horses, the equivalent of a sports car, and in December 1718 he
told Lord Newcastle that his driving was 'none of the Slowest'.
In his later years he owned several vehicles of quite diverse
character. Four weeks after his death his widow recorded in
the Account Book the receipt of sixteen guineas for the sale of
some of these: 'for a chariot a calash a travelling caridge for a
coach & harness for 4 horses'; perhaps the low price not only
indicates a desire for a quick sale but also suggests that these
conveyances were no longer in prime condition. Although it is
not clear whether there were four of them or only three, the
calash was certainly distinct from the four-wheeled chariot.
Like his uncle William, Vanbrugh developed a taste for rural

life, building himself a second home at Esher in 1709-10 and later renting and then building houses at Greenwich. In the early days of his Comptrollership Vanbrugh's usual circuit began at Whitehall and extended, taking in the theatres at Lincoln's Inn Fields and Drury Lane, as far as the College of Arms; he also visited Kensington as a matter of course, and the 1703 letters tell of dining at Windsor and Hampton Court on occasions which combined the serious and the frivolous interests of the Kit-Cat circle.

When he went up to Barn Elms on 14 June 1703 it was by river, and 'under a tylt (as everybody has done that has gone by water these three weeks, for the Devils in the sky)'. A tilt was specifically an awning over a boat, and it was a wet devil rather than a fiery one; a day earlier Evelyn had written of

raines . . . so greate, continual, & unseasonable, as have hardly ben known in the memory of any alive; The weather now neere Midsomer cold & so Wet, as threatens a famine, after our murmuring at the Cheapnesse of Corne.

But the English weather was as unaccountable then as it is now: a week later it was still variable and endangering the hay harvest, but in another week it was 'tollerably seasonable', and on 11 July, as Vanbrugh told Tonson two days later,

We remember'd you . . . at Hampton Court, as we were sopping our Arses in the Fountain for you must know we have got some warm weather at last, a Week ago I was in furs still, and so were most Folks; but the Farmers are like to be all undone for all that; for in spight of this bantering ill Season, they are likely to have a Swinging Crop at last; terrible complaints they make about it; they don't say 'twill produce a Famine, but they say 'twill ruin the Nation.

For once Vanbrugh draws a picture that outdoes anything on the stage, of three mature gentlemen (the other two seem to have been Congreve and Lord Halifax) letting down their breeches to cool off over the rim of the fountain basin. But more bad weather was to follow, culminating in the 'Great Storm' which swept the south of England on Friday and Saturday 26 and 27 November 1703.

A great wind came from the south-west, accompanied by thunderstorms. Orchards were destroyed, many thousands of oak trees were felled in the New Forest and the Forest of Dean, their roots often raising huge mounds of earth as they were wrenched out of the ground. Many of the surviving trees in agricultural areas were festooned with the remains of hay-stacks caught up in the whirlwind. Church spires were blown down, and in the City pinnacles were taken off some of the new churches and the roof works of the still unfinished St Paul's were damaged. Houses lost their roofs or were even blown down, and the sheet-lead roofs of churches were rolled up by the gale. Falls of soot were everywhere, and at Wells the Bishop and his wife were killed as they lay in bed when a chimney stack collapsed on them. In the Channel many ships were sunk or damaged and sailors drowned. London was filled with rubbish of all kinds, while the centre of Bristol was clogged with wrecked ships raised from the port basin by the combined forces of high wind and high tide. Congreve wrote to a friend that at Whitehall some of the big sash-windows, only recently installed in the Banqueting House, were sucked out and blown away.

Outside Plymouth Sound, on the Eddystone Rocks, the storm took both the new lighthouse and its inventor, Henry Win-stanley, who also has a calmer place in architectural history. He was born at Saffron Walden, Essex, and was for many years Clerk of Works at Audley End, the great Jacobean house nearby which between 1669 and 1701 belonged to the Crown.* It was during his years there that Winstanley made a series of large engravings of the palace, which he collected together with a dedication to James II in 1688, and which are important documents for the history of the house. Winstanley was also the inventor of the Water Theatre in Piccadilly, which remained in business for some years after his death. This was a series of indoor fountains with many jets, and figures of sea-gods, nymphs, and so forth, presented in a succession of staged arrangements. But in 1696 Winstanley agreed with the Corporation of Trinity House to build a lighthouse on Eddystone, to his own design. In June 1697 he was carried off by a French

* p. 331

privateer and the work destroyed; he was soon exchanged, and began all over again. The structure was finished by 1700, and on the day of the storm the unfortunate designer had gone out to supervise some repairs. A few years later, in 1708, Vanbrugh would work at Audley End, but there is another family connection with Eddystone through the Carletons: that same year, 1708, a new lighthouse was opened, built by Colonel John Lovett, the brother-in-law of Vanbrugh's first cousin Edward Pearce and the uncle of the architect Sir Edward Lovett Pearce. Lovett's lighthouse was of sounder construction, but like its precursor it was mainly built of wood and it burned down in 1755.

On 16 December 1703 the Society for the Promotion of Christian Knowledge debated whether the staging of Shakespeare's *The Tempest* at Lincoln's Inn Fields on 1 December had been 'proper or seasonable'. We might say today that it was a gesture of defiance, especially as the scribblers were already at work. 10 December is the date of *Dissuasive from the Play-House, in a Letter to a Person of Quality, Occasioned By the Late Calamity of the TEMPEST*; the pamphlet was actually published, with two others in similar vein, in time to be handed free of charge to Londoners as they came out of church on 19 January 1704, the public fast day appointed by the Queen after the disaster. The author of the *Dissuasive* was Jeremy Collier, who perhaps predictably interpreted the storm as 'a sad instance of God's judgements'. He was also outraged because there had been a performance of *Macbeth* at Drury Lane on the very night of 27 November. John Dennis produced a long but amusing reply, pointing out that as a judgement the storm was both singularly ill timed, since it had waited until the stage had already undergone considerable reformation, and also ill placed, since it had continued on its path of destruction to 'the very Innocent. Not only the poor Inhabitants of *Cologn*, but the very *Hamburgers* and *Dantzickers*, and all the People of the *Baltick*.'

The year 1703 saw Vanbrugh failing to interest Lord Newcastle in his design for a new house at Welbeck. Talman had written to the Duke on 17 April, a few days before setting out for Welbeck, explaining his recourse to the law:

I am sorry to have the occation of suing any Person, but iff right

is not to be had without I must submitt to what is most contrary
to my inclinations to obtaine itt. Iff I undertake Your Grace's
Buildings I shall act as an honest Man iff not Your Grace shall
have noe Reason to complane off me.

Vanbrugh must have felt that Talman's arguments, if not his
designs, were persuasive; otherwise he would not have put so
much effort into his account of the lawsuit and the catalogue of
those who had met with 'vexations' from his rival.* But in dis-
suading Newcastle from employing Talman he seems to have
put him off the idea of building altogether. The surviving
drawing he sent to the Duke is of such importance in the
development of Vanbrugh's architecture that it is better considered in the context of a later chapter.†

The only Vanbrugh letter that is securely dated in 1704 is one
which he wrote in his capacity as Comptroller, to Godolphin,
the Lord Treasurer who had appointed him. Once again
Talman was involved, although only indirectly through his
favourite mason Benjamin Jackson, but the letter also concerns Vanbrugh's relationship to Wren, the superior upon
whom it was his function in theory to act as a control.

In the course of examining the Works accounts for the year
ended on 31 March 1698, it occurred to Edward Harley, Auditor
of Imprests and younger brother of Lord Oxford, that the
allowances claimed in them had no adequate authority in law.
For the instructions to the officers of the Works, issued in 1663,
had automatically lapsed on the death of King Charles II and
had not been renewed or replaced. In July 1705, therefore, the
Treasury ordered the preparation of new instructions, which
were issued on 12 October. In general they confirmed the procedures and authorities of the 1663 orders which themselves
were copied from the very practical and sensible orders of
1609. No doubt Wren was aware of an irregularity of twenty
years' standing, but then it might be said that Wren had, after
all, taken up architecture – and become a great architect – because he was more interested in things that worked than in the
theoretical bases underlying their working. The same might

* p. 208
† p. 273

be said of Vanbrugh, but he was over thirty years younger than the Surveyor and undoubtedly anxious to justify the confidence so recently placed in him.

The chief innovation of the new instructions was a paragraph to the effect that in future officers of the Works were not to undertake any Crown building works themselves, or to have any advantage either directly or indirectly from such works; they were only to oversee such works as were entrusted to their particular care and inspection. The penalty for infringement was to be dismissal. This affected the Queen's Master Mason and Master Carpenter as members of the managing board of the Office of Works. By a tradition of centuries they had been able, like other royal warrant-holders, to carry on their trades in contracts for the Crown; now they were placed at a disadvantage. As was observed in 1713, 'no Artificer of any repute or consideration would quit his Trade and business for the Office-salary and allowance'. Their presence on the managing board, on the other hand, which put them in the position of both supervised and supervisors, dated only from a reorganization of the board in 1564. Nevertheless successive royal masons and carpenters seem to have exercised this anomalous privilege for 140 years before anyone considered seriously that it might be to the disadvantage of the Crown.

The person to whom this at last occurred seems to have been Vanbrugh, who mentioned it to Godolphin almost a year before the new instructions were ordered. He wrote to Godolphin on 9 November 1704, suggesting that 'a long Letter may easilyor find a convenient time of being read; than a Long Speech of being heard', but the substance of his claim – which in fact was erroneous – was already known to the recipient:

> Before I acquainted yr L'dship this Summer with that shamefull abuse in the Board of Works; of those very officers doing the Work themselves, who rec'd Sallarys from the Queen to prevent her being imposed on by Others; I made severall attempts upon Sr Chr. Wren to perswade him to redress it himself without troubling yr Lordship; putting him in mind; that besides its being utterly against common Sense, it was contrary to an Express Direction to the Board upon the Establishment after the Restoration. He always own'd what I urg'd him to was right . . . but when I press'd him to the execution, he still evaded it, and

that so many times, that at last I saw he never intended it, and so I gave your L'dship the trouble of a Complaint.

Your Lordship was pleas'd upon it to send us a Letter, in as express Terms as it could be penn'd, that no such thing for the future should be Suffer'd.

Vanbrugh was mistaken, common sense or not, because the clause is not in the 1663 instructions. However, he was not concerned merely with a matter of principle but also with a specific instance. Work began in July 1704 on the new greenhouse or Orangery at Kensington; how far Vanbrugh was involved in the design of this fine building is a question to be examined in a subsequent chapter,* but he was, for whatever reason, taking a particular interest in it. He discovered, by asking questions, that the stonework was being undertaken by Jackson, who usually worked on Talman's outside commissions and had been appointed King's Master Mason in December 1701 on the death of John Oliver. The Orangery is mainly built of brick, with stone dressings, and although it has a stone floor and is fronted by a Portland stone terrace the amount of mason's work involved was relatively small. But Vanbrugh pestered Wren until the Surveyor agreed to place the work with another mason, Thomas Hill, whose firm had worked at Kensington for some years as well as at Hampton Court, St Paul's, and elsewhere. It may indeed have been the small size of the contract involved that prompted its allocation to Jackson rather than an independent mason in the first place.

Hill was reluctant to start on the Orangery; Vanbrugh asked more questions and discovered that Hill was 'frighten'd with some hints of what shou'd befall him if he durst meddle with the Master Masons business'. Vanbrugh then went back again to Wren, who 'said the Man was a Whimsicall Man, and a piece of an Astrologer, and would Venture upon nothing till he had consulted the Starrs ... I desir'd he would employ Somebody that was less Superstitious which he said he wou'd.' The next day Vanbrugh went away on his summer trip to Castle Howard; on his return he found a mason named Palmer, who turned out to be Jackson's deputy. When taxed with the matter

* p. 291

the Surveyor told Vanbrugh that 'Jackson wou'd not be quiet without he let him do the work'.

The affair was still under discussion by the Treasury Board in July 1705, but Jackson managed to retain the post of Master Mason until his death in 1719, when he was succeeded by an engineer, Nicholas Dubois, thus ending the succession of practical masons in the office. Vanbrugh's opinion, if perhaps coloured, was certainly unequivocal:

> As for Jackson my Lord, Besides this Crime the highest the nature of his Office will admit of I must acquaint your L'dship He is so Villainous a Fellow and so Scandalous in every part of his Character; and that in the unanimous opinion of all Sorts of People and to everybody that is oblig'd to be concern'd with him.

Vanbrugh told the Treasury Board that Jackson had used a deputy named Kidwell. The next garden building at Kensington was the large pedimented alcove or summer house which originally stood south of the palace but was later rebuilt at the north end of the Serpentine River; in 1706 over £500 was paid for work on it to a mason named John Smoute. In the later seventeenth century *smout* was trade slang for a casual substitute worker, especially in the printing trade, and it is not difficult to imagine that the use of this otherwise unrecorded name was another of Jackson's tricks.

At the time of the Orangery incident Wren was seventy-two; he would officially remain Surveyor for another fourteen years until his dismissal in 1718 as a result of political and personal animosity. Wren was undoubtedly stronger in mind than in body, and these years were clouded by a series of allegations of incompetence, prejudice, irregularity and weakness. In the latter part of their association Vanbrugh developed a protective attitude towards his venerable chief, but in 1704 he was frank:

> As for Sr Chr. Wren I don't in the least believe he has any Interest in his part of it; but yr L'dship will see by this decisive proof the power those Fellows have over him wch they never made so effectual a use of as when they prevail'd with him (against your L'dships Directions) to let 'em have a Clerk of the Works of Whitehall, whom he himself own'd but a Week before he cou'd put no trust in: one who by nature is a very poor

Wretch; and by a many years regular Course of morning Drunckenesses, has made himself a dos'd Sott.

It has been supposed that this was Leonard Gammon, who for many years (and until his death in 1713) held the clerkship at Whitehall. However, Vanbrugh writes as if the appointment had been made in Godolphin's period of office as Lord Treasurer, and in the absence of any other evidence in official papers of Gammon's misconduct or inadequacy it would be wiser to remove this slur from his character to some other, unknown, person whose far briefer career in the Works has left no other resonances.

Before the end of 1704 Vanbrugh had embarked on two other great enterprises. On 18 April the foundation stone was laid, preliminary site work being well advanced, of the new Queen's Theatre in the Haymarket; at Christmas time, on a casual meeting at the Drury Lane playhouse, the Duke of Marlborough 'told him he designed to build a house in Woodstock Park . . . and further said he must consult [Vanbrugh] about the design'. In their different ways the theatre in the Haymarket and the theatre of Blenheim would for over a decade try both his ingenuity and his patience to the full, and to the end of his life he would never be entirely free of them.

22

Towards a New Theatre

Anne R.

WHEREAS We have thought fitt for the better reforming the Abuses, and Immoral[i]ty of the Stage That a New Company of Comedians should be Establish'd for our Service, under stricter Governmt and Regulations than have been formerly

We therefore reposing especiall trust, and confidence in Our Trusty and Welbeloved John Vanbrugh and Willm. Congreve Esqs. for the due Execution, and performance of this our Will and Pleasure, do Give and Grant unto them the sd. John Vanbrugh, and Willm. Congreve full power and Authority to form, constitu[t]e, and Establish for Us, a Company of Comedians with full and free License to Act & Represent in any Convenient Place, during Our Pleasure all Comedys, Tragedys, Plays, Interludes Operas, and to perform all other Theatricall and Musicall Entertainmts Whatsoevr and to Settle such Rules and Orders for the good Govermt of the said Company, as the Chamberlain of our Household shall from time to time direct and approve of.

When this licence was issued by Henry Grey, Earl of Kent, on 14 December 1704, less than seven years had passed since Collier's *Short View*, and only twelve months since his return to the fight in the wake of the Great Storm. Since the ostensible reason for the new licence was the establishment of a repertory company effectively controlled and purged of smut and profanity (of which the licence makes no mention), the choice of two of Collier's principal targets as its managers seems curious. Congreve had given up writing plays after *The Way of The World* (1700) and Vanbrugh had turned to adaptations, but neither had done public penance for the sins with which Collier had charged them. The most versatile genius cannot make more than twenty-four hours in the day, and although Congreve seems to have settled for the quieter life of such administrative backwaters as the Commission for Hackney Carriages, Vanbrugh still aspired to change rather than to rest.

The real reason behind the issue of the licence was that Vanbrugh was building a new theatre in the Haymarket, to be known as the Queen's Theatre and to be managed by himself and Congreve. In order to be managed it required a licence, in accordance with the legal fiction that the players were Her Majesty's servants. And whereas Collier would have reformed the stage in order to abolish it, the new licence, like the patents issued to the early Restoration companies, embodied the idea that the stage should be supported in order to reform it. According to Colley Cibber the third manager was to be Betterton, who had not made a great success of his company since its breakaway to Lincoln's Inn Fields in 1695; but 'when this House was finish'd' Betterton and his fellow actors dissolved their agreement and 'threw themselves upon the Direction of Sir *John Vanbrugh and Mr Congreve*'.

Vanbrugh had told Tonson on 15 June 1703,

> I have finished my purchase for the Playhouse, and all the tenants will be out by Midsummer-day; so then I lay the corner stone; and tho' the season be thus far advanced, have pretty good assurance I shall be ready for business at Christmas.

On 13 July he wrote further:

> Mr Wms has finish'd all the writings for the ground for the Playhouse they will be engross'd and I believe Sign'd on friday or Satterday; wch done, I have all things ready to fall to work on Munday. The ground is the second Stable Yard going up the Haymarket. I give 2000 for it, but have lay'd such a Scheme of matters, that I shall be reimburs'd every penny of it, by the Spare ground; but this is a Secret lest they shou'd lay hold on't, to lower the Rent. I have drawn a design for the whole disposition of the inside, very different from any Other House in being, but I

have the good fortune to have it absolutely approv'd by all that have seen it.

Vanbrugh perhaps had still to learn that optimism by itself will only carry a project so far. The site was the subject of legal wrangles with the owner of the houses occupying most of the Haymarket frontage, which were not settled until the summer of 1704. Although Vanbrugh had originally intended to demolish them he decided that the rent or the accommodation they could provide might be more valuable than a wide open approach to the highway. Work in the 1703 building season was' thus limited to site clearance and foundations, and the theatre took three times as long to build as its designer had hoped.

In the early stages Vanbrugh sank undisclosed sums of his own money into the new building, and he seems to have been the driving force behind the whole project. The conclusion of Judith Milhous, its most recent historian, that he saw it as a means of re-uniting the London companies, is the more convincing because it accords with Vanbrugh's character as a reformer in whatever area he entered. Nevertheless the new theatre was certainly viewed at the time as a Kit-Cat venture. Tonson was evidently party to events from the start, and some of the contemporary satires on the club imply that groups of its members could often be seen and identified as parties at the playhouses. The Kit-Cat Club was to be a major source both of moral support and at least of financial promises. Cibber saw the foundation stone laid – by the Duke of Somerset on 18 April 1704 according to an inscription discovered during repairs in 1825; on the same stone, says Cibber, 'was inscrib'd *The Little Whig*, in Honour to a Lady of extraordinary Beauty, then the celebrated Toast, and Pride of the Party'. This suggests that a less friendly account, published a month after the opening of the playhouse, is substantially correct. The Jacobite journalist Charles Leslie wrote in *The Rehearsal of Observator*, No. 41 (5/12 May 1705):

The Kit-Cat Club is now grown *Famous* and *Notorious*, all over the *Kingdom*. And they have Built a *Temple* for their *Dagon*, the new *Play-house*, in the *Hay-Market*. The *Foundation* was laid with great *Solemnity*, by a Noble Babe of *Grace*. And over or

under the *Foundation Stone* is a Plate of *Silver*, on which is
Graven *Kit Cat* on the one side, and *Little Whigg* on the other.
This is in *Futuram rei Memoriam*, that after *Ages* may know by
what *Worthy Hands*, and for what good *Ends* this stately *Fabrick*
was Erected. And there was such *Zeal* shew'd, and all *Purses*
open to carry on their Work, that it was almost as soon *Finish'd*
as *Begun*. While *Paul's* Work [the still domeless cathedral] is
become a Proverb.

The 'Little Whig' was the twenty-year-old Lady Anne, second
daughter of the Duke of Marlborough and wife of the third Earl
of Sunderland, the son of William III's drawling Lord Chamberlain. Cibber states that Vanbrugh raised a subscription
from thirty persons of quality at £100 each; a note in Vanbrugh's autograph in the Portland Papers (Nottingham University Library) refers to a hundred guineas, to be paid in four
equal stages between the signing of the lease to the ground and
the roofing of the building, and confirms that the privilege
offered to those who completed their subscriptions was that 'of
seeing all Plays and Operas Gratis'. This note carries a list of
twenty-nine names: twenty-five are peers, thirteen are known
Kit-Cats, including Lords Essex, Halifax, and Manchester, and
three are Berties (Vanbrugh's friends Robert and Peregrine
and Lord Abingdon). The thirtieth was perhaps to be either
Congreve or Vanbrugh himself. One payment of £25 from Lord
Carlisle is recorded in those of his accounts that survive, and
the Portland (Harley) Papers in the British Library include an
agreement with the Duke of Newcastle, signed by Vanbrugh
and Congreve, and dated 8 May 1704, as well as Vanbrugh's
receipt of the following day for the first payment. Three out of
four payments are recorded in the diary of Lord Hervey, later
Earl of Bristol, who is not known to have been a Kit-Cat
although he was a confirmed Whig; no doubt other payments
are hidden in archives. Defoe devoted a whole four-page issue
of the *Review* (No. 26, 3 May 1705) to attacking the new playhouse with a vehemence that must have pleased Collier, if
with a coarseness that could not have done so. He suggested,
both in prose and in verse, that the building was under-
subscribed:

The Fabrick's Finish'd, and the Builder's part

▲ 3. Castle Howard. South front.

▼ 4. Hawksmoor's drawing of the bow room.

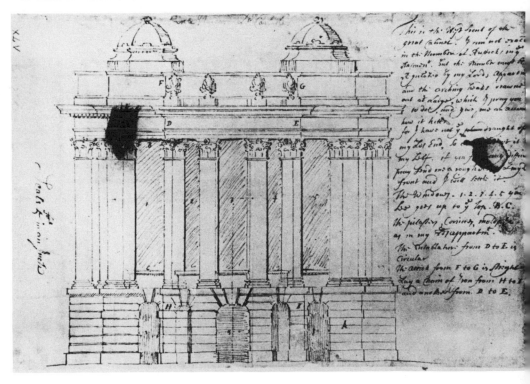

▲ 5. Castle Howard from the north.

▼ 6. Castle Howard. Bird's eye view.

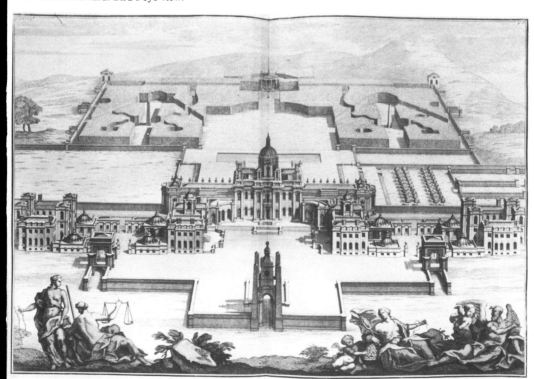

▶ 7. Robert Smythson.
Wollaton.

▼ 8. William Talman.
Chatsworth.
South front.

▼ 9. Hawksmoor.
Easton Neston.
West front.

10. Burley-on-the-Hill. North front. ▲

► 11. William Talman.
Drayton. Hall front.

▼ 12. Hawksmoor. Kensington Palace.
The Orangery.

▲ 13. Le Vau. Paris. Collège des Quatre Nations.

▲ 14. Vincennes. North side.

▼ 15. Vincennes. The castle from the south, c.1700.

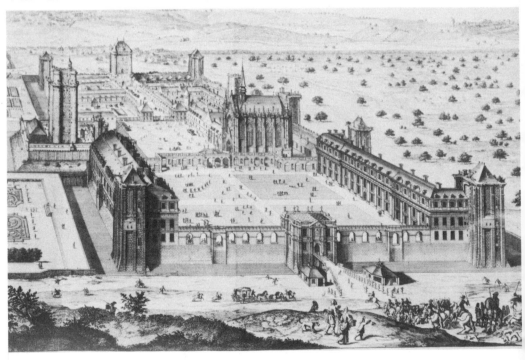

▲ 16. Old Woodstock Manor, *c.*1700 (British Library).

▲ 17. Blenheim. East gate.

▼ 18. Blenheim. North court.

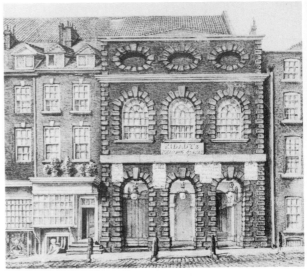

▲ 19. The bust of Louis XIV.

▲ 20. The Haymarket Theatre (British Museum).

▲ 22. Kimbolton Castle. West front.

▶ 23. A stage set
at the Haymarket
Theatre (British
Museum).

◀ 21. Blenheim.
The Hall.

▲ 24. Claremont, *c*.1750. (Royal Library, Windsor Castle).

▼ 25. Castle Howard, Pyramid Gate.

▼ 26. Vanbrugh Castle. South front.

▲ 27. Lumley Castle. West front.

▼ 28. Kings Weston. South front.

▲ 29.
Seaton Delaval.
North court.

◀ 30. Blenheim
Gateway to the
kitchen court.

▲31. Eastbury. Entrance front.

▼32. Seaton Delaval from the south-west.

Grimsthorpe Castle
◀ 33. The hall.

▼ 34. North-east pavilion.

▼ 35. Door to chapel.

The Garden front of Grimsthorp in the County of Lincoln the Seat of his Grace the Duke of Ancaster and Kesteven Hereditary Lord great Chamberlain of England. Design'd by Sr. John Vanbrugh K.

1723

▲ 36. Grimsthorpe.
Design for
south front, 1723.

▶ 38. Castle Howard.
The Temple.

▼ 37. Skelbrooke.
Robin Hood's Well.

▶ 39. Vanbrugh *c*.1719.
Attributed to
Thomas Murray
(National Portrait Gallery).

▼ 40. Blenheim.
The Bridge.

Has shown the Reformation of his Art.
Bless'd with Success, thus have their first Essays
Reform'd their *Buildings*, not *Reform'd* their *Plays* ...

Never was Charity so Ill Employ'd,
Vice so Discourag'd, Vertue so Destroy'd;
Never Foundation so abruptly laid,
So Much Subscrib'd and yet so little Paid.

Nevertheless the persistent financial troubles of the theatre seem to have stemmed from more than the default of sub-scribers.

Not long before this time [wrote Cibber], the *Italian* Opera began first to steal into *England*; but in as rude a Disguise, and unlike it self, as possible, in a lame, hobling Translation, into our own Language, with false Quantities, or metre out of Measure, to its original Notes, sung by our own unskilful Voices, with Graces misapply'd to almost every Sentiment, and with Action, lifeless and unmeaning, through every Character.

Opera is an Italian word, whose basic meaning is work, and as a work of entertainment it was an Italian invention. Evelyn described an opera he saw in Rome devised by the great sculp-tor, architect, and designer Bernini in 1644, and on 5 January 1674 he witnessed in London 'an *Italian Opera* in musique, the first that had ben in *England* of this kind'. This was probably a run-through of a French work, *Ariane, ou le Mariage de Bacchus*, with words by Pierre Perrin and music by Louis Grabu, eventually staged at Drury Lane on 30 March. There seems to have been a distinction in Evelyn's mind between this and Davenant's works, one of which he had seen, rather un-willingly, on 5 May 1659 and described as 'a new *Opera* after the *Italian* way in *Recitative, Music & Sceanes*'. The art-form was more clearly defined by Dryden in the Preface to *Albion and Albanius*, written in collaboration with Grabu and finally staged at Dorset Garden on 3 June 1685. Opera was, wrote Dry-den, 'a poetical Tale or Fiction, represented by Vocal and In-strumental Musick, adorn'd with Scenes, Machines and Dan-cing'. The best – and best known – English operas of the seventeenth century were by the undisputed genius of the age,

Henry Purcell: *Dido and Æneas* and *King Arthur*. The hour-long *Dido*, with words by Nahum Tate, was apparently first performed at (rather than by) Josiah Priest's boarding school for young ladies in Chelsea in the summer of 1689. *King Arthur*, produced at Dorset Garden in May 1691, belonged to a category for which Roger North coined the name 'semi-opera', separating spoken scenes from sung ones; here Purcell set – and often altered – a libretto written by Dryden several years earlier.

If Purcell, who was only five years older than Vanbrugh, had not died at the age of thirty-six, the history of opera in London would undoubtedly have been very different, and Handel, arriving in 1710, would have found himself continuing rather than initiating a tradition of first-rate musical works for the stage. By Handel's time the *Italian* opera had become identified as one in which singers and librettists, and some of the composers, were Italian; the first work of this kind to be staged in London was *Arsinoe, Queen of Cyprus* (Drury Lane, 16 January 1705). This was precisely the sort of hobbling polyglot concoction described by Cibber, for the singers were English, the words were translated from Italian, probably by Peter Motteux, and the music was arranged by Thomas Clayton, a member of the royal band in the reign of King William, from a string of songs he had recently collected in Italy.

It was in response to this work that Joseph Addison produced an *English* opera, *Rosamond* (Drury Lane, 4 March 1707), also with music by Clayton; according to contemporaries it was the poverty of Clayton's invention that sank the work after three nights. The last attempt at an English grand opera for many years was *Calypso and Telemachus*, with words by John Hughes and music by John Galliard, first given at the Haymarket Theatre on 17 May 1712. The cast was a mixed one: Proteus was sung by Leveridge, but the part of Calypso was taken by 'Signora Margarita', the soprano Margarita de l'Épine; she had come to London in 1692 with the German Jakob Greber, with whom she lived for many years, being known as 'Greber's Peg'. This was the context in which, in Cibber's words,

To strike in, therefore, with this prevailing Novelty, Sir *John*

Vanbrugh and Mr *Congreve*, open'd their new *Hay-Market Theatre*, with a translated Opera, to *Italian* Musick.

If Vanbrugh's new theatre had been available earlier he might have secured *Arsinoe* to open it. In fact the building was first used for a concert, about the end of November 1704; this was attended by Queen Anne (as *The Diverting Post*, 25 Nov. – 2 Dec. reported), and this occasion probably explains her absence from the opening operatic production the following spring. Congreve had written to a friend on 3 February 1705, 'I know not when the house will open, nor what we shall begin withal; but I believe with no opera.' Nevertheless the theatre officially opened, on Easter Monday, 9 April, with an opera, *The Loves of Ergasto* by Greber, who appropriately italicized his first name to Giacomo. The principal singers were newly imported from Italy, and the libretto (whose author is unknown) was printed with alternate pages in Italian and English for the benefit of an audience unused to the Italian tongue. The performance was framed by a prologue and epilogue, spoken by Mrs Bracegirdle and written respectively by Sir Samuel Garth and Congreve. Cibber says that the opera (which he misidentified) ran for three nights and was moderately well attended; the five nights for which other sources say it ran may include the two performances later in the month.

By the end of the season on 29 June there had been thirty-one further performances of sixteen plays, most of them accompanied – to the distaste of critics like Dennis – by music, singing or dancing. Some productions were brought by the company from Lincoln's Inn Fields, where they had been in the repertory; only *The Conquest of Spain* by Mary Griffith Pix was entirely new, though several other plays were advertised as the first performances for several years. Two were by Beaumont and Fletcher and three, more or less adapted to contemporary taste, were from Shakespeare. The season ended in a blaze of travesty with three performances of Congreve's *Love for Love* by an all-female cast; it had been less of a failure than might be concluded from Cibber, whose memory tended to the detriment of the Haymarket Theatre. But the managers' optimism was misplaced: neither the novelty of the building and its location nor the rather confused and eclectic policy of direction succeeded in building an adequate allegiance among the London public.

From July until the end of October 1705, spanning the summer recess, Betterton's company were back at Lincoln's Inn Fields, and the Queen's Theatre was closed; the original opening, so long awaited, had yet been premature, with the contractors' men still inside, and that extra time was needed for the finishing touches. *The Daily Courant* for 19 July 1705 reported that the comedy would continue to perform at Lincoln's Inn Fields 'till Her Majesty's Theatre in the Hay-Market be intirely finish'd'. Vanbrugh, preoccupied though he was that summer and autumn with the start of Blenheim, made his own contribution to the theatre with two new adaptations, *The Confederacy*, based on Dancourt's *Les Bourgeoises à la Mode*, and *The Mistake*, a close prose translation of Molière's *Le Dépit Amoureux*, first produced in 1656. And it was with *The Confederacy* that the theatre re-opened on 30 October, running for five nights. During the period up to 26 December there were thirty-eight further houses, including on that day the eighth performance of *The Confederacy*. It was a popular play, but neither its success nor the production of *The Mistake* (six nights from 27 December to 2 January) could make the new theatre into a wild success. Vanbrugh's difficulties were only augmented by Congreve's resignation at the end of the year, leaving him with sole responsibility for the management.

Audiences are fickle and lazy, and many a good production has failed for, apparently, no better reason than that it was in the wrong place at the wrong time. The new West End was close to Whitehall, St James's Palace, and the court suburb that still shares the name of that palace with its parish church in Piccadilly. But it was over half a mile from Drury Lane, and from anywhere to the east it seemed to be on the edge of town. This was one of three reasons offered by Cibber forty years later for public coolness towards the new Queen's Theatre:

for at that time it had not the Advantage of almost a large City, which has since been built, in its Neighbourhood: Those costly Spaces of *Hanover*, *Grosvenor*, and *Cavendish* Squares, with the many, and great adjacent Streets about them, were then all but so many green Fields of Pasture, from whence they could draw

little, or no Substance, unless it were that of a Milk-Diet. The
City, the Inns of Court, and the middle Part of the Town, which
were the most constant Support of a Theatre, and chiefly to be
rely'd on, were now too far, out of the Reach of an easy Walk;
and Coach-hire is often too hard a Tax, upon the Pit, and gallery.
But from the vast Increase of the Buildings I have mention'd, the
Situation of that Theatre has since that Time receiv'd consider-
able Advantages: a new World of People of Condition are nearer
to it, than formerly, and I am of the Opinion, that if the auditory
Part were a little more reduc'd to the Model of that in *Drury-
Lane*, an excellent Company of Actors would now, find a better
Account in it, than in any other House in this populous City.

Thus Cibber's second and far more significant reason is that
the auditorium was, even in 1740, too large to be easily filled.
Although he does not say so, this was less a matter of economic
overheads than of psychology, because a house half full is also
half empty, and profits depend on the floating part of the public
who are attracted by reports of a full house. Although in the
exceptional circumstances of a benefit performance for
Handel on 28 March 1738 an observer estimated the house at
1300 persons, the comfortable capacity has been calculated as
about 900, as against 600 or 700 at Drury Lane.

Neverthless the vastness of Vanbrugh's theatre, on which
many writers have remarked, was partly illusory. Much of the
greatly increased external size of the building was due to the
front-of-house and other ancillary spaces and to the large
assembly room that ran along the west edge of the site; nevertheless the theatre itself was significantly larger than that of
Drury Lane. In an engineer's terms of cubic capacity the auditorium alone was about twice that of Drury Lane, taking the
width as 60 feet, depth from gallery back to pit front as 46, and
height from pit to ceiling as 41, against figures at Drury Lane of
51, 33 and 33. And especially in its original form the interior of
Vanbrugh's playhouse did appear – as he must have meant it to
appear – bigger and better than any previous London theatre.
But the architecture itself of the playhouse is Cibber's third
reason for its failure:

As to their other dependence, the House, they had not yet discover'd, that almost every proper Quality, and Convenience of a

good Theatre had been sacrific'd, or neglected, to show the
Spectator a vast, triumphal Piece of Architecture! And that the
best Play, for the Reasons I am going to offer, could not but be
under greater Disadvantages, and be less capable of delighting
the Auditor, here, than it could have been in the plain Theatre
they came from. For what could their vast Columns, their guil-
ded Cornices, their immoderate high Roofs avail, when scarce
one Word in ten, could be distinctly heard in it? Nor had it, then,
the Form, it now stands in, which Necessity, two or three Years
after reduc'd it to: At the first opening it, the flat Cieling, that is
now over the Orchestre, was then a Semi-oval Arch, that sprung
fifteen Feet higher from above the Cornice: The Cieling over the
Pit too, was still more rais'd, being one level Line from the
highest back part of the upper Gallery, to the Front of the Stage:
The Front-boxes were a continued Semicircle, to the bare Walls
of the House on each Side . . . The Tone of a Trumpet, or the
Swell of an Eunuch's holding Note, 'tis true, might be sweeten'd
by it; but the articulate Sounds of a speaking Voice were
drown'd, by the hollow Reverberations of one Word upon another.

In consequence, even Vanbrugh's admirable adaptations

> however well executed, came to the Ear in the same un-
> distinguished Utterance, by which almost all their Plays had
> equally suffer'd: For what few could plainly hear, it was not
> likely a great many could applaud.

[23] The appearance of the great half-oval arch is probably recorded in a scene design by an Italian hand in the Burney Collection (British Museum); it cannot have risen fifteen feet above
[21] the cornice as Cibber says, because the top of the cornice was
only ten feet from the main ceiling. Nevertheless the crown of
the arch was about thirty-three feet above the stage and the opening door about forty feet wide: compared with the great arch
in the Hall at Blenheim that frames the doorway to the Saloon,
it was about the same height but twice as wide. This 'piece of
architecture' was, like most of the interior, executed in wood
and plaster, and some of its decorative features were probably
painted in *trompe-l'oeil*. It seems to have been the first true
proscenium *arch* in England, for previous openings had been
rectangular; Vanbrugh's vision of a dramatic arched frame for

the stage looked forward to the future of playhouse architecture, but after only three years its visual splendour was sac-
rificed in the cause of auditory improvement.

At the Queen's Theatre the scene-stage and vista-stage
(those parts behind the arch) extended back about forty-five **[J]**
feet, or twenty feet further than at Drury Lane. These figures
exclude the rooms at the back of both stages which, although
in theory potential extensions of the vista-stage, were of little
use because of the narrow sight-lines they offered the
audience; nevertheless the increased depth allowed more elaborate scenic perspectives to be envisaged. The forestage originally extended about equally far in both theatres, although
both were reduced in depth for reasons that were distinct from,
but consonant with, the eighteenth-century abandonment of
the forestage. Almost all the action was gradually withdrawn
from that spatially and dramatically ambiguous area and taken
within and behind the proscenium arch.

J Reconstruction of the Haymarket Theatre. The hatched portion of the stage
was removed in 1708 to enlarge the orchestra pit.

Writing shortly before 1740, Cibber comments on this
change in staging, and illustrates it by a reference to Drury
Lane which was quite clear to his original readers who could
go and look at the building itself. He describes changes made
there by 'the old Patentee', that is Rich, and with the motive
'to make it hold more Mony'. These changes are assumed to
have been made either in or before 1696, but in the present
context the date is not important, especially as all modern in-
terpretations of his words are based on the assumption that we
know exactly what the 1674 theatre looked like. It does, however, seem certain that originally there were two doorways on
each side of the forestage, and that the latter had a curved
front, projecting 'in a semi-oval Figure, parallel to the Benches
of the Pit'. Rich enlarged the pit by cutting 'about four Foot' off
the forestage; to make this financially worthwhile he probably
took four feet off straight across from side to side, making a
straight instead of a bowed front and thus reducing the forestage on the centre-line by more like eight or ten feet. The two
pairs of doorways were turned into side-boxes and a new,
single, doorway was made on each side as part of a new deep
side jamb added to the proscenium opening, where 'there formerly stood two additional Side-Wings, in front to a ful Set of
Scenes'. Cibber's account of Drury Lane continues:

> By this original Form, the usual Station of the Actors, in almost
> every Scene, was advanc'd at least ten Foot nearer to the Audi-
> ence, than they now can be; because, not only from the Stage's
> being shorten'd, in front, but likewise from the additional Inter-
> position of those Stage-Boxes, the Actors (in respect to the
> Spectators, that fill them) are kept so much more backward
> from the main Audience, than they us'd to be: But when the Ac-
> tors were in Possession of that forwarder Space, to advance
> upon, the Voice was then more in the Centre of the House, so
> that the most distant Ear had scarce the least Doubt, or
> Difficulty in hearing what fell from the weakest Utterance; All
> Objects were thus drawn nearer to the Sense; every painted
> Scene was stronger; every Grand Scene and Dance more exten-
> ded; every rich, or fine-coloured Habit had a more lively Lustre.

At the Haymarket in 1708 there were no performances between 20 May and 14 December; although for the last seven

weeks of this period the theatres were in mourning for the death of Prince George, the original delay in re-opening was made to allow changes to the internal architecture. Their effect was similar to those at Drury Lane insofar as the single forestage doors were replaced by boxes and the forestage was shortened. But there the similarities end, and it should be remembered that whereas in the case of Drury Lane Cibber was complaining that the changes *impaired* the speech acoustics, the primary need in Vanbrugh's theatre was for changes to *improve* them. The curtailment of his forestage was not in order to enlarge the house, which was already difficult to fill; it must therefore have been in order to improve and extend a feature that was quite lacking at Drury Lane – the orchestra pit.

From 13 January 1708 until it closed on 20 May, the Haymarket had been used only for operas, altogether ten performances of *Thomyris* (arranged by Pepusch from Alessandro Scarlatti, Giovanni Bononcini, and others), nine of *Camilla* (arranged by Nicolino Haym from Marcantonio Bononcini with a libretto translated by Owen Swiney), and eight of *Love's Triumph*, the composer of which may have been Giovanni Saggione, whose wife sang in some of the performances. The last alone was a new piece; *Thomyris* and *Camilla* had been presented at Drury Lane in 1707 and 1706 respectively. Ideally an opera orchestra of the time would consist of between twenty and thirty musicians, and space was also needed for at least one keyboard instrument and on occasion a pair of kettle-drums. Whereas in previous London theatres the musicians had been placed either in a gallery above the stage or in a room to one side of it, Vanbrugh had provided from the start an orchestra pit in front of the stage. But orchestra pits are always too small, and no doubt the manifold criticisms of the new theatre that came to its architect included complaints about space from the musicians who played in the 1708 spring season. Modern orchestra pits extend backwards under the stage, often to the detriment of acoustical balance; this was not the case at the Haymarket, but by curtailing the forestage the musicians' space was effectively doubled.

The audience's most serious matter of complaint was the loss and confusion of speech in the lofty auditorium. In the 1708 alterations this was considerably improved by construct-

ing a new flat ceiling over the truncated forestage, across and
below the great arch, with a new sloping ceiling descending
from the back of the upper gallery to meet the new ceiling over
the forestage.

Vanbrugh's short-lived great arch was indeed prophetic of
much later theatres, but the seating in the house also seems to
have reflected the change in staging which Cibber describes.
[E] He makes it clear that at Drury Lane the pit seats were arranged in shallow concentric arcs in such a way that anyone
sitting straight in his seat would face towards a point on the
centre line of the stage somewhere behind the proscenium
arch. The boxes and galleries must have been similarly concentric; thus every spectator had a sense of sharing a common
viewpoint well upstage, beyond the greater part of the action,
and the ambiguity of the forestage was maintained between
the worlds of both audience and actors. Vanbrugh's seats, on
the other hand, were arranged in deeper arcs, so that their
common focal point was at the front of the pit, and separated
from the stage by the orchestra. Thus even an actor standing
right at the front of the stage, addressing the audience directly,
was seen to inhabit a world adjacent and physically similar to
the spectator's but distinct from it; the gap could be bridged
only by dramatic suggestion. Vanbrugh was not the first to
design an auditorium on this geometrical basis, which after all
is to be found in the theatres of the Ancients. But coupled with
the other differences the arrangement seems to reflect an understanding of contemporary staging rather than a desire to
imitate Antiquity.

The architecture of a theatre has to be functional: to adapt Le
Corbusier's famous phrase, a *machine* for the showing and
seeing of plays. What matters is that as many people as possible can be placed so as to see the stage with an acceptable
degree of discomfort; they must be protected from the weather,
and if some of the audience are stacked in boxes and galleries
those structures must carry their weight without the supports
spoiling the sight-lines of those below them. They must have
convenient access to and exit from their seats, including staircases to and from the upper levels, and – although little is
known about it – there must even in the seventeenth century
have been some provision for the calls of nature when a per-

formance lasted up to four hours: a provisional list of staff in
the Lord Chamberlain's papers, now identified as for Vanbrugh's new theatre, includes three 'necessary women' or
sanitary attendants. The glitter of the decoration and the
sparkle of the lights, which enhance the audience's sense of
being transported into another world, are desirable but not indispensable additions to this prescription.

Backstage, in another world again, the requirements are different. Behind the scenes nothing at all is decorated, and there
must be space for making, storing and moving the scenes and
their machinery. The accommodation for the actors, who are
paid to be in the theatre, will be more spartan than for the audience, who pay to be there. The whole theatre has to be
functional because it is full of people engaged in different and
interlocking activities that require exact timing; and the
drama – let alone opera – is so expensive that every component
must pay its way or at worst not be a drain on money. Thus in
designing the Queen's Theatre Vanbrugh had to deal with a   [20]
range of practical requirements that were quite new in his
experience.

Only in its street front does the theatre become part of the
outside world, and the idea of the façade as an advertisement
did not arise as long as theatres were converted halls or tennis-
courts and, although fashionable, a little disreputable. The
purpose-built Drury Lane of 1674 was still approached by an
alley and surrounded by other buildings, and in this respect
the new theatre in the Haymarket was little better. Defoe in the
Review, not without malice, found it indistinguishable from 'a
French Church or a Hall, or a Meeting-House, or any such
usual Publick Building'; yet for the early eighteenth century
the three-bay brick and stone loggia facing the street was a
quite satisfactory statement about what lay behind. The best
view we have of it is a water-colour made shortly before the
theatre was rebuilt after the fire of 1789; probably the stone
rustication of the arches and the oval windows above them originally looked more crisp and precise, and thus more like the
front of Vanbrugh's own house in Whitehall.

The story of Vanbrugh's attempts to manage the theatre and
the opera, and to earn rather than lose money thereby, is a long
and chequered one; it is therefore appropriate to defer it to a

later chapter,* and to end this one with the two adaptations he made, already mentioned, in the autumn of 1705. *The Confederacy* was deservedly popular throughout the eighteenth century, and was reprinted in 1779 with a few changes as *The City Wives' Confederacy*. The wives, Clarissa and Araminta, are married to two City scriveners (investment brokers), Gripe and Moneytrap: already in the *dramatis personæ* Vanbrugh departs from Dancourt's original by giving the men comic type names while their wives retain names whose elegance suggests the society to which they aspire and sharpens the contrast between the atmospheres of the City and St James's. When the ladies, who have run up debts at cards and at the dressmaker's, discover that each husband covets the other's wife, they contrive to extract a few hundred pounds as tokens from their illicit admirers.

The secondary plot concerns Mrs Amlet and her son Dick. Vanbrugh refashions Dancourt's Madame Amelin, a *marchande* or tradeswoman, into Mrs Amlet, 'a Seller of all Sorts of private Affairs to the Ladies'. Other characters specify her as 'A Gin of all Trades; an old daggling Cheat, that hobbles about from House to House to Bubble the Ladies of their Money', and 'a Pedlar . . . who carries her Shop under her Arm'. Some of her wares are mentioned as 'Paint and Patches, Iron-Bodice, false Teeth', hip bolsters and wire and lace head-dresses. She has 'Two Thousand Pounds owing me, of which I shall never get Ten Shillings' — one of the undercurrents of the play is the relation between lack of ready money and capital sums tied up — but she is willing to act as pawnbroker and moneylender. Her son is a gamester, a climber, and a cheat, who robs his own mother, poses as a colonel, and seeks the hand — and the money — of Gripe's daughter; he is meanwhile blackmailed by Brass, his companion *alias* valet.

The bones of the story are indeed in Dancourt's original, but Vanbrugh consistently expands the dialogue, bringing humour and colour to Dancourt's rather straight and plain citizens, and expanding downwards their social spectrum. Some of the characters swear by heaven and hell, or blood and thunder, and others are shocked by such oaths. Three scenes

* p. 322

are completely Vanbrugh's own, including the opening one in which he dreams up Mrs Cloggit, a neighbour of Mrs Amlet in Covent Garden, whose brief appearance allows him to set the scene in one of those doorstep exchanges of gossip that the whole world loves to overhear.

The two plots are bound together by a diamond necklace which Clarissa at first pretends to have lost in order to get money from her husband Gripe. She then pawns it to Mrs Amlet; Dick steals it from his mother's strong-box; Brass extorts it from Dick by threatening to spoil his marriage plans, and tries to sell it to Clip, a goldsmith. But Gripe had warned the London goldsmiths to look out for it after the original 'loss', and when Clip calls on Gripe to return it and incriminate Brass the whole tangle of intrigues is revealed: the lustful husbands, the extravagant wives, the dishonest young men. The conclusion is the nearest thing to the irresolution of a modern farce; as the wives admit, 'we are to go on with our Dears, as we us'd to do' and 'while you live, every thing gets well out of a Broil, but a Husband'. Yet although Vanbrugh shows people 'what they shou'd do, by representing them upon the Stage, doing what they shou'd not', *The Confederacy* can hardly be called a morality, for not everyone is left in the mess they have conspired to make. Mrs Amlet is only too eager to forgive her son:

> *Amlet.* If he is not a Gentleman, he's a Gentleman's fellow. Come hither, *Dick*, they shan't run thee down neither, Cock up thy Hat *Dick*, and tell 'em tho' Mrs *Amlet* is thy Mother, she can make thee amends, with 10000 good Pounds to buy thee some Lands, and build thee a House in the midst on't.
> *Omnes.* How!
> *Clarissa.* Ten thousand Pounds, Mrs *Amlet?*
> *Amlet.* Yes Forsooth; tho' I shou'd lose the hundred, you pawn'd your Necklace for. Tell 'em of that, *Dick*.

In *The Mistake* Vanbrugh transports the characters and the setting from the Paris of Molière's *Le Dépit Amoureux* to Spain; this has led to false associations with Dryden's *An Evening's Love*, whose plot is quite different. Molière's play, which derives from an earlier Italian one, is concerned with the complex consequences of a simple deception. Camillo and Leonora are the children of Don Alvarez, and the audience soon

learns that Camillo, though brought up as a man in order to
secure an inheritance, is in fact Leonora's sister. Camillo falls
in love with, and secretly marries, Lorenzo, who believes himself to be wedded to Leonora. The gradual discovery of this
situation by the various characters causes havoc between
Lorenzo, Leonora, and her sweetheart Carlos, as well as between the fathers of the two families. All ends well, however,
with the touching discovery of Camillo's true identity, the
transfer of the inheritance to Lorenzo who had been deprived
of it by the deception, and the promise of a double wedding.

The Mistake, a lively play, follows Molière's original scene by
scene and almost speech by speech, but no further. Whereas
Molière's characters speak throughout in rhyming hexameter
couplets, Vanbrugh's speak prose, and even when they lapse
from time to time into blank verse they seem to speak with the
natural ease for which Vanbrugh was renowned. The play was
revived periodically until the 1760s, but it lacks the excitement
and the comic business of *The Confederacy*. Of Vanbrugh's
other two adaptations little can be said, for nothing of substance survives. *Squire Trelooby* was translated from Molière
by Vanbrugh, Congreve, and William Walsh, each taking one
act and working at great speed; it was produced at Lincoln's
Inn Fields on 30 March 1704. It has been established beyond
reasonable doubt that the subsequent printed translation is by
another hand. The *Cuckold in Conceit*, also from Molière, was
first staged as the after-piece to Lord Lansdowne's *The British
Enchanters* on 22 March 1707; it was never printed. On that
occasion, about a year after the première of Lansdowne's play,
new scenes were advertised, including 'particularly the intire
front prospect of Blenheim Castle'. Surely the architect was in
the house that night; if he looked back then over eleven years
in the theatre he must have recognized the supremacy of his
first two, quite original, plays, over everything he had written
since. For they alone were totally new, indebted perhaps in
particulars to previous authors, drawing on the range of char-
acterization of the Restoration, but without precedent in plot,
language, and structure. They were, and still are, remarkable
too for the interplay of 'jest and earnest' which turns the stock
figures of comedy into real people and builds an emotional
bridge between their world and ours. As far as the stage was

concerned, although it would remain in his blood, he had in a sense said everything in the first couple of years; the alchemy of architecture, on the other hand, would continue to work in him, more slowly and more weightily, to the end of his life.

_ 23 _

Towards a New Architecture

As to what your Grace says against building at all, I have very little to answer ... he's a fool that lays out his money in what he don't like ... I believe if your Grace will please to consider of the Intrinsique vallew of Tytles and Blew Garters, and Jewells and Great Tables and Numbers of Servants & in a word all those things that distinguish Great Men from small ones, you will confess to me, that a Good house is at least upon the Levell with the best of 'em.

When Vanbrugh wrote thus to the Duke of Newcastle on 15 June 1703 he hoped to turn him away from Talman but not from building altogether.* The Duke was already inclining to leave old Welbeck as it was, and Vanbrugh's account of the complexities of commissioning a great house evidently confirmed him in his inertia. A few days later Talman, undeterred by his brush with Lord Carlisle and perhaps even spurred on by Vanbrugh's conduct in court, asked himself down to Welbeck a second time. His Grace did not reply to him in person, but sent a message that

If you come down, my Lord hopes you will Come to Welbeck, but he will by no means encourage your Workmen to Come down when there's such a difference between You & his Grace.

* p. 208

If you do not approve of his Graces Termes my Ld desires it may not hinder you of any other business.

Careful consideration of the surviving letters and drawings suggests a sequence of events rather more complex than has hitherto been supposed, and also more indicative of the importance of Welbeck in Vanbrugh's artistic development. Vanbrugh prefaced his account of the court case with 'I hear Mr Talman and Jackson intend to be at Welbeck very soon'; but whether he knew it or not Talman had been there in April. Already before that visit, as we have seen, Talman had tried to reassure the Duke that his recourse to the law was neither unreasonable nor to the Duke's disadvantage.* As a result of that visit, or perhaps during his stay there (as Vanbrugh and Hawksmoor would do in 1707 at Kimbolton) he produced the three elevations, all drawn on one sheet of paper, that are now in the Soane Museum.

No plan survives, but from the north (garden) and south (entrance) fronts and one end elevation we can deduce that the house would have been rectangular, 150 by 250 feet, with either a central courtyard or two small courts to give light like those in the main block at Blenheim. The house was to be on two floors but, as with the long orangery-like south wings of Castle Howard, these comprised an above-ground basement and a single main storey over it. Even the slightly taller corner pavilions have no attic windows, and the upper lights in the middle bays of the south front imply a lofty and well-lit entrance hall rather than attic rooms over it. This distribution of living spaces on one main floor is extravagant, because it occupies a great deal of ground, foundations and roof in proportion to the number of usable rooms. It seems in history to be more often associated with villas or garden houses than with principal residences; at Castle Howard house, garden and landscape were considered as a unity from the start. Since at Welbeck in 1703 Vanbrugh also made designs for the garden and lake,† perhaps what the Duke wanted – if he knew his own mind – was a villa, the ducal equivalent of a weekend cottage.

* p. 247
† p. 461

He may also have specified the projections and recesses of the south front so as to take account of foundations surviving from old Welbeck Abbey, for they appear not only in both Vanbrugh's and Talman's drawings but also in the early twentieth-century rebuilding of this front, and something similar is already implied in a plan for Welbeck made by Robert Smythson about 1600.

Vanbrugh's design, made as three separate elevations, would thus seem to be a revision of Talman's single paper of three drawings – the reverse of what has usually been supposed. Only Vanbrugh's south front survives, and his letter of 15 June confirms the internal evidence of draughtsmanship that Hawksmoor was certainly making the drawings. This drawing, or one like it, was already in the Duke's hands, together with a plan for the garden. The end elevation, west or east, Vanbrugh enclosed with the letter, although 'not drawn as I propose it'. As for the north (garden) front,

> if your Grace has not tother Mr Hawksmoor has it, and I'll get it from him, but I remember how it was, it was with Dorique Pillasters all along except the two Pavillions wch were Rustick like

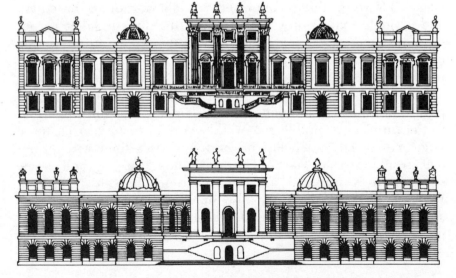

K   Welbeck. Talman's (above) and Vanbrugh's (below) elevations compared.

the rest but Your Grace directed Mr Talman to draw it with Corinthian instead of the Dorique, which I suppose he has done and shewn your Grace, but I never saw it.

Talman and Vanbrugh seem thus to have known they were in competition, and according to the Duke's message to Talman of 26 June the garden front pleased His Grace least: 'my Ld did intend as Mr Vanbrook had drawn it with the Dorique Order, Your Front should be with the Corinthian pillars in the Same places as his was the Dorique'. Since Talman's north front in the Soane Museum does not have pilasters 'all along' but only in the middle three bays, this is the clearest indication that Vanbrugh was revising Talman, the latter now being asked to match his rival's pilastered version. Whether he ever did so, whether he returned to Welbeck with or without Jackson, we do not know, although it seems that the Duke was not prepared to accept his estimate of cost. But a comparison of the two south fronts is instructive. **[K]**

Talman's elevation depends for its effect on the extent and variety of surface enrichment: on plain and rusticated areas, on the fluted half-columns in the centre bays, the fish-scale tiling of the little cupolas, and the elaborate window frames, of which those in the end and centre pavilions are close derivations from seventeenth-century Roman examples, specifically the architecture of Bernini. Windows are the principal features of most elevations, both in the appearance of the building and in the relationship between the façade and the rooms behind it which the windows illuminate. As by the decorative details, Talman charms the eye also by a slight and easy elasticity in the rhythm of his windows, a little faster in the end pavilions and a little slower in the turrets under the cupolas. This elevation is not conventional, but something of its beguiling character can be gauged from the hall front he designed at Drayton, **[11]** Northants, for whose construction Jackson signed a contract in 1702.

Vanbrugh's elevation is no more conventional, but it is simpler, bolder, more limited in vocabulary, and more dramatic. Except for the three bays in the middle, the whole façade is evenly textured with banded rustication of the kind used on the north front and wings at Castle Howard, and this is even

lightly suggested in the centre. The Doric pilasters are unfluted, and the cupolas are lead-covered, with ribs which emphasize their rotundity rather than their texture. The windows
have no architràves, being simply punched or gouged out of
the walls; this also means that, without framing devices, all the
windows are identical in form.

But instead of Talman's easy rhythm the pace is abruptly
quickened in the recessed sections of the façade, and the
graceful curves of Talman's approach staircase to the main
floor are replaced by straight flights parallel to the house front.
Finally the centre bays are thrown into dramatic relief by curving the wall back into quadrants on either side – the circular
corridors mentioned in Vanbrugh's letter. Thus fewer elements are used to produce a building which already shows, in
the words of Robert and James Adam about Vanbrugh seventy
years later, 'the rise and fall, the advance and recess, with
other diversity of form, in the different parts' of a building, so as
to add greatly to the picturesqueness of the composition'.

Four years later Vanbrugh would write of his design for
Kimbolton as proof of his belief that 'tis certainly the Figure
and Proportions that make the most pleasing fabrick, And not
the delicacy of the Ornaments'.* His letter to Newcastle refers
to the addition of Doric pilasters, and these are roughly
sketched in on the left half of the surviving drawing. Pilasters,
we recall, are among the features which redeemed the early
Castle Howard design from the appearance of an orange-
house. Over Kimbolton, Vanbrugh found it necessary to defend
his belief in writing to Lord Manchester; at Welbeck Lord
Newcastle seems to have found the design too plain and perhaps not lordly enough. Who, then, wanted Castle Howard and
Welbeck to be more elaborate?

One possibility might seem to be Hawksmoor, who in his
final design for Easton Neston, about 1695, dressed Lord
[9] Lempster's house in a close jacket of giant Composite pilasters.† But nothing could be further from the truth than the idea
that Hawksmoor designed Vanbrugh's early buildings. When
Vanbrugh wrote in 1707 of the skyline features of Castle

* p. 336
† p. 200

Howard, 'I'll get Mr Hawksmoor to Add them', he referred to his draughtsman in the same terms as one might refer to one's tailor or one's master bricklayer. Moreover there are signs that Lempster had aspirations to grandeur and may have asked Hawksmoor, who designed a number of very plain buildings both earlier and later, to make his house more noble in appearance.

The discovery by Charles Saumarez-Smith that Lord Carlisle intended some sort of overall programme for the decoration of Castle Howard, in which the statues on the north front are individually identifiable, suggests that Carlisle also found Vanbrugh's first design not grand enough. Carlisle had been in Padua at the beginning of 1690 and, since England and France were at war, his return journey if not also his outward one will have been through the Netherlands, the Rhineland, and Switzerland or Austria. While there are those who believe, against the evidence of their eyes, that Castle Howard was inspired by an engraved design by Jean Marot for the Electoral Palace at Mannheim, it is worth considering that Carlisle's experience of European architecture is likely to have included, besides northern Italy, the earliest examples of Baroque palaces in the southern Germanic lands. And by the time Marlborough spoke of commissioning Blenheim in the winter of 1704–5 he too had journeyed almost as far as Munich and back. Whatever Vanbrugh did in subsequent commissions, even the first known design for Blenheim has an Imperial profusion of giant pilasters. In our own day architects sometimes claim, in the face of popular criticism, that it is the client who chooses the appearance of his building. This is disingenuous; nevertheless, Vanbrugh quickly learned how important it was that the patron should believe it to be true. In the cases of Castle Howard and Blenheim the outward appearance must have been the result of co-operation between patron and architects, but it is also important to note that even the earliest recorded design for Castle Howard with its 'Ornaments of Pillasters and Urns'* was more Italianate than Kimbolton. Castles were the end, not the beginning, of Vanbrugh's stylistic journey.

In the lawsuits which clouded the later years of building

* p. 212

Blenheim Vanbrugh made, between 1718 and 1724, three separate but consistent statements about the origin of the commission. The Duke had told him of his intention to build in
Woodstock Park, which had been granted to him by the Queen
as a reward for winning the battle of Blindheim on the Danube
the previous August. Vanbrugh clearly remembered that Marlborough was prepared to spend up to £40,000 and that

> Viewing a Modell wch Dep[onen]t then had in Wood of the Earle
> of Carliles House the Duke said that was the sort of House he
> liked ones with some alteracõns and addicõns as a Gallery &c.
> and concluded that Dept should prepare a design ... Lord
> Trea[sure]r Godolphin was with him who both viewed and con-
> sidered the same ... and at last ... fixt on that design but after-
> wards several Draughts more Correct were made and from time
> to time shown to his Grace who at length vizt. in Feb. 1704[/5]
> desired Dept would meet him at Woodstock to fix upon the Situ-
> acõn wch Dept accordingly did.

Vanbrugh's statements were made at a time of acrimonious
forensic questioning about who had given instructions for the
building of Blenheim and who was legally obliged to pay for it.
His own position was, to him at least, clear: he acted first on the
Duke's instructions and subsequently under a Treasury
warrant appointing him Surveyor to the project. But his evidence is also of considerable historical value. It tells us that
Marlborough initially was prepared to pay for the house himself and – on whose recommendation we know not – chose
Vanbrugh to design it. He wanted a house similar to Lord Carlisle's but with some additions such as a gallery; the wooden
model that had served to launch Vanbrugh's architectural
career now acted as an advertisement and a pattern. Moreover,
Marlborough was willing to spend a very large sum of money.
Lord Nottingham's Burley-on-the-Hill cost about £19,000 between 1696 and 1704, although in the following six years a
further £10,000 or so was spent on gardens, outbuildings and
decoration. Carlisle himself spent £35,000 on his house up to
1713, and if we allow that houses always cost more in the end
than the first estimate, then it seems clear that Marlborough
began with the intention of having a grander house than Castle
Howard.

For Vanbrugh Marlborough was, and would remain, a hero, and he would always believe in the Duke's altruism; for him Blenheim was to be a monument to the doer, not the deed. He told the Duchess in 1710 that 'tho' ordered to be a Dwelling house for the Duke of Marlborough, and his posterity' it was 'at the Same time by all the World esteemed and looked on as a Publick Edifice, raised for a Monument of the Queen's Glory through his great Services'. But Marlborough was at least as vain as Carlisle and far more ambitious, and that he considered Blenheim as no more than his due is apparent from two of its principal decorative features: Thornhill's painting of his **[2]** glorification on the Hall ceiling and the carved trophies surmounted by a colossal bust of Louis XIV which he removed entire from the Citadel at Tournai and set up over the south front. **[19]**

Woodstock's royal connections go back beyond Henry I, who stayed at his house there on many occasions; but in history and in legend it is most particularly associated with his grandson Henry II, who founded the town of New Woodstock half a mile away in order to accommodate his courtiers, and who kept his mistress Rosamund Clifford at Everswell, a sizable 'Trianon' or garden house two or three minutes' walk away from the manor house. In geological pre-history the River Glyme cut a wandering valley through the area on its way to the Thames. Woodstock Manor stood north-west of one of its bends, and at Everswell a natural spring in the valley-side was augmented by a well (later known as Rosamund's Well) and a series of carefully constructed pools and channels which provided the romantic setting for Henry's infidelities and which survived long enough to be sketched by Aubrey in the reign of Charles II.

The topicality of the place no doubt influenced the choice of subject for Addison and Clayton's opera of 1707.* The book of *Rosamond* was dedicated to the Duchess of Marlborough, and at the beginning of Act III King Henry was presented by angels with a vision of the future palace:

Behold the glorious pile ascending!
    [Scene changes to the plan of Blenheim castle]

* p. 258

Columns swelling, arches bending,
Domes in awful pomp arising,
Art in curious strokes surprising.

This display, at Drury Lane on 4 March 1707, may have prompted the advertised 'intire front prospect' of Blenheim eighteen days later at the Haymarket.*

The Duchess of Marlborough was perhaps less than enchanted with the subject of *Rosamond*. Some years later the Duke proposed to erect an obelisk in the park to commemorate its earlier history, and suggested that a site near the old Manor 'would please Sr John best, because it would give an opportunity of mentioning that King whose Scenes of Love He was so much pleas'd with'. The Duchess wrote on his letter, 'but if there were obelisks to bee made of what all our Kings have don of that sort the countrey would bee stuffed with very odd things'.

The possible phallic associations of obelisks should not be overstressed, for in Vanbrugh's day those of Ancient Egypt had other well defined meanings. Their original function as solar markers and ray catchers was unknown then, and the hieroglyphs were undeciphered, but because we tend to consider clever what we do not understand they were seen as repositories of ancient wisdom. And because they were known to be extremely old they were also seen as emblems of the passage of history, past, present, and future; as such they appear on Elizabethan and early Stuart funeral monuments. For Hawksmoor, and undoubtedly therefore for Vanbrugh too, they also made splendid focal points in a city or a park; Hawksmoor was an expert on this use of the obelisk, which started with the re-erection of the ancient monoliths in Rome in the 1580s as part of Pope Sixtus V's programme of urban renewal and was described in a book by Sixtus's architect Domenico Fontana. But as Marlborough stood with his architect on the field of Woodstock in February 1705 Tournai and Thornhill, Henry and Rosamund, were yet in the future, and their principal concern that day was the siting of the house.

[L]   Woodstock Park lies on a gentle slope, rising slightly towards the north and bisected by the Glyme valley. As they stood facing north of north-west, the valley lay immediately before

* p. 270

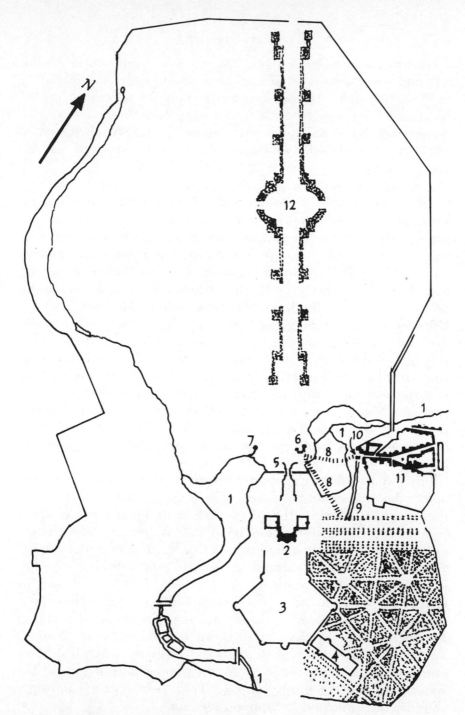

L   Blenheim Park, as designed by Vanbrugh and Henry Wise. 1. River Glyme. 2.
Blenheim Palace. 3 Formal gardens. 4 Kitchen garden. 5 The Great bridge. 6
Woodstock Manor. 7 Rosmund's Well. 8 Remains of causeways to Woodstock
and Oxford. 9 Modern approach road. 10 Hawksmoor's Triumphal Arch. 11 New
Woodstock. 12 The Avenue.

them, the town to their right, Everswell in front a little to the
left and the rambling buildings and walls of the old Manor a
little to the right. Behind them stretched the southern half of
the estate, basically level though not quite as level as the gardeners were to make it. The old Manor was approached by two
causeways across the valley, one north of eastwards to the
town, and the other south-east towards Oxford.

The plan of campaign which the general's architect outlined
to him was to site the house in the direction they were facing,
smoothing out a formal garden behind to the south, and using
the surplus earth to extend the 'irregular ragged ungovernable
hill' (as Vanbrugh later called it), building embankments to
narrow the valley before the house. The two banks would be
joined by a huge bridge so as to form the main approach to the
house. Visitors from the north would enter the park by the
Ditchley Gate and ride down the long avenue and straight across the Bridge. But most people would come, as they still do,
through Woodstock town, and the intention was that they
should follow the causeway up to the old Manor, catching their
first sight of the Bridge and the house distantly to the left. Passing the Manor and coming to the end of the avenue nearest
the house, they would turn on to the line of the Bridge; having
first viewed it as landscape they would now cross it to reach the
house.

Fifty years later Capability Brown dammed the river and
made the marsh into a lake, drowning the Bridge's feet and
flooding the lowest of the rooms within its great piers. So perfect does this transformation seem that it requires some effort
to imagine the original intention; in order to do so it is important to realize that Vanbrugh envisaged a land-bridge, or what
in the nineteenth century would be called a viaduct. It was, in
Cibber's phrase, to be a 'vast triumphal piece of architecture'
or even of engineering, and whereas Brown's enchanting
landscape uses artifice to suggest the triumph of Nature,
Vanbrugh's intention was to show the triumph of Artifice. Certainly Brown's master-stroke was the simple one of raising the
water-level, but he must share the credit for it with Vanbrugh,
who literally prepared the ground for him.

Brown conceived buildings as parts of the landscape; Vanbrugh still saw the gardens of Blenheim as extensions of the

house. But in the act of taking in the valley and the ruins on the far side of it Vanbrugh revealed a new conception of buildings in relation to landscape that is much closer to Brown's. The great drama that is jointly their creation could only be dreamed up on the site, but the house itself had already been designed, as indeed houses often are, without reference to the ground on which it was to stand. It had been possible to work out the plan and elevations before choosing the exact position and direction, because it was taken for granted that the front would be approached perpendicularly by an avenue and through a forecourt and that the back would overlook a formal garden of parterres and gravelled walks. But the extent to which Blenheim was to be like the Earl of Carlisle's house can still be seen by comparing the two.

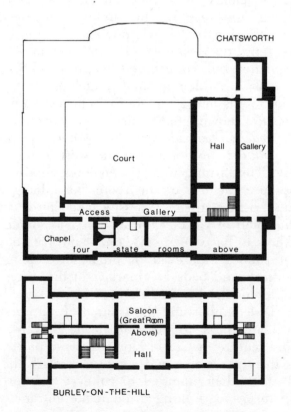

M   Sketch-plans of Chatsworth and Burley-on-the-Hill, showing arrangement of state rooms.

[M] As a piece of house-planning Burley-on-the-Hill is far more typical of its time than Chatsworth, and not only because it was designed as a whole rather than piecemeal. It is symmetrical both outside and, almost entirely, inside: that is to say, in both the way it looks and the way it was to be used. Burley is also typical of its time in being a 'double pile', that is two rooms thick, but it is exceptional in the provision of a corridor along the middle of the house between the two ranges of rooms. At Castle Howard Vanbrugh had adopted the corridor and the left-right symmetry, but abandoned the compactness of the double pile.

The arrangement of matching sets of apartments on either side of central halls and 'great rooms' derived, earlier in the seventeenth century, from the kind of house that, although not actually a royal palace, was intended to be suitable for entertaining a king and queen. The imitation of royalty by the nobility, the diffusion of French notions of state, comfort and convenience, and the examples in the second book of Palladio's *Architettura* all contributed to an ideal in which the great house of a nobleman had matching state suites. At Blenheim the rooms along the south front are named in *Vitruvius Britannicus*, moving outwards, as *ante-chamber, drawing room, great bedchamber*, and in the corner only on the east side, *grand cabinet*; the corner on the west is one end of the great gallery. This arrangement is no longer clear to the visitor, first because the use of the rooms has changed and sec-
[N] ondly because visitors are of necessity taken on a circular tour. The *Vitruvius* plan of Castle Howard does not name the rooms which we know to have been *My Lord's* and *My Lady's*, but the sequence of shapes and even of projections along the south front is identical, and beds are marked in the same positions.* The only difference is the inclusion of some extra little rooms between the bedchamber and the cabinet on either side, and in this respect Blenheim is simpler than Castle Howard.

The second feature of Castle Howard is the pair of corridors, one behind the state rooms and running through the inner end of the Hall, the other intended to connect the north-east and north-west wings and running through the entrance end of the

* p. 219

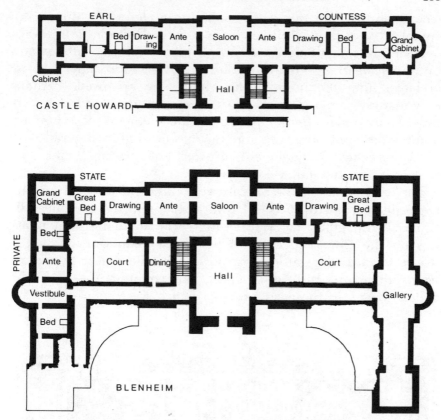

N   Layout of the main rooms at Castle Howard and Blenheim.

Hall. At Blenheim the corridors occupy the same positions, but the addition of the great gallery means that the second corridor is on the middle cross axis of the whole block; this block includes both the private apartments on the east and the gallery on the west. Thus from three sides the exterior of Blenheim looks more like a great enclosed courtyard house than the long-drawn-out Castle Howard.

From the north, however, Blenheim seems to have an open courtyard: quadrants frame the centre part much as they do in the earlier house, but the combination of corner towers, framing quadrants and entrance hall owes a good deal to the Welbeck elevation. The resemblance was indeed more marked in the original design, before Vanbrugh added the pro-

jecting portico and raised the Hall into a clerestory. But in the
complexity of its plan Blenheim was new. Visitors have always
been impressed (though not always pleased) by its vast extent,
but much of that is due to the huge service courts added by its
architect after the initial design had been approved. Perhaps
only a study of the plan on paper shows the logic and compactness of the main house, in which the elements of symmetry
and the sense of order they produce seem to grow naturally out
of the practical arrangement of state and private rooms, entrances, stairways and access corridors.

The elevations of Blenheim were also intended from the
beginning to outstrip Castle Howard. It would not even be ridiculous to imagine that Marlborough wanted more giant pilasters on the front and back of his house than Carlisle had —
twelve towards the garden instead of ten, and ten or twelve towards the court instead of eight, not counting those on the
[O]   corner towers in the early designs, which were soon discarded.

O   Blenheim. South front of the first design.

Moreover, in recognition of Blenheim's martial origins, Vanbrugh not only proposed the Doric, the most masculine of the
orders, for both fronts, but also — perhaps at the Duke's behest
— introduced heroic ornaments of the kind to be found at Versailles and Hampton Court: trophies of arms and figures blow-
[K]   ing trumpets and writing in chronicles. Apart from these features the elevations are similar in components and
arrangement — especially in the corner towers — to the
Welbeck design.

But there is as yet no hint of the extraordinary variety of
rooftop objects that give Blenheim its famous skyline, those
gratuitous masses of masonry once aptly described by Hawks-

moor as 'eminencies', and for the last forty years attributed almost universally to his imagination as well as to his pencil. On their account alone it is desirable to return to the question of Hawksmoor's contribution to Vanbrugh's early works.

There are several references in letters to drawings for Blenheim by Hawksmoor, but they are about drawing rather than designing; how far the latter was his responsibility is a question the documents do not answer. But a useful working hypothesis can be built from a study of what Hawksmoor *drew* in the light of what Vanbrugh *said*. Not only was Vanbrugh unconcerned about 'the delicacy of the ornaments'; he had also told Lord Newcastle that he was satisfied 'in generall' with the drawing he sent but 'as to the perticulars, I am scarce determined in any thing'. In the early days of Castle Howard he had indeed to rely on Hawksmoor for all the particulars, but what he first believed and afterwards found to be true was that he had a gift for imagining buildings which did not depend on being able to draw them. Today we are so used to the idea of drawing as a means of research towards a design that we need to imagine how architects worked before drawing became a normal part of office practice and the standard method of designing, something that only happened gradually during the sixteenth and early seventeenth centuries. In this context Vanbrugh, whether they realized it or not, belonged to an older tradition than Hawksmoor, who had learned from Wren to think with pencil or pen in hand. Indeed Vanbrugh's account of how at Kimbolton in July 1707 he, Hawksmoor, the local builder Coleman, and the Countess of Manchester had 'all Agreed Upon' the design which he then enclosed to the Earl, sounds very like the practice sometimes found in the Renaissance which might be called design by house party.

We also tend to think that there is nothing more to building than the making of a design, its approval, and its execution. In fact the essential difference between designing machines, which go through the stages of making mock-ups and prototypes, and designing buildings, which do not, is in the factor of cost: a building is too large and expensive for an experimental version to be feasible. Nevertheless, during the building of Blenheim we do find experimental procedures: both the erection of temporary ornaments to judge their effect seen from

below and the dismantling of portions of the structure because
the design has been changed.

In fact the complexity of Blenheim's plan could not have
been worked out or transmitted in the old way; the many particulars of shape and position that it embodies were essential if
the intuitive idea of stateliness and order was to be realized in
terms of material, workmanship, and measurement, and these
[4]   details could only be put into execution through the use of detailed drawings.* Hawksmoor's study for the Bow Window
Room at Castle Howard is a good example of the process in operation, for his written notes on the sheet show those points
that still need clarifying. The best example for Blenheim is a
plan (which he later turned over in order to make a design for
Greenwich Hospital on the back) which is concerned with the
precise location of chimney-pieces and flues on the east side of
the house. It would also take all Hawksmoor's knowledge and
skill to accomplish the increase in height, and the consequent
change from a Doric to a Corinthian exterior, that occurred
during the winter of 1706–7.†

Yet even if no later Vanbrugh house was as complex as
Blenheim, he learned to work these things out himself. He
learned to draw, and we cannot say that, because no working
sketches survive, he made none; some people are as obsessive
about destroying their marginal work as others are about
keeping it, and in any case the survival of drawings is a matter
of chance. But at Blenheim, if only because he had secured
Hawksmoor's paid services to do so, he still left the particulars
to him. It often happens, too, that in a successful twosome the
partners cannot always remember which of them conceived a
particular idea. So the two questions remaining are first, what
is the origin of Vanbrugh's vision; second, how far do such
things as the Blenheim 'eminencies' belong either to the gene-
rality of that vision or to the particulars of Hawksmoor's.

There is general agreement that the later works of Vanbrugh
such as King's Weston and Seaton Delaval, and those of
Hawksmoor such as the 'Queen Anne' churches, are independent and exclusive to their respective creators; yet it is not at

* p 297
† p. 309

all easy to demonstrate by formal analysis what we fortunately know from documents to be the case. The difficulty can be appreciated by the experiment of imagining the authorship of all these buildings to be the other way round and asking first how it would alter our perception of their work and secondly whether it would be necessary to bring back the idea of collaboration in order to explain them. For the basic ingredients are often remarkably similar; huge prismatic blocks of masonry, plain surfaces, simple mouldings, arcades of round-headed windows, even such devices as exaggerated projecting keystones, not to mention the adoption by both architects of one of the trademarks of early Palladianism, the three-light 'Venetian' window as it is correctly called in English.*

Formulas such as 'Vanbrugh's architecture is basically simple, Hawksmoor's basically complex' (which is generally true) turn out to be of little more use than the vague feelings and impressions of connoisseurship, because to explain terms like *simple* and *complex* requires a short course in philosophy, whereas feelings asserted with confidence carry the stamp of authority until the documents are found. What the documents show in this case is that Hawksmoor was making designs in this common style while Vanbrugh was still in the Bastille: the new Writing School at Christ's Hospital in the City was built in 1692–5 to a humbler version of Hawksmoor's design than the one for which his drawings survive, and those drawings show most of the characteristics (though not such details as large keystones) of the later 'Hawksmoor–Vanbrugh' style.

It was in fact the *Hawksmoor* style, and his own invention. A great conductor may have no talent for composition but can bring another's music to life: the analogy is limited but nonetheless useful, if one thinks of Toscanini and Beethoven or Beecham and Delius. It was Hawksmoor's style, and Vanbrugh found it both exciting and usable. Hawksmoor tended to overlay it with details and meanings out of his extraordinary range of vocabulary and metaphor; Vanbrugh on his own did not have, and realized that he did not need, that range. Their successful collaboration was the result not only of mutual respect and congenial feelings but also of an understanding by

* p. 455

both men of what they were doing.

Supplementary to this first question is that of how Vanbrugh met this style in the first place. From what we have seen of his career so far the most likely time is 1698 and the most likely channel his cousin William Vanbrugh's concern with Green-wich Hospital: on one side William must have known Hawksmoor, and on the other, being on the staff of the Lord Chamberlain he must have seen John quite often in the com-pany of Vice-Chamberlain Bertie.

An answer of this sort to the first question suggests that both architects were responsible for the Blenheim skyline. This is undoubtedly true but does not go far enough. As part of that 'rise and fall, advance and recess' noted and praised by the Adam brothers, and in their affinity with the fantasy houses of a century or so earlier like Wollaton, the towers and finials of Blenheim, like the great clerestory in the centre, are Van-brugh's. But in their particulars another mind can be seen at work.

The 'delicacy' of the mouldings – at least in comparison with those on the bastions of the Bridge – tells us only that Hawksmoor was responsible for the detailing. This leaves the question whether in these structures the detailing is insepar-able from the whole, and here the elaborateness of the forms suggests that it is. Comparison with Hawksmoor's churches, and with his unexecuted designs for Oxford colleges, argues very strongly that it was his wit and love of metaphor that pro-duced the finials on the corner towers which symbolize victory over France: as the building accounts confirm, they consist of ducal coronets on top of upside-down fleurs-de-lys, supported by cannon balls. The rest of the various rooftop urns and pin-nacles also have a complexity and diversity of form unmatched in any later Vanbrugh houses. But what principally dis-tinguishes the 'eminencies' is their geometrical abstraction.

Taking first the plan of one of the corner structures: from a square the corners were cut off to make an octagon. Then buttress-piers were added, two on each cardinal face to make a miniature triumphal arch, and one on each diagonal face to support the fleur-de-lys finial. But then the cornice at the top was made continuous and curved, so that the octagon with buttresses became a kind of curvilinear square, a mass with

[2]

[18]

[7]

[40]

four concave curved faces each framing a triumphal arch. These shapes, like all geometry, take longer to describe than recognize. Moreover, their life began and developed on a drawing board.

Something similar happened in the two intermediate chimney towers that stand above the ends of the north corridor. They began as cylinders composed structurally from **[18]** double-ended arches but decoratively from a giant interlace which other architects sometimes used instead of a balustrade. Buttresses added at the corners produce an equivalent, but quite different, combination of straight and curved lines and planes, framing and projecting masses. Finally the towers over **[30]** the archways to the kitchen and stable courts, designed about 1708, are built up from semicircular arches, segmental pediments, scrolls, and brackets, and buttressed by piers set diagonally into the side faces so that they appear to be triangular in plan. There is nothing like any of these in the simple balustraded or battlemented square and octagonal towers of Vanbrugh's later houses.

With these distinctions in mind we may return to the Orangery at Kensington, where we found Vanbrugh in the autumn of 1704 in pursuit of contractual irregularities.* Officially the architect of the Orangery was Wren, because officially the Surveyor designed all the Queen's buildings. But when art-historians began about fifty years ago to look for the work of a **[12]** younger generation in the Surveyor's office this long low building was an obvious starting point, for its ringed columns and triple keystones, the curious abstractions on the roof and the reiterated semicircles of blind arches and niches are, singly or in combination, unlike anything we know certainly to be Wren's. As Clerk of Works at Kensington his pupil Hawksmoor would seem a possible candidate, although Wren would be held responsible for the design as he was for the choice of a stonemason. But while arguments from the payroll may confirm an attribution, they cannot be relied on to establish it in the first place; on the other hand there is now a fashion for re-attributing the Orangery to Vanbrugh as a 'documented' work. It is therefore desirable to look again at the design to see how it is put together.

* p. 250

Four features make the Orangery more than a plain long low mostly brick building with large south-facing windows: the circular rooms inside the two ends, the attic ornaments in the centre and ends of the façade, the meticulous handling of the orders, and the repeated triple-bay design both outside and within. The circular rooms, which have plaster domes within the high-pitched roof, can be entered each by glazed doors on two sides as well as from the main hall. Each room is lined by a ring of eight engaged Corinthian columns, between which large arches and smaller niches alternate; the elegance of this pattern stems partly from the detailing of the order and partly from the *geometrical* regularity of the plan. If Vanbrugh were the architect of the Orangery, he would in 1704 surely have needed Hawksmoor to devise these rooms. The attic features again derive their character from geometry, especially those at the end; these can only be interpreted, in terms of things we already know, either as the beginning of huge niches or as arches that have fallen over, and it is more satisfactory to call them abstractions without further definition.

The Doric order in the central applied portico, like the Corinthian order inside, is the work of a designer who understands the niceties of detailing; part of the building's emotive character indeed comes from the knowing contrast between such attention to 'correct' details and the unconventional novelties of other parts of the design. Contrasts of this kind in the use of architectural language are typical of Hawksmoor. Moreover, the decorative details of the outside cornice and of the eaves-board into which it turns at the ends of the building betray a mind obsessed with the particularities of detailing. Finally the triple-bay design forms a set of ingenious variations on a simple theme. Stated boldly and simply between the pillars of the portico, it takes a different form in the end bays of the façade and again in the end elevations of the building; inside, it is adapted to the wall opposite the central doorway and again to the ends of the hall. Pillars, piers, arches, niches, recessed panels, and pediments are all used in different patterns and combinations of shape with a thoroughness as well as an economy that are, again, typical of Hawksmoor, not of Vanbrugh.

Treasury Papers do provide some evidence about the building of the Orangery; initially they suggest that the Treasury's control of events was less effective than Comptroller Vanbrugh can have desired. On the other hand, Queen Anne took a great interest in the building; she used it as a supper room and also for the ceremony of 'touching for the evil' (the laying on of royal hands) in order to keep both afflicted and spectators out of her own house. The Orangery's creation and progress must have received her personal sanction and indeed her encouragement. On 17 June 1704 an estimate of 10 June was approved, but the following month, on 10 July, according to Treasury Minutes, Her Majesty's pleasure was 'signified to the officers of the Works to make the greenhouse at Kensington pursuant to the alteration of the draft proposed by Mr Vanbrugh'. Two months later, on 8 September, Richard Stacey the contracting bricklayer sent a petition for a part payment for work he had carried out; it was returned to the Treasury five days later with the approval of the officers, Wren, Jackson, and the Master Carpenter Matthew Bankes. Stacey reported that he had laid out over £800 in materials and wages without receiving any advance, and had completed one third of his contract. The total sum for which he had agreed was £1560, that is more than twice the £697. 12s. for brickwork included in the June estimate.

Work had proceeded rapidly during the longest days of the building season. Clearly the design had become either considerably larger or more elaborate or both, and clearly several people – the Surveyor, the Comptroller, the Clerk of Works, the contractors, and not least the Queen – knew what was going on. They also must have known whether it was the draft that Vanbrugh had proposed and the Queen had accepted, or the alteration of it. In this instance the documents as they stand remain ambiguous, and the stylistic case for Hawksmoor's authorship is still a good one.

At Woodstock on Monday 18 June 1705, at about six o'clock on a warm evening, as a newspaper cutting of the time relates,

was laid the first stone of the Duke of Marlborough's house, by Mr Vanbrugge, and then seven gentlemen gave it a stroke with a hammer, and threw down each of them a guinea; Sir Thomas Wheate was the first, Dr Bouchel the second, Mr Vanbrugge the

third; I know not the rest. [Hawksmoor was perhaps one of
them.] There were several sorts of musick: three morris dances;
one of young fellows, one of maidens, and one of old beldames.
There were about a hundred buckets, bowls and pans, filled
with wine, punch, cakes, and ale. From my lord's house all went
to the Town-hall, where plenty of sack, claret, cakes &c. were
prepared for the gentry and better sort; and under the Cross
eight barrels of ale, with abundance of cakes, were placed for
the common people. The stone laid by Mr Vanbrugge was eight
square, finely polished, about eighteen inches over, and upon it
were these words inlayed in pewter – *In memory of the battel of
Blenheim, June [1]8, 1705, Anna Regina.*

This was exactly ten weeks after the opening of the Haymarket
Theatre; in the next few years these two enterprises would
bring Vanbrugh both fame and trouble such as he could hardly
have imagined. And as the curtain rose on the first scene of the
Blenheim drama his opening line would be a knock-out.

— 24 —

Building Blenheim

Marlborough had returned to the Continent early in April 1705. On 22 June, having been for some time 'in dayly hopes of being Able to acquaint you the first stone was Layd', Vanbrugh could at last do so, four days after the event. Although there was little to see – 'few stones lay'd one upon an other' – much more work had been done than the Duke might have imagined, 'in Digging Foundations, making of Contracts, perfecting the Design, and getting Materialls, the most difficult of which has been Stone'. The park afforded rough stone for 'inside walls', but hardly any freestone for fine ashlar masonry and none suitable for outdoor weathering. Lord Rochester at Cornbury, five miles away, offered good stone free for the quarrying; Sir Thomas Wheate at Glympton, two miles closer, offered a reasonable price as a concession to the Duke. Vanbrugh, no doubt with the help of a master mason, explored a considerable number of quarries within a radius of about twenty miles, and altogether about twenty were used; special kinds of stone also came from Portland, Plymouth and Ross-on-Wye.

Before the end of June almost a thousand men would be at work; two months later there would be nearly fifteen hundred on house, gardens, and quarries, that is five times the number reported at Castle Howard a couple of years before. The formal garden walls and those of the kitchen garden away to the south were already well advanced, so that by the following spring both gardens would be fully planted; preparations were also being made for the arrival of substantial trees for the avenues.

The drawings Vanbrugh had earlier sent to the Duke were 'not (nor cou'd not be) perfect in little perticulars'; more recent drawings, of the kind that 'took up a vast deal of pains and time' (in the words of Vanbrugh's evidence against Talman), had been made and 'more thoroughly consider'd'. Thus perfected, the design embodied one alteration 'worth mentioning to your Grace': it was

> in the first entrance of the House; where by bringing the break forwarder, the Hall is enlarg'd, and from a round is brought to an Ovall, figure, a Portico added and Yet the Room much better lighted than before. And the top of it rises above the rest of the building regularly in the middle of the four great Pavillions. I hope your Grace will like this alteration for it adds wonderfully (I think) to the Beauty, regularity and Magnificence of the Building.

Vanbrugh's use of *round* and *oval* cannot be taken literally, for there is no parallel anywhere in his work for such shapes. The inaccuracy may seem very amateurish for someone who had spent six years making himself into a professional; such vagueness was meant to reassure the Duke that what he had not yet seen could now be approved with a mere nod. Marlborough seems to have acquiesced, although the form and depth of the portico were not settled until April 1708 when he wrote to the Duchess, 'I am advised by every body to have the Portico, so that I have writt to Vanbrook to have itt'. But the effect of the altered hall design was as dramatic as the addition of the dome to Castle Howard. Whether seen from the garden or the courtyard or from farther away over the bridge, the clerestory gave extra height to the sprawling design and a central focus which the portico reinforced on the courtyard side. It also solved, with sixteen upper windows added to those on the entrance wall, the problem of lighting what would otherwise have been a very dark north-facing room. The extra distance from the floor as well as the far better illumination were also ideal for the allegorical ceiling painting that was perhaps already envisaged and would be painted by Thornhill in 1716.

[18]

[21]

Blenheim is unusually well documented for a house of its time; besides the many letters, reports, and other papers recently acquired from the house archive, the British Library already possessed the books of accounts and numerous other documents that were collected as evidence in the lawsuits about who should pay for the building. Not the least valuable are the files of Henry Joynes, the young Clerk of Works on the site, who had entered the Office of Works in 1700 as a store-keeper at Kensington Palace and who probably received his training from Hawksmoor as Clerk of Works there. Joynes kept the letters sent him by both Vanbrugh and Hawksmoor, with drafts of his replies, and they cover a wide range of subjects: drawings, materials, organization, money, labour relations, site visits by important persons, and in Hawksmoor's letters good advice both professional and occasionally moral. 'I heard you was at Oxford', he wrote in June 1706, 'which (except busness calls) may as well be lett alone.' Joynes became a proficient draughtsman, and during 1707 corresponded with both architects about drawings of Castle Howard as well as of Blenheim.

On 26 July 1705 Hawksmoor wrote to Joynes that Mr Castle the stationer was sending down a supply of writing books and drawing paper, and asked him to make three copies of 'the great plan of the house on a scale of 10f in one Inch'. Two of them he was to draw 'in black lead only, that when I come down I may settle the plann of the cellar and Attick storys'; in the third he was also to pencil in 'My Laydy Duchess's appart-emt lying next the East'. Evidently much of the disposition of rooms other than those of state was worked out on site, as it would have been before the days of architectural drawing; nevertheless a year later, having established the plan in com-plete detail, Hawksmoor would send down sketches on the back of a letter to Joynes, showing which rooms were to be paved and vaulted and which to have timber floors and ceilings. Even in December 1709 Vanbrugh was writing to Joynes:

pray speak to Kit: Cash to send me the Exact demensions that the Bed chamber next the Gallery will be of; if the Back wall be carry'd up but 18 Inches thick, and the Front Wall Two ft and half; for I fancy the Joyners have made Some Mistake in the Acct: they give me. Or I believe it wou'd not do Amiss, if he sent

me the exact plan, of the Anti Room, drawing Room And Bed
Chamber of the great East Appartmt: with the Walls figur'd (as
to the thicknesses) as they now are: And then I can tell what to
do in Thining the Walls of the West Appartmt.

But by then many other changes had been made. On 28 July
1705 Hawksmoor wrote again to Joynes with a message for
Henry Bankes the mason:

tell him that the disposition of the chapell kitchin and colonade
is by m Ld Treasurer's appointmt quite alter'd from the designs
he has. Soe that befor he proceeds he must have a new Draught.

Vanbrugh did not inform Marlborough of this 'considerable'
alteration until four weeks later (24 August):

it appear'd to my Lord Treasurer so clear for the best that he
thought there was no need of delaying the Work while your
Graces Opinion might be knowing, And so we have gone on as I
propos'd it to him. The Chappell by this change is (instead of
lying behind the Collonade) now at the end of it, in part of the
Stable Wing, and the Kitchen the same on the other Side, there is
Six or eight Thousand pound Sav'd by this, and the Figure both
of the Building and Court much improv'd by it, so I hope 'twill
find your Graces approbation.

Vanbrugh could also tell the Duke that the foundations of the
main house were up to the cellar floor, and those of the chapel,
kitchen and colonnades relocated by Godolphin were almost
to ground level.

This was the first occasion on which the design grew in area
rather than height, and probably the last alteration before the
making of 'a very large, Exact, And intelligible Model of the
Building' which, as Vanbrugh later related, 'was set in the Gallery at Kensington' for the Queen to see. The suggestion that
this model had been made and approved by April 1705 seems
to derive from a misunderstanding of a passage in Coxe's *Memoirs of the Duke of Marlborough*; however, it was on 7 September that the Duke told the Duchess in a letter that

I did in my former letters forgett to approve of what Sr Chri:

Wren propos'd which was that no time shou'd be lost in ordering Mr Vanbrook to have a model of the house made, so that
every thing might be resolv'd, to prevent alterations.

It must therefore have been in September or October 1705, and
this is confirmed by an account for £125. 11s. 5d. in the last
quarter of the year for a new shed at Kensington 'for Joyners to
make the Modells of Woodstock House'. What happened to it
afterwards is unknown, but in 1710 Vanbrugh wrote that the
model was still at Kensington, where he had kept it as a proof
that he had followed it exactly.

Standards of exactness were not then as rigorous as ours –
for example the liberties taken by Wren with the approved
design of St Paul's – but Vanbrugh's claim is easier to accept for
a model made in the autumn than for drawings made the previous spring. These niceties are important because memories
were in conflict ten or fifteen years later, when anything to do
with Blenheim was a matter of acrimonious dispute and a
great deal was found never to have been written down. The
Duchess would maintain, against Vanbrugh, that the Queen
had commissioned the model. She would also maintain that
the estimate for the building given by Sir Christopher Wren
was made without seeing the site, he having made 'an excuse
for not being able to attend it from his old age and the distance
it was from London'. In this case she was probably right,
although Vanbrugh not only stated that Wren was 'sent down
for the purpose' but also implied that this was after the model
had been made. In July 1705 Hawksmoor had told Joynes to
expect Wren at the end of the month, but Joynes's draught letters give no sign that Wren, who in general disliked travelling,
ever arrived. Indeed since on 14 August Hawksmoor asked
Joynes to return some papers urgently 'that I may have 'em
again, to go to Sr Chr Wren with', it looks as if there was some
difficulty in getting an opinion from the old Surveyor.

Wren's estimate, again according to Vanbrugh, was for
ninety or a hundred thousand pounds – twice Marlborough's
proposed outlay on a private commission – for the house and
offices alone, without 'the Back Courts, Garden Walls Court
Walls, Bridge, Gardens, Plantations & Avenues, ... which I
Suppose nobody cou'd Immagine cou'd come to less than as

much more'. In the end the cost was nearer three times than
twice Wren's upper figure; in the end, too, it was nearly all paid
by the Treasury. Vanbrugh only received his arrears as architect on the day of his 'asthma' attack in August 1725. The
Crown was a slow payer, if usually a good one, but the
Treasury was chronically short of money and no accountant
could take kindly to a project whose cost limits had not been
determined at the outset because nobody put a set of figures to
the royal bounty. For five years money arrived, fitfully, irre-
gularly, always late, and in competition with other demands of
Government. Not the least of these were the expenses and the
loan interest of the very war that had occasioned the Battle of
Blenheim and still engaged most of Marlborough's attention.

Not all his attention, however, even when he was on campaign. In September, in Flanders, he proudly showed the
designs to Lord Ailesbury, the Jacobite contact he cultivated as
an insurance in case the Pretender, Prince James Edward
Stuart, should regain the throne:

> in pointing out the apartments for him and lady, &c., [he] laid his
> finger on one and told me '*that* is for you when you come and see
> me there,' ... I asked him who was his Architect (although I
> knew the man that was). He answered 'Sir Jo. Van Brugg.' On
> which I smiled and said: 'I suppose my Lord you made choice of
> him because he is a professed Whig.' I found he did not relish
> this, but he was too great a Courtier for to seem angry. It was at
> my tongues end for to add that he ought as well to have made Sir
> Christopher Wren the Architect Poet Laureate. In fine, I under-
> stand but little or nothing of this matter but enough to affirm (by
> the plan I saw) that the house is like one mass of stone, without
> taste or relish.

During his winter vacations from the field Marlborough visited
the site. Fifty-five when Blenheim was commissioned, he was
torn between the prospects of retirement and of properly finishing the war. In August 1707 Vanbrugh, on his annual visit to
Henderskelfe, wrote to Joynes that the Duke was 'mighty des-
irous to have the Building that is up made habitable' but there
was no hope of anything before the next summer. In July 1708
he told Lord Manchester that 'We have made a Vast Progress
... but it will Still take up two Seasons More to finish'. Never-

theless this estimate, which proved wildly optimistic, was for a
habitable house, not a completed palace, for just before Christmas he told Joynes that the Blenheim office 'shou'd now be
fix'd in some place where it may Stand these Seaven Years'.

Early in 1709 Vanbrugh was alarmed by reports of frost damage to the masonry, even though the new work had been
covered for the winter as usual. On 13 November 1708 Hawksmoor had written to Joynes, 'I hope stone may come in this
hard Drye weather, unless the defect of Mony proves more
fatall than the frost.' It was already cold (being in any case eleven days later by the sun than the English calendar); on the
30th Vanbrugh urged Joynes 'to continue to Secure the Work
all you can against the Frost', and the winter of 1708–9 turned
out to be one of the coldest ever recorded. As in the hard winter
of 1683–4, the Thames froze over and a fair was held on the ice;
an enterprising printer again set up a press on the ice to print
souvenir handbills.

Narcissus Luttrell records the progress of the weather. On 26
December 'it began to freeze, and so continued with snow
every day, more or less, till about Thursday, the 6th of January'.
Luttrell's notes are cautious and factual, but an interesting
sidelight is thrown on the Great Frost and on popular reaction
to it by a letter of 4 January from Peter Wentworth to his
brother Lord Raby in Berlin:

> My ink has been fros, and tho I writ with it as it comes boiling
> from the fire, it's white. If I might tell you all the stories are daily
> brought in of accidents accationed by the great frost I might fill
> sheets, as childern drown upon the Thames, post-boys being
> brought in by their horses to their stages frose to their horses
> stone dead, and we are obliged to the horses for having our let-
> ters regular. There are several stories trump'd up that happen'd
> the last great frost in 1684 and told as now; they begin to build
> booths upon the Thames, it begins to a little to thaw, so I hope it
> will not last so long as that did, for 'twill make all provission very
> dear and I that have a family must think of that.

On the evening of 9 January Luttrell noted a 'great fog' and the
beginning of a thaw, but the next day 'the weather began to
freeze again as hard as ever, it having not been a thorough
thaw, but only some of the snow melted'. Three days later it

again turned milder in the evening, but a cold rain ensued, and 'before the snow was quite gone, it began to freeze again'. Vanbrugh wrote to Joynes on 13 January:

> This unusual weather has prevented my Coming downe; but as soon as the Ways are tollerable I shall come: I shou'd in the Mean time be glad to know what effects this Sharp frost may have had Upon the Building, for this will be a thorough tryall.

In London it again snowed all day on 25 January, but most of the ice disappeared between 28 January and 1 February. However, there was another violent frost on 7 February, followed by 'a pretty deal' of snow. On 10 February Vanbrugh wrote again to Joynes:

> I rec'd One Letter from you, and an Other from Mr Bobart some time Since: in wch you told me the Damage by the Frost was but Small. Mr Banks the Mason was with me Since, And gave me a dismall Account of his Worke being torn all to peices by the Second Frost, But by yours of the 5th, I find no such thing, So hope he told me wrong.

On 15 February, according to Luttrell, parts of the Thames were again frozen. Two days later Vanbrugh told Joynes:

> I have yours of the 13th and am glad Mr Bankes's Information was wrong as to his Work being torn ... This return of the Frost has made me put off my coming downe a little longer, but shall be with you as soon as the Weather alters.

The thaw finally set in on 19 February, but whereas 1684 turned into a dry summer with a good harvest, 1709 continued wet and cold; a poor harvest doubled the price of corn at home and led to a famine in France.

In the management of Blenheim, as in that of the Haymarket Theatre, Vanbrugh was becoming something of a juggler; and how several thousand pounds could be saved by expanding the building is something he never explained. Any saving was in any case more than absorbed by another extension which, as Vanbrugh reminded the Duchess in a memorandum of 8 July 1709, the Duke had approved on site eighteen months earlier.

This consisted of two large rectangular courts behind the kit-chen and stable blocks, with covered arcades connecting the various extra offices: store-rooms, bakehouse, laundries, coach houses, staff quarters, and on the south flanks 'Two Green houses, which Answer one another in the Genll. view of the South Front of the whole Building'. That on the east, 'inten-ded purely to preserve the trees in Winter', was actually built; its full-length round-headed sash-windows overlook the south-east formal garden. It now has a glass roof carried on iron pillars, but there are again some orange trees growing in it. That on the west, Vanbrugh told the Duchess,

> having a very beautiful Situation (the West end . . . looking dir-ectly down the Valley and River) may perhaps be thought proper for a distinct retired room of Pleasure, furnished with only some of the best Greens, mixd with pictures, Busts, Statues, Books and other things of ornament and entertainment. These kind of De-tached Buildings have ever been extremely valued, where there has happened any thing particularly fine for their Situation, And I believe there is not in Europe a finer than this.

Vanbrugh had proposed 'a little kind of Salon' at the end, facing the valley, and a pair to it on the east, reminiscent of the cab-inets at the ends of Castle Howard. The Duke had rejected this in favour of one large room, but the more Vanbrugh thought about the orangeries the better he liked them. Four days after his letter to the Duchess he wrote from Blenheim – evidently to Lord Ryalton, her son-in-law and at that time the likely inher-itor of Blenheim – in the hope of gaining support for the western one:

> I find your Ldship Seems to think the Greenhouse on the West Side, will take off too much of the View from the Gallery . . . but I believe there is as little of that misfortune here, as ever happen'd in any Situation. All the most Valluable parts of the Views, lying to the most Significant Rooms in the Building. Nor is there any thing hid by this Greenhouse; from the Bow window in the Gallery, but the bleak naked part of the Park. And that, to One of the Worst points of the Compass, which is the North-west . . .

There is another thing, I think worth yr Ldships remark too in this Case, which is, that this Greenhouse will keep off the Westerly Sun from the end Garden. And Grott under the Gallery at a time in the Summer evening when the West Side of a house is intollerable ... Nor will there be so pleasant a Room for View Nor so cool (yet all the Same Gay and light) in the Whole house, as that Greenhouse or Detach'd Gallery, for that indeed is what I take it to be, And not a Magazine for a parcell of foolish Plants. I don't see why this shou'd not be the Room for the Tytian hangings which it will just hold. And Since there is no Library in the House, that may be the business (or pretended business at least) of this Galery The Books dispos'd in Presses made handsome like Cabinets, And plac'd Regularly along with the Chairs, Tables and Couches, This, my Lord has allways been my Notion of this Room: And I shou'd be mighty glad to find your Lordship come into it, for it Seems clearly to me the most Valluable Room in the Whole Building, And I never saw any one of this kind Abroad (which scarce any fine Place is wthout) that cou'd compare with it, for the Extreame pleasantness of its Situation.

This letter later came into the Duchess's hands and was endorsed by her:

The second green house, or a detached gallery I thank God I prevented being built; nothing, I think can be more mad than the proposal, nor a falser description of the prospect.

Ultimately it was never built in any form because the west court was abandoned, the work at Blenheim proceeding, like that at Castle Howard, from east to west. But Vanbrugh's enthusiasm for this gallery is as understandable as its rejection by everyone else. As for greenhouses, the family would argue, one was surely enough; as for a gallery, the provision of one within the house had been the essential difference in the Duke's mind between Lord Carlisle's palace and his. With a length of one hundred and eighty feet and a height of over thirty, with six great mirrors opposite the windows and with Kneller's projected life-size allegory framed at the upper end, the great gallery in the main house was going to be a room to challenge most in Europe. On 3 March 1710 the States General of the Netherlands issued a pass for the duty-free export of the mirrors to England. Macky wrote of the intention to place them in the gallery at Blenheim, but its completion as the Long Library left nowhere to put them. Kneller's sketch for the painting survives, as does his explanation of it, from which we learn that Queen Anne authorized it in 1708 and that Marlborough desired that her figure alone should be a portrait. Thus the sketch depicts her presenting an elevation drawing of Blenheim not to the Duke but to 'a warlike Vigorous Figure representing Millitary Merit'. Kneller never painted the picture, 'State Difference happening', as the fourth Duchess noted on Kneller's paper, 'betwixt the Queen and the Duke of Marlbrough'.

Perhaps one of the ideas in Vanbrugh's mind was a memory of the Electoral residence at Herrenhausen on the outskirts of Hanover; although the journey there hardly passed through the most rewarding part of Germany for the student of architecture, his trip to Hanover in the summer of 1706 must have given him a new kind of confidence in making comparisons with foreign buildings. The *Festsaal* or Gallery next to the Elector's villa-palace faced south on to an orange garden, and doubled as an orangery in the winter; it had been recently completed and decorated with wall-paintings by Venetian artists, and was by far the grandest and biggest of the rooms. In any case, for Vanbrugh two galleries must be better than one, at least as far as Blenheim was concerned. For, as long as the royal favour lasted, Blenheim was an architect's dream. His frequent references to things which would save money or justify its expenditure were made in the context of a commission to which no price had been set; his very confidence surely covers a slight uneasy suspicion that it was too good to last.

In the security of his Warrant (dated 9 June 1705) as 'Surveyor of all the Works and Buildings' at Woodstock, Vanbrugh seems to have made the most of his privileges and perquisites, even if he did not quite overstep them. In May 1709 the accounts include £12. 9s. 4d. for joiner's work in the front upstairs room of his Whitehall house, in fitting up presses, a drawing board and a writing table to make him an office 'for the Service of Blenheim Castle'. More questionably, in the same month Robert Wetherill charged £50. 7s. 10d. for plastering of ceilings and walls 'done at the Mannor House in Wood-

stock park for his Grace the Duke of Marlborough'. This was a
formula of convenience, if not actually a fiction since, unlike
Vanbrugh, the Marlboroughs had no interest whatever in the
old Manor. Moreover, the previous year some of the roof had
been re-leaded. Nevertheless on 14 September 1708 the architect assured the Duchess

> That there has been such Husbandry in the Design (which is the
> Chief Concern) as well as in the Execution, That the Whole will
> by all People be judg'd to have Cost full twice as much as will be
> paid for't.

On that occasion he was reinforcing the argument he had
already offered two months earlier in a letter, evidently addressed to Arthur Maynwaring and intended for her information
and Godolphin's. He was asking for the same salary in respect
of Blenheim as that awarded to Edmund (or William) Boulter,
the Blenheim Comptroller at the time. It is the artist's claim to
be valued equally with the administrator:

> 'Tis impossible it can be refus'd me. If it be; 'Tis purely from the
> misfortune, of my Sort of Service in this Business, not being
> rightly Understood: which is indeed what I have always App-
> rehended, Since I saw so much Stress laid upon an officer in Mr
> Boulters Post: But in this. My Ld Treasurer is so very wrong
> Appris'd, That 'tis most certain the good Husbandry of the
> Money in the most Essentiall and Significant part, lys as entirely
> upon the Surveyor, as the Designing of the Building: All that
> comes in the Way of a Comptroller or a Clark of the Works, is to
> See, That the Prices are right, And that there is no more work
> allow'd for than is done . . . But in the great Article of Manage-
> ment, they have no sort of Concern, Which is, in so casting
> things in the Execution of the Building, And disposing the mat-
> erialls that nothing may be Superfluous, or Improperly
> Apply'd; But that the Appearance of every thing may exceed the
> Cost . . . The Case is exactly Parralell to that of keeping a Frugall
> and yet a Creditable Table; Which I suppose nobody will say de-
> pends in any measure so much upon the Cheap buying in of the
> Provisions, as in a Right management and Distribution of 'em
> Afterwards . . . I confess there must Pass two Years more, before
> it can be clearly Seen, whether I have done right, in this great
> Point or no: But this may be known at present; That I take Ten

times the Pains to Succeed in it, that Others in this kind of Business usually do ... there is not one part of it, that I don't weigh
and Consider a hundred times, before 'tis put in Execution; And
this with two ends, one of trying to do it better, And tother of
giving it Some other turn that may be as well and yet Come
Cheaper. And 'tis this that makes me when I am here, Avoid all
Company, And haunt the Building like a Ghost, from the Time the
Workmen leave off at Six a Clock, till tis quite Dark.

Maynwaring's comments to the Duchess were shrewd, even if
they do betray a fawning self-interest:

I have read Mr Van's letter, and can only say I am sorry for him,
because I believe he is unhappy through his own folly, and I can
see no reasonable way to help him. What I mean by his folly, is
his building the play-house, which certainly cost him a great
deal more than was subscribed; and his troubles arise from the
workmen that built it, and the tradesmen that furnished the
cloaths, &c., for the actors. But I am now in your Grace's service
(in which I will die). I cannot advise you to do any thing for him
out of your own estate, from which I may hope for a subsistence
myself after I am grown old and good for nothing, though for the
last reason I am afraid I might pretend to it already.

But the Duchess was almost always Vanbrugh's adversary. Ten
years younger than the Duke and four years older than his
architect, Sarah Jennings was devoted to her husband, whom
she married at eighteen; she was practical, thrifty, managing,
fearless, and sure of her own rightness in everything, and she
had a poor opinion of all architects.* In July 1707 Vanbrugh
had told Lord Manchester, that the Duchess was

so entirely pleas'd, that She tould me, she found She shou'd live
to Ask my pardon, for ever having Quarrell'd with me, And I find
she declares the same to My Lord Treasurer and every Body. So
I hope I shall come Off in her good graces at last.

The following March he told Manchester,

* p. 199

Blenheim is much Advanc'd, and to My Ld Dukes entire satisfaction, nor have I any Quarrells with my Lady Dutchess About it. There will be a great deal done this Summer, And one Summer more I hope will Cover it all.

But although the Duchess was civil to Vanbrugh for over ten years, and even on occasion complimentary, she had quickly decided for herself that he and his ideas were extravagant. She would have preferred Wren to design the house at Woodstock, although she referred on other occasions than that of the Blenheim estimate to Sir Christopher's inability, in his seventies, to keep his staff in order. Wren was a diplomatist and a man of few words, and she felt a little sorry for him; nevertheless he seems to have outwitted her over the designing of Marlborough House, the London residence she began at the back of St James's Palace in 1709, the year before her irreparable quarrel with the Queen. For although her dealings were with Sir Christopher, most of the work was delegated to 'Mr Wren', his son Christopher, Chief Clerk of the Queen's Works.

The Duchess also respected Hawksmoor enough to be willing to write a testimonial for him in December 1715; she described him as capable, modest and honest, and a man in whose ability to cut costs she believed as firmly as she doubted Vanbrugh's. Her description of the latter as 'perhaps the only Architect in the World, capable of building such a House' was, in the circumstances, a brickbat rather than a bouquet. She was a fluent – and exceptionally illegible – correspondent and a constant annotator of documents. Above all, as we shall see, she detested the two features at Woodstock that Vanbrugh, as if wilfully, seemed to care about most: the great Bridge and old Woodstock Manor. Yet it seems to have been her own desire for domestic amenity that precipitated the biggest change, visually, in the exterior of Blenheim.

Lady Marlborough thought of Blenheim as her house and a home for the Duke; later she would make it his memorial. She cared to make it comfortable, and she had a passion for light rooms. In April 1707 the masons were paid for pulling down the whole garden front between the corner pavilions and the central portico: two stretches of ninety-seven and a half feet, some of it as high as the upper floor; other demolitions followed. The added expense came less in taking down work than in cutting and setting fine masonry all over again. Although Vanbrugh and Hawksmoor might have decided that Blenheim was going to be excessively low, resorting to such costly demolition and rebuilding would have struck them as a desperate and unprofessional solution. Vanbrugh's only reference to the change, in a letter to the Duchess (11 June 1709), implies that the idea was not his. Seeking to allay her 'uneasyness about the New Building', and especially about cost, he mentioned two extra expenses together, as if neither was within his control:

> Then there happen'd One great disappointment. The Freestone in the Park Quarry not proving good, which if it had wou'd have saved 50 p. Cent in that Article; And besides this, the House was (since the Estimate) resolv'd to be rais'd About Six ft higher in the principal parts of it.

Nevertheless it is possible that the requirement of more light thus offered a justification for a change in appearance that by itself would have been reckless. Good architecture aims to provide a single solution to all the problems of a design. A com- [0] parison of the early drawings with the building shows three principal changes in the elevation: in windows, overall height [2] and choice of order. The ground-floor windows in the long intermediate sections, previously flat-headed, were raised two and a half feet into round-headed arches, and the upper windows were also lengthened by a smaller amount; this gave appreciably better illumination on both floors. But raising the windows meant also raising the walls around them, and consequently raising the corner pavilions and the central block to preserve the balance between taller and lower parts.

Now the central nine bays of the house have a giant order of pilasters and columns. The grammar of Classical architecture allows only two ways of lengthening columns: since the height is proportional to the diameter, either the diameter must also be increased or the order must be changed to a slenderer one. In this case there was no room for sideways expansion, so the squat Doric with its martial and masculine associations had to be changed to something taller in proportion to its width. One drawing shows that the Ionic was considered, but eventually the architects – and Vanbrugh will have valued Hawksmoor's expert knowledge in the matter – chose the extra richness of the Corinthian.

Other detail features of the design were regarded as no more than provisional until the last moment. The demands of quantity surveying, cost accountancy and planning regulations have made it necessary today – and developments in architectural drawing and document copying have made it possible – for every detail of a design to be fixed before work begins, but this was seldom so in the past. There was nothing so very unusual, except the scale of the operation, about the experimental way in which the corner lanterns and other 'eminencies' were evolved, partly on Hawksmoor's drawing board and partly by experiment (what he later referred to as 'experience and trials, so that we are assured of the good effect of it'). Full-size models and cut-outs of all sorts of particulars were hoisted up to see how they looked from below – whether they were large or bold enough – before being finally settled. The first lantern, on the north-east corner, was completed in 1708. The same year Marlborough approved the final design of the north portico with its upper pediment set back in the middle like a cleft rock. At about the same time the gate towers to the side courts were finalized; they were also embellished with a device too emphatic for Addison's taste in *The Spectator* [30] (No. 59, 8 May 1711). It was

> a *Rebus*, which has been lately hewn out in Free stone, and erected over two of the Portals of *Blenheim* House, being the Figure of a monstrous Lion tearing to pieces a little Cock. For the better understanding of which Device, I must acquaint my *English* Reader that a Cock has the Misfortune to be called in *Latin* by the same Word that signifies a *French*-Man, as a Lion is the Emblem of the *English* Nation. Such a Device in so noble a Pile of Building looks like a Pun in an heroic Poem; and I am very sorry the truly ingenious Architect would suffer the Statuary to blemish his excellent Plan with so poor a Conceit: But I hope what I have said will gain Quarter for the Cock, and deliver him out of the Lion's Paw.

In 1709 Marlborough himself had found an emblem more startlingly primitive in its associations, a formalized version of the severed heads on stakes that were still sometimes raised above Temple Bar in the Strand. At the beginning of September he captured the Citadel at Tournai, over whose great gate stood a colossal bust of Louis XIV flanked by carved trophies of arms. The equestrian victor and the heroic virtues that his architects had outlined in designs to surmount the south front of Blenheim gave way to this massive piece of booty. In 1711 it was seen and sketched, still *in situ*, by the painter Thornhill, but by April 1712 the bust (weighing four or five tons) and six cases of trophies had arrived at the Works wharf in Scotland Yard in preparation for being shipped by barge up the Thames to Abingdon or Oxford. But by that time, and long before it was finally set up, Blenheim had become (in a phrase coined by **[19]** Vanbrugh and taken over by the Marlboroughs) 'a monument of ingratitude'.

Sarah Jennings and the Princess Anne had known each other since they were ten and five respectively, but became close friends about 1683, the year of the Princess's marriage to Prince George of Denmark. In a few years Sarah, a lady of the bedchamber and a successful and expert mother, became almost indispensable to the Princess, whose efforts at maternity resulted in a string of misfortunes. By 1691 the ladies were on nickname terms and Sarah was receiving a pension of £1000 a year. Her fatal mistake, unseen at the time, was to persuade her royal friend in 1697 to employ a needy relative in the lower but familiar office of bedchamber *woman*: this was Abigail Hill, Sarah's first cousin whom she had earlier nursed through smallpox.

By 1703 the Duchess was telling the Queen (as they now were) that the Tories were no more than Jacobites in disguise: Sarah saw the world in black and white without half-tones, and neither her presumption nor her arrogance improved relations with a monarch of one year's standing who, herself a Tory, was still feeling her way through a minefield of political dissension in the hope of bringing her subjects to unity. The Duchess became importunate, repeating her charge in the aftermath of Blenheim; for most of 1705 she was absent from court, but the estrangement was hidden from public awareness by the Queen's continued support of Marlborough and Godolphin.

But by 1707 five years of monarchy had toughened the Queen; she was ready to stand on her own, and she was tired of the Duchess's jealous and paranoid attacks. Some time between April and June, as the Blenheim masons rebuilt the demolished south front, Abigail Hill secretly, at Kensington, married Samuel Masham. Having entered royal service aged thirteen in 1692, as a page to Prince George, Masham had risen by 1706 to the rank of groom of the bedchamber to the Prince and the following spring to the absentee colonelcy of an Irish regiment. We know little about Abigail except that she wrote a good hand; the Duchess was obviously not to be a reliable witness, but as matters stood by 1707 Abigail would have needed only to be ordinarily civil in order to be preferable to Sarah in the Queen's eyes. But in addition Abigail was a second cousin of the Tory Robert Harley. In the struggle for party political influence Marlborough and Godolphin forced Harley's resignation as Secretary of State in January 1708 by threatening the Queen that they would not serve while he remained in the Cabinet; in these circumstances Harley saw in his cousin a way of continued access to the Monarch.

The Duchess meanwhile continued to overplay her hand. Adding insult to familiar licence, in July 1708 she accused – as she would continue to accuse – the Queen and Mrs Masham of lesbianism. Vanbrugh had told Manchester on 11 May that 'My Lady Marlborough go's now very often to Court, & is in perfect good humour. I hope all will keep right.' On 27 July he wrote, 'She is very much at Court, and mighty well there, but the Qs: fondness of tother Lady, is not to be expressd.' The Queen was angry at the accusation, and she was hurt. The 'tateling' (as she called him) former Vice-Chamberlain Bertie – who put it about that Vanbrugh was going to design Marlborough House – informed Arthur Maynwaring – who told the Duchess – that after 'two terrible Battles . . . her Eyes were red, & it was plain she had been crying very much'; nevertheless she maintained her dignity. Her greatest dilemma was between the Duchess and the Duke, for she depended on Marlborough for the successful conduct of the war. The Duchess ranted on, apparently insensible, as she busied herself with Marlborough House, that the breach was irrevocable. By September 1709 the victor of Tournai was dragged into her private war, writing a complaining letter to Anne about her treatment of Sarah.

On 6 April 1710 the Duchess had her last tearful interview with the Queen, who refused all discussion or comment. Vanbrugh seems to have been too preoccupied with other matters to realize that three weeks after that interview was an inopportune time for the Duchess to receive his letter, asking her once more to persuade the Queen that because Blenheim was a national monument his Surveyor's salary ought to be increased. But the next few months would see changes in government that would indeed be momentous for the country, for the Marlboroughs and for Blenheim alike.

It is of great significance that three of the principles of modern British government were not yet established: first, that the Cabinet is drawn from only one party; second, that it is drawn from the majority party in the House of Commons; thirdly, that the monarch is apolitical.* Harley, Abigail, and the Duke of Shrewsbury (one of the kingmakers before the 1688 Revolution) now encouraged the Queen in her idea of a Cabinet 'above party'. Harley and Shrewsbury hoped, in G.M.Trevelyan's words,

> to govern the land by favour of the Queen and by the goodwill of the many moderate men among her subjects. They intended to lean on the Tories as much perhaps as Godolphin had leant on the Whigs five years back, but no more. As late as September ... Harley wrote to the Duke of Newcastle: 'As soon as the Queen has shewn strength and ability to give the law to both sides, then will consideration be truly shewn in the exercise of power without regard to parties only'.

In August the Queen was persuaded – with great reluctance – to dismiss Godolphin from the Treasury, and his office was put into commission, being administered for the time being by the Treasury Board. Harley was made Chancellor of the Exchequer; not until the following May, newly created Earl of Oxford, would he be promoted to be Lord Treasurer. But by September 1710 the quiet and gradual change in the political complexion of the Cabinet had gone so far that agreement with a Whig House of Commons was impossible. The desire for

* p. 234

peace, a passion for the principles of the High Church, the very
fact of the changes in the political ministry, and the glamour of
the Queen's name all contributed to a Tory landslide in the
October election which ironically, in Trevelyan's words,
'bound the Queen and Harley to the chariot wheels of the High
Tories ... and proved once more that Parliamentary Government could only mean Party Government'.

The effect of the Cabinet changes on Blenheim had been immediate. A week after Godolphin's dismissal Henry Joynes
wrote to Samuel Travers at the Treasury:

> The ill news of my Lord Treasurer being out causes a Mighty
> Talk here and I am Affraid will make people in the Country not
> give such Creditt as the worke will require if we continue going
> on as we have without theirs [there's] such Supplys to Convince
> them that the Building is in all likelyhood to proceed as it has
> done for the time past.

Early in September 1710 the mason Edward Strong laid off all
his men. There were fears of sabotage, and some capitals
awaiting setting were damaged. The Duchess's nightmare had
always been that the Duke himself would have to pay for the
monstrous house on which he had set his heart; with the
Treasury in Tory hands the waking reality drew dangerously
close. On 28 September she stopped all work until either the
Duke returned or the Treasury sent money.

Vanbrugh persuaded Harley to issue £7000, on grounds not
of hardship to the work force but of the safety of the fabric over
the winter. Harley agreed less for the sake of a public monument than to avoid a Whitehall scandal and to keep
Marlborough at the war front. Nevertheless it took the whole of
October to get the cash drawn and conveyed to Woodstock.
Writing to inform the Duke of what he had achieved, Vanbrugh
asked no longer for such money 'as might have made me toler-
ably easy the rest of my life' but 'only to Save me from a Ruin, I
must afterwards Struggle hard to Avoid'.

The halcyon days had gone for ever. The original spirit of
optimism and goodwill had forsaken Blenheim, and the
Marlboroughs' days of favour were numbered. On 23 November Swift published a swingeing attack on them in *The Ex-*

aminer. Early in 1711 the Duke's hopes of winning Paris were finally dashed by the opening of secret peace initiatives with France. He had returned to England the day after Christmas 1710; he met the Queen two days later and was in her words 'very humble and submissive'. On 17 January he took her a letter of apology from his lady, but it was too late; the Queen was adamant, and the next morning he returned the Duchess's golden key of office. On the last day of 1711 Anne rid herself of the Duke also: he was dismissed from all his offices on suspicion of financial misappropriation.

A year earlier the whole main block and east court of Blenheim had been roofed except the two west corner towers. Vanbrugh wrote to Harley on 12 February 1711: 'The Duke of Marlborogh has order'd me to beg you'd give me leave to wait upon you with something relating to Blenheim before he go's away.' He saw Harley on 23 February, and secured further money from the Treasury for 1711. Work continued indoors into the early months of 1712, but on 1 June Treasury payments stopped. On 23 August 1712, at about the time Lord Carlisle moved into Castle Howard, Marlborough visited Blenheim and told Joynes he was going into voluntary exile.* On 10 November he made a new will; Vanbrugh was one of the witnesses. None of the great house was habitable, but the garden was flourishing. 'All Woodstock knows', wrote the Duchess later, 'that they made Hay in it and sold it.' There was precious little else for Joynes and his office colleagues and the watchmen and gardeners to do.

For Vanbrugh himself worse was yet to come, as the shadow that had fallen on the Marlboroughs extended also over him. He was deeply in debt, and only in his most optimistic moments could he believe that the opera would ever make money. Castle Howard was a success, if still far from complete, and there were others. But in the valley at Woodstock the great Bridge stood marooned, useless for want of embankments at either end; beyond it smoke could sometimes be seen curling from a chimney in the habitable remains of the old Manor.

* p. 349

_ 25 _

Venture and Vacation

In the early summer of 1706, as the walls of Blenheim began to rise above ground level, both Vanbrugh's commitment to the office of a herald and his sense of the theatrical were put to a more severe test than he can have anticipated. He was chosen to carry the insignia of the Most Noble Order of the Garter to the young Prince of Hanover who would – it might already be hoped by some and feared by others – one day become King George II. As a serious Kit-Cat, this move in the strategy of safeguarding the Protestant succession was welcome to him. In his official capacity the opportunity for pomp and ceremony was matchless. But his eye for the comic and the ridiculous must never for a moment betray him: whatever life had taught him about keeping a straight face, he needed it now.

Most of our information about the Hanover visit comes not from Vanbrugh himself but from the account written by Samuel Stebbing, Somerset Herald, for old Sir Henry St George, Garter Herald. Properly speaking, it was Sir Henry's duty to undertake the investiture, but at eighty the long journey would have been very taxing for him, and the task therefore fell to Vanbrugh as the next in rank although the most junior in length of service. Stebbing's account was composed as the report of a junior to his superior; it therefore tells us more about the particulars of the ceremonies than about the people concerned, and says almost nothing about Stebbing's own part; we must therefore imagine him (and others) as the silent witnesses to all that took place.

The party included Lord Halifax and Vanbrugh, appointed by the Queen 'Commissioners for this Solemnity', Stebbing as Vanbrugh's assistant, Joseph Addison as Halifax's secretary, the young Earl of Dorset, and Pierre de Falaiseau, the unofficial Hanoverian representative in London. Lord Dorset was eighteen, the son of the Kit-Cat Earl, whom he had only recently succeeded in the title, and a Kit-Cat himself; Falaiseau acted as guide and interpreter (French being the current diplomatic language) although Vanbrugh's familiarity with both written and spoken French will have been a great asset to the visitors. Lord Halifax and Addison were Kit-Cats, and Halifax was an old friend of Vanbrugh's, three years his senior. He had been, according to Cibber, the first audience for the draft of *The Provok'd Wife* 'in its looser Sheets', and it was he who implemented the reinstatement of Vanbrugh as Comptroller in 1715.* It was for him that Vanbrugh asked Tonson to find an elegant set of mathematical instruments the following year, and he was one of the original subscribers to the new theatre.

On 26 April the Duke of Montagu, who had heard it that morning from the Duchess of Marlborough, wrote to Halifax that Vanbrugh's departure was likely to be delayed because he was 'now upon making an agreement betweene the two playhouses'. Having taken on the businesses of play-writing and architecture he evidently conceived some sort of great plan for the London stage that would not only bring profitability to the Queen's Theatre but also heal the rift caused by Betterton's defection from Drury Lane to Lincoln's Inn Fields in 1695. Cibber remembered or represented the purpose of the new playhouse as providing for Betterton's 'elder Actors', to 'recover them . . . to their due Estimation'; but Vanbrugh seems to have envisaged a joint company, for the theoretical establishment list of *c.* 1703† includes names of actors from both companies. Moreover, only *The Provok'd Wife* was written for Lincoln's Inn Fields, and Vanbrugh had no special affection for that company in preference to Drury Lane. Congreve wrote to a friend (Joseph Kealy) on 30 April 1706: 'I believe the Play house cannot go on another Winter. Have heard there is to be a Union of the two houses as well as Kingdoms'. The process of

* p. 235
† p. 267

uniting England and Scotland was indeed accomplished in
1707, but Vanbrugh left for Holland without any success; all the
problems of both the Haymarket and Blenheim would await
his return.

Vanbrugh had received a money order for £300 for his
expenses on 7 May; Halifax had crossed to Holland almost
three weeks earlier, having other business there, bringing as
he did an official copy of the recently passed Regency Act
which legalized the Protestant Succession to the throne, and
also deeds of naturalization for the electoral family. Vanbrugh
was still in London on 10 May, when Harley gave him a letter
for Halifax; he set out for Gravesend the following day, Saturday. But although Harley wrote to Halifax on the 17th, 'I doubt
not but Mr Vanbrugh is come to Your Lordship in good time',
he did not reach Hanover until nine days later, on Sunday
evening, 6 June (New Style; 26 May in England). His journey
was not free from anxiety, for although he and Stebbing travelled in the comfort of a private coach they carried a considerable amount of valuable luggage: besides their own ceremonial robes and insignia (and perhaps Lord Halifax's as
well) they were bringing the 'Habit and Ensigns of the Order
for the Prince Electoral'.

On Monday morning at a respectable hour Halifax and Vanbrugh delivered their letter of credentials to Baron Goertz, the
Elector's Minister of State, and requested an audience of the
Prince. The Elector had received the Order five years earlier
from Lord Macclesfield. He 'would by no means hear', wrote
Stebbing, 'of having it done with more Ceremony than he had
himself, and to make a distinction would not permit that the
Prince should receive the Habit under a Canopy as he did but
only to have an arm'd Chair'. To understand the extreme form-
ality of the proceedings, as well as the Elector's concern not to
be upstaged by his son, it is important to know something of
their relationship at the time.

At the end of 1694 the elder George had divorced his wife
Sophia Dorothea on the grounds of adultery with Count Philipp
Christoph von Königsmarck, notwithstanding his own misalli-
ance with Melusine von der Schulenberg. Sophia Dorothea
was banished to the castle of Ahlden in Celle where she remained a virtual prisoner, and the young George was brought

up by his grandparents. Believing his mother to be innocent, he was estranged from his father, the rift only being patched over on the latter's accession as George I of England in 1714. In 1706 there were three princely households within the palace at Hanover, for three generations. First there was the elder George's mother, the Princess Dowager Sophia of the Palatinate, widowed in 1698 and the grand-daughter of James I; it was through her that the English succession was to pass to her son on the death of Queen Anne, whom she pre-deceased. Secondly there was her son, the ruling Elector, the future George I; thirdly his son, the Prince Electoral, now twenty-three and recently married to Caroline of Ansbach, and the object of Vanbrugh's mission.

The Queen's commission turned out to give the Elector the option, as a Knight Companion of the Order, of conducting the investiture himself – which would have reduced the English party to the function of delivery men – and his wish in the matter had first of all to be discovered. 'At length', wrote Stebbing, nicely understating the tedium of the occasion, it was intimated that His Electoral Highness would leave the whole affair to the Commissioners, whose next task was thus to agree the programme of ceremonies with court officials. The requisite number of coaches was ordained to carry the party between their lodgings and the court, and Friday 11 June (New Style) was appointed for presenting the Prince with 'Her Majesties Credential Letter, the Book of Statutes and afterwards to Invest His Hs. at the same time with the Blew Ribbon Garter and George'; this combined two separate acts, saving the Prince – not to mention his visitors – the trouble of a second audience in the afternoon.

Shortly before midday on Friday the Lord Chamberlain, Thomas Grote, and several other courtiers came with two six-horse and six two-horse coaches to take the party to the 'castle'. It is tempting, because it is picturesque, to suppose that this was the summer-palace of Herrenhausen, which the family used mainly between May and October. But the scale and number of rooms to which Stebbing's account refers suggest very strongly that the scene of events was the Residence in the town. Moreover, Stebbing implies that the coaches were furnished more for pomp than for the distance involved:

As they generally have Eat at the Electors Table ever since the
time of their first Audience, their Retinue are likewise treated at
the Electors charge, and the same Honours paid them in all respects as are allowed to those who have the Character of Ambassadors.

One of the grander coaches was for Halifax, the other appears
to have been for Dorset, who was lodged in the same house.
Alighting in the inner courtyard, they were welcomed at the
foot of the stairs by the *Hofmarschall*, Christian von Hard-
enberg (who was about Vanbrugh's age) and a great number of
officers; at the top of the stairs they were greeted by Baron
Goertz and led through the gallery to a large antechamber
'where the Company falling off on each hand made a lane for
the Commrs to pass through into the Chamber where His Hs.
staid to receive them'. Lord Halifax handed over his letter to
the seated Prince, and then 'Mr Vanbrugh address't himself to
his Hs. in a few words, and presented him with the Book of
Statutes. Then he withdrew into the Antichamber, and there
putting on his Mantle of the Order took with him the Blew
Ribbon Garter and George, and Repaired again to His Hs.'

The Prince declared his acceptance of the conditions and
returned the book to Vanbrugh, 'who thereupon presenting the
Blew Ribbon Garter to my Ld Halifax, and the Prince reposing
his left Leg on a Footstool the Commrs together tyed it on, Mr
Vanbrugh reading the proper Admonition'. Then with a similar
admonition they both put the ribbon of the Diamond George
'about His Hs. Neck vizt over his left shoulder and under his
right Arm'. The party then proceeded to the apartment of
'Madam the Electrice' — the Princess Dowager, where they
joined the other members of the electoral family for an early
afternoon dinner. At about five o'clock the procession of
coaches returned the party to their lodgings in the town.

On Sunday at six in the evening the identical journey took
place, with the same welcomes and leading to the same room,
where the Prince received them as before. There 'Mr Vanbrugh having Habited himself in his Mantle, the Commrs entred the Room, where His Hs. was' and removed the ribbon
George, the Prince's upper coat and his sword and belt. Vanbrugh handed to Halifax the surcoat and the sword and belt of

the Order, which had previously been laid out on a table, 'and they together Invested his Hs. therewith; Mr Vanbrugh reading the usual Admonitions'; the ribbon George was then replaced, the Prince signed an acceptance of the Order, already sealed, and they all proceeded to the 'great Room'. Vanbrugh, assisted by Stebbing, walked in front of the Prince, carrying the rest of the insignia on a crimson velvet cushion.

Lord Halifax's instructions ordained that the ceremonies should take place in a setting as similar to Windsor Castle as possible. In fact nothing at Hanover was at all like Windsor with its curtain walls and its great late Gothic chapel. Stebbing, anxious to confirm that the setting had been appropriate, translated the rooms into English terms while saying little about their appearance or arrangement.

In the great hall they found the Electress and other members of the family, though not the Elector, with 'a great number of Persons of Quality of both Sexes' and members of the court and of foreign embassies. At the upper end of the hall were three armchairs for the Prince, Lord Halifax on his right, and Vanbrugh on his left. Vanbrugh placed the cushion on a table and all three sat down and 'a while reposed themselves in their Chairs' with, no doubt, that vacant gaze that hides both satisfaction and slight anxiety in participants on such occasions. Then they all stood up, and Vanbrugh held the Commission while Halifax made a short speech. The Prince sat down again and put out his leg on a couple of high cushions; Halifax took off the blue garter and, assisted by Vanbrugh, replaced it with the diamond one, which they both buckled, 'Mr Vanbrugh reading the accustomd Admonition'.

The Prince stood up again, the George was removed and he was clothed in the mantle, hood and collar and the George was replaced, Vanbrugh reading the appropriate formula for each action. They put on his head the ostrich-feathered cap 'which the Prince had before Orderd to be Enricht with Diamonds' and he sat down and promptly stood up again. Vanbrugh made 'a short congratulatory Compliment' and Halifax another short speech, the Prince remaining standing. Then Vanbrugh gave him the two stars and two ribbons and they all sat down for a while before returning to the Prince's apartment. The English party were driven back to their lodgings, but only for long enough to prepare for the supper and ball which concluded the proceedings.

After that the visitors seem to have been at leisure, for it was not until 18 June that Stebbing wrote his report. But what they did, whom they saw and what they talked about he did not relate. The gardens at Herrenhausen were large, elaborate, and very pleasant, but the idea of Vanbrugh as an eager architectural tourist is hard to sustain. It was known that he was both a poet and an architect, so he probably had to answer more questions than he was able to ask. And when most topics of interest had been exhausted the news came that it would not be possible – or at least not polite – to leave so soon. 'The Commrs have not yet recd. their Presents', wrote Stebbing; moreover the King of Prussia had arrived with his son Friedrich Wilhelm, a 'well set youth, large limbs, but little shape, yet has a very good face, above 18 years old'. He was to be married at once to the Prince's younger sister Dorothea Sophia, a beautiful young lady of eighteen. The wedding took place on the day Stebbing wrote, and there was a great ball 'with cannons' in the evening. Halifax left about a week later and made a fairly leisurely return home, stopping to visit Marlborough in camp at Helchin in the latter part of July and not reaching England until 18 August. Vanbrugh had travelled out separately and must surely have returned separately. Whatever the attractions of a tour in northern Europe, the style of his next designs seems to have come not from the Continent but rather from within him. Moreover, he must have indicated that he would be home soon. A week after the Prussian wedding (12 June in England) Hawksmoor wrote to Edmund Boulter at Blenheim that 'Mr Vanbrugh will not be long before he comes from Holland so that I woud have us give him satisfaction of our care and forwardness in his absence.'

The Lord Chamberlain's papers in the Public Record Office contain a note of agreement of 14 August 1706 with Owen Swiney by which Vanbrugh was 'to put into the Hands of Mr Swiny the Direction and Government of the Queens Company of Actors in Her Majesty's Theatre in the Haymarket, for the Space of Seaven Years'. Swiney was to receive the profits and among other extras the 'fruit money' from sales in the playhouse; he was to hire any actors he thought fit, but could dismiss them only with the Lord Chamberlain's consent. Congreve, originally joint manager with Vanbrugh, had 'quitted the affair of the Hay-market' by 15 December 1705, having (as he wrote then) 'got nothing by it'. Left as sole manager, Vanbrugh evidently had too many irons in the fire, and he must have been relieved to find that Swiney would take on the management and pay him for the privilege a rent of £5 a night up to a maximum of £700 a year towards the recovery of his original outlay on the construction. However, his sense of relief was premature, and the next two years would see an extraordinary succession of schemes and crises in the Haymarket, involving both the management and finances of the theatre and the kind of entertainments presented there. Almost at once, on 10 September 1706, Congreve told Keally that

> The play-houses have undergone another revolution; and Swinny, with Wilks, Mrs Olfield, Pinkethman, Bullock, and Dicky, are come over to the Hay-Market. Vanbrugh resigns his authority to Swinny, which occasioned the revolt. Mr Rich complains and rails . . . My Lord Chamberlain approves and ratifies the desertion: and the design is to have plays only at the Hay-Market, and operas only at Covent Garden [Drury Lane].

As a result, according to Cibber,

> such a Detachment of Actors, from *Drury-Lane*, could not but give a new Spirit to those in the *Hay-Market*; not only by enabling them to act each others Plays to better Advantage; but by an emulous Industry, which had lain too long inactive among them, and without which they plainly saw, they could not be sure of Subsistance. Plays, by this means began to recover a good Share of their former Esteem, and Favour.

Nevertheless Vanbrugh soon found that the arrangement was not what he had wanted. The unsolved problems of both production and acoustics at least balanced, or even outweighed, the separation of the audiences for plays and for operas. The division of *genre* had been so framed as to prohibit at the Haymarket any of the songs and dances or other musical pieces with which it had been customary both to embellish plays and to round out the evening's programme. George Granville, Lord

Lansdowne, was so alarmed that his *The British Enchanters** should be thus mutilated that with the help of his brother-in-law Sir John Stanley, who happened to be the Lord Chamberlain's secretary, he managed to prevent the revival advertised for 9 December 1706 from taking place. But the acoustic defects were even more serious. As we have seen in the discussion of Vanbrugh's Haymarket building, speech simply got lost under the vast ceiling. In Cibber's account,

> The greatest Inconvenience they still labour'd under, was the immoderate Wideness of their house; in which, as I have observ'd, the Difficulty of Hearing, may be said to have bury'd half the Auditors Entertainment. This Defect seem'd evident, from the much better Reception several new Plays (first acted there) met with when they afterwards came to be play'd by the same Actors, in *Drury-Lane*.

This unsatisfactory state of affairs continued into 1707, and when the new season opened in October of that year little had changed. But before the end of the year Rich at Drury Lane was again faced with trouble, this time the mutiny of some of his singers over money. On 1 December the Lord Chamberlain gave permission for fourteen first-class musicians 'to perform in the Operas at the Queens Theatre in the Haymarket' and the theatre papers of Vice-Chamberlain Coke (the successor to Peregrine Bertie) contain a draft proposal for the engagement of singers. The first division by kinds had come to an end. The *Order of Union* of 31 December, signed by the Earl of Kent, ratified a complete reversal of the functions of the two theatres, and gave the official reason for the change:

> Whereas by reason of the Division of her Majestys Comedians into two distinct houses or Companys the Players have not been able to gain a reasonable Subsistance for their Encouragemt in either Company nor can plays always be Acted to the best Advantage And Whereas the charge of maintaining a Company of Comedians with pformers of Opera in the Same House is now become too great to be Supported Therefore to remedy those inconveniences and for the better regulation and Support of the

---

* p. 270

Theatres I do hereby Order & require

That all Operas and other Musicall presentmts be perform'd for the future only at her Majestys Theatre in the Hay Markett undr the direction of the Managr. or Managrs thereof, wth full power and Authority to receive Admitt and Employ any pformrs in Musick Dancing &ca whom he or they shall judge fitt for their Service and I do hereby strictly charge and forbid the sd Manager or Managrs from & after the 10th day of Janry next to represent any Comedys Tragedys or other Entertainmts of the Stage that are not set to Musick or to erect any other Theatre for that purpose upon pain of being Silenced for breach of this my Ordr.

There was a significant difference in the arrangements for plays at Drury Lane, in that music was permitted when it was necessary to the production.

From the Coke papers it also appears that by the beginning of 1708 Vanbrugh, not Swiney, was again in control at the Haymarket, seeking favourable contracts with singers and, as the season progressed, estimating costs and sitting down again and again with his pages of figures in the hope of extracting from them a forecast of solvency if never of profit. He worked closely with Coke, and we learn from Vanbrugh's letter to Lord Manchester of 24 February that other friends had also helped him. In order to exchange plays for operas at the Haymarket, he had 'got the Duke of Marlbor: to put an end to the Playhouse factions, by engaging the Queen to exert her Authority'. And 'Mr Bertie and my Self' were 'now the Sole Adventurers and Undertakers of the Opera, for I have Bought Mr Swiney quite out: Only pay him as Manager'. Peregrine Bertie had shared with him in this transaction; now, looking towards the next season, they hoped that in Venice Lord Manchester could secure a man and a woman star to sing during 1708-9, each for £500 – or better, since it came to less, for 500 pistoles.

Since very few of the audience understood the language, the words of Italian operas were not of great significance, but the same could not be said for settings of English words. In the autumn the roof would be altered and the orchestra pit enlarged.* Nevertheless, the removal of plays to Drury Lane immediately benefited the drama, while the size and the scenic

* p. 265

and musical facilities at the Haymarket were of advantage to the opera. But competition now came from another source, and Vanbrugh made a determined effort to stifle it. He wrote to Coke on 20 January 1708:

> There will be another misfortune, a great one if not nip'd in the Bud. I mean musick meetings. There is one given out to morrow at York Buildings . . . I'm told (and believe) Rich is in the Bottom on't. But I hope you'll move My Lord Chamb: for an Order to stop their Performance.

The concert room at York Buildings, off Villiers Street near Charing Cross, was just over 30 feet square and 21 feet high, with a gallery at one end and at the other a platform for the performers in a recess 17 feet wide and about 15 feet deep. It could not seat more than about two hundred people uncomfortably crowded, and it was less the diversion of audiences than the effect on the musicians that alarmed Vanbrugh. For if they were in demand for concerts they would, he feared, want more money to perform for him. His bid was of course unsuccessful, but on 21 February he was able to report to Coke and the Lord Chamberlain that the new arrangement between the two theatres had not only put an end to recent rivalries but had also put 'both houses into a capacity of supporting themselves very tollerably'. Only one thing was wanting – and that was the reason for his memorandum – namely that the Queen should exercise her patronage to the extent of a thousand pounds in order to bring over for the next season two Italian soloists at £400 each and a concert-master to lead the orchestra at £200.

The hard facts that were beginning to come home to him were that operas cost twice as much to stage as plays and that two performances a week were as much as the available public could support. If the expense of the costumes, about which the artistes were fussy, was overshadowed by the cost of even the small orchestra of about twenty-five players, it was dwarfed by the fees of the principal singers. But the success of the Italian opera did not depend on the credibility of the plot or the realism of the production but on the singers. The celebrities were what the public came to see and hear: they were foreign, they were flamboyant and they were temperamental, and the *castrato* singers aroused an interest that was largely auditory but also contained a certain element of titillation. Without these attractions there would virtually be no opera, and in this combination of conditions – as indeed at the present day – the opera could not pay its way without subsidy.

On 7 April Vanbrugh provided Coke with figures: twenty-three opera performances at an average cost of £116. 4s. 2d. brought in average receipts of £127. 18s. 5d. But 'extra' costs of over £800 for costumes and scenery, £334. 10s. for the new opera (*Love's Triumph*), £147. 10s. extra for musicians and so on, turned this very modest profit into a loss of £1146. 14s. 2d. even before the end of the season. Even if the Queen were pleased to allow a thousand a year and if 'the Towne shou'd by Subscriptions take off the Load of Cloaths & scenes', at £100 a day the opera would still barely break even. A week later he thought of something else: a profit-sharing scheme. If Valentini, Mrs Tofts, Mlle de l'Epine, and the three principal musicians Dieupart, Haym, and Pepusch took shares instead of salaries, the daily expenses (excepting costumes and scenery 'which must be furnish'd by subscription') could be reduced to £70. If next season the receipts were 'to be £115 the Profitts wou'd then be £45 per day'. Two-thirds of this profit over sixty performances would give £1800, or £450 each to the three singers and £150 each to the musicians.

There is at least one flaw in this optimistic forecast, for he had already stated the present season's average receipts as £125; they needed therefore to rise to £170. In trying to check Vanbrugh's calculations one soon senses that they are incomplete: he could not solve the problem, and probably he knew it. Almost at once it was compounded by one of cash flow: he wrote to Coke of his

> Entire disposition to comply with whatever you think right in this unhappy affair . . . You are Sensible the daily Receipts of the Opera are not sufficient to answer the Daily and monthly demands and whenever they fail, there will be a full Stop. So that I am forc'd to apply all other money I have, to keep touch in that point and this Distresses me to the last Degree.

His only hope of ready money was now from agency sales of

tickets which had not yet come in. Therefore, 'if ever my Lord Chamberlain will move the Queen, now should be the time'. His only hope of saving himself was to find someone with money to spend. On 11 May he told Lord Manchester,

> I have parted with the whole concern to Mr Swiney: only reserving my Rent: So that he is entire Possessor of the Opera And most People think, will manage it better than any body. He has a good deal of money in his Pocket; that he got before by the Acting Company; And is willing to Venture it upon the Singers.

Three days later he still had to explain to Coke that he would pay Valentini what was owing to him as soon as Peregrine Bertie returned to London from Grimsthorpe. But his letter to Manchester continued full of enthusiasm for the future: Swiney was prepared to offer two singers £500 a year each for two seasons, and it was hoped that by word of mouth London would come to be known as an opera-loving capital.

When the season ended early on 20 May Vanbrugh must, privately at least, have been relieved, even if he was at once involved in the alterations to the Queen's Theatre. On 27 July he told Manchester, 'I lost so Much Money by the Opera this Last Winter, that I was glad to get quit of it; And yet I don't doubt that Operas will Settle and thrive in London.' In the circumstances his account of the reasons for the season's failure is almost euphoric:

> The Occasion of the Loss was three things, One: that half the Season was past, before the Establishmt: was made. And then, My Ld Chamb: Upon a Supposition that there wou'd be Immence gain, Oblig'd us to Extravagant Allowances; An Other thing was, That the Towne having the Same Notion of the Profits, wou'd not come into Any Subscription; And the 3d was, That tho' the Pitt and Boxes did very near as well as usual the Gallery People (who hitherto had only throng'd out of Curiosity, not Tast) were weary of the Entertainment: so that Upon the Whole, there was barely Money to Pay the Performers & Other daily Charges; And for the Cloaths & Scenes they fell upon the Undertakers. I might Add a Fourth Reason which is, That I never cou'd look after it my Self, but was forc'd to Leave it to Managers.

Vanbrugh had finished with management. With the imminence of Manchester's return the letters to him cease. Steele
wrote to Keally on 7 October,

> Mr Congreve is at Newmarket. Mr Addison is your servant. The
> taste for Plays is expired. We are all for Operas, performed by
> eunuchs every way impotent to please. Lord Manchester is
> returning from Venice with a singer of great expectation.

Nicolini Grimaldi made his London début on 14 December
1708 in *Pyrrhus and Demetrius*; Lady Wentworth, whose spelling is a joy although also a reflection of her times, wrote on the
10th to her son Lord Raby in Berlin:

> Your Brother Wentworth had almoste persuaded me to have gon
> last night to hear ther fyne muisick, the famous Etallion sing att
> the rehersall of the Operer, which he asured me it ws soe dark
> none could see me. Indeed musick was the greatist temtation I
> could have, but I was afraid he deceaved me, soe Betty only went
> with his wife and him; and I rejoysed I did not, for thear was a
> vast deal of company and good light – but the Dutchis of
> Molbery had gott the Etallion to sing and he sent an excuse, but
> the Dutchis of Shrosberry made him com, brought him in her
> coach but Mrs Taufs [Tofts] huft and would not sing becaus he
> had first put it ofe, though she was thear yet she would not, but
> went away.

The alterations to the Haymarket auditorium had improved
the acoustics for plays but did not make them ideal. At Drury
Lane Rich's mismanagement continued, and Swiney had been
able by the end of March 1709 to engage some of Rich's actors
at the Haymarket. Vanbrugh's plan for a united theatre had
come to an end. On 16 November 1710 Swiney once more
agreed to pay him £700 a year, out of the proceeds of the opera;
however, two years after that Swiney was bankrupt, and went
abroad suddenly in the middle of January 1713 to avoid his
creditors, remaining away for over twenty years. Vanbrugh
kept some financial interests in the Haymarket until 1720, but
the troubles and successes of the managers and producers, the
advent of John James Heidegger as manager and the establish-

ment of Handel as not only the leading opera composer of the day but by far the greatest, are only marginal to Vanbrugh's story. The conditional *if only* that had been prospective in his letters to Coke became retrospective in his analysis of the failure for Manchester: he never lost the belief in himself as a good manager. Maybe, he must have told himself, if he had haunted not only Blenheim but the theatre like a ghost, things would have been different.

One of the marks of the professional is the ability to survive shipwreck or to salvage it. Vanbrugh learned the hard way, as others would do, that the theatre was tricky and the opera ruinous. For several years his finances would grow yet worse before eventually improving. In August 1711 Samuel Travers of the Treasury informed the Duke of Marlborough of

> Mr Vanbrughs importuning me for more mony, by way of Advance on account, by reason of the great expense he has bin at 3 days ago in burying his mother.

This has been taken to mean that her funeral was accompanied by such signs of pomp as (in Wren's description of 'the Fashion of the Age') 'a Train of carriages (even when the Deceased are of moderate condition)'. But Mrs Vanbrugh chose to be buried in a sleepy Thames-side village; and, as any executor knows, while funeral directors' bills are rendered in the expectation of dilatory payment, the pressing need is for ready cash to deal with incidental expenses and the provision of affidavits and certificates.

But the letters to Lord Manchester also deal with Vanbrugh's architectural success at Kimbolton. In future everything he did would have to be to a budget, saving money before the work began, not during it as he claimed at Blenheim. As for the prodigality of that great palace, that was something that came, if ever, only once in a lifetime. But already Vanbrugh had become what in the end he most wanted to be, an architect, and that was what, in the end, would best and most fully exercise and express his talents.

26

The Castle Air

'All the world are running Mad after Building, as far as they can reach', wrote Vanbrugh to Lord Manchester on 27 July 1708. Blenheim, he said, was 'beyond all Comparison more Magnificent' than Chatsworth – as indeed both he and Marlborough had intended it to be; at Castle Howard 'My Ld Carlisle has got his whole Garden Front up And is fonder of his Work every day than Other'. The Duke of Shrewsbury's house, Heythrop, a few miles north of Woodstock and designed by Thomas Archer, 'will be About half up this Season', and 'My Ld Bindon is busy to the Utmost of his Force in New Moulding Audley end'. Vanbrugh's south front at Kimbolton provided the occasion for this survey, which turns out with the exception of Heythrop to comprise only works of his own.

Henry Howard, first Earl of Bindon and later sixth Earl of Suffolk (1670-1718) was a remote cousin of Lord Carlisle and another of Vanbrugh's distant kinsmen. Audley End, an enormous symmetrical Jacobean mansion on the outskirts of Saffron Walden, had been bought by Charles II from the third Earl of Suffolk because it was near Newmarket, and sold back by William III to the fifth Earl, Lord Bindon's father, in 1701. During its period of Crown ownership Henry Winstanley, the ingenious but unlucky creator of the Eddystone lighthouse,* had been responsible as Clerk of Works for a certain amount of repair and maintenance work, but the house was in a fairly

* p. 246

run-down state when Lord Bindon bought out his co-heirs in 1702. Moreover it still had no great staircase although a roughly cubical space had been left for one next to the south end of the two-storey great hall.

The first stage of Bindon's 'new moulding' seems to have been the demolition of most of the outer court; the remaining entrance side of this court was taken down in the early 1720s either by his son or by his younger brother, leaving the block containing the hall and stair space at the front of the house. Work was needed to make the remainder wind and water tight. In several rooms on the upper floor windows were altered and plaster friezes were extended in a style imitative of the original work; the other important addition was the provision of a great stair to give a suitably grand access from the hall, by then only an entrance and not a living room, to the suites above. In 1762 Horace Walpole, on a visit to Audley End, was told that the demolitions were on Vanbrugh's advice, but there is no supporting evidence for this; if the story is true his reasons must have been practical ones since he cannot have supposed that his relatively impoverished kinsman could commission a new palace. The evidence for his more positive involvement at Audley End is in a petition of about 1715 from John Anstis, who was engaged in a wrangle with Vanbrugh for the post of Garter Herald. The Earl of Bindon, he wrote,

> did by some Instruments under his hand & seale dated in or about the year 1707 nominate yr Orator to be Garter when a Vacancy should first happen in that office ... but the said Earl notwithstanding his frequent assurances by letters and otherwise of recommending yr Orator to Her Majesty, was pleased however to continue to delay doing the same, having about this time employed one Mr Vanbrugh Clarenceux King of Armes (i.e. Sr John Vanbrugh) about altering the said Earls Mansion House at Audley End.

Thus much of Vanbrugh's employment must have been on those practical matters of building that he had set out early to master. What *looks* most like his work is the screen of two rows of pilastered arches which replaces the wall between the hall and the staircase. The upper part was rebuilt later in the eighteenth century; nevertheless the screen is still a remarkable and significant piece of work.

There is something basically attractive to the human eye in looking through arches or other openings at a further space beyond; Vanbrugh had already used this device at both Castle Howard and Blenheim, where the staircases are placed to **[33]** either side of the hall; at Grimsthorpe he would use it again to great effect, also at the ends of the hall. But besides the excitement of the view through it the Audley End screen is important as Vanbrugh's first known attempt at archaism: the pilasters and the sections of entablature they support conform to Jacobean patterns rather than to the more 'correct' neo-Roman ones of his own time.

Many years ago Sir Nikolaus Pevsner, who was something of a connoisseur of Jacobean work, suggested that the plaster relief ceiling over the staircase was also Vanbrugh's pastiche work; this has recently been disputed, but it is unusual in form and the question remains open. The staircase itself seems to have been inserted about 1725 by someone else at the price of some violence to the structure of the screen, perhaps because the original 'new moulding' programme ran out of money and Vanbrugh's design for the stair was not recorded.

Vanbrugh's first sight of Audley End and of Kimbolton must have been at about the same period, but it would be as unwise as it is unnecessary to suggest that the first influenced his attitude to the second. Elizabethan and Jacobean buildings stood in relation to his day as Victorian ones do to ours, and the great houses of that age were inescapably numerous in both London and the country. They included not only examples like Wollaton and Longleat, whose elevations are visibly based on **[7]** the local version of the Classical orders, but also mansions like Hardwick, Audley End, and the original Elizabethan Chatsworth, in which the orders hardly appear although they may have dictated the proportions of heights and widths: the exteriors of these buildings depend for their effect on their proportions and on the advance and recess of particular parts, the repetition of identical or similar groups of rectangular mullioned windows, and often on a varied skyline with towers, turrets, parapets, and sometimes battlements.

These are, except for the preference there for arched

[K] windows, the principal elements of Vanbrugh's Welbeck
[2] design and they are also, if one thinks away all the 'particulars',
[22] the underlying elements of Blenheim. What Vanbrugh did at
Kimbolton was to give a name, a concept and an identity to his
own version of this style – if it can be called a style: it is no accident that he referred to it as an *air*. He seems to have anticipated that Lord Manchester's Venetian acquaintances at least
would not consider it a style, precisely because (to introduce a
linguistic confusion) it was *astylar*, that is without pilasters or
columns.

> As to the Outside, I thought 'twas absolutly best, to give it
> Something of the Castle Air, tho' at the Same time to make it
> regular. And by this means too, all the Old Stone is Serviceable
> again; which to have had new wou'd have run to a very great
> Expence; This method was practic'd at Windsor in King
> Charles's time, And has been universally Approv'd, So I hope
> your Ldship won't be discourag'd, if any Italians you may Shew
> it to, shou'd find fault that 'tis not Roman, for to have built a
> Front with Pillasters, and what the Orders require cou'd never
> have been born with the Rest of the Castle: I'm sure this will
> make a very Noble and Masculine Shew; and is of as Warrant-
> able a kind of building as Any.

This was in his first letter of 18 July 1707. The Countess of Manchester had insisted on writing to her husband before Vanbrugh did, to tell him the reason for the new design. Kimbolton
is about ten miles from the old county town of Huntingdon and
is now in Cambridgeshire; it is about five miles from the Great
North Road. The house followed, as it still does, the plan of a
semi-fortified medieval courtyard house. The elevations to the
court, and the rooms behind them, had been rebuilt quite recently, probably in the early 1690s and by Henry Bell of King's
Lynn, a provincial architect-builder of considerable talent and
versatility. This work also included the reconstruction of the
outer face of the gateway in the middle of the west range and
the replacement of its Gothic arch by a Classical one. Vanbrugh was called down to Kimbolton, taking Hawksmoor with
him, because of a crisis: the south front, facing the garden, collapsed, and what did not fall had to be taken down for safety's
sake. The Countess, wrote Vanbrugh to her husband when she

gave him leave to do so, 'did me the honour (when she saw it must do) to, ask my Advice in carrying it up Again'. Her local adviser, William Coleman, was an accomplished carpenter and joiner who would undertake all the new work in those trades in the house, but the architectural design of a new front was beyond him. In particular, 'he had not brought the Door of the House into the Middle of the Front'.

The problems were first to make a symmetrical front to a rather irregular old quadrangle, and secondly to make its centre line coincide with that of the garden and the short ornamental canal. Vanbrugh solved both problems by extending the front to the west so that the centre lines coincided, and by inserting a large extra room, domestically superfluous, in the middle of the range between the drawing room and the bedchamber. He would have liked to make this room 'a reall Salon, by carrying it up into the Next Story', but that would have lost bedroom space above; thus instead of a smaller version of the two-storey saloon of Blenheim he had to be content with a suite of rooms eighteen feet high, 'which is no contemptible thing, tho' not what in Strictness One wou'd wish'.

At this stage Vanbrugh said nothing about further rebuilding; indeed he presented the idea of conformity with 'the rest of the Castle' as one of the bases of his design, which he promoted as a package of solutions to the needs of appearance, economy, firmness, and conformity. Nevertheless the Castle Air itself was more than an inspired response to a particular set of circumstances. The most obvious 'castle' element is the battlements along the top, which happen to be one place where stones from the old building have been traced. And clearly Hugh May's remodelling of the Upper Ward at Windsor Castle in the 1670s was a source, although Vanbrugh placed his windows near the outer wall surface, eschewing the deep recesses that gave chiaroscuro and high relief to May's fronts and which still survive as a feature of Wyattville's Gothic redressing.

But Kimbolton was also, although strange to an Italian eye, to be regular in comparison with the building it replaced; that meant not only perhaps rhythmical or symmetrical but also according to rules. As with Hardwick, or with Queen Anne and Georgian Street fronts, the shapes and sizes of windows and the areas between them were determined by a range of proportional formulas that are *ultimately* Classical in origin and which experience has shown to be visually effective or pleasing. It was in his next letter (9 September), intended to allay various fears of his patron, that Vanbrugh predicted that Kimbolton's 'Manly Beauty' would demonstrate the aesthetic importance of 'the Figure and Proportions' rather than 'the delicacy of the Ornaments'.

Six months later he was prepared to predict that, even with the use of old stone from the nearby ruined Stonely Priory, the work could 'be made handsomer than Any Gentlemans house in Huntingdon Shire'. He was anxious to reassure Manchester, who had seen no more than a drawing, that this was no mere repair job; but his own conviction went further. This was the new architecture he had begun to work out for himself in the Goose-Pie House and the Welbeck project. It was, almost by definition, English and un-Italian, modern and un-Antique. One unequivocal sign of its modernity was the tall sash-windows, examples of the technology of the age of Wren, which could be – and often were – used in place of their original cross-mullion windows to make seventeenth-century buildings look like Georgian ones.

It is dangerous to argue from negative evidence, but the limited part played by Hawksmoor at Kimbolton must be significant. Vanbrugh took him down there on his first visit, and in 1710 Coleman's accounts mention drawing paper 'used by Mr Hawcksmoore' and postage on drawings sent by him from London. But Vanbrugh never quotes his opinions to Lord Manchester, and the letters throughout give the impression that Kimbolton, unlike Castle Howard or Blenheim, was Vanbrugh's building alone. It is not even necessary to attribute to Hawksmoor the projecting keystones over alternate lower windows on the south front. There are also interesting differences more generally between Vanbrugh and Hawksmoor as letter writers, especially in the early 1720s when both were writing to Lord Carlisle. Both show very clearly and unaffectedly their knowledge and their practical experience, but Vanbrugh never mentions written sources. Hawksmoor on the other hand often refers to Antiquity, and says on one occasion:

I wou'd not mention Authors and Antiquity, but that we have so
many conceited Gentlemen full of this science, ready to knock
you down, unless you have some old father to stand by you. I
dont mean that one need to Coppy them, but to be upon the
same principalls.

Vanbrugh makes no such claims; although he discusses in
detail his own design for the Temple at Castle Howard* it is not
he but Hawksmoor who tells Carlisle that it is 'founded upon
the Rules of the Ancients'. Hawksmoor can write as a theorist
or as the learned architect he was recognized to be; Vanbrugh's opinions show a manager's confidence rather than a
scholar's.

It begins to look as if Vanbrugh thought of himself as a
Modern architect not only in the sense of believing that art
could make progress and the ancients could be surpassed, but
also in the sense of returning Antiquity to the past rather than
trying to revive it. And if that is the case then he admired the
great houses of a century earlier not only for their picturesque
and dramatic massing; not only for the visual or romantic
associations, which they shared with some of his own buildings, of turreted castles of a yet earlier age; but also for their
'manly beauty', their rationalistic plans and elevations, one
might say for their Englishness. Hardwick Hall, 'more glass
than wall' in the popular rhyme, and the other tall gaunt
houses of Robert Smythson were, after all, the late Elizabethan
equivalent of the Modern glass and concrete frame building
that it has in recent years become fashionable to decry. When
Evelyn visited Audley End in 1670 he admired it and called it
'antico-moderno'.

Vanbrugh's supervision of the work at Kimbolton was close:
he made several visits to the site, and was in 'a Constant Correspondence' with Coleman, who came to London to confer
with him before the start of the 1708 building season. Their respect was mutual. 'I must do Coleman the Justice', Vanbrugh
told Manchester, 'that he has manag'd the Old Materials to
Admirable Advantage, And executed the Directions he has
had, extreamly well.' And in July he added, 'If we had Such a

* p. 466

Man at Blenheim he'd Save us a Thousand pounds a Year'. Coleman in his turn wrote of the architect, 'If their is anay Credet Gayned In this Bulden, I beg that he may have it'. The new range of building was roofed when Lord Manchester returned in October, but by then the architect, and soon afterwards the patron, entertained thoughts of a more complete modernization. Vanbrugh had introduced the subject on 22 March:

> I Apprehend but One thing from the Whole, which is, That your Ldship will two or three years hence find your Self under a violent Temptation to take down and rebuild (suitable to this New front) all the Outside Walls round the Castle, But I'll say no more of that, 'till I see you at home and Secretary of State again.

[22] By the end of the 1710 season the west range too had been rebuilt, incorporating the existing gateway arch; Vanbrugh also, for economy, took advantage of the solid old foundations for the flanking walls on either side, which recede a little inwards towards the centre at a slight angle to each other. This geometrical irregularity is so skilfully handled that it is only perceptible on close inspection: economy and regularity were again reconciled. Part of its success is due to the framing of these splayed walls by projecting end pavilions; that on the south was of course what Vanburgh had added to make the south front symmetrical, and it was a relatively simple matter for him to extend the northern range to match the new length of the southern.

The east side was left to the last; its centre was the old great hall, and Vanbrugh designed a projection to front it containing a concealed staircase from the outside, lit by three open arches above. For some reason Lord Manchester did not proceed with this, and about 1718 he was introduced to the young Florentine architect Alessandro Galilei who was then being passed from one English nobleman to another with vague promises of commissions.* The enormous balustraded Doric portico that overtops the rest of Kimbolton used to be considered another Vanbrugian afterthought, but Galilei's careful signed drawing

* p. 450

survives for both the portico and its curved approach steps, and
there can be no doubt that he designed both. It seems that the
desire for an 'Italian' front proved stronger for Manchester,
who was raised to a Dukedom in 1719, than something 'suitable' (in Vanbrugh's word) to the rest, and he took the opportunity when it was offered, to employ an Italian to provide
it.

We might expect an architect's ideas to be particularly well
expressed in a house built for himself or his immediate family.
Vanbrugh in fact built three in this category: Whitehall, Chargate, and the Castle at Greenwich. On 13 May 1709 he obtained
a seventy-year lease of a brick house with a sixty-acre farm
called Chargate in the parish of Esher in Surrey, including permission to rebuild the house to the same size and standard, and
to fell trees in order to make walks and views – perhaps the
germ of Bridgeman's garden at Claremont.* In October 1714
he sold the house and estate to the young Earl of Clare, later
Duke of Newcastle, who renamed it Claremont and appointed
Vanbrugh to incorporate the little house into a great new mansion. At the same time Vanbrugh was engaged to modernize

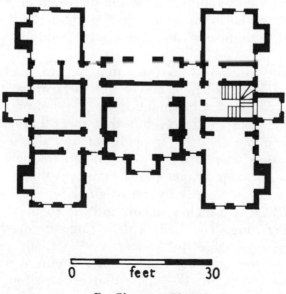

0   feet   30

P   Chargate. Plan.

* p. 461

Newcastle House at the north-west corner of Lincoln's Inn
Fields, which was both the Duke's London residence and the
management centre of all his estates.

Apart from a couple of views of Claremont all we know about
[P] the appearance of its original nucleus is from Vanbrugh office
[Q] drawings. It stood on rising ground ('built under an hill' according to a tourist of 1762); its H-shaped plan could well have
repeated that of a substantial Tudor or early Stuart farmhouse,
allowing the use of the old foundations. One of the two surviving plans is dated 14 August 1711 and the other, a slight variant in Vanbrugh's own hand, has a pencilled instruction to a
draughtsman to copy it leaving out the beds and the figures
(i.e. the dimensions). Both plans show beds, though both as far
as one can tell show the ground floor; it was quite usual even in
yeomen's houses to have 'parlours' with beds in them, like
modern bed-sitting rooms, on the ground or main living floor.
The 'cross-bar' of the H between the wings contained a
roughly square hall surrounded on all sides except the entrance by a corridor which gave access to the staircase and the
four rooms in the ends of the wings. There were beds in three
of these rooms and another in the middle room of the left-hand
wing. Only in the front room on the right, longer than the
others, facing south-east and getting the morning sun, is no
bed marked.

But among the unanswered questions are whether this was a
living room or the kitchen, and if not then where the kitchen
was. Later views of Claremont show the house raised on a
[24] podium or basement storey, but this must have been made
during the enlargement by scooping out the sloping ground at
the front, using what originally was no more than a cellar to
make the house appear one storey higher at the front than behind. None of the rooms in the original house was very big,
most being 10 feet 6 inches square and the room without a bed
about 18 feet long. The hall, with a huge fireplace on either
side, was about 13 feet by 15 feet, and perhaps extended up
through two storeys; none of the other rooms can have been
more than 8 feet high. We know that at least four were bedrooms, perhaps more. These questions are the more important
because we do not know why the house was built or who, or
how many, were to live there. In particular there is no known

reason why Vanbrugh should have had any attachment to that part of Surrey.

A possible answer to the last questions occurs when we ask how Chargate can have been paid for. Vanbrugh was in increasing debt in 1709-10, and in March 1713 he told the Duke of Marlborough that he was 'loaded with between three and four Thousand Pound debt (besides what the Playhouse is charged with)'. If even part of this sum was on account of Chargate then the whole undertaking was inconceivably foolish; after all, there had been no ready money to pay Valentini in May 1708.

But on the other hand, it was at Chargate that Vanbrugh's mother Elizabeth died, aged about seventy-four, on 13 August 1711, the day before the date on one of the plans. As we have seen,* Mrs Vanbrugh was careful to conceal her last wishes

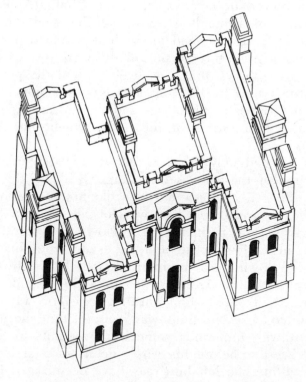

Q   Chargate. Perspective reconstruction.

* p. 7

from the world, not to mention future historians, but it seems probable that it was she who paid for the estate and the new house, placing them in John's name; that she intended to make a home there with some of her unmarried daughters, or with her sister Dorothy (1636-1713), the widow of William Van-brugh – Dorothy had witnessed her will in 1707 – and that she chose the location because it was near the one-time Carleton house at Imber Court where she and Dorothy had spent part of their childhood. We know nothing about the house for the next three years, but its purchase by Lord Clare on 14 October 1714 probably marks the recovery of Vanbrugh's finances that is so evident when the Account Book begins the following year.

Roque's engraved view of Claremont of 1738 shows the centre of the house with a triangular pediment and a straight parapet, but Vanbrugh's drawings show that his intention, whether achieved or not, was to make Chargate like a small brick version of Kimbolton, crowning the whole house with battlements. These extended to the hall part which rose above the rest like a miniature version of the clerestory at Blenheim. A perspective shows that the lively silhouette produced by these features and by the tall chimneys was matched by the advance and recess of the wings and the entrance porch; there were also square turrets at the ends, which may have con-tained privies.

Almost immediately (that is about 1710) Vanbrugh dev-eloped some of these ideas on a larger scale in the design of Kings Weston, a compact but sizeable house overlooking the Avon valley near Bristol. This was for Sir Edward Southwell, Bt, a barrister and politician of Anglo-Irish descent, who had inherited an earlier house and its estate from his father in 1702. The following year he married Lady Elizabeth Cromwell, whose mother Lady Ardglass was in 1699 caught shoplifting fans from Mrs Tombs's shop. On that occasion Lady Betty, who was in the coach at the time, was so upset that she took to her bed.* Southwell undertook some improvements to the garden at Kings Weston before his wife's death in March 1709; the moderate estate she left him may have encouraged him to re-build the house.

* p. 226

At Kings Weston Vanbrugh arranged access corridors on both main floors and in the attic storey round a central hall containing the main staircase. Old foundations may be the reason for the U-shaped plan, with the recess at the back providing a windowed outside wall to the stair-cage (now lit by a glass roof). On the skyline Vanbrugh combined two of his favourite features, arcades and battlements, to make the extraordinary skeleton of a clerestory which distinguishes Kings Weston; this is not, however, mere ornament, for the piers between the arches contain all the chimneys of the house. Domestic architects were constantly aware of the problems of flues which did not draw properly, but there is very direct evidence that Vanbrugh also considered the chimneys part of the appearance of a house, since in a number of sketches he drew, rather child-like, smoke rising from them.

[28]

Three letters from Vanbrugh to Southwell have been found, all from the autumn of 1713, and all mentioning the chimneys, which were evidently a matter of great concern to him. Southwell was different from Vanbrugh's previous patrons not only in social standing but in background and aspiration. He was a man of considerable education quite apart from his legal training, and the journal he kept on his visit to Holland in 1696 shows an interest in and understanding of architecture. He not only patronized Vanbrugh but also supported Colen Campbell, who arrived in London from Scotland about 1712: in the first volume of his *Vitruvius Britannicus* (1715) Campbell calls Southwell 'the Angaranno of our Age, to whom my Obligations are so deep, that to repeat the least Part of them, would offend the Modesty of my Benefactor.'* This lofty and fulsome allusion to Giacomo Angarano, to whom Palladio dedicated his *Quattro Libri dell'Architettura*, probably means that Southwell gave money to Campbell, although the latter subsequently made at least one design for work at Kings Weston. The design of Penpole Gate, an archway with a square gazebo room over it (demolished in 1950), was built about 1723 from a design that combines elements from drawings by both Campbell and Vanbrugh, and this also says something about Southwell's attitude to architects. Vanbrugh's letters to him mention a Mr Henley

* p. 447

and a Mr Clark, and Southwell seems, rather like Roger North, to have thought of architects as little different from other specialists such as masons, engineers and stewards whom he could call upon and pay for their advice and experience.

On 28 September 1713 Vanbrugh wrote to Southwell from Chester, in some doubt 'whether I shou'd wish the Chimneys up this Season or not'. The prospect of seeing 'the whole Shell clear of Scaffolds' was offset by his desire 'to make some tryalls with boards about height, &c, before they are carryed up'. A month later, at Castle Howard, he was glad to find Southwell of the same opinion, 'tho' you had not yet recd my letter; for I would fain have that part rightly hit off'. Southwell apparently thought the front door too small; 'if an alteration be thought necessary', wrote Vanbrugh, 'I can show you how to do it; but of these particulars it is better to talk than to write'. The last letter (4 December) shows how much was left in this project to Southwell's discretion:

> As to the retrenching your vaults under the great Parlour and bedchamber, I can't say 'tis of much consequence; but on tother side what you save by it is so little, that I think it wou'd be worth the money only to have it said the whole ground floor is vaulted besides the good look of Vaults in that floor and the Security from fire. But I cannot see how you can well avoid Vaulting under the great Stairs, because the paving wont ly steady upon Timber But perhaps you have in View, the contenting Mr Clark, by letting those stairs rise from below. which I have no objection to if you find it necessary. but that you will be the best judge of, when you see the little stairs finish'd.
>
> I see no harm in using the Vault under your bedchamber for a present Kitchen tho' I hope you will let the offices be built after the last Design.

Brick vaults are of course a better fire-stop than wooden floors; no design is known for the separate offices. The chimneys were left until the spring, but the house was structurally complete by the end of 1714. But as Member for Kinsale in the Irish Parliament until his death in 1730 Southwell had only limited time to spend at Kings Weston, and although work continued on gardens and garden buildings the interior decoration of the house was never completed in his lifetime. Evidently, like Lord

Manchester, he had wanted something 'Italian' for the exterior, and Vanbrugh provided a giant temple-front portico – or
at least the relief image of one – in the pilasters and pediment   **[28]**
of the south (entrance) front.

Nevertheless the exteriors of Kings Weston show him still
simplifying. The pilasters are Corinthian, but they are plain
and not fluted as is usual, and the mouldings of the entablature
are of the simplest and plainest. Moreover, at Chargate Vanbrugh had discovered that it was possible to dispense with
even the simple window architraves he had used at Kimbolton,
simply punching the openings, figuratively speaking, out of the
plain wall surface. At Kings Weston, working again in stone instead of brick, he gave the same treatment to many of the
windows, and where there are architraves they are broad, flat,
and in very low relief.

In the often quoted – and often misunderstood – *Tracts* by Sir
Christopher Wren, on which most of our knowledge of his
architectural theory depends, clear distinctions appear between the principles and the principals of architecture and the
basis of beauty. The principles of architecture, says Wren, are
those of Vitruvius: Beauty, Firmness, and Convenience (or, as
they are most often quoted today in Sir Henry Wotton's translation from Vitruvius, in reverse order, Commodity, Firmness,
and Delight). The principals, on the other hand, are for Wren
the Five Orders: these are the formative components rather
than the creative ends of architecture upon which a design is
based; Wren is also clear that latitude rather than pedantic
precision is needed in their use.

But for Wren the essential basis of beauty or delight is geometry, the only visible demonstration of perfect forms free
from all errors and accidentals. It was Hawksmoor who first, in
his plainer buildings, put into practice Wren's emphasis on
solid geometrical purity to the exclusion of surface enrichment: as pupils sometimes will do, he took literally and
developed in one direction an idea which his master had entertained only in a more general way.

Vanbrugh arrived at a similar plainness by a different route,
based less on aesthetic theory than on what he saw and
decided he liked. In later years he twice set down principals of
architecture (in Wren's sense), and although in both cases the

identification of the components was only incidental to his argument – perhaps indeed for that very reason – the distinction between them is significant. Writing in 1719 of 'the Great expensive part' of architecture as understood by history painters like Thornhill, he listed columns, arches and bas reliefs.* This was the kind of architecture that, in Kimbolton and Chargate and Kings Weston, he had very largely avoided. Three years later, writing to Lord Carlisle about his little son Charles, the emphasis is different:

> I fancy your Lordships Godson will be a Professor that way [in architecture], for he knows Pillars & Arches and Round Windows & Square Windows already, whether he finds them in a Book or in the Streets, and is much pleas'd with a House I am building him in the Field at Greenh: it being a Tower of White Bricks, only one room and a Closet on a floor.

This was not a toy house but one of the two White Towers that formed part of Vanbrugh's family colony near Vanbrugh Castle, successors of Chargate in both form and function.

Vanbrugh's letters so often place stress on Commodity and Firmness that Delight seems overshadowed, but this impression is wrong. It could have been corrected in his day, as it can in ours, by a return to Woodstock Park, where some way back we left the great Bridge unfinished and the derelict manor house mysteriously tenanted.

On 31 May 1709 Vanbrugh had written to Godolphin denying a report that £3000 had been spent on the manor:

> I find I was not mistaken in what I believ'd the Charge had been; which do's not yet amount to Eleaven hundred; nor did there want above two more to Compleat all that was intended to be done the Levelling and Planting Included, And I believe it will be found, that this was by a thousand pound the Cheapest way that cou'd be thought on to manage that Hill, so as not to be a fault in the approach. I am very doubtfull whether Your Lordship (or indeed My Lord Duke) has yet rightly taken the Design of forming all that side of the Valley; where severall Irregular things are to have such a regard to one an Other, that I much

* p. 203

fear the Effects of so quick a Sentence as has happen'd to pass
Upon the remain of the Manour. I have however taken a good
deal of it downe; but before tis gone too farr, I will desire your
Lordship will give your Self the trouble of looking Upon a Picture I have made of it, which will at one View explain the whole
design, much better than a thousand Words.

The Duchess of Marlborough, gathering evidence a decade
later, wrote on the paper, 'All that Sir J.V. says in this lettr is
false. The Manor house had cost near £3000'. Whatever the
true figures, the cost was substantial, and repairs had begun as
early as the spring of 1708, although as soon as the Marlboroughs heard about it they ordered work to stop and the
ruins to be taken down.*

On 9 June 1709 Vanbrugh told the Duchess he had 'set Men
on to take downe the Ruins at the Old Manour', but he left room
for equivocation here in deciding what was ruined and what
was not. Two days later, sending her a long letter about
Blenheim, he enclosed a paper of *Reasons* for preserving 'the
Small Remains of ancient Woodstock Manour'. This paper has
earned him a place as one of the fathers of conservationism;
his arguments, like many of those put forward today, involved
the presentation of sincere feeling in the guise of logic, and
there can be little doubt that if he had considered the old buildings an obstacle, or a quarry like Stonely Priory for Kimbolton,
he would have been as strongly in favour of their demolition.
In fact, in an age when such buildings were both common and
little appreciated, he had taken an inordinate fancy to the
Manor, both for itself and as part of his overall plan for
Blenheim.

His first reason was historical: he suggested that, just as
visitors came in his day because of the associations of Woodstock with Henry II, they would come in future ages to see the
house built by Queen Anne for Marlborough. The Manor was
not, he conceded,

Erected on so Noble, nor on So justifiable an Occasion; But it
was rais'd by One of the Bravest and most Warlike of the English

* p. 305

Kings; And tho' it has not been Fam'd, as a Monument of his Arms; it has been tenderly regarded as the Scene of his Affections. Nor amongst the Multitude of People who come daily to View what is raising to the Memory of the Great Battle of Blenheim; Are there any that do not run eagerly to See, what Ancient Remains are to be found, of Rosamonds Bower. It may perhaps be worth some Little Reflection Upon what may be said, if the Very footsteps of it Are no more to be found.

His second reason, which he supported with 'a Picture to Explain what I endeavour to Describe', was aesthetic:

That Part of the Park which is Seen from the North Front of the New Building, has Little Variety of Objects Nor dos the Country beyond it Afford any of Vallue, It therefore Stands in Need of all the helps that can be given, which are only Two; Buildings, and Plantations These rightly dispos'd will indeed Supply all the wants of Nature in that Place: And the Most agreable Disposition is to Mix them: in which this Old Manour gives so happy an Occasion for, That were the inclosure fill'd with Trees (principally Firrs, Yews and Hollys) Promiscuously Set to grow up in a Wild Thicket. So that all the Building left, (which is only the Habitable part and the Chappel) might Appear in Two Risings amongst 'em, it wou'd make One of the Most agreable Objects that the Best of Landskip Painters can invent. And if on the Contrary this Building is taken away; there then remains nothing but an Irregular, Ragged Ungovernable Hill, the deformitys of which are not to be cured but by a Vast Expence; And that at last will only Remove an Ill Object but not produce a good One, Wheras to finish the present Wall for the Inclosures, to forme the Sloops and Make the Plantation (which is all that is now wanting to Compleat the Whole Designe) wou'd not Cost Two Hundred pounds.

[16] Vanbrugh's 'picture' is lost, but a contemporary pen-and-ink drawing, which was afterwards engraved, shows how the Manor looked. The buildings were very extensive, and it was possible for some time for the architect and Henry Joynes to keep up an elaborate pretence that nothing irregular was afoot, while in some places demolition was in progress and in others – those in the best condition – repairs secretly continued.

Hawksmoor would perhaps have attempted to draw a parallel between the Manor and Antiquity in the villas of the Younger Pliny, discussion of which had recently entered the literature of architecture; Vanbrugh on the other hand was only concerned with the medieval associations of the particular site. Exactly when he decided to make the old building again habitable is impossible to discover, but the decision relates to the historical element in the Castle Air. Nor do we know when he first took to living in it himself. In 1716, before the Duchess of Marlborough evicted him, he told her that he had been there with Godolphin's permission for three years, but although he can only have stayed intermittently he may have started to do so rather earlier. This is implied by her later account of how he had laid out upon it

> a good round Sum of money (Tho' he had before made an expence in his former house at the expence of the Crowne) to make a Habitation for Himself, and a great Expence there was to lead it [the roof], and a Closet in the midle, as if he had been to study the Planets. As soon as I discovered this I put a Stop to it, till my Ld Marlborough came out of Flanders.

Now Vanbrugh told her it was convenient, 'and very pleasant too, altho in the middle of Rubbish'; certainly there were worse habitations, and the view from the windows was spectacular. It was true that, on his last visit to Blenheim before exile, Marlborough had taken Joynes into the room next the Saloon and, putting a hand on his shoulder, entrusted to him the care and the keys of the house. Yet it can have been no bad thing for the architect to keep an eye on the deserted and unfinished palace; besides, Vanbrugh had also a special affection for the Bridge.

In the end, that is in 1721, the earthworks at either end of the Bridge were complete and it could at last be crossed on foot or in a carriage. The Duchess had once written, 'one may goe under it, but never upon it no more than one can goe into the moon'. But she was a practical woman: if a thing existed it might as well be used, and the following year she was so far reconciled to it that she ordered the stream that flowed under the central arch to be dammed and widened into a broad canal. Later still, in 1730, she gave it a new purpose – since it was never used to approach the house – by placing the Duke's memorial column to the north of it. But the Bridge itself was never completed with the covered arcades that would have made it a more obvious emulation of Palladio's design in his *Quattro Libri* for the Rialto Bridge in Venice.

[40]   When Capability Brown dammed the canal into a lake and drowned the bottom five or six feet of the Bridge, the only access to the rooms within became by rowing boat, a perilous journey that few have had the opportunity to make. These rooms are a mystery, for some have fireplaces and chimneys; can they have been intended for use in drying out the structure? The Duchess counted thirty-three chambers, and Vanbrugh told her that 'if at last, there is a house found in that Bridge, Your Grace will go and live in it'.

Originally, when in April 1706 a competition was held with designs and stone models, Marlborough chose Vanbrugh's project in preference to others by Wren, Hawksmoor, and Henry Wise the gardener; he found it the best combination of grandeur and practicality to manage the rugged ungovernable hill. But there is a revealing passage in Vanbrugh's memorandum of 8 July 1709* describing the Duke's visit to Blenheim 'last winter was twelvemonth', that is about January 1708. Among the features of the big kitchen and stable courts he then proposed to the Duke (and for which he gained approval) was

A Tower to raise the Great Cistern upon, which receives the Water from the Engine, And from Whence the pipes go into the Gardens, Offices, and other Places in the East end of the house, This Tower is at the same time a Gateway for an entrance to the House from the east Avenue: which will be the constant way of approach from London and Oxford.

In the northern side arch of the Bridge was installed the paddle pump designed by Robert Aldersea, a specialist in such machines; by means of a mill-race it raised the water to the great cistern. But the passage in Vanbrugh's memorandum contains the admission that the usual way of approach was already

* p. 303

going to be along the south side of the valley from Woodstock **[L]**
town and not across the Bridge at all. Thus even before the
main arch was turned the gigantic structure had become more
a ceremonial than an everyday approach.

There are no sound logical reasons for Vanbrugh's attachment to it, either as homage to Palladio or defiance to the
Duchess or as a pun on his own name, *Van Brug*. Such reasons
may be sought in the library or the lecture room; but in the
park, on a dewy spring morning or a warm autumn afternoon,
even in the heat of summer midday or a cold moonlit night, the
truism becomes meaningful that if you need to ask the question you have missed the point. In the late eighteenth century
the design of vast triumphal bridges became a subject for
architectural prize competitions and set pieces. The sparse but
gargantuan detailing of Vanbrugh's Bridge owes nothing to
Hawksmoor; it recalls, if anything, the coarse vigour of late
Tudor attempts at Renaissance work. It marked the end of Vanbrugh's apprenticeship: in the correct and original sense of the
word, it was his master-piece.

27

Out of Office

On the night of 28 November 1710 the roof of the old parish
church at Greenwich collapsed in a gale. The parishioners had
for forty years paid a tax on the coal they burned, which went to
pay for the rebuilding of St Paul's Cathedral and the City
churches. It occurred to some of them that any odd money left
over from this enterprise, which was now complete, might be
worse spent than on rebuilding their church, and they accordingly sent a petition to Parliament on these lines. In the previous month's general election the Tories had won a sweeping
victory, and in Whitehall several ideas quickly came together.

Since the Great Fire, London and Westminster had grown
rapidly, spreading not only into prosperous suburbs like May-
fair and Bloomsbury but also to the east and south of the river,
where the poor had long tended to congregate and where
trades and industries were concentrated. These new suburban
populations were poorly served, if at all, for churches; in the
absence of proper places of worship there was no check to the
spread of non-conformism, seen by the Tories as a danger to
both the religious and the political stability of the capital. St
Paul's was indeed virtually complete, and to prolong or renew
an old tax for a further period into the future was easier and
less contentious than inventing a new one. What better way
could there be of honouring Almighty God, their own victory,
the Queen's Majesty and her sovereignty over the Church of
England, than the provision of fifty new churches in the suburbs!

An Act was passed in 1711 and to administer it a Royal Commission was set up, composed of leading statesmen, churchmen, and London citizens and including, with unusual good sense, several architectural gentlemen. Two of them were Sir Christopher Wren, the Queen's Surveyor, and his son Christopher, who was chief clerk at Whitehall and had recently been responsible for Marlborough House. A third was Thomas Archer, then building Heythrop for the Duke of Shrewsbury; he had travelled in Austria and Italy in the early 1690s and was knowledgeable about the recent architecture of those countries. Officially Archer was an amateur since he lived on a sinecure connected with the control of gaming at court. The fourth was Mr Comptroller Vanbrugh, who thus found himself officially involved in a Tory project. On 10 October 1711 the Commission set up a working committee which included all four, together with the two Surveyors or salaried architects it had just appointed; these were Hawksmoor and another Wren pupil named William Dickinson.

Hawksmoor and Dickinson were entrusted with the routine work of the project, assessing sites, finding contractors and monitoring construction; designs for the new churches were submitted by a number of architects outside as well as within the Commission. Only a dozen churches were built, partly because they cost far more than the £10,000 each that was originally planned; the six that Hawksmoor had the good fortune to design and see completed, including the new church at Greenwich, are among the mainstays of his reputation today. Vanbrugh submitted several designs but none was chosen, and his principal recorded contribution to the Commission's work was a paper of *Proposals* or recommendations, which survive in his autograph and in one of the many manuscript copies that must have been circulated among his colleagues.

Wren also produced a paper of advice to his colleagues, and it is customary to say how practical his remarks are and how unpractical are Vanbrugh's; this does justice to neither. Wren was content in his eightieth year to offer the benefit of his experience which included the design and building of fifty churches in earlier decades. Vanbrugh on the other hand was promoting his own ideas about architecture, and perhaps wished to pave a way for his own designs; probably he was also promoting Hawksmoor, who had worked for some years in Wren's team on the City churches and whose fertile imagination broke out in drawings for any kind of proposal at the slightest encouragement.

Writing to Lady Marlborough in 1709 – and therefore about some other scheme – the obsequious Arthur Maynwaring throws some light both on Hawksmoor's character and on his relationship with Vanbrugh after ten years of collaboration:

> I hope . . . that my friend Mr Vanbrugh is very good and tractable. He has often mentioned a request which he would have me make to you in behalf of Mr Hawkesmore, and I beg you will please to let him tell it you yourself, now they are both together. I would not take this liberty, but that I have often heard you wish for some opportunity to do him good: which he is the more worthy of because he does not seem to be very solicitous to do it for himself: but has two qualities that are not often joined, modesty and merit.

Hawksmoor indeed tended to put forward his designs rather than himself, and he was never a Commissioner. It is proper, normal and often necessary for members of such appointed or elected bodies to consult with their salaried officers, and for officers to seek the help of individual members in putting forward suggestions informally. Vanbrugh was not the rabid anticlerical that is sometimes presented, and the irony of a Whig architect on a Tory commission must have amused him. He may indeed have thought long and carefully about the problems and requirements of the new churches. Nevertheless the *Proposals* may be the joint work of himself and Hawksmoor, and one phrase is especially significant for what it implies about the way the document was composed. In the opening paragraph, 'the following Considerations are humbly offer'd, to the Commissioners', and there is no indication that Vanbrugh is writing to his fellow members; Wren's paper on the other hand was addressed to a friend on the commission and contains an acknowledgement that the writer is himself a member of it.

The *Proposals* certainly do emphasize that the new churches should not only be practical for worship but also 'remain Monuments to posterity' of the Queen's 'Piety & Grandure And by consequence become Ornaments to the Towne, and a Credit to the Nation'. The congregation should be able to hear but not be 'disturb'd in their devotions by one an Other'. The churches should not be 'too much crowded with Pews' – Wren makes this point too – and a broad central aisle should be left, with some benches so that those who could not afford the rent of a pew seat might 'repose themselves by Turns'. The windows should be small in order to protect the worshippers from extremes of heat and cold, although also in order to increase the solemnity of the interior, which ought not to resemble a lantern full of window lights. This last comment was not entirely new, for a similar observation had been made almost a century before by Sir Henry Wotton in his *Elements of Architecture*.

Other comments are more concerned with Firmness and Beauty. In order to be a credit to the town the churches should stand on island sites, each with a portico (the advice of both Alberti and Palladio), and they should have a grace 'express'd in a plain but Just and Noble Stile' without 'such Gayety of Ornaments as may be proper to a Luxurious Palace'. The provision of a tower for each church was specified in the 1711 Act, but the paper recommends fireproof construction, presumably ruling out leaded steeples, and adds, 'That in a Church of Ten thousand pounds cost, it turns upon five hundred, whether it shall be crippled in a hundred Years, or stand like a Rock a Thousand'.

Almost a third of the paper concerns cemeteries, and the 'barbarous' custom of burials under the church floor (burial in a vault, such as the Vanbrughs owned at St Stephen Walbrook, was a different matter). Instead, as Wren also recommends, ground should be bought where it is cheap, 'in the Skirts of the Towne'. These suburban places should be walled, planted with trees and divided with walks, where 'the Richer sort of People' may build 'Lofty and Noble Mausoleums' rather than ordering 'little Tawdry Monuments of Marble, stuck up against Walls and Pillars' in the churches.

Here Vanbrugh provided a little sketch of such buildings with a note in the margin: 'This manner of Interment has been practic'd by the English at Suratt and is come at last to have this kind of effect'. Some seventeenth-century monuments survive

in the English cemetery at Surat, including the domed mausoleums built by the East India Company for Christopher
Oxinden (d. 1659) and his brother Sir George, Governor of
Bombay (d. 1669). Exotic architecture of this sort fascinated
Hawksmoor as well as Vanbrugh, but in this instance the latter's family contacts with Eastern trade were probably the
source of information.

Very shortly after this Vanbrugh seems to have decided to try
his hand at the design of a 'luxurious palace', or rather two. In
the Royal Library at Windsor are several plans, but no
elevations, of St James's Palace, ranging by stages from a
survey 'as it now is 1712' to a completely new palace, about
twice as big as the main block at Blenheim, with a great enclosed court 120 feet by 140 feet and eight minor courts, a gatehouse sixty feet square, a chapel as big as the nave of St James,
Piccadilly, and a theatre almost as large as Drury Lane. The
drawings are titled in Vanbrugh's hand, some in French, and
there is also a plan for a rather smaller rebuilding of Kensington Palace with the addition of stables for about two hundred horses.

One drawing refers to the King, and the titles in French, the
common language between George I and his court, imply that
the drawings were submitted to him and therefore date from
after his accession in August 1714; on the other hand the dated
survey plan was made two years earlier and Queen Anne's
health was then already very poor. Vanbrugh would have had
access in the office to Wren's ideal plans for a new Whitehall
made after the 1698 fire, and probably to some of those made
for Charles I and Charles II by John Webb. He had made contacts and perhaps friends on his trip to Hanover in 1706, and he
may have been looking ahead in the hope of interesting the
future king not only in building in London but specifically in
building to his design.

But in March 1713, with Blenheim at a standstill and the
Marlboroughs in exile, Vanbrugh's fortunes sank. An election
was in the offing, and Woodstock was in crisis. Most of those
with a vote would normally have loyally supported the Duke of
Marlborough and therefore voted for the two Whig candidates;
but the Marlboroughs were abroad and all sorts of tradesmen
in the district were owed money on account of the suspension

of work at Blenheim. On 25 January Vanbrugh wrote to the Mayor of Woodstock:

> Having long had it at heart, to see the Towne of Woodk so improved in Buildings and other things, as to bear some proportion with what strangers may reasonably expect to find in a Borough Towne, joining to so great a Palace as Blenheim; I several times spoke to my Lord Duke about paving the Market Place, which he seemed well inclin'd to, and I believe had done e'er now –

This was immaculate, but in writing to a friend Vanbrugh thought it safe to continue:

> – but for the continual Plague, and bitter persecution he has most barbarously been followed with, for two years past. However, upon his going away, I mentioned this thing to him again; And he left such directions with those who take care of his Affairs, that I have at last Commission to tell you, it will be done, and that I am desired to take some care of it, and to consult with you and the Corporation about the manner and extent of it: which I design to do, as soon as I can possibly come downe.

The letter was not delivered. According the the Duchess, 'The cause of his Misfortune . . . proceeded purely from his want of good Spelling'; the letter destined for the Mayor 'was carried to one Major by which means my Ld Oxford was acquainted with it'. The Duchess was in no position to talk about want of spelling, and Vanbrugh addressed his letters clearly. Nor need the Duchess have been quite so smug about the delivery of letters; after the Duke's death her mail and her daughter's were often confused.* Vanbrugh's own account to the Duke was that the letter 'being Opened at the Posthouse by the Opposite Party, Coppys were sent up to My Lord Trear: and others'. Soon the news of Vanbrugh's indiscretion was public around Woodstock; Joynes wrote to him on 7 March, 'Wee are here very much concern'd that your Letter should be made so publick and they are so base as to take a Coppy of it, but Mr Mayor takes it very ill at their hands'.

* p. 409

On 20 February Vanbrugh had been to see Robert Harley, now Lord Treasurer Oxford, taking him his own fair copy of the offending document; the next day he sent Harley an anxious letter confirming what he had told him then. He believed that the offences imputed to him were 'meddleing an Election, and reflecting on some body or other in behalf of the Duke of Marlborough'. As to the first, even in a private letter he had been wise enough not to mention any bearing the paving plan might have on votes, and no case could be made out of a coincidence. As to the second charge,

> I can only repeat what is true, That I meant nothing more than the Persecution of Pamphlets, News Papers and Storys, which daily gall'd him, and kept him in an improper Temper, to be press'd, for Imbellishing of Townes. If I had meant any thing farther, I shou'd certainly have used the word Prosecution, as it was reported I had.

He ended up hoping that 'by your favourable Construction the Queen may not take a very bad Impression from it'. But the damage had been done, even among those who had seen the letter or an accurate copy and did not credit the *Prosecution* story. The Queen had finished with the Marlboroughs and she had, in the phrase she later used, done with Vanbrugh. It looks as if someone in Woodstock first of all was his enemy, and there were some at court willing to represent to the Queen that her Comptroller had impugned one of her ministers. The offending letter was printed in *The Post Boy* on 24 March with a smug editorial warning to others; a week later a Treasury order was issued for the revocation of his Comptroller's patent, with effect from 15 April. On the 14th, 'being oblig'd to go out of Towne for some time', he thought a courteous note to Lord Oxford more appropriate than a personal leave-taking.

> I beg leave by this Short Letter, [he wrote] to declare, That I am very far from thinking the Queens present displeasure towards me, is owing to your Self . . . I cannot think, had it been quietly left to your own decision you wou'd ever have judg'd it Criminal. I take my Self to be cast by a Jury of True English Foxhunters, The whole business of whose Lives it is to hallow downe Creatures, who do them very little injury tho they never are fond of their Company.

Insignificant people then, he told himself (and Oxford): people of the kind he later pilloried in the character of Sir Francis Headpiece in *A Journey to London*. It may have been, as Laurence Whistler suggested, that Oxford was friendly enough to Vanbrugh to ignore the petitions that quickly fell on his desk, one from Talman for his old job back as Comptroller and another from Archer for the post. But among the other papers that reached him at this time was 'A Scheme proposed for the Office of her Majesty's Works' which described the Comptrollership as a needless sinecure and recommended its abolition as one of a number of reforms. At any rate, the post was not filled.

The story had other twists. Vanbrugh had told Marlborough on 18 March that

> the true rage I found against me, for this Letter, was; that it occasion'd the Mayors taking some Vigorous Resolutions relating to the Election which otherwise there was litle hopes of his doing. This made the Gentlemen, who set up the new Pretender there [the Tory candidate], press my Ld Trer: to turn me out, which when they had got him to consent to, it was intimated to me, That I might save my Self, if I cou'd prevail to have the opposition to them drop't. This I never mentioned to my Lord Godolphin, or anybody else till now . . . but now they have actually turnd me out, I acquaint your Grace, with what they wou'd have had me endeavour, to save my Place, which indeed I cou'd badly afford to lose, it cutting me off at the same time, from all hopes of succeeding either Sr Chr: Wren, or Sr Harry St George.

The future looked black indeed, and Vanbrugh took no comfort from the Queen's mortality. Moreover his debts still exceeded the £3000 owing to him in arrears for Blenheim and the Comptrollership. On 2 April he wrote to a relation (so called but unnamed in the surviving copy):

> I don't Know whether you have heard, that I am turn'd out of my place in the Works, for writing a Letter to the Mayor of Woodstock in which I say the Duke of Marlborough has been bitterly and barbarously persecuted, for these two Years past, in which I only meant the Continuall and Daily Libels and Pamphlets which pelted him, but some High-Church Members of Parliament wou'd needs have it, I meant the House of Commons and

so have push't the Matter to my being turn'd out, I believe I cou'd have prevented it, if I wou'd have made my Submission to those High-Church Blockheads, but that I wou'd on no terms do.

However, I wou'd not have you Concernd at it, for if the Pretender comes in, I shall gett more by it then they that made it their business, or were imploy'd to turn me out.

Interference with the mail was so widespread as to be considered a normal hazard by many correspondents. This letter also miscarried; at least a copy of part of it was sent on 26 June to Lord Oxford by one J.S. (unknown to him) from Liverpool. Four weeks later J.S. learned that his communication had been received, and offered to send the remainder of the letter. But Lord Oxford was not to be misled into thinking Vanbrugh, of all people, a secret Jacobite even – indeed especially – at a time when the succession to the throne was again in contention and many secret allegiances were being made or kept warm in case the political wind should one day blow from Saint-Germain.

Woodstock market-place was paved on the Blenheim account. The amenity was much appreciated in the town, and the Whig candidates were returned to Parliament. Vanbrugh also proposed a new front for the Town Hall: Joynes wrote to him on 3 September 1713:

I have drawn your Designe for the Front of the Town Hall Larger, and have made an Estimate of the same, if it be Executed According to that Designe and all of Freestone, Including Steps &c will cost for Workmanship & Materialls About 200£. I believe Sr. if you wou'd think of something that is more plain & strong, and that the Material near the spot would serve, and only freestone for Cornices & Embellishments would reduce the Expence to near half the Sum, for Pillasters or any such like made of Blaydon Stone, I believe will not cost above 5s. a perch.

This design was never carried out. Joynes addressed his letter to Vanbrugh in Chester; at the end of September he left there for Castle Howard where, as he told Edward Southwell, Lord Carlisle had at last arrived after having 'staid much longer at the Bath than he design'd which has kept me in this country thus long'.

From Chester Vanbrugh had been to Cholmondely Castle 'a second time ... and concerted a generall scheme for what is left to do'. Most of this house had recently been rebuilt, and probably designed, by William and Richard Smith, and Vanbrugh's design for the north front, made at this time and recorded in *Vitruvius Britannicus*, was not executed. From Castle Howard he went with the family to the Assemblies in York, where he met the Yarburghs of Heslington, one of whom was to be his destiny.* He wrote enthusiastically of Castle Howard to Edward Southwell and to James Craggs. He told the former it was so agreeable he thought of staying over Christmas. As the autumn weather began to bite he had 'a fair trial' of the house, and found that 'in corridors of 200ft long there is not air enough in motion to stir the flame of a candle'. He told Craggs, who duly passed the letter to the Duchess of Marlborough, that she

must find the same conveniency in Blenheim, if ever She comes to try it ... For my Lord Carlisle was pretty much under the same Apprehensions with her, about long Passages, High Rooms &c. But he finds what I told him to be true. That those Passages woud be so far from gathering & drawing wind as he feared, that a Candle wou'd not flare in them of this he has lately had the proof, by bitter stormy nights in which not one Candle wanted to be put into a Lanthorn, not even in the Hall, which is as high (tho not indeed so big) as that at Blenheim. He likwise finds, that all his Rooms, with moderate fires Are Ovens, And that this Great House do's not require above One pound of wax, and two of Tallow Candles a Night to light it, more than his house at London did Nor in Short, is he at any expence more, whatsoever than he was in the Remnant of an Old house, but three housemaids and one Man, to keep the whole house and Offices in perfect cleanliness ... If you think the knowledge of this, may be of any Satisfaction to my Lady Marlborough, pray tell her what you hear.

Three pounds of candles a day and four staff are substantial increases, but Lord Carlisle was pleased. Vanbrugh then referred to the Duchess's 'Generosity: in urging my Lord

* p. 376

Marlborough in my favour'. The Duchess later commented:

> What he calls Generosity was getting the Duke of Marlb: to give
> him two hundred pounds a year, which appears in the accounts.
> This was order'd upon the Duchess of Marlborgh's being told
> that my Lord Oxford had taken some Employment from him
> upon account of his having been faithful to the Duke.

How much of this he ever received there is no way of knowing.

From Castle Howard Vanbrugh also began a correspondence with the Lord Chamberlain's Office that would drag on
throughout the following year. When the Haymarket Theatre
opened he had paid £900 for the wardrobe at Lincoln's Inn
Fields. 'All that was added to it upon the first opening the Haymarket house ... and what was in a most profuse manner
added farther, when Mr Swiny brought all the Chief Actors
thither from Drury Lane' combined with this to make 'the
Richest and compleatest Stock, that ever any Company had in
England'. When, as a later letter puts it,

> Mr Swiny by Order, carryed the Players from the Haymarket to
> Drury Lane (leaving the Opera to Mr [William] Collier) the
> whole Stock of Cloaths &c belonging to Plays, and even a great
> deal belonging to the Opera, was removed thither; Mr Swiny
> having the command of them, as remaining still my Tenant by
> Lease, and the Rent he paid me, being in consideration of the
> Stocks, as well as the House.

The movement of players and costumes, and the compensa-
tory changes in the rents, became extremely complicated, and
most are set out in surviving letters to the Vice-Chamberlain.
But Vanbrugh's principal points were that the stock was his
and should revert to him in 1714 in good condition even
though Swiney had absconded, and that if anyone was benefit-
ing from abated rentals it was not he. Eventually, in January
1721 the Drury Lane managers agreed to pay him £1000 in in-
stalments, but in the five years up to his death they had only
paid £800.

One small ship came home at the end of 1713, when he received nearly three years' arrears as Comptroller, amounting
to £734.17s. Apart from this the only income left to him, as far

as we know, was his salary and fees from the College of Arms, and even these were in danger. On his return to 'uncomfortable things' in London he applied, with the help of Lord Bindon, now Earl of Suffolk and Deputy Earl Marshal, for the official grant of a coat of arms, something he had managed to do without for ten years as a herald. His father and his uncle William had used a device no doubt brought by their father from the Netherlands. The arms granted by the College on 15 April 1714 were: *Gules, on a Fesse, Or, three Barrulets, Vert: in Chief, a Demy Lion. For a Crest, a Demy Lion, issuant from a Bridge composed of three reversed Arches, Or.* So the rebus on *Van Brug* finally appeared, and perhaps none too soon: on 2 April Anstis had been granted the reversion of the Garter post. On 29 May Vanbrugh wrote to Marlborough, enclosing a drawing of the hundred-foot obelisk Lord Carlisle was raising in his honour, and ending with a postscript:

> The Queen has at last pass'd a Patent (even without my Lord Suffolks concurrence in it) to Mr Anstis for the reversion of Garter. She said, she had been under an Obligation to me, not to consent to it; but my behaviour had been such, in writing that Letter to Woodstock, That now she had done with me   That was her expression.

That was the lowest ebb. Vanbrugh told Marlborough, 'your Grace is held in Strong Suspicion, of having wholy embark'd in the Pretenders Interest and that you are to bring him over'. But two months later the Queen was on her deathbed, and on 2 August, the day after she died, the Marlboroughs landed at Dover. Prince George of Hanover was proclaimed King, and the Pretender would have to resort to arms the following year in a bid to carry his claim. The Duke, and then Vanbrugh, were reinstated, and Vanbrugh was knighted. When old Sir Henry St George died in mid August 1715 Lord Suffolk refused to recognize Anstis as Garter, saying that the decision had been made by the Queen without his knowledge. Anstis was then in prison, on suspicion of complicity in plotting a Jacobite rising in his native Cornwall; the wrangle dragged on until 1718 when he finally won his case, and in the meantime Vanbrugh was Acting Garter.

Royal Commissions do not outlive the sovereign who appoints them, so the accession of George I meant a new Commission for building churches. The return of the Whigs to power at the next election meant ironically that Vanbrugh, like his fellow architects, was excluded from it. For the new commissioners were as keen to save money as the old, apparently, had been to spend it; it was made clear that their business was only to provide places of worship and not monuments to the late Queen.

[24] On 14 October 1714 Lord Clare bought Chargate complete with its furniture and household goods. For the five years from 1715 Vanbrugh was engaged in turning it into Claremont, adding long wings that stretched along the contour of the park, punctuated by tall chimneys, towers, and turrets. The first work in 1715 was the Belvedere, a miniature neo-Norman brick castle on top of the hill behind the house; this is the only building that survives. In former days it was possible to climb to the roof platform to admire the view over the Surrey hills. The last work (in 1719-20) was the Great Room, a hundred feet long and two storeys high, which Newcastle used for great dinners and the entertainment of foreign ambassadors; this stood behind the right-hand wing and was the largest room Vanbrugh ever built apart from the Queen's Theatre.

With the improvement of his finances Vanbrugh began a new account book or journal – the one that survives – although the old one was not full. He started with several memorandums to himself about the Haymarket Theatre:

> Memd: I have accepted of Mr Swinys Resignation of his Lease of the Playhouse as on the 10th of May last, to wch time having settled the Account between us (with Mr Sexton his Agent, he himself being in France) I paid him part of the Ballance, and Sign'd a note to him payable at Michaelmass next, of £125 for the remainder, which is in full, of All Accounts between him and me. The Surrender of his Lease is only by a Writing sent from France; the lease it self being lock'd up with things of his at Leyden as likewise a Mortgage he had upon the Playhouse for £1000 . . .
>
> Memd: I have let the Vaults under the Play house to Mr Maes and Partners, for £30 a year, the Rent to commence from December the 25th 1714.

May the 10th 1715. I took up my Sisr Garrencieres [his half-sister] Mortgage for £600 on the Playhouse (of which at Severall times there had been £300 of the Principal paid her) and gave her a Bond for the remaining £300 ...

I mortgag'd the Playhouse to my Brother Charles for £2500. the Int[erest] to Commence June the 25th 1715.

I let the Chocolate Room &c to Mr Bowden for £60 a year, to begin from Michaelmass 1714.

The incompleteness of Blenheim and the affair of the Wood-stock letter do not seem to have deterred private patrons. By 1715 Vanbrugh was making the first designs for Eastbury in Dorset, for George Doddington. That year he also visited Grimsthorpe, one of the Lincolnshire houses of the Berties be-longing to his old friend Robert, fourth Earl of Lindsey and re-cently created Duke of Ancaster. He took a draughtsman down with him, for a survey plan is titled in his hand *Principal Floor, as it now is, 1715*; thus the work done from 1723 onwards for Robert's son, the second Duke, may have been designed some years earlier. In November 1715 Vanbrugh had a letter from Baron Goertz in Hanover asking about accommodation for ministers in London; he replied explaining that none was pro-vided and ministers were expected to have or acquire their own houses.

In March 1716 the Treasury paid the Blenheim creditors a third of their dues on account, and Vanbrugh got the first £800 of his surveyor's salary; within three weeks he had paid most of this over to Peregrine Bertie's executors 'In full Discharge of Principal & Interest of three Bonds'. Peregrine had died of apo-plexy on Tuesday 20 July 1711, and this was probably the money he had advanced to help buy out Swiney in 1708.

Very slowly Blenheim returned to activity. Marlborough was sixty-five and wanted above all to live there; that was reason enough for the Duchess to want to make a home there for him. One of the staff in the building office, Tilleman Bobart, annota-ted a plan of the principal floor to show what was yet to be done: no upper windows, paving or painting in the Hall, no floor or ceiling in the Saloon and only one of the four marble doorcases, many rooms without chimneypieces, no ceiling in the Gallery, no steps to either front, many rooms simply marked 'nothing done'. Some people, wrote the Duchess later with her characteristic hyperbole, 'said it was a chaos, and that no body but God Almighty could finish it'.

In May 1716 the Duke suffered a stroke. As if to compensate for her worries over his illness the Duchess threw herself into the details of habilitating the great unfinished shell. She questioned the new prices quoted by the masons, and the cost of plastering. 'The Plaistering done at Blenheim', Vanbrugh replied, 'is all after the Dutch manner which no body is got into the practice of here in England', but there was 'as much difference as between fine Paper and coarse, besides its being much more lasting'.

It was necessary to ask her agreement to every detail, and clearly although she knew what she wanted – a house that worked – she had not the slightest idea what had to be done or how. In June 1716 when the Marlboroughs were at Bath, Vanbrugh wrote to the Duchess from Blenheim, reminding her that the bakehouse, laundry and cistern gate, all essential for running the house, were as yet unroofed, but adding, 'The beauty of this place at this time is hardly to be conceiv'd'. Again in early July she questioned the cost of plastering. And what did he mean by the phrase 'painting the Wainscot in the Corridores'? What, she seems to have asked, is a *corridore* anyway. He explained the sequence of works and added, a trifle testily, 'The Word Corridore Madam is forreign, And signifys in plain English, no more than a Passage, it is now however generally us'd as an English word'.

Every so often he would refer to the lack of progress in finishing the Bridge, and at the end of July she responded by questioning the authority for the embanked causeways leading to it. Vanbrugh recalled in detail the competition between different designs, in which

> that of Sr Chr: Wrens, Stuck full of Pins, by which he pretended to lessen the charge, was quite rejected, and that I propos'd was resolv'd on, which has never been alter'd since that ever I heard of, and is the same now pursued. – Besides this my Lord Duke has never I believe, in Ten Years time, been once at Blenheim, without going to the brow of the Hill by the Bridge, and talking of the Causeway &c Which I thought he as properly understood as I did.

There had been, he continued, 'no whimsy or secret in this matter . . . I have no humour or desires of my own in it . . . As to going on without a contract I can only repeat what I have said before I did not go on without a contract'. And then,

> As to the computations of the Expence of this and the other works, I can only say, that they were made with a great deal of pains and care, and will I believe prove so. I wonder your Grace should think they were only done by random Guess. –
>
> As to the difference between the Estimate which was made of the House in general and the money it has cost I can give your Grace a very reasonable account whenever you have a mind to have it.

From Bath the Duchess drove out to Kings Weston; this led to a protracted correspondence about the stone front steps there in comparison with those intended for Blenheim. In August she asked about the various clerks at Woodstock, in particular about William Jefferson, who had been in charge of the paper-work since Joynes's departure in June 1715 to be Clerk of Works at Kensington. Vanbrugh told her:

> The Person yr Grace desires an account of at Blenheim, is one Jefferson, he was there from the Beginning at 15 Shillings a Week. And did the Business of an Assistant Clark of the Works, in taking an account of all Matterials as they come in, which requires a constant attendance from morning to Night But he neither measures the Work, nor Inspects the Execution of it, which is the great Business of a Clark of the Works. I found this man there now, he having been continued in pay by my Lord Duke to take care of the Building &c ever since the Work was Stop'd.

An idea perhaps began to form in the Duchess's mind. When she quizzed the juniors at Blenheim they confirmed Vanbrugh's opinions, and one of them might well be as knowledgeable as Sir John and a great deal less tiresome. Or perhaps an outsider? In October the Marlboroughs made a tour of inspection with Vanbrugh and Hawksmoor, attended by some of the others. On the 15th Jefferson wrote for Joynes in London a detailed account of what had passed. He had been ordered 'from the Dukes own Hand to deliver up all Bookes and Papers whatsoever and all Building Stores till I heard further from him'. He had asked the advice of Thornhill, painting the Hall ceiling, who told him 'it was certain that I must obey'. In return he had asked for his money. He went on:

Sir John has been Extreamly my friend. So has Mr Hawsmoor Mr Thornhill all of them, faith to a wonder. I was to waite on Mr Hawsmoor when he went of, he told me that he wou'd Doe what Laid in his power for me, and that few words was best, but what Disturbs me is and what I am heartily Sory for, that I beleive Sir John will never See Woodstock more, notwithstanding the pretended favour she had for Sir John when he was here. She has alter'd all againe and has put of all the Men at the Mannour house, notwithstand it was told her that Sir John paid them himself She Carry'd the Duke to the Mannour into Every Roome and Order that they shou'd put up no more Hangings or any thing Else, that Sir John had nothing to Doe there. This is truth and Matter of fact. She thought that she had pleasd Sir John with Carrying him Round the where it was Ready for Furniture, and As soon as Mr Hawsmoor had Set Downe Every thing wanting, then order'd Moor to have a Coppy, & he had one, the very next Day she alter'd her mind Entirely and Said Come Mr Moor I will leave all to you and you shall Doe every thing as you think fit, and tho Sir John has Contracted with several Workemen if you Can Get any Body to Doe it Cheaper they shall be turn'd out notwithstanding the progress they have made in the Workes, which makes Sir John of Great Use to 'em and in order to this he has begun Calling in the Contracts, which has sunk the Spirits of Fletcher Reade ever one of them, are all flat. Bradsall lys Ready and will take what they Refuse.

On 18 October Vanbrugh attempted in a letter to the Duchess to ·explain once again what he had been doing with the old manor, at his own expense, 'to make the place just habitable'. The Duchess later wrote, as sure of herself as always, that what she did next was only meant to have 'converted him and given me some quiet'; but it is difficult to give the benefit of the doubt to a woman who could pick a quarrel with Lord Bristol over a game of cards (as she did in 1724) and then accuse him of having started it the previous evening. She sent some papers to one I was very intimate with, Old Mr Craggs, and who I knew to be a great friend of Sr Johns, and I desired him with his Brother [in-law] Mr Richards to invite Sr John to dinner, And to read the Papers I sent them which wou'd make them Laugh over a botle of Wine.

Concurrently with the Blenheim correspondence Vanbrugh had been acting, to the Duchess's apparent satisfaction, to negotiate a marriage between her granddaughter Harriet (Henrietta) Godolphin and Lord Clare, now Duke of Newcastle. But at Bath she had come across Peter Walter, a leading London scrivener, who not only seems to have had a professional interest in marriage broking but also had been for some years adviser and attorney to Newcastle.

On 5 November Vanbrugh was called down to Claremont to see Newcastle, and found there Walter, from whom he learned that the Duchess of Marlborough had taken the affair out of his hands. On the 6th or the 7th he met Brigadier Richards who

shew'd me a Packet, he had recd, from her Grace, In which (without any new matter having happend) She had given herself the trouble, in twenty or thirty Sides of Paper, to draw up a Charge against me, beginning, from the time this Building was first ordered by the Queen, And concluding upon the Whole, That I had brought the Duke of Marlb: into this Unhappy difficulty Either to leave the thing Unfinishd, And by Consequence, useless to him and his Posterity; or by finishing it, to distress his Fortune, And deprive his Grandchildren of the Provision he inclin'd to make for them.

This is from the full account he sent Lord Carlisle some months later. But immediately he sat down to address the Duchess for the last time:

Whitehall. Nov: the 8th. 1716

Madam,

When I writ to your Grace on Tuesday last I was much at a loss, what cou'd be the ground of your having drop't me in the Service I had been endeavouring to do you and your Family with the Duke of Newcastle, Upon your own Sole motion and desire. But having since been shewn by Mr Richards, a Large Paquet of

Building Papers Sent him by your Grace, I find the reason was, That you had resolv'd to use me, so ill in respect of Blenheim; as must make it Impracticable to employ me in any other Branch of your Service.

These Papers Madam, are so full of Far fetch'd, Labour'd Accusations, Mistaken Facts, Wrong Inferences, Groundless Jealousys, and Strain'd constructions: That I shou'd put a very great Affront upon your Understanding, if I suppos'd it possible you cou'd mean any thing in earnest by them, but to put a Stop to my troubling you any more. You have your end Madam; for I will never trouble you more, Unless the Duke of Marlborough recovers so far, to shelter me from Such Intolerable Treatment.

I shall in the mean time, have only this Concern on his Account (for whom I shall ever retain the greatest Veneration) That your Grace having like the Queen thought fit to get rid of a Faithfull servant; The Torys will have the Pleasure, to See your Glassmaker Moor, make just such an end of the Dukes Building, as her Minister Harley did of his Victorys for which it was Erected.

> I am your Graces most Obedt
> Sert.
> J Vanbrugh

If your Grace will give me leave to Print your Papers I'll do it very exactly; And without any Answer or Remarks but this Short letter tack'd to the Tayle of them, That the World may know, I desir'd they might be Publish'd.

Two days later the Duke had a second stroke, possibly induced by the violence of the Duchess's reaction. He rallied enough, and the house progressed far enough, for them to move into the east side late in 1719. He had his great house, but the cost had been far more than financial. The Duchess now relied not on any architect, or on any of the old Blenheim office, but on Moore the cabinet-maker, to whom she referred as her 'oracle'. The next two years were also clouded by massive lawsuits between the Duchess and the workmen and others concerned with the building of Blenheim.* In April 1722, two months before the Duke's death, Hawksmoor wrote to the Duchess in concern about major architectural matters that,

* p. 399

after nearly six years, even she was beginning to recognize were quite beyond the competence of a 'glassmaker'. She accepted his offer of service, and for three years, with letters, drawings and personal visits, he was responsible for the design and execution of the Gallery, the Woodstock Gate and other works. Then, as quietly as he had come, he disappeared again from the Blenheim story. If he consulted Vanbrugh, there is no record of it.

When the Duke died Vanbrugh suggested to Godolphin the building of a mausoleum in the park; but in effect the Duchess on her own turned the whole place into a vast triumphal monument, with inscriptions, a tomb in the chapel designed by William Kent and executed by Rysbrack, and the pillar designed by Lord Herbert from which the Duke's statue still waves victoriously over the park and the Stratford road that skirts it. Only the old Manor played no part in the programme: a year after Marlborough's death not one stone of it remained upon another.

28

A Chatelaine

On 1 August 1716 Sir Christopher Wren retired as Surveyor or architect to the Royal Naval Hospital at Greenwich, and Vanbrugh, previously Deputy Surveyor, was appointed to succeed him. After twenty years' work, parts of the four courts were complete and in use while others were scarcely begun. It used to be thought that Vanbrugh was responsible for the design of King William Court and also for a number of very grand schemes for enlarging the hospital and adding a huge courtyard and domed chapel on its central axis. But modern research has established that King William Court is Hawksmoor's work, designed before Vanbrugh 'turned to architecture' and that the drawings for courts and chapels represent the unfulfilled dreams, again, of Hawksmoor. In fact the erroneous beliefs about the nature and the date of Vanbrugh's responsibility for Greenwich Hospital go back to the nineteenth century and to a period when biographers and archivists had not yet managed to distinguish between Sir John and his less famous cousin William, the original Secretary to the Hospital Commissioners.

Construction was still going on slowly according to the designs of Wren and Hawksmoor approved before 1700, its pace determined by the availability – or rather the scarcity – of funds; Greenwich was a charitable enterprise which enjoyed the patronage of successive monarchs but was not paid for by the Treasury. The Surveyor's duties were thus chiefly administrative, and it is Hawksmoor, as Clerk of Works, who is named in the Directors' minutes as the designer in 1715 of the charming little end loggias inside Queen Anne Court. But the Surveyor's attendance, for which he received expenses, was required at the Directors' meetings. He was also allowed the use of an official house, although Vanbrugh chose not to live in it.

Sited on almost level ground by the Thames, opposite the Isle of Dogs, the Hospital was built on the site of the Tudor Palace of Placentia and its garden, five miles down river from London Bridge. The Office of Works also had a wharf there and a landing stage, which was sometimes the point of entry or departure for distinguished travellers. The most recent of these to arrive was King George I, who disembarked on 18 September 1714 at the end of his journey from Hanover to take the throne.

'The first knight that King George made', wrote the crusty Oxford gossip Thomas Hearne in his diary a week later, 'is one Vanbrugh, a silly Fellow, who is the Architect at Woodstock.' Officially the honour was for Vanbrugh's journey to Hanover in 1706 to bring the Garter to the future George II, but this was the 'something lasting' for which Marlborough had advised him to wait and which, restored to favour at the death of Queen Anne, the Duke was now able to arrange for him. The investiture was at Greenwich, and the same honour was conferred on William Saunderson or Sanderson, Captain of the *Peregrine*, the ship in which the new King had crossed the North Sea to England. Saunderson was also one of the Directors of Greenwich Hospital and lived in the neighbourhood.

It was at Greenwich, the green village, that Saint Alphege, Archbishop of Canterbury, had been martyred by the Danes on 19 April 1012. The new parish church, dedicated to him and designed by Hawksmoor as the first of the proposed 'Fifty New Churches', was in 1716 being fitted and furnished. In the later Middle Ages there had been a royal house at Greenwich with a deer park. Henry VIII and his two daughters Queen Mary and Queen Elizabeth were born in the palace. In 1605 James I settled the estate on his queen, Anne of Denmark, who eleven years later commissioned Inigo Jones to design the Queen's House, ingeniously built astride the road from Deptford to Woolwich with doors on one side to the park and on the other to the palace garden. But the house was only completed in 1635 for the next queen, Henrietta Maria, who had few occasions to use it before the outbreak of the Civil War. After the Restoration plans were made to enlarge it and the central bridge connecting the two halves over the road was augmented by two others at the ends of the house. But the Queen Mother decided to return once more to her native France, and Charles II commissioned John Webb to design a new palace by the river on the site of Placentia. The single range built of the three planned by Webb was begun in the year of Vanbrugh's birth but abandoned as a carcase in 1669; it was only completed thirty years later as part of the Hospital.

Charles II kept his yachts at Greenwich although he never lived there. In 1676 the Royal Observatory built by Wren on the hill in the park was opened, and in the 1680s the Huguenots established a community and a chapel in the village. As the area's associations with the Crown declined it became more important first as a convenient and then as a fashionable place to live within easy reach of London. Moreover development also took place at the top of the hill nearer to the London-Dover road running across Blackheath, and also in the next village, Charlton, where in 1721 lived and died two of Vanbrugh's friends, Brigadier Michael Richards and his brother-in-law the elder James Craggs, Postmaster General; contrary to general belief, however, the painter Sir James Thornhill did not live there.

Vanbrugh already knew the district quite well. He had long since sold his little house at Chargate in Surrey and he had lost his ruin in Woodstock Park. It was thus for a variety of reasons that he decided to take a weekend house at Greenwich. On 9 March 1717 he wrote in his Account Book:

> Memd: I Sign'd a Lease this day to Sr Wm Saunderson, for his House at Greenwich, for three years Certain, for more if I desire it; or to purchase it out at £800. The Rent £40 pr Anm to commence from Ladyday next.

He also recorded the payment of one pound to the attorney for drawing up the lease. Saunderson's principal house was on top of the hill in the direction of Charlton, and among the Vanbrugh drawings at Elton Hall is an undated sketch showing proposals for alterations to it. But the house that Vanbrugh leased was probably the one down towards the river, near the old palace tiltyard, which until Midsummer 1715 Saunderson had leased to Dr Oliver, the Physician to Greenwich Hospital.

At Ladyday (25 March) 1717 Vanbrugh and his younger brother Charles moved out of the house in Duke Street, St James's, which had been rented mainly for Charles's benefit when he was ashore, and into Saunderson's house. This was the 'country morsell' as one of his friends called it, from which he wrote to the Duke of Newcastle a few days before Christmas 1717, but by that time he was beginning to consider new ambitions in respect of both his house and his life-style: a little castle and perhaps a chatelaine.

In October 1713 the young Lady Mary Wortley Montagu had written from York to a friend a letter full of gossip:

> I can't forbear entertaining you with our York Lovers . . . In the 1st form of these Creatures is even Mr. Vanbrug. Heaven no doubt compassionateing our Dullness has inspired him with a Passion that makes us all ready to die with laughing. Tis credibly reported that he is endeavouring at the Honourable state of matrimony and vows to lead a sinfull life no more.

Vanbrugh indeed was enjoying an autumn vacation at Castle Howard, and was often to be seen at the York assemblies. The previous Monday,

> there were 200 peices of Woman's flesh (fat and lean), but you know Van's taste was allways odd; his Inclination to Ruins has given him a fancy for Mrs Yarborrough. He sighs and ogles, that it would do your heart good to see him; and she is not a little pleas'd, in so small a proportion of men amongst such a Number of Women, a whole man should fall to her share.

Lady Mary, whose father Lord Kingston was a Kit-Cat, had been the toast of the Club at the age of ten, and at twenty-three she had married Edward Montagu for love instead of the husband arranged by her father. She was writing with personal knowledge of Mr Vanbrug, although this is the only comment on his bachelor habits, and her remarks are neither very kind nor very clear. *Mrs* did not necessarily indicate a married woman, being the title of all but the very young and the doubt-fully virtuous for whom *Miss* was used. Mrs Yarborough was either Faith, the daughter of Sir Thomas and Henrietta Maria Yarburgh of Heslington, York, an unmarried lady of thirty, or her niece of twenty, also named Henrietta Maria, the daughter of Faith's brother Colonel James Yarburgh. He was the same age as Vanbrugh and had been aide-de-camp to Marlborough.

Vanbrugh's inclination to ruins of masonry, in the form of old Woodstock Manor, was certainly well known in Kit-Cat cir-cles. He himself used the word *ruin* facetiously to mean marri-age (to Newcastle, 24 January 1719), but since Lady Mary was twenty-four and Vanbrugh was forty-nine it would not have been difficult for her to find his conduct amusing, however he behaved.

Vanbrugh was in Yorkshire again in April 1715 and August 1716; the latter visit was crucial, as we can deduce from a letter he wrote on 30 April 1717. The signature is missing, but the letter is in his characteristic hand. The recipient, whose name is also missing, must have been one of Lord Carlisle's daugh-ters, who had written to tell Vanbrugh of the Earl's departure from Yorkshire to London in order to patch up the rift in the Whig Party. She had Vanbrugh's confidence to an unusual degree, although later, when its contents were history, it was passed to the Duke of Newcastle, probably because it refers among other topics to the latter's own recent marriage; Van-brugh felicitated both the Duke and himself on the success of a match he had helped to promote.

But Vanbrugh also revealed that he himself had gone 'into a Sort of retirement here at Greenwich', and that 'this is your Heslington Ladys doing still; she keeps me from your gay meetings at York, by [being] there; and from those at London, by being absent'. The letter then makes clear to us, in the dis-cussion of Newcastle's marriage, what was already clear to Vanbrugh's correspondent – the lady's identity. She was the second cousin of the new Duchess of Newcastle, 'and not much unlike her, especially in Temper and manners'. She was Hen-rietta Maria Yarburgh, now twenty-four.

So acute an observer of people as Vanbrugh cannot have failed to notice the reactions of bystanders and gossips to his

conduct at the York assemblies of 1713, or to appreciate that
the deeper he became involved the faster tongues would wag.
The courtship – for that is what it had become by 1717 – was at
its most delicate stage, even within the elaborately contrived
etiquette of the time. During his northern holiday of 1716 his
feelings had become undeniably clear to himself if not, perhaps, to anyone else. The letter from Greenwich suggests that
they were still unknown to the young lady; at the very least, if
they were known they had not been reciprocated. Vanbrugh
was pleased with his rented house at Greenwich, and he now
added, 'were I young enough, to make it as agreeable to that
Lady, I shou'd certainly desire you to invite her to it'.

In fact the next thing we know with certainty is that over
Christmas 1718, which Vanbrugh spent at Castle Howard, the
arrangements for the wedding were made. On Christmas Day
itself Sir John wrote to Newcastle that "tis so bloody Cold, I
have almost a mind to Marry to keep myself warm'. This was
the only hint, although a heavy one, that he was to give the
Duke; his next letter (4 January) made it clear that the cold at
Castle Howard was only out of doors, for

> this Place where I am now, has since I remember been Shiver'd
> at, when Nam'd for a Winter habitation. And yet, is now so very
> comfortable a One, that in this sharp Season, there has not past a
> day, without setting Open severall times, the door and Windows
> of the Room My Lord Car: and the Ladys constantly use; it has
> been so much too hot: And all the rest of the house, is so in pro-
> portion.

There spoke the architect; he went on to refer to the refurbishment the Duke had asked him to design at Nottingham Castle,
a grandiose block built forty years earlier by Samuel Marsh.
The exterior walls of Marsh's building still stand, but the
interior was rebuilt after a fire in 1831. 'And so may Nottingham Castle be made', wrote Vanbrugh, 'by the same care
and Methods'. Although he advised the Duke not to come up
until the weather was better, Newcastle arrived with his estate
managers soon after Christmas. On 29 December he wrote
home to his Duchess:

I am very busy here every Moment of the Day, The House is in
the Main very Noble & pretty convenient. The Apartment below
Stairs will be made very handsome for to live in Every Day, That
above is very magnificent, but out of Repair but we may shift wth
it as it is. The State Bed Chamber is well furnished wth Velvet
Bed, & good Tapistry, Our Rooms must all be new fitted up &
furnished, but they will be very handsome, and convenient,
above & below there will be great conveniencies for servts &
seven spare Apartemts for Strangers. wch is more than we expected.

Newcastle saw no reason not to employ a furnishing consultant who was no great friend of his architect.* He told his
Duchess:

Mr Moore, I must say does wonders. So I hope My Friend the Ds
of M. will forgive my keeping him here. Van is a creature we
have not seen but want. The Maried part of our company, as we
do Every post Night, are retired to write to our Wives.

On 11 January Vanbrugh moved to the George Inn in York,
from whence the following day he wrote again to Newcastle,
telling him only that Lord Carlisle, 'the Idol here', and his
family were about to join him. His account of future movements is indeed a little confusing, but the register of St
Lawrence's, York, records that on 14 January 1719 the marriage took place between Henrietta Maria Yarburgh, now
twenty-six and of that parish (in which she had been christened) and Vanbrugh, described as of Castle Howard. Probably
Lord Carlisle not only gave him a temporary address but also
acted as best man. That day or the next, the party moved to
Temple Newsam just north of Leeds, the seat of Carlisle's son-
in-law Viscount Irwin, the husband of Lord Carlisle's daughter
Anne; by the 24th the Vanbrughs had reached Nottingham, the
Carlisles being by then in Stamford. For part of the time (and
probably for the wedding day) the Vanbrughs had the hire of a
coach, for which the Account Book later records a payment of
£13. 18s.

From Nottingham Vanbrugh again wrote to Newcastle, at

* p. 370

last telling him of his choice of a wife 'whose principall Merrit in my Eye has been some small distant shadow of those Valuable Qualifications in her, your Grace has formerly with so much pleasure heard me talk of', a roundabout compliment to the Duchess. Having professed himself a bachelor for so many years, he was not going to expatiate on his new pride and happiness; nevertheless it is clear that the whole affair was both deeper and more premeditated than he admitted to any but his closest friends. Between the letter of 30 April 1717 and that of Christmas 1718 there is one possible occasion for a flying visit to York to win the Heslington lady's consent and to ask that of her father; the Account Book records, without destination, an absence from home of eight nights and hire of six horses from 26 June to 3 July 1718, when the days were at their longest. Comparison with other recorded journeys, in which the destination is stated in addition to the number of horses and their cost, suggests that the expense in particular was variable, most probably according to the kind of vehicle Vanbrugh was driving. It also confirms that, whereas the short days and bad roads stretched the journey to Nottingham in December 1718 to four days, even in his light calash, at midsummer he could have made the return trip to York comfortably and cheaply in the recorded length of time.* The six nights from 15 to 20 July were, as not the Account Book but the Earl of Bristol's Diary records, for a visit to Ickworth in Suffolk, where Vanbrugh made and left for the Earl a plan for a new or re-styled house.

One of the more dubious legacies of Sigmund Freud to civilization has been the doctrine that everyone has a sex-life. In fairness it must be said that, although this idea may have been accepted by society in general, it is not supported without qualification by the findings of those professionally involved with this sphere of human behaviour. After all, to take a modern 'scientific' view, the sexual drive is biologically necessary for the continuance of the human race but not for the survival of the individual. Unless some even more revealing document comes to light, it is pointless to speculate on Vanbrugh's sexual inclinations and experience before his courtship and marriage. Nobody at the time seems to have taken seriously the lam-

* p. 244

poon on Goose-Pie House which insinuated that he was homo-
sexual; such allegations have been made of gregarious
bachelors often enough, with a fairly consistent measure both
of malice and inaccuracy, in eras both of permissiveness and of
repression.

Lady Mary Wortley Montagu's reference to a vow 'to lead a
sinful life no more' must, in its context, be taken as the sort of
jocular remark that is often, even usually, made about – and
even to – a lively unattached male with a ready wit and an eye
for the ladies. Without delving more generally into seventeenth-century demography it is worth considering Vanbrugh's siblings. Four of his sisters – discounting the elusive
Elizabeth – lived unmarried to ages between thirty-six and
ninety-six, and his youngest brothers married at thirty-three
and forty-one. In the years covered by the Account Book he was
close to all of these siblings except Lucy who had died, and
clearly celibacy was not unfamiliar to their generation.

Vanbrugh gave some of his stage characters the opportunity
to discover real and noble emotions, and in those still mysterious formative years he must have pondered the choice between rakery and true love. If the former had been his choice
we might at least expect to have found more evidence of it. But
if indeed he waited for true love – for that 'one inestimable lot,
in which the only Heaven on Earth is written', he took to the
duties of both matrimony and fatherhood with relish and success. Sir John and his lady began as Uncle William and Dorothy had done, 'a Bit of a Girle popping into the World', as he
told Newcastle in August 1719, 'three months before its time'.
But three years later he wrote to Tonson:

> I am now two Boys Strong in the Nursery but am forbid getting
> any more this Season for fear of killing my Wife. A Reason; that
> in Kit Cat days, wou'd have been stronger for it, than against it:
> But let her live, for she's Special good, as far as I know of the
> Matter.

On 30 January 1719 he had introduced his bride to the
agreeable rented house at Greenwich, and the next day he
recorded a gift to her of fifty guineas. For a moment indeed he
forgot who she had become, writing in his accounts *pd to Mrs Y*

and amending it to *Given my Wife*; a similar gift on 7 March was correctly entered.

Lady Vanbrugh had already discovered what was entailed in being the wife of a successful architect, for the stop in Nottingham without the Carlisles was in order for him to give directions to ensure that the Castle would be 'fit for habitation sooner than one cou'd have imagin'd'. But Nottingham was not the only castle on which he was by now engaged. On 3 March 1718 he had taken a ninety-nine year lease from Sir Michael Biddulph of 'a Field & other Grounds' at Greenwich. From June onwards there are payments on account to Richard Billinghurst, a well-known master bricklayer whose firm was big enough to have contracts at St Paul's Cathedral and Greenwich Hospital. It appears from the Account Book that Billinghurst dealt with the whole construction of Vanbrugh Castle from foundations to roof, Vanbrugh paying separately for bricks and some other materials and trades. One Sunday towards the end of 1719 Vanbrugh heard that in his absence Newcastle 'was pleas'd to Storm my Castle'. By December it was finished, and by Ladyday (25 March) 1720, when the agreement with Saunderson expired, the family had moved in: Gale the upholsterer was paid £28. 7s. on 4 March and on the 17th Vanbrugh gave Mr Demetrius (probably his kinsman Abraham of Laurence Pountney Lane) £18 for '4 peices of Tapistry'. Possibly these were the depreciated remains of Peter Matthews Baldwin's 'Flower Pots'.*

Vanbrugh's lease, which has recently been rediscovered, shows that the 'other grounds' mentioned in it included a detached plot of land on the north side of the coach way which is now the west end of Westcombe Park Road; it was on this plot that Vanbrugh built his castle. The lease also shows that the area, although rural, was not unpopulated. At the corner with Maze Hill was a long house divided into three dwellings, and nearby were houses occupied by William Davies, a blacksmith whose services Vanbrugh used on several occasions, and William Deakins or Deacons, victualler. There was also a property known as The Three Tuns, but as the lease mentions

* p. 11

only land the hostelry, if there was one of this name, was not on the Biddulph estate.

[26]   Vanbrugh Castle still stands at the top of Maze Hill just east of Greenwich Park. The original building into which the family moved early in 1720 is three-cornered and symmetrical. The south front, facing the twelve-acre field and looking beyond it towards Blackheath, has a projecting circular tower in the centre and square towers at the corners. All three towers rise a whole storey above the body of the house, that is four storeys instead of three above the basement which is half over and half below ground. The corner towers have battlements, and all around the upper walls run a corbel table like a pie-edging. Most of the windows have semicircular heads, arched in the same brown London stock brick as the rest of the walls. The round tower, which is filled by a spiral staircase, is topped by a conical cap much like the one Vanbrugh later proposed for one of the mock bastions at Castle Howard, derived (as he told Lord Carlisle) from one he remembered on the old walls of Chester.

Each floor of the building consists basically of three rooms, one at each corner. The south-west and south-east rooms, flanked by the battlemented towers which provide cabinets or closets to them, look out both south to the field and north towards the Essex marshes. On each floor a corridor joins these rooms to each other and gives access to the spiral staircase and to the third room, which takes up the whole centre of the north side and opens into a central semicircular bay. This bay has three arched windows which, until the trees to the north grew so high, provided between them a panoramic view across the park and village and further away west to the Thames and the City, east to Woolwich and the beginning of the Thames estuary. Even from the ground floor the views on a fine day were remarkable; from the top floor they were breathtaking, and it was even possible, as it used to be at the Claremont Belvedere, to go out on the lead roof and see all the way round the horizon.

It is surely part of Vanbrugh's design that the south elevation of the Castle fits almost into an exact square; that is, the corner towers are as high as the distance encompassing them is wide. Nevertheless the way in which the walls break forward and backward into towers, bays, and recesses, the placing of windows in vertical tiers, and the virtual absence of continuous horizontals, all contribute to an appearance of tallness. This was the ultimate, the simplest form of the Castle Air, and the proof of Vanbrugh's claim that, for him at any rate, the figure and proportions, not the delicacy of the ornaments, are the essence of architecture. This is the third of the little houses he built for himself – not counting the repaired Woodstock – and the only one that survives. Part of its appeal is in the ironic contrast between the monumental grandeur of its sheer external surfaces and clean lines and the small actual size which makes it both rather toy-like and comfortable to live in. Vanbrugh saw very clearly the difference between his own castle and Blenheim, of which he wrote in retrospect to Tonson in November 1719, 'one may find a great deal of Pleasure, in building a Palace for another, when one shou'd find very little living in't ones Self'.

Today the Castle presents a very different appearance from the original. It is once again lived in, sensitively and sensibly converted into apartments after many years as a private school, but it has suffered both additions and losses. Some of the additions were Vanbrugh's own, others were made later and some as recently as the beginning of this century. The most serious losses are of almost all the out-buildings with which Vanbrugh surrounded the Castle, so that it rose like the keep in the midst of a fortress, a reminder to nobody more than the architect himself of Calais, Vincennes, and the building which many years later was to give the Castle the popular name of Bastille House. These buildings were already beginning to disappear when John Carter wrote a long account of the Castle in the *Gentleman's Magazine* for 1815; they included a big one-storey kitchen, a circular tower over the well in the forecourt that supplied the Castle with water, a crenellated gateway, and curtain walls. But Vanbrugh began almost as soon as he moved in to make plans for an addition to the Castle itself that would virtually double its size, and even that was not all. For this most solid of children was to be given its own family of dependants in the twelve-acre field.*

* p. 433

— 29 —

The Cuckoo in the Nest

[39]   At about the time of his marriage Vanbrugh sat for his portrait a
second time, probably to Thomas Murray. Whereas his Kit-Cat
face looks beyond the spectator, in the later likeness the gaze
of his dark grey eyes is direct and shrewd. He wears a coat of a
colour known to painters as Indian red, a waistcoat of blue and
gold. His wig is blond rather than the brown of the earlier portrait, perhaps because his own hair now tended towards silver
or white. By a device admired by artists in his day and still used
in modern portrait photography, he is shown about to speak;
although it is an artifice the effect is so convincing that we can
almost see in the mouth the formation of one of those well-
formed phrases that characterize his apparently artless style of
writing. He no longer rests his arm on a table or holds a pair of
dividers; moreover the attitude of what we can see implies that
he is not seated but standing, head turned to the left and his left
shoulder forward, hand in waistcoat, with the swagger of a
man displaying his new and well-fitting suit in the tailor's
mirror.

   This portrait once had a companion of the same size by a less
distinguished painter, showing Lady Vanbrugh wearing a
yellow dress and a blue shawl; this has not been traced since it
was sold at auction fifty years ago. One of the Yarburgh family
portraits now at Ampleforth College is traditionally supposed
also to represent her, but fashionable young ladies usually try
to look alike more than do gentlemen in their fifties, whether
or not the painter is required to adjust the reality to fit the norm

of the day. For these reasons more is left to the imagination concerning her appearance.

On 8 June 1721 Vanbrugh began his reply to a letter from Lord Carlisle by expressing sympathy that

> you shou'd owe any Stroaks of Philosophy to a fit of the Gout. I hope it will prove only a Summer fit, and so be soon over. But I, without the Gout to incline my Philosophy, have every day of my Life Since twenty years old, grown more and more of opinion, that the less one has to do, with what is call'd the World, the more Quiet of mind; and the more Quiet of mind, the more Happyness. All other delights, are but like debauches in Wine; which give three days pain, for three hours pleasure. It has however been my chance, to lead a Life quite against my Sentiments hitherto; But I have made a Virtue of Necessity, from Some rebuffs I have met with in this Reign, and lessen'd my concern in things I was tempted before to be busy about which has cas'd me a good deal, and I hope will Still do more.

This is the clearest statement we have not only of the gravity of mind that underlies that portrait but also of how early that mind had been formed. If Vanbrugh meant the age of twenty literally and precisely then something happened in 1684 of which we know nothing. But looking back over the best part of forty years he might well, and very understandably, have used an approximation for his *early twenties*: he was just twenty-two when he joined Huntingdon's regiment, and he celebrated his quarter-century as a prisoner in Calais. Writing to Tonson in November 1719, he had specified one rebuff: being twice passed over for the Surveyorship in favour of unqualified persons, the first being eighteen years his junior and the second a man of sixty-five who in the event would outlive him by only a fortnight. What galled him most was that the appointment had once been his for the asking.

Early in 1715 Lord Halifax had brought about a reorganization of the Office of Works. It was probably then that either Halifax or Carlisle, who succeeded him for a time later in the year, offered Vanbrugh the Surveyorship, that Vanbrugh refused it out of 'tenderness' towards Wren, and that instead of being persuaded to retire Wren was given the 'support' of a new and larger Board of Works which in effect took decisions

on his behalf. Wren, in his own words, was left with his title but
'no power to over-rule, or give a casting vote'. But whether or
not that was the occasion on which Vanbrugh turned down the
offer, his expectations went back several years earlier: since
he already thought himself out of the running after his letter to
the Mayor of Woodstock, he must have expected earlier than
that to succeed Wren in due course.

A further irony in the situation was that Halifax's re-ordering
of the Works was based at least partly on Vanbrugh's advice: on
29 November 1714 he had, at Halifax's invitation, sent him a
paper of recommendations. This was before his reinstatement
as Comptroller; it may be that uncertainty in the Treasury,
whether the post should be retained or abolished, was not
resolved until the decision was made to issue a new patent to
him on 24 January 1715. In Vanbrugh's paper, however, the
Comptroller's office was clearly to be no sinecure. The offices
of Master Mason, Master Carpenter 'and all the other master
Workmen, with the Purveyour, and Clark Ingrosser' were to be
'Sunk, and their Allowances Saved to the Crown'. The Paymaster and the Comptroller, the two financial officers of the
Works, were to provide a check on the Surveyor, making contracts, passing bills, and signing the books. The number of
clerks was to be reduced from seven to two, the separate
establishment for Windsor Castle was to be abolished, and new
checks were to be provided against the execution of private
works on the Office's charge. All clerks were to be skilled in
'Drawing, Measurements, Workmanship and Materials', and
finally Vanbrugh's own remuneration, like that of the Surveyor, was to be cleared of its traditional components of fees,
perquisites and allowances and put 'on the foot of a Salary certain'.

In March 1715 Vanbrugh submitted a further paper of detailed comments on the Treasury's draft proposals. From these
papers it is clear that he had undertaken a desirable cost-
cutting exercise of the kind that would find approval today;
moreover, he had found out what each officer did and needed
to do, and which posts the long-term changes in royal building
patronage and Office procedure had rendered unnecessary
and expendable. But the changes authorized by a warrant of 29
April were less sweeping, and less likely to 'Save the King, a

very great Sum of Money' than those which Vanbrugh had proposed. The most significant changes were therefore first an
improvement in the calibre of the clerks, and secondly the
establishment of the new Board comprising, besides Wren, the
Comptroller and Paymaster and four outsiders. Two of these
were Treasury Secretaries, one of whom attended only the first
meeting on 6 May and the other none at all. The other two were
Surveyors General of other offices: Hugh Cholmley of Crown
Lands and Thomas Hewett of Woods and Forests. Hewett
would be the one to watch.

In the next three years, up to Wren's dismissal on 26 April
1718, Vanbrugh attended 204 meetings of the Board and
missed only 32; as he told Lord Newcastle, 'I (in effect) presided at the Board of Works' to the saving of £10,000 a year.
Vanbrugh had learned something about juggling with figures
in his Haymarket Theatre days; nevertheless there is no doubt
of his intention to save the Crown money and there is some
substance to his claim to have succeeded. Just before Christmas 1717 he had told Newcastle

> that there is a most thorough Care and Strickt management in
> the Board of Works, And no Sort of Ground upon Earth, for the
> Suggestion to the Contrary, And upon this one point (I beg your
> Grace will frankly say to the king) I desire to have his Favour or
> Abandon any pretence to it for ever.

The appointment of William Benson in Wren's place on 26
April was the second blow for Vanbrugh within a week, for on
the 20th his period as Acting Garter and the long wrangle with
Anstis over the post came to an end. In spite of all Vanbrugh's
lobbying and letter-writing to Newcastle, Anstis's claim was
finally accepted. And with Benson's arrival in Scotland Yard
the Works entered a period of chaos such as it had never
known.

Benson (1682-1754) was the son of a prosperous iron merchant; on his marriage in 1707 he acquired estates in Wiltshire,
and in 1715 he got himself elected Member of Parliament for
Shaftesbury in Dorset. One reason for his electoral victory was
his provision of a piped water supply for the town, and the following year he was with George I at Herrenhausen for which

he designed hydraulic apparatus. In 1718 George ordered that Benson's pumping engine for the big fountain there was to be bought 'whatever the cost'; evidently Benson enjoyed the ear and the favour of the King. Besides his concerns with water engineering and Whig politics Benson had aspirations to literary patronage – he commissioned a monument to Milton in Westminster Abbey in 1737 – and to the patronage and practice of architecture. On his Wiltshire estate he began building a villa for himself, basing the elevation design on a reduced version of the nearby Amesbury, of which he had a lease, and which although designed by John Webb was then believed to be the work of Inigo Jones.

Subsequent statements by Vanbrugh and Hawksmoor are strongly worded, but their truth is confirmed by other records; much of the story can thus be told in their words. Being, as Hawksmoor later wrote to Lord Carlisle,

in extream Need of an employment [Benson] could find nothing at that time, but the Office of Workes, to fall upon, soe disguising himself under the pretence of an Architect, got himself made Surveyour Generall, and also power ... to Destroy the Settlement of the Office, to Turn out Sir Chrisr Wren and several others, clerks and officers, and me in particular ... and made his brother, a very young man clerke of the Workes, and Secretary in my place, which quite defeated the good intended to the Publick, by the Lord Halifax, your Lordship and Sr J. Vanbrugh.

Halifax was succeeded as Lord Treasurer in turn by Carlisle, Lord Stanhope and, on 20 March 1718 by Charles Spencer, third Earl of Sunderland. He was the son of William III's drawling Lord Chamberlain and the husband (and already widower) of Marlborough's daughter Anne Churchill. In November 1717 Benson had obtained the reversion of one of the two Auditorships of the Imprest, to succeed whichever Auditor died first (one being Edward Harley whose enquiries had led to the revised orders for the Office of Works in 1705).* Benson's interest in architecture, and the fact that Wren, now eighty-six, held his

* p. 248

appointment not for life but 'at the pleasure' of the sovereign, suggested to him or his friends that the Surveyorship would be a convenient employment – putting in a deputy – until one of the Auditors should die. He promoted himself to the attention of Lord Treasurer Sunderland as an expert to rival Vanbrugh in management efficiency, sending him a critique of the 1715 orders that the latter had framed with Lord Halifax.

In view of the dissensions within both the Marlborough family and the Whig party it would be wrong to suppose that Sunderland agreed to Benson's appointment as Surveyor because of Vanbrugh's quarrel with the Duchess. We can only say that Sunderland was less committed to Vanbrugh's support than Carlisle or Halifax, that neither Benson's ambition nor his incompetence was foreseen, and that three years later Sunderland supported Vanbrugh in the House of Lords over the Blenheim lawsuit. On 21 August 1718 the new Surveyor dissolved the Board set up three years previously, and nine days later Vanbrugh told Newcastle that

> my Ld Sund: has been so good to me, as to Assure me of the Utmost of his Friendship: And indeed I am far from having the least doubt of his good Intentions to me.

With the blind obstinacy of a hatchling cuckoo Benson proceeded to lay about him in every direction in an attempt to dislodge all opposition; Hawksmoor did not exaggerate. The reconstitution of the Board of Works restored to Benson all the powers Wren had enjoyed as Surveyor before 1715. As Clerk Ingrosser he appointed Colen Campbell, an ambitious Scottish architect with a legal training, some claim to professionalism, and, according to Hawksmoor, a nose for sinecures. By also making him Deputy Surveyor, Benson obtained a deputy to do his work not at his own expense but at the Crown's; it was partly in reply and partly to keep a salary for Thomas Kynaston, another clerk dismissed by Benson, that a fortnight later Vanbrugh made Kynaston Deputy Comptroller. Benson also revived the offices of Master Carpenter and Purveyor, and can only have added to Vanbrugh's anger by giving the latter post to James Moore the Blenheim cabinet-maker. Vanbrugh takes up the story in a paper of *Remarks on the Conduct of William*

Benson which he submitted to the Treasury in March 1719:

> For the first 6 Months no Business was done in the Office, nor
> any Tradesmens Bills stated, wch before that time us'd to be
> done monthly.

The Minutes of the Board show that it held no meetings in May
1718, only eight between 10 September and 7 November, and
none at all between then and 5 February 1719. After seven
meetings in February it met only six times in the following four
months. Vanbrugh's account continues:

> And the Pallaces being in good repair, He forms a Project of
> keeping them so under pretence of having cost his Majesty &
> former Crowns for the Ordinary Repairs 28000£ p. Ann: (but
> wch was not commun[i]s ann[i]s the 3d prt of that sum, but occa-
> sion'd by Buildings and Repairs of Lodgings by Warrants from
> the Treasury call'd Extraordinarys) for the sum of 12000£ pr
> Annm.

Benson suggested an annual maintenance contract for this
sum

> in the Names of the Kings Mason, Carpenter & Bricklayer, who
> were to declare a Trust to his two foremention'd Instruments B.
> Benson & C. Campbell, but realy in Trust for himself; by which
> 1000£ pr Month was to be receiv'd of the Treasury for 4 years, of
> wch the said Mason, Carpenter & Bricklayer was not acquainted
> till the Contract was ripe, & then they were told by this new Sur-
> veyr that they should have each of them sallaries of about 200£
> pr Ann: Each, for the use of their Names, wch was either for
> Bribes or Hush money.

Benson was to be both Surveyor and contractor. Moreover the
scheme excluded the other Patent Artisans: joiner, plasterer,
glazier, painter, and plumber. It also excluded the worst-kept
palace, Somerset House, and any repairs to fire and storm
damage.

> This Contract was accordingly sign'd by the 3 Workmen ... in
> which it is expressly said that all doubts or disputes should be

settled by 3 Persons one to be chosen by the Lords of the Treasury, One by the said Surveyor, & the 3d by the Contractors, so that He had 2 Arbitrators against the Treasurys one, and consequently as little money might be expended as he pleas'd, And by the same Contract he is made Judge what Buildings are necessary or fit to be repaird, or pulled down & rebuilt, whereby to save himself 50£, he might put the Crown to 500£. And call it Extraordinarys.

But at the eleventh hour the conspirators fell out among themselves. The Master Mason, the same Benjamin Jackson whose activities at Kensington had started Vanbrugh on the path of reform in 1704, wondered whether a Surveyor prepared thus to defraud the Crown could be trusted to reward his accomplices. In spite of very ungentlemanly threats from the two Benson brothers he revealed the plot to the excluded Artisans, who informed the Treasury.

At Castle Howard over Christmas 1718, as he told Newcastle, Vanbrugh had received

> a wild strange Acct: of the rout my Friend and Superiour Officer, Benson, makes at The Treasury. I find poor Dartiquenave [the Paymaster] scar'd out of his Witts about a Memoriall given in by Campbell and Benson the Young, to decry the Managements of former Boards, and exalt this precious New One. I have no Copy of this honest Memll: so can say little to it from hence, but that I know of no fault I have committed that a Jurey in Westminster Hall wou'd fine me half a Crown for. And so, having good reason to believe my Lord Sund: so much my Friend, that he will never Suffer me to be trickt into a Criminall I am easy; Let me be but protected from any dark Stroaks in the Kings Closet, and I have nothing to fear To defend me from which, I know I may depend upon Your Graces usual kindness, And I have writ a Short Letter to my Lord Sund to beg the Continuance of his.

It was probably after his return to London that he sent Newcastle a note to the effect that

> I have reason to believe, the King has had such an unfair Account given him secretly of my Management, both of his Houses and Gardens; As must make me Appear a very bad

Officer in the Employments he has been pleas'd to intrust me with.

And I am inform'd, This Representation has been follow'd, with an Attempt to have me remov'd from his Service: And that this Attempt, is in a way of Succeeding.

For in January 1719 Benson wrote to the Treasury charging the former Board with failing to keep records, allowing private work in Crown buildings, and incurring extravagance by dispensing with the Purveyor's controls on purchases. These allegations were not difficult to refute, but the same month saw Benson's grossest and most famous blunder. In a paper signed jointly with Campbell and another of his creatures, the Master Carpenter Robert Barker,

> the said new Surveyor Alarum'd the King, Lords & Commons, with the immediate and imminent danger of the falling of the House of Lords, Painted Chamber, Court of Requests &c. And by his own Orders were set up Shores & Props, found and reported by the Ablest Builders and Workmen to be more dangerous to the Buildings than their own decay.

Benson even refused to remove the props and 'oppos'd & Quarreld with the Workmen for so doing'. On 16 March the Lords formally notified the King of their displeasure, and a month later, when he himself had admitted that the Office of Works was 'in very great Disorder', Benson was suspended and warned of prosecution. He still did not go easily, only giving up his office on 17 July; the dismissal of Campbell followed, and Barker was replaced before the end of the year. Vanbrugh attributed Benson's behaviour to 'his Ignorance & obstinacy if not worse'; he never was prosecuted, and eventually succeeded Edward Harley as Auditor. But during the whole of 1742 he was insane, and those specialists prepared to make a psychiatric diagnosis in the absence of the patient may detect the beginnings of his disorder almost a quarter-century earlier.

In little over a year, having received in Hawksmoor's estimation more '(for confounding the kings Works) than Sr Chrisr Wren did in 40 years, for his honest endeavours', Benson had wrecked the instrument fashioned by Wren and tuned by

Halifax and Vanbrugh. He also offered a precedent for treating the Surveyor's office as a sinecure for which political allegiance counted and not distinction or experience of any other kind. And so Vanbrugh was passed over a second time, not for Thornhill, who had been recommended – perhaps partly out of spite – by Benson and the Duchess of Marlborough, and whose candidature he had ridiculed to Newcastle, but for Thomas Hewett, amateur architect and a Whig, who had as Surveyor of Wood served on the 1715 Board of Works. Hewett's knighthood followed in November.

Hewett had travelled to Italy and elsewhere, had offered (but not given) patronage to Alessandro Galilei,* and in 1719-20 designed and built the library of Sunderland's house in Piccadilly. In his rivalry with Vanbrugh this connection with the Lord Treasurer and his knowledge of the most tasteful examples of Italian architecture probably counted most. Hawksmoor, who was kept out of office until Hewett's death in April 1726, was understandably outspoken, calling him 'that Reptile Knight' and on another occasion telling Lord Carlisle that 'we are most of us made of Clay; but that sad wretch was made of *Kennell Dirt* as my Ld pembroke use to say of sad fellows'. Nor had he a good word to Lord Carlisle for Lord Kingston's stables at Thoresby, 'the only piece of Building that Sr Thomas Hewett was Guilty of, dureing his being Architect Royall'.

Vanbrugh told Newcastle on 11 August 1719:

> I am not one of those, who drop their Spirits, on every Rebuff: if I had, I had been under ground long ago. I shall therfore go on; in hopes Fortune will one day or other, let those help me, who have a mind to it: And that as I Am past over, where my Pretentions are good, And I cou'd be of Use; I may chance to be taken notice of, where my Pretentions Are nothing, And I can be of no Service at all.

He kept his Comptrollership, but for him the rebuff reflected both on his ability and on his vision of what the Works could again be; but what in the end he talked about was money. He

* p. 450

hoped for a time at least to be next in line to Hewett; on 6 August 1719, when Hewett's patent was not 'yet past (tho' pasing)', he told Newcastle:

> I'm sorry my Project of the Reversion won't do, 'Tis a very hard matter for me to find out any thing, 'till 'tis over late to ask for't; but they know of every thing time enough to help their humble Servants. (without their Aid) when they are quite determin'd to take care of them. Which is Hewets Case now, and was once before, when Ld Halifax made him Surveyr: of the Forrests, without his ever dreaming of it.

George I granted pensions on occasion to those who had been removed from office for political reasons: one of them was Addison, who resigned as Secretary of State in 1718. Vanbrugh must have been aware of this when, in an – admittedly undated – note, he asked that the King

> wou'd please to Grant me, What I now have [the Comptrollership], for Life. And, that the Person he thinks fit to make Surveyour, may make me some Compensation by money, Which, I have been honest enough in my Station, to stand very much in need of.

The idea of a pension seems to have recurred to him as he approached sixty, for in July 1722 he told Carlisle of his hopes of the King's

> doing something of advantage to me, tho' not as an Architect; which is not a Trade I believe for any body to recommend themselves to at Court.

And a year later he was asking Newcastle's leave

> to remind you, of what you told me not long since, of your favourable Intentions towards me, for that Sinecure, The Reversion of which, I now take the Liberty to ask of you.

Since the request seems to have some connection with Sir Richard Steele, whose patent at Drury Lane had been the subject of a long battle between himself and Newcastle, this may be the sinecure on which Vanbrugh had his eye. Certainly he believed that, if the Works had become a haven for personal ambition, it was no longer a place for architectural vision; indeed early in 1724 Surveyor Hewett himself would complain of 'nothing but repairs' and 'no prospect of fine new buildings'. Crown building was in the doldrums. The palaces were, as Vanbrugh had said, in quite good repair, and even with the loss of Whitehall there were enough royal residences. Since George I had consigned his wife to Ahlden* the royal household was divided between himself and the Prince of Wales – to whom Vanbrugh had brought the Garter in 1706 – and his family. The new King's contribution to English architecture was modest.

St James's Palace was George I's principal residence when he was not away in Hanover, with Kensington intended as a summer palace. In June 1718 he finally decided, after much consideration, on an economical project for completing the state rooms at Kensington Palace. This was probably the work of Colen Campbell on Benson's behalf. The work was not finished until about 1727, and apart from the Water Tower on the Palace Green, for which Vanbrugh was separately responsible, he seems not to have been involved with Kensington.

The King shared St James's with his son's family, who were fond of entertaining, and the palace kitchens proved inadequate – or at least inconvenient – for supplying two establishments and their guests. In 1716 also, therefore, the Lord Chamberlain (Newcastle) requested Vanbrugh to design a new kitchen for the Prince's service. 'Here happens to be severall very pressing things to be done at St James's', Vanbrugh told Lady Marlborough on 3 August, 'against the Princess comes, to Towne to Ly in. which she keeps me running too and fro, between St James's and Hampton Court about.' (Princess Caroline was delivered of a stillborn son in November.) Vanbrugh's great kitchen survives: it is lit by big arched windows at one end, by roundels between the corbels at the top of the walls, and by a large rectangular lantern overhead.

At Hampton Court the princely family moved into the Queen's Side, on the east front of Wren's building, in the

* p. 318

summer of 1716. 'I am to attend the Prince to Hampton Court to morrow', Vanbrugh told Lady Marlborough on 13 July, 'where he go's to View the House, distribute the Lodgings, and direct (I believe) all the Unfinish'd rooms to be compleated.' The unfinished rooms were the suite at the north-east corner of Wren's building, known today as the Prince of Wales's Rooms; they contain several of Vanbrugh's characteristic chimneypieces, boldly cut and scrolled from squared blocks of marble. Similar examples are found at Blenheim, Grimsthorpe and elsewhere. He must also have designed the chimneypiece in the Prince's Guard Chamber, where the mantel is supported by two 'Beefeaters' or Yeomen of the Guard, whose vigorous and probably deliberately archaic carving recalls the supporting figures of Jacobean fireplaces.

In December 1717 discord between King and Prince came to a head once more, and the Prince and his family were virtually banished from the palaces for over two years, retiring to Richmond. At about this time Vanbrugh designed an open courtyard to the north of Hampton Court, bounded by long ranges of court lodgings, framing Henry VIII's Great Hall and facing the avenue through Bushy Park; this was probably for the King, who took more interest in Hampton Court during his son's enforced absence. It may have been a model of this project that Vanbrugh arranged to discuss at Kensington with the King and Lord Newcastle. Nothing came of it, but in the late summer of 1718 the Great Hall was converted into a proscenium theatre, and seven plays were performed there between 23 September and 25 October.

The scenery, which probably included the proscenium arch, was the work of Thornhill, but the massive wooden structure inside the hall and the division into stage, scenes, auditorium, galleries, and front-of-house space, must have been entrusted to a specialist and Vanbrugh is the obvious candidate. The stage was similar to that at Drury Lane, with one door opening on each side of a wedge-shaped forestage 36 feet wide at the front and 16 feet deep; behind it the vista stage extended back 24 feet. The dimensions of the Great Hall, about 112 feet by 40 feet, left room for an auditorium of the same depth as the total stage, three dressing rooms behind the scenes, and a front house about 20 feet by 40 feet wide for foyer and gallery stairs.

Vanbrugh's letters of the time mention arrangements to meet Newcastle at Hampton Court, and it can only be presumed that he was indeed responsible for the theatre.

The seven plays performed at Hampton Court that autumn were all in the current repertory at Drury Lane, and none of them was at all new. Although the King preferred French, the polite language of court and society in Europe, his understanding of English was by no means as poor as legend makes out. The season opened with Farquhar's *The [Beaux'] Stratagem* (1707), and three earlier Restoration comedies were presented: Farquhar's *The Constant Couple* (1699), Crowne's *Sir Courtly Nice* (1685), and D'Urfey's *Love for Money* (1691). The other three plays were even older: Shakespeare's *Henry VIII*, Jonson's *Volpone*, and Beaumont and Fletcher's *Rule a Wife and Have a Wife*. So much for Early Georgian Taste!

30

Friends at Court

'I have dam'd luck', Vanbrugh told Newcastle, referring to Anstis and Benson, 'to have two Such Fellows get over me'. The quarrel with Anstis had been long, bitter and personal and on Anstis's part, Vanbrugh believed, underhand. But why was he defeated by such nonentities as Benson and Hewett? There is no easy answer to this question. Changes in taste and in patronage, and Vanbrugh's own professionalism, all played a part. Although Lord Ailesbury had been mistaken in suggesting that Vanbrugh got the Blenheim commission because he was a Whig*, there is no doubt that his Kit-Cat associations contributed to his early architectural success. But as the Whigs came closer to being a party (in Swift's hostile but perceptive phrase) 'patched up of heterogeneous inconsistent parts', suppositions such as Lord Ailesbury's became not merely simplistic but untenable. Vanbrugh seems to have owed his knighthood, and perhaps his reinstatement as Comptroller in 1715† to Marlborough's advocacy with the new King, but the Duke was by no means the universal hero of the Whig party. The world of patronage is of its nature insecure, because it revolves around the patron's right to do as he likes: Vanbrugh suffered, either side of 1720, from the very same system that had promoted him either side of 1700.

By habit if not by nature, Vanbrugh was outspoken only to his

* p. 300
† p. 235

closest friends, and it cannot have been the strength of his
opinions that disqualified him. On the other hand, the knowledge and experience to which he and Hawksmoor laid claim –
usually with justice – distinguished them from the newcomers
to the Office of Works, and may, paradoxically, have turned to
their disadvantage. Moreover, while neither his allegiance to
Marlborough nor his quarrel with the Duchess perhaps did
any lasting damage to Vanbrugh's cause, the Blenheim lawsuits of around 1720 gave the architect the least welcome kind
of publicity; the changing critical reputation of Blenheim was
also serious.

In 1718 Edward Strong, the Blenheim mason until work
stopped in 1712, filed in the Court of Exchequer a suit for over
£12,000 in arrears, against Marlborough, or alternatively
against Vanbrugh as his architect and agent. The case took the
best part of three years to come to court; in November 1719
Vanbrugh told Tonson that the Duchess was trying to turn the
debt on to himself, and in the meantime other creditors
decided to take similar action. Eventually, in February 1721 a
three-day hearing ended in a judgement against the Duke –
and against the Duchess, who was the driving force in all the
proceedings. Vanbrugh kept Lord Carlisle informed. On 20
February 1721 he wrote:

> My Lady Marlborough has been cast by the Workmen ... She's
> Outragious at it, She accuses the Judges, and says I have for-
> sworn myself. I am told one of them said there was no more in
> the Cause, but a Rich man on one Side and a poor man on tother
> or something to that effect.

The Duchess appealed to the House of Lords. In April Vanbrugh was

> told She is handing about, a Sort of Case (in writing) in which
> She lays me on. I am but newly come to Towne, and han't yet
> been able to get a Sight of it. She only sending it to Lords to read,
> & so getting it back again that I may'nt see it before the Tryal,
> when I suppose 'twill come out in print. I don't know whether I
> am rightly inform'd, but I heard it said yesterday, She had writ to
> your Ldship, wishing you cou'd be at her Cause ... By all I See I
> believe she'll hardly get any of her own Family to Vote for her.

The Judges were mighty clear against her, in the Excheqr Court, and if Right won't help her, I fancy affection won't. She's a Vile Woman.

In a postscript he added:

The Dutchesses Cause I hear is put off, to Wednesday senight. The Workmens Spirits are very Low from the fear they are under, that She and her Family, will at least be Able to keep a great many Lords away, who wou'd not Vote for her if they were in the House.

Lord Bristol had written to the Duchess on 12 April:

The pending point will solely turn upon the proof of the Duke of Marleboroughs privity or consent to the warrant given by my Lord Godolphin to Sir John Vanbrugh, which for fear of the fatal consequences that may happen to any other man in the same scituation, I should think ought to be most plainly & fully made before it should affect the Duke of Marleborough's estate.

During March and April 1721 the Duchess of Marlborough wrote four times to Carlisle denouncing Vanbrugh. On 9 May the architect called on Carlisle's daughter Lady Lechmere; as an attendant of the Duchess, her view of Vanbrugh was perhaps rather different from that of her father, to whom she wrote:

he has sent you a printed paper (which I fancy you would not approve); he is now frighted about it, for he has made himself liable to severe punishment, by being guilty of a breach of the House of Lords, in printing a libel upon a peer, while a cause is depending before them in judgment, in which Sir John himself is a witness; how he'll come off, I can't tell, but he has given the Duke of Marlborough the advantage of having a full blow at him if he pleases.

This danger passed. In spite of his evident caution (as befitted a man who accepted that any of his letters might be opened) Bristol voted for the Marlboroughs. Lord Carlisle, who wrote to the Duchess advising caution in the appeal, evidently did not

consider his vote vital for the rescue of Sir John. The hearing
was twice postponed; the delay gave the Exchequer judges an
occasion 'to declare upon the Bench, That they were extreamly
glad there was an appeal to the Lords, That the World might
See, how just a Decree they had made'. Vanbrugh also managed to read the Duchess's 'Vile manuscript' and to prepare
and have printed a *Justification* of which he sent copies to Carlisle, to 'all the Lords in Towne' and to the King, Prince and
Princess. This showed, among other things, that from his
warrant of appointment it was clear that he acted on the
Duke's behalf and therefore could not be held responsible for
the debt. Both Vanbrugh and Carlisle thought the case, thus
delayed, would be dropped, but it was finally heard on 23-24
May 1721.

> It went for the Workmen 41. to 25. People talk a little freely of
> those 25. Especially, the Cause appearing so clear to others, that
> even the Dukes own Family cou'd not bring themselves to Vote
> for him, except Lord Bridgewater. My Lord Sund: wou'd not so
> much as hear the Cause. The Duke of Montague, Duke of New-
> castle and Ld Godolphin heard it quite thorough, and then left
> the House ... When the Tryall was over, the Duke of Wharton
> complain'd to the House of the Paper I had Printed, & was secon-
> ded by my Lord Falmouth. It was presently propos'd, by those
> who were inclin'd to favour me, To defer it till after the Holydays
> wch was agreed to. I find my Self much Stronger on this occa-
> sion, than I cou'd have Imagin'd almost every Lord in the House
> showing by Some expression or other, they are not inclin'd to let
> me Suffer this way.

Vanbrugh was at a loss to know how the Duchess managed to
engage two of Lord Carlisle's daughters to accompany her to
the hearings. He believed that the inconsistencies she had
found in his depositions were invisible to anyone else, and
concluded that 'if I have Stretcht my evidence in favour of the
Workmen, it has been to cut my own Throat; for my Lord
Marlb: being decreed to pay them, I may be pretty Sure, he will
never pay me'.
    When the Lords met a fortnight later to consider Vanbrugh's
Justification he had more or less bidden farewell to his fee,
although the ruling at least made him 'safe from being pull'd to

pieces by the Workmen'. As for his printed paper, the Duchess found their Lordships

> so generally well dispos'd to me, on this occasion, That [when] the day Set came . . . She went out of Towne, and so did the Duke of Wharton too. My Lord Falmouth was in the House, grumbled much, but did not think fit to Speak aloud, So nobody calling for the order of the day, my Ld Sund: mov'd to adjourn. I hear the Dutchess do's not think of trying her Strength in West[minste]r: Hall against me; She says, She can have justice nowhere.

Nevertheless the Duchess prepared a bill in Chancery, suing Vanbrugh, Hawksmoor and 399 other named persons who, she alleged, had 'combined and confederated together to load the Duke of Marlborough with the payment of the debt'. The case came to Macclesfield, the Lord Chancellor; Archdeacon Coxe, the Duke's first serious biographer, expressed the pious hope that Macclesfield had not been unduly swayed by the Duchess's wealth. We know three things: that in 1725 Macclesfield was relieved of office and fined £30,000 by the House of Lords for a long list of charges of bribery, fraud and corruption in the execution of his Chancery; that he was to be imprisoned in the Tower until the fine was paid, and that he wrote to thank Sarah Duchess of Marlborough for bailing him out. But however he reached his decision Macclesfield could not do very much for the Duchess. He ordered all the work at Blenheim to be measured again – a gargantuan and extravagant task in itself – and issued a perpetual injunction against Vanbrugh's claiming any money from the Marlboroughs on the grounds that he had been appointed not by them but by Queen Anne.

Having disposed of the architect as far as she could, the Duchess turned her wrath towards Henry Joynes, whom she sued unsuccessfully for fraud. In September 1724 Vanbrugh tried to persuade the Duchess's agent Guidott that his due could be conveyed to him without passing through the Duchess's hands, but that letter ended up, like all the others, on her writing table. Finally the following year, with the support of Sir Robert Walpole, Vanbrugh approached the Treasury. His petition makes the case in formal language, but his summary to Tonson in October is more colourful:

being forc'd into Chancery, by that B.B.B.B. Old B. the Dutchess of Marlbh: and her getting an Injunction upon me, by her Friend the late Good Chancelr, who declar'd I never was employ'd by the Duke of Marlbh: and therefore had no demand upon his Estate, for my Services at Blenheim, I say since my hands were tyed up, from trying by Law to recover my Arrear, I have prevail'd with Sr Rob. Walpole to help me, in a Scheme I propos'd to him, by which I have got my money in Spight of the Huzzys teeth, and that out of a Sum, She expected to receive into her hands towards the discharge of the Blenheim Debts, and of which She resolv'd I shou'd never have a farthing. My carrying this point enrages her much.

The legal wrangles displayed to the world the great expense of Blenheim, although they also showed the reasonableness of its architect in contrast to the fury and spitefulness of his adversary. The aesthetic inadequacy of Blenheim by the standards of the eighteenth century, and the decline from fashion of the whole English Baroque style, were demonstrated more subtly, but nevertheless from within the very philosophy that had produced the Whig Hanoverian settlement of 1714.

Early in 1712 the third Earl of Shaftesbury, living in Naples for his health, wrote *A Letter Concerning the Art or Science of Design*, which he addressed to the Whig elder statesman Lord Somers,* one of the elder statesmen of the Whig party. Although an enterprising and misleading bookseller later stitched some printed copies into his back stock of the second (1714) edition of Shaftesbury's *Characteristicks*, the open letter was not in fact published until the fifth (1732) edition; nevertheless it must have been circulating in manuscript in London soon after Shaftesbury's death in the spring of 1713. His thesis was that since Britain had solved the political problems of uniting England and Scotland and of tempering the monarchy's power by the will of Parliament, it was time for the most enlightened nation on earth to take a lead in promoting the arts. He attacked by name Wren and some of his buildings as the products of an absolutist monarchy and of the long monopoly which he supposed Wren, as architect royal, to have exercised over architectural taste. Claiming the predictive insight to

* p. 83

which writers of manifestos pretend, he urged the formation of
a new national style, which he defined only by default as not
French, not Baroque (though he did not use the word) and not
like the works of Wren. And although he did not name them,
the Fifty New Churches and Blenheim surely came as clearly
into his readers' minds as they do into ours when he wrote on
the one hand,

> since a Zeal of this sort has been newly kindled amongst us, 'tis
> like we shall see from afar the many Spires arising in our great
> City, with such hasty and sudden growth, as may be the occasion
> perhaps that our immediate Relish shall be hereafter censur'd,
> as retaining much of what Artists call the *Gothick* Kind

and on the other,

> when a great Man builds, he will find little Quarter from the
> Publick, if instead of a beautiful Pile, he raises at a vast expence,
> such a false and counterfeit Piece of Magnificence, as can be
> justly arraign'd for its Deformity by so many knowing Men in
> Art, and by the whole People, who, in such a Conjunction,
> readily follow their Opinion.

Shaftesbury offered his noble and gentle readers, who made up
the government and the electorate of the day, the mirage of a
cultivated taste formed by consensus. The attempt to realize
this ideal is part of a larger story, and its relevance to Vanbrugh's later architecture belongs to another chapter.* What is
important for the moment is that, although Shaftesbury made
no positive recommendations, his strictures encouraged in his
readers the belief that Vanbrugh and Hawksmoor, as much as
Wren, were lacking in the magic ingredient of Taste.

The Spectator had found the use of puns – the craze of the
age – unsuitable to heroic architecture.† It was against this
background that the huge cost of Blenheim, the spasmodic
progress of its construction, and the squabbles about money
and responsibility were discussed in coffee-houses and drawing rooms. A poem *Upon the Duke of Marlborough's House at
Woodstock* first published in 1714, variously attributed to Pope

* p. 449
† p. 310

and Swift (among others), ended with the lines:

> Thanks, sir, cried I, 'tis very fine,
> But where d'ye sleep, or where d'ye dine?
> I find, by all you have been telling,
> That 'tis a house, but not a dwelling.

In a letter of 1717 Pope found similar faults. Although he admired the Hall, he 'never saw so great a thing with so much littleness in it ... the most inhospitable thing imaginable'. He disliked the 'ill effect' of the roof-line which made 'the building look at once finical and heavy', and he concluded, 'In a word, the whole is a most expensive absurdity; and the Duke of *Shrewsbury* gave a true character of it, when he said, it was a great *Quarry of Stones above Ground*'. Since Shrewsbury's own house at Heythrop was Thomas Archer's version of a huge monolithic Berninesque *palazzo*, his objection must have been to those same qualities of 'rise and fall ... advance and recess' that, two generations later, Robert and James Adam would find so praiseworthy. Pope later adapted this phrase for the tasteless Timon's Villa in his *Epistle to Lord Burlington* (1731), and in 1736 Horace Walpole called Blenheim 'a quarry of stone, that looked at a distance like a great house'. And it could never be forgotten that Blenheim, however imperfect and ungracious it became, was the nation's gift to a hero, not a private but a public monument. There were surely some who for that reason considered Vanbrugh an unsuitable candidate for the Surveyorship.

The three largest collections of Vanbrugh letters are those to Lord Carlisle, the Marlboroughs, and Lord Newcastle. Thomas Pelham succeeded to the estates of his uncle, the Duke of Newcastle of Vanbrugh's 1703 letter, in 1711. He assumed his uncle's surname of Holles, and as Thomas Pelham-Holles was created Earl of Clare (hence Claremont) and then in 1715 Duke of Newcastle. He was twenty-nine years younger than Vanbrugh, whose fifty-one surviving notes and letters between 1715 and 1724 reveal in the writer both the affection and the authority that a man in middle age might show towards a nephew. They also often deal, if briefly, with different topics from those discussed with Lord Carlisle far away in the north, for the young Newcastle was at Court and met his architect on both business and social occasions.

In October 1718 Sir John enclosed to the Duke an admonitory letter to Charles William Howard, who was the same age as Newcastle and had just succeeded to Audley End as seventh Earl of Suffolk; Vanbrugh impressed on the new Earl his duty to attend the House of Lords on the first day of Parliament and to make a 'warm and generous appearance at Your setting out'. A few months later Vanbrugh wrote to Newcastle about the famous Holbein Gateway in Whitehall, which he knew very well because he passed it on the way to his Whitehall house. The increasing use of coaches by Members of Parliament to travel to Westminster had led to a traffic problem, and Vanbrugh's colleagues in the Works had told a House of Commons committee that, whereas the King Street Gateway at the south end of Whitehall Street could be enlarged to allow the passage of coaches, the Holbein Gateway at the north end near the Banqueting House could not. Accordingly in July 1719, after Benson's dismissal, Newcastle as Lord Chamberlain was instructed to arrange for its demolition. But on 6 August, while there was still no Surveyor and therefore no Board of Works to act, Vanbrugh wrote to Newcastle about the matter:

> In the mean time I may Observe to your Grace, That I find many people Surpris'd there shou'd be no other Expedient found to make way for Coaches &c, than destroying One of the Greatest Curiositys there is in London as that Gate has ever been esteem'd, and cost a great Sum of money the Building; And so well perform'd, that altho' now above 200 Yrs Old, is as entire as the first day. The Chancellr: of the Excheqr: said much of this to me last night being entirely of the Opinion it ought not to be destroy'd, if an other Expedient can be found And there is a very easy one, with Small expence Which is, To Open the Wall of the Privy Garden, near Lord Rochesters, And turn the Passage, thorough a Slip of that wast ground Coming out into the Street again, between Mr Vanhulse's And the Banquetting house.

Five days later, he even suggested the possibility of paying for the passage himself, if its cost turned out to be the sticking point. As a result the gateway was reprieved for forty years; Canaletto's *View of Whitehall* at Goodwood shows it with the by-pass cut through according to Vanbrugh's suggestion.

On several occasions Vanbrugh asked Newcastle's help with the patronage of appointments. Late in 1717 he forwarded a recommendation from the Rector of Swallow in Lincolnshire, 'a True Whig Clergyman, a Favourite of the late Duke of Newcastles', for his curate, Ralph Baynes, to succeed him in the living; this he did. A later attempt to gain the Prebend of Southwell for 'my Friend and Kinsman Garencieres' was unsuccessful.* In November 1719 he sent a letter, enclosing one to Lord Stanhope, on behalf of another true Whig, Philip Ayscough, High Master of St Paul's School, who was approaching sixty and felt that the vacant Prebend of Canterbury would be more restful than caring for 300 scholars. Whether as a result of Vanbrugh's application or not, in 1722 Ayscough was given by the Crown the Rectorship of St Olave's, Southwark, which he held for the next twenty years.

Newcastle's failure to help in a matter of patronage produced one of Vanbrugh's sharpest letters in 1722, when he wrote:

My Lord Duke

I never was more Surpris'd, at any disagreeable thing, has happen'd to me in my Life; than to find (a day or two ago) your Grace had thrown aside a Small Domestick of mine, to make way for an other in the Kings Musick.

When I ask'd your Favour for him, I was so far from designing to press you, if I found the least Unwillingness; that if you had not granted it me (as you did) in an easy kind way, at the first word; you had never heard any more of it . . .

I must own my Lord, I did think I had as much pretention to your Favour & Friendship, as almost any humble Servant you had, And that which made me think so, was, That you us'd to tell me so. How I therfore come to fall so low in your Regards, I can't conceive; because, I am quite sure I have done nothing to forfeit them . . .

As I cou'd not forbear, saying Something to your Grace on this Occasion, And had not a mind to say very much; I rather chose to do it by writing than otherwise; And shall be very glad if your Grace pleases, that we may never have any sort of discourse about it.

* p. 444

At first glance 'a small domestic' might appear to be a servant, such as Jack Jones who had lessons on the bass viol. But *domestic* can mean a member of one's family, and a much more plausible candidate is George Vanbrugh, his musical cousin.*

In April 1722 Sunderland died; Marlborough followed him two months later, and at the age of forty-one his elder surviving daughter the friendly Henrietta Godolphin† thus became second Duchess of Marlborough in her own right. Vanbrugh was far from being the only person with whom Sarah the first Duchess picked a quarrel: she alienated her own children, and the bond of sympathy between Vanbrugh and Duchess Henrietta as fellow sufferers was confirmed by the fact that the latter was also the young Lady Newcastle's mother. Among the Blenheim papers in the British Library there is an amusing letter (and intentionally so) written by Vanbrugh to the second Duchess shortly after the great Duke's death, about a meeting with Dean Jones. Barzillai Jones, who had been appointed Dean of Lismore in County Waterford in 1683, was as a Non-Juror denied preferment, but saw the son to whom he passed on his Old Testament name become a Fellow of All Souls, Oxford. The Marlboroughs gave the Dean shelter as a kind of domestic chaplain, though Duchess Sarah mistrusted him. The new Duchess sent the Dean his mourning money by the hand of Vanbrugh, who described to her the circumstances of its delivery; the letter is neither headed nor signed, but the hand is Vanbrugh's:

Winchester, July the 26th: 1722

I did your Grace the Justice, to acquaint the Dean, with the first movement of your heart, towards him: upon observing his Old Black Coat, grown Gray with years, when you expected to find him in the Freshest Mourning, for so good a Friend as the World took the Duke of Marlborough to be to him.

I then told him, your Graces farther reflections on that matter, And that they had produc'd a Letter to him from you, which I had in my Pocket, with a Hundred pounds, to dry his Tears up.

* p. 77
† p. 235

> At which, (Astonisht), he repeated the Words – A hundred
> pounds. Then Vail'd his Reverend Hatt, and Slowly raising it up
> to his Melting Eyes, he with true Devotion, ask't Gods Blessing
> on your Bounty.

The two duchesses had trouble with their mail. Fate miscarried both Vanbrugh's note and the Dean's letter of thanks to
the Dowager Duchess, and the same volume of Blenheim
papers contains her letter of January 1725 to the Commissioners of the General Post Office, complaining about the
delivery of her mail to her daughter. Similarly phrased letters
are still today received by the Post Office, which still sends
similarly patient replies. The Commissioners answered that
they took every care with letters, but that 'unless your Graces
letters are directed to you as Dowager' mistakes could not be
prevented.

Vanbrugh's visit to Winchester may have had some connection with political events of 1722. In the spring a Jacobite plot
had been uncovered, centring round Francis Atterbury, Bishop
of Rochester. King George was to have been killed on his way
to Hanover, the Bank of England and the Royal Exchange
seized and the principal ministers of the government arrested.
For a time it was feared that France (under the regency of Phil-
ippe II, Duke of Orléans while Louis XV was a minor) or Spain,
and Russia might be involved, with serious implications for
foreign policy. On 10 May Vanbrugh told Lord Carlisle:

> Your Ldship will see by the Gazette and other papers, the main
> that is known of the present affair; all I can tell you farther of it
> is, That altho' the Ministers had some Intimation of a Scheme on
> foot, they neither knew it certain, nor any thing material of it till
> within this Week. Nor do they yet know, as I am (I think) well
> inform'd, that the thoughts of attempting the design, is yet over;
> Only they are easy, as to France or Spain taking any part in it.
> Having the most direct and positive assurances from the Regent,
> that he can express in words. But they know of more money re-
> mitted from hence, than one wou'd imagine, to carry on this De-
> sign; & they say, they have already sufficient matter to lay before
> the Parliament, to obviate any thing that may be Surmis'd,
> against the reality of a deep Design to overset the present Gov-
> ernt:

Carlisle thereupon offered to go to London, but was told by
Lord Townshend that his presence in the country would be
more useful. The King decided not to go to Hanover in 1722,
and as a precaution against disturbances in the Capital he ordered the Guards' regiments to London, encamping them in
Hyde Park, 'a very expensive place to all the officers, and I believe very unpleasant' as Lady Lechmere told Lord Carlisle.
The King also decided to take a short summer excursion
through southern England. On 17 August Lady Bristol wrote
from Richmond to her husband that during the King's progress
he would stay on Monday at the Duke of Bolton's (Hackwood,
near Basingstoke), on Tuesday and Wednesday at Salisbury,
where he would review his army, and on Thursday at Winchester. On Friday he would visit Portsmouth, staying with
Lord Scarbrough at Stansted (Sussex), and return to Kensington on Saturday. But Vanbrugh had already told Lord Carlisle on 19 July that

> The King is much pleas'd with Kensington and the Easy way of
> living he is fallen into there. He go's however to Hampton Court
> the beginning of Next month, and 'tis thought will make some
> little Tour toward Salisbury and back by Winchester & Ports-
> mouth.

Vanbrugh himself was 'Out of Towne' between 26 July, when
he spent 5s. on lavender drops for Dean Jones, and 3 August.
Besides Winchester we know that he visited Amesbury and
Salisbury, where he bought scissors and a razor. The silence of
the Board of Works's Minute Book rules out an official advance
visit by the Comptroller in preparation for a royal progress;
nevertheless the timing and places of Vanbrugh's journey may
involve more than coincidence.

In 1722 the writing of plays seemed to be an activity which
Vanbrugh had tried with great success and afterwards abandoned for other things. But a new comedy by Steele, discussed
all that summer and produced in November, was probably the
cause of his returning – briefly but significantly – to writing for
the theatre.

_31_

Unfinished Business

On 18 June 1722 Vanbrugh wrote to Tonson, rusticating in Herefordshire:

> the Opera has been Supported at half a Guinea, Pit and Boxes, and perform'd 62 times this last Season. And withall this, the fine Gentlemen of the Buskin in Drury Lane, ride about in their Coaches. The Remnants of Rich, have play'd Something and Somehow, Six times a Week. And Aron Hill has set up a New Play-house, to come in for a Snack with them in the Haymarket where the french acted.
>
> But with all this encouragement from the Towne, not a fresh Poet Appears; they are forc'd to Act round and round upon the Old Stock, though Cibber tells me, 'tis not to be conceiv'd, how many and how bad Plays, are brought to them. Steel however has one to come on at Winter, a Comedy; which they much commend.

Steele's new play, *The Conscious Lovers*, was to be his last. But it was not written to remedy the dearth of good new plays, for Steele had been talking and writing about it for years. The scant internal evidence which is all there is suggests Vanbrugh began to write his *A Journey to London* (which he never finished) in the early 1720s, probably as a reaction not only to the state of the theatre in general but also particularly to Steele's play, which was finally staged in November 1722. The three short Acts and the opening of Act IV are no more than a torso,

but yet much more than the series of sketches they are sometimes held to be.

Finishing another's play, as Cibber tried to do when he
turned *A Journey to London* into *The Provok'd Husband*, is
rather different from finishing another's building. We have a
fair idea of Vanbrugh's intentions for Eastbury, but Cibber
printed Vanbrugh's play with his own in order to show how different they were, and the only hints he gave about Vanbrugh's
intentions contradict each other. Steele's play was very successful; Vanbrugh's fragment cries out to be staged but, ending
as it does in mid-scene, this could only be done as an experiment. But there is another difference between the two. Steele's
is a Georgian play. Vanbrugh's would have been the last brilliant flare of Restoration comedy. In their different ways each
has a bearing on our judgement and understanding of Vanbrugh as a dramatist.

The Conscious Lovers concerns Mr Sealand's two daughters,
Indiana and Lucinda, and their suitors. Lucinda, his daughter
by his second wife, is in love with Myrtle, but a marriage has
been arranged for her with young Bevil, and in addition her
mother wished to marry her to the coxcomb Cimberton, whose
'strongest Biass is Avarice; which is so predominant in him,
that he will examine the Limbs of his Mistress with the Caution
of a Jockey, and pays no more Compliment to her personal
Charms, than if she were a meer breeding Animal'. Sealand,
once an East India Merchant, had changed his name and started a new life after his first wife had died tragically at sea on the
way to join him in the Indies with their daughter,
Indiana. His sister Isabella, who was also on the voyage,
brought up Indiana, but at a nubile age the girl found herself at
the mercy of a Toulon lawyer, from whom she was rescued by
purchase and brought back to London by young Bevil. During
the play the identity of Indiana (originally played by Ann Oldfield) as Sealand's elder daughter is known to none, not even to
herself. She loves Bevil, but believes him indifferent to her and
about to marry Lucinda.

Bevil, a dutiful son, will not marry without his father's
approval; the problems in the play are therefore how to get old
Sir John Bevil to accept Indiana, whom the world takes to be
his son's mistress, and how to break Bevil's engagement to

Lucinda and bring her and Myrtle together. Bevil's secret exchange of letters with Lucinda, by which she agrees not to marry him, is misinterpreted as treachery by Myrtle, who challenges Bevil to a duel. According to Steele's Preface the whole play 'was writ for the sake of the Scene of the Fourth Act, wherein Mr *Bevil* evades the Quarrel with his Friend'. This he does by showing him Lucinda's letter of rejection.

In the last Act Sealand goes suspiciously to investigate the mysterious Indiana, and her tearful account of her misfortunes leads, with aunt Isabella's timely help, to a recognition between father and daughter and the revelation to her of Bevil's love for her. When Cimberton discovers that Lucinda's fortune now has to be shared with her new-found sister he loses interest, and the two pairs of happy lovers are united.

The main action is supported by the genteel courtship of the bearers of letters, Lucinda's maid and young Bevil's servant Tom, and by the wise counsel of Sir John Bevil's old retainer Humphrey. Some comic business is provided when, in order to thwart Cimberton and Mrs Sealand, Myrtle and Tom dress up and appear as lawyers and Myrtle afterwards disguises himself as Cimberton's decrepit uncle. The solution of the plot, however, depends not on these personations but on the revelations of Indiana, Isabella, and Sealand.

The successful comic passages derive amusement not from the servants – who like all the characters speak the refined prose of *The Spectator* – but from 'middle class' gentility. Tom (originally played by Cibber) makes a stuttering Serjeant, and the whole of the mock lawyers' consultation at the end of Act III is a witty parody of legal jargon. In the previous scene Steele pokes fun at Mrs Sealand's prudery. Cimberton tells her that among the Spartans

> their Meetings were secret, and the Amorous Congress always by Stealth; and no such professed Doings between the Sexes, as are tolerated among us, under the audacious Word, Marriage. *Mrs Sealand.* Oh! had I liv'd, in those Days, and been a Matron of *Sparta*, one might, with less Indecency, have had ten Children, according to that modest Institution, than one, under the Confusion of our modern, barefac'd manner.
> *Lucinda.* [*Aside*] And yet, poor Woman, she has gone thro' the whole Ceremony, and here I stand a melancholy Proof of it.

In this scene Steele characteristically toned down during the run of the play Cimberton's catalogue of Lucinda's charms. Enough remains in the published play, however, from 'the Vermilion of her Lips' and her 'forward Chest' to her breeding potential, to send Lucinda off the stage in a fury.

In Act V the Foot-Boy (played by the young Theophilus Cibber) offers a lesson in diplomacy:

> *Boy.* Nay, nay. I'm not such a Country Lad neither, Master, to think she's at home, because I see her: I have been in Town but a Month, and I lost one Place already, for believing my own Eyes.
> *Sealand.* Why, Sirrah! have you learnt to lie already?
> *Boy.* Ah! Master! things that are Lies in the Country, are not Lies at *London*---I began to know my Business a little better than so so---but an you please to walk in, I'll call a Gentlewoman to you, that can tell you for certain---she can make bold to ask my Lady her self.

When Isabella tells Sealand that she is 'as a Mother' to Indiana he temporarily misunderstands:

> As a Mother! right; that's the old Phrase, for one of those Commode Ladies, who lend out Beauty, for Hire, to young Gentlemen that have pressing Occasions.

A similar confusion occurs, with infinitely more justice, in Vanbrugh's *A Journey to London*, when Uncle Richard quickly makes up his own mind about the accommodation his country nephew has secured on arriving in London from Mrs Motherly, 'one that lets Lodgings':

> *Sir Francis.* Very kind and civil truly; I believe we are got into a mighty good House here.
> *Uncle Richard.* [*Aside*] For good Business, very probable.

Steele's concern to influence public opinion against duelling and 'the Force of a Tyrant Custom, which is misnamed a Point of Honour' was almost obsessive; it extended from *The Christian Hero* and *The Lying Lover* in the first years of the eighteenth century to *The Conscious Lovers*, by way of a series of articles in *The Tatler* in the summer of 1709 and Nos. 84 and 97 of *The Spectator* in June 1711. One bloody tragedy the following year became a political scandal: the Kit-Cat Lord Mohun spent most of his life fighting either in battle or for 'honour' until in November 1712 he and the fourth Duke of Hamilton killed each other in a duel in Hyde Park. Nevertheless Steele's motives for writing *The Conscious Lovers* involved the reform of taste as much as that of morals. By 1713, if not earlier, he was thinking about a play based on one of Terence's comedies, stories of mistaken identities and the conflict of paternal and filial wishes.

In *The Spectator*, No. 502 (6 October 1712) he discussed Terence's *Heauton Timorumenos (The Self-Tormentor)*, which he had been reading; however, in the end he chose Terence's first play, *Andria* or *The Lady of Andros* as a model for his own. He wrote of *The Self-Tormentor*:

> It is from the Beginning to the End a perfect Picture of humane Life, but I did not observe in the Whole one Passage that could raise a Laugh. How well disposed must that People be, who could be entertained with Satisfaction by so sober and polite Mirth!

How very different, in other words, from the comedies of the last age! Moreover, Steele was commending his chosen example entirely without irony. His choice of Terence rather than Plautus is significant, for it was already a commonplace by the time of Henry Peacham's *The Compleat Gentleman* (1622) that *Scaliger* willeth us to admire *Plautus* as a Comoedian, but *Terence* as a pure and elegant speaker'. In Plautus we find low wit, low characters, and low expressions. And it is in reference to Plautus that Pope's comment on Vanbrugh, always quoted out of context, may be properly understood; for it comes from his *First Epistle of the Second Book of Horace Imitated* (1737) and paraphrases a passage that refers to Plautus:

> Some doubt, if equal pains or equal fire
> The humbler Muse of Comedy require?
> But in known Images of life I guess
> The labour greater, as th'Indulgence less.
> Observe how seldom ev'n the best succeed:

Tell me if Congreve's Fools are Fools indeed?
What pert low Dialogue has Farqu'ar writ!
How Van wants grace, who never wanted wit!
The stage how loosely does Astræa tread,
Who fairly puts all Characters to bed.

Vanbrugh had written to Lord Manchester in 1707 of the *Gusto* of his design for Kimbolton; he used the Italian word that was then still synonymous with *Taste* – but not for much longer. There is no better key to the nature of Taste in the eighteenth century than the change it brought about in the use of *Gusto*, which now has almost the opposite meaning. Steele's aim was to write a play with *Taste*.

In basing *The Conscious Lovers* on Terence, Steele took over from his source the arranged marriage, the long-lost sister in the keeping of the bridegroom, the wise old servant, the revelation between father and daughter, and the double wedding at the end. He also improved on the morality of the original: there the action turns on the birth of a child to the bridegroom and his mistress, whereas Steele scarcely allows Bevil to speak to Indiana without a chaperon.

The Spectator was widely read both in its original daily form and in the collected edition that began to appear even before the end of the paper's original run of publication. Notwithstanding the Kit-Cat allegiance of Addison and Steele, it was almost apolitical, its concerns being social, moral, and literary. Addison's early articles included attacks on the new Italian Opera; Steele paid more attention to the drama – both to the defects, as he saw them, of older plays currently revived and to the virtues of the more sentimental productions to which he wished to direct public taste. In No. 22 (26 March 1711) an anonymous correspondent (perhaps Steele himself) objected to the mad scenes in *The Pilgrim*, which Vanbrugh had enhanced from Fletcher, as examples of 'the false Taste the Town is in, with Relation to Plays as well as Operas'. In particular the writer pointed out that these scenes, including the addition of a licentious she-fool, did not represent 'the Disturbance of a noble Mind' as in Shakespeare's mad scenes, but were designed to evoke laughter.

A month later (No. 51, 28 April) Steele used the letter quoted

in a previous chapter about passionate phrases in *The Funeral*
as the springboard for an attack on 'Luscious Expressions'.
There is nothing, he said mockingly, like a little smuttiness for
enlivening a flagging text: 'I will answer for the Poets, that no
one ever writ Bawdry for any other Reason but Dearth of
Invention.' He continued, referring to a recent revival at Drury
Lane:

> This Expedient, to supply the Deficiencies of Wit, has been
> used, more or less, by most of the Authors who have succeeded
> on the Stage; tho' I know but one who has professedly writ a Play
> upon the Basis of the Desire of Multiplying our Species, and that
> is the Polite *Sir George Etherege*: if I understand what the Lady
> would be at, in the Play called *She would if she could.*

In a later issue (No. 502) Steele would note the tendency of the
gross audience in the Pit to chuckle at 'a Scene tending to Pro-
creation'. Going on (in No. 51) to discuss the suggestibility of
the audience (always a major argument of reformers), he took
the example of the scene in Mary Griffith Pix's tragedy *Ibrahim*
in which the Turkish Emperor 'throws his Handkerchief as a
Signal for his Mistress to follow him into the most retired part
of the Seraglio ... but, methought, we made but a sad Figure
who waited without.' Yet this was, said Steele, a refinement on
Aphra Behn

> who, in the *Rover*, makes a Country Squire strip to his Holland
> Drawers. For *Blunt* is disappointed [having lost his belongings
> but not his virginity before he is dumped through a trap-door]
> and the Emperor is understood to go on to the utmost.

The Rover himself, Willmore, 'is very frequently sent on the
same Errand; as I take it, above once every Act'. Mrs Behn was
generally adept both in the use of stage properties and in getting her characters into either nightclothes or 'an Undress':
The Lucky Chance (1686) is the prototype of modern bedroom
farce.

On 15 May (No. 65) Steele expressed his intention of examining 'some of our most Applauded Plays [to] see whether they

deserve the Figure they at present bear in the Imagination of
Men, or not'. His attack on Etherege's *Sir Fopling Flutter, or the
Man of Mode*, recently revived at Drury Lane, is better aimed
than Collier's on *The Relapse* although, like most attacks of the
kind, its value lies more in what it says about the theories of the
critic than about the work criticized. But that was just what
Steele wanted:

> I will take it for granted, that a fine Gentlemen should be honest
> in his Actions, and refined in his Language. Instead of this, our
> Hero . . . is a direct Knave in his Designs, and a Clown in his
> Language. *Bellair* is his Admirer and Friend, in return for
> which, because he is forsooth a greater Wit than his said Friend,
> he thinks it reasonable to perswade him to Marry a young Lady,
> whose Virtue, he thinks, will last no longer than 'till she is a
> Wife, and then she cannot but fall to his Share, as he is an irres-
> istible fine Gentleman . . . As to his fine Language; he calls the
> Orange Woman, who, it seems, is inclined to grow Fat, *An Over-
> grown Jade, with a Flasket of Guts before her*; and salutes her
> with a pretty Phrase of, *How now, Double Tripe?*. . .
>
> This whole celebrated Piece is a perfect Contradiction to good
> Manners, good Sense, and common Honesty . . . there is nothing
> in it but what is built upon the Ruin of Virtue and Innocence . . .
> To speak plainly of this whole Work, I think nothing but being
> lost to a Sense of Innocence and Virtue can make any one see
> this Comedy, without observing more frequent Occasion to
> move Sorrow and Indignation, than Mirth and Laughter. At the
> same time I allow it to be Nature, But it is Nature in its utmost
> Corruption and Degeneracy.

In No. 141 (11 August 1711) Steele attacked the use of flying
figures and other contrivances in Shadwell's *The Lancashire
Witches* (1681), another recent Drury Lane revival. He also
printed a letter by John Hughes, a critic whose historical sense
was strong enough for him to commend, elsewhere, Spenser's
Faerie Queene as the best of its kind. But Hughes observed that
witchcraft was in no way the matter of comedy:

> Subjects of this kind, which are in themselves disagreeable, can
> at no time become entertaining, but by passing thro' an Imagin-
> ation like *Shakespear's* to form them; for which Reason Mr *Dry-*

den wou'd not allow even *Beaumont* and *Fletcher* capable of imitating him.

Moreover, wrote Hughes, there was

something else in this Comedy, which wants to be exorcis'd more than the Witches. I mean the Freedom of some Passages, which I should have overlook'd, if I had not observed that those Jests can raise the loudest Mirth, tho' they are painful to right Sense, and an Outrage upon Modesty.

We must attribute such Liberties to the Taste of that Age, but indeed by such Representations a Poet sacrifices the best Part of his Audience to the worst, and, as one wou'd think, neglects the Boxes, to write to the Orange Wenches.

Steele's discussion of Drury Lane revivals continued a few months later with *The Scornful Lady* of Beaumont and Fletcher (No. 270, 9 January 1712). Once again the shadow of Collier can be seen, for although Steele found much to praise

I must confess I was moved with the utmost Indignation at the trivial, senseless, and unnatural Representation of the Chaplain ... The meeting between *Welford* and him shews a Wretch without any Notion of the Dignity of his Function; and it is out of all common sense, that he should give an Account of himself *as one sent four or five Miles in a Morning on Foot for Eggs*. It is not to be denied, but his part and that of the Maid whom he makes Love to, are excellently well perform'd; but a thing which is blameable in it self, grows still more so by the success in the Execution of it ... an Audience should rise against such a Scene, as throws down the Reputation of any thing which the Consideration of Religion or Decency should preserve from Contempt ... This very one Character of Sir *Roger*, as silly as it really is, has done more towards the Disparagement of Holy Orders, and consequently of Virtue it self, than all the Wit that Author or any other could make up for in the Conduct of the longest Life after it.

In August 1712 (No. 446) Addison took up the theme of proper subjects, and drew specific support from the Ancients for a view of reform which goes right back to the early Restoration Patents:

It is one of the most unaccountable things in our Age, that the Lewdness of our Theatre should be so much complained of, so well exposed, and so little redressed. It is to be hoped, that some time or other we may be at leisure to restrain the Licentiousness of the Theatre, and make it contribute its Assistance to the Advancement of Morality, and to the Reformation of the Age . . . A Father is often afraid that his Daughter should be ruined by those Entertainments, which were invented for the Accomplishment and Refining of Human Nature. The *Athenian* and *Roman* Plays were written with such a regard to Morality, that *Socrates* used to frequent the one, and *Cicero* the other.

Infidelity, says Addison, was always a matter for tragedy, not comedy. The Ancients never chose an inappropriate subject for ridicule, such as one that

is apt to stir up Horrour and Commiseration rather than Laughter. For this Reason, we do not find any Comedy in so polite an Author as *Terence*, raised upon the Violations of the Marriage Bed. The Falshood of the Wife or Husband has given Occasion to noble Tragedies, but a *Scipio* or a *Lelius* would have looked upon Incest or Murder to have been as proper Subjects for Comedy.

In October 1714, as Cibber related, Steele obtained a licence as Governor of Drury Lane, which was converted into a Patent the following January. This was financially rewarding; nevertheless in petitioning the King to have the Patent for life he pointed out its practical value for the improvement of morality:

That the use of the Theatre has for many years last past been much perverted to the great Scandal of Religion and Good Government.

That it will require much time to remedy so inveterate an evil, and will expose the Undertaker to much Envy and Opposition.

That an affair of this Nature cant be accomplished without a lasting Authority . . .

That your Pet[itione]r did not desire this Favour in so ample a manner as your Majtie was graciously disposed to bestow it upon him, till he had taken a View of the State of the Theatre.

The exercise of his Patent was not easy, especially after the young Duke of Newcastle, appointed Lord Chamberlain in April 1717, sought to exercise his authority with unusual energy. Early in 1720 Newcastle managed to get Steele's licence revoked, and it took him over a year of lobbying and petitioning to recover it. In March 1724 Steele tried to have his Patent changed to a perpetual one for himself and his heirs, as Davenant and Killigrew had had; in support he claimed

> That he did not then desire it for a Longer Time, not knowing whether he could make a Dispositon for the Amendment of Theatrical Entertainment or not.
>   That Your Petitioner by writing the Comedy of the Conscious Lovers, has found by Experience, that more Regular and Vertuous Entertainment would take place if he had duration of time in which to Establish Rules and make Contracts accordingly.

Meanwhile Steele had finally completed and produced *The Conscious Lovers*. From January to April 1720, under the pseudonym of Sir John Edgar, he had run a twice-weekly paper, *The Theatre*, to draw attention to his fight over Drury Lane. He devoted two numbers to the characters and plot of his already long-promised new play, which was then still called *Sir John Edgar* when, in the last number of *The Theatre* (No. 28, 5 April), Steele dropped his pseudonym and undertook to print it 'forthwith'. Other hints were dropped about both its imminence and its quality:

> Advertisements have been sent to the News-Papers to this Effect, That the Comedy now in Rehearsal, is, in the Opinion of excellent Judges, the very best that ever came upon the *English* Stage.

Moreover, before it at last opened on 7 November 1722, the play had

> trotted as far as *Edinburgh* Northwards, and as far as *Wales* Westwards, and [had] been read to more Persons than will be at the Representation of it, or vouchsafe to read it, when it is publish'd.

These remarks come from the Preface to Dennis's *Defence of*

Sir Fopling Flutter, published five days before Steele's première. Twenty years earlier Dennis and Steele had been firm
friends, but the circumstances of first a monetary loan and
more recently the failure of Dennis's tragedy *The Invader of
His Country* at Drury Lane had turned their relationship to en-
mity; nevertheless Dennis wrote the truth, for Steele was in
Edinburgh in the autumn of 1720 and again a year later, and
newspaper advertisements have been found from November
1721.

Dennis knew in advance from Steele's own publicity, that
the new play would be in every way the reverse of Etherege's,
and his pamphlet, produced so long after the *Spectator* article,
was designed more as an attack on Steele than a defence of
Etherege. Dennis wrote with deliberate controversy, and with
a passion, vigour, and wit that invite wholesale quotation.
Steele had, he said, 'scurrilously and inhumanly ... attack'd
one of the most entertaining Comedies of the last Age', and he
turned Steele's own phrase against him: 'a perfect Contradic-
tion to good Manners and good Sense'. Conceding that ridicule
in Etherege's play was 'an Imitation of corrupt and degenerate
Nature', he asked whether *anything else* could be the proper
subject of ridicule, and whether anything but ridicule could be
the proper subject of comedy. But once Steele's play had opened it became the focus of Dennis's attention, and his *Remarks on the Conscious Lovers* was published on 24 January
1723.

Dennis's emphasis on the dearth of good plays agrees with
Vanbrugh's remarks quoted at the head of this chapter. The
burden of his criticism of Steele's comedy was that it was no
comedy at all. Starting with Steele's Preface, he dismissed as
meaningless the contention that the chief design 'was to be an
innocent Performance'. He then proceeded to a destructive analysis of the play, character by character and almost scene by
scene, pointing out inconsistencies and improbabilities with a
literal-mindedness that, in other circumstances, would have
earned the admiration of Jeremy Collier – the same Collier he
had answered with so much good sense twenty years earlier.
How in the civilized world, asked Dennis, could the identity of
Sealand and Indiana have remained so long unknown, and
why had they not taken steps earlier to trace each other? 'Does

Sir *Richard* believe', he asked, 'that *Toulon*, is situate under one of the Poles, that neither Ship nor Passengers were heard of in so many Years?'

But the crux of Dennis's attack, in which he showed his old common sense, is a passage referring to Steele's Preface. The quarrel in Act IV and 'the Case of the Father and Daughter', Dennis claimed, were not the proper subjects of comedy.

> When Sir *Richard* says, that any thing that has its Foundation in Happiness and Success must be the Subject of Comedy, he confounds Comedy with that Species of Tragedy which has a happy Catastrophe. When he says, that 'tis an Improvement of Comedy to introduce a Joy too exquisite for Laughter, he takes all the Care that he can to shew, that he knows nothing of the Nature of Comedy . . . Let Sir *Richard*, or any one, look into that little Piece of *Moliere*, call'd, *La Critique de l'Ecole des Femmes*, and he shall find there, that in *Moliere*'s Opinion, 'tis the Business of a Comick Poet to enter into the Ridicule of Men, and to expose the blind Sides of all Sorts of People agreeably; that he does nothing at all, if he does not draw the Pictures of his Contemporaries, and does not raise the Mirth of the sensible Part of an Audience, which, says he, 'tis no easy Matter to do . . . When Sir *Richard* talks of a Joy too exquisite for Laughter, he seems not to know that Joy, generally taken, is common like Anger, Indignation, Love, to all Sorts of Poetry, to the Epick, the Dramatick, the Lyrick; but that that kind of Joy which is attended with Laughter, is the Characteristick of Comedy; as Terror or Compassion, according as one or the other is predominant, makes the Characteristick of Tragedy, as Admiration does of Epick Poetry.

Dennis was right. But *The Conscious Lovers*, although not universally approved, ran for a remarkable eighteen nights, with eight more during the season; it brought profit to the author, who dedicated the published text to King George I. It was much to mid-century taste: in the next forty years it had 280 performances in London. Steele had done what Farquhar believed impossible: he had shown, by doing it, that a good comedy could indeed be written according to rules.* Moreover he had prepared for this consummation over more than a decade, and where Collier failed he had succeeded. Vanbrugh's biographers would, however, give Collier the credit and the

* p. 186

blame: he had made all the noise, although much of it was in the wrong quarter, and to so little immediate effect that he received only two brief references in the whole of *The Spectator*, and his *Short View* none at all. But in the process Steele changed not only the definition of comedy but its very nature, to such a degree that Farquhar would no longer have recognized it any more than Dennis was prepared to do.

Steele succeeded because he was a writer of great talent. *The Conscious Lovers* is a good play; but it is not funny and was not meant to be. In 1749 Henry Fielding, who had abandoned the writing of plays for novels, asked in the prefatory chapter to Book V of *Tom Jones*:

> Hath any one living attempted to explain what the modern judges of our theatres mean by that word *low*, by which they have happily succeeded in banishing all humour from the stage, and have made the theatre as dull as a drawing-room!

The stage would continue to resist efforts to reform it, even after the reading and licensing of every play by the Lord Chamberlain's Office became legally enforceable in 1737, as it would remain for over two hundred years. Nevertheless a comparison of Dennis's remarks with Farquhar's shows how far ideas and tastes had changed in two decades. The analogy is a dangerous one, but it provokes thought: there is the same degree of difference, over the same span of years, between Castle Howard or Blenheim and Campbell's Wanstead or Lord Burlington's Chiswick. *The Conscious Lovers* is, as its author claimed, an innocent play and a moral play. *Moral* is far more than the opposite of *immoral*; a few years later Pope's *Epistle to Lord Burlington*, which is a poetic essay on Taste, would appear in a group which he entitled *Moral Essays*. And insofar as Palladianism was, at heart, less about Palladio or Inigo Jones than about taste – moderation in all things that show, never being noticeably out of step with one's neighbours or above one's peers – Steele's play is, even in its indebtedness to a Classical prototype, the equivalent of early Palladian architecture.

It is surely no accident that twentieth-century enthusiasm has run parallel for Restoration theatre and the architecture of

Vanbrugh and Hawksmoor, for both have the excitement that goes with bending rules, making experiments and rejecting moderation. Moreover, the case of Steele does suggest that the 'Georgian' values that made *The Relapse* and *The Provok'd Wife* seem unrefined were the same as those that turned Blenheim into an architectural reproach.

Between the first season of the Haymarket Theatre and the production of *The Conscious Lovers* Vanbrugh's concerns with the stage were those of management and finance, not of writing; nevertheless he was well aware of the changes that had taken place. The fact that *A Journey to London* was found unfinished among his papers does not prove by itself that it comes from his last years, but the text offers a few clues. Mention of a seven-year term for Parliament places it after the Septennial Act of 1716, and references to the game of quadrille and to toupees (the man 'with the strange Perriwig' in the last sentence of the manuscript is named Toupee) must be of the early 1720s. Although it cannot be proved, a direct connection seems likely between Vanbrugh's original and his remarks to Tonson of 18 June 1722; the state of the theatre and the character of Steele's comedy do provide the strongest reasons for his return to creative writing.

Any description of Vanbrugh's play takes the word *catastrophe* out of its original dramatic sense into that of our everyday usage; as relentlessly as a Greek chorus, witnesses in succession announce one off-stage disaster after another. Meanwhile on the stage the principal characters blunder into snares from which, it seems, only a near-miraculous last Act could ever disentangle them. Sir Francis Headpiece, a country gentleman of forty-two, has been elected to Parliament, and as the play opens he is about to arrive in London with his family. In the course of the play he also hopes to pick up a lucrative sinecure which will both increase his standing and solve his problems in living up to it. For he exceeds his means, has drunk an estimated thirty-two tons of ale in his life, and has spent much of it 'in persecuting all the poor four-legg'd Creatures round, that wou'd but run away fast enough from him, to give him the high-mettled pleasure of running after them'; this pursuit has brought him many falls and injuries, all of which he has survived. We learn all this from his uncle Richard, who considers him – like most of the rest of the family – a fool. The family arrive in their coach, drawn by a team of four old geldings augmented by two cart-horses 'because my Lady will have it said, she came to Town in her Coach and Six'; they have brought their own cook and such a vast load of provisions of every kind that the coach broke down and delayed them by a day*.

Lodgings have been found for them by Sir Francis's servant, who is perhaps not the best judge of 'the Gentlewoman, her two Maids, and a Cousin' to be found there, for 'he never was in *London* before, you know, but one Week, and then he was kidnapp'd into a House of ill Repute, where he exchang'd all his Money and Cloaths for a-----um'. But before they are fully installed in Mrs Motherly's dubious house the cook has been mugged and robbed of 'the Goose Pye', and before the coach can be safely parked it is demolished by 'a great Luggerheaded Cart, with Wheels as thick as a good Brick Wall' – everything in this play is larger than life. Another second-hand coach is promptly bought 'for present use', but before the end of Act III it too is smashed. On the way to the playhouse it is overturned, spilling the party out into the muddy street; Lady Headpiece, her daughter, Martilla (the niece – an equivocal term – of Mrs Motherly) and Colonel Courtly, who received no 'Damage in his Services to the Ladies' beyond that from 'some Pins I met with about your Ladyship'.

> *Lady Head.* I am sorry any thing about me should do you harm.
> *Col.* If it does, Madam, you have that about you, if you please, will be my Cure. I hope your Ladyship feels nothing amiss?
> *Lady Head.* Nothing at all, tho' we did rowl about together strangely.
> *Col.* We did indeed. I'm sure we rowl'd so, that my poor Hands were got once---I don't know where they were got. But her Ladyship I see will pass by Slips.   [*Aside.*

Against this turbulent background Vanbrugh outlines a series of uneasy relationships. Sir Francis and his lady are only interested in what London can offer them. Their naïve daughter Betty and their fourteen-year-old son Humphry, who eats his

* p. 232

way through the play, are set to be as foolish as their parents. Then there is the Colonel, who has seduced Martilla and probably has an eye on Lady Headpiece, and there are Lord Loverule and Arabella, his lady. Her aims in life are to spend his Lordship's money and to act against his wishes whatever they may be, and we are led to suspect that her past is not above reproach: at the beginning of Act II Loverule tells her that if she cannot keep reasonable hours he will lock her out for good. In contrast to these ill-starred couples Vanbrugh seems to have envisaged a quiet story of true love between one Sir Charles and Clarinda, a young unmarried lady, though he develops it no further than one courteous conversation and Sir Charles's admission to Loverule that, though tired of society ladies, he believes 'there's yet one Woman fit to make a Wife of'. Had the playwright here his own lady in mind?

The unfinished Act IV opens with Lady Arabella's disgraceful treatment of her creditors. Her purse is empty after an evening's gambling, so she cheats the mercer Short-yard of the money her steward had put aside for him – at his seventeenth application – on the pretext that he should have come for it earlier. But we should not be too sorry for the mercer, for his name shows that he is no more honest than her Ladyship. In the next and last scene she sits down to a game of Hazard with Lady Headpiece, Betty, and Captain Toupee, who is a new arrival not found in the *Dramatis Personae*. Sir Francis Headpiece enters and quickly realizes that the Captain's dice are loaded. Violence is surely near.

> *Capt.* There's Two for you, Miss.
> *Miss Betty.* I'll at 'em, tho' I dye for't.
> *Sir Fran.* Ah my poor Child, take Care.   [*Runs to stop the Throw.*
> *Miss Betty.* There.
> *Capt.* Out . . . twenty Pounds, young Lady.
> *Sir Fran.* False Dice, Sir.
> *Capt.* False Dice, Sir? I scorn your Words . . . twenty Pounds, Madam.
> *Miss Betty.* Undone, undone!
> *Sir Fran.* She shan't pay you a Farthing, Sir; I won't have Miss cheated.
> *Capt.* Cheated, Sir?
> *Lady Head.* What do you mean, Sir *Francis*, to disturb the Com-

pany, and abuse the Gentleman thus?
Sir Fran. I mean to be in a Passion.
Lady Head. And why will you be in a Passion, Sir *Francis*?
Sir Fran. Because I came here to Breakfast with my Lady there, before I went down to the House, expecting to find my Family set round a civil Table with her, upon some Plumb Cake, hot Roles, and a cup of Strong Beer; instead of which, I find these good women staying their Stomachs with a Box and Dice, and that Man there, with the strange Perriwig, making a good hearty Meal upon my Wife and Daughter.---

The rest is lacking. Cibber claimed in his Preface that Vanbrugh considered the scenes 'yet undigested, too long, and irregular'; he tried to impose what he believed was a more coherent shape on the play by developing a sequence of three quarrels between the Townlys (as he renamed the Loverules, raising them to the status of title characters). Vanbrugh's structure seems to have been architectural in a similar way to *The Provok'd Wife*, working by pairs of characters rather than by development in time. But we cannot guess how the last Act would have pulled the whole thing together, as it surely would have done, as securely and as unexpectedly as in his first two original plays. Our inability to make predictions can be gauged by asking how we should complete either of those if the text had run out at the same point.

In his Dedication (to Queen Caroline, the wife of George II) Cibber described the design of his adaptation as 'chiefly to expose, and reform the licentious Irregularities that, too often, break in upon the Peace and Happiness of the Married State'; if Vanbrugh had finished the play he could no doubt have made the same claim. Cibber confessed both to reducing the scenes 'of the Lower Humour' in the course of editing and, although he printed them, to taking out a couple more after the first night. Fielding, again in *Tom Jones* (Book XII), mockingly depicted a puppet show of 'the fine and serious parts' of *The Provok'd Husband* which lacked 'any low wit or humour, or jests; or, to do it no more than justice . . . anything which could provoke a laugh'. Fielding also provides the clue to the fuss that was made over the lines about a 'broiled bone'; since the words were of Vanbrugh's invention and the associations are obscure it is perhaps worth gathering what is known about this example of eighteenth-century suggestibility.

Early in Act III Vanbrugh makes Lady Headpiece suggest to her children that, when their father returns from the House of Commons, they might 'eat a broil'd Bone together'. Cibber moved the incident to Act IV.i., where Sir Francis has returned, and has Mrs Motherly ask him, 'Will you give me leave to get you a broil'd Bone, or so, 'till the ladies come home, Sir?' Timing, inflexion, and tone of voice can overlay the proper meaning of the most innocent of words, and on the first night the reception of this line brought the play to a standstill. Cibber printed the line in his first edition, and careful readers were able to see that its originator was not Cibber but Vanbrugh. However, in the second edition he changed the words to 'a little something', although not before he had become identified in satirical writing with the bladebone of a shoulder of mutton. Johnson's *Dictionary*, the paragon of decent English, has an entry for *bladebone* and a quotation from Pope about 'the broiled relicks of a shoulder of mutton', and it seems that only Fielding leads to any improper connotation. He refers in Act III of his *Author's Farce* to Sir Farcical Comick, a parody of Cibber, as having 'had once an Intention to introduce a Set of Marrow-bones and Cleavers upon the Stage'.

> *Sir Farcical.* 'Tis true: And I did produce one Bone, but it stuck so confoundedly in the Stomach of the Audience, that I was obliged to drop the Project.

Fielding undoubtedly knew the phallic meaning of *marrow-bone and cleaver*. The same meaning must have been attached by the first-night audience to the broiled bone; what was in Vanbrugh's mind we shall never know, but Cibber must at first, and perhaps always, have been quite innocent.

In his Prologue Cibber suggested that Vanbrugh had changed his mind about comedy, and that most of what he had done was to complete the unfinished play according to Vanbrugh's intentions:

> *This Play took Birth from Principles of truth,*
> *To make Amends for Errors past, of Youth.*
> *A Bard, that's now no more, in riper Days,*

Conscious review'd the Licence of his Plays:
And though Applause his wanton Muse had fir'd,
Himself condemn'd what sensual Minds admir'd.
At length, he own'd, that Plays should let you see
Not only, What you Are, but Ought to be:
Though Vice was natural, 'twas never meant
The Stage should shew it, but for Punishment!

Such a change of heart was indeed necessary if Cibber was to make out of Vanbrugh's ideas the kind of play he thought suitable for the late 1720s. But in the Preface he admitted to the reader that he had no warrant for this; indeed his impression from talking to Vanbrugh had been rather the reverse:

All that I could gather from him of what he intended in the *Catastrophe*, was, that the conduct of his Imaginary Fine Lady had so provok'd him, that he designed actually to have made her Husband turn her out of his Doors. But when his Performance came, after his Decease, to my Hands, I thought such violent Measures, however just they might be in real Life, were too severe for Comedy, and would want the proper Surprize, which is due to the end of a Play. Therefore with much ado (and 'twas as much as I could do, with Probability) I preserv'd the Lady's Chastity, that the Sense of her Errors might make a Reconciliation not Impracticable.

Vanbrugh, on the other hand, seems to say that there are several kinds of fools and knaves, and that if they have changed at all over twenty-five years it is in the greater refinement of their describer's perception, not in their own behaviour. Vanbrugh seems indeed to have learned nothing from the theatrical controversies of his time. But did he need to learn anything?

The signs are, especially in the light both of Vanbrugh's early original plays and of his adaptations, that the last state of most of his characters would have been worse than the first. The romance of Sir Charles and Clarinda is certainly something different, for these good people with real feelings would surely have made their match at the end with a naturalness that it was beyond the capacity of a Cibber or a Steele to bring about. For the rest, Vanbrugh is as far as ever from showing 'not only what you are, but ought to be'. As Sir Charles says, 'bad Examples (if they are but bad enough) give us as useful Reflections as good ones do'.

The incompleteness of *A Journey to London* is a loss that Cibber was quite unable to remedy, although we are much in his debt for preserving what he found. The fragment has all the speed and apparent spontaneity of Vanbrugh's first plays, and he perhaps wrote it quickly in response to some immediate stimulus such as Steele's play, putting it aside when other things claimed his attention.

Sir John at Home

The pages of Vanbrugh's Account Book allow us to build up a fair picture of family life in the early 1720s, divided between Whitehall during the week and Greenwich at weekends and when business required Sir John's presence at the Royal Hospital there. It also gives details of all his travels 'out of town', a phrase reserved for journeys farther afield than Greenwich. On occasion Vanbrugh refers in letters to moving to either Greenwich or Whitehall 'for good', but the two are of course mutually exclusive and this phrase simply means a period of two or three weeks; in fact for the most part the two houses are treated in the accounts without distinction, and it is not clear how, for example, the servants were divided between them. One of the functions of household staff was to be at home when the master and mistress were elsewhere, to prepare for their return and to open the door to them when they arrived: outside keys were not generally carried except when a house was to be entirely closed up. This could lead to unfortunate con-sequences, as when the owners of one country house returned after a few days away to find that their staff had drunk a whole month's supply of home-brewed ale and were sleeping off the effects in broad daylight.

In the language of modern economics the average number of Vanbrugh's domestic staff during seven years of married life was 1·43 male and 4·25 female servants, according to the re-cords of their pay in the Account Book. This ranged from about £5 to £10 a year, sometimes with a bonus of a few shillings; the bonuses may have been tokens of appreciation or on occasion a compensation for late payment, to which the employed were as much subjected as was their employer. They also received their board and lodging and their livery or daily apparel; several pairs of buckskin breeches for the men servants appear in the accounts. But these figures should not be taken as more than a rough guide. Jack Jones, for example, who served Vanbrugh before the Account Book opens, may have been paid by Lady Vanbrugh after the marriage, for although payments to him are not recorded after Midsummer 1717 he witnessed signatures in 1719 and 1721 and worked for Lady Vanbrugh after Sir John's death. Alternatively, since the Greenwich family extended to other members and increasingly to other houses nearby, there may have been interchanges of servants. As a user and creator of apt names for stage characters Vanbrugh must have had some innocent amusement from servants like Mary Helps (1715-16) and Mary Whitwood (1718-19), if not also from Mrs Ruffle the cornchandler and Mr Spark the brazier.

Early in 1720 Vanbrugh extended the ground-floor accommodation of the Whitehall house by adding one-room wings on either side; he also obtained for the first time a lease **[I]** to the site and therefore the legal title he had not previously possessed. Marriage and the expectation of a young family also brought additions at Greenwich. Before June 1721, when the antiquary William Stukeley sketched it, Vanbrugh Castle had already acquired a crenellated gateway and an assortment of low out-buildings and turrets,* but soon after Stukeley's visit the architect decided on more substantial additions. All the rooms in the original castle were small like those at Whitehall and Chargate - the largest, about fifteen feet by twelve feet was the middle room facing the garden, with a semicircular bow window in the centre (the big bow-fronted room at the north-west corner was added by someone else later in the eighteenth century). Now Vanbrugh extended the castle by an addition on the east, of the same height and arrangement as the original work, with a ground-floor room about fifteen feet by twenty-five feet. At the east end he built a big fireplace with a tall out-

* p. 383

side chimney, and facing the garden he added on each floor a rectangular recess; this addition, symmetrical in itself, combined with the original symmetrical building to make a group that foreshadows the studied asymmetry of picturesque castles of sixty or a hundred years later. How far the practical needs which Vanbrugh always stressed to others were affected by aesthetic considerations in the composition of his own house it is impossible to say.

Vanbrugh probably decided to build more houses at Greenwich soon after his marriage, and even before the original castle was completed. On 27 March 1719 he leased to a neighbour, Thomas Dorrell, the right to graze a cow on the twelve-acre field, and it was a condition of the agreement that Sir John could carry on building operations as he thought fit. The first of the new houses on the east side of the field, three or four minutes' walk from the castle, was 'The Nunnery', as it was already known when Stukeley sketched it on 16 June 1721. This was a bungalow with two flanking rooms separated from the main block by walled yards. It was probably built for Vanbrugh's youngest brother Philip, who lived in it when on leave from the Navy, first renting it from him from Christmas 1720. Philip was born in 1682, seven when his father died and ten when John returned from the Bastille. At the age of fourteen he went to sea as a volunteer on board the *Deal Castle*; by 1710 he commanded the *Speedwell*. He was later captain of several other ships, until in 1739 he became a Commissioner of the Naval Dockyard at Plymouth. His rather brief marriage produced a surviving son and daughter; his wife had probably died by 1720, but although the name of the Nunnery must have been a family joke the reason for it is unknown. In 1743, after Philip had moved to Plymouth, the architect's son Charles was living in this house.

When Stukeley visited Greenwich again on 15 August 1722 he drew another house which he called *Castellulum Vanbrugiense* or 'little Vanbrugh castle'. This stood at the north-east corner of the field and was newly finished. Vanbrugh's brother Charles (born 1680) bought this outright from him at cost price. It had round towers at the ends, joined by a corridor running through the middle of the house, and a thirty-foot room with a bow window facing the back garden; it was later known variously as Vanbrugh House or Mince-Pie House.

Charles was also a sailor, becoming a captain in 1709. He had some of the spirit of enterprise shown by his father and his uncles William and Peter, and accumulated a useful sum of money which, among other things, enabled his son Edward (1722-1802) to live comfortably with his wife for many years in the fashionable Brook Street, Bath. (His obituary notice in the *Gentleman's Magazine* wrongly called him 'an immediate descendant of the celebrated Sir John Vanbrugh'.)

In 1714 Charles Vanbrugh was, while captain of the *Sorlings*, involved in liquor-running from the French colony of Martinique to the British one of Barbados. This was not an uncommon activity, and since it offended only against a trade agreement with France there was no great enthusiasm to deliver to Captain Vanbrugh the reprimand requested by the French authorities; indeed he seems not to have received it. He was also an investor: in February 1713 while he was at sea his architect brother used his power of attorney to draw a dividend on Charles's stock in the South Sea Company. As the note at the front of the Account Book shows, in 1715 Vanbrugh got a mortgage for £2500 from Charles on the Haymarket Theatre,* and this is the first recorded event in a series of transactions in which large sums of money passed between the two brothers.

At the end of December 1716 John repaid part of the mortgage on the playhouse and two years later (24/31 December 1718) the remainder, at the same time borrowing back half the amount on a bond, which he repaid a year later. On 29 November 1719 Vanbrugh had written to Tonson:

I'm much oblig'd for the advice you give me, to dispose of some money, where you have Succeeded so well. And 'tis not out of fear, I do not follow it. But to tell you the Truth; I have no money to dispose of. I have been many years at hard Labour, to work thorough the Cruel Difficultys, the HayMarket undertaking involv'd me in; notwithstanding the aid, of a large Subscription Nor are those difficultys, quite at an end yet. Tho' within (I think) a tollerable View.

I have likewise had a very hard Disappointment of not being

---

* p. 365

made Surveyour of the Works; Which I believe you remember, I
might have had formerly, but refus'd it, out of Tenderness to Sr
Chr: Wren, And I have a farther misfortune, of losing (for I now
see little hopes, of ever getting it) near £6000. due to me for
many years Service, plague and Trouble, at Blenheim, Which
that wicked Woman of Marlb: is so far from paying me, that the
Duke being Sued by some of the Workmen for work done there,
She has try'd to turn the Debt due to them, upon me. for which I
think she shou'd be hang'd.

Nevertheless Vanbrugh's fortunes improved, as the ensuing
transactions make evident. On 31 December 1719 Sir John
mortgaged the newly built Vanbrugh Castle to Charles for
£2000, signing the papers four weeks later. But the following
May Charles also paid Sir John £2406 on account towards the
purchase price of the playhouse. In October 1720 Sir John repaid the mortgage on the castle and at the same time received
from Charles the balance of the price of the theatre, which the
Land Registry document gives as £6544.

In fact the situation was not so simple: on 31 December 1720
Vanbrugh entered in his journal:

Memd: I made a Lease to John Potter Carpenter, of Five Houses
fronting to the Haymarket, for the Term of 46 yrs: 2 Months: 20
days To commence at Christs: 1719.
The Rent Seaventy Six pounds pr Anm: Rent Charge. And afterwards, made over the said Rent, to my Siss: Eliz: and Robina, for
their Lives, in considera[tio]n: of Two bonds they had from me,
of £400 each. The Rent to commence to them, from Chrs: 1719.
Memd: I sold the Playhouse (with some Tenements adjoining)
to my Brother Charles, for £8581 - Which he has paid me. But the
said Playh: still stands Charg'd with Three annuitys to my Siss:
·Mary, Victoria & Robina of £20 pr Annm: each and £2000. Settled
on my Wife in marriage.

What emerges from all this is that both brothers were solvent
and had money to use. Sir John invested in South Sea stock,
and later (in 1723) in the Chelsea Waterworks Company.
When in July and August 1725 he sold his herald's office and
received his Blenheim arrears (£1600) he put the greater part
into South Sea stock; all these investments enabled his widow,

who survived him for fifty years, to live in tolerable comfort.

It is still difficult or impossible to find out the sources of Vanbrugh's wealth; ironically his letters tell us more about Charles's. In July 1719 the latter was on his way back to England through France, where he observed in Paris, and afterwards gave Sir John an account of, the speculation in the Mississippi Company. This company had been set up in France in 1712 to trade with the French colony of New Orleans, but soon came to nothing. In 1717 it was acquired by John Law, a Scottish businessman who had taken French citizenship and introduced to France the system of promissory bank notes that still forms the basis of paper currency today. By May 1719 Law had a fleet of twenty-one ships and the monopoly of all the French trading companies from China to Peru. Many foreigners went to Paris to speculate in shares, including Lady Mary Wortley Montagu. Charles Vanbrugh apparently did not do so, perhaps advisedly since the company collapsed in May 1720. But, as we have seen, he had shares in the British South Sea Company soon after its establishment in 1711 to trade with South America.

The idea of shareholding in companies by private citizens, as opposed to members of a family, partners or close associates, was still unfamiliar to most people. The ideas that money could generate more money, and that in the form of shares in a company it could be bought and sold at a profit, were not only novel; they were so little understood that there seemed to be something magic in them. Companies of all sorts were floated, and there was a craze for patents to be exploited. Sir Richard Steele tried to promote a tanker ship of his own invention to bring live Irish salmon to London, and Vanbrugh himself became involved in the manufacture of a new kind of brick.* As for speculation on the share market there were scarcely any controls because very few people, and no government, had yet seen the pitfalls.

The success of the Mississippi speculation encouraged a boom in the South Sea. Vanbrugh told Tonson (who was in Paris) on 18 February 1720 of Charles's business achievement:

---

* p. 439

Our South Sea, is become a Sort of a Young Messissippy, by the
stocks rising so vastly; I am however only a looker on, and a
Rejoycer, not an Envyer, of other peoples good Fortune. In particular my Brother (who was with you at Paris) who had about
£5000 there, which is now near doubled.

Shares in the company reached their highest in June 1720,
only a few weeks after the collapse of the Mississippi Company. But as one share issue was followed by another a situation developed in which there were too many shares for any
dividend payable to be worth having. The cautious and the
shrewd pulled out with their profit before the crash: they included Charles Vanbrugh and the Duchess of Marlborough.
Few were so fortunate; the first suicide directly attributable to
the failure was early in September.

Nevertheless the company survived, after a rescue operation
worked out by the Bank of England (itself an institution of only
twenty-five years' standing) and the Treasury. Moreover, on a
new unadventurous footing it paid dividends. Vanbrugh told
Lord Carlisle (25 March 1721):

The South Sea is so hatefull a Subject one do's not Love to name
it; And yet it do's so interfere with almost every body's Affairs
more or less, that all they have to do, is in some degree govern'd
by it. Even I, who have not gain'd at all, Shall probably be a Loser
near £2000. I wou'd however fain See an end on't before I come
away if I cou'd; for when I know the worst of any thing, I can
make my Self tollerably easy.

Sir John had in fact become more than a looker on, for he had
invested £2000, from the first instalment of Charles's purchase
of the Playhouse, in May 1720; this money he seems to have
lost as he feared. On 7 October he paid £1050 for a further £400
in shares, and the following April he was no doubt delighted to
receive half a year's dividend of £20. He put further money into
the company, noting in September 1722 that he had altogether
£1511. 2s. 2d; at his last relevant entry (19 February 1726) he
had £3802. 15s. 11d. in stock, and it was still paying.

The three Greenwich houses so far built were of London
stock brick, which starts its life yellow and ends up brown. On

9 June 1721 Vanbrugh signed an agreement with Thomas Miller of Fulham, who had invented a new method of burning bricks, tiles and lime and who hoped with Vanbrugh's help to get a patent for fourteen years. The help was clearly financial, for according to the agreement Vanbrugh could sell his interest during the first two years for £1000. Miller took out a patent (No. 440) in March 1722 for burning bricks evenly hard, and he also supplied the white bricks which distinguished from the others the last two houses to be built. These were the two White Towers which stood on either side of the Nunnery; one was built in 1722-3 and the other started and finished a few months later. The first, on the north, is the house Vanbrugh had told Lord Carlisle he was building for his son Charles,* and there is a reference in the Account Book to 'Charles's House' and 'Jack's House'.

Little Charles, named after his godfather Lord Carlisle, had been born on 20 October 1720 – Sir Christopher Wren's eighty-eighth birthday - when Mrs Jefferys the midwife was paid £3. 9s. Jack, or rather John, was almost certainly born on 14 February 1722 when the midwife and nurse were paid £4. 12s., and new clothes, including a lot of pins, were bought for his elder brother. (Lady Vanbrugh's Bible, now in the possession of Lady Mowbray, has an inscription giving the birth date as 14 January, but the reliability of this as evidence is questionable since neither it nor the record of Charles's birth was made at the time. Henrietta Godolphin, Duchess of Marlborough, Charles's godmother, did not succeed to the title until June 1722. The Mrs Vanbrugh who gave this Bible to Henrietta Maria in 1720 cannot have been Sir John's mother, who died in 1711.)

Sir John's relationship to his young brothers was near to that of an uncle; he showed his own young son some of the doting attention of a grandfather. Writing to Lord Carlisle about the White Tower and the two-year-old boy, he told him, 'He talks of everything, is much given to Rhyming, and has a Great turn to dry joking. What these Seeds may grow to, God knows.' Other pleasant pictures are only hinted at in the pages of the Account Book, but it is not difficult to imagine Sir John sitting with the

* p. 346

lad on his knee, turning the pages of Blaeu's *Atlas Major*, which Tonson had had bound for him, or weaving carefully edited stories around the engraved illustrations in Tonson's folio English edition of Ovid's *Metamorphoses*, the purchase of which on 11 January 1726 is recorded, by a slip, as 'a Horace's Metas, for Charles'.

John, the younger boy, did not live long. He was sent at three months old to Walton-on-Thames, where Vanbrugh had taken over, as principal creditor, the house of his late cousin William (and probably the house that had belonged to the elder William Vanbrugh). Nurse Wintour cared for him there, and there are payments for coal to warm the house. But at just over a year old he died, and was buried at Walton on 28 March 1723.

In May 1723 Vanbrugh paid ten guineas to 'Mr Amyand, for Inoculating Charles'. The practice of inoculation for smallpox by scratching the skin and administering a mild strain of the disease was common in Turkey; it was described to the Royal Society in 1713 and become popular with the well-to-do English a few years later through the reports of Lady Mary Wortley Montagu, who had visited Turkey. Interest also grew after an epidemic in 1721 which claimed among others Lord Irwin, the Vanbrughs' host on their journey home in January 1719. There was as yet no understanding either of clinical hygiene or of the principles of antibodies. The procedure was not always successful, and indeed it was dangerous: some people died as a result, and it was later considered that the practice had done more to spread the disease than to control it. Claudius Amyand, surgeon to George I and George II, inoculated the daughters of the latter as Prince of Wales in April 1722. Vanbrugh wrote to Lord Carlisle on 18 February 1724:

> There has dyed of the Small Pox in Paris this last year above 14000 people whereas there never dyed in London in the worst years above 3000. This has occasion'd the Physitians at Court there, writing over hither, to Sr Hans Sloan & Mr Amyand the Kings Surgeon ... to know what Success that practice has realy had here − their enquiry has been in regard to the King of France. But the Priesthood presently Stept in, and had the matter sent to the Sorbonne, Whose wisdome and Piety do not think fit to allow of it. I don't hear of any of our Clergy but high Church, who are of opinion with them.

When the King was at Hanover Prince Frederick hinted something to him as if he shou'd not be unwilling to be inoculated if the King thought it right. The King told him, he shou'd not care to direct it, but that he himself had a good opinion of it and the Prince knew how it had Succeeded with his Brother and Sister. But that he look't upon him to be now of an Age proper to determine such things himself, and so left it to him to think farther of it. The result of which at last is, that here is a Person just arriv'd from the Prince to the King, to desire his Leave that he may be Inoculated, which I Suppose will be agreed to.

Vanbrugh's reference to the clergy suggests that objections were moral – against 'interfering with Nature' – rather than medical. He seems to have thought the risk worth taking, for on 2 March he recorded a double fee – twenty guineas – to Amyand, presumably for his wife and himself.

The Account Book makes only three references to music. In February 1716 Vanbrugh paid 'for Stringing a Dulcimer'; in April he gave 15s. 'for a flute for Arthur' (who will be discussed presently), and in February 1717 he paid 21s. 6d. to 'a Bassviol Master for Jack Jones'. It is not easy from these references to imagine what part, if any, music played in the household. Vanbrugh was apparently not a gambler, though the gaming scene in *A Journey to London* shows that he understood the more hazardous kinds of card game. But Henrietta Maria wrote on one of his letters to Tonson, a few months after her marriage,

> & if you will make one at cards as I understand you have often done, with much finer Ladys than I am I give you my word that I will neither cheat nor wrangle. Yr Sernt
>
> Hariot V.

Few books are mentioned in the accounts, and some of those are subscriptions before publication - to Addison's collected works for example, and to Giacomo Leoni's translation of Alberti on architecture, which did not appear before Vanbrugh's death but which his widow received. But regular payments show that he subscribed a guinea a quarter to Hartley's the bookseller, and what he borrowed or acquired there is not specified.

After Vanbrugh's death his widow kept an account of major expenses in a book started and discarded by her husband. A loose sheet inserted into this contains two separate attempts, in Vanbrugh's hand, at a *Computation* for the year 1723. The calculations are not consistent, but they give some idea of the cost of the household. Housekeeping was reckoned at £25 a head, including all food and drink, coal, candles, laundry, and utensils. Coal is separately costed at £20, wine at £50, small beer and ale at £28. In addition servants' wages amounted to £50 and their livery to £48. Horses (four) and coach mainten- ance cost £145. Clothes for Vanbrugh and his wife and Charles came to £200. Doctors' and apothecaries' bills were £33. The total he calculated at about £1000; this did not include any of the expenses of his professional activities or travelling.

The household figures are based on the surprising number of fourteen heads, and it is not possible to discover how this number was determined. A complement of seven known ser- vants, a nurse, two adults and a child make eleven. A twelfth was probably Solomon, who first appears in the accounts in January 1719 when 5s. 6d. was spent on 'things' for him and Will Curtis. On 25 August 1722 Vanbrugh paid seven guineas 'to bind Solomon Prentice', but to whom he was apprenticed or indeed who he was there is no clue. The other entries are for medical attention, and he died, probably still in the household, in March 1725.

A slightly more tangible figure is Arthur, for whom the flute was bought. In 1716-17 he appears as a servant, receiving £5 a year and a pair of buckskin breeches. But he was still attached to Vanbrugh in August 1725: the notes at the back of the ac- count book used later by Lady Vanbrugh show that he was re- imbursed in 1722 and 1725 for toll charges, and he must have accompanied Vanbrugh on some of his business journeys. His talents had taken him out of the servant category, for Vanbrugh wrote to Newcastle in November 1723 that Arthur was copying the design for the Newcastle Pew in Esher Church.

It is clear from surviving drawings that Vanbrugh used sev- eral draughtsmen besides and after Hawksmoor; one was Henry Joynes in the Blenheim days, and another was Thomas Kynaston, who also paid Vanbrugh's Hartley's subscription for 1719 and was reimbursed. In that year Vanbrugh told Newcastle that he had employed Kynaston for fifteen years, but the first substantive reference we have is in a letter written the day after Christmas 1708 to Joynes. Vanbrugh was sending Kynaston down to Blenheim 'to See the Manner of Measurements . . . in Order to Qualify himself the better for future business'. He told Joynes that Kynaston had worked for several years for his cousin William but was now moving to the Office of Works. In the disordered state of the Works following Wren's dismissal from the Surveyorship in 1718 Vanbrugh made Kynaston Deputy Comptroller in order to keep him on the payroll.

An office had been fitted up in the Whitehall house in 1709 on the Blenheim account, but undoubtedly Vanbrugh took some of his work, public or private, wherever he went, and used assistants wherever he found them. The album of architectural drawings at Elton Hall contains the work of both Vanbrugh and Sir Edward Lovett Pearce, who between 1726 and his death in 1733 had an architectural practice in Dublin. In some of the drawings it is difficult to distinguish between Vanbrugh and Pearce, and it is possible that Pearce was for a time in the early 1720s a pupil-assistant of Vanbrugh. This seems the more likely because Pearce, the nephew of Colonel John Lovett who built the successor to Winstanley's Eddystone Lighthouse, was also the grandson of Vanbrugh's aunt Mary Carleton.

The Account Book shows that, besides his brothers Charles and Philip, Vanbrugh was in touch with his sisters Elizabeth, Mary, Robina, and Victoria, with his half-sister Elizabeth Garencieres and with Anna Maria Van den Bush, daughter of his first cousin Anna Delboe. To all these ladies at various times he paid interest on bonds. The accounts do not show what payments were made in person, but Mary lived in Chester and Anna Maria probably in Southwell, a town which seems to have attracted several of the women of the family.

In 1789 John Byng, Lord Torrington, described Southwell as 'a well-built clean town such a one as a quiet distressed family ought to retire to'. The Minster has only been a cathedral since 1884, but in the Middle Ages it had been a collegiate church and a regional centre, and the Archbishop of York had a house there. In Vanbrugh's time there were several clergy and there was a Minster school. His elder sister Lucy and his nearest younger sister Anna Maria were in Southwell before 1700: Lucy was buried at the Minster in 1699 and Anna Maria married there a schoolmaster, the Rev. Thomas Hesleden, in 1698. But she too died in 1700 though not in Southwell. The profession of her husband, the earlier Garencieres connections in Chester, and the existence of the Minster school raise the question whether some of Vanbrugh's sisters were concerned with teaching. But nothing more is known until 1714, when Anna Maria Van den Bush's mother Ann moved to the Nottinghamshire town, dying there before the end of the year. If it was not pure coincidence, there must have been some enduring family connection with the town that drew her from London and other relatives after her.

In the early 1720s Athanasius Garencieres, son of Vanbrugh's half-sister and by then a London merchant, figures in the Account Book. In 1724 his brother Theophilus, Vicar of Scarborough and Master of the Grammar School in that town, learned that the Prebend of Southwell was vacant. It was only worth £7 a year but brought the prospect of much better remuneration. Before setting out for the North Vanbrugh wrote to Lord Newcastle, asking him to recommend Theophilus for the Prebend; on his way home again he called in at the vicarage in Scarborough and afterwards sent a reminder to Newcastle — so much for his supposed anti-clericalism — but the application was unsuccessful. Vanbrugh sent tea 'to Southwell' in March 1724 and 'Fans & Handkerchers to Southwell' the following January, according to the Account Book, and further connections ensued.

Vanbrugh's sister Robina made a will in Southwell in 1745, and referred in it to her two sisters buried there. One of them was of course Lucy, the other must be Elizabeth. It is very probable that all the following were one person: Elizabeth Vanbrugh, sister of the architect and born in 1671; Sister Betty of the Account Book, to whom Vanbrugh gave sums of money after 1716; Elizabeth the widow and administratrix of Cousin William Vanbrugh of the Royal Household and of Walton-on-Thames (d. 1716);* Mrs Vanbrug who in 1722 was allowed to

* p. 201

build over land overlooking the Minster churchyard; Elizabeth Vanbrugh of Southwell, widow, who signed a lease for the Archbishop's Palace or Courthouse there in 1726; and Mrs Elizabeth Vanbrugh, widow, whose death at Southwell a Cheshire diarist recorded on 1 January 1731.

Two of Vanbrugh's aunts lived into the 1720s. Lucy, who left her husband Thomas Breton and had two children whom he disowned, appears as Aunt Breton;* Vanbrugh sent her money and a 'token'. Mary Pearce, the grandmother of Sir Edward Lovett Pearce, went to live in the Lower Close at Norwich, and it would seem that she was the object of a visit to Norwich by Vanbrugh's three sisters Betty, Robina, and Victoria, in May 1719, for which he gave them money for their journeys. He seems not to have gone with them, even though he had a newly acquired wife to parade.

Most of Vanbrugh's designs were for places far from London. Instead of Woodstock he travelled, in his last ten years, to other places: Grimsthorpe, Stowe, Ickworth, Amesbury, Eastbury, Seaton Delaval. He also went to the spas at Bath and Scarborough, and until 1724 he continued his habit of taking a summer or autumn vacation at Castle Howard, where he could also watch the progress of the outworks and the park. Then there were trips to Claremont, where a room was kept for his use, to Windsor and Hampton Court, and to the house at Walton. Sometimes he took Lady Vanbrugh with him: to Bury St Edmunds in October 1719, where they met Lord Bristol and also an aunt of hers who was married to Sir Marmaduke Wyvell, and two years later to Yorkshire. On that occasion they took little Charles in 'a heavy coach', visiting both Castle Howard and Heslington. They spent a week in York, where Vanbrugh's view of the company was a brighter one than Lady Mary Wortley Montagu's had been eight years previously: 'A Race every day, and a Ball every night; with as much well look'd Company, as ever I got together The Ladies I mean in Chief'.

There was for Vanbrugh a particular pleasure in coming home down the Dover road, turning into the drive through the towered archway at the south end of the field, passing on the

* p. 6

right first the White Tower, then the Nunnery, then the other tower, and finally turning left by Mince-Pie House into the last stretch to the Castle gate. All that remains of this today is the Castle, bereft of some of its ancillary buildings but, by a curious irony, endowed with some later additions in a similar style. After many years as a school it is now once more lived in; of the rest of Vanbrugh's field only the line of the drive persists in the streets now known as Vanbrugh Fields and Westcombe Park Road. The tall trees around the Castle were certainly part of his intention, although it is doubtful whether any of them is as old as the building: in 1815 John Carter looked at a great oak in the Castle forecourt and considered from its girth that it was 'coeval with the pile, no doubt of the knight's planting'. It was surely with a memory of Greenwich and its mixture, by then, of buildings and mature trees, that Sir Joshua Reynolds wrote in his *Thirteenth Discourse* (1786) of the delight given by

whatever building brings to our remembrance ancient customs and manners, such as the castles of the barons of ancient chivalry ... hence it is that towers and battlements are so often selected by the painter and poet to make a part of the composition of their landscape; and it is from hence, in a great degree, that, in the buildings of Vanbrugh, who was a poet as well as an architect, there is a greater display of imagination, than we shall find perhaps in any other.

— 33 —

A Portico Each Way

The Act of Union of 1707 established commercial equality between England and Scotland, which James I and VI had joined
politically a century earlier. One of its consequences was the
emigration of enterprising Scots from Edinburgh and Glasgow
with the intention of beating Londoners at their own trades;
among them was Colen Campbell, whom we have already met
as the agent and sometime Deputy of Benson in the Office of
Works.* In April 1715 Campbell and a consortium of London
booksellers published the first of three volumes of *Vitruvius
Britannicus, or the British Architect,* a folio of 100 engraved
plates which had been advertised some months previously,
and of which by 25 March 370 copies had been sold to 304 advance subscribers. Campbell's name had to be squeezed into
the title-plate after the rest of it had been engraved, but it
appears large and clear on the florid calligraphic dedication to
George I that forms the second plate. Campbell's contributions
were the short descriptive notes to the plans and elevations, a
two-page Introduction, and some of the illustrations.

Referring in his Introduction to the 'general Esteem that
Travellers have for Things that are Foreign', he observed that
the Grand Tour, an increasingly popular way of completing a
young gentleman's or nobleman's education, was the privilege
of the young and ignorant and impressionable. His declared
aim was therefore to offer such a collection of British buildings

* p. 389

of the preceding hundred years as would 'admit of a fair comparison with the best of the *Moderns*', the works of Antiquity being, he said, beyond comparison. In a masterpiece of compacted prose which certainly reveals the talents of the Scottish lawyer's mind, he then introduced, by implication rather than by direct statement, further comparisons: between the modern Italians (unfavourably) and those of the sixteenth-century Renaissance; between 'the Famous *Inigo Jones*' (favourably) and 'the Renowned *Palladio*', and between the works of Wren, Vanbrugh, Hawksmoor, Archer, Talman, and others (unfavourably if with a glove of velvet) with both a number of buildings by Inigo Jones or John Webb and several designs of his own that were visibly indebted to Jones and Palladio. The book also contained two promises of a second volume which would include further works by Jones, among them 'the incomparable Designs he gave for *WHITE-HALL*'.

It has recently been established by Eileen Harris that the originators of *Vitruvius Britannicus* were the group of booksellers, who engaged Campbell at a late stage of preparation, first as a draughtsman and secondly to alter the complexion of their volume. This was in response to a competing project whose forward state of preparation had come to the booksellers' notice, namely the first complete English translation of Palladio's *Quattro Libri dell'Architettura* by Nicholas Dubois, a French (probably Huguenot) military engineer turned architect, who later became one of Hewett's acolytes in the Office of Works. The illustrations, on engraved copperplates instead of the original wooden blocks, were provided by Giacomo (or James) Leoni, a Venetian architect who had recently arrived in London by way of the Rhineland and was seeking to turn the fashion for things Italian to his own profitable employment as an architect.

Leoni, the first of whose four volumes appeared in September 1713, correctly judged the value of Palladio's book as not only a practical manual but also a compendium of architectural exemplars, a matter on which Vanbrugh, devoted as he was to his copy of Fréart's faithful 1650 French edition, would have agreed with him. Leoni also saw, as a consequence, the commercial viability of a large-paper English edition up to date in typography and illustrative techniques.

Vanbrugh never aimed to reproduce any of Palladio's designs literally, whereas one of the underlying assumptions of the style that came to be known as Palladianism was that the examples in the *Quattro Libri* were reproducible, either integrally or eclectically from parts of several designs. Why this kind of architectural plagiarism should have become attractive is too large and complex a question to be explored here, but that is what began to happen in the second decade of the eighteenth century, and it increased the potential demand for the Leoni-Dubois edition of Palladio. The publishers of *Vitruvius Britannicus*, who had already invested heavily in engravers' work with the intention of producing no more than a fine picture book of architecture (mainly English rather than British) of the preceding fifty years, now decided to make their own project more topical and thus more competitive, by the inclusion of references to Palladio and to his follower, as he was made out to be, 'this great Master', Inigo Jones.

This was the purpose of Campbell's introductory text, and to the same end a number of plates originally commissioned were relegated to the second (1717) or third (1725) volumes and replaced by the 'Palladian' designs of Jones or Webb or of Campbell himself. Campbell's Introduction has ever since been rightly regarded as one of the most important polemical statements in eighteenth-century architecture. What he aimed to do, and what − at least in the eyes of his readers ever since − he succeeded in doing, was to offer a sound and positive basis for the national style for which Shaftesbury's prescription in the *Letter Concerning Design* had been merely negative.*

Shaftesbury's appeal to patriotism centred on a rejection of French taste, appropriately at the close of Marlborough's war; Campbell, appreciating the virtues of brevity, saw no need to re-engage an aesthetic battle with France that by 1715 could be regarded as won. His target was different and subtler, for he singled out for censure the Italian 'Productions of the last *Century*', that is of the seventeenth, in which 'the *Italians* can no more relish the Antique Simplicity, but are entirely employed in capricious Ornaments, which must at last end in the *Gothick*'. He continued:

* p. 403

How affected and licentious are the Works of Bernini *and* Fontana? *How wildly Extravagant are the Designs of* Boromini, *who has endeavoured to debauch Mankind with his odd and chimerical Beauties, where the Parts are without Proportion, Solids without their true Bearing, Heaps of Materials without Strength, excessive Ornaments without Grace, and the Whole without Symmetry? And what can be a stronger Argument, that this excellent Art is near lost in that Country, where such Absurdities meet with Applause?*

Many of the designs of buildings such as Chatsworth, Blenheim, Castle Howard, and Easton Neston had been supplied for *Vitruvius Britannicus* by their architects, and Campbell was careful not to spoil his case by any adverse comment on the works illustrated in the volume. But *Gothick* was the word Shaftesbury had applied to the then unbuilt steeples of the Fifty New Churches; Blenheim was regularly termed a quarry of stones, and it is perhaps worth remembering that Jeremy Collier had called *The Relapse* a 'heap of irregularities'. To those who could make the comparison – and that meant to a growing number of educated and informed persons – the relevance of Bernini, Fontana and Borromini (whom even Bernini had called a madman) to designs like Castle Howard and Blenheim was inescapable; the antithesis to the simple shapes, inert plane wall surfaces and standardized door and window frames of the Palladian exemplars was equally clear.

But the backcloth to the last decade of Vanbrugh's architectural career contained yet further strands. The politicization of the Office of Works and its decline as a centre of architectural design have already been considered. Another thread involves, unlikely though it may appear, both Alessandro Galilei and Thomas Hewett,* and a third is the change of direction in Vanbrugh himself from France towards Renaissance Italy. Little is known about Hewett and Galilei, except that the former was one of those potential patrons who tempted the latter with schemes for great country houses, London churches and even a colossal new royal palace. But it is noteworthy that Galilei's executed works have an urbanity and a freedom from

* p. 393

excess (except in scale) that distinguish them from the architecture censured by Campbell.

Moreover it seems probable that Hewett and his friends saw
Galilei, if only for a short time, as the figurehead for their own
attempt to fill Shaftesbury's stylistic prescription. In 1715 the
third Earl of Burlington, just twenty-one, returned from the
Grand Tour to read Campbell's remarks and to find them to his
taste; four years later he went back to the Veneto specifically to
study Palladio's buildings and to acquire as many of the master's drawings as possible, and from then on Burlington
assumed the leadership of architectural taste. 'Chiswick', his
country estate west of London became in artistic and literary
matters what 'Bloomsbury' would be two centuries later. But
Galilei's English sojourn occupied roughly the years between
Burlington's two Italian trips, and in that period Hewett and his
associates were known as 'the new Junta for Architecture', the
word meaning a self-electing committee or council, generally
with political intentions or overtones.

As far as so broad a generalization is feasible, it can be said
that one of the characteristics of French exterior architecture
from the late Middle Ages to the end of the nineteenth century
is a concern with surface enrichment. The effect of Wren's stay
in France in 1665-6 was to modify his conception of architecture as a geometrical demonstration by the addition, as it
were, of a decorative outer skin: St Paul's and Hampton Court,
the two buildings which Shaftesbury adversely criticized by
name, are the best examples of this. Castle Howard and, to a
lesser extent, Blenheim, still show this attitude to the external
wall surface; Vanbrugh's later works, from Kimbolton onwards, generally do not. But while Kimbolton and Chargate
and the Greenwich houses look as if they were designed largely out of Vanbrugh's head without reference to pattern books
or earlier buildings, his major house designs from about 1715
onwards suggest not only that he had found the Castle Air unsuitable for some applications but also that he was either using
a new pattern book or looking again at an old one; moreover,
that in either fact or intention it was closer to Italy than to
France.

Vanbrugh's first designs for Eastbury, a few miles from
Blandford in Dorset, were made about 1715 for George

R 'New design' for Eastbury. Front elevation.

S 'New design' for Eastbury. Side elevation.

Doddington of the Admiralty, who had bought the estate in 1709. The Account Book records two visits to Eastbury in July and October 1716, but it was two or three years before any work began. Several preliminary designs are known from drawings and one, described as 'A New Design for A Person of Quality', was engraved in *Vitruvius Britannicus* II (1717). It seems that Doddington was living in the new kitchen wing before he died in March 1720 but that the main house had never been started. His nephew and heir George Bubb added the name of Doddington to his own, and the main house was begun for him about 1722, when Vanbrugh expected work 'from this time . . . to go on without any Stop'. This was to a plan whose reduced area was made to appear larger by the placing of square towers at the corners.

Vanbrugh made further site visits in July and October 1723, June 1724 and May 1725, and George Bubb Doddington paid him £1000 in 1722-3 and a further £275 to his widow in July 1726. Since the house, together with the enormous gardens laid out by Charles Bridgeman, cost about £140,000 these amounts are roughly in proportion to Vanbrugh's receipts from Blenheim. But when he died Eastbury was far from complete, and to finish it Bubb Doddington employed Roger Morris, the professional 'ghost' of the amateur architect the ninth Earl of Pembroke. Work continued until 1738, and Morris did what he could to give Eastbury a more Palladian appearance by leaving off the huge clerestory and adding a pediment to Vanbrugh's portico.

But most of our knowledge of Vanbrugh's Eastbury comes from the engravings in *Vitruvius Britannicus* III. Lord Temple of Stowe, who inherited the estate on Bubb Doddington's death in 1762, found the house unsuitable to his taste, and after thirteen years of neglect he set gunpowder to the main block, brutally returning it to the condition of a 'quarry above ground'. Most of the wings and courts were dismantled, and the stones and bricks of Eastbury now lie embedded in foundations and walls of the neighbourhood. Some of Bridgeman's garden layout survives, part of the stable wing was kept and made into a dwelling house, and one of the courtyard gateways still stands, a picturesque and indeed fantastic sight with two mature trees growing from its roof.

Eastbury was far smaller than Blenheim, yet with its
ancillary courts and its deep forecourt 210 feet by 160 feet it
was a 'great house' in the same sense. The plan of the 'New
Design' was rigidly symmetrical, and conformed to the princi-
[T]   ples Vanbrugh had absorbed from his study of Palladio's house
plans: a hall and saloon on the main axis, flanked by staircases,

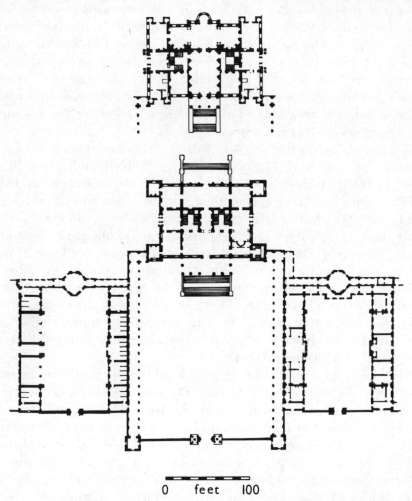

T   Eastbury. 'New design' (above) and final (below) plans.

with the sides of the house taken up by matching suites of
rooms each ending in a state bedchamber on the entrance
front. The saloon in this 'New Design' is divided by clusters of

columns into three sections, similar in shape to the central
three-fifths of the gallery at Blenheim and with a similar bow
window in the middle. The two open-newel staircases were to
be lit from above by octagonal lanterns hidden on the roof [R]
among the enormous arches containing the chimneys. These
arches were to be twenty-five feet high, or rather more than [S]
the main storey: their huge size suggests an element of what
seems like self-parody in the design, as do the deep arches that
frame the end windows of the main fronts and the middle ones
of the side elevations. But in both this design and the preliminary ones Vanbrugh introduced the three-light Venetian
window that came soon afterwards to be one of the trademarks
of English Palladianism.

In the final design Vanbrugh intended to light the staircases [31]
from a huge clerestory which, with the corner towers, would
have made Eastbury very like a re-interpretation of Wollaton.
In reducing the plan area he abandoned the matching state
suites in favour of a greater variety of use. The hall, saloon, and
staircases remained, but there were two drawing rooms and
only one state bedroom on the main floor; a big room on the
right-hand side, which has an apse at one end and looks as if it
ought to be the chapel, is marked as the 'Great eating Room' in
the *Vitruvius* plan.

On the outside Vanbrugh again used Venetian windows, this
time at the top of the towers. These towers and some other features of Eastbury give it a curious resemblance to some of the
buildings in the landscapes of Claude Lorrain, and since
Claude's ideal vision of Antiquity was one of the sources of inspiration for eighteenth-century landscape gardeners it may
be tempting to wonder whether there is any connection between Claude and Vanbrugh. But the answer can only be that,
as Sir Joshua Reynolds recognized, both were interested in the
skylines and the textures of buildings and both drew on similar
examples. Vanbrugh also made extensive use at Eastbury of
the window with a blocked or rusticated surround that only
occurs once in Palladio but became a favourite with the
English Palladians. (Nikolaus Pevsner, finding no ready-made
name for this, rather arbitrarily named it 'Gibbs surround' for
his *Buildings of England* series, although it is by no means individual to James Gibbs.)

The last distinctive motif at Eastbury was the ringed columns of the portico. Attempts have been made to trace these to the Villa Sarego at the end of Chapter XV of Palladio's second book, but the precise and regular grooving of Vanbrugh's columns is quite different from Palladio's deliberately rustic order. The Eastbury columns derive ultimately from seventeenth-century France, and are an extension of the horizontal banded rustication of the entrance wall (and, for example, of the north front of Castle Howard) from wall to column. The motif is in fact common, like a number of others, to both Vanbrugh and Hawksmoor: it occurs in the side gate **[30]** towers of Blenheim, the Kensington Orangery, flattened into **[12]** pilasters at the corners of Kimbolton, in Hawksmoor's St Mary Woolnoth in 1718, and last of all at Seaton Delaval a couple of **[22]** years later.
[29] In the early 1720s Vanbrugh developed a relish for the North-East of England: he enjoyed the clear air and wide skies, took the medicinal waters at Scarborough with Lord Carlisle, and watched the Castle Howard plantations and outworks grow year by year. 'Two Years more', he wrote from there in August 1721,

> tho' they won't compleat all the Building, will so Beautify the Outworks, of Gardens, Park &c, That I think no Place I ever Saw, will dispute with it, for a Delightfull Dwelling in generall, let the Criticks fish out what particular faults they please in the Architecture.

In the same letter he told Brigadier Watkins that he had been at Lumley Castle, outside Chester-le-Street, the seat of his Kit-Cat friend Richard Lumley, soon to be second Earl of Scarbrough. He found Lumley Castle.

> a Noble thing; and well deserves the Favours Lord Lumley designs to bestow upon it; in order to which, I stay'd there near a Week, to form a General Design for the whole, Which consists, in altering the House both for State, Beauty and Convenience, And making the Courts Gardens and Offices Suitable to it; All which I believe may be done, for a Sum, that can never ly very heavy upon the Family. If I had had good weather in this Expedition, I shou'd have been well enough diverted in it; there being

many more Valluable and Agreeable things and Places to be Seen, than in the Tame Sneaking South of England.

In April 1722 Lord Scarbrough (as he had become the previous December) asked Vanbrugh 'to propose some things for him in order to begin his Works there. What I shall be able to do, I don't yet know.' The Earl expected to reach Lumley at the end of May, but although Vanbrugh's desires were 'strongly North-ward, especially to Castle Howard', there is no evidence from the Account Book of a northern journey that summer or autumn. However, the start of work did not require his pres- **[27]** ence. It comprised the refurbishment of the south range into a suite of modern living rooms, general refacing of the exterior, and the replacement of the old late Gothic windows by re-gularly spaced rectangular ones with the new sash frames. There are no further references to Lumley, but the work was carried out over several years, and Vanbrugh may have been there in 1724 on his way to or from Seaton Delaval. Lumley is now a hotel.

Seaton Delaval has fared somewhat better than Eastbury, for although gutted by fire in 1822, blackened by soot and des- **[29]** poiled of its gardens by open-cast mining it stands proud and gaunt on its plateau, re-roofed and re-glazed, near the North-umberland coast. The Delavals had owned Seaton since the twelfth century; in 1717 the sixty-year-old Admiral George De-laval bought from his cousin Sir John an existing house, which by the spring of 1719 he was hoping to get Vanbrugh either to alter or rebuild. He must have engaged Vanbrugh in London later that year, for in October stone was being quarried and oak beams were being sought in York.

During March 1720 there is a gap in Vanbrugh's attendances at the Board of Works and a corresponding paucity of entries in the Account Book, and it is possible that the Admiral took him up to the site then; otherwise (or in addition) Seaton may have been the cause of his absence from London for the whole of December 1720. He was certainly there for some days in August 1721, when he told Watkins:

The Admiral is very Gallant in his operations, not being dispos'd to starve the Design at all. So that he is like to have, a very fine Dwelling for himself, now, and his Nephew &c hereafter.

That, apart from a reference earlier in 1721 to 'Some things I have to send Mr Etty very Soon of Admll: Delavals', is the only reference in letters, but there must have been a considerable amount of correspondence both with the Admiral and with William Etty of York, the Clerk of Works at Castle Howard. Etty made several recorded site visits, and a letter of advice of August 1722, addressed to the mason George Cansfield, is probably his; it is certainly not Vanbrugh's in either handwriting or spelling. Etty met Vanbrugh at Seaton on the architect's last visit in August 1724 when the house was roofed. By then the nephew, Captain Francis Blake Delaval, had succeeded his uncle, who died after a riding accident in June 1723. Joiners were at work in 1727 and a scratched date of 1729 on the northwest tower suggests that the building was by then finished. How far Vanbrugh was responsible for the internal fittings is doubtful, but enough remains of the structure to show, with imagination, that Seaton was as fine a building as any he designed.

Seaton Delaval is small by Vanbrugian standards, although like Eastbury it has a deep forecourt. The main block has only four principal rooms on the ground floor: the hall and two flanking parlours on the north and a great tripartite saloon 70 feet by 121 feet along the whole south side. But the four octagonal corner turrets each contain a room on each floor. These turrets, and the larger side towers containing oval staircases, make the complete plan an inseparable amalgam of Palladian axial symmetry and the richness of projection and recess of late Tudor castellated houses.

In its massing and its skyline Seaton Delaval is the ultimate expression of Vanbrugh's Castle Air; however, it is more than that. The north front has the martial severity of the corresponding front at Castle Howard, with banded rustication, heavy keystones and ringed columns supporting a full Doric entablature very similar to that at Castle Howard and perhaps designed in detail by Etty. But the stair towers are lit by Venetian windows, and the south front to the garden is as different from the north as are the two fronts of Castle [32] Howard. Rectangular windows are surmounted by cornices and pediments based on sixteenth-century Italian models; the garden portico, two bays deep, is fronted by four fluted Ionic columns of the

utmost elegance. It is a building full of contrasts not only in shapes
and shading but in the assured way Vanbrugh uses his varied and
carefully selected vocabulary.

The entrance hall, two storeys high, is lined with round-
headed arcades not unlike those of the hall at Blenheim,
except that those are open and these are blind. Before the
building was gutted a great attic room on the top floor ran the
whole depth of the house, a more dramatic and indeed closer
reminiscence than Eastbury's of Wollaton, where a similar
room still stands over the hall. From Wollaton the Tudor coal   [7]
magnate Francis Willoughby looked out over the coalfields on
whose profits he had built his mansion; had he lived to see it
finished Admiral Delaval would from his own great room have
scanned the North Sea with an old sailor's eye.

Strong contrasts between Italianate elegance and rustic
vigour also lie at the heart of Vanbrugh's partly executed
design for Grimsthorpe, the seat of his old friend Robert Bertie.   [34]
As we have seen,* Vanbrugh had a survey made of the old
courtyard house, part medieval and part Tudor, as early as
1715, the year in which Robert was raised from fourth Earl of
Lindsey to first Duke of Ancaster; this may even be the date of a
drawing for re-fronting the north range, which had last been
rebuilt only about thirty years earlier with a great two-storey
room, 40 feet by 106 feet, as its centrepiece. Vanbrugh called at
Grimsthorpe on political business in December 1718 on his
way to Nottingham, Yorkshire, and marriage, and we may
wonder whether he told his old friend the Duke then of his intentions. In the winter of 1722-3 he made a 'General Design'
for the Duke, which was also approved by his eldest son and
heir. The Duke died in July 1723 and early in September the
architect took in Grimsthorpe on his way south in order 'to
consult about his Building', believing the new Duke 'inclin'd to
go on upon the General Design'. Vanbrugh was at Grimsthorpe
again in September 1724 and in September-October 1725, and
Vitruvius Britannicus III (1725) includes a complete plan and
elevations for the north, south and west fronts, dated variously   [36]
1723 and 1724.

In the event only the north range of the 1680s was refaced

* p. 365

and refurbished. Vanbrugh inserted staircases from ground
[33] level up to the main floor at each end of the great room, divid-
ing them from the centre hall by double screens of arches
which continue the superimposed arcades around all four
sides. These arcades also appear in the middle seven bays of
the exterior; thus the hall is reduced from 106 feet to 57 feet in
length, and the whole centre of the range is based on one
simple arch motif. The most interesting features of the interior
[35] are the pedimented doorcases with downward tapering pilasters at the top of the staircases; these are, as was first pointed
out by Rudolf Wittkower over forty years ago, based by way of
an engraving on those designed by Michelangelo for the side
palaces of the Capitol in Rome. Vanbrugh's exploration of the
Italian *Cinquecento* was no more bound by the protocols of
contemporary taste than anything else he did.

Vanbrugh's respect for Palladio and his sense of scenery
came together most remarkably in the last of his designs to be
carried out, the Temple (which Hawksmoor called the Belvedere) at Castle Howard, begun the year before his death. But
we must arrive there, as Vanbrugh did, by way of 'a good
agreeable Expedition' though other pleasant parks and gardens.

The architect's comment of 1721 on the beauties of the Henderskelfe estate reflects more than two decades of journeying
almost every year to Yorkshire. Over the years these trips became as much vacations as professional visits, and in the company of his patron Vanbrugh must have crossed and re-crossed
the fields and plantations of Henderskelfe until they both knew
every fold and ridge and clump of trees from many different
aspects. As we have seen, Lord Carlisle and his daughter Lady
Irwin wrote as if the landscape of Castle Howard was the Earl's
own invention and not that of a professional gardener, but that
cannot be an accurate statement of the case. And although it
was probably Carlisle's idea to move Henderskelfe village it
was almost certainly Vanbrugh's to turn the house to face
north and south and extend sideways along the ridge.*

Very early in his explorations Vanbrugh must have looked at
George London's designs and decided that, as with so many

* p. 210

other activities, he could do that sort of thing too. In June 1703 Sir Godfrey Copley, whose new mansion at Sprotborough near Doncaster had recently been completed, wrote to Thomas Kirk of Arthington near Leeds:

> I pray give my Service to All at *Arthington* and to Mr *Dyneley*. I am glad the Canalls & Ponds go on so Well, but I am told great Lakes are now the mode. *Vanbrook* set out one for the D: of *Newcastle* to front his new house of 40 acres.

Nothing came of either house or garden at Welbeck, and although Vanbrugh had quickly developed an eye for what he might have called the 'Figure and Proportions' of gardens, the professional niceties of their design remained an area which in practice he usually left in other hands: those of London and Switzer at Castle Howard, of Henry Wise at Blenheim, and of Charles Bridgeman at Claremont, Eastbury, and Stowe. However, if King George I had shown the same enthusiasm for the gardens of Kensington and Hampton Court that he devoted to those of Herrenhausen, Vanbrugh as a gardener would have been quite a different story. For on 15 June 1715 he was appointed Surveyor of Gardens and Waters, 'a place (your Lordship knows)', Hawksmoor told Carlisle eleven years later, 'was made for Sr John V--'; and indeed Carlisle did know, for in his second term of office as Lord Treasurer he was not only party to the appointment but most probably the instrument or even the instigator of its making.

His instructions (preserved in a book of Works patents) were to make draughts and designs, with estimates, for all new works or alterations; to oversee the care of pleasure gardens, kitchen and fruit gardens, and of rivers, conduits, pipes and hydraulic engines. Estate records were probably inadequate or out of date, for he was also to survey the royal gardens with an indication of their contents and their acreage; in September 1715 he wrote to tell the Treasury that he had not yet had time to perform this complicated task. Later correspondence concerns, among other matters, the hopeless state in 1717 of the pumping engine installed at Windsor many years earlier by Sir Samuel Morland; as a result a new engine was commissioned from Robert Aldersea (who had built the one under the Bridge at Blenheim)* and Vanbrugh probably designed for it the new pump house that survives near the tow-path at Windsor.

U   Kensington Water Tower, from an illustration in the *Gentleman's Magazine*.

It was in this capacity too that Vanbrugh designed the water tower on Kensington Palace Green, for which an estimate was **[U]**   made in 1716, and which William Stukeley drew in 1722. This brick building resembled one half of the Claremont Belvedere. It housed a horse-wheel which raised water from wells on the green to a huge cistern above; the tower was demolished about 1850 after the construction of a sewer nearby had unexpectedly drained almost all the wells.

At Stowe, for Lord Cobham, Vanbrugh designed several garden buildings; he also proposed alterations to the late-

* p. 350

seventeenth-century house and probably designed the existing north portico. In June 1719 he found Cobham 'much
entertain'd with (besides his Wife) the Improvements of his
House and Gardens, in which he Spends all he has to Spare'.
The Account Book records further visits in September 1722,
October 1723, October-November 1724, and July 1725 when, as
a letter tells, the Vanbrughs took Lord Carlisle and his daughters on a tour from London, by way of Lord Portland's (Bul-
strode), Colonel Tyrrell's (Shotover), Oxford (two nights in a
Whig inn), Woodstock and Rousham. The Carlisles stayed four
nights at Stowe before turning north for home, and the Vanbrughs spent a further fortnight there.

Cobham was an old Kit-Cat friend, and Vanbrugh's description of the visit in a letter to Tonson is full of nostalgia for 'the
first Supper in the Kitchen at Barns' and other Kit-Cat memories:

> You may believe me, when I tell you, you were often talk'd of
> both during the Journey, and at Stowe; and our former Kit Cat
> days, were remembered with pleasure. We were one night reck-
> oning who was left, and both Lord Carlisle & Cobham exprest a
> great desire of having one meeting next Winter, if you come to
> Towne, Not as a Club, but old Friends that have been of a Club,
> and the best Club, that ever met.

Vanbrugh also found Stowe 'a Place now, so Agreeable, that I
had much ado to leave it at all'. Yet the number and length of
his visits there suggest that they combined pleasure with business. Lord Perceval went there in 1724 and wrote categorically
that 'Bridgeman laid out the ground and plann'd the whole,
which cannot fail of recommending him to business'. But the
garden layout which Bridgeman had very largely carried out in
the previous five years seems to have been conceived around,
and to be seen from, the Rotondo, an open circular temple **[V]**
designed by Vanbrugh with a hemispherical dome which was
later reduced in profile. All Vanbrugh's buildings at Stowe
have been either demolished or altered, and Cobham continued to alter and extend the gardens for years to come. Vanbrugh and Cobham discussed the setting of Castle Howard as
they must have discussed Stowe; Bridgeman's work must have

V   Stowe. The Rotondo before the dome was lowered, from an illustration in the *Stowe Guide*.

been subject to the controlling opinion of both of them; nevertheless Stowe is now so overlaid with successive ideas and
meanings that Vanbrugh's *persona* is difficult to identify there.

Castle Howard and its surroundings are out of the ordinary
in many respects. One of their unusual, though not unique,
features is the large scale of the park and the outworks. It is
half a mile from the house to the Pyramid or the Temple,
almost a mile to Hawksmoor's Mausoleum or from his
Carrmire Gate on the approach road to the great obelisk. The
curtain wall punctuated by towers, for which Vanbrugh drew
inspiration from the ancient walls of Chester,* runs for nearly a
mile across the park. Another remarkable feature, especially
for us today, is the extent to which the life of the estate has remained constant over two and a half centuries. The great
formal parterre garden on the south front has been replaced by
a more modest arrangement of lawns, walks, and hedges, and
modern tourism and the private automobile have brought

* p. 382

more and diverser visitors than came in the eighteenth century; but the farming and forestry which Carlisle developed on the estate as not only a source of income but also a moral duty still continue, even around and between the outworks designed for him by his architects. And in 1985 Lord Howard of Henderskelfe, who did so much in forty years to conserve and restore Castle Howard, was laid to rest with his forebears in one of the *loculi* in the crypt of the Mausoleum.

Castle Howard is perhaps unique in the calibre of its architects and the constancy of their patron's support. And finally there is surely no other landscape north of the Alps in which the traveller has the same feeling of being watched by the spirits of the past; for this feeling is due less to the historical associations of the buildings (Lady Irwin identified the Obelisk, Temple, Mausoleum, and Pyramid with the *'Grecian, Roman* and *Egyptian* Form') than to the gently rolling terrain which, as one moves about, gives these and other structures the effect of suddenly disappearing and reappearing in the pattern of little hills on which most of them are placed.

Many observers have noted felicitous alignments between one feature and another; their significance is neither geometrical nor symbolic but even more fundamental. They are in the right place for their setting to suggest that they grew naturally from it and indeed that they have always been there. As with certain places in Greece or the Roman Campagna, it would be the most natural surprise to meet a group of nymphs and satyrs or, as Lady Irwin's poem implies, Diana herself coming from the wood.

Yet almost every feature except the hills themselves was constructed for Lord Carlisle. The straight approach road 'over hill, over dale' from Welburn and York suggests that the Roman legions came that way, but it did not yet exist when London made his layout plans and its origin lies rather in the straight rides of forestry. The gently curving but level grass walk from the house to the Temple preserves the line of the old [F] street village of Henderskelfe. Lord Oxford's chaplain commented on 1 May 1725 that the village had not been moved but dispersed: 'the Present Ld has scatter'd the farm-houses into other places, & clear'd all for the Park'. Vanbrugh was certainly aware of the lie of the land: in 1721-2 the correspondence reveals a project to people the gardens with a varied collection of obelisks, and he commented:

> I don't apprehend any thing amiss, from the Obelisks falling gradually with the ground from North to South as long as those which are on the Same line from East to West stand on the Same Levell; The Case being no more than in a regular plantation up a Hill, where nothing more is endeavour'd or wish'd, than that the Trees may grow of a pretty equal height in regard to one another; but not that the Tops of them shou'd be of one dead level; nor wou'd they be half so beautifull if they cou'd be so, their rising one above another having a much better effect; and so it is in the View of Townes which ly on the Side of Hills, as Constantinople and (in a good degree) London doe, by which means the Towers Steeples and other Eminent Buildings, produce a much finer effect, than if they stood all upon one natural flat; So that I think your Lordship need be in no manner of pain, upon your Obelisks appearing from the farthest parts of the Garden, one above another, tho' they really are of equal height.

The most artificially 'natural' feature of all was Wray Wood immediately north-east of the house, walled and bastioned on the west and north, and created by Stephen Switzer from a forest plantation of beeches. Lord Oxford's chaplain indeed noted, adjacent to Wray Wood and the house, 'a small plantation of young obelisks . . . which are in number four. & have a fluted pillar in their centre'. In the wood he saw 'some waterworks . . . but there seems too great a poverty of that Element to make any thing fine of that kind: But the *close walks*, when it is dryer & warmer than it was at our passing through them, must be very Pleasant & Delightfull'. Wray Wood survives today only as an overgrowth of trees and bushes which Nature has taken back to herself, but originally it was a magical place, a 'paradise' in Lady Irwin's word, with winding paths or 'meander walks' leading to fountains, statues, a little open temple of Venus and a gilt sculpted flame that recalled the magic spring of Dodona at Epirus whose waters ignited torches. And at the south-east corner of Wray Wood Lord Carlisle chose to build the Temple.

'I know Sr J Vanbrugh is for a Temple of smooth freestone', **[38]** wrote Hawksmoor to Carlisle on 7 January 1724, 'with a portico each way, and Dom'd over the centre, & it woud indoubtedly be beyond all objection, but as yr Lordship desired a drafft of one, made of the common Wall stone, I have done this accordingly.' A week later Carlisle wrote to Vanbrugh, who was forced by an unspecified illness to celebrate his sixtieth birthday in bed at Whitehall, and was not well enough to reply, 'out of Bed but not downe Stairs', until 11 February. Carlisle thought that a rough stone building would be cheaper, but Vanbrugh estimated that 'the first Design I sent, with the 4 Porticos will be found very near (perhaps quite) as cheap, as any Gothick Tower, that has yet been thought of'. In open, if friendly, competition with his old partner, Vanbrugh added that Lord Morpeth, the Earl's eldest son and heir, had already 'declared his thoughts utterly against anything but an Italian Building in that Place, and entirely approv'd the first Design'.

A week later, 'in a Condition at home, to do some of my Sort of business', Vanbrugh was 'very glad to find your Lordship at last incline to the Temple with the four Porticos'. He also pointed out

> That since the Situation requires it shou'd be open to look out every way, were there no Porticos, the Sun wou'd Strike in so full, as to make it quite dissagreable, whereas these Porticos will keep the Sun almost always out of it, and yet leave it quite light of the most pleasing kind. And for the Porticos themselves nothing can be more agreeable than the Seats under them. As to husbanding the Stone by Rusticks, I do not think they wou'd by any means do in this Case the whole turn of the Design being of the more delicate kind; but another expedient will husband the Stone, better than Rusticks, and be but what ought to be in this Design, and that is to flute the Pillars, which do's so much disguise the joints, that one may use almost what Stones one will.

By 11 April the drawings were almost ready to post, but Vanbrugh had

> some doubts about the Name of Belvedere, which is generally given to some high Tower; and such a thing will certainly be right to have some time and in Some Place, tho' I can't say I do at present think of one about the Seat, where the View is better

than this, But this Building I fancy wou'd more naturally take the Name of Temple which the Situation likewise is very proper for.

[6] The correspondence then turned to other matters, in particular to the north forecourt and gateway, work on which actually began, as crop-marks revealed from the air in the dry summer of 1976. But Vanbrugh was more concerned with the unbuilt west wing of the house. In November 1724 he wrote

> As much as I love a Gateway, and by consequence Shou'd be glad to See one up at Castle Howard; I must own, I think the Wing of so much more weight to the Credit of the house, both in regard to the outside and the in, that as far as my Wishes or Opinion may go in the determination, I give them clearly for the Wing. Nay, tho the consequences shou'd be such as to occasion the finishing the Wall in the front of the Court, where the Gate is design'd in such a manner as may leave it doubtfull, whether a Gate need hereafter be made or no. And Such a Design I have to offer.
>
> I don't yet find Mr Etty wants any farther Instructions for advancing with the Wing, than the Designs he has; if he thinks he do's, and will send his Querys they shall be answer'd.

Vanbrugh's concern was justified, for in the 1750s the fourth Earl commissioned his brother-in-law Sir Thomas Robinson to complete the west side to his own design. In December 1725 Vanbrugh was even 'sorry to find by a letter yesterday from Mr Etty, your Ldp is going on in the Temple instead of the West Wing'; nevertheless in his last letter (8 March 1726) he was glad to learn that Etty 'is so far prepared towards the Temple'.

Three weeks later Vanbrugh was dead, and it was left to Hawksmoor and Etty to carry out his design, faithfully except for 'a small alteration in the cap' which Hawksmoor proposed in August; the masonry was finished in 1727-8, with unfluted columns. The interior decoration, however, was delayed another ten years; its fine plasterwork, executed and perhaps designed by Francesco Vassali, complements Vanbrugh's conception but is not part of it. Lady Oxford's companion noted in 1745 'the floor not finish'd but is to be Inlaid'.

One of Hawksmoor's sketches for the Belvedere has the four corners marked *Books, Chimny, Drains and A bot wine*; his other annotations overlay with Classical learning, but do not contradict, the basic function of the building as a summer house for reading, refreshment and contemplation. But as Fiske Kimball was the first to observe, the description of an earlier building by its architect is singularly appropriate:

> The site is as pleasant and as delightful as can be found; because it is upon a small hill, of very easy access . . . it enjoys to every part the most beautiful views, some of which are limited, some more extended, and others that terminate with the horizon; there are loggia's made in all the four fronts . . . In the extremity of the pedestals, that form a support to the stairs of the loggia's, there are statues.

The description in Palladio's Second Book of his suburban Villa Almerigo or Rotonda, outside Vicenza, was as familiar to Vanbrugh as it was to Lord Burlington, who began to build his villa at Chiswick the same year (1725), or to Campbell who began Mereworth a couple of years earlier. Those buildings, like the now destroyed Foots Cray and Nuthall Temple, were self-consciously sophisticated rural villas based on Palladio's formula of a square plan with a central round or octagonal domed hall and porticoes on each side.

But alone among Palladio's imitators it was Vanbrugh, who had never seen the original, who understood and reproduced the Rotonda's hillside position and its occasional function – for it was not intended for daily habitation. Vanbrugh alone produced a design of complete symmetry with all four porticoes rather than one or two. Moreover, its geometry is simpler and clearer, the building being not only square in plan but a cube in shape. And for all its relative plainness, its elegance seems to reconcile those components of a design that he had earlier separated and contrasted, the figure and proportions and the delicacy of the ornaments.

Hawksmoor had written of this design in 1724:

> What Sr John proposes is very well, and founded upon the Rules of the Ancients I mean upon Strong Reason and good Fancy, Joyn'd with experience and tryalls, so that we are assured of the good effect of it, and thats what we mean by following the Antients, if we contrive or invent otherways, we doe but dress things

in Masquerade which only pleases the Idle part of mankind, for a Short Time.

Hawksmoor's prescription of reason, intuition, and empirical testing was the one which he believed to underlie the architecture of Antiquity and therefore of all good architecture. In offering his own project for a different kind of building, he was careful not to deny his colleague's design its due praise. He was quite right. It is the best garden temple in England, and the closest to the Classical spirit. And here again Vanbrugh took a current idea, that of selective architectural plagiarism, and showed that he could do it better than others.

— 34 —

Between Jest and Earnest

The carriage accidents in *A Journey to London* were not exaggerated. Many London streets were too narrow to accommodate hauliers' carts with comfort, and even those of the cobbled surfaces that were in good repair were hardly adequate for the weight or the amount of traffic that used them. The results were ruts and potholes, arguments, scrapes and collisions, and a carriage could be overturned even at moderate speed as a result of entering a deep rut. John Barker wrote from the City to Lord Fermanagh in June 1716:

> The Streets are so very bad in London especially about Stocks Markett, and just before our doore, that we have severall Coaches overturned every day, and severall full of ladies! by which means we have an opportunity of helping them out and seeing the Coulour their stockings are of.

None of the safety regulations developed during a century of life with the internal combustion engine had even been imagined in an age when the term *horse-power* was precisely literal.

The numbers of hired and private coaches, hackney carriages, carts, and wagons led to constant congestion and traffic jams, and a collision even in a major street could lead to an entanglement of axles and horses that was difficult to clear; the effects were quickly felt over a large area. There was no rule of the road, and a pedestrian who made an unconsidered step backwards could fall fatally under the wheels of a wagon or a carriage, or equally seriously could be run over by a sedan chair and its carriers; these conveyances, which became very fashionable in the reign of Queen Anne, moved at a trot and had no effective braking system. Moreover, even a minor tumble was a messy experience, for the streets were full of rubbish and filth of every imaginable kind; in many places this provided the top surface of the street and thus also made the ruts and holes beneath impossible to anticipate.

Vanbrugh himself had a more serious response to the problems, namely the invention, before its time, of the road fund licence tax for vehicles. The *London Journal* of 11 March 1723 reported that

> Sir John Vanbrugh, in his Scheme for new Paving the Cities of London and Westminster, amongst other Things, proposes a Tax on all Gentlemens Coaches; to stop all the channels in the Streets, and to Carry all the Water off by Dreins and Common Sewers under Ground.

Almost a year later (11 February 1724) he wrote to Lord Carlisle that his Lordship's son and heir had agreed to help:

> I am glad I can acquaint your Ldship, that we have prevail'd with my Lord Morpeth, to take under his Conduct the Bill for Reforming the Streets. I finding at last that Mr Walpole was come to think a little Seriously of the matter, as a thing quite fit for the Governmt: to take some care of, concluded, if he engag'd any body of Note to take the Chair He wou'd certainly take care he shou'd be Supported in it; So my Ld Morpeth being nam'd by Mr Frankland and others and Mr Walpole saying nobody wou'd be better, I ask't him whether he wou'd be so good, to Speak to him himself, he said with all his heart . . . He at last resolv'd to take all the pains he can, to carry so good a Publick Work thorough.

On 26 March, however, he wrote:

> My Lord Morpeth is often low Spirited about this Paving Bill; and often much Inclin'd to give it up, till another Sessions, thinking the Great Men don't appear in it, as he expected they

wou'd. But for my part, I see no rubs or delays, more than what I reckoned upon, from the natural Course of everything moving in Parliamt: thats worth having ... But I think nothing is to be carryed of this kind but by Resolution and Pushing on with Vigour ... And tho' there Shou'd not be time to get it through this Sessions, I shall be glad to have it lodged in the House, that People may know what it is; and by Consequence that it is not liable to the reflections of a Pack of Rogues without doors, cast upon it in order to Stir up the People to come with Clamorous Petitions against it; For this Bill is quite a fair thing, without the least trace of a Bubble or jobb of any kind; and so may bear the light.

But although Lord Morpeth was expected to move a second reading in the House of Lords in mid April the bill seems to have come to nothing. Opposition stemmed not only from inertia and an antipathy to new taxes but also from fatalism, since it was a common view that the constant excavation of the streets by the water companies to lay or more often to repair their pipes prevented any real and lasting improvement in the carriageways. Vanbrugh was still trying to raise support shortly before his death, for the Account Book records on 9 March 1726 a payment of two guineas 'for Carrying about the Paving Petition'.

This was not the first instance of Vanbrugh's concern for public amenity. Many years earlier he had appeared before a House of Lords Committee discussing the 1709 London Building Act 'for the better prevention of mischiefs that may happen by fire'. One clause prohibited the use of timber foundations for front, party or partition walls, with the exception of piles and plank bases in marshy and unsound ground; this was a precaution against not only fire but also 'constant decay and ruin'. On 13 September 1709 Vanbrugh gave evidence that the difference between wood and stone was no more than five shillings for a house.

Vanbrugh may also have had some influence on the next clause in the Act, which required all doors and windows to be set back at least four inches from the wall surface; although the main purpose was the prevention of fire the specific intention here was protection from the weather and thus from rot. Certainly he must have shared the strong views on this matter

which Hawksmoor expressed in a letter to the Fellows of All
Souls, Oxford in 1715 – a letter in which he also roundly condemned the London speculative builders of the day. He gave
examples in Oxford of 'the Scandalous Effect that Chass [sash]
windows have, by putting them flush (as Workmen call it) to
the outside of the Wall'. He attributed this practice to the widespread but mistaken belief that this 'gains more Light, than
when it Receds'. For since the glass is transparent it passes the
same amount of light 'no matter in what part of the Wall you
place it'; moreover there were both practical and aesthetic
advantages:

> The more the Chasse frame of wood, and Chass stands from the
> out face of the Wall, it is the better. because the Wooden Worke
> is defended from the rain and more Strongly fix'd, besides the
> beauty it gives the Overture by receding.

A Parliamentary committee would expect to draw on the
expert opinion of the Queen's servants before that of private
individuals, and the obvious person to testify on such points
would be her Surveyor, Sir Christopher Wren, whose advice
had contributed so much to the earlier London Building Acts
passed after the Great Fire. The fact that Vanbrugh was called
suggests not only the extent of his friendships within the House
of Lords but also the seriousness of his interest in the practical
and social aspects of architecture. One of the undercurrents of
this book has been the seriousness of a character more often
considered a joker than a thinker, an epicurean rather than a
stoic. And of course he was both. *The Relapse* and *The Provok'd
Wife* are still played because they make an audience laugh –
which is still the business of comedy.

Nevertheless a good deal of the critical attention these plays
have received in the twentieth century has focused on the serious social and moral issues they raise with such apparent lack
of effort; ironically such criticism has tended both to under-
value Vanbrugh's skill as a writer and dramatist and to blame
him for not being a whole-hearted preacher as Steele became
in *The Conscious Lovers*. Of course Vanbrugh laughed, sometimes uncontrollably, and he saw the incongruities of life as
readily and as broadly as anyone; but, just as there is an un-

spoken sense of tragedy in every clown's act, so his sense of humour was based on the unspoken seriousness of the human condition. He was after all bred to be serious and to use to the full the talents God had given him; his character was also hardened and tempered by the experience of captivity for almost half of his twenties – a captivity that was not only undeserved but also the more painful because there was no set or ascertainable term to it.

Vanbrugh was not a spy. At the age of twenty-four he was still too naïve, and there is no reason whatever to suppose, either, that he was the unwitting tool of someone else who was. Lord Nottingham's papers show conclusively that his misfortune in France was that he was of no interest whatever. He told his mother, in the letter smuggled from Vincennes, that 'du Livier finds he had not well inform'd himself of me nor my friends, but this he dares not owne'. And in September 1692, when things were at last beginning to move, Nottingham told Blathwayt that there was *no colour for such hardship* towards Vanbrugh and his companions, whereas Forvall might *justly be hanged and would at any time redeem any man who might be sent to France upon the like account.* Indeed, he went on, it might be *dangerous to those gentlemen to offer Forvall in exchange*, since *it might give a fair praetext to France to treat them as spyes, tho' hitherto there be no ground for the suspicion* [author's italics].* And it was personal influence, not a reward for secret services, that gained Vanbrugh the site for his Whitehall house. There was an element of bravado in that project, and for that reason perhaps it qualifies for that phrase of which he was rather fond, *between jest and earnest.*

Lincoln B. Faller used this phrase some years ago as the title of a perceptive essay on Vanbrugh's comedy, remarking that

> his delight in Foppington's ripe folly is mellowed with a certain sympathy, and his pleasure in Brute is tainted with disgust. In the case of Sir John especially Vanbrugh displays a sensibility exceptional among the comic writers of his age. Perhaps this is so because he very nearly is not a comic writer, or to put it differently, his plays are comedies by default. How else are we to

* p. 74

respond to Sir John, we might ask, how else can we respond to
him, but with laughter? To suggest that Vanbrugh in some mar-
velous way foreshadows the modern sensibility would be fat-
uous; still, to an audience acquainted with 'black' comedy, the
darkness that penumbrates jolly Sir John should not seem unfamiliar.

The indignities to which Lord Foppington and Lady Brute are
subjected are indeed laughable, yet 'beyond such farce there is
often something to complicate and contain, even to embarrass
our laughter.'

Faller also points to some of Vanbrugh's remarks on Loveless and Amanda in his *Vindication* which are usually overlooked by commentators, perhaps 'because they seem such
blatant concessions to Jeremy Collier's attack'. They seem,
Collier or no, devoid of the levity which informs much of the
Vindication; one has already been quoted.* And referring to
Berinthia, Vanbrugh says:

> When Fate (here's Blasphemy again) so disposes things, that the
> Temptation's brought home to his Door, and his Wife has the
> misfortune to invite it into her House ... This I design'd for a
> natural Instance of the Frailty of Mankind, even in his most fixt
> Determinations; and for a mark upon the defect of the most
> steady Resolve, without that necessary Guard, of keeping out of
> Temptation. But I had still a farther end in *Loveless's Relapse*,
> and indeed much the same with that in *The Provok'd Wife*,
> though in different kind of Characters ... There the Provoca-
> tion is from a *Brute*, and by consequence cannot be suppos'd to
> sting a Woman so much, as if it had come from a more Reason-
> able Creature ...
>
> But in the Adventures of *Loveless* and *Amanda*, the Caution is
> carri'd farther. Here's a Woman whose Virtue is rais'd upon the
> utmost Strength of Foundation: Religion, Modesty, and Love, de-
> fend it. It looks so Sacred, one wou'd think no Mortal durst app-
> roach it; and seems so fix'd, one wou'd believe no Engine cou'd
> shake it: Yet loosen one Stone, the weather works in, and the
> Structure molders apace to decay.

There is relevance here also, though Collier would as usual

* p. 120

have missed the point, in a general observation of T.S. Eliot's about Restoration drama. Asking what was the moral attitude of Dryden's *The Kind Keeper*,* he answered:

> Impeccable. The morality of our Restoration drama cannot be impugned. It assumes orthodox Christian morality, and laughs (in its comedy) at human nature for not living up to it. It retains its respect for the divine by showing the failure of the human. The attitude of Restoration drama towards morality is like the attitude of the Blasphemer towards Religion. It is only the irreligious who are shocked by blasphemy. Blasphemy is a sign of Faith. Imagine Mr Shaw blaspheming! He could not. Our Restoration drama is all virtue. It depends upon virtue for its existence. The author of *The Queen was in the Parlour* does not depend upon virtue.

Faller also prompts the question how many of us remember that the middle of *The Provok'd Wife* contains a vicious and senseless – if off-stage – murder. It occurs at the beginning of Act IV, and in the excitement of a change of scene (to Covent Garden) and of persons, the audience may miss the significance of the brief event, especially if it is hurried or underplayed. But it is there:

> *Enter Lord Rake, Sir* John, *&c.* with *Swords drawn.*

> *Lord Rake.* Is the Dog dead?
> *Col. Bully.* No, damn him, I heard him wheeze.
> *Rake.* How the Witch his Wife howl'd!
> *Bully.* Ay. She'll alarm the Watch presently.
> *Rake.* Appear, Knight, then; come, you have a good Cause to fight for, there's a Man murder'd
> *Sir John.* Is there? Then let his Ghost be satisfied: For I'll sacrifice a Constable to it presently; and burn his Body upon his wooden Chair.

The two scenes in which Sir John Brute assumes the disguise of the costume he steals from the tailor in Covent Garden (IV.i and iii) were the subject of a revision which has always – and

* p. 102

no doubt rightly – been accepted as Vanbrugh's own, although
the first printed text of the re-written version is a Dublin edition of 1743. Vanbrugh kept the opening lines quoted above,
but changed the habit from that of a clergyman to that of a lady
– and according to Sir John that of his own wife. It is supposed
that he made the alteration in response to Collier's objections
to what he saw as an attack upon the Cloth; this may indeed be
the case, but the revision very probably dates from the last
months of Vanbrugh's life. *The Provok'd Wife* was advertised
with alterations in 1706, 1715 and on 11 January 1726, but only
the last production was billed as 'Revis'd by the Author', and
Cibber's dating of the changes to 1725 (which lasted until 25
March 1726 in the Old Style calendar) confirms this conclusion.

In fact the introduction of the travesty part and Sir John's satirical account of the life of a fashionable lady enrich the
texture of the play, inviting the audience to compare the grotesque caricature not only with the real Lady Brute but also
with Lady Fancyfull. In Vanbrugh's own mind, moreover,
there was a further parallel with that other spoiled and wilful
society lady, Arabella Loverule in *A Journey to London.*

Vanbrugh never designed scenery for the stage, not only because his own settings were the conventional streets, gardens
and rooms of comedy which could be left to the experts or
made up from stock, but also because it would have been out of
character. For what had drawn him to the theatre was a concern with the real – real people and situations – and not the
illusory world of the vista stage; and what drew him to architecture was the possibility of making real buildings, not pictures or illusions of them. If perhaps he first entered either
writing or building in jest, he very soon found himself in
earnest.

Between jest and earnest is a phrase used by Vanbrugh himself on several occasions. It is implied in a letter to Joynes of
September 1711, after the Blenheim money had stopped:

As to the Tower on the Stable Wing, its a jest to Mention it. there
is not a Stone for it, nor is it a thing can be done in four months
time, the expence too I am sure will be near £2000.

Elsewhere it is stated in full. In *The Relapse* (IV.ii) Amanda and Berinthia, the two contenders for Loveless, engage in a discussion full of irony for the audience:

Am. Phu, will you never learn to talk in earnest of any thing?
Ber. Why this shall be in earnest, if you please; for my part, I only tell you matter of fact, you may take it which way you like best, but if you'll follow the Women of the Town, you'll take it both ways; for when a Man offers himself to one of them, first she takes him in jest, and then she takes him in earnest.
Am. I'm sure there's so much jest and earnest in what you say to me, I scarce know how to take it; but I think you have bewitched me, for I don't find it possible to be angry with you, say what you will.

In *The Provok'd Wife* (III.iii) when Lady Brute and Bellinda are plotting an assignation with Constant and Heartfree in Spring Garden, Lady Brute suggests making 'an Appointment 'twixt jest and earnest';* Vanbrugh himself uses the phrase in his *Vindication* against Collier, where he applies it to the discussion earlier in the same scene between aunt and niece about 'the Smuttiness of some Plays'. They 'let fall a Word between Jest and Earnest, as if now and then they found themselves cramp'd by their Modesty'.† But the best-known passage is in the letter of 25 October 1725 in which he told Lord Carlisle of his disposing in earnest of the Herald's place he had obtained in jest.**

What is less well known is the impression his sale of the post left not on Carlisle but on the other Heralds. A draft brief in the Earl Marshal's papers at Arundel Castle shows that Peter Le Neve and others tried to stop the grant of the post to the buyer, Knox Ward, of whom it was elsewhere claimed that he had 'no genius to Heraldry'. Ward was only twenty-two at the time; the money was provided by his father, a wealthy Hackney merchant whose own grant of a coat of arms is recorded in the Account Book in December 1722. Young Ward's main qualification was his ambition, which led him into strange places; in

* p. 150
† p. 169
** p. 241

1729 he married Elizabeth Nettleton, and was promptly sued
for breach of promise by a Miss Holt of Hackney. The case was
dismissed because the plea described him as *Esquire*; however, Miss Holt persisted, suing him successfully for £2000
three years later in his title of Clarenceux.

Vanbrugh had hoped either for the extension of his Comptrollership from an appointment 'at His Majesty's pleasure' to
one for life, or else for the licence of the Drury Lane Theatre;*
architecture at court was no longer a field for his talents. When
he died he left unfinished business at Castle Howard, Grimsthorpe, Eastbury, and Seaton Delaval, and there were no signs
that if he had been able to retire from regular employment on a
pension he would have given up architectural design. But patronage was uncertain. Lord Carlisle seems to have been constant to his architect, but his son Lord Morpeth and later his
son-in-law Sir Thomas Robinson were concerned with their
own taste. Vanbrugh worked for Newcastle at Claremont, at
Nottingham, and in Lincoln's Inn Fields, but he could no more
expect a monopoly than he could rely on the Duke to find a
place for his musical cousin: Newcastle employed glassmaker
Moore at Nottingham and he obtained designs, never executed, for a house from Galilei.†

Yet Vanbrugh's stoical side perhaps protected him from fret-
ting, as Hawksmoor fretted, over lost commissions and un-
realized dreams. In 1733 Hawksmoor was dismissed, at the
hands of the Palladian Thomas Ripley and Sir Robert Walpole,
from the care of Greenwich Hospital on which he had spent
such devoted effort over nearly forty years. In February 1736
he wrote, with this principally in mind: 'the World is determined to starve me, for my good services'. But earlier he had
also mourned the decay of a great vision:

> There is imperiall Mischief (as Alexander says in the play) don
> to Greenwich Hospitall since Sr John dy'd; and I need not say by
> who, yr Lordship knows it well enough; I once thought it wou'd
> have been a public Building but it will sink into a deformed
> Barrac.

* pp. 394-5
† p. 378

Indeed Vanbrugh was unsparing in his support and admiration for the man to whom, architecturally, he owed almost everything. More than once he wrote on Hawksmoor's behalf; in 1719 to Newcastle in the hope of 'his being restor'd to the Station Mr Benson turn'd him out of',* and again six years later to Carlisle when there were premature reports of Hewett's death. There is also a letter of 26 August 1721 that contains a passage often quoted but always worth quoting again, not only for what it tells us of the writer and the subject but also for its context. Three weeks earlier the carver Grinling Gibbons had died, and the appointment had just been reported of Ripley to succeed him as Master Mason to the Crown, one of the posts that Vanbrugh had persuaded Lord Halifax to abolish but which Benson had revived. As the protégé of Walpole, Ripley would succeed Hewett as Surveyor in 1726, and it was his appointment as Surveyor to Greenwich Hospital three years later that led to Hawksmoor's dismissal first as Assistant Surveyor at Greenwich and in 1733 even as Clerk of the Works. Vanbrugh wrote in 1721 from Yorkshire to Brigadier General William Watkins, who as Keeper of the King's Private Roads had sat since 1717 on the Board of Works; after recounting his doings in the North, he went on:

Here are Several Gentlemen ... that are possess'd with the Spirit of Building. And Seem dispos'd to do it, in so good a Manner, that were they to establish here a sort of a Board of Works to conduct their Affairs, I do verily believe, they wou'd sooner make Hawksmr: a Comissioner of it, than that Excellent Architect, Ripley. When I met with his Name, (and Esquire to it) in the News paper; Such a Laugh came upon me, I had like to have Beshit my Self. Poor Hawksmoor, What a Barbarous Age, have his fine, ingenious Parts fallen into. What wou'd Monsr: Colbert of France have given for Such a Man? I don't Speak as to his Architecture alone, but the Aids he cou'd have given him, in almost all his brave Designs for the Police. A thing I never expect to hear talk'd of in England, Where the Parts of most of the Great men I have Seen or read of, have rarely turn'd to any farther Account, Than getting a Great Deal of Money, and turning it through their Guts into a House of Office, And now I think of

* p. 393

eating Pray do me the favour to get a Warrant from his Grace, for an other Buck instead of that he sent for a Stag, for I find that will be of no use to me here. the Buck I have had, and very good. The sooner you can Send me this, the more you will Oblige, Yours Dear Brigadr:

J Vanbrugh

Jean-Baptist Colbert (1619-83) was Louis XIV's finance minister and the archetype of the loyal, altruistic, and incorruptible servant of the state. Vanbrugh abhorred the absolute power of the French monarchy, believing that it made subjects into slaves; nevertheless the brave designs for the Police (the management of the state) were Colbert's, and Vanbrugh's admiration embraced equally Hawksmoor's practical wisdom and Colbert's skill as an administrator. To adapt a phrase of Shaftesbury's,* we should scarcely see another Hampton Court treated like a Versailles, or the great chapel and oval forecourt dreamed up by Hawksmoor for Greenwich Hospital treated like St Peter's and its piazza, because only a pope or a Bourbon, not a democracy modelled on the Athenian or Roman republics, could command the resolution and the finances necessary to their realization. In this light the unfinished Blenheim was a monument not to the whims of monarchy but to the indecisions of democracy.

Vanbrugh did not, and could not, supply the national style that Shaftesbury had desired, and to which, for a time, Hewett and his friends also hoped, through Galilei, to offer an Italianate alternative. Nevertheless he himself may well have believed that *he could have done so*. The essential difference for him between Versailles or St Peter's and Greenwich or Blenheim was that the latter were the work of free men; it was ultimately a political difference, not a stylistic one. His remark about Colbert implies that he believed such a man would have been good for Britain, provided of course that he had a Hawksmoor — and without doubt a Vanbrugh too — at his side. Their style was in his eyes perfectly acceptable for the Whig Britain described by Shaftesbury, and if they had been in control of the

* p. 403

Office of Works Vanbrugh would, surely, have defended himself ably against the sort of charges of absolutism that Shaftesbury had made against Wren.

The clever publicity of Campbell in *Vitruvius Britannicus* and the piracy of the Office of Works by himself, the Bensons, Hewett, and others, ensured that Vanbrugh's belief was never put to the test. The term 'Vanbrugh school' is thus a misnomer. His influence can be seen in the work of William Wakefield, notably at Duncombe Park, Yorks. (some of whose Vanbrugian features are due to Sir Charles Barry), and probably the Debtors' Prison in York (now part of the Castle Museum), as well as in some of the houses of Francis Smith of Warwick. The Blenheim correspondence suggests that Henry Joynes was closer to Hawksmoor and learned more from him than from Vanbrugh. But none of these can be considered his pupils, and although Edward Lovett Pearce probably worked with him for a time in the early 1720s* – some of the drawings at Elton Hall are difficult to apportion between the two of them – Pearce's own buildings are polished examples of Palladianism. Town houses such as Vanbrugh House in St Michael's Street, Oxford (probably designed by the Oxford mason Bartholomew Peisley) and Hope House, Woodstock, show that local builders had an eye for the style of Blenheim.

Designs for houses by Vanbrugh were also copied and collected in the early 1720s. An album of drawings formerly at Kings Weston, bought in 1973 by the Bristol Civic Trust, contains about a dozen designs – plans and elevations – for small houses which clearly belong to the same architectural family as the Nunnery and the White Towers at Greenwich, as well as some of the Vanbrugh drawings at Elton and in the Victoria and Albert Museum. But none of those in the Kings Weston album is in Vanbrugh's own hand, and neither the draughtsman nor the compiler of the album has been convincingly identified.

The largest group of Vanbrugian buildings, both in number and in individual size, is of those constructed for the Board of Ordnance in the period of unusually great expenditure immediately following the Jacobite rising of 1715. They include

* p. 443

the new Barracks at Berwick-on-Tweed (begun 1717), the Ordnance Board Room, Foundry and other buildings at Woolwich, the Gun Wharf at Devonport (of which the domestic and office terrace survives), the Great Storehouse at Chatham (begun 1718, demolished some years ago) and the main dockyard gateway there, which is a larger version of the gatehouse Vanbrugh built at the south-east corner of his Greenwich field.

No documentary evidence, however, has been found which would decide whether any of these buildings stem from Vanbrugh's authorship rather than his influence. However, the Ordnance was under the control of his friends. Marlborough was promptly reinstated as Master of Ordnance by George I, and one of his officers, Brigadier General Michael Richards (to whom the Duchess sent her tirade against Vanbrugh in 1716)* was appointed Surveyor-General of Ordnance and was nominally responsible for any new military architecture. When Andrews Jelfe, a stonemason and His Majesty's Clerk of Works at Newmarket since 1715, was appointed Architect and Clerk of Works to the Board in January 1719 most of the Vanbrugian buildings had already been designed; the exception is the Gun Wharf at Devonport, begun under Jelfe's supervision the following year. But another mason, Christopher Cass, had business connections with Jelfe, had worked at Blenheim under Edward Strong, and became Master Mason to the Ordnance. The missing link between all these figures would appear, although without proof, to be Vanbrugh.

From the historian's point of view the absence of any designer's name from the surviving records is all the more unsatisfactory when so much is known both about the Ordnance's administration and buildings and about Vanbrugh's activities in the period covered by the Account Book. The observable fact remains, however, that this group of buildings is quite distinct not only in kind but in architectural quality from the general run of Ordnance constructions during the first half of the eighteenth century; what they owe to Vanbrugh may be difficult to define but it is nevertheless substantial.

Although it was a private document, the Account Book of

* p. 369

course only tells us what Vanbrugh chose to record in it. It says
nothing about the death of his cousin William in November
1716 except that Sir John spent £1. 4s. 6d. on a journey to
Walton-on-Thames and paid the village baker a bill for 10s.
William died intestate at the age of fifty-eight, leaving a widow
named Elizabeth; Sir John, as the principal creditor, took over
William's house at Walton, and his ailing younger son was
nursed and died there in 1723.* 'Mr Vanbrugh, K[nigh]t' was
described as a resident of Walton in an episcopal visitation of
1724-5 and he spent two nights there in May 1725. The silence
suggests tragedy around William, but the nature of it cannot
even be guessed.

Nor does the Account Book refer to what seems to have been
the last isolated meeting of the Kit-Cat Club which according
to Steele (who missed posting a letter on account of it) took
place on 30 March 1717 with the Duke of Newcastle in the
chair. This may have been in the nature of a discreet stag party
for the Duke, who was married three days later. Did they perhaps regale themselves with Sir John's cup? Pope told Spence
that it consisted of

> Water or small beer; mead; port – two glasses each; rum, saffron
> – a very little of each; nutmeg, poker, orange or lemon-peel in
> winter; balm etc. in summer.

In July 1725 Vanbrugh and Lord Carlisle talked, on their visit to
Stowe,† of Tonson and former Kit-Cat days. As he told Tonson
on 12 August:

> We were one night reckoning who was left, and both Ld Carlisle
> & Cobham exprest a great desire of having one meeting next
> Winter, if you come to Towne, Not as a Club, but old Friends that
> have been of a Club, and the best Club, that ever met.

The club had served its purpose and, they must all have
agreed, served it well, with a Protestant on the throne and the
succession assured for two generations to come; in fact Van-

* pp. 440, 444
† p. 463

brugh never saw any of them again. The previous October he
[37] had for the last time watered his horse at Robin Hood's Well in
Skelbrooke, five miles north of Doncaster, where on 28 April
1725 Lord Oxford's chaplain noted that

> close by the road's side, is a Famous Spring, called, *Robin
> Hood's Well*, with a New Stone Building, that covers it over,
> raised at the Expence of the Earl of Carlisle, under the peculiar
> Direction of *Sr John Vanbrugh* . . . This Structure would make a
> cube of abt 8 foot, the Spring is 1 foot deep in the centre, its Dia-
> meter 16 inches, and a poor old man attends here constantly,
> and reaches it in a black pot with great Liberality to all Pas-
> sengers, and we accordingly tasted of his cup both to our own &
> his satisfaction.

The spring has long since disappeared, but Vanbrugh's well-
head still stands, not far from its original position, in a parking
area off the southbound carriageway of the Great North Road.

Vanbrugh saw little of Blenheim on that last summer excursion. Visiting Stowe in June 1719, he had taken 'Blenheim in
my way back, not with any affection, (for I am thoroughly
wean'd) but some curiosity, the Dutchess of Marlb: having
taken a Run at last to finish in earnest'; but that was before the
infamous lawsuit and the alleged libel. Six years later Lord
Carlisle thought it courteous and perhaps prudent to address
the Duchess thus:

> Designing to see Bleinheim in my Way to the North & Sr John
> Vanbrugh proposing to goe part of the way with me, I would not
> Take the liberty to carry him thither without first acquainting
> your Grace therewith & haveing your leave for the same.

So, as Vanbrugh afterwards told Tonson, when the party
arrived a few days later,

> There was an order to the Servants, under her Graces own hand,
> not to let me enter any where. And lest that shou'd not mortify
> me enough, She having some how learn'd, that my Wife was of
> the Company sent an Express the Night before we came there
> with orders, if she came with the Castle Howard Ladys, the Ser-

vants shou'd not Suffer her to see either House, Gardens, or even to enter the Park, which was obey'd accordingly, and She was forc'd to Sit all day and keep me Company at the Inn.

One of the Blenheim gardeners afterwards reported the whole incident to the Duchess, adding that on being refused admission to the park Vanbrugh had replied 'I thought so', had asked for Dr Cockes, the Rector, had been up the Stratford Road to Old Woodstock 'and there look'd over the wall to See the water, and I do believe he was in Dr Coxes Garden where he could See some of the other works'. If, as seems likely, the East Gate [17] and the windowless outer wall of the kitchen court embody a reminiscence of the curtain wall and north gateway of Vin- [14] cennes, the full force of the resemblance now came home to the architect. In reply to Lord Carlisle the Duchess wrote that she had acted not

upon the worthlessness of his character, nor for any abuses in the building occasioned by him, but in the life of the Duke of Marlborough he had the impudence to print a libel both of him and me for which his bones ought to have been broke ... besides this his behaviour was so saucy to me and of me, that one should wonder at any other person after such proceedings should desire to come within my walls.

The story spread, for a month later a correspondent wrote to Lord Oxford:

The Dutchess has given out a list of persons that may not see the house, among wm are two of her own daughters and Sir Jo Vanbrugh. It is very hard that these Ladys may not come to see their Mamma, and that the Dutchman may not visit his own Child, who, however he may appear a meer lump and mishapen to others, may seem beautifull in his eyes that begot him.

Lady Marlborough had alienated her own daughters, and for a time those of Lord Carlisle acted as substitutes for them, especially Elizabeth, wife of Mr (and from 4 September 1721 Baron) Lechmere. Two weeks after her husband's elevation to the peerage Lady Lechmere wrote to the Duchess:

I had a letter tother day from my sister Mary, who says Sr John
Vanbrugh, his Wife & Child, are at Castle Howard. I find all his
Works are large, for I hear his Child is the biggest that ever was
seen of its age; I think you may the easier forgive him, his Vast
designs at Bleinheim since it appears to be so much the tendency of his Nature.

Less than a year later the Duchess endorsed one of Elizabeth
Lechmere's fawning letters:

this leter La: Lechmere writt when I am sure she felt nothing for
me, for I have discovered her to bee very insincere but without
being false my self I design to let her deceive her self in thinking
that I don't see it & I will never say anything to her . . . for her
h[usban]d is the worst man that I ever knew in my life, & she will
allways bee a slave to him, & perhaps in some time bee made by
him as bad as himself.

But we have Vanbrugh's own comments on the Castle Howard
visit of 1721. 'Of the House I say nothing', he wrote to Newcastle in August, but the gardens

I may commend, because Nature made them; I pretend to no
more Merit in them than a Midwife, who helps to bring a fine
Child into the World, out of Bushes Boggs, and Bryars.

A few weeks later he wrote to an unknown recipient about the
therapeutic effect of little Charles, only eleven months old,
upon Lady Irwin, young, widowed and childless,* who was
sharing a floor of 'the office wing' with her unmarried sister
Mary and the Vanbrughs:

Our being there . . . proved of some small relief to her; for she
came at last not only to vent herself pretty much to my Wife but
to pass a great deal of her time with the Child whom she grew
mighty fond of, declaring she never felt any thing of the kind for
her Brothers Children or any other. And her Woman (who has
attended her from her Cradle; and enters deep into her Afflictions) said this was the first thing She had observ'd her take the

* p. 440

least pleasure in, since my Lords death. Lady Mary was as fond
of him as she; going twenty times a day into the nursery, and
Sitting an hour together by her self, at the Cradle foot, to see him
sleep; then carrying him about in her arms as long as she was
able, from whence he was handed from one to another round
the family of all Degrees, and a favourite every where, because
he never cry'd . . . Green[wic]h [Lady Irwin] likes better than
any other village, and before we came away begun to think in
earnest of building there So I shall send her some Designs, to
amuse her at least.

In June 1722, thanking Tonson for a gift of cider and telling of
his satisfaction in being 'two Boys Strong in the Nursery', he
teased him:

Have a Care of this retir'd Country Life we shall hear of some
Herefordshire Nymph, in your Solitary walks; bounce out upon
your heart, from Under an Apple Tree and make you one of us.

The last remaining bachelor replied:

You hint the danger of my heart being .rapt by a Bait from an
Aple Tree. The first *tete a tete* club was in Paradise, & the minute
the woman (tired with having the onely conversation of her, to
be sure, deare Spouse) took in a spruce Prig . . . & upon onely
saying Countryman, will you eat a pippen? We have been all – as
we are – The Club from *Tate a tate* was soon turnd to Corps au
Corps – and this if true is certainly a better excuse for a Herefordshire mistake than for some other Countrys . . . in the Ordinary sort, there is no Scruple of taking a liken as children say at
trapball without any notice taken otherways than the product be
noe charge to the Parish – and soe much for the Naturall History
of Herefordshire.

The following month when Vanbrugh was building the White
Tower in the field as 'Charles's House' he told Lord Carlisle of
the progress the Earl's godson, not yet two years old, was making in the study of architecture.* He went on:

* p. 346

He talks every thing, is much given to Rhyming, and has a Great turn to dry joking. What these Seeds may grow to, God knows. they being of a kind, that may do his business, uphill, or downe hill, so perhaps upon the whole, he were as well without them. They serve however to make himself and other people Sport at present. If my Lady Irwin ever has a House under the Cannon of this Castle, I shall be glad to see him some amusement to her.

Surely the games in the field were the father's rather than the son's, and the rhymes too and the dry jokes. The father was the life and soul of the little community on the hilltop, and it was when he died that the joy went from it.

The lad certainly inherited a good deal of his father's charm. He was brought up by his mother, and the occasional visits of his sailor uncles Charles and Philip, with their tales of adventure, will have made a great impression on him. By the time he was eight he was lodging, according to his mother's account book, with Mr Le Plas or Le Play, a tutor or private schoolmaster; at twelve he went away to a school run by a Mr Bourne. In his sixteenth year (February 1736) he entered the Temple; by then he had taken lessons in French and Italian and in dancing. But the idea of a business or legal training, which the Inns of Court provided for young gentlemen, soon lost its appeal and he went within a few months to Lausanne to learn to be a soldier. Early in 1740 he was back in England, and entertained Baron Bielfeld, showing him 'not only all the designs of his father, but also two houses of his building, one near Whitehall, and the other at Greenwich'. Bielfeld's judgement is uncomfortably close to the truth:

The son of this able artist inherits the genius of his father; but as it is opportunity that makes a man famous, I doubt whether the war [at that time with Spain] will enable him soon to acquire a name equally celebrated.

Charles became an ensign in the Coldstream Guards, and went to fight the French in the War of the Austrian Succession. At the battle of Fontenoy on 11 May 1745 he was wounded, and he died soon after midnight; his friend Joseph Yorke sent the news, in a noble and moving letter, not directly to Lady Vanbrugh but to Mr Jones, the same Jack Jones who had served his father. Charles was not yet twenty-five when he died; he was remembered by the men of his regiment for his friendship and his bravery, but in the histories he is only the son of a famous father. Had John Vanbrugh died in the Citadel of Calais at the same age, he would have left scarcely a ripple on the sands of time.

Vanbrugh was absorbed in his many interests until shortly before he died on 26 March 1726 of quinsy, an acute and fever-ish complication of tonsillitis. He was probably ill for about ten days, for his last entry in the Account Book was on the 15th. Lady Vanbrugh survived him by fifty years and one month, leading a life as private as her husband's had been public. The many rooms and outbuildings of Vanbrugh Castle did not suit her purse, nor perhaps her taste, and she moved very soon to Whitehall; in 1728 the Castle was let to the first of a succession of tenants, Viscount Tyrconnel.

Within a month of Sir John's death his widow also engaged a local joiner, William Pomeroy, to build for her use a small house, possibly based on one of her husband's designs. How-ever it was probably not the building in Vanbrugh Fields later known as Beechcroft and demolished about 1960, but one im-mediately south of it, later known as the Manor House; this was inhabited from 1743 onwards by John Moor, the gardener who had kept the Castle grounds, and it is mentioned in her will. The Greenwich rate books show that from 1743 to 1757 Lady Vanbrugh occupied the Nunnery when she was not at White-hall; from then until 1767 she lived in the northern White Tower, and from then until her death in the southern one. Her chief interests were friends, clothes, theatres, and her son; after his death she turned to religion, but after her account book stops in 1757 we know little about her. In October 1773 her nephew Edward Vanbrugh wrote from Bath of the shorten-ing days 'which to you, who pass so much of your time alone, must be tedious'. Two and a half years later she died at White-hall; on 3 May 1776 she was buried, as she directed, with her husband in the family vault in St Stephen Walbrook.

Pope and Tonson told Joseph Spence that 'Garth, Vanbrugh and Congreve were the three most honest-hearted, real good men of the poetical members of the Kit-Cat Club'. These quali-ties shine out from many of Vanbrugh's letters, which are today our closest links with the person behind the works. His own sense of history appears in his plea for the preservation of Woodstock Manor, in which he suggested future visitors would come there both for Henry II and for Marlborough.* The Manor is long since gone and almost forgotten, but many visitors now come to Vanbrugh's houses for him rather than for anyone else. And what he wrote of Blenheim and its hero may bear a more general application to its creator and all his works. Recognizing that his building would not always be to everyone's taste, Vanbrugh referred to those who,

tho' they may not find Art enough in the Builder, to make them Admire the Beauty of the Fabrick they will find Wonder enough in the Story, to make 'em pleas'd with the Sight of it.

* p. 347

Bibliography and References

Errors, like Straws, upon the Surface flow:
He who would search for Pearls must dive below.
Dryden, Prologue to All for Love.

This section is divided into two parts. The first is an alphabetical list, by author or keyword, of works and documentary sources mentioned in the text or cited in the second part and in the appendixes. The second part consists of author and keyword references to entries in the first part and to other sources. It is divided, in accordance with the main text, into individual chapters, and as far as possible in the same order within each chapter as the topics to which they relate. It also includes a few supplementary notes containing information that could not be incorporated into the text. I have read or consulted many other works, to which no reference is given because the matter in them is either self-evident, or outdated, or marginal, or valueless.

The following general abbreviations are used:

Account Book = Vanbrugh's Account Book or Journal, 1715–26 (printed in Downes, 1977).

BIHR = Vanbrugh and Yarburgh papers in the Borthwick Institute of Historical Research, York.

BL = British Library.

Bodl. = Bodleian Library, Oxford.

CSPD = *Calendar of State Papers, Domestic.*

CTB = *Calendar of Treasury Books.*

CTP = *Calendar of Treasury Papers.*

HMC = Historical Manuscripts Commission Reports.

PRO = Public Record Office, London and Kew.

PROB = Probate documents of the Prerogative Court of Canterbury, now in PRO.

RCHME = Royal Commission on the Historical Monuments of England.

RIBA = Royal Institute of British Architects, London.

RO = Record Office.

VCH = Victoria County History.

Wren Soc. = *The Wren Society*, Vols. I–XX (Oxford 1924–43).

Part 1 BIBLIOGRAPHY

Adams, J.Q., *The Dramatic Records of Sir Henry Herbert*, 1917.

Addison, William, *Audley End*, 1953.

Ailesbury, Thomas, Earl of, *Memoirs*, ed. W.E. Buckley, 1890–91.

Alberti, Leone Battista, *Ten Books on Architecture*, translated . . . into English by James Leoni, 1726 (reprinted 1955).

Allen, R.J., *The Clubs of Augustan London*, Cambridge (Mass.), 1933.

Alvensleben, Udo von, and Hans Reuther, *Herrenhausen*, Hanover, 1966.

Andrews, C. Bruyn, *The Torrington Diary*, 1938.

Anthony, Sister Rose, *The Jeremy Collier Stage Controversy 1698–1726*, Milwaukee, 1937.

Archdale, Martin, 'An East Anglian Original', *Country Life*, CXL, 1966, 614–16.

Avery, Emmett L., 'The Capacity of the Queen's Theatre in the Haymarket', *Philol. Quarterly*, XXXI, 1952, 85–7.

Baker, David Erskine, *Biographica Dramatica*, 1812.

Beard, Geoffrey, *The Work of John Vanbrugh*, 1986.

Bennett, J.H.E., 'The White Friars of Chester', *Journ. Chester and N. Wales Archit. Archæol. and Hist. Soc.*, NS.XXXI/1, 1935, 5–54.

Bill, E.G.W., *The Queen Anne Churches: a Catalogue of the Papers in Lambeth Palace Library of the Commission for Building Fifty New Churches in London and Westminster*, 1979.

Bingham, Madeleine, *Masks and Façades*, 1974.

Blome, Richard, *Britannia*, 1673.

Breman, Paul and Denise Addis, *Guide to Vitruvius Britannicus*, New York, 1972.

Brown, Horatio F., *Inglesi e Scozzesi all'Università di Padova*, Venice, 1921.

Browne, Tom, *A Description of Mr D––––n's Funeral: A Poem*, 1700.

Burne, R.V.H., *Chester Cathedral*, 1958.

Campbell, Colen: see *Vit. Brit.*

Carmarthen: Osborne (Peregrine Hyde, Duke of Leeds) A Journal of the Brest-Expedition, 1694.

Carswell, John, *The South Sea Bubble*, 1961.

Carter, Charles, *The Complete Practical Cook*, 1730.

Carter, John, 'Architectural Innovation', *Gentleman's Magazine*, LXXXV/1, 1815, 326–8, 517–9.

Cast, David, 'Seeing Vanbrugh and Hawksmoor', *Journ. Soc. of Archit. Historians*, XLIII, 1984, 310–27.

Chalmers, Alexander, *General Biographical Dictionary*, 1816.

Chaney, Edward, 'The Road to Rome' [letter], *Country Life*, CLXXIX, 1986, 1446.

Chester Rolls: Rolls of the Freemen of Chester. I. 1392–1700. *Lancs. and Cheshire Record Soc.*, 1906.

Cibber, Colley, *An Apology for the Life of Colley Cibber*, ed. B.R.S. Fone, Ann Arbor, 1968.

Cibber, Theophilus, *Lives of the Poets*, 1753.

Coleman: Vanbrugh (Sir John), *The Provok'd Wife*, ed. Anthony Coleman. Manchester, 1982.

Colvin, H.M., *Biographical Dictionary of British Architects 1600–1840*, 1978.

Colvin, H.M., 'Grimsthorpe Castle, the North Front', in Colvin and J. Harris, ed., *The Country Seat* (1970), 91–3.

Colvin, H.M. and M.J. Craig, *Architectural Drawings in the Library of Elton Hall* (Roxburghe Club), Oxford, 1964.

Companion: Pepys, Samuel, *Diary*, ed. R. Latham and W. Matthews, Vol. X, Companion, 1983.

Congreve, William, *Letters and Documents*, ed. John C. Hodges, 1964.

Connely, W., *Sir Richard Steele*, 1934.

Connor, Timothy, 'Grimsthorpe Castle', *Archæol. Journ.*, CXXXI, 1974, 330–3.

Connor, Timothy, 'The Making of Vitruvius Britannicus', *Archit. History*, XX, 1977, 14–30.

Cressy, David, *Education in Tudor and Stuart England*, 1975.

Cummings, W.H., 'The Lord Chamberlain and Opera in London 1700–1740', *Proc. [Royal] Musical Assoc.*, XL, 1914, 37–71.

Cunningham, Alan, *Lives of the Most Eminent British Painters, Sculptors and Architects*, IV, 1831.

Dalton, Charles, *English Army Lists and Commission Registers*, 1892–

Davies, Thomas, *Dramatic Miscellanies*, 1784.

Davies, J.H.V., 'The Dating of the Buildings of the Royal Hospital at Greenwich', *Archæol. Journ.* CXIII, 1956, 126–36.

Defoe, Daniel, *A Tour through England and Wales*, 1725.

Dennis, John, *Works*, ed. E.N. Hooker, Baltimore, 1939.

D'Israeli, Isaac, *Curiosities of Literature*, 1858.

Dixon: Cibber (Colley) and Sir John Vanbrugh, *The Provok'd Husband*, ed. Peter Dixon, 1975.

Dobrée: Vanbrugh (Sir John) *Works*: I–III, *The Plays*, ed. Bonamy Dobrée, 1927.

Downes, Kerry, *Hawksmoor*, 1959.

Downes, Kerry, *English Baroque Architecture*, 1966.

Downes, Kerry, 'The Kings Weston Book of Drawings', *Archit. History*, X, 1967, 9–88.

Downes, Kerry, 'The Little Colony on Greenwich Hill', *Country Life*, CLIX, 1976, 1406–8.

Downes, Kerry, *Vanbrugh*, 1977.

Downes, Kerry, 'Vanbrugh's Heslington Lady', *Burlington Mag.*, CXXIV, 1982, 153–5.

Downes, Kerry, 'The Publication of Shaftesbury's "Letter Concerning Design" ', *Archit. History*, XXVII, 1984, 519–23.

Downes, Kerry, [Review of Girouard, 1983] *Burlington Mag.* CXXVII, 1985, 98.

Downes, Kerry, 'Hawksmoor's House at Easton Neston', *Archit. History*, XXX, 1987.

Drury, P.J., ' "No Other Palace in the Kingdom will Compare with it": the Evolution of Audley End 1605–1745', *Archit. History*, XXIII, 1980, 1–39.

Drury, P.J. and others, *Audley End (Official Handbook)*, 1984.

Dryden, John, *Essays*.

Edye, Lourenço, *The Historical Records of the Royal Marines*, 1893.

Eliot, T.S. *Selected Essays*, 1934.

Evelyn, John, *Diary*, ed. E.S. de Beer, Oxford, 1955.

Everett, Sir Henry J., *The History of the Somerset Light Infantry 1685–1934*, 1934.

Faller, Lincoln B., 'Between Jest and Earnest: the Comedy of Sir John Vanbrugh', *Modern Philology*, LXXII, 1974–5, 17–29.

Farquhar, George, 'A Discourse upon Comedy in Reference to the English Stage' (1702), in *Works* (1728), I, 79–105.

Festeau, Paul, *Nouvelle Grammaire Anglaise*, 1675.

Finch, Pearl, *History of Burley-on-the-Hill*, 1901.

Fluchère: Vanbrugh (Sir John), *L'Épouse Outragé*, ed. Marie-Louise Fluchère, Paris, 1981.

Fowler, L.H., and E. Baer, *The Fowler Architectural Collection of the Johns Hopkins University*, Baltimore, 1961.

Fraser, Lady Antonia, *The Weaker Vessel: Women's Lot in Seventeenth-Century England*, 1984.

Fremantle, Katharine, 'A Visit to the United Provinces and Cleves in the Time of William III', *Nederlands Kunsthist. Jaarboek*, XXI, 1970, 39–68.

Fremantle, Katharine, *Sir James Thornhill's Sketch-Book Travel Journal of 1711*, Utrecht, 1975.

Friedman, Terry, *James Gibbs*, 1984.

Gatty, Charles T., *Mary Davies and the Manor of Ebury*, 1921.

Gibbon, Michael 'Stowe, Buckinghamshire: the House and Garden Buildings and their Designs', *Archit. History*, XX, 1977, 31–44.

Gildon, Charles, *Lives and Characters of the English Dramatic Poets*, 1699.

Gildon, Charles, *A Comparison between the Two Stages*, ed. Staring B. Wells, Princeton, 1942.

Girouard, Mark, *Robert Smythson and the Elizabethan Country House*, 1983.

Godfrey, Walter H., and others, *The College of Arms*, 1963.

Green, David, *Blenheim Palace*, 1951.

Green, David, *Queen Anne*, 1970.

Habbakuk, H.J., 'Daniel Finch, Second Earl of Nottingham', in J.H. Plumb, ed., *Studies in Social History*, 1955, 139–78.

Harley, Graham D., '*Squire Trelooby* and *The Cornish Squire*: a Reconsideration', *Philol. Quarterly*, XLIX, 1970, 520–9.

Harris: Vanbrugh (Sir John), *The Relapse*, ed. Bernard Harris, 1971.

Harris, Bernard, and J.R. Brown, ed., *Restoration Theatre* (Stratford upon Avon Studies, 6), 1965.

Harris, Eileen, ' "Vitruvius Britannicus" before Colen Campbell', *Burlington Mag.*, CXXVIII, 1986, 340–6.

Harris, John, *William Talman*, 1982.

Harris, John, *The Design of the English Country House*, 1985.

Hatton, Ragnhild, *George I*, 1978.

Hervey, John, First Earl of Bristol, *Diary*, Wells, 1894.

Hervey, John, First Earl of Bristol, *Letter-Books*, Wells, 1894.

Hewlings, Richard, 'James Leoni', in R. Brown, ed., *The Architectural Outsiders*, 1985, 21–43.

Heywood, T., ed., *The Moore Rental*, (Chetham Soc. XII), 1847.

Hobson, M.G., ed., *Oxford Council Acts 1665–1701* (Oxford Historical Soc.

N.S.2.), Oxford, 1939.

Holland, Peter, *The Ornament of Action: Text and Performance in Restoration Comedy*, Cambridge, 1979.

Holme, Randle, *The Academy of Armory*, Chester, 1688 (reprint Menston 1972).

Hopkins, Paul, 'John Vanbrugh's Imprisonment in France 1688–1693', *Notes and Queries*, N.S.XXVI, 1979, 529–34.

Hotson, Leslie, *The Commonwealth and Restoration Stage*, Cambridge (Mass.), 1928.

Hughes, T., 'Sir John Vanbrugh', *Notes and Queries*, ser. 2,I, 1856, 116–7.

Hunt, Leigh, ed., *Dramatic Works of Wycherley, Congreve, Vanbrugh and Farquhar*, 1840.

Huseboe, Arthur R., 'Vanbrugh: Additions to the Correspondence', *Philol. Quarterly*, LIII, 1974, 135–40.

Huseboe, Arthur R., *Sir John Vanbrugh*, Boston, 1976.

Johnson, Samuel, *Lives of the English Poets*, Oxford, 1905.

Jones, R.F., and others, *The Seventeenth Century: Studies in the History of English Thought and Literature from Bacon to Pope*, Stanford, 1951.

Jordan, R.J., 'Vanbrugh at Sea', *Notes and Queries*, N.S. XXVI, 1979, 527–9.

Josselin, Ralph, *Diary*, 1976.

Kelch, R.A., *Newcastle: A Duke without Money*, 1974.

Keller, Fritz-Eugen, 'Christian Eltester's Drawings of Roger Pratt's Clarendon House and Robert Hooke's Montague House', *Burlington Mag.*, CXXVIII, 1986, 732–7.

Kenyon, J.P., *Robert Spencer, Earl of Sunderland*, 1958.

Kern, R.L., 'Documents Relating to Company Management 1705–11', *Theatre Notebook*, XIV, 1959/60, 60–65.

Kieven, Elisabeth, 'Galilei in England', *Country Life*, CLIII, 1973, 210–12.

Kimball, Fiske, 'Romantic Classicism in Architecture', *Gazette des Beaux-Arts*, per. 6, XXV, 1944, 95–112.

King's Works (1963): Colvin, H.M. and others, *The History of the King's Works*, II. *The Middle Ages*, 1963.

King's Works (1975): Colvin, H.M. and others, *The History of the King's Works*, III. *1485–1660, Part I*, 1975.

King's Works (1976): Colvin, H.M. and others, *The History of the King's Works*, V. *1660–1782*, 1976.

King's Works (1982): Colvin, H.M. and others, *The History of the King's Works*, IV. *1485–1660, Part II*, 1982.

Krutch, J.W., *Comedy and Conscience after the Restoration*, New York, 1924.

Lang, S, 'Vanbrugh's Theory and Hawksmoor's Buildings', *Journ. Soc. of Archit. Historians*, XXIV, 1965, 127–51.

Lang, S., [Review of Downes (1977)]. *Journ. Soc. of Archit. Historians*, XXXVIII, 1979, 208–10.

Leacroft, Richard, *The Development of the English Playhouse*, 1973.

Lees-Milne, James, *English Country Houses: Baroque*, 1970.

Links, J.G., *Canaletto*, Oxford, 1972.

Loewenberg, Alfred, *Annals of Opera 1597–1940*, Cambridge, 1940.

London Stage: The London Stage 1660–1800: I. 1660–1700, ed. William van

Lennep, Carbondale, 1965. *II. 1700–1729*, ed. Emmett L. Avery, Carbondale, 1960.

Luttrell, Narcissus, *A Brief Relation of Historical and State Affairs*, Oxford, 1857.

Lynch, Kathleen M., *Jacob Tonson, Kit-Cat Publisher*, Knoxville, 1971.

McCormick, Frank, 'Vanbrugh's Imprisonment in France: More Light', *Notes and Queries*, N.S.XXIX, 1982, 57–61.

Macky, John, *A Journey through England*, 1714; 2nd ed. 1722.

Macnamara, F.N., *Memorials of the Danvers Family*, 1895.

Marlborough, Sarah, Duchess of, *Private Correspondence*, 1838.

Marsh, Emilia Field Cresswell, *The Plays and Architecture of Sir John Vanbrugh* (Ph.D., Northwestern University), Ann Arbor, UMI, 1985.

Meekings, E.A.F., *Surrey Hearth Tax 1664*, Surrey Record Soc. XVII, 1940.

Milhous, Judith, 'New Light on Vanbrugh's Haymarket Theatre Project', *Theatre Survey*, XVII/2, 1976, 143–61.

Milhous, Judith, 'Five New Letters by Sir John Vanbrugh', *Harvard Library Bulletin*, XXVII, 1979, 434–42.

Milhous, Judith and Robert D. Hume, *Vice-Chamberlain Coke's Theatrical Papers 1706–1715*, Carbondale, 1982.

Mitchell, R.J., and M.D.R., Leys, *A History of London Life*, 1963.

Montagu, Lady Mary Wortley, *Letters*, ed. R. Halsband, Oxford, 1965.

Mueschke, P, and J. Fleisher, 'A Re-evaluation of Vanbrugh', *Publ. Modern Language Assoc.* XLIX, 1934, 848–89.

Mullin, D.C., 'The Queen's Theatre, Haymarket', *Theatre Survey*, VIII/2, 1967, 84–105.

Murdoch, Tessa, and others, *The Quiet Conquest: the Huguenots 1685–1985*, London, 1985.

Newton, Evelyn Legh, Lady, *The House of Lyme*, 1917.

Nicoll, Allardyce, *History of English Drama 1660–1900: I. 1660–1700, II. The Early Eighteenth Century*, 1961.

North, Roger, *On Music*, ed. John Wilson, 1959.

North, Roger, *Of Building*, ed. H.M. Colvin and John Newman, Oxford, 1981.

Oldmixon, John, *History of England*, 1735.

Olleson, Philip, 'Vanbrugh and Opera at the Queen's Theatre, Haymarket', *Theatre Notebook*, XXVI, 1972, 94–100.

Oswald, Arthur, 'Kimbolton Castle, Huntingdonshire', *Country Life*, CXLIV, 1968, 1474–8, 1584–7, 1644–8, 1696–9.

Parker, Geoffrey, *The Dutch Revolt*, 1985.

Peacham, Henry, *The Compleat Gentleman*, 1622.

Pepys, Samuel, *Diary*, ed. Robert Latham and William Matthews, 1970–76.

Pevsner, Sir Nikolaus, *The Buildings of England: Bedfordshire and the County of Huntingdon and Peterborough*, 1968a.

Pevsner, Sir Nikolaus, *Studies in Art, Architecture and Design*, 1968b.

Pinks, W.I., *History of Clerkenwell*, 1865.

Piper, David, *Catalogue of Seventeenth-Century Portraits in the National Portrait Gallery*, Cambridge, 1963.

Pope, Alexander, *Works*, ed. Elwin and Courthope, 1882.

Pope, Alexander, *Correspondence*, ed. G. Sherburn. I. Oxford, 1966.

Powell, Jocelyn, *Restoration Theatre Production*, 1984.

RCHME, *North Dorset*, 1972.

RCHME, *Wilton House and English Palladianism*, 1988.

Reddaway, T.F., *The Rebuilding of London after the Great Fire*, 1940.

Reresby, Sir John, *Memoirs*, ed. Andrew Browning, Glasgow, 1936.

Revels: Loftis (John) and others, *The Revels History of Drama in English: V. 1660–1750*, 1976.

Reynolds, Sir Joshua, *Discourses*.

Rhind, Neil, *Blackheath Village and Environs 1790–1970*, II, 1983.

Richards, K., 'A Classical Borrowing in Vanbrugh's "The Relapse" ', *Notes and Queries*, N.S.XXVI, 1979, 534–5.

Roberts, H.D., *Matthew Henry and his Chapel 1662–1900*. Liverpool, 1901.

Rogal, S.J., 'John Vanbrugh and the Blenheim Palace Controversy', *Journ. Soc. of Archit. Historians*, XXXIII, 1974, 293–303.

Rogers, Pat, 'An Unpublished Vanbrugh Letter', *Scriblerian*, V, 1972, 41.

Rose, Giles, *A Perfect School of Instructions for the Officers of the Mouth*, 1682.

Rosenberg, Albert, 'New Light on Vanbrugh', *Philol. Quarterly*, XLV, 1966, 603–13.

Rubens, Sir Peter Paul, *Letters*, transl. and ed. R.S. Magurn, Cambridge (Mass.), 1955.

Ryan, A.N., 'William III and the Brest Fleet', in Mark A. Thomson, *William III and Louis XIV, Essays 1680–1720*, Liverpool, 1968, 49–67.

Saxl, Fritz, and R. Wittkower, *British Art and the Mediterranean*, 1948.

Silcox-Crowe, Nigel, 'Sir Roger Pratt', in R. Brown, ed. *The Architectural Outsiders*, 1985, 1–20.

Slack, Paul, *The Impact of Plague in Tudor and Stuart England*, 1985.

Smith: Vanbrugh (Sir John), *The Provok'd Wife*, ed. James L. Smith, 1974.

Smithers, P. *Life of Joseph Addison*, 1954.

Spence, Joseph, *Observations, Anecdotes and Characters of Books and Men*, Oxford, 1966.

Steele, Sir Richard, *Letters*, ed. Rae Blanchard, 1941.

Steele, Sir Richard, Tracts and Pamphlets, 1944.

Steele, Sir Richard, *Plays*, ed. Shirley Strum Kenny, Oxford, 1971.

Sullivan: Cibber (Colley), *Three Sentimental Comedies*, ed. Maureen Sullivan. New Haven, 1973.

Summers, Montague, *The Restoration Theatre*, 1934.

Summers, Montague, *The Playhouse of Pepys*, 1935.

Survey: London Survey Committee, later Greater London Council. Survey of London. XXIII (1951); XXIX (1960); XXXV (1970).

Swift, Jonathan, *Poems*, ed. H. Williams, Oxford, 1937.

Swift, Jonathan, *Journal to Stella*.

Thompson, A. Hamilton, *The Premonstratensian Abbey of Welbeck*, 1938.

Thompson, Francis, *A History of Chatsworth*, 1949.

Thomson, Mrs A.T., *Memoirs of Sarah Duchess of Marlborough*, 1838.

Thomson, Gladys Scott, *Life in a Noble Household 1641–1700*, 1937.

Thomson, Gladys Scott, *Letters of a Grandmother*, 1943.

Timbs, J., *Curiosities of London*, 1885.

Tipping, H.A. and Christopher Hussey, *English Homes*, IV.ii. *The Work of Sir John Vanbrugh and his School*, 1928.

Toesca, Ilaria, 'Alessandro Galilei in Inghilterra', *English Miscellany*, III, 1952, 189–220.

Tong, William, *Account of the Life and Death of Mr Matthew Henry*, 1716.

Tour: A Tour through Great Britain by a Gentleman, 1762.

Trevelyan, G.M., *England Under Queen Anne*, III. *The Peace*, 1934, (new ed. 1965).

Uffenbach, Zacharias Conrad von, *London in 1710*, trans. W.H. Quarrell and Margaret Mare, 1934.

Verney, Lady Margaret, *Verney Letters of the Eighteenth Century*, 1930.

Vit. Brit.: Campbell (Colen), Vitruvius Britannicus, or the British Architect. I (1715); II (1717); III (1725). Facsimile reprint New York, 1967. *See also* Breman and Addis.

Wagner, Sir Anthony, *Heralds of England*, 1967.

Walpole, Horace, *Anecdotes of Painting in England*, ed. R.N. Wornum, 1888.

Walpole, Horace, *Letters*, ed. Mrs Paget Toynbee, Oxford, 1903–5.

Ward, Edward, *The Secret History of Clubs*, 1709.

Webb: Vanbrugh (Sir John), *Works*. IV: *The Letters*, ed. Geoffrey Webb, 1928.

Webb, Geoffrey, 'The Letters and Drawings of Nicholas Hawksmoor Relating to the Building of the Mausoleum at Castle Howard', *Walpole Soc.* XIX, 1931.

Westrup, J.A., *Henry Purcell*, 1947.

Whinney, Margaret, 'William Talman', *Journ. Warburg and Courtauld Inst.*, XVII, 1955, 123–39.

Whistler, Laurence, *Sir John Vanbrugh, Architect and Dramatist*, 1938.

Whistler, Laurence, *The Imagination of Vanbrugh and his Fellow Artists*, 1954.

Whistler, Laurence, 'Stowe in the Making', *Country Life*, CXXII, 1957, 68–71.

Whistler, Laurence, 'Vanbrugh's Work at Stowe', *Country Life*, CXXV, 1959, 352–3.

Whistler, Laurence, 'Deeds of Partnership', *Times Literary Suppl.*, 17 Feb. 1978, 205.

Wilkinson, T., 'Crumbling Monuments of the Raj', *Country Life*, CLX, 1976, 606–8.

Willis, Peter, *Charles Bridgeman and the English Landscape Garden*, 1977.

Wittkower, Rudolf, *Palladio and English Palladianism*, 1974.

Wood, Anthony, *Fasti Oxonienses*, Oxford, 1721.

Wood, Anthony, *Fasti Oxonienses*, Oxford 1820.

Wood, Anthony, *Life and Times*. III. (Oxford Historical Soc. XXVI). 1894.

Woods, Charles B., 'Cibber in Fielding's *Author's Farce*', *Philol. Quarterly*, XLIV, 1965, 145–51.

Wren Society, Vols. I–XX. Oxford, 1924–43.

Zimansky: Vanbrugh (Sir John), *The Relapse*, ed. Curt Zimansky, 1970a. Vanbrugh (Sir John), *The Provok'd Wife*, ed. Curt Zimansky, 1970b.

Part 2 REFERENCES

General

Vanbrugh's architecture was first brought to a larger public by Tipping (1928), which was based on a long series of articles in *Country Life*. The first serious full-length biography was Whistler (1938); it was not superseded by Bingham (1974) which, although described by one critic as a re-writing of it, is often sketchy, inaccurate or misleading, and contains many statements that cannot be substantiated. Both works now need to be checked against more recent research. Whistler (1954) comprises a series of studies of then recently discovered drawings and documents relating, for the most part, to Vanbrugh as an architect. Huseboe (1976) is primarily a study of Vanbrugh as a writer; most of the biographical material has been superseded, and the shadow of Collier overhangs this author's estimation of Vanbrugh.

Downes (1977) was concerned primarily with architecture, but also included a great deal of new material on the history of the Vanbrughs and related families and an extensive series of genealogical tables. Individual references are not given in the present work to family matters covered in that book, which may be found by recourse to its index. It also contains a complete transcript of the Account Book or Journal kept by Vanbrugh from 1715 until his death.

Beard (1986) attempted to synthesise the existing literature on Vanbrugh's life and architecture, and consequently lacks a consistent viewpoint. Moreover his eclectic use of sources necessitates the checking of all statements.

References to the extensive literature on Vanbrugh from the point of view of the student of English will be found under subsequent chapters.

The Nonesuch collected edition of Vanbrugh's own writings (1927–8) consists of the plays in three volumes (cited as Dobrée, 1927) and (with Geoffrey Webb's pioneer introduction to the architecture) the letters in Volume IV (cited as Webb, 1928). Letters whose date is quoted are not always cited by page reference.

As a rule, references are not given for general historical matters, or to those mines of general information, Johnson's Dictionary and the Oxford English Dictionary, or to articles in the Dictionary of National Biography (DNB), the Complete Peerage and the Complete Baronage which, although sometimes in need of amendment from more recent research, remain basic equipment for historical biography.

With the exception of a few odd words, passages from Vanbrugh's plays have been quoted from the earliest known edition, since the re-punctuation of later printers and modern editors is not always to the advantage of either sound or sense. A similar principle has been followed with passages from other early works. Many letters are quoted from Webb (1928) or other printed sources, but some passages have been amended against the originals. Appendix B in the present work incorporates revisions to the list of Vanbrugh's letters in Downes (1977), 267–73.

In quotations the graphical convention of y for *th* has been disregarded in all cases, and *yt* has been expanded to *that*. Other contractions have been either kept or expanded in square brackets. Vanbrugh's eccentric use of initial capitals, stops and commas has been retained.

Chapter 1

The autograph of Vanbrugh's will is PROB 1/61, but the normal reference for the copy will is PROB 11/608, fol.84.

Chapter 2

Restoration London: see especially the diaries of Evelyn and Pepys, and in particular *Companion*. Flemings: Parker (1985). The Huguenots: see most recently Murdoch (1985). Weather on Vanbrugh's birthday: Josselin (1976), 504–5.

Chapter 3

See in general Downes (1977). Antwerp: Rubens (1955), 185, 279. W. Noel Sainsbury, *Rubens* (1859), 11 (the future Lord Dorchester in 1616). Giles Vanbrugh in Rome: Chaney (1986); in Padua: Brown (1921), 160.

Chapter 4

The Plague: in addition to sources for Chapter 2 see Slack (1985). The Fire: Reddaway. Sugar refiners' case: CSPD 1671, 117. Sugar costs at Woburn: Thomson (1937), 165–6. Allyn Smith: Macnamara (1895), 436–7, 448–51. Moore: Heywood (1847): 76–8. Jacobsen and Kalthof – VCH *Surrey*, IV, 52; CSPD 1666–7, 218–9, 527. Meekings (1940). Will of Caspar Colthoffe, aged gentleman, 1679, PROB 11/362, f.36.

Chapter 5

Chester: Bennet (1935), 36–9; *Chester Freemen* (1906), 178, 180. Hearth tax and quarter sessions records in Chester City RO; Register of Holy Trinity Church, Chester (transcript in Chester RO). Tong (1716), 94–9; Roberts (1901), 87. Blome (1673), 354–6. Sir Willoughby Aston's Journal (Liverpool RO, MD 172–3). J. Davies's article, 'Sir John Vanbrugh at Chester', in *Cheshire Life*, Dec. 1958, 55, is a mixture of fact and legend, as indeed is Hughes (1856). Vanbrugh family: Downes (1977). Grosvenor Estate: Gatty, 210 (lead); Grosvenor accounts at Eaton Hall (corn).

Theophilus Garencieres: DNB; Pinks (1865), 94–5, Wood (1721), II.c.113; Wood (1820), IV.c.196. Dudley Garencieres: Downes (1977), 157–8; Festeau (1675); allegations for marriage licences: 1678: *Harleian Soc.* XXIV (1886), 142; 1669: ibid. XXIII (1886), 171. Burne (1958).

Education: Cressy (1975). Giles Vanbrugh to the Bishop of London: Downes (1977), 245–6. The incident at Mons to which Giles refers was occasioned by the French blockade of the previous summer.

Chapter 6

Openings for a young man of talent: Whistler (1938), 21. Supposed visit to France: Cibber (1753), IV, 99–100. Born in the Bastille: D'Israeli (1858), III, 102–11.

London and Westminster in 1681: Ogilby and Morgan's map of 1681–2. The stage: Holland (1979); also *Companion*.

Chapter 7

Letter to Huntingdon: HMC Hastings II, 181; Rosenberg (1966), 603–4. Chester Castle: *King's Works*, (1963), 607–12; (1975), 238–42. Justice in Eyre: Luttrell, I.367; CSPD 1686–7, 315. Huntingdon's Regiment: Everett. This, like earlier histories, is based on some of the material to be found in PRO WO 5/2 (marching orders). See also WO 25/3, 25/4, 25/7 (commission books); Dalton, *passim* and with caution. Vanbrugh's commission: CSPD 1686–7. 20, 243. Macarty on his arrival: Rosenberg (1966), 611. Hales's case, Luttrell, 16 June 1686; CSPD 1685, 391. Macarty: CSPD 1685, 363, 391, 395; 1686–7, 23. Obligation to Skipwith: Cibber (1968), 120. Skipwith's commission, 20 June 1685: PRO WO 25/3, 195; his resignation: CSPD 1686–7, 165 (in error as captain of horse). Reresby (1936), 444–5. Wren to Fermor: Wren Soc. XII, 23 (misdated); Whinney (1953), 210. Shearing of hogs: HMC Lindsey (suppl.), 271–2. Oxford Council Acts: Hobson (1939), 191, 196. Berties dismissed: Wood (1894), III.171; HMC Downshire, I.i, 77.

Berties in Paris: HMC Lindsey, 50. Skelton: Luttrell, and Vanbrugh's letter of 26 August 1692 (Downes, 1977, 249).

Chapter 8

The abstracts in Downes (1977), 247–52, are further explained and amplified with much new material by Hopkins (1979); McCormick (1982) does not add significantly to the latter.

Chapter 9

Vanbrugh family: Downes (1977). Captain Dudley: PRO WO 25/3, 223; 25/4, 93, 161; Downes (1977), 161. *Lysander:* BL (Music) H.1652.t(21).

Legros: Downes (1977), 16. Previously Quartermaster to Prince George's Regiment, 1685 (PRO WO 25/3, 10). Some papers concerning Legros and Vanbrugh are in PRO DL42/90 (ff.105–15, 155, 190v) and DL13/41. E. Smith to Henry Tomlin: Downes (1977), 253; the fourth line should read: 'by any of My Lord Lindsees servants'.

Dryden's funeral: Browne (1700); a second edition was expanded. Kit-Cat Club: the account in Lynch (1971), 37–65, supersedes Allen (1933). Renaut's bill: Bingham (1974), 90 (misdated in caption). Wycherley's alcoholic supper: Spence (1966), I, 37. John Charlton to Lady Granby, HMC Rutland II, 177. Oldmixon, *History of England* (1735), 479, quoted in Lynch (1971), 38. Walpole (1888), II.207. Lord Dorset: Macky, I (1714), 188.

War at sea: Ryan (1968). Marine regiments: Edye (1893). Camaret Bay: Jordan (1979); Carmarthen (1694). Proposal for Vanbrugh's transfer, CSPD 1695, 46. Warrants to Vanbrugh as John Brooke: PRO SP 44/168, 171 (31 January 1696); CTB 1697–8, 445 and CSPD 1698, 380 (20 Aug. 1698).

Chapter 10

For the Restoration stage in general, see *Revels* (1976). This does not supersede Nicoll (1961), which is nevertheless now dated and whose conclusions need considerable revision. See also Pepys, *passim*; Hotson (1928); Summers (1934) and (1935); Harris and Browne (1965); Leacroft (1973); Powell (1984). For details of performances see *London Stage*, which also has much useful material in the introductions to each volume.

'No better than you should be': Beaumont and Fletcher, *The Coxcomb*. Patent of 21 Aug. 1660, in Herbert Papers: Adams (1917).

Drury Lane: Southern in *Revels*, (1976), 85–6; *Survey* (1970); Leacroft (1973), 83–92. The Wren drawing: Wren Soc. XII, Pl. XXIII, and elsewhere. English and foreign theatres compared: Macky (1722), I, 170–1. Richard Legh: Newton (1917), 240. Proclamations against persons on the stage: PRO LC7/3, no.1 (1673–4); CSPD 1689–90, 321. Thomas Killigrew, *Comedies and Tragedies*, 1664 (reprint New York 1967).

Chapter 11

The principal source for Cibber is his autobiography (Cibber, 1968). His plays: in the 1721 edition he altered the style and punctuation of his works to make them more literary, and this edition was used by Maureen Sullivan for hers of *Love's Last Shift* and other comedies (Cibber, 1973). Quotations here, from the first edition (BL 11775.e.1(1)), make better dramatic sense; as is very evident in his *Apology*, his later style is peppered with gratuitous and often obstructive punctuation.

Gildon on the secession: Gildon (1942), 7. Rich's elephant: Cibber (1968), 184. The philosopher's stone: Gildon (1942), 16.

Mueschke and Fleisher (1934) is still one of the best critical articles on Vanbrugh as a playwright.

Chapter 12

Vanbrugh's transfer: last reference in Chapter 9. John Brooks: a John Brook and Dudley Vanbrugh were both commissioned captains in Colonel Beveridge's foot regiment on 28 February 1689 (PRO WO 25/4, 171, 161), when our subject was imprisoned at Calais. A John Brooke or Brookes, commissioned ensign in Colonel Farington's regiment on 16 February 1694, was promoted to lieutenant on 24 December 1695 (WO 27/7, 23, 81) and to captain on 10 March 1702, the same day as John Vanbrugh's final commission as captain in the new Huntingdon regiment (WO 25/7, 120, 122).

Lord Berkeley's will, PROB 11/437, f.70. *The Relapse*: Cibber (1968), 120–1. Lady Morley: Hotson (1928), 306–7, 377–9. Vanbrugh's style: Pope to Swift and Spence: Spence (1966), I.206 and note; Cibber (1968), 122; Holland (1979), 112. Marsh (1985) attempts to compare Vanbrugh's architecture with his plays (and specifically the 'figure and proportions').

Collier: Krutch (1924); Anthony (1937). Stychomythia: Fluchère (1981), 76, 79, citing Eliot (1934): 'Seneca in Elizabethan Translation'. See also Richards (1979).

A Journey to London: Cibber's Preface to *The Provok'd Husband*, in Dobrée (1927), III and Dixon (1975).

The Relapse: Zimansky (1970a) and Harris (1971). Sunderland: Kenyon (1958), quoted by Harris (1971), xviii.

Chapter 13

Æsop was first published in two parts in 1697. The first edition of *The Country*

House is 1715 (BL 642.b.4(4)). The copy at 11735.e.49(1) is the 1740 edition. *Æsop* designed for Drury Lane: Huseboe (1976), 117. The Green Sickness and Mrs Sharp: Fraser (1984), 55–6; see also *Spectator* No. 431.

Chapter 14

Modern editions of *The Provok'd Wife*: Zimansky (1970b); Coleman (1982). The first edition in BL, 841.d.18(2), is incomplete; a complete copy is Bodl. Vet.A3.e.682. Spring Garden: see Appendix F. Death a leap in the dark: Smith (1974), 101, quoting John Wilkins, *Characteristic Anecdotes of Men of Learning and Genius* (1808), 276; Coleman (1982), 154–5, quoting Anthony Wood.

Chapter 15

Dennis (1939). Collier: Krutch (1924); Anthony (1937). Earl of Dorset, 1696: Krutch (1924), 180 (PRO LC7/1). Sunderland, 1697: ibid. 181. Bertie to Killigrew, 1699: ibid. 182. Jersey, 1704: ibid. 183–4. Censorship (including Steele's part): Cibber (1968), 188, 152–3.

Chapter 16

Vanbrugh's *Short Vindication*: Dobrée (1927), I, 193–215. Waitwell and Small-well: Downes (1959), 127.
Ancients and moderns: Jones (1951). Remarks on *The False Friend*: Gildon, (1942), 95.

Chapter 17

Midnight Masque: *Spectator*, No.8.
  Steele's plays: the best edition is by S.S. Kenny (1971).

Chapter 18

Castle Howard: printed in Downes (1977), 263–6. A defective copy was followed there; the first eight lines should read:
. When happy Plenty, the Effect of Peace,
  Improves our Arts, makes Sciences encrease;
  Then may an humble Muse essay to sing,
  And try in tim'rous Flights her tender Wing:
  So the gay tuneful Choir, who haunt the Grove,
  From the small Linnet to the Cooing Dove,
  In Consort joyn, their Melody to raise.
  When the Creative sun his Pow'r displays:
Mrs Hawksmoor's bill: Downes (1959), 266–9. Vanbrugh to Carlisle on Hawksmoor: Webb, 6–7. Vanbrugh's account of the Talman-Carlisle lawsuit: Whistler (1954), 35–8. *Of Building*: North (1981). Duchess of Marlborough on artists: Thomson (1943), 134. Alberti on overseers: Bk.IX, ch.11 (Alberti, 1726, 207). Hawksmoor's copy of Perrault's edition of Vitruvius is in the Canadian Architectural Centre, Montreal. 'A loving nurse': Hawksmoor to Lady Marlborough, 17 April 1722 (Green, 1951, 309). Easton Neston: Downes (1987). William Vanbrugh: Downes (1977), 159–61. *Vanbrug's House*: Swift (1937).

Chapter 19
Leland: quoted in Whistler (1954), 26. Site of old Henderskelfe: Barley (1978). Carlisle at Padua: Brown (1921), 172. York: Defoe (1725). Chatsworth: Thompson (1949). Prior's snub: Johnson (1905), II, 184. Burley-on-the-Hill: Downes (1966), 12, 63–5; Finch (1901); Habakkuk (1955). Talman at Castle Howard: Whistler (1954), 32–6; Whinney (1955), 132–4. The Henderskelfe fire and Thomas Worsley's letter: information from the late Lord Howard of Henderskelfe. Hawksmoor's letter of 1701: Downes (1959), 234–5. Early drawings for Castle Howard: Whistler (1954), 40–6. Pratt: Silcox-Crowe (1985). May's staircases: Downes (1966), 19–20.

Oranges: Pepys (19 April 1664); Evelyn (14 July 1664, at Eltham; 29 March 1688, Sir Henry Capel's orangery at Kew). For the price, see Hotson (1928), 291; Pepys (26 March, 11 May 1668); Swift, *Stella*, 10 Feb. 1710/11. Inigo Jones noted, c. 1636–8, a preparation of oranges as a remedy 'for the spleene and winde' (B. Alsopp ed., *Inigo Jones on Palladio*, Newcastle, 1970, 72).

Economy of Castle Howard: Webb (1928), 55 (to Southwell), 56 (to Craggs), 99 (to Newcastle). Hawksmoor on diversity of elevations: Downes (1959), 254. Draft mason's contract of 1719: Tipping (1928), 22. Work on Castle Howard for his heir: Macky (1722), II, 214. Sir Thomas Robinson married Elizabeth Howard, Lord Carlisle's eldest daughter and the widow of Baron Lechmere, in 1728. Lady Marlborough's bow window: Whistler (1954), 229. Lady Oxford's tour (1745): BL. MS. Loan 29/234, f.75.

Chapter 20
Fires: Mitchell and Leys (1963), 222–7.

Thoresby fire (Hawksmoor's letter of 1731): Webb (1931), 126. Burley-on-the-Hill: Evelyn (11 March 1705). Montague House: Evelyn (19 Jan. 1686); Downes (1966), 57–8; Keller (1986). Vanbrugh and Hawksmoor at St James's Square: *Survey* (1960), 84; Webb (1928), 172. Hawksmoor's comments on this and other house fires: Green (1951), 311. Wren's survey of Whitehall underlies a plan for a new palace (Wren Soc. VIII, Pl.II). *A True Character*: see Appendix D. First introduced into the literature by Cast (1984), 313. Goose Pie: Downes (1977), 11–14; Rose (1682); Carter (1730); Earl of Mar (HMC Stuart VI, 162).

Vanbrugh's patent as Comptroller: CTB 1702, 33. Duchess of Marlborough on his Comptrollership: *King's Works* (1976), 36 (letter to 2nd Duke of Devonshire, 1721). But in 1721 she also told Lord Macclesfield that Craggs introduced Vanbrugh to Marlborough as a potential architect for his house (Whistler, 1954, 84), implying that they had not met before 1704.

Additions to Vanbrugh's office 1702–3: PRO Work 5/53.

Chapter 21
Half-pay to Dec. 1701: CTB 1702, 1141, 478; CTP 1702–7, 46. Military Entry Books PRO WO 25/4, 25/7; references as in Chapters 9 and 12.

Shelton's shorthand: Pepys (1970–76), I, xlviii–xlix. The symbol for *My wife* appears on the first page of the *Diary* (plate f.p.xlv) and on f.45 of Vanbrugh's Account Book (Downes, 1977, Pl.3).

Kneller's portrait: Piper (1963), 356. Heraldry: Godfrey (1963); Wagner (1967),

326. Warrant for Vanbrugh's costume: CTB 1704–5, 221, 281. Sale to Knox Ward: Webb (1928), 170; Account Book f.57v. Spence on Barn Elms: Spence (1966), I.52. Halifax's mathematical instruments: Webb (1928), 9. Lord Essex's Palladio: Fowler (1961), 179. Hervey's Caesar: Hervey, *Diary*, 97. Winstanley's Water Theatre: Uffenbach (1934), 50–1; *Tatler*, No.74. Great Storm: Luttrell; Evelyn; Congreve (1964), 26–7; newsletters in CSPD 1703; Anthony (1937).

Talman to Newcastle April 1703: Wren Soc. XVII, Pl.I. Reform of Office of Works: *King's Works* (1976), 47–8; CTB 1704–5, 40, 307; 1705–6, 21,136,271.

Chapter 22

Haymarket Theatre: *Survey* (1960), 223–33; Leacroft (1973), 99–105; Milhous and Hume (1982); Cummings: Loewenberg (1943); *London Stage*.

Warrant of Dec 1704: Krutch (1928), 186 (PRO LC5/154, 35). Cibber (1968), 172. Vanbrugh's note of subscribers: Nottingham University Library, MS. Pw2.571, f.64; agreement with Newcastle: BL MS. Loan 29/237, f.71; receipt, f.71v. Spence (I, 51) quotes Pope to the effect that Lord Halifax gave £400 to the Haymarket in 1707. Hervey, *Diary*, 157.

Opera: Evelyn, 19 November 1644. Purcell: Westrup (1947). Semi-opera: North (1959), 274, 353. Cibber (1968), 175. Congreve (1964), 35 (3 Feb. 1705). Disadvantages of the new theatre: Cibber (1968), 173–4. Its capacity: Avery (1952). Scene design with proscenium arch: BM Print room, Burney Theatrical Portraits, IX, 65, No.101. Mullin (1967) reproduces an improbable engraving purporting to show a Vanbrugh design for a grand exterior front. Changes in stages: Cibber (1968), 224–6. Staff list: Milhous and Hume (1982); Nicoll (1961), II. 276–8. *Squire Trelooby*: Congreve (1964), 29; Harley (1970). No text survives for *The Cuckold in Conceit*.

Chapter 23

Newcastle to William Talman: Whistler (1954), 38–9. Talman's Welbeck drawings: Wren Soc. XII, Pl.XL; Harris (1982), 38, 39 (and Pl.66) also suggests that Talman's drawings preceded Vanbrugh's. Smythson plan for Welbeck: Girouard (1983), 183; 18th-century views: Thompson (1938), f.pp.78, 106, 108. Vanbrugh's 'draught': Wren Soc. XVII, Pl.XIV; Downes (1977), 27–30 and Pl.18; Harris (1985), 103. Drayton: Downes (1966), 65–6. Figure and proportions: Webb (1928), 15. Adding the Castle Howard skyline: Webb (1928), 209 (6 March 1706/7). Castle Howard programme: Charles Saumarez-Smith's paper at the Society of Architectural Historians' 'Annual Symposium' on 6 March 1982, amplified in his Warburg Institute thesis (1987). Mannheim: this hare, which is all that it can be considered, was started by John Shearman in about 1953.

Marlborough's original approach to Vanbrugh: BL. MS. Add. 38056, f.101. Other versions are on f.70 and in MS. Add. 19616, ff.16v–19. Woodstock: *King's Works*, (1963), 1009–17; Green (1951), 23–36. Marlborough's 'great services': Whistler (1954), 237, misquoted in Downes (1977), 58. An obelisk to Henry II: Green (1951), 170. Keyed plan of Blenheim: *Vit. Brit.* I (1715), 56. Eminencies: BL MS. Add 19607, f.44. Hawksmoor's plan of Blenheim: Green (1951), Fig.20.

Christ's Hospital designs: Wren Soc. XI, Pls.XLVIII–LI; Downes (1959), Pl.1a; Downes (1977), Pl.83. Kensington Orangery: Colvin (1978) remained cautious and indeed equivocal, but other writers have interpreted his reference to Treasury documents as a 'discovery' of Vanbrugh's authorship: most strongly of all, Green (1970), 137n. See CTB 1704–05, 40, 53, 279, 299, 352, 378; Wren Soc. VII, 184–5; PRO Work 6/14, 65, 70; T27/17, 407. On the 'originality' of Vanbrugh and Hawksmoor see Cast (1984).

Foundation stone of Blenheim: the passage quoted has for the past fifty years been cited in error, following Whistler (1938), as from William Upcott's Diary. Thomson (1838), 443, alone gives the true source: it is (as one might expect from its style) a cutting from a contemporary newspaper which belonged to Upcott (1779–1845) and was communicated by him to Mrs Thomson. Hawksmoor told the Duchess of Marlborough in 1722 that he 'had the honour to see the first Stone layed' (Green, 1951, 309).

Chapter 24

Blenheim stone: Green (1951), 59, 193–5. Blenheim papers: there are now two major collections in the British Library: MSS. Add. 19591–19618, originally compiled in conjunction with the Marlborough lawsuits, and the much more extensive MSS. Add. 61101–61710, acquired from the Blenheim Estate by the Treasury in 1978 in settlement of inheritance tax, and referred to in literature before that date by Blenheim index letters and numbers. Printed catalogue 1985. Rogal (1974) is a synthetic study based almost entirely on the letters in Webb (1928).

Hawksmoor to Joynes: BL. MS. Add. 19607 (Downes, 1959, 235–40). Exact plans: Webb (1928), 226 (6 Dec. 1709). Blenheim models: Downes (1977), 255; Coxe's *Marlborough*, I.252 (Green, 1951, 43 and n.). Wren's estimate according to Vanbrugh: Webb (1928), 31. Vanbrugh's *Reply on Behalf of the Workmen* at the time of the lawsuits stated that Wren was sent down to Blenheim 'and made his Report accordingly' (Webb, 1928, 199).

A professed Whig architect: Ailesbury (1890–1). 586–7. P. Wentworth: Cartwright (1883), 68. Frost: Luttrell; Timbs (1885), 361–2. Mirrors for Marlborough: Macky (II, 1722), 115; Wren Soc. VII, 227, quoting A.H. Beavan, *Marlborough House* (1896), 233. Kneller sketch: Downes (1977), 58 and Pl.50; Green (1951), 298–9. Herrenhausen: Alvensleben and Reuther (1966). Vanbrugh's Warrant: Green (1951), 300. Joiner's bill 1709 at Whitehall: BL MS.Add.19596, f.44. Plasterer's bill: Sotheby Sale, 30/31 Jan. 1956 (444). Lead roofing: Webb (1928), 215, 218. Vanbrugh to Maynwaring: Webb (1928), 22–3. Maynwaring sorry for Vanbrugh: BL. MS. Add.61459, f.88. Mr Wren and Marlborough House: *King's Works*, (1976), 36–7. Raising the elevation height: Whistler (1954), 93–4. Tournai: Fremantle (1975), 56–7; Downes (1977), 66. The bust was set up probably about 1721–2, and certainly by 1725 when Lord Carlisle viewed it (Green, 1951, 316). 'Tattling' Bertie: BL MS. Add.61459, f.118. Harley and Shrewsbury: Trevelyan (1934), 62–3; (1965), 85. Joynes to Travers on Godolphin's dismissal: Green (1951), 118. Joynes as keeper of Blenheim: Green (1951), 130. Marlborough's will: Webb (1928), 53. 'Made hay in it': Green (1951), 130.

Chapter 25

Account of the Hanover trip: BL. MS. Add.6321 (copies of Stebbing's letters);

Smithers (1954), 106–8, implies that Vanbrugh travelled with Addison and Halifax, but this is not borne out by letters in PRO SP 104/48 (Harley's letter-book). £300 expenses to Vanbrugh: CTB 1705–6, 634. Vanbrugh's delay on account of the theatre: Milhous and Hume (1982), 5. Congreve to Keally on the union: Congreve (1964), 40. Theatre management: Milhous (1976) and Milhous and Hume (1982); the latter largely supersedes Cummings (1914), Kern (1959/60) and Olleson (1972). *London Stage, passim.*

Hawksmoor to Boulter: BL MS. Add.19607, f.15. Agreement with Swiney: PRO LC7/2, f.1 (Milhous and Hume, 1982, 7). 'Another revolution': Congreve (1964), 43; Cibber (1968), 182. Lansdowne to Stanley: Milhous and Hume (1982), 15. Acoustics: Cibber (1968), 182, 173, 224. Order of Union: PRO LC5/154, 299–300 (Milhous and Hume, 1982, 49). York Buildings: Steele (1941), 115 n.2. Steele to Keally: ibid.25. Lady Wentworth: Cartwright (1883), 66. Travers to Marlborough, Whistler (1954), 145. Wren on funerals: Wren Soc. IX, 15.

Chapter 26

Audley End: Addison (1953); Drury (1980), 27–9, modified in Drury (1984). Anstis 1715: Bodl. MS. Rawl. C.335, f.11–15. Staircase ceiling: Pevsner (1968b), 157–8. Kimbolton: Archdale (1966); Oswald (1968); Whistler (1954), 131–42. May at Windsor: Downes (1966), 16–17. Hawksmoor's 'old father': Downes (1959), 244. Hardwick: Girouard (1983), 145–62 and Downes (1985). Evelyn at Audley End: 22 July 1670. Vanbrugh on Coleman: Webb (1928), 20, 24. Coleman on Vanbrugh: Pevsner (1968a), 277. Galilei: Toesca (1952)), 214; Kieven (1973); Oswald (1968), 1696–8; Downes (1966); the drawing, initialled AG, is repr. by Oswald, 1697, and by Lees-Milne (1970), 106. Chargate: Downes (1977), 50–51. Kings Weston: Downes (1967); Downes (1977), 79–80. Southwell's travels: Fremantle (1970). Wren on principals and principles: the Orders are the Principals, 'Beauty, Firmness and Convenience are the Principles' (Tract I, from C. Wren, *Parentalia*, 1750: Wren Soc. XIX, 126). Little Charles: Webb (1928), 149. *Reasons*: BL MS. Add.61353, ff.62–3. Vanbrugh's original differs substantially from all printed versions. Drawings of Woodstock: BL. K.35.28.e. Expenditure on the Old Manor: Green (1951), 141. 'goe into the moon': BL. MS. Stowe 751, f.205. Competition for approach to the house: Whistler (1954), 111–3, 230–1; Wren's memorandum on the subject: ibid. 253.

Chapter 27

The Fifty New Churches: Bill (1979); Downes (1959), 156–70; Downes (1966), 98–105. Maynwaring on Hawksmoor: Marlborough (1838), I, 263–7. Vanbrugh's *Proposals* are most recently reprinted in Downes (1977), 257–8. For Wren's (from C. Wren, *Parentalia*, 1750) see Wren Soc. IX, 15–18. Suratt: Wilkinson (1976). Plans for Kensington and St James's: Downes (1977), 88–90 and Fig. 11. See also *King's Works* (1976), 195–6, 239.

Woodstock letter: Webb (1928), 53–5. Vanbrugh's own copy in Harley papers, BL. MS. Loan 29/217, ff.613–14, endorsed *R from Mr Vanbrugh himself Febr: 20.* Other papers, ff.615–20. 'The Letter to his Relation' MS. Loan 29/200; the last sentence ('However . . . turn me out') is marked by a large cross in the copy. Lord

Oxford well disposed to Vanbrugh: Whistler (1954), 129. Talman's petition ('the only person in that Office turned out to make room for Mr Vanbrooke, who enjoys a very good place in the Office of Armes'), MS. Loan 29/217, f.506. Archer's petition, ff.617–18. The new scheme for H. M. Works, ff.637–42; another copy (ff.649–52) is endorsed with date of receipt 11 March 1712/13; this suggests that the document was composed after, and maybe partly prompted by, Vanbrugh's dismissal. On 13 September 1713 James Gibbs, hoping to succeed Dickinson as Hawksmoor's co-surveyor to the Fifty New Churches, wrote to Lord Oxford, 'Only my friend Mr Vanbrugh was against me, I suppose because I was recommended by your Lordship, and got the Commission to defer the nomination of a surveyor these two months as yet, and it may be longer, which I believe may be dangerous'. After a ballot on 18 November Gibbs was appointed (Friedman, 1984, 9–10).

Woodstock Town Hall: Joynes to Vanbrugh, BL MS.Add.19605, f.175. Comptroller's house at Whitehall to be kept wind and water tight, CTB 1714, 199. Cholmondeley: Vanbrugh's unexecuted project for the north front, c.1713, in *Vit. Brit.* II, 32 (Downes, 1977, Pl.95). The limits of Vanbrugh's concern with executed work at Cholmondeley were previously stated in Downes (1977), 92 n.41, and 278 (under both 'unexecuted projects' and 'attributions rejected'); some writers remain confused.

Correspondence with Lord Chamberlain's Office: Webb (1928), 57; Rosenberg (1966), 608–10. The Yarburgh papers (BIHR) include an agreement of 15 October 1706 by which Betterton and others are to sell clothes, properties etc. from Lincoln's Inn Fields to Vanbrugh for £500. Drury Lane payments: Account Book, ff.35, 35v, 41, 46, 51, 61.

Claremont building accounts: BL. MS. Add. 33442. Claremont in 1762: *Tour* (1762), I.243. Grimsthorpe survey: Colvin (1970), Fig.61. Baron Goertz: Hatton (1978), 147, 343. Peregrine Bertie's death: HMC Rutland II, 192. See also Whistler (1954), 240.

'Nothing done' plan: Green (1951), 146 (Fig. 68). Vanbrugh on Jefferson: Webb (1928), 78. Jefferson to Joynes: BL. MS. Add.19610, f.12; postmarked 16 October. Peter Walter: Kelch (1974), 25, 29, 47, 53. Lady Marlborough's quarrel with Lord Bristol: Hervey, *Letters*, II, 342–3. Her provocation of Vanbrugh: Webb, 89–92 (June 1717, wrongly as to Godolphin). Vanbrugh's resignation: BL. MS. Add.61353, f.213. The Duchess was archly surprised and 'wished to have had the civility I expressed . . . back again, and was very sorry I had fould my fingers writing to such a fellow' (Thomson, 1838, II, 540).

Chapter 28

Greenwich Hospital: Davies (1956); Downes (1959), 83–98. Directors' Minutes: PRO Adm 67. Greenwich Palace: *King's Works* (1982), 96–123. Greenwich residents: Rhind (1983), 256. The common statement that Thornhill lived in the area appears to be based on an error in Hasted's *Kent*. Vanbrugh at York in 1713: Montagu (1965), I,201; in 1715: *Architectural Review*, CXXXVIII (1965), 379 (letter from Hawksmoor to Henry Joynes, 12 April 1715). The Heslington lady: Downes (1982). Newcastle to his Duchess: BL. MS. Add.33073, ff.3–5. Two boys in the nursery: Webb (1928), 146. Vanbrugh's Greenwich lease: Rhind (1983),

240–2. History of the Castle: ibid.245–7. The Vanbrugh estate in 1815: Carter (1815).

Chapter 29
The Murray portrait at present forms part of the National Portrait Gallery's display at Beningbrough. See Piper (1963), 357. Two versions are known of a late portrait attributed to Jonathan Richardson: in the College of Arms and in the RIBA. The latter was still under restoration in 1987.

Halifax and the Works: *King's Works* (1976), 51–5; Webb (1928), 247–50. Board of Works attendances: Downes (1977), 260–1. Vanbrugh to Newcastle: Webb (1928), 96. The Herrenhausen engine: Hatton (1978), 262, 364. Benson's villa at Wilbury: RCHME (1988) will supersede all previous accounts. Hawksmoor on Benson: Downes (1959), 245–7. Vanbrugh's *Remarks on William Benson*: Downes (1977), 262. The King's unfair account of Vanbrugh: Webb (1928), 98. Robert Barker's paper on Benson: *King's Works* (1976), 62–3. Hawksmoor on Hewett: Webb (1931), 126; Downes (1959), 249. Addison's pension: Hatton (1978), 369; CTB 1718, 32, 264. Grant for life: Webb (1928), 114, 115, 149, 151. That the Drury Lane patent was Vanbrugh's goal is stated as fact by Connely (1934), 394. Work at St James's: *King's Works* (1976), 239-40. Hampton Court design: ibid. 178. A volume of drawings, probably made by Thomas Fort. Clerk of Works at Hampton Court during the period, was last recorded as in the Department of Environment Library. (*King's Works*, 1976, 171). Plays at Hampton Court: *London Stage*. A plan of the theatre is in the Fort volume. An estimate for its construction was approved by the Board of Works on 11 September (PRO Work 4/1).

Chapter 30
Anstis and Benson 'got over me': Webb (1928), 104. Lord Bristol to Lady Marlborough: Hervey, *Letters*, II, 144. Lady Marlborough to Lord Carlisle: HMC Carlisle, 32. Lady Lechmere: ibid. 34. Carlisle to Lady Marlborough: BL. MS. Add.61465, f.40. Vanbrugh's *Justification*: Webb (1928), 177–92. *House of Lords' Journal*, XXI, 508, 522, 528, 529; no further reference was made after the Whitsun recess.

Shaftesbury's *Letter* is often discussed. For the date of publication see Downes (1984). *Upon the Duke of Marlborough's House*: Pope (1882), IV, 451. Comments on Blenheim: Pope, *Letters*, I, 431–2. Walpole (1903), I, 15. Canaletto's view of Whitehall: Links (1982), 155–6. Baynes of Swallow: Webb (1928), 155. Small Domestick: Webb (1928), 140. Vanbrugh on Dean Jones: BL. MS. Add.61432, f.128. Duchess of Marlborough to the Post Office: ibid.f.135. Townshend to Carlisle: HMC Carlisle, 39 (19 May 1722). Atterbury: Hatton (1978), 256; HMC Carlisle, 43. Vanbrugh refers obliquely in two letters to Lord Carlisle (Webb, 1928, 143–4). George I's Progress: *London Gazette*, No. 6091 (1–4 Sept. 1722); Hervey, *Letters*, II, 224.

Chapter 31
See Krutch (1924). The recent publication of *The Rover* (1986) is an acting edition made for the Swan Theatre at Stratford-upon-Avon and is substantially altered

from the original. Steele's licence: Cibber (1968), 237–8, 270–2; Steele (1941), 524–5. Petition for perpetual licence: BL. MS. Add.32685, f.42. (Steele, 1941, 533–4). Steele's *The Theatre* was republished by John Loftis, Oxford (1962). *A Journey to London* was printed in Dobrée (1927), III, 131–68. Blade-bone: Woods (1965), 149–51.

Chapter 32

Account Book: Downes (1977); a second book was kept by Lady Vanbrugh from April 1728 to November 1757; it had, however, been started by her husband from the other end and used for some domestic and petty cash items from February 1722 to the end of 1725. Vanbrugh's Greenwich houses: Downes (1976); Downes (1977), 93–100; Rhind (1983), 245–54. Philip and Charles Vanbrugh: Downes (1977), 170–2. South Sea Company: Carswell (1961). Steele's fish pool vessel: Steele (1941), *passim* (indexed s.v. *Steele*). Miller's bricks: Downes (1977), 177. Payments to the midwife: Account Book. The inscription in the family bible: Beard (1986), Pl.2 (the caption should be compared with his pp.53 and 28, where n.60 misquotes Whistler, 1938). Reading matter: many assumptions have been made (Lang, 1965) about Vanbrugh's reading. He may have read almost anything that was printed, but few conclusions are 'obvious'. One of the least self-evident is that of Lang (1979), 210, that, coming from 'Flanders', Giles Vanbrugh's family was French-speaking; many a visitor to Antwerp has found to his or her cost the unlikeliness of this conclusion. An example in Dr Lang's own experience is not irrelevant. She believed (Lang, 1979) that in 1977 I had 'accepted, albeit anonymously' her 'contention' (Lang, 1965, 138) that the Temple at Castle Howard is based on Palladio's Rotonda (see chapter 33 here). This might seem obvious, but this contention is not only previously stated in Downes (1966), 125 (written before the publication of Dr Lang's paper) but is to be found (as is rightly acknowledged in her paper) in Kimball (1944), 100 ('the earliest of British adaptations of Palladio's Villa Rotonda').

Little Charles: Webb (1928), 149. Kynaston described to Newcastle: Webb (1928), 118. Elton Hall drawings: Colvin and Craig (1964). Southwell: Andrews (1938), IV, 142. The family at Southwell: Downes (1977), 167–9. Visit to Ickworth in 1719: Hervey, *Letters*, II, 95–6. The great oak: Carter (1815), 517.

Chapter 33

Vitruvius Britannicus: E. Harris (1986); date of Leoni's Palladio: Connor (1977), 20 n.38; Facsimile ed.

Leoni: Hewlings (1985). The new Junta: *King's Works* (1976), 71 n.2. Eastbury: Downes (1977), 114–8; RCHME (1972), 90–93; Kimball (1944). Palladian clichés: Wittkower (1974), 155–74. Seaton Delaval: Downes (1977), 102–6. Papers in the Northumberland RO (NRO 650) include a letter from James Mewburn, agent, to Delaval, 23 Jan. 1722. A bill from Robert Keating to Mr John Vernbergh, and receipt from Madam Apreece, executrix of Mr Vernbergh deceased, 20 April 1724, are evidently not connected with Sir John Vanbrugh. The letter exhibited in the house at Seaton Delaval, concerning the top lunette on the north front and addressed to the builder, George Cansfield, is not Vanbrugh's. See Appendix B.

Grimsthorpe: Downes (1977), 118–21; Colvin (1970); Connor (1974); Saxl and Wittkower (1948), 66. Sir Godfrey Copley on Welbeck: BL. MS. Stowe 748, ff.9–10. Bridgeman: Willis (1977). Vanbrugh's instructions as Surveyor of Gardens and Waters: PRO Work 6/11, 31–2. Kensington Water Tower: *King's Works* (1976), 195 (wrongly as 1722–4); Timbs (1885), 288. The engine 'to work with two men' was ordered from John Rowley on 8 January 1717 (PRO Work 4/1). Stowe: Whistler (1957, 1959); Gibbon (1977). Lord Perceval at Stowe: BL MS. Add.47030, ff.156–9. Lord Oxford at Castle Howard 1725: BL MS. Loan 29/233, ff.87–9. Obelisks: Webb (1928), 130–1. Hawksmoor on the Belvedere: Downes (1959), 243–4. Crop marks revealing the north court: Whistler (1978). Hawksmoor's sketch for the Belvedere: Downes (1959), 244 and Pl.87. Following the Ancients: Downes (1959), 40–2.

Chapter 34

London traffic: Mitchell and Leys (1963), 161–6. John Barker to Lord Fermanagh: Verney (1930), II, 27. 1709 Building Act: HMC House of Lords, N.S. VIII, 305. Hawksmoor's *Explanation*: Tipping (1928), xliv-xlviii. A reprint as a pamphlet was issued by All Souls College in 1960.

Uncontrollable laughter: Vanbrugh to Watkins (quoted below). Jest and earnest: Faller (1974). In *A Journey to London* (I.i) Lady Headpiece 'will be extremely courteous to the Fops who make love to her in jest, and she will be extremely grateful to those who do it in earnest'. Restoration morality: Eliot (1934), 45 (*A Dialogue on Dramatic Poetry*). Date of the altered scenes in *The Provok'd Wife*: Cibber (1968), 308–9; Zimansky (1970b), 123–4; Smith (1974), 112–4. Knox Ward: *Harleian Soc.* CXV–CXVI (1963–4), 63; Godfrey (1963).

Galilei's design for Newcastle: Kieven (1973), fig. 5; Toesca (1952), 216–7. Imperial mischief at Greenwich: Webb (1931), 153. Vanbrugh to Watkins: Webb (1928), 137–8. Shaftesbury: 'Hardly, indeed, as the Publick now stands, shou'd we bear to see a *Whitehall* treated like a *Hampton-Court*, or even a new Cathedral like St Paul's' (*Characteristicks*, 1732, 401). A statement in Downes (1977), 90–91, that Vanbrugh 'could have supplied Shaftesbury's national style', has been widely misunderstood: the conditional construction referred to Vanbrugh's own opinion, not the author's.

Duncombe: information from the York staff of RCHME. Vanbrugh House, Oxford: Downes (1966), 97. King's Weston Album: Downes (1967). Ordnance: Whistler (1954), 212–26; Dr Nigel Barker's Reading Ph.D. thesis returned to the conclusion that the Vanbrugian buildings are so different from the general run of Ordnance architecture that Vanbrugh must have been concerned in some way. Jelfe: Colvin (1978), 456–7. Appointed Clerk Itinerant to the Works, 13 August 1715: CTB 1714–15, 686.

William Vanbrugh: Downes (1977), 159–61. Last known meeting of the Kit-Cat: Steele (1941), 336. Vanbrugh's cup: Spence, I, 207. Robin Hood's Well: Downes (1977), 124; Lord Oxford's tour: BL. MS. Loan 29/233, f.62. Lord Carlisle's letter about visiting Blenheim: BL. MS. Add.61465, f.170. The Duchess's reply: Webb (1928), 271. Vanbrugh to Tonson: ibid. 167. Report of Vanbrugh's exclusion: Green (1951), 316. William Dowdeswell to Lord Oxford: Webb (1928), 271. Lady Lechmere on Vanbrugh: BL. MS. Add.61465, f.57v.

Lady Marlborough on Lady Lechmere: ibid. f.157. Bushes, bogs and briars: Webb (1928), 136. Lady Irwin and the Vanbrughs: Vanbrugh's letter in BIHR. Tonson's reply to Vanbrugh: Lynch (1971), 164–5.

Young Charles Vanbrugh: Lady Vanbrugh's account book (BIHR). Bielfeld's account: Downes (1977), 275. Charles's death: Whistler (1938), 293–5. The original letter from Joseph Yorke to Jack Jones (first published in *The Genealogist*, II, 1878, 239–40), is in BIHR. Beechcroft: Rhind (1983), 245–56; Lady Vanbrugh's will: PROB 11/1020, f.250. Edward Vanbrugh to Lady Vanbrugh: BIHR. Pope and Tonson: Spence (1966), I, 50. Abel Evans's facetious (and, some would now have it, scatological) epitaph on Vanbrugh is included here solely to obviate a charge of suppression:

Lie heavy on him, Earth, for he
Laid many a heavy load on thee.

There are no separate notes to the Appendices.

Appendix A

List of Works

Plays   Dates are of first productions.

The Relapse, 1696.
Æsop, 1696/7, from Boursault. *Æsop II*, 1697.
The Provok'd Wife, 1697.
The Country House, 1698, from Dancourt.
The Pilgrim, 1700, from Fletcher.
The False Friend, 1702, from Le Sage.
Squire Trelooby, with Congreve and Walsh, 1704, from Molière. *LOST*.
The Confederacy, 1705, from Dancourt.
The Mistake, 1705, from Molière.
The Cuckold in Conceit, 1707, from Molière. *LOST*.
A Journey to London. Unfinished, printed 1728.

Buildings wholly or partly executed
   † destroyed or rebuilt, * attributed

Castle Howard, Yorks., 1700–12. West wing by Sir Thomas Robinson 1753–9.
†Vanbrugh ('Goose-Pie') House, Whitehall, London, 1701.
†*Barn Elms, Surrey, ?room for Jacob Tonson, 1703.
†The Queen's Theatre, Haymarket, London, 1704–5.
Blenheim Palace, Oxon., 1705–25; Vanbrugh resigned 1716.
Kimbolton Castle, Hunts., 1707–10. East portico by Galilei 1719.
Audley End, Essex, screen and ?staircase, 1708.
†Chargate, Esher, Surrey, 1709–10.
Kings Weston, Glos., c.1710–14. Interior finished by Robert Mylne.

Castle Howard, Great Obelisk, 1714.

†Newcastle House, Lincoln's Inn Fields, London, refitting, 1714–17.

*Morpeth, Northumb., Town Hall, 1714.

†Claremont, Esher, Surrey (incorporating Chargate), 1715–20.

Claremont, Belvedere, 1715.

Orford House, Chelsea Hospital, London, alterations, 1715.

*Naworth Castle, Cumb., ?alterations for Lord Carlisle, partly destroyed. (G. Worsley, *Country Life*, CLXXXI, 1987, 74–9).

Hampton Court, Middx., Prince of Wales's Rooms, 1716.

*St James's Palace, London, Great Kitchen, 1716–17.

†Kensington Palace, Water Tower, 1716–18.

Vanbrugh Castle, Greenwich, London, 1718–21.

*Windsor, Berks., Pump House, 1718.

†Eastbury, Dorset, 1718–38.

*Duncombe Park, Yorks., Rotondo, c.1718.

Castle Howard, Pyramid Gate, 1719.

†Nottingham Castle, Notts., refitting, 1719.

†Stowe, Bucks., additions to house, and garden buildings, c.1719–24. The north portico and (in part) Rotondo survive.

Seaton Delaval, Northumb., 1720–8. Gutted.

†Vanbrugh Fields Estate, Greenwich, London, 1719–25.

Robin Hood's Well, Skelbrooke, Yorks., c.1720.

Lumley Castle, Co. Durham, remodelling, 1722–

*Somersby Hall, Lincs., 1722.

Grimsthorpe Castle, Lincs., north range (1715?), 1722–6.

Esher, Surrey, Old Church, Newcastle Pew, 1723–5.

Castle Howard, Temple, 1725–8. Interior by Francesco Vassali 1738–9.

*Swinstead, Lincs., Belvedere or Old Summer House.

†*Middleton Park, Oxon., alterations for Henry Boyle, Lord Carleton, c.1715? (but in August 1722 Vanbrugh probably visited Carleton at Amesbury: notes in back of Lady Vanbrugh's Account Book).

†*Sacombe Park, Herts., garden walls and pavilions for Edward Rolt (d.1722).

†Vine Court, Sevenoaks, Kent, c.1720?

†*Brompton Park, London, house for Henry Wise.

†*Peckham, London, Hanover House.

†*Kingston, Surrey, house in London Road.

This list is based on that in Downes (1977), 277–8 with additions from Colvin (1978), 854. For Ordnance buildings attributed to Vanbrugh, and for unexecuted or lost designs and untenable attributions, see Downes (1977), 278.

Appendix B

Vanbrugh's Letters

There has been no complete edition of Vanbrugh's letters since Webb (1928). The transfer of the Blenheim archives to the British Library has made available the originals of many letters which Webb printed from copies. A further twenty-four letters, most of them previously unknown, were published in Whistler (1954), and some thirty have been discovered since then. The list of known letters in Downes (1977), 267–73, requires amendments and additions in the light of recent discoveries, as well as the correction of some errors. The immediate need is for an up-to-date list with the indication of one (not necessarily the only) printed source; this list therefore supersedes that of 1977.

In the following list of sources, numbers, unless otherwise noted, are those of documents rather than pages.

Webb = Webb (1928), main sequence.
Webb II, III = Webb (1928), Appendices II, III.
Whistler = Whistler (1954).
Downes = Downes (1977), by page No.
Huseboe = Huseboe (1974).
Milhous = Milhous (1979)
Milhous/Coke = Milhous (1982), by page No.

Other sources, for single letters only, are traceable in the Bibliography. Details for unpublished letters are indicated in square brackets.

1685

28 Dec.	Earl of Huntingdon	Chester	Rosenberg (1)
1691			
7 July	Henry Browne	Vincennes	Hopkins (1979)
9 Nov.	Mrs Vanbrugh	Vincennes	Downes, p.249
1692			
26 Aug.	William Blathwayt	Bastille	Downes, p.249

1699

25 Dec.	Earl of Manchester	London	Webb (1)
1700	Earl of Carlisle	Tadcaster	Webb (2)
1703			
15 June	Duke of Newcastle	London	Whistler (1)
15 June	Jacob Tonson	London	Webb (3)
13 July	Tonson	London	Webb (4)
30 July	Tonson	London	Webb (5)
1704			
9 Nov.	Lord Godolphin		Webb (6)
1705			
22 June	Duke of Marlborough		Whistler (2)
24 Aug.	Marlborough	London	Whistler (3)
1706			
1 Jan.	Boulter		Webb II (1)
8 Nov.	Boulter	London	Webb II (6)
19 Dec.	Henry Joynes	London	Milhous (1)
1707			
11 Jan.	Boulter	London	Webb II (2)
c.23 Jan.	Boulter		Webb II (3)
6 Mar.	Joynes		Webb II (4)
7 Mar.	Boulter	London	Webb II (5)
15 July	Marlborough	Blenheim	Whistler (4)
18 July	Boulter	London	Webb II (7)
18 July	Manchester	London	Webb (7)
25 July	Marlborough	London	Whistler (5)
Aug.	Joynes	Henderskelfe	Webb II (24)
9 Sep.	Manchester	London	Webb (8)
16 Oct.	Peter Le Neve		Milhous (2)
11 Nov.	Boulter	London	Webb II (9)
18 Nov.	Boulter	London	Webb II (10)
18 Dec.	Boulter	London	Webb II (11)
1708			
7 Jan.	Vice-Chamberlain Coke		Whistler (6)
15 Jan.	Coke		Milhous/Coke, p.72
20 Jan.	Coke		Huseboe (1)
21 Feb.	Coke		Milhous/Coke, p.83
24 Feb.	Manchester	London	Webb (9)
16 Mar.	Manchester	London	Webb (10)
22 Mar.	Manchester	Stevenage	Webb (11)
29 Mar.	Boulter	London	Webb II (12)
1 Apr.	Boulter		Webb II (13)
7 Apr.	[opera account]		Milhous/Coke, p.97
c.14 Apr.	[proposal to singers]		Milhous/Coke, p.99
mid Apr.	Coke		Milhous/Coke, p.100
25 Apr.	Boulter	Henley	Webb II (14)
1 May	Boulter	London	Webb II (15)

11 May	Manchester	London	Webb (12)
14 May	anon.		Rosenberg (3)
19 June	Joynes	London	Webb II (16)
24 June	Joynes	London	Webb II (17)
8 July	?Arthur Maynwaring	Blenheim	Webb (13)
27 July	Manchester		Webb (14)
17 Aug.	Manchester	Biggleswade	Webb (15)
14 Sep.	Duchess of Marlborough	Blenheim	Webb (16)
21 Sep.	Joynes	London	Webb II (18)
28 Sep.	Joynes	London	Webb II (19)
6 Nov.	Joynes	London	Webb II (20)
30 Nov.	Joynes	London	Webb II (21)
9 Dec.	Joynes	London	Webb II (22)
26 Dec.	Joynes	London	Webb II (23)
1709			
13 Jan.	Joynes	London	Webb II (25)
10 Feb.	Joynes		Webb II (26)
17 Feb.	Joynes	London	Webb II (27)
5 May	Hopkins		Whistler (7)
31 May	?Godolphin	Blenheim	Webb (17)
9 June	Duchess of Marlborough		Webb (18)
11 June	Duchess of Marlborough		Webb (19)
11 June	Duchess of Marlborough		Webb (20)
8 July	[Memorandum]		Webb (21)
14 July	Duchess of Marlborough	London	Webb (22)
18 July	?Lord Ryalton	Blenheim	Webb (23)
25 July	Duchess of Marlborough		Webb (24)
29 Sep.	Joynes	London	Webb II (28)
1 Nov.	Duchess of Marlborough	Blenheim	Webb (25)
22 Nov.	Joynes	Oxford	Milhous (3)
30 Nov.	Samuel Travers	Whitehall	Webb II (26)
6 Dec.	anon.	London	Webb II (29)
18 Dec.	Joynes	London	Webb II (30)
20 Dec.	Joynes	London	Webb II (31)
1710			
10 Feb.	[Memorandum]		Appendix G
14 Mar.	Joynes	London	Webb II (46)
1 Apr.	Joynes and Bobart		Webb II (32)
28 Apr.	Marlborough	London	Whistler (10)
29 Apr.	Joynes	London	Webb II (33)

6 May	Joynes	London	Webb II (34)
27 May	Duchess of Marlborough		Whistler (11)
27 May	Duchess of Marlborough		Whistler (12)
6 June	Duchess of Marlborough	London	Webb (28)
6 June	Joynes and Bobart	London	Webb II (35)
8 June	Joynes	London	Webb II (36)
24 June	Duchess of Marlborough	London	Webb (29)
1 Aug.	Marlborough	Blenheim	Webb (30)
31 Aug.	Duchess of Marlborough	London	Webb (31)
7 Sep.	Joynes	London	Webb II (37)
21 Sep.	Joynes	London	Webb II (38)
22 Sep.	Marlborough	London	Webb (32)
30 Sep.	Marlborough	Blenheim	Webb (33)
30 Sep.	Lord Poulet	Blenheim	Webb (33a)
30 Sep.	Robert Harley	Blenheim	Webb (33b)
3 Oct.	Marlborough	Oxford	Webb (34)
10 Oct.	Treasury		Webb (33d)
10 Oct.	Marlborough	London	Webb (35)
10 Oct.	Joynes and Bobart	London	Webb II (39)
12 Oct.	Joynes	London	Webb II (40)
19 Oct.	Joynes	London	Webb II (41)
25 Oct.	Joynes	London	Webb II (42)
25 Oct.	Maynwaring	Chargate	Webb (36)
2 Nov.	Joynes	London	Webb II (43)
28 Nov.	Joynes	London	[Huntington Library]
[1710]	Marlborough		Whistler (13)
1711			
9 Jan.	Joynes	London	Webb II (44)
12 Feb.	Robert Harley		Whistler (8)
17 Feb.	Joynes	Whitehall	Webb II (45)
23 Feb.	Marlborough	London	Whistler (9)
22 Mar.	Joynes	London	Webb II (47)
17 May	Joynes	London	Webb II (48)
10 Aug.	Marlborough	London	Whistler (14)
11 Sep.	Joynes	London	Webb II (49)
15 Sep.	Joynes	London	Webb II (50)
25 Sep.	Joynes	London	Webb II (51)
30 Sep.	Joynes	London	Webb II (52)
27 Oct.	Joynes	London	Webb II (53)
13 Nov.	Joynes	London	Webb II (54)
22 Nov.	Joynes	London	Webb II (55)
1 Dec.	Joynes	London	Webb II (56)

3 Dec.	Joynes	London	Webb II (57)
27 Dec.	anon	Whitehall	Webb (38)
1712			
3 Aug.	Earl of Oxford		Webb (39)
30 Oct.	Joynes	London	Webb II (58)
4 Nov.	?Marlborough		Webb (40)
10 Nov.	[Memorandum]		Webb (41)
1713			
25 Jan.	Mayor of Woodstock	Whitehall	Webb (42)
21 Feb.	Earl of Oxford		Whistler (15)
24 Feb.	John Grigsby		Milhous (4)
18 Mar.	Marlborough	London	Whistler (16)
2 Apr.	[a relation]		Webb (44)
14 Apr.	Earl of Oxford	Whitehall	Whistler (17)
28 Sep.	Edward Southwell	Chester	Whistler (19)
23 Oct.	Southwell	Castle Howard	Webb (45)
29 Oct.	James Craggs	Castle Howard	Webb (46)
20 Nov.	Coke	Castle Howard	Webb (47)
4 Dec.	Southwell	Castle Howard	Huseboe (2)
1714			
29 May	Marlborough	London	Webb (48)
6 July	Lord Chamberlain		Rosenberg (6)
13 Aug.	Lord Chamberlain		Rosenberg (7)
29 Nov.	Lord Halifax		Webb III (1)
7 Dec.	Lord Wharton		[Portland Papers, Nottingham Univ.]
27 Dec.	Lord Chamberlain		Rosenberg (8)
1714–15	Earl of Clare		Webb (50)
1715?	Tonson		Webb (53)
1715			
16 Jan.	Duchess of Marlborough		Webb (49)
Feb.	Lord Chamberlain		Rosenberg (5)
5 Feb.	Earl of Clare	Whitehall	Webb (51)
9 Feb.	anon.		Webb (52)
31 Mar.	Treasury		Webb III (2)
3 May	Joynes	London	Webb II (59)
5 May	Joynes	Whitehall	Webb II (60)
7 May	Joynes	Whitehall	Webb II (61)
1 June	Lowndes	Whitehall	Appendix G
Oct.	Robert Walpole		Downes, p.274
17 Oct.	Robert Walpole		Webb (54)
23 Nov.	Baron Goertz		[Darmstadt: Hatton (1978), 147,343]
1716			
5 Apr.	Joynes		Webb II (63)
19 Apr.	Marlborough		Webb (55)
1 May	Joynes		Webb II (64)

14 May	Henry Wise		Appendix G
25 May	Marlborough		Webb (56)
12 June	Duchess of Marlborough	Whitehall	Webb (57)
19 June	Duchess of Marlborough	London	Webb (58)
30 June	Duchess of Marlborough	Blenheim	Webb (59)
10 July	Duchess of Marlborough	London	Webb (60)
13 July	Duchess of Marlborough	London	Webb (61)
21 July	Treasury		Appendix G
27 July	Duchess of Marlborough	Blenheim	Webb (62)
3 Aug.	Duchess of Marlborough	London	Webb (63)
19 Aug.	Duchess of Marlborough	Castle Howard	Webb (64)
21 Aug.	Duchess of Marlborough	Scarborough	Webb (65)
27 Sep.	Duchess of Marlborough	Blenheim	Webb (66)
30 Sep.	Treasury		Appendix G.
18? Oct.	Duchess of Marlborough	London	Webb (67)
20? Oct.	Duchess of Marlborough	Whitehall	Webb (68)
6 Nov.	Duchess of Marlborough		Webb (70)
8 Nov.	Duchess of Marlborough	Whitehall	Webb (71)
10 Nov.	Duke of Newcastle	London	Webb (72)
15 Nov.	Newcastle	Whitehall	Webb (73)
27 Nov.	Newcastle	Whitehall	Webb (74)
15 Dec.	Bobart	London	Webb (75)
1716	Marlborough		Whistler (20)
1716–	[Memorandum]		Whistler (25)
1717			
26 Apr.	Treasury		Appendix G
30 Apr.	[a Carlisle daughter]		Downes (1982)
27 June	Marlborough		Whistler (21)
June	Carlisle		Webb (76)
3 July	Newcastle		Webb (77)
9 Oct.	Newcastle	Bath	Webb (78)
14 Oct.	Treasury	Bath	Webb (79)
Nov.	Newcastle	Whitehall	Webb (151)

21 Dec.	Newcastle	Greenwich	Webb (80)
—	Newcastle		Webb (81)
—	Newcastle		Webb (82)
—	Newcastle		Webb (83)
—	Newcastle	Greenwich	Webb (84)
—	anon		Webb (85)
1717–18	Newcastle	Whitehall	Webb (152)
—	Newcastle		Webb (153)
—	Peter Le Neve		Milhous (5)
1718			
4 July	Peter Forbes	Greenwich	Webb (86)
31 July	Earl of Sunderland		Whistler (22)
7 Aug.	Newcastle	Whitehall	Webb (87)
30 Aug.	Newcastle		Webb (88)
17 Sep.	Newcastle	Greenwich	Webb (89)
—	Newcastle	Greenwich	Webb (90)
Sep.	Newcastle	Greenwich	Webb (91)
—	Newcastle		Webb (92)
30 Oct.	Earl of Suffolk	Whitehall	Webb (93)
—	Newcastle		Webb (94)
—	Newcastle		Webb (95)
29 Nov.	Newcastle	Greenwich	Webb (96)
17 Dec.	Newcastle	Nottingham	Webb (97)
25 Dec.	Newcastle	Castle Howard	Webb (98)
1718	Newcastle	Whitehall	Webb (149)
1719			
4 Jan.	Newcastle	Castle Howard	Webb (99)
12 Jan.	Newcastle	York	Webb (100)
24 Jan.	Newcastle	Nottingham	Webb (101)
March	Treasury		Downes, p 262
5 May	Newcastle		Whistler (23)
1 July	Tonson	London	Webb (102)
23 July	Newcastle	London	Webb (103)
6 Aug.	Newcastle	Whitehall	Webb (104)
—	Newcastle		Webb (105)
11 Aug.	Newcastle	London	Webb (106)
15 Aug.	Newcastle		Webb (107)
10 Sep.	Sunderland or		
	Stanhope	London	Webb (108)
—	Newcastle	Whitehall	Webb (109)
—	Newcastle	Greenwich	Webb (110)
5 Nov.	Tonson	Whitehall	Webb (111)
23 Nov.	Newcastle	Whitehall	Webb (112)
—	Stanhope		Webb (113)
29 Nov.	Tonson	Whitehall	Webb (114)
31 Dec.	Tonson	Whitehall	Webb (115)

1720

18 Feb.	Tonson	London	Webb (116)
15 Sep.	Newcastle	London	Webb (117)
24 Nov.	Mauduit		Webb (118)

1721

2 Feb.	Carlisle	London	Webb (119)
7 Feb.	Carlisle		Webb (120)
18 Feb.	Carlisle		Webb (121)
20 Feb.	Carlisle		Webb (122)
25 Mar.	Carlisle	Greenwich	Webb (123)
22 Apr.	Carlisle	London	Webb (124)
5 May	Carlisle	London	Webb (125)
25 May	Carlisle	London	Webb (126)
8 June	Carlisle	London	Webb (127)
6 July	Carlisle	London	Webb (128)
8 Aug.	Newcastle	Castle Howard	Webb (129)
20 Aug.	Brigadier Watkins	York	Webb (130)
20 Sep.	anon.	Heslington	Appendix G
16 Nov.	Carlisle	Whitehall	Webb (131)
18 Nov.	Joynes	Whitehall	Webb (132)

1722

11 Feb.	Newcastle		Webb (133)
13 Feb.	Duke of Ancaster		[Sotheby sale 28 Mar. 1972(330)]
6 Apr.	Carlisle		Webb (134)
24 Apr.	Carlisle	London	Webb (135)
5 May	Carlisle	London	Webb (136)
10 May	Carlisle	London	Webb (137)
30 May	Treasury		Webb (138)
June?	Sir Hans Sloane		Appendix G
18 June	Tonson	London	Webb (139)
19 June	Carlisle	London	Webb (140)
19 July	Carlisle	London	Webb (141)
26 July	2nd Duchess of Marlborough	Winchester	Appendix G

1723

19 Jan.	Newcastle	Greenwich	Webb (142)
30 July	Newcastle	Greenwich	Webb (143)
3 Aug.	?Forbes	Greenwich	Webb (144)
20 Aug.	Newcastle	Castle Howard	Webb (145)
1 Nov.	Newcastle	Greenwich	Webb (69)
11 Nov.	Joynes	Greenwich	Webb (146)
26 Nov.	Carlisle	London	Webb (147)
22 Dec.	Newcastle	Greenwich	Webb (148)
—	Newcastle		Webb (150)

1724

11 Feb.	Carlisle	Whitehall	Webb (154)

18 Feb.	Carlisle		Webb (155)
24 Feb.	Le Neve	Whitehall	Milhous (5)
26 Mar.	Carlisle	London	Webb (156)
11 Apr.	Carlisle	London	Webb (157)
10 July	Newcastle	Greenwich	Webb (158)
23 Aug.	Newcastle	Scarborough	Webb (159)
28 Aug.	Newcastle	Castle Howard	Webb (160)
4 Sep.	Guidott		Whistler (24)
21 Nov.	Carlisle	London	Webb (161)
10 Dec.	Carlisle	London	Webb (162)
1725			
26 Apr.	Treasury		Webb (163)
4 May	Treasury		Webb (164)
12 Aug.	Tonson	London	Webb (165)
19 Aug.	Treasury		Appendix G
4 Sep.	Carlisle	Greenwich	Webb (166)
11 Sep.	Carlisle	Greenwich	Webb (167)
25 Oct.	Tonson	Greenwich	Webb (168)
16 Dec.	Carlisle	London	Webb (169)
1726			
8 Mar.	Carlisle	London	Webb (170)

The unsigned letter of 16 August 1722 at Seaton Delaval addressed to George Cansfield, reproduced and transcribed by Bingham (1974), 345, 363, is not by Vanbrugh as claimed there and by Beard (1986), 169. Not only is the handwriting not Vanbrugh's, but the possibility of its being a copy is excluded by the format, which overlaps a pencil sketch and finishes sideways. Moreover the style and spelling are unlike Vanbrugh's.

Appendix C

Vanbrugh's Coat of Arms

Randle Holme's *Academy of Armory* (1688) gives Giles's arms as *Argent a Fesse Barry of ten Or and Azure, a Lion Issuant Sable*. William Vanbrugh's arms appear graphically in a similar form in the heraldic frontispiece to Thomas Fuller's book on the Holy Land, *A Pisgah-Sight of Palestine* (1650), to which William, and also Peter Matthews Baldwin, subscribed with thirty-one other knights, gentlemen and merchants whose arms appear there.

The seal Vanbrugh used on his agreement of 1704 with Newcastle for the Queen's Theatre shows the lion issuant quartered with part of the Carleton arms. But on a number of Blenheim letters in BL MS. Add. 61353 (for example f.88v of 28 April 1710) he used a different seal in which the lion issuant and bars are halved with the arms of Clarenceux, namely *Argent, a Cross Gules, and on a chief Gules a Lion Passant Guardant crowned with an open Crown, Or*; the crown forms a crest to the shield.

According to Mark Noble, *History of the College of Arms*, 1804, Vanbrugh's arms as incorporated in 1714 were *Gules on a Fesse Or three Barrulets Vert; in chief a Demy Lion, with for the Crest a Demy Lion issuant from a Bridge of three Reversed Arches, Or*. They appear in this form, including the bridge which is literally upside-down, below the plate (No.62) which Vanbrugh sponsored for Tonson's 1712 publication of Julius Cæsar's works. Noble also states that the Earl of Suffolk, as Deputy Earl Marshal, was not fully satisfied with the 'truth of the premises' of Giles Vanbrugh's origins, nor of the authenticity of the arms in the frontispiece to Fuller's book of 1650. Lord Suffolk accordingly referred the matter to Garter and Clarenceux, who in 1714 were respectively Sir Henry St George and Vanbrugh himself. Perhaps in the circumstances not surprisingly, they confirmed the arms and the crest, the arms to be quartered with those of Vanbrugh's Carleton mother. They also declared that the Vanbrugh arms were to be borne by all surviving descendants of Gillis Vanbrugh.

A volume of Wardrobe papers in the Royal Archives at Windsor Castle (RA.87910) contains a pasted-in water-colour drawing (RA.87910A) of the new tabards issued to Heralds in 1717 which bore for the first time the Saxon horse; the document is not personal to Vanbrugh as suggested by R. Hatton, *George I* (1978), 303, 367. The reference given there is not now applicable.

Appendix D

A True Character of the Prince of Wales's Poet

This defamatory composition survives, apparently, in a unique copy in the Beinecke Library of Yale University (Broadsides Quarto, By 6 1701). It is reprinted here, by kind permission, in order to spare the Library further enquiries, rather than for any merit whatsoever in the document beyond the historical fact of its existence.

The Prince of Wales was Prince James Francis Edward, proclaimed King James III in exile at Saint-Germain on the death of his father, on 5/16 September 1701. Since he was only thirteen, the notion of his having a poet is no more than a roundabout way of branding Vanbrugh as a Jacobite.

Vanbrugh's claim of loyalty to James II, written from prison, must have been an embarrassment to him in retrospect, for nothing was farther from the truth of his allegiance. Whether or not the writer of the verses knew anything about Vanbrugh's false claim, made under expediency, cannot be determined.

The imputation that Vanbrugh and Peregrine Bertie were homosexuals and living in unnatural sin at Whitehall is not supported by evidence of any kind, and two instances are worth mentioning of the inaccuracy of the document. First, as contemporary accounts make clear, the Whitehall fire did not begin in the area of Bertie's lodgings but in the King's Lodgings. Secondly, it is not true that Vanbrugh's house had no front entrance. On the other hand, Whitehall as a scene of more conventional misbehaviour was already a cliché some years earlier, and is referred to as such in *The Relapse* (V.ii), when Berinthia places Loveless's assignation 'somewhere about that *Babylon* of Wickedness, *White-Hall*'.

A TRUE
CHARACTER
Of the Prince of *WALES*'s Poet, with a Discrip-
tion of the new erected *Folly* at *White-Hall*.

I Sing the Man, who n'ere *Distinction* knew,
Till he had *Din'd* 'tween *Christian*, *Turk* or *Jew*:
No *Sense* of *Friend*, or *Foe* can on him steal:
Who all *Regards* renounces for a *Meal*

In Love, and Friendship false; to all unjust:
Active, and *Passive*, in *both Sexes Lust.*
Pregnant of Vice; he hath supply'd the stage
With Characters to improve the Basest Age,
By his loose Pen, still are Lewdest shown;
His *Foppingtons*, and *Worthy's* are his own:
For Fools and Knaves, others may stretch their Wits,
He needs not to himself, he only fits.
As *Painters* their own *Pictures* by a *Glass*,
So he but *viewes himself*, and *draws* the *Asse*:
Exactly drawn, 'twould merit praise from all:
For its an *Exquisite Original.*

Bereft of fortune, slave to Vanity,
He Scrible's the fine Fool, he cannot be,
With secret liking he doth *Fopton* write:
And to *Disguise himself in't, makes him Fight*:
For he forlorn to honour, and his Word:
To Wear his *Pen unpunish't* quits his *Sword.*
Quick is his Hand with Libels to defame,
But is to *Vindicate the scandal lame.*

With Vilest Arts into your House he'l creep:
Secrets for his own sake, not thine, hee'l keep,
But thence to be Impower'd to give the Strife,
Thy Daughter to suborn, or Whore thy Wife;
For such low ills, with him alas are small:
Who Dares no more, he can a *worthy call.*

Look for this thing of mixt Preposterous kind,
And by these markes you may the Monster find;
Find did I say? forgive my zeal that run
Too fast, you may by these the Monster shun.

If yet you know him not: When 'ere you see,
A thing, that's in its Nature mean? tis he,
In *Conversation, Building, Poetry*,
He knows no *Sense, nor Place, nor Unity*:
How shall I the Pretending Thing Define:
Builder, and *Poet* too, without *Design*:

Yet must this Abject Tool, this Wretch so Base:
A Mansion from a *Ruin'd Palace raise*:
So let it be, *Vengeance wee'l now excuse;*
This all the Vice for which 'twas burn't Renewes.
The *Wondrous Gimcrack* only stands to tell;
That there was once *White-hall* and *why it fell*:

The Fire which laid that Noble Pile in Dust,
Begun where *P——* us'd to *burn in Lust*,
Such was the *Sin*, so great the *Punishment.*
Which *angry Heaven* in its fury sent.
Whose heart but his, would it not make relent?

Forbear! unthinking foolish Man forbear!
Nor farther the *incestuous Building* rear:
With Modesty Great *WILLIAMS* favour use;
Robb not his *Chappel* to Erect your *Stewes*:
Stewes said I? But *Bare Stewes!* were it no more
It might be Born: But————————

Why even the *Buildings* by itself *betray'd*,
Itself *confesseth* for what use 'twas made.
It self's the *Emblem* of your *Darling Sin.*

No other way but only Backwards in,
Betrayes your Genius, and too plainly shows,
Within your *Veines*, what *Beastly Passion* flowes.

You might retire to your *Fulsome sport*,
To some Dark Cave, where only Beasts resort,
And not have made a *Sodom of the Court.*
Down with this Infant Nurssery of Sin,
E're yet the Infection does to spread begin:
Or pull it Down, or else for times to come.
When *War and Danger Drawes our Fleets from Home*:
When *Strangers* to our *Men of War* shall call,
For *shame*, no longer be the word *White-hall.*
The Place will now no better Style afford.
But *B————s Shoving House* must be the *Word.*

Reader from him thy self with care defend,
He's never terrible but when a Friend;
But Satyr's lost on him, do what you can,
He act's the Woman oft, but ne're the Man.

FINIS

LONDON, Printed in the Year 1701.

Appendix E

The Bow Window Room at Castle Howard

The King's Maps in the British Library include a drawing in Hawksmoor's hand for the bow window room built at the west end of the south range, and destroyed by Sir Thomas Robinson (KTC xlv.18.c). This was first published (in a cropped illustration) by Lang (1950). Although the drawing has since been discussed elsewhere in the Vanbrugh literature, notably (and with different conclusions) by Whistler (1954), Dr Lang has more recently resurrected the opinions put forward in her article (Lang, 1979). Since they can be shown to be erroneous, the questions raised by this Socratic paper are here discussed at some length.

The drawing, in pen and ink, is inscribed by Hawksmoor with a scale of 5 ft to an inch and a long note which reads (allowing for a blot and a rough edge) as follows:

> *This is the West front of the great Cabinet. I am not exact in the Number of Rusticks in the Basment. but the number must be Regulated by my Lords Appartmt and the arching heads drawne out at Large, which I pray you to doe, and give me an account how it hitts.*
> *For I have not the draught of my Lds End, so cannot adjust it my Self, if you find any difficulty pray send me a rough sketch of my Lds front and I will settle it.*
> *The windows. 1. 2. 3. 4. 5 you See goes up to the top. B. C.*
> *The pilasters, Cornices, molds &c. as in my Lds appartmt.*
> *The entablature from D to E is circular*
> *The attick from F to G is straight*
> *Lay a Chain of Iron from H to I and another from D to E.*

On the back is a simple sum, the subtraction of 1662 from 1707 to leave 45; this appears to be in the same ink and hand as the rest of the sheet. Even if it is not a calculation of Hawksmoor's age – he died in his 75th year and thus may have been born in early 1662 rather than 1661 – its implications for dating the drawing will be discussed later.

The early plan designs in the Victoria and Albert Museum show the two south wings differently divided up inside; thus from the start they were designed for similar but not identically interchangeable functions. The general plans of the house in *Vitruvius Britannicus* (I, Pl.63) have a key on which all the south rooms are shown as two principal apartments; although it is not stated, the implication is that one was for the Earl and one for the Countess, on the model of king's side and queen's side in a royal house. Failure to take account of this designation led Lang (1950), 130, to identify the room in the drawing as 'My Lord's Great Cabinet' (misquoting the inscription, which only refers to 'the Great Cabinet') and thereby introducing a false antithesis with 'My Lord's Apartment' at the east end.

It follows from this that My Lord's Great Cabinet was part of My Lord's Apartment, and was at the east end, and that the west end shown in the drawing was My Lady's Cabinet and part of her apartment.

Lang also assumed that the similarity between the two ends, implied by the inscription, extended to the existence of a bow window room at the east end. This in turn led her first to find in the drawing 'a proof of the accuracy of the engravings in *Vitruvius Britannicus* which one finds so often questioned', and secondly to speculate on when the supposed eastern bow was removed.

Not only does the drawing not prove 'the correctness of Colen Campbell's representation of Castle Howard' (Lang, 1979, 208), but the question is begged of which representation is under discussion. In various impressions Campbell presented several different versions of the plan, of which one at the most can be correct.

The 'accepted' version of the main house and wings (as in the New York 1967 reprint) shows the bow room on the west and the rectangular room on the east as built (Pl.64) but the general plan (Pl.63) is entirely reversed, with stables and chapel, as well as the one bow room, on the east. Breman and Addis illustrate a variant of the keyed general plan, Pl.63, the right way round but with two bow rooms (their pp.73a–b, presumably the evidence of Campbell's 'correctness') and right-angled passages behind the quadrant arcades, and two variants of Pl.64. One differs only in having some rooms dimensioned and an off-centre title (73c–d); the other shows two bow rooms and right-angled passages (73e–f).

Since Breman and Addis comment (p.74) that 'it is surprising that nobody has yet drawn attention to the existence of different versions of the main ground plans given by Campbell in succeeding issues of the book', the attention of historiographers may be drawn to the (admittedly summary) warning in Downes (1966), 76, n.74.

In fact there is no satisfactory evidence that there was ever an eastern bow. On the contrary, the rectangular end is shown on the 1727 estate map (Whistler, 1954, fig.20) as well as in a painting by de Cort (at Castle Howard) of the house with the Mausoleum in the foreground. These documents take the existing east end back before Robinson's work and indeed to Vanbrugh's own lifetime. Moreover, when the fabric was examined after the 1940 fire there was no trace of either bow or alteration.

Hawksmoor's inscription says of the east end only that it must be used to regulate the number of rustic courses on the west, and it should be noted that if the two ends were the same he would not have needed to prepare a new drawing for the western one.

Whistler (1954, 47–8) discussed the bow window and its relation to those on the sides of the main block of Blenheim, and concluded from documentary references (see below) that the west bow there was designed after, and therefore in imitation of, those at Blenheim, in particular of that on the east which Vanbrugh referred to as the Duchess of Marlborough's favourite (Whistler, 1954, 229). He made no mention of the date 1707 on the back of the drawing, but referred to payments in the 1706 Castle Howard accounts for the west wing in 1706 in respect of the 'Circuler Basement' and the 'Circuler Front of the 3 Windows'. Since the bows at Blenheim feature in the earliest designs, which were made early in 1705, the conclusion of their significance for the addition at Castle Howard seems justified.

Whistler further suggested (48), in order to explain Hawksmoor's concern with the rustication, that the builders made a fresh start at the west end rather than working continuously from the east, with the result that the rusticated courses would not necessarily join up exactly. This may indeed have been so, although it is known that at St Paul's Cathedral Wren had sufficient faith in his contractors to divide construction not merely between different firms but on the centre lines of windows or doorways; in any case Lang's contention (130) that work proceeded continuously is based on false premisses.

The 1705 accounts show that the flat east end was considerably ahead of the west. Samuel Carpenter's account of November 1705 included carving in wood of 125 'Cartozzas' or modilions in 'My Lords Grand Cabinett', which was therefore already roofed. In stone he charged 50s. each for '27 Pilaster Capitalls of the Corinthian Order' and, also 50s. for 'A Shield and Cherabin head Over the window', probably the lower rather than the upper window in the centre of the south front (Tipping, 1928, 12). Tipping and Hussey concluded that the capitals 'will have included those of the Main Pile', but this raises the difficulty that these capitals are larger than those in the wings and would certainly have commanded a higher price; they are also several feet higher from the ground and therefore may have been carved later. This remains a possibility even though Nadauld was paid the same year (ibid.) both for woodwork in the Grand Cabinet and for the tritons, lions and 'tropheas' in the main frieze of the south front – that is, above the main capitals. Arguments from negative evidence are always perilous, but the fragmentary nature of the Castle Howard accounts leaves no alternative; certainly it cannot be proved by default that work on the south front went unbroken from east to west. In fact twenty-seven capitals of equal size can be accounted for within the south-east wing as follows:

South front	7
South end of east room	4
North end of east room	4
East front	8
West returns of east room (two each, north and south)	4
	27

Failure to understand the significance of the two principal apartments, however, led Tipping and Hussey to conclude (20) that while the 'Grand Cabinet' at the west end was unfinished in 1706 (which is true) 'the east end of the south front . . . will have been completed early'. This is true only if 'early' does not mean earlier than 1706, since in 1706 Carpenter and Nadauld were still being paid for further work in 'My Lords appart' and in 'My Lords Grand Cabinett', which Tipping and Hussey (16) correctly assumed were all on the east side. The reference to a bow window in the 'Grand Cabinett' in John Bagnall's bill for plastering (19–20) indicates that the bow window room was plastered at some time between 1711 and 1714. The suggestion by Tipping and Hussey that there was once a bow window on the east has been ruled out in the preceding paragraphs.

There remains the puzzle of the date on the back of the drawing. Since the account quoted by Whistler shows that work on the bow window was going on in 1706 the drawing cannot be as late as 1707. Either the date was predictive (for example, it will be forty-five years since 1662) or it was added later. It cannot be proved *either* that Hawksmoor sent this particular drawing to Castle Howard rather than a copy of it *or* that, if he did send it, it was not returned to him by the recipient, probably William Etty, who was working at Castle Howard by 1705. In fact the presence of two large blots on the surface suggests that, with a fair degree of annoyance, he was obliged by a last-minute accident to make and send a clean copy. In either case the drawing in the British Library may have come, as others in the King's Maps seem to have done, from the 1740 sale of his collection. They include the preliminary drawings for the page of Hawksmoor's two designs, sent by him to Lord Carlisle in 1724 and still at Castle Howard, for the Belvedere Temple.

Appendix F

Spring Garden

Spring Garden was the name of several pleasure gardens noted as places of assignation and intrigue. The original, named from a mechanical spring or fountain which could be used to sprinkle spectators, was made in the late sixteenth century at the north-east corner of St James's Park, towards Charing Cross, and is marked today by a street of the same name. After being opened to the public it was more than once closed and re-opened: on 10 May 1654 Evelyn reported it closed by Cromwell, but by 23 May 1658 it was again open, when he 'collationed' there with his brother.

Soon after the Restoration there was a 'New Spring Garden' in Lambeth near the glassworks, on the estate known as Foxhall or Vauxhall, which Evelyn described on 2 July 1661 as 'A pretty contriv'd plantation' and which according to the French traveller Monconys two years later was laid out in squares with gooseberry hedges, beans, roses and asparagus (*Survey*, 1951, 146). The sequence of Pepys's account of a visit on 29 May 1662 has led to the inference that there were both an old and a new garden at Lambeth, although elsewhere Evelyn in 1661 distinguished clearly between the new Spring Garden at Lambeth and the old one at Charing Cross (de Beer's editorial note to Evelyn, 2 July 1661). If there were indeed two gardens at Lambeth they were so near together as to be contiguous. Certainly what was generally known as the New Spring Garden was named after the original but had no mechanical spring, and came in the eighteenth century to be known, and further developed, as Vauxhall Gardens.

Sir Roger de Coverley's wish for 'more nightingales and fewer Strumpets' in Spring Garden (*Spectator*, No. 383, 20 May 1712) is taken to refer to Lambeth. Uffenbach in 1710 (Uffenbach, 1934, 131) unequivocally described the Lambeth garden, where he saw 'vast crowds . . . especially females of doubtful morals, who are dressed as finely as ladies of quality'.

The garden at Charing Cross is often said to have been built over after the Restoration, and this assertion and the later reputation, good and bad, of Vauxhall have led many writers, including some of Vanbrugh's editors (e.g. Smith, 1974), to place Act IV.iv of *The Provok'd Wife* at Lambeth; this was a mile and a half away and the journey involved a boat ride across or up the Thames. But Roque's London Map of the mid 1740s shows that the planted garden survived at St James's at least until then, and there are good reasons to suppose that Vanbrugh and his original audience understood this to be the location.

The characters in *The Provok'd Wife* would have lived in Westminster, north or north-east of St James's Park, and the whole action would appear to have occurred between St. James's Square and Covent Garden. In Act II.i Lady Fancyfull is lured by Heartfree to St James's Park. Locket's, the eating house frequented both by Heartfree and Constant and by Lord Foppington in *The Relapse*, looked on to the garden, and the Blue Posts, to which Lord Rake and Colonel Bully invite Sir John Brute, is variously described as in the Haymarket or in the Spring Garden street. This would also make sense of the premature arrival of Sir John, still drunk and mistaking his wife and niece for a couple of whores, near the beginning of the garden scene. Before her violent entanglement with Constant later in the scene, Lady Brute is invited by her niece to take 'a turn in the Great Walk', which is clearly ('It's almost dark; nobody will know us') an open walk like those flanking the Mall in St James's Park and, unlike Spring Garden itself, one that offers no cover in daylight.

Appendix G

Letters, Mostly Unpublished

1 BL MS. Add.61353, f.137.

February the 10th 1710

My Lord Duke has been pleas'd to approve the Request I made to Him: That the £1300, I have had, Shou'd stand in the Books as allow'd me for Travelling Expences: And that I shou'd charge besides, a Salary of Five Hundred pounds a Year, for my Service in the Works.

J Vanbrugh

2 PRO T 1/190, No.158 (First published by Rogers, 1972)

Whitehall. June the 1st 1715

The Duke of Marlborough desires the favour of you, to move the Lords of the Treasury, for a fresh Order (if such Order be necessary) for delivering out of Whittlewood Forrest, such Trees as were formerly cut for the use of Blenheim House, and still remain lying on the ground. The whole number Orderd to be felld, was   248   Trees

of which brought away   127

Remains in the Forrest   121

I am Sr
Your most humble
Servant J Vanbrugh

The Trees are numbered from No: 1 to 248.

Endorsed by a clerk: D. Marlbo: Ref to Survr of woods to examine by what warrant these Trees were felld, how much & what Remaynes.

[As the endorsement suggests and is made clear by the covering letter of 17 June from Thomas Hewett, Surveyor of Woods, Vanbrugh's note was addressed to the Secretary to the Treasury, William Lowndes; Hewett's letter shows that Lowndes had forwarded Vanbrugh's note to him on 7 June and indicates that no further order is necessary for the removal of the remaining trees.

Hewett refers to *Mr Vanbrugh* although the latter had received his knighthood nearly a year earlier; it is impossible to say with confidence whether this was an oversight or a deliberate snub. Hewett did not become Sir Thomas until 1719.]

3   PRO Work 6/113, f.2 (Copy)

To the Rt Honble The Lords Comrs of His Majts Treasury

May it please Your Lordps,

In obedience to Your Lordps Commands Signified by Mr Lowndes, on Mr Wises Petition, hereto annexed, I beg leave to represent.

That in the Genll Contract for keeping the Gardens, That belonging to the little house at Windsor is not included.

That I find entred in the Cofferers Office, an Agreement made with Richd Watts dated the 6th of Augt 1702, to keep the said Garden for 180£ a year, and that the said allowance, was paid to Mr Watts to the last of Novr 1712, at which time, Mr Wise by the Queens Verball Order, without any new Agreement tooke that Garden into his care, and has continued to keep it ever Since in good Order and Condition, together with a large Greenhouse furnished with Plants, my humble opinion therefore is, That it may be reasonable to allow him for the time past the same Salary of 180£ p Ann. for his charge of keeping the said Garden & Greenhouse which by Contract has been paid to Mr Watts.

But since the Genll Contract with Mr Wise for the other Gardens is calculated upon the foot of £20 an acre, That the allowance of 180£ p Ann. for this Garden is above that proportion, and that there are Additions at Hampton Court not yet included in the aforesaid Contract which the said Mr Wise has kept in order this 5 years without any allowance, I humbly offer to your Lordps consideration whether it may not be proper, that the Garden at the little house at Windsor, & the Additions at Hampton Court be measured, and for the future allow'd for, at the rate of £20 an Acre p Ann. as the other gardens are.

I have in pursuance of your Lordps farther Commands examined into the demand made by Mr Wise for keeping the Mall, and do find that by agreement with the late Lord Fitzharding beginning at Midsr 1711 he was to receive fifty pounds a year for that service, and was paid the said Salary accordingly to Christmas 1712, and no farther.

All which is humbly Submitted &c
J: Vanbrugh

July 21st 1715

4 PRO Work 6/113, f.2v (Copy)

To the Rt Honble The Lords Comrs of His Majts Trea[su]ry

May it please Your Lordps,

His Majty having been pleased in the Instructions to me, as Surveyour of the Gardens and Waters belonging to the Severall Royall Palaces, to direct That I should lay before your Lordps an exact plan of the said Gardens, as likewise the contents of them in Acres Roods or Perches respectively, together with a description of the Conduits Rivers Rivulets or Streams of Water that are used for Supplying as well the said Gardens as the Severall Palaces with water, I have in obedience to his Majts Command here annext the Contents of each respective Garden, as I find it upon a new and exact Admeasurement, But have not yet been able to prepare the Severall Plans, they requiring a good Deal of time and pains, nor to give your Lordps so full an account of the State of the Waters, as may be necessary for your Satisfaction, they being in very great disorder, and under Severall difficultys, wch I hope in a Little time to offer to your Lordps some expedient for.

> All wch is humbly submitted by
> J Vanbrugh

Septr 30th 1715

5 PRO Work 6/113, f.3v (Copy).

Whitehall May 14th 1716

Sr

This is to acquaint you That I have rec'd His Majts Command to give leave to the Hautbois in his Service to perform in the Gardens at Kensington during this Summer. I am

> Sr
>
> Yours &c
> J Vanbrugh

To Mr Henry Wise

6 PRO Work 6/113, f.4 (Copy)

To the Rt Honble The Lords Comrs of His Majts Treasury

The Memoriall of Sr John Vanbrugh Knt, Surveyour of His Majtys Gardens and Waters.

May it please yr Lordps,

The Great Engine at Windsor erected by Sr Samll. Moreland, to serve the Castle with water from the Thames, after a very great expence for many years past in mending and supporting it, is at last so faulty and worn, that it is incapable of any farther repair to make it answer the Service for wch it was design'd, so that there seems an absolute necessity for an entire new Engine, the water wch is furnished at present by other means being in no degree sufficient for the common use of the House, much less in case of any accident by fire.

Which is humbly submitted to yr Lordps
by your most obedient humble servant
J Vanbrugh

26 Aprill 1717

[Agreement with John Rowley to make a new engine: Board of Works Minutes, 7 June 1717 (PRO Work 4/1).]

7 BIHR (Autograph letter, incomplete. *Partly printed on pp.188-9.*)

Heslington 20 Sept 1721

We return'd hither but on Saturday last, finding both business and entertainment to keep us at Castle Howd. twice as long as we design'd. We were disposed of there with much convenience having four or five Rooms in the office Wing all together, and upon the same floor, the rest of which floor, serves Lady Erwin & Lady Mary. Who by their Neighbourhood, soon fell into quite an easy manner of conversing wth La: Van: without any manner of Stiffness or reserve; only making allowance for the true sorrow Lady Irwin cannot avoid Shewing. tho' she do's all she can, to keep it in bounds before Company. Our being there however proved of some small relief to her; for she came at last not only to vent herself pretty much to my Wife but to pass a great deal of her time with the Child whom she grew mighty fond of, declaring she never felt any thing of the kind for her Brothers Children or any other. And her Woman (who has attended her from her Cradle: and enters deep into her Afflictions) said this was the first thing she had observ'd her take the least pleasure in, since my Lords death. Lady Mary was as fond of him as she; going twenty times a day into the nursery, and Sitting an hour together by her self, at the Cradle foot, to see him sleep; then carrying him about in her arms as long as she was able, from whence he was handed from one to an other round the family of all Degrees, and a favourite every where, because he never cry'd.

Tho my Lord Irwin (and the King too) intended a considerable advantage to Lady Irwin, by the Sale of the Regiment; it so falls out by South Sea and other Circumstances, that not one penny comes to her, so that she is left without even her Jewells, or any thing else but her bare Joynture. She is like to be at Castle Howd. till she can save enough to build her a small house near London, for in it, she will never live, nor cou'd ever endure it. Greenh: she likes better than any other village, and before we came away began to think in earnest of building there So I shall send her some Designs, to amuse her at least.

We were to have gone on Friday to carry Mrs Norcliff home to her Mother and to have spent a . . . [*page missing*]

[*deleted passage*: That she might write her word, I wou'd not pay a farthing, unless I was sued for it, So this I reckon will puzzle the Clmant cruelly.] Lady Van: bids me say, She intended to tell you her Self (but her head Achs, so she bids me do it) that Ld Car: has equipt his Godson with a £25 peice of Plate, and his Nurse with a Couple of Guineas She writ to you totherday

Watkins own's his marriage, is gone home to his Wife, And has got a Dead Son – I'm sorry things so Fall out, we can't see you at Christ[ma]s in London.

[The recipient is unknown, but possibly someone in the Newcastle circle. Mrs Norcliffe was probably Lady Vanbrugh's first cousin Frances (1700–70) whose mother, Mary, had been widowed in 1720. Viscount Irwin had died of smallpox on 10 April 1721; Vanbrugh sent condolences to Lord Carlisle on 22 April (Webb, 1928, 132). Lady Irwin decided in the end to live in London, where No. 5 New Burlington Street was built for her by Hawksmoor in 1735 (*Survey of London*, XXXII, 1963, 490). Vanbrugh's Account Book records on 1 March 1723 the receipt of £25 'from the Earl of Carlisle to buy a Cup for Charles', and its actual cost, £33.12s.]

8   BL MS. Add.4061, f.223

Whitehall. Thursday Noon.

Sr

Having acquainted Dr Slare, that you wou'd be glad to talk a little with him on my Wifes Indisposition; he has sent me a Letter just now, that he is in Towne, And desires I wou'd send to you, that if you can you wou'd be so good to meet him here this afternoon; He begs if possible, it may be between four and five, he being Oblig'd at five to return to Greenwich on pressing Occasion. I am

Sr
            Your most humble
                Servant
                J Vanbrugh

To Sr Hans Sloan
  In Southampton Square

[Account Book, 14 June 1722: To Sr Hans Sloan & Dr Slare 2–2–0.]

9   BL MS. Add.61432, f.128. To the 2nd Duchess of Marlborough. *Printed on pp.408-9.*

10   PRO Work 6/113, f.6v (Copy)

To the Rt Honble The Lords Comrs of His Majts Treasury

May it please your Lordps

Mr Scrope having by a Letter of the 18th Instant, Signified to me your Lordships pleasure, that I should lay before you the particulars of the work done by Mr Carpenter and Mr Wise in the lower Wildernesse at Hampton Court with my opinion of the rates charged in their bill, I here transmit to your Lordships a Copy of it, which I have examined, and find this work has been done, and that the Rates charged for the Plants are not higher than what is usually paid by private persons. which is humbly Submitted to your Lordships by

                    your most humble
                  and most obedient Servant
                    John Vanbrugh

Whitehall Augt
the 19th 1725.

Glossary

Architrave. The lowest section of an **entablature**, below the **frieze**. Of a window, a moulded band framing the opening on the outside.

Attic. The topmost storey of a building, understood as being above, and usually smaller in height than, the main storey or storeys.

Banded rustication. A form of **rustication** in which the vertical joints are smooth and concealed but the horizontal ones (or those between the stones of an arch) are marked by regularly spaced grooves.

Basement. In architectural design, a visible storey or half-storey immediately above ground level and seen to support the principal storey or storeys.

Capital. The 'head' of a **column** or **pilaster**, at the top of the shaft and immediately below the **entablature**. The capital more than anything else gives each **order** its identity and character.

Classical. Art of, or emulating that of, ancient Greece and Rome, especially considered as an exemplar of style, reason and taste.

Clerestory. A top storey, usually rising from the central part of a building above the surrounding parts and consisting mostly of windows, provided so as to give abundant daylight within the building.

Composite. The most ornate of the Roman and Renaissance orders, combining the acanthus leaves of the **Corinthian** with the volutes of the **Ionic**.

Corbel table. In medieval architecture, a connected row of corbels or support blocks projecting from the wall, immediately below the roof or parapet.

Corinthian. One of the **Classical orders**, next in richness to the **Composite**. Its **capital** consists of an inverted bell-shaped centre surrounded by rows of acanthus leaves and shoots.

Cornice. The uppermost section of the **entablature**, above the **frieze**. More generally, a projecting horizontal moulding of similar form, over a door or window, or at the top of a storey.

Doric. The oldest of the Greek **orders** and the simplest of the Roman ones except for the consciously primitive Tuscan. Its **capital** is a simple round cushion-like stone.

Engaged column. A fully rounded **column** of which a small segment is attached to or engaged in the wall which it fronts.

Entablature. The whole horizontal part of an **order**, originally a structural beam and resting on the **capitals**.

Forestage. That part of the Elizabethan and Restoration stage which projected into the domain of the audience, unencumbered by vertical supports or framing devices.

Frieze. The middle section of an **entablature**, basically a continuous horizontal band, either plain or enriched with relief work or, in the **Doric**, by alternating metopes and triglyphs.

Giant order. An **order** which clearly spans two storeys, sometimes used simultaneously with a second smaller order in the lower storey.

Ionic. An **order** intermediate in richness between the **Doric** and **Corinthian**, distinguished by large volutes or scrolls at the corners of the **capital**.

Keystone. The central wedge-shaped stone of an arch which locks its structure together. Vanbrugh and Hawksmoor liked the dramatic effect of exaggerated or tripled keystones.

Loggia. An open gallery on the outside of a building, in which the roof is carried on columns, piers or arches.

Neo-Classical. Used by students of English Literature in the sense of **Classical**; used by art-historians for the style and attitude prevalent after c.1750 in which specifically Greek rather than Roman or Renaissance art provided the exemplars and prototypes.

Order. In **Classical** architecture, a system of parts, originally those of the Greek Doric temple, from which a complete design can be generated, according to formulas of proportion and decorative detail. A complete order consists of **columns** (vertical members) and an **entablature** (the horizontal member). The Greek orders, **Doric, Ionic** and **Corinthian**, were developed at different times and in different places; the Romans adopted them and added the Tuscan and (in Imperial times) the **Composite**. Thus a geographical and historical distribution gave way to a linguistic and expressive one.

Palladian. A style of architecture or an attitude to style, consciously and retrospectively based on the buildings and publications of Andrea Palladio (1508–80).

Pavilion. (French *pavillon*). A projecting sub-division of a secular building, usually in the centre or at a corner, and distinguished by a separate roof.

Pediment. Originally the low-pitched gable-end of a Greek or Roman temple or **portico**, resting on the entablature and framed by the cornice below and by similar mouldings over the sloping edges. It was also used decoratively above doorcases and window frames. Although originally pediments were low triangles in shape, segmental ones, in which the upper edge is a continuous curve, usually an arc of circle, have been used since Roman times.

Pilaster. A high-relief equivalent of a **column**, affixed to the surface of a wall or a pier to serve the decorative and expressive functions of an **order**.

Portico. Properly the open area at the front of a Greek or Roman temple, defined by free-standing **columns** and usually surmounted by a **pediment**.

Proscenium (Latin) = **Forestage**.

Proscenium arch. The framing aperture at the *back* of the **forestage**, which from the end of the seventeenth century came increasingly to mark the boundary between the world of the stage and that of the audience.

Rustication. A style of masonry in which the surface is artificially made rough or irregular or the joints are emphasized or recessed in grooves, for an effect of grandeur, reference to Nature or decorative enrichment.

Saloon. (Italian *salone*, augmentative of *sala*, a hall.) The principal formal living room when the hall had ceased to be one and was used only for entrance and exit.

Surveyor. (Medieval Latin *supervidere*, to oversee.) Used in the seventeenth and eighteenth centuries both in the modern sense and, instead of *architect*, for the designing manager of a building project. The title survives in use for the consultant architect in charge of many cathedral fabrics.

Tennis court. An oblong hall designed and set out for the game of tennis (known as *real tennis* since the invention of lawn tennis in the late nineteenth century).

Triumphal arch. Properly a free-standing solid masonry structure traversed by a central arch, erected solely for ceremonial entry or transit. In medieval, Renaissance and later architecture, an arch of this kind used decoratively as part of an elevation design.

Venetian window. Wrongly called *Palladian window* and correctly, by those who wish to air their Italian, *Serliana*. A window in three sections, framed by columns or pilasters, with the central section rising above the others into a semi-circular arch.

Index